Street
LONDON

2nd edition June 2002

© Automobile Association Developments Limited 2002

Ordnance Survey® This product includes map data licensed from Ordnance Survey® with the permission of the Controller of Her Majesty's Stationery Office.
© Crown copyright 2002. All rights reserved. Licence No: 399221.

Published by AA Publishing (a trading name of Automobile Association Developments Limited, whose registered office is Millstream, Maidenhead Road, Windsor, Berkshire SL4 5GD. Registered number 1878835).

The Post Office is a registered trademark of Post Office Ltd. in the UK and other countries.

Schools address data provided by Education Direct.

One-way street data supplied by:

Tele Atlas ◄ © Tele Atlas N.V.

Mapping produced by the Cartographic Department of The Automobile Association. A01423

A CIP Catalogue record for this book is available from the British Library.

Printed by GRAFIASA S.A., Porto, Portugal

Ref: MN037z

Key to map pages	ii-iii
Key to map symbols	iv-1
Enlarged scale pages	2-49
Street by Street	50-163
Index – towns & villages	164-168
Index – streets	169-323
Index – featured places	324-370

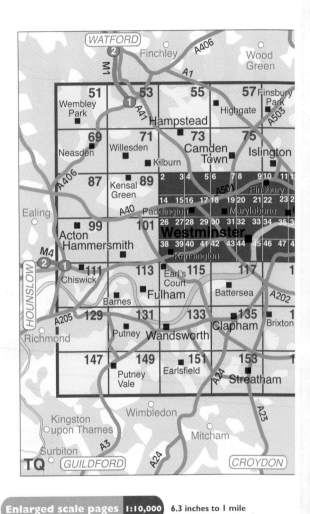

ii

51 Wembley Park
53
55
57 Finsbury Park
Highgate
Hampstead
69 Neasden
71 Willesden
73 Camden Town
75 Islington
Kilburn
87
89 Kensal Green
2 3 4 5 6 7 8 9 10 11
14 15 16 17 18 19 20 21 22 23
Paddington
Finsbury
Marylebone
99 Acton
Hammersmith
101
Westminster
26 27 28 29 30 31 32 33 34 35
38 39 40 41 42 43 44 45 46 47
Kensington
111 Chiswick
113
Barnes
115 Earl's Court
Fulham
117
Battersea
129
131 Putney
133 Wandsworth
135 Clapham
Brixton
147
149 Putney Vale
151 Earlsfield
153 Streatham

WATFORD
Finchley
Wood Green
M1
A406
A1
A41
A406
A40
A501
A503
Ealing
M4
HOUNSLOW
Richmond
A205
Kingston upon Thames
Wimbledon
Mitcham
A202
A24
A23
Surbiton
GUILDFORD
A3
A24
CROYDON
TQ

Enlarged scale pages 1:10,000 6.3 inches to 1 mile

0   miles   1/4

0   1/4   kilometres   1/2

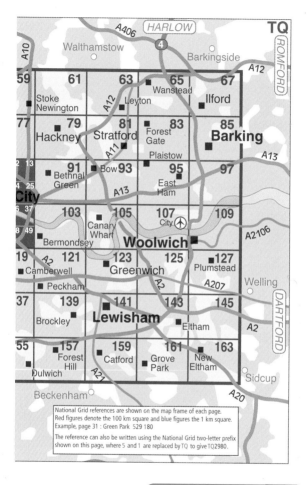

National Grid references are shown on the map frame of each page.
Red figures denote the 100 km square and blue figures the 1 km square.
Example, page 31 : Green Park 529 180

The reference can also be written using the National Grid two-letter prefix
shown on this page, where 5 and 1 are replaced by TQ to give TQ2980.

3.2 inches to 1 mile Scale of main map pages 1:20,000

iv

Junction 9	Motorway & junction	Underground station
Services	Motorway service area	Light railway & station
	Primary road single/dual carriageway	+++++++ Preserved private railway
Services	Primary road service area	LC Level crossing
	A road single/dual carriageway	●—●—● Tramway
	B road single/dual carriageway	- - - - - Ferry route
	Other road single/dual carriageway	·············· Airport runway
	Minor/private road, access may be restricted	County, administrative boundary
← ←	One-way street	Mounds
	Pedestrian area	**93** Page continuation
- - - - - -	Track or footpath	River/canal, lake, pier
	Road under construction	Aqueduct, lock, weir
]- - =[	Road tunnel	465 ▲ Winter Hill Peak (with height in metres)
AA	AA Service Centre	Beach
P	Parking	Coniferous woodland
P+	Park & Ride	Broadleaved woodland
	Bus/coach station	Mixed woodland
	Railway & main railway station	Park
	Railway & minor railway station	

	Cemetery			Theme park
	Built-up area			Abbey, cathedral or priory
	Featured building			Castle
	City wall			Historic house or building
A&E	Hospital with 24-hour A&E department	Wakehurst Place NT		National Trust property
PO	Post Office			Museum or art gallery
	Public library			Roman antiquity
i	Tourist Information Centre			Ancient site, battlefield or monument
	Petrol station Major suppliers only			Industrial interest
†	Church/chapel			Garden
	Public toilets			Arboretum
	Toilet with disabled facilities			Farm or animal centre
PH	Public house AA recommended			Zoological or wildlife collection
	Restaurant AA inspected			Bird collection
	Theatre or performing arts centre			Nature reserve
	Cinema		**V**	Visitor or heritage centre
⚑	Golf course			Country park
▲	Camping AA inspected			Cave
	Caravan site AA inspected			Windmill
	Camping & caravan site AA inspected			Distillery, brewery or vineyard

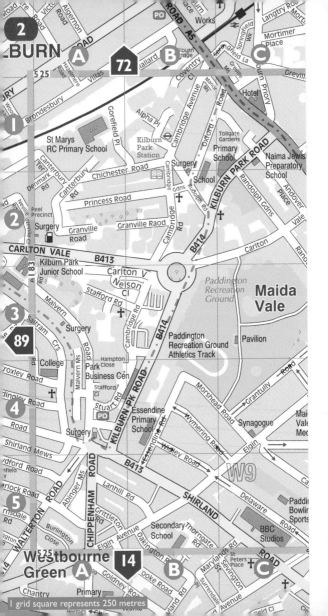

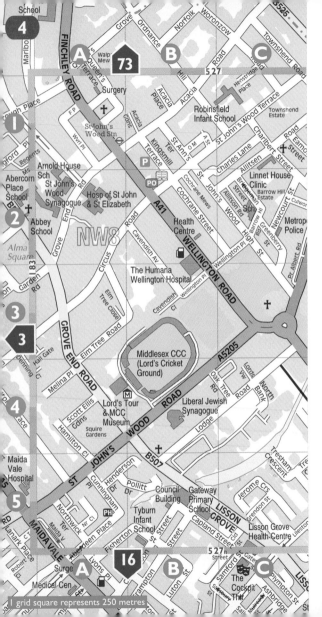

1 grid square represents 250 metres

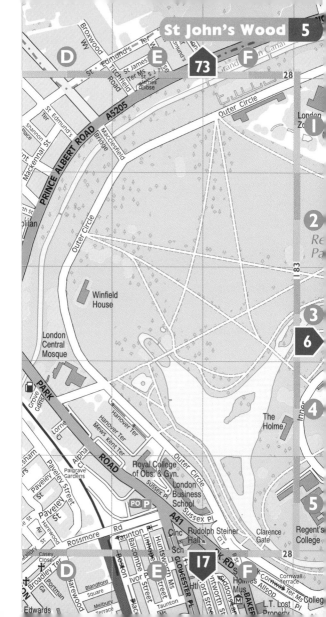

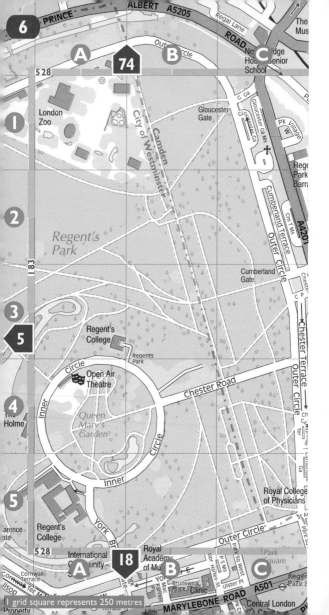

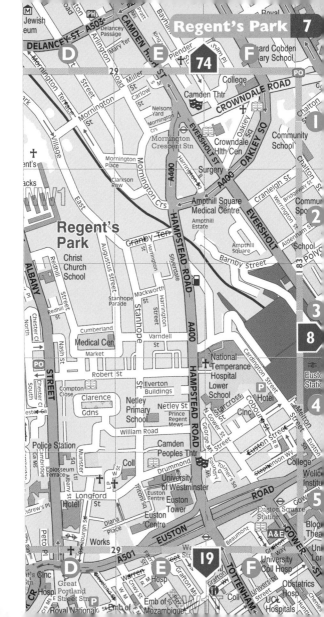

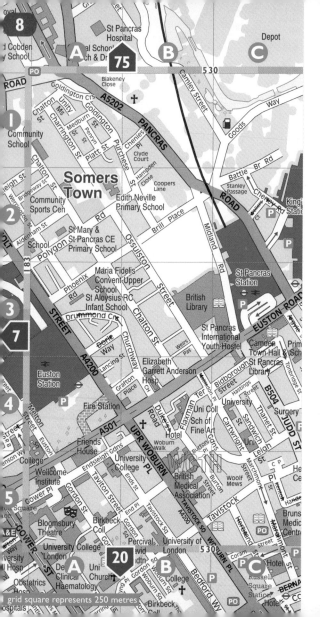

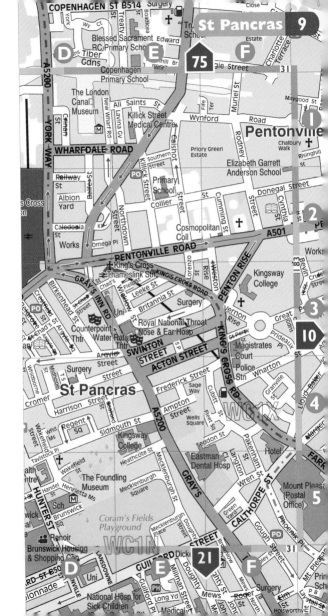

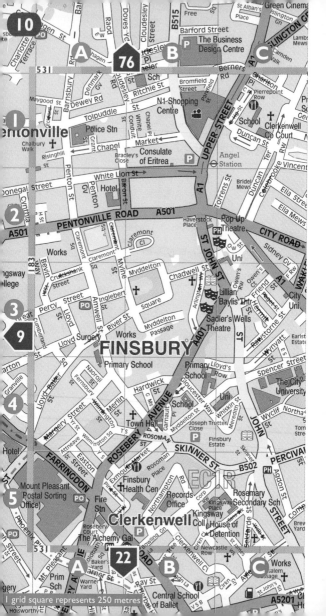

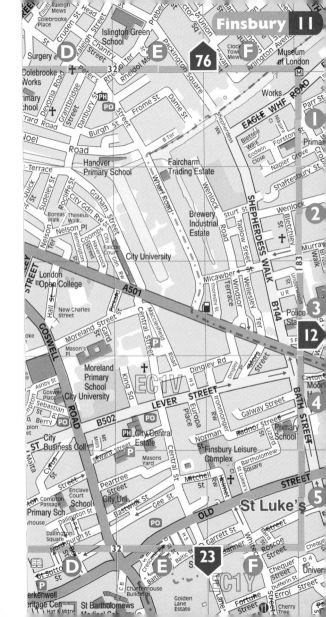

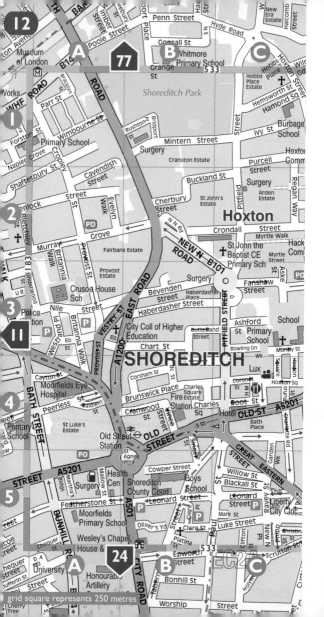

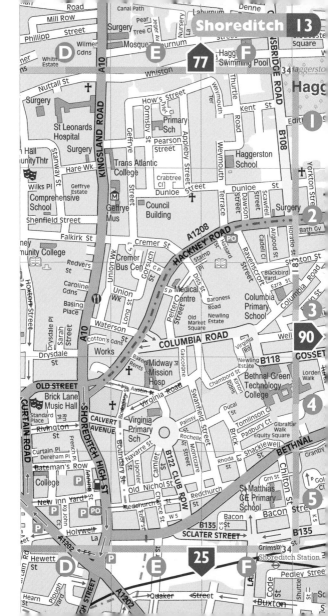

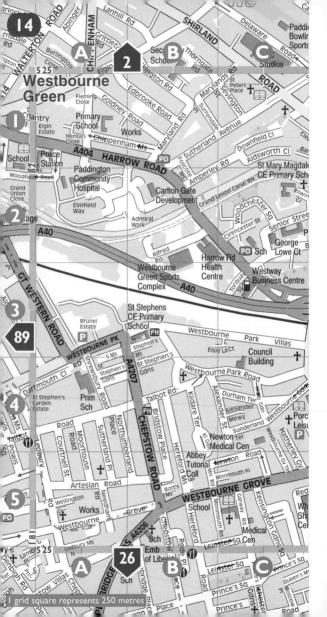

1 grid square represents 250 metres

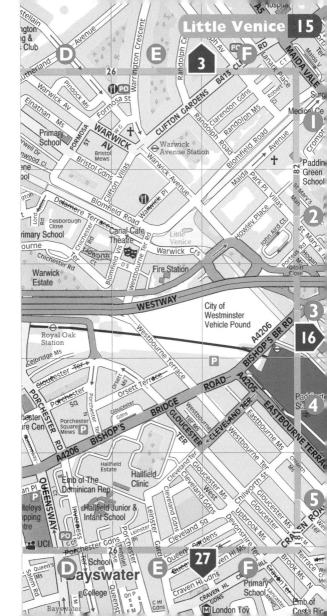

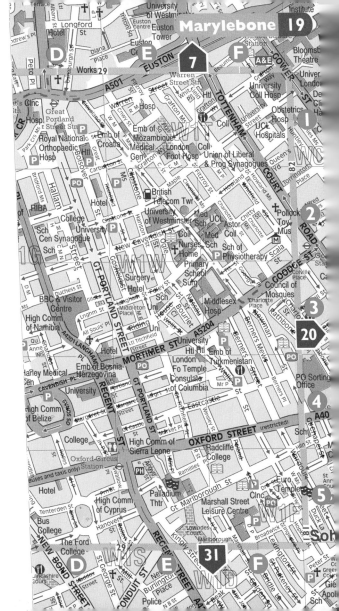

1 grid square represents 250 metres

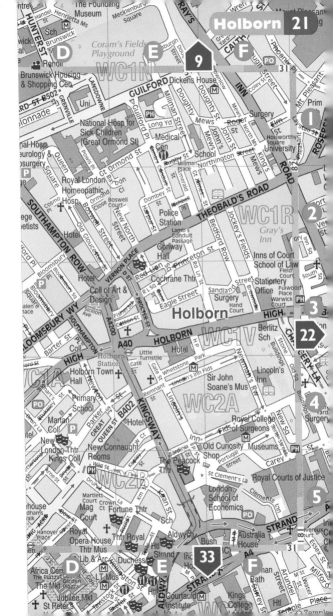

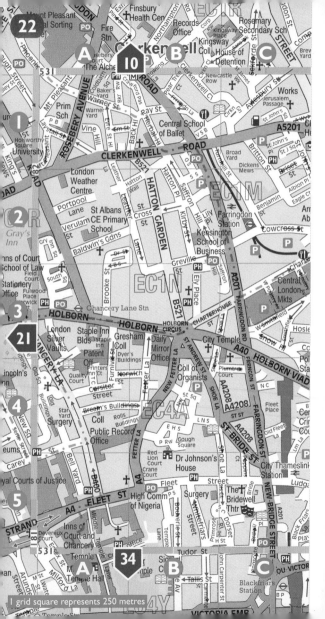

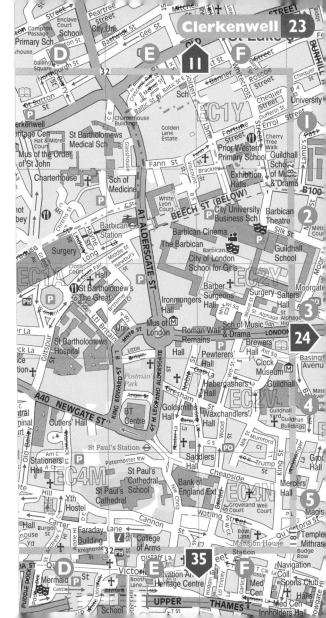

Peartree Street
Enclave Court
City Uni
Bastwick St
Gee St
Mitch
St Luke's
STREET
BUNHILL

Compton Passage
Northburgh St
D
E
F
Banner
Roscoe Street
Chequer
University
Errol Street
Lamb's Pas

Primary Sch
32
II
Golden Lane
Whitecross St
Chequer Street
Dufferin St
B100
I

Gt Sutton St
EC1Y
Fortune Street
Cherry Tree Walk
Guildhall Sch of Music & Drama

Clerkenwell Heritage Cen
Hat & Mitre Court
St Bartholomews Medical Sch
Charterhouse Buildings
Golden Lane Estate
Prior Weston Primary School

Mus of the Order of St John
Fann St
Brackley St
Exhibition Halls

Charterhouse
Sch of Medicine
White Lyon Court
BEECH ST (BELOW)
City University Business Sch
Barbican Theatre
Silk St
2
Milto Court

Barbican Station
Barbican Cinema
Guildhall School

Surgery
Middle St
Newbury
The Barbican
Barbican
City of London School for Girls
EC2Y
Moorgate

EC1A
Cloth Court
Cloth Fair
Hall
Ironmongers Hall
Barber Surgeons Hall
Surgery
Salters' Hall
3

St Bartholomew's The Great
Bitthin
Mus of London
M
Sch of Music & Drama
LONDON

Uni
Roman Wall Remains
Brewers' Hall
24

St Bartholomews Hospital
Little Britain
Pewterers' Hall
Oat La
Clock Museum
M
Basing Avenu

Gresham
Haberdashers La
Guildhall
Maso

A40 NEWGATE ST
KING EDWARD ST
Postman's Park
Angel St
Goldsmiths Hall
Waxchandlers' Hall
EC2V
Guildhall Yard
Guildhall Buildings
4

Cutlers' Hall
BT Centre
Carey La
Wood St
Mumford Ct

St Paul's Station ⊖
Paternoster Rw
Saddlers Hall
Cheapside
Trump St
Groc Hall

Stationers Hall
EC4M
Bank of England Ext
EC4N
Mercers' Hall
5

St Paul's Cathedral School
Bread St
Groveland Well Court
Magis

Hill
Yth Hostel
Cannon
Watling Street
Victoria St
Temple

Carter La
Faraday Building
College of Arms
Bow Lane
Mansion House Station
Mithras
Budge Row

Knightrider St
Distaff La
35
T Clk Tostle
Trinity
Navigation
LaColl

Mermaid
Castle
Victoria
Salvation Army Heritage Centre
Garlick
Med Cen
Sports Club

PUDDLE DOCK
School
Booth Lane
UPPER
THAMES
Innholders Hall

D
E
F

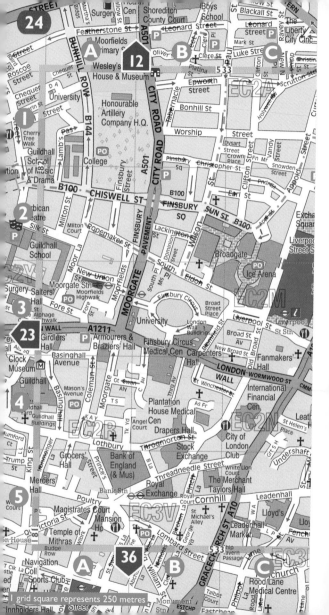

grid square represents 250 metres

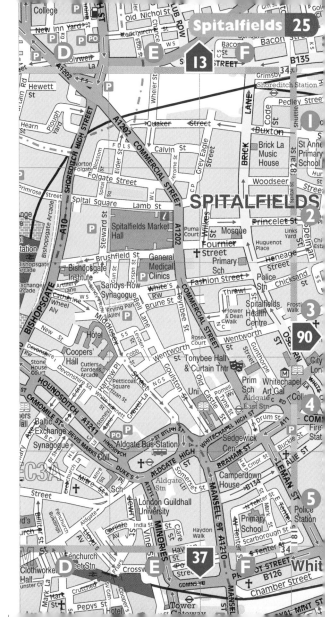

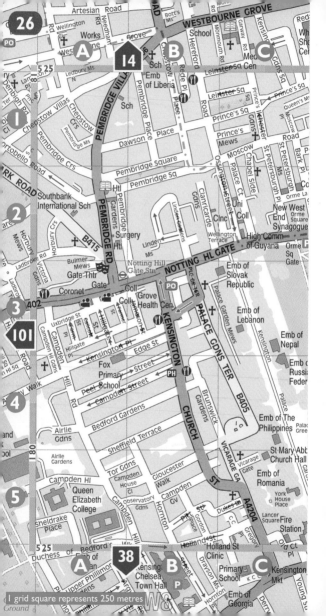

1 grid square represents 250 metres

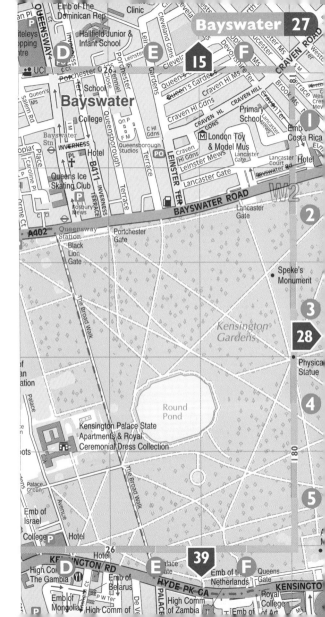

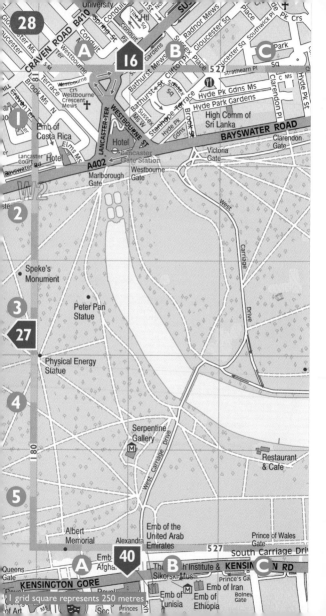

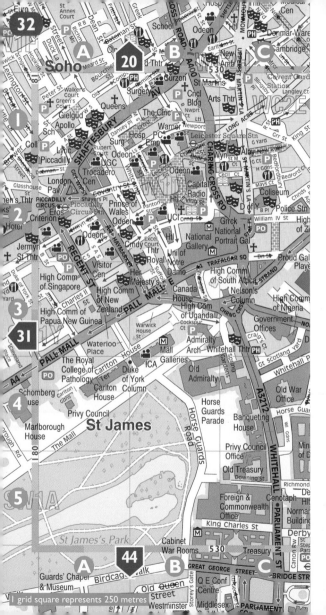

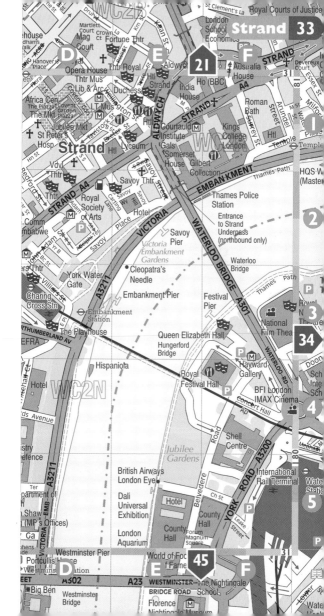

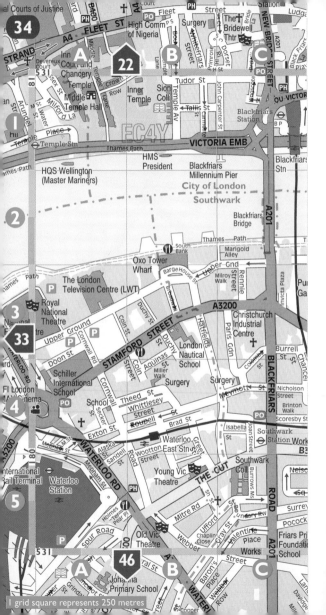

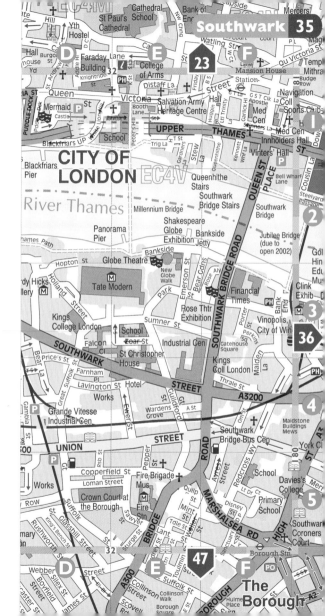

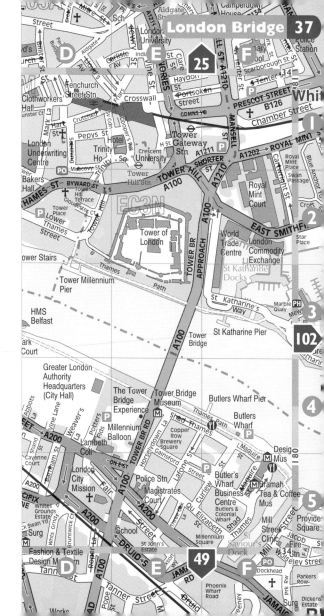

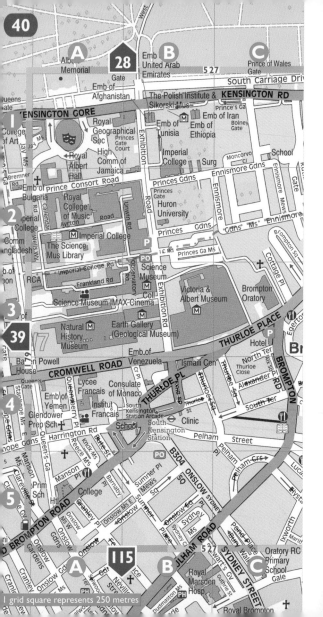

A Albert Memorial

28

B Emb United Arab Emirates

5 27

C Prince of Wales Gate

South Carriage Dri

Gate

Emb of Afghanistan

The Polish Institute & Sikorski-Mus

KENSINGTON RD

I

KENSINGTON GORE

Prince's Ga

Queens Gate

College of Art

Royal Geographical Soc

Princes Gate Court

Emb of Tunisia

Emb of Iran Bolney Gate

Emb of Ethiopia

Jay Ms

High Comm of Jamaica

Imperial College

Surg

Moncorvo Cl

School

Royal Albert Hall

Ennismore Gdns

Ennismore Mews

Bremner Rd

Emb of Prince Consort Road

Princes Gdns

Ennismore

Ennismore Gate

Emb of Bulgaria

Royal College of Music

Princes Gdns

Huron University

Gdns Ms

Ennismore

2

Imperial College

Ayrton Road

Unwin Rd

Princes

Gdns

Brompton sq

Comm Bangladesh

Wells W.

The Science Mus Library

Imperial College

Princes Ga Ms

Cottage Pl

RCA

Imperial College Rd

I C Rd

P

b-of on

Frankland Rd

Observatory Rd

PO

Science Museum Coll

Exhibition Rd

Victoria & Albert Museum

Brompton Oratory

Edentton

3

of

Science Museum IMAX-Cinema

39

Natural History Museum

Earth Gallery (Geological Museum)

THURLOE PLACE

P

Hotel

Br

Ba-n Powell House

Emb of Venezuela

Ismaili Cen

North Ter

Thurloe Close

BROMPTON RD

Queen's Gate

CROMWELL ROAD

THURLOE PL

Alexander Pl

4

Sta-e Ms

Emb of Yemen

Queensberry Pl

Lycee Francais

Consulate of Monaco

South

South Ter

Harrington Rd

Institut Francais

Kensington Station Arcade

Clinic

Glendower Prep Sch

Hope Gdns

Harrington Rd

Reece Ms

School

South Kensington Station

Pelham

Street

Manson Ms

Manson Rd

Knox Ms

Bute St

Pelham Cres

Lucas

5

Clareville Gv

Prim Sch

Manson Pl

College

Barnaby

Sumner Pl

PO

B304

Sumner Mews

ONSLOW SQ

SYDNEY

Pelham Pl

Onslow M E

Cranley

Onslow Ms W

Onslow Rd

Sydney Pl

Sydney Ms

Ixworth

Onslow Gdns

BROMPTON ROAD

Onslow Gdns

Onslow

Onslow

FULHAM ROAD

Sydney St

Stewart's Gv

SYDNEY STREET

Oratory RC Primary School

Cranley

A

Onslow Gd

115

B

Ice

Royal Marsden Hosp

Dudmaston Ms

C

Gale

Neville

PH

Dovehouse

PH

Royal Brompton

I grid square represents 250 metres

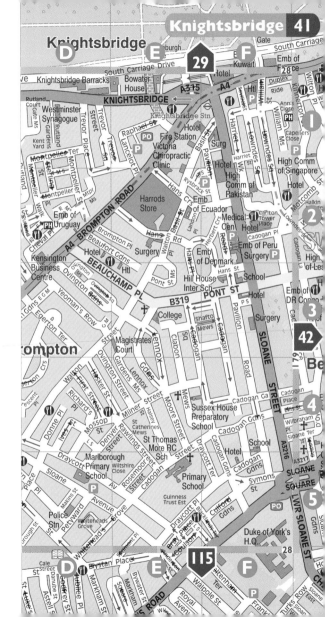

42

30

41

116

South Carriage Drive

Emb of Fran

528

duplex Ride

Ann's Close

Capeners Close

High Comm of Singapore

Emb of Portugal

Emb of Syria

High Comm of Malaysia

Emb of Luxembourg

Emb of Turkey

Hotel

Headfort Pl

A302

Emb of Ireland

European School of Economics

Wellington Arch

DUKE OF WELLINGTON

GROSVENOR PLACE

Chapel St

Groom Place

Chester Cl

Chester St Ltd

Chester Ms

Wilton Street Ms

Dorset

Chester Place

London Tourist Board

B31

GROSVENOR CRS

Wilton Crs

Wilton Rw

Barrack Ms

Grosvenor Ms

Wilton Pl

Hotel

Halkin Arcade

W Halkin St

Motcomb St

High Comm of Austria

Emb of Germany

Emb of Norway

Belgrave Ms South

Eaton Place

Eaton Ms N

Eccleston Mews

Eccleston Square

Wilton Ms E

Grosvenor Gdns Mews Nth

BELGRAVE SQ

High Comm of Lesotho

Emb of Finland

Emb of Spain

Chesham Place

Lyall St

Lyall Ms

Cadogan Lane

Emb of Hungary

Emb of Belgium

Emb of Bolivia

KING'S ROAD

HOBART PL

Eaton Rw

Mews E

Grosvenor Gdns Mews Nth

Hotel

High Comm of Singapore

Surgery

Eaton Ms S

EATON SQUARE

Eaton

Eaton Square

Eaton Ms

Chester Sq

Chester Mews

ECCLESTON ST

Ebury Ms E

Ebury

Prep School

PO

Eccleston Pl

Belgravia

A3217

Cadogan Place

Emb of Iceland

School

Surgery

Eaton Square

Eaton Ms W

Boscobel Place

Elizabeth St

Gerald Rd

Ebury Ms

Chester Sq

Ebury Mews

Surgery

Eccleston Place

BUC

Cadogan Place

Grosvenor Cottages

Eaton Cl

Holy Trinity CE Primary School

Minera Ms

Caroline Terrace

Eaton Row

Burton Ms

Eaton Terrace

Ebury Street

Victoria Coach Station

The Colonna Shoppi Centre

SLOANE SQUARE

A3216

Royal Court

Sloane Sq Stn

Graham Terrace

Chester Terrace

Whittaker St

School

Cundy St

Ebury Sq

Semley Pl

A3214

SW1W

LWR SLOANE

of York's

528

Holb

Whittaker

Passmore

Ranelagh Grove

Police Station

PIMLICO ROAD

Council Building

Blm Ter

St Barnabas CE Prim Sch

Surgery

BR RD

PIMLICO RD

ROAD

Abb Man

Abb Est

A   **B**   **C**

I grid square represents 250 metres

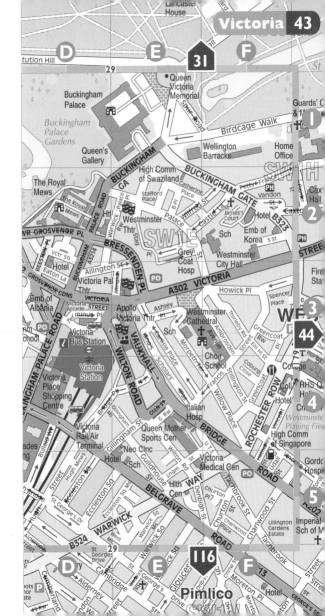

Lancaster House

D   E   31   F

tution Hill   29   St

Queen Victoria Memorial

Buckingham Palace

Guards' C & M

Buckingham Palace Gardens

Buckingham Palace Gardens

Birdcage Walk

Wellington Barracks   Home Office

SW1H

Queen's Gallery

The Royal Mews

The Royal Mews

High Comm of Swaziland

Stafford Place

Petty France

PH Vandon

Cax Hall

Caxto   St

BUCKINGHAM GATE

BUCKINGHAM GA

BUCKINGHAM ROAD

PALACE ROAD

Warwick Place

Palace St

Catherine Place

Wilfred St

Castle Lane

St James's Court

Hotel B323

2

Htl

Westminster Thtr

SW1E

Sch   Emb of Korea   St

STREE

NR GROSVENOR PL

BRESSENDEN PL

Grey Coat Hosp

Westminster City Hall

Fire Sta

BEESTON

Eaton La

Hotel

Allington St

Victoria Pal Thtr

PO

A302   VICTORIA

Howick Pl

Spencer Place

3

GROSVENOR GDNS

Emb of Albania

Victoria Arcade   VICTORIA STREET   minus PL

Apollo Victoria Thtr

Ashley

PH

Westminster Cathedral

Thirleby Road

Greencoat

WE

F

KINGHAM PALACE ROAD

PO

im school

Victoria   i   Bus Station

VAUXHALL

Sch

Ambrosden Ave

Morpeth

44

RW

Howick Pl

College

RHS Q

WILTON ROAD

Victoria Station

KINGS

Scholars

Choir School

Francis

Coburg Close

Stillington

Greencoat

Coll

Hotel

4

Victoria Place Shopping Centre

Italian Hosp

Willow Place

Westminste Playing Fie

High Comm of Singapore

ROCHESTER ROW

Victoria Rail/Air Terminal

Gillingham St

BRIDGE

Vincent St

Gordo Hospi

Hotel   Sch

Neo Clnc

Queen Mother Sports Cen

Victoria Medical Cen

PO

Guildhouse

Churton

ROAD

Hlth Cen

Denbigh St

5

Bullieid

High Mews

Eccleston Sq

WAY

Lngm

Churton St

Lillington Gardens Estate

Imperial Sch of M

Eccleston St   Eccleston Sq Ms

BELGRAVE

Charlwood St

Tachbrook St

St George's Dr

WARWICK   Warwick Sq

West Warwick Pl   St George's

ROAD

Cambridge St

B324

Cumberland

Alderney

bots nor ate   P

SW1V W

Moreton Pl

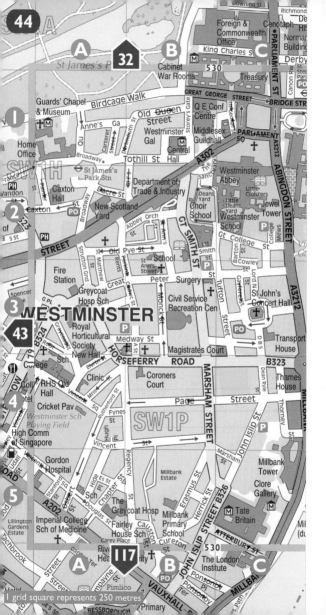

32

A   B   C

Richmond
Foreign &
Commonwealth
Office
King Charles S   Derby
Cabinet
War Rooms   530
Treasury

Guards' Chapel
& Museum   Birdcage Walk   GREAT GEORGE STREET   BRIDGE STR
Old Queen   Q E Conf
Anne's Ga   Street   Centre
Home   Westminster   Middlesex
Office   Gal   Guildhall   PARLIAMENT
Broadway   Central   SQ
SW1H   Tothill St   Hall
St James's   Westminster
Park Stn   Abbey   Little
Caxton   Department of   Cloisters
Hall   Dacre St   Trade & Industry   Deans   Jewel
Yard   Tower
New Scotland   Abbey Orch   Choir   Westminster
Caxton   Yard   School   School
St   Ann's   Gt College   SW1
PH   Old Pye St   St
STREET   St   Smith   St John's
School   Surgery   Concert Hall
Fire   Peter
Station   Civil Service
Greycoat   Recreation Cen   PO
Hosp Sch
WESTMINSTER   Transport
Royal   Monck   House
Horticultural   P
Society   Medway St   B323
New Hall   HORSEFERRY   ROAD
Coroners   Thames
College   Court   Dean Ryle   House
RHS Old   Clinic   MARSHAM
Hall   Page   Street   P
Cricket Pav   Rutherford St   STREET
Westminster Sch   SW1P
Playing Field   Hugh   Marsham
High Comm   Vincent   St
of Singapore   Millbank
Gordon   Tower
Hospital   Millbank   Clore
Hide   Estate   Gallery
Regency   Erasmus St
Imperial College   A202   The   Millbank
Sch of Medicine   Greycoat Hosp   Primary   Tate
Lillington   Fairley   School   Britain
Gardens   Douglas St   House Sch   Cureton
Estate   Carey Place
River   The London
Hea   ity   Institute
Pimlico   530
A   B   C
VAUXHALL   MILLBANK
BESSBOROUGH

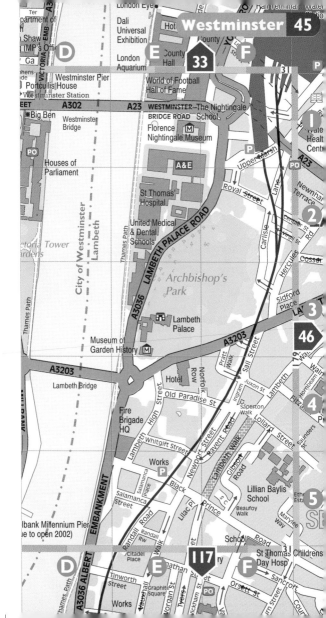

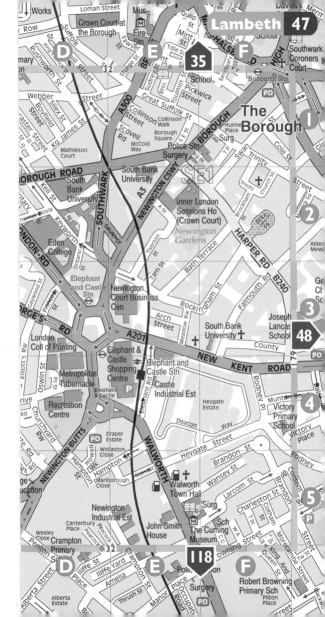

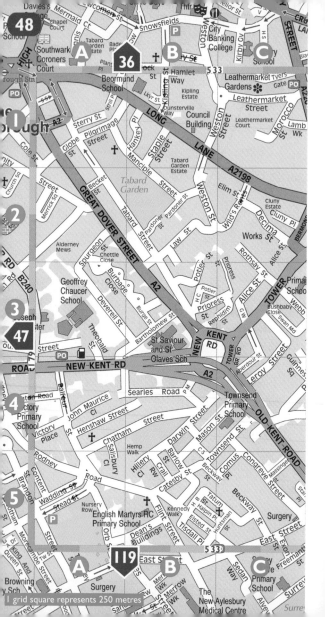

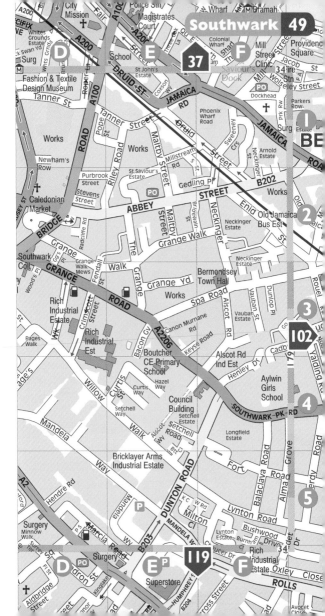

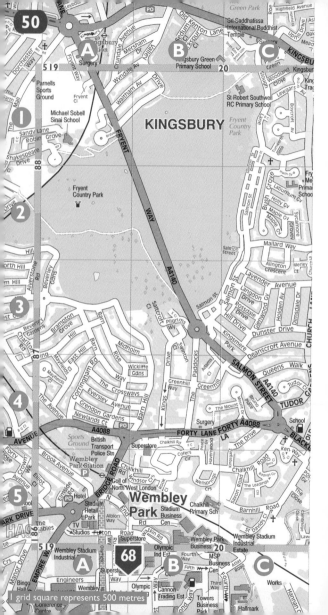

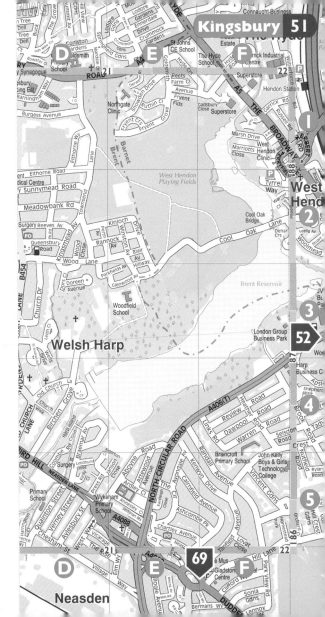

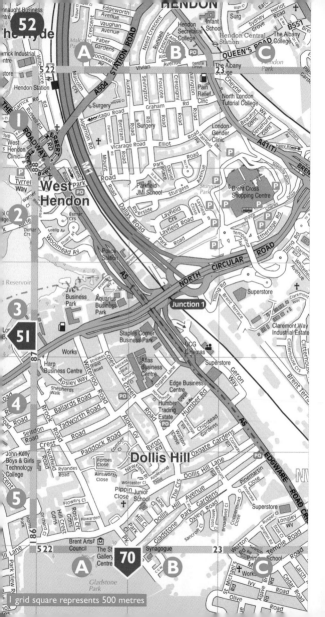

I grid square represents 500 metres

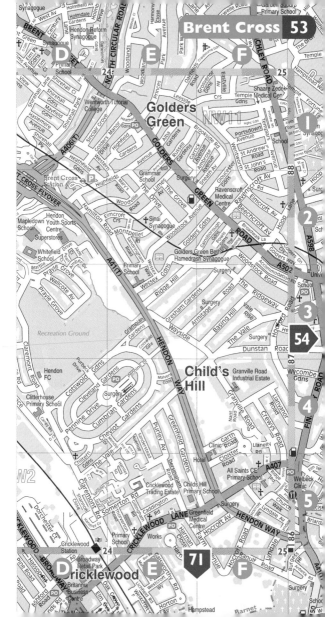

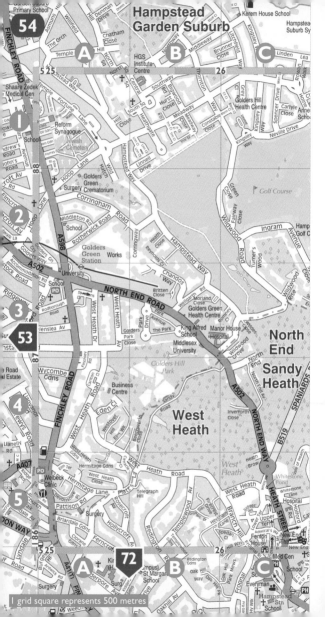

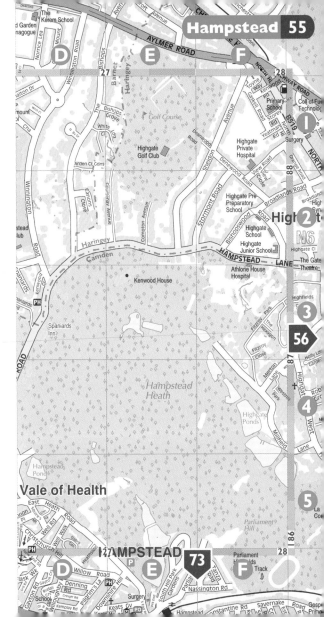

The Kerem School

d Garden
nagogue

AYLMER ROAD

D Mount

E

F

27

Norrice Lea

Wildwood Road

Bishops Avenue, The

Barnet

Haringey

Golf Course

Highgate
Golf Club

White
Cl

The Bishops Grove

Arden Ct Gdns

Winnington Road

Courtenay Avenue

Eatons Close

Compton Avenue

Deansway
Road

Sheldon
Road

Denewood Road

View Road

Towne
Kenwood
Highgate
Primary
School

Coll of Fuel
Technology

Storey

yeatman

Surgery

I

NORTH HILL

HIGHWAY ROAD

28

Grange Road

B519

NORTH

88

Highgate
Private
Hospital

Highgate Pre-
Preparatory
School

Broadlands Road

Highgate

High
Syn

N6

2

stead
Club

Winnington
Road

Haringey

Camden

Spaniards
Road

Kenwood

PH

Spaniards
Inn

Kenwood House

Bishopswood
Road

Stormont Road

Highgate
School

Highgate
Junior School

HAMPSTEAD LANE

Highgate Cl

The Gate
Theatre

Athlone House
Hospital

Highgate

Sheldon
Road

Fitzroy Park

The
Elms

Highfields
G

3

Fitzroy
Close

56

Holly Lde

Garden

87

Highgate Road

West

4

Merton
Lane

Westhill
Park

Millfield Lane

Hampstead
Heath

Highgate
Ponds

WEST

HILL

Hampstead
Pond

Vale of Health

East
Heath
Road

Well Rd

Well Walk

Christchurch Hill

PH

Spaniards
Road

86

5

La
Co

Parliament
Hill

28

Gayton Rd

Flask Wk

Cayton

PH

School

Denning

Pilgrim's La

Willoughby

Kemplay Rd

D Willow Road

Downshire Hill

Keats Gv

Surgery

PO

Gainsborough Gdns

HAMPSTEAD

P

E

South Hill Park

South Hill Park Gardens

Tanza

Parliament

73

Nassington Rd

Parliament
Hill Fields
Track

F

Constantine Rd

Savernake Road

Gosp
Prime

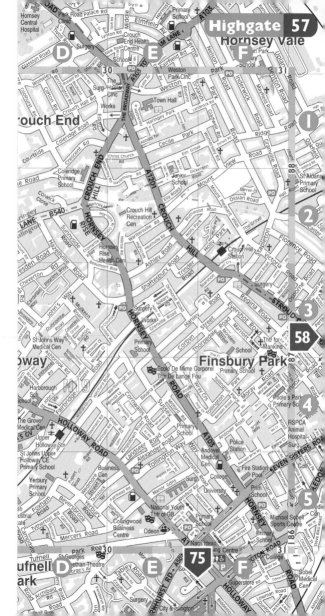

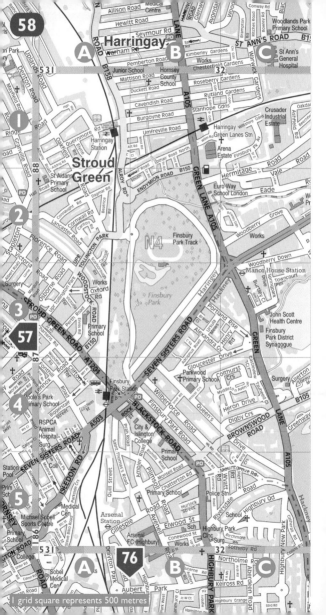

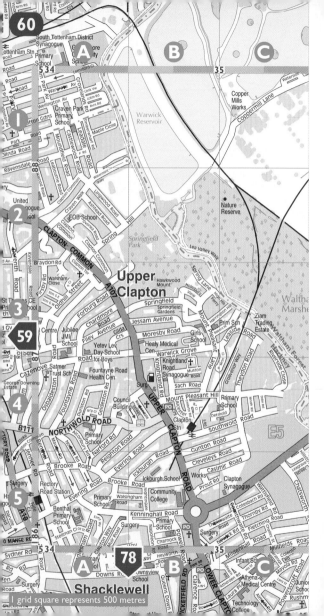

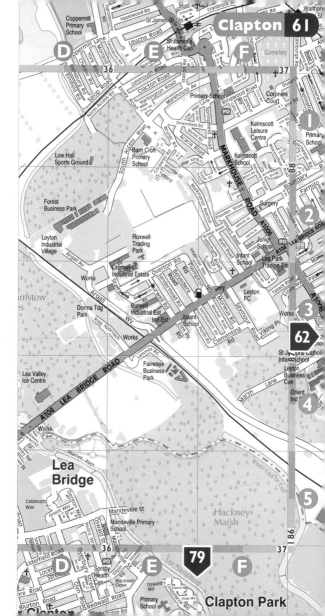

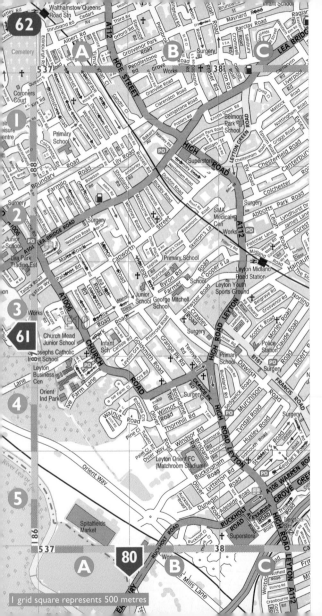

I grid square represents 500 metres

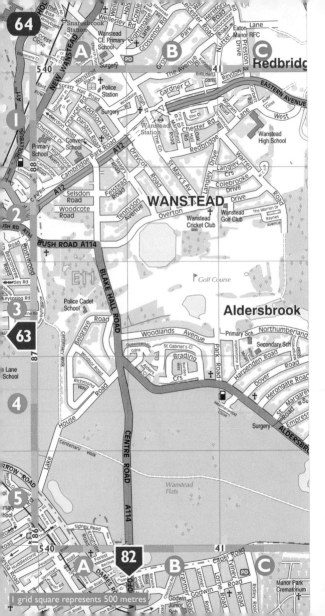

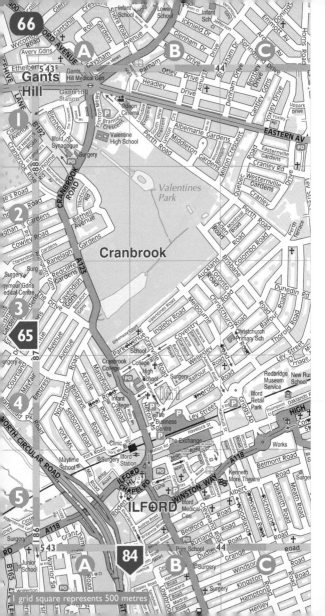

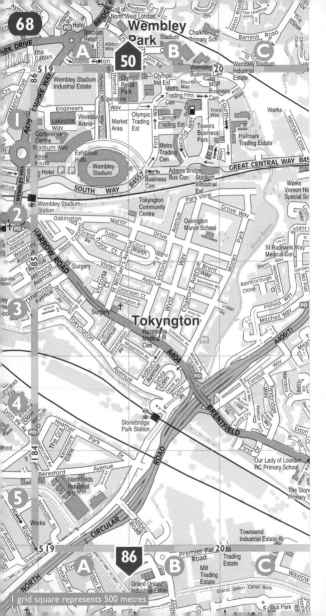

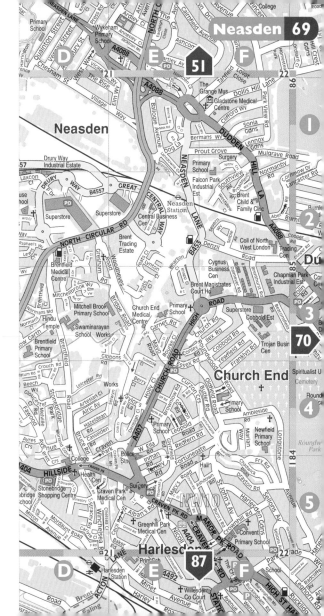

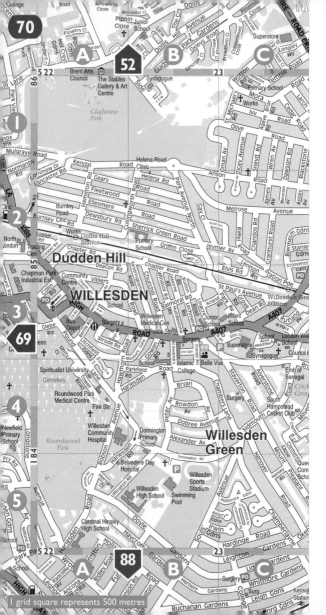
I grid square represents 500 metres

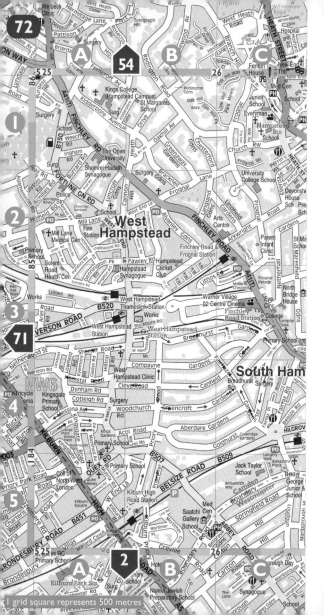

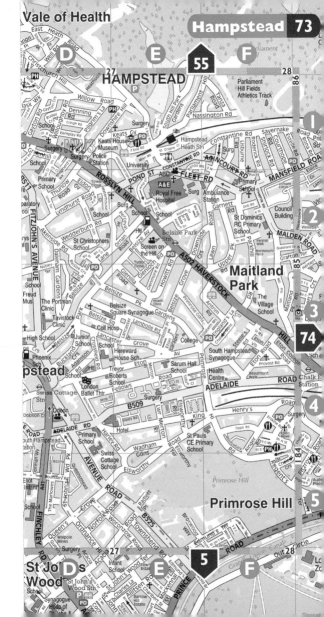

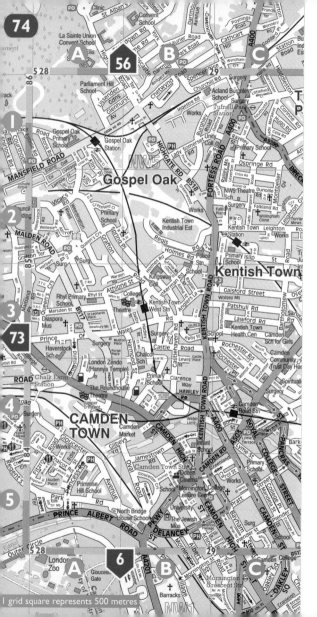

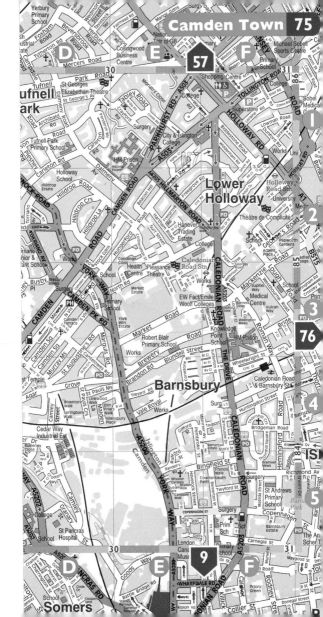

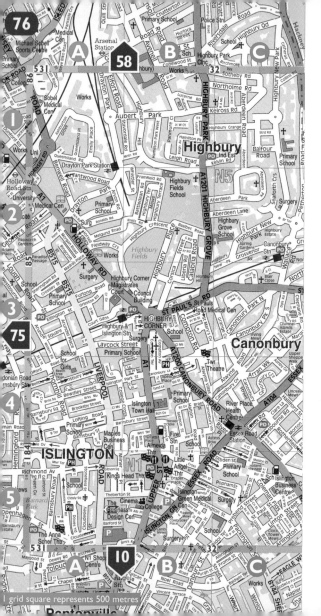

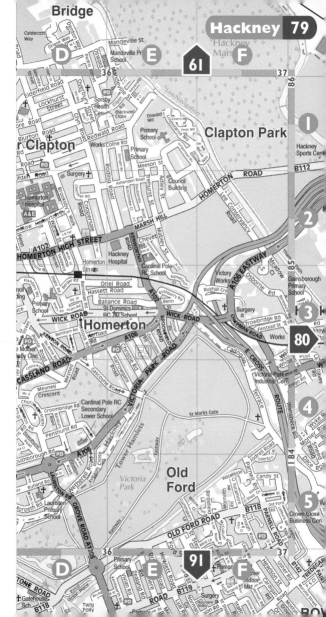

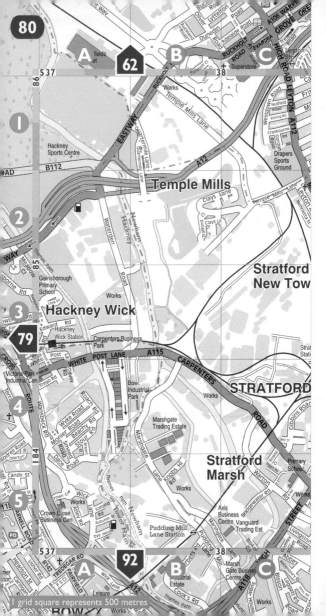

I grid square represents 500 metres

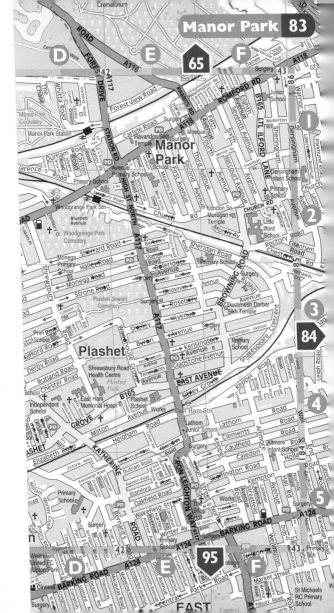

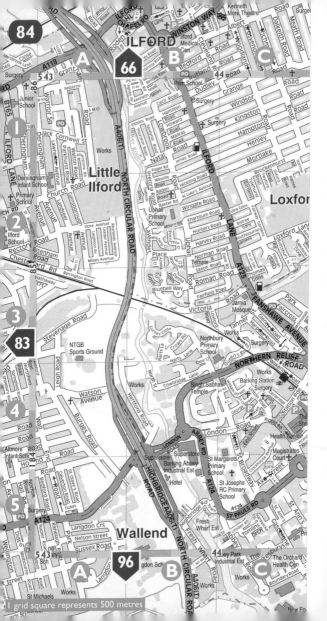

I grid square represents 500 metres

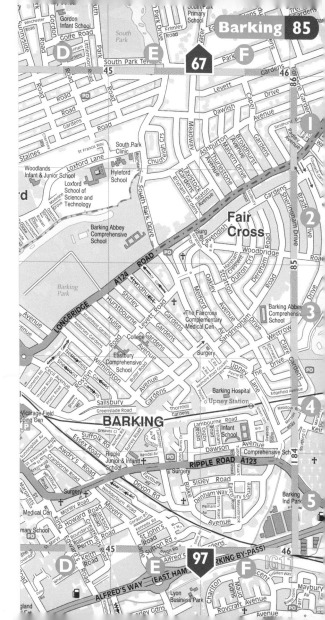

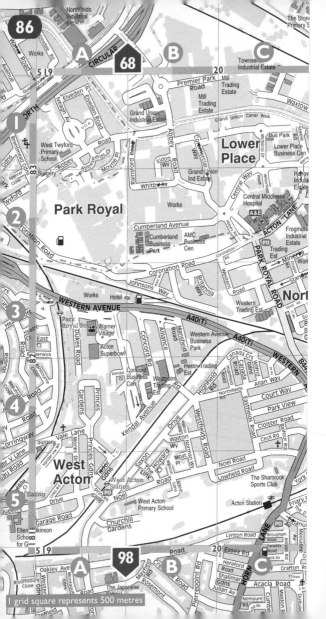

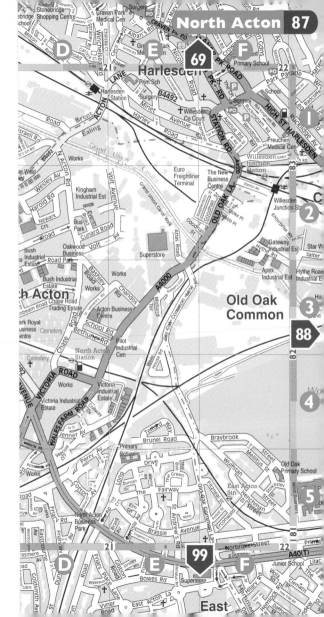

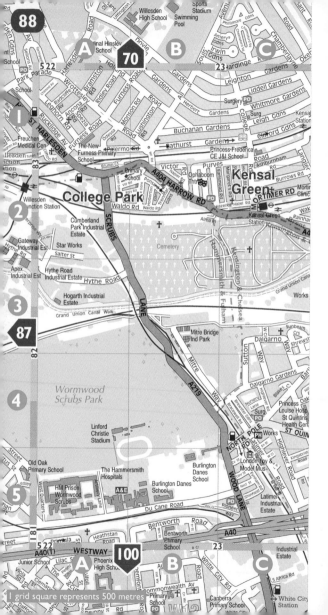

I grid square represents 500 metres

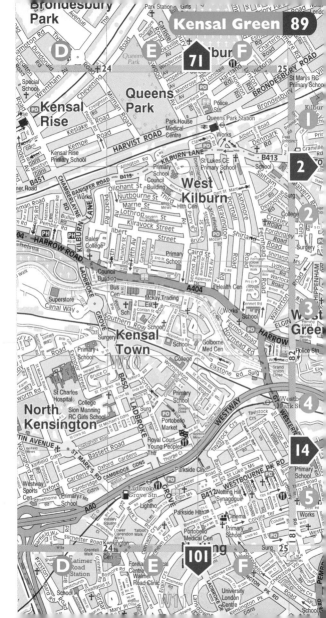

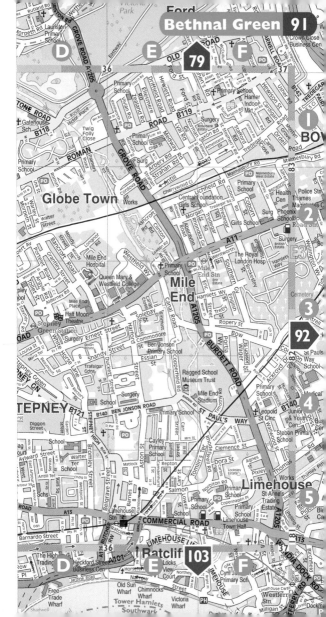

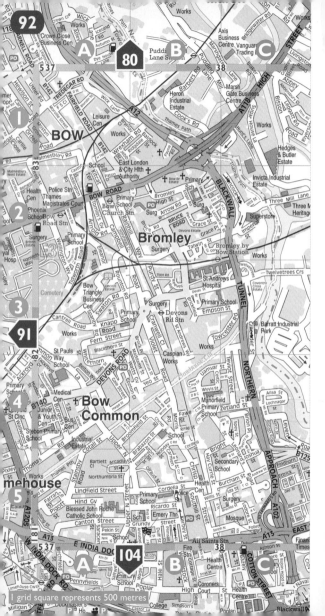

1 grid square represents 500 metres

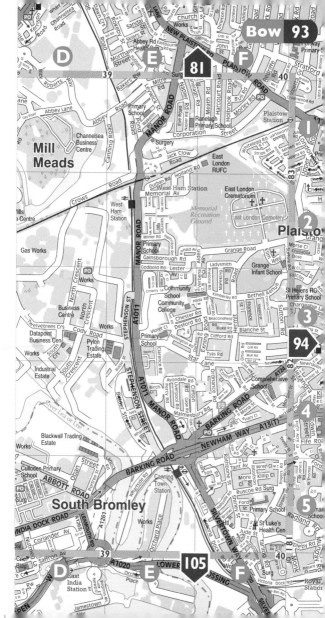

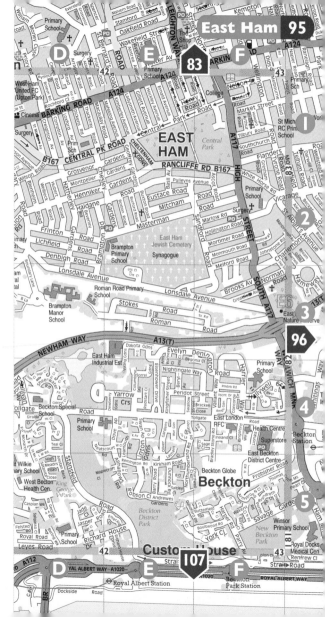

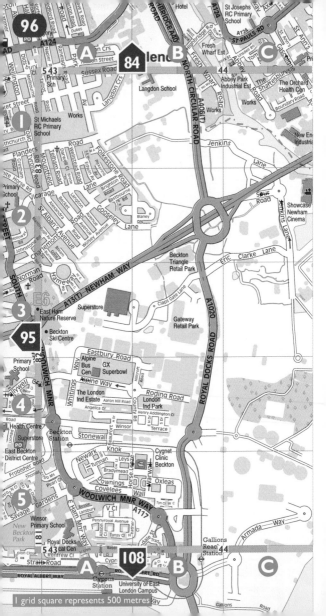

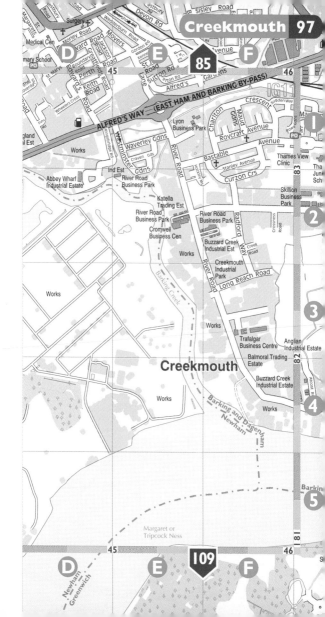

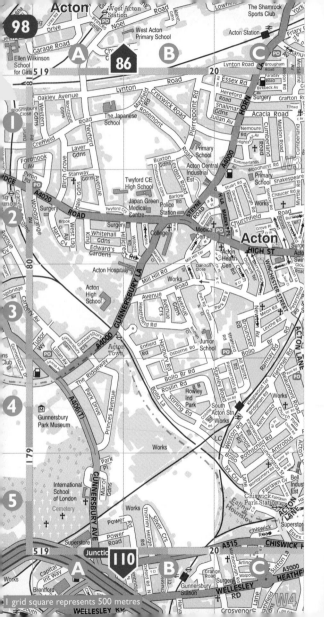

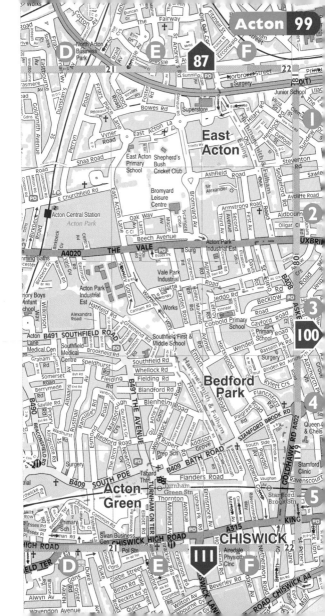

grid square represents 500 metres

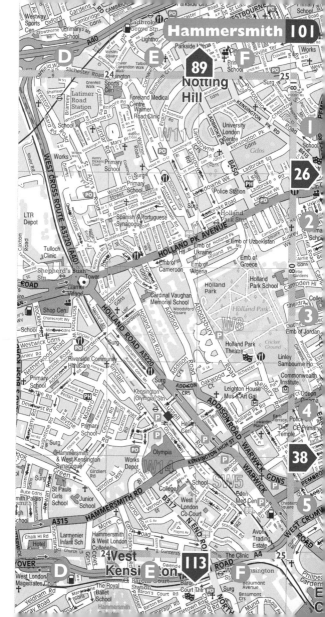

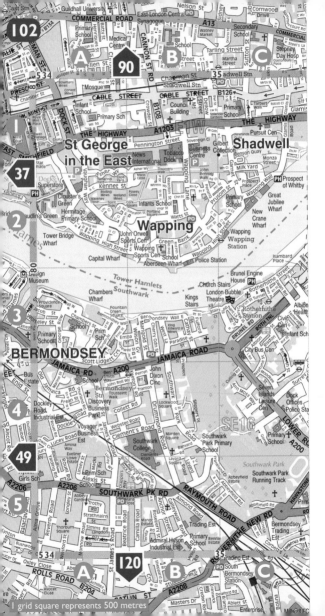

91

Ratcliff

I

2

104

WESTFERR

3

4

5

121

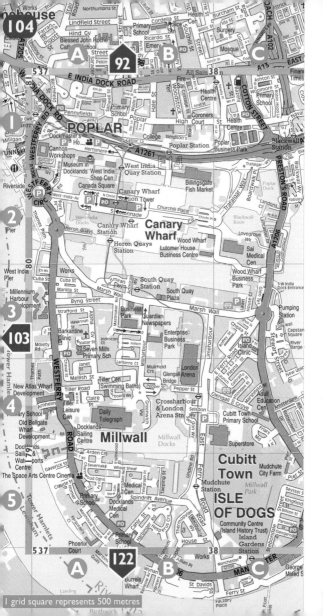

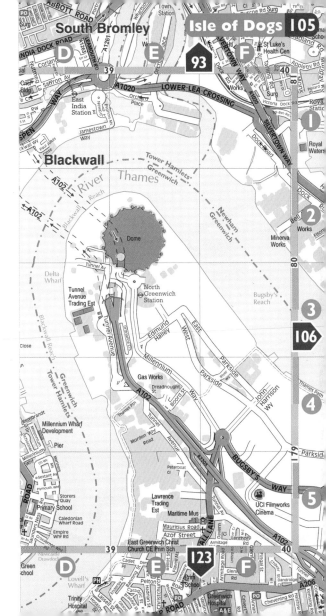

ABBOTT ROAD

Town Station

Buscoe Rd

Surg

Radland

Scho

St Luke's Health Cen

Appleby Rd

D **E** **93** **F**

39

A1261 LEAMOUTH RD

LOWER LEA CROSSING

A1020

East India Station

Orchard Place

Works

Victoria Dock

Surg

Jamestown Way

Blackwall

Tower Hamlets

River Thames

Greenwich

A102

Blackwall Reach

Reach

Newham

Greenwich

Royal Station

Royal Waters

I

Dock Road

Bell

2

Minerva Works

Dome

80

Delta Wharf

Tunnel Avenue Trading Est

North Greenwich Station

Bugsby's Reach

3

106

Blackwall Reach

Tunnel Avenue

Edmund Halley

West Parkside

East Parkside

Thames Path

Close

Millennium Way

John Harrison Wy

4

Gas Works

Dreadnought St

Greenwich Tower Hamlets

A102

Thames Path

Boord St

179

Parksid

Millennium Wharf Development

Pier

Morden Wharf Road

Tunnel Avenue

BUGSBY'S WAY

5

ROAD

Millennium

sextant av

Plymouth whf

Storers Quay

Primary School

Caledonian Wharf Road

Empire Whf Rd

Peterboat Cl

Lawrence Trading Est

Maritime Mus

UCI Filmworks Cinema

A102

40

Green School

Newcastle Drawdock

39

Lovell's Wharf

PH

East Greenwich Christ Church CE Prim Sch

D **E** **123** **F**

Mauritius Road

Azof Street

MILLANE

Armitage Rd

Lenthorp Rd

Glenf St

A206

Trinity Hospital

Greenwich Hospital

A&E

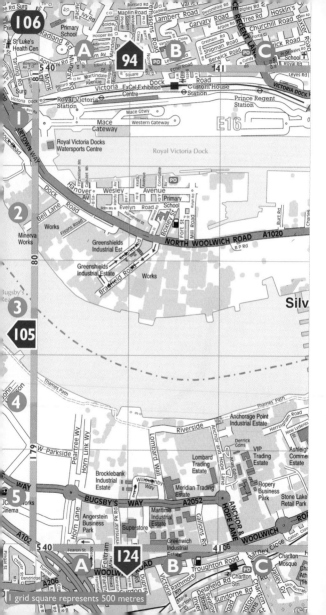

1 grid square represents 500 metres

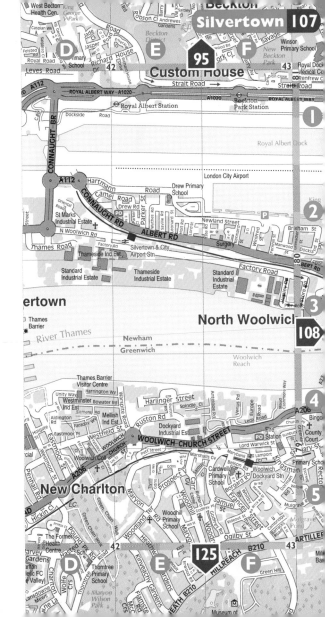

grid square represents 500 metres

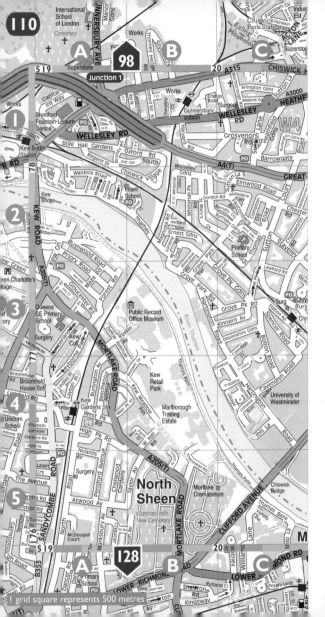

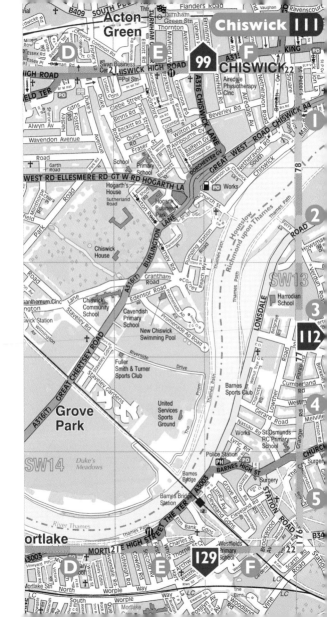

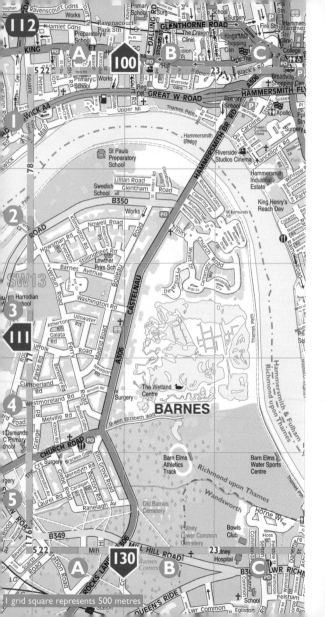

I grid square represents 500 metres

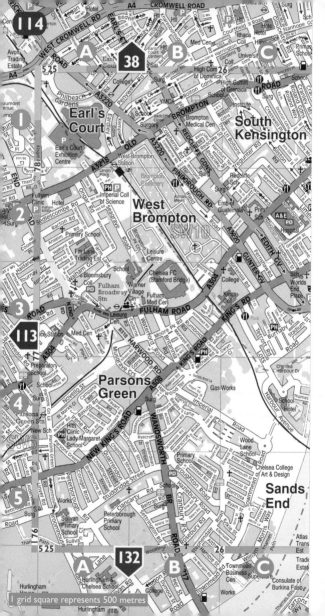

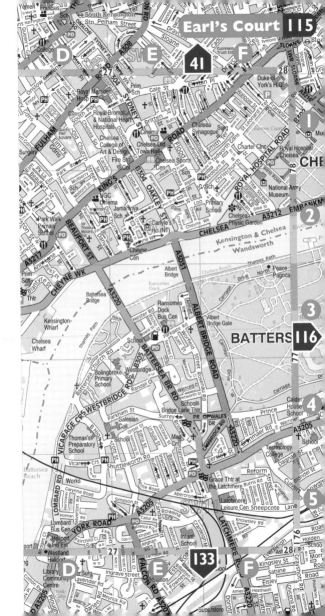

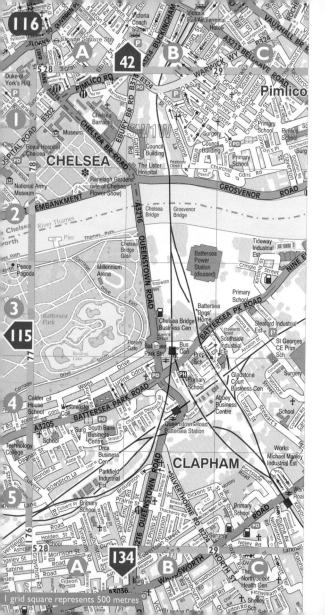

I grid square represents 500 metres

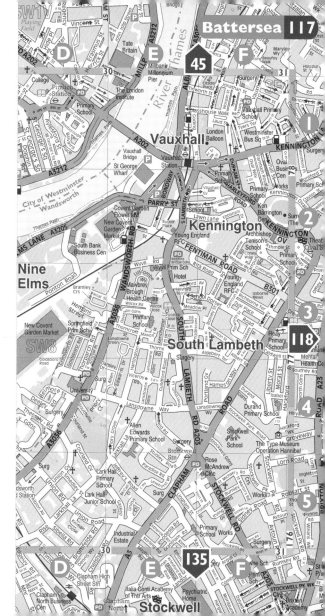

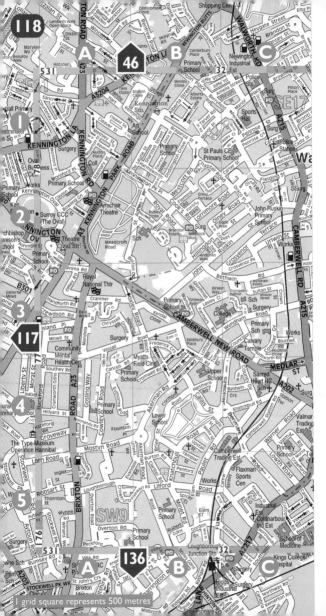

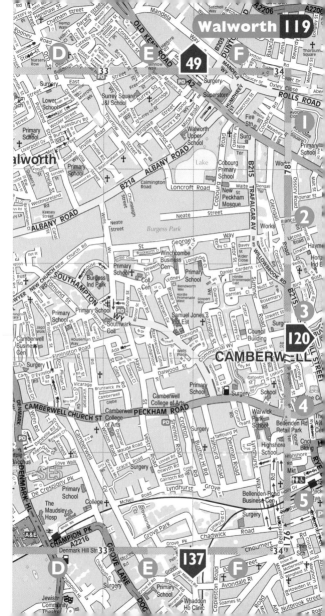

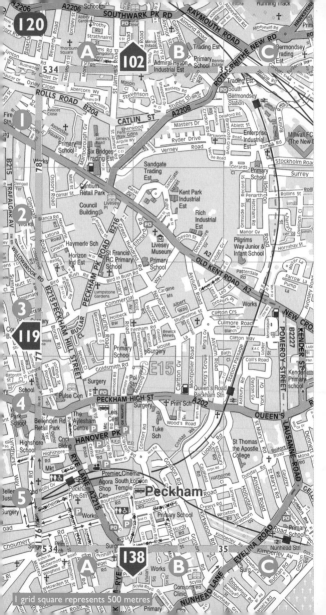

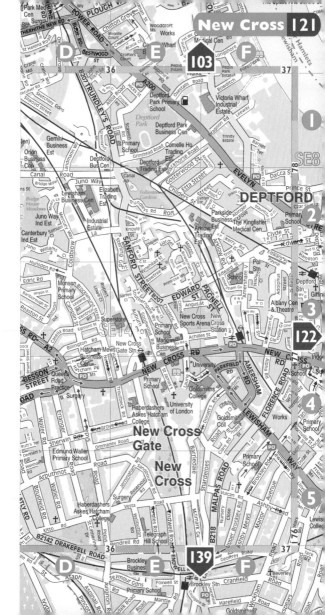

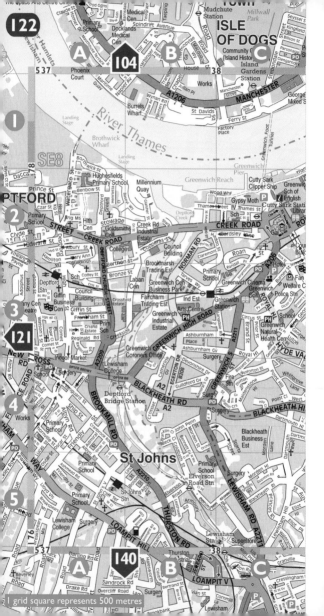

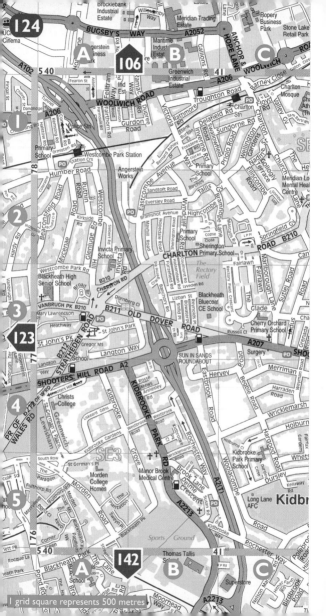

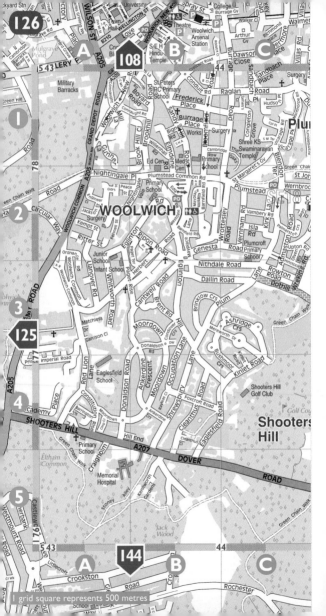

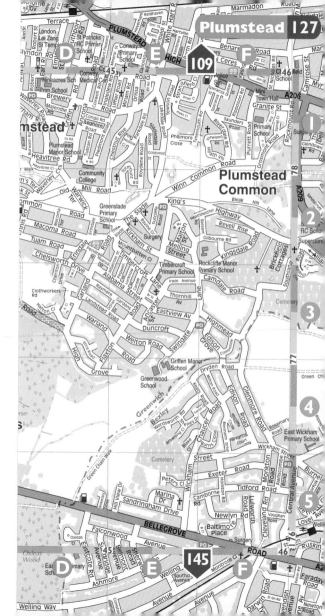

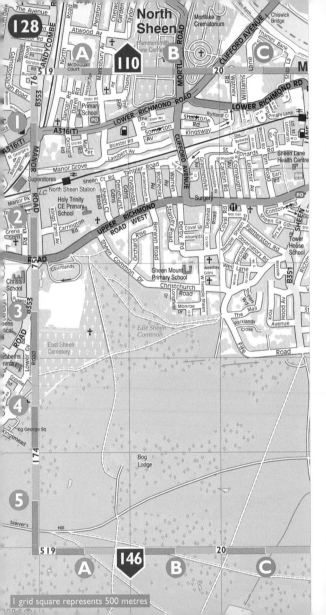

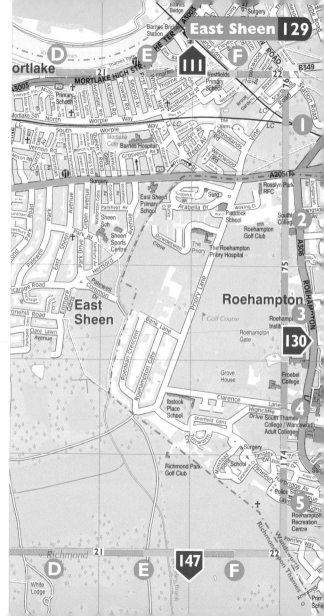

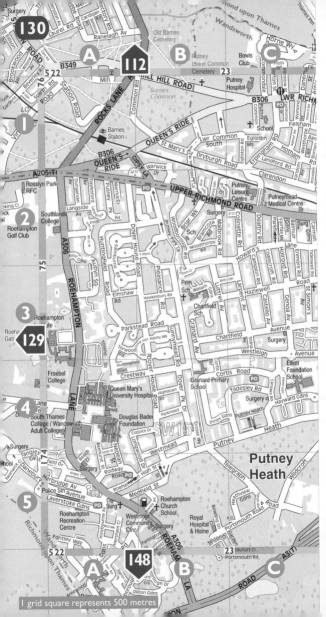

1 grid square represents 500 metres

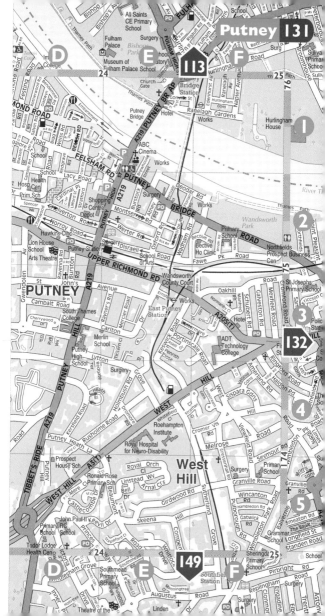

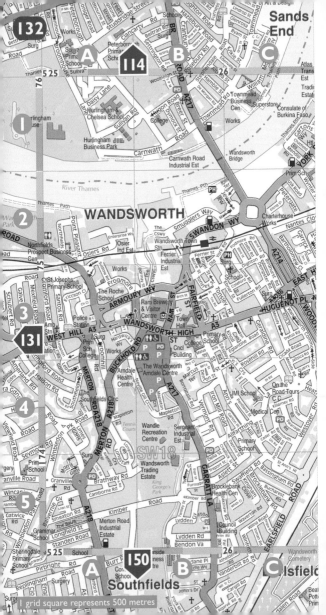

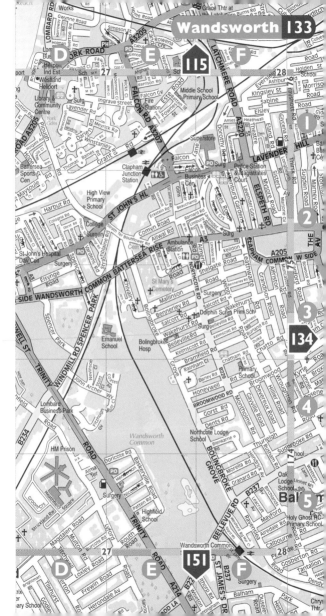

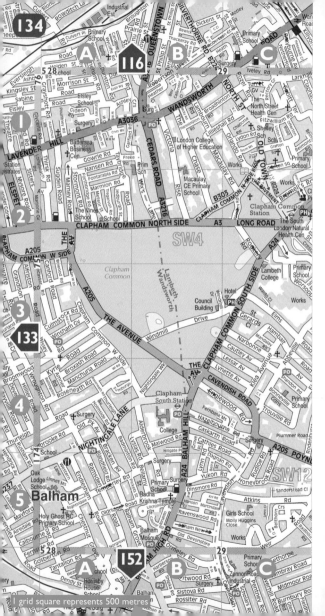

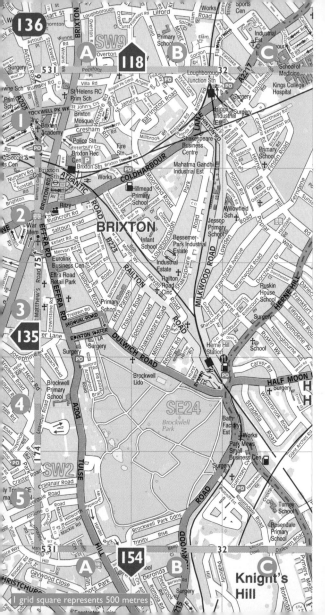

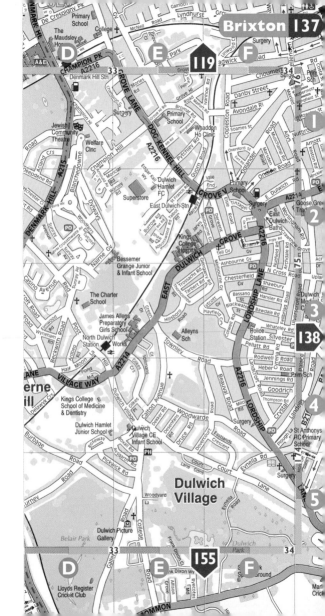

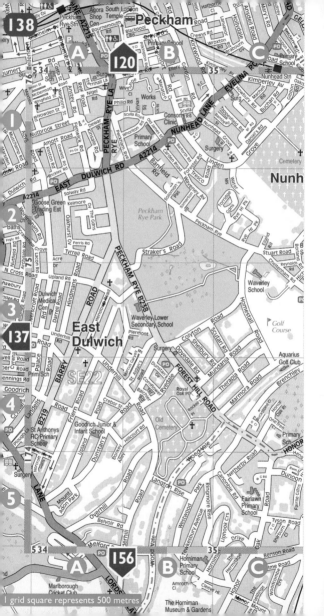

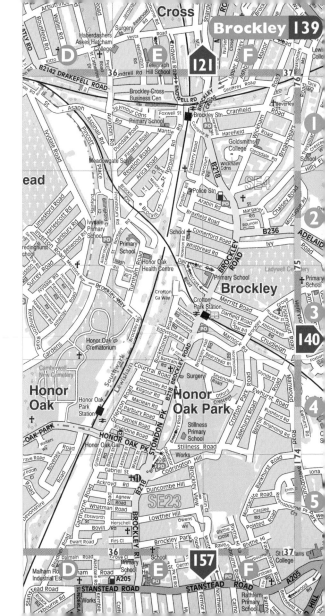

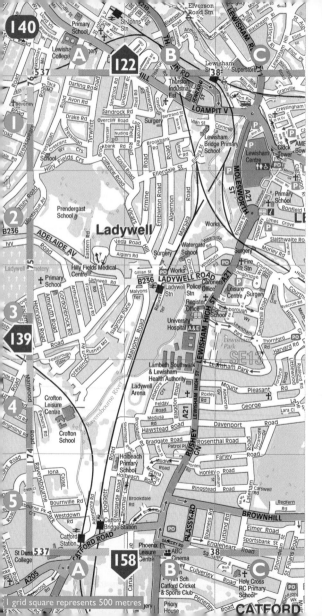

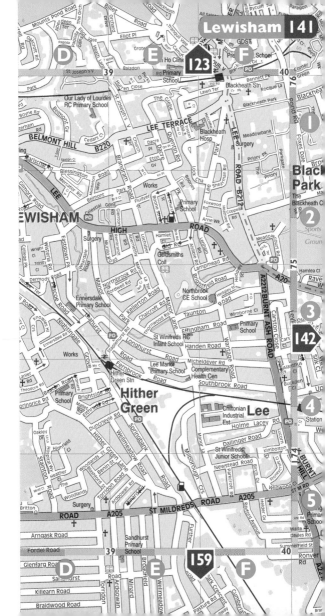

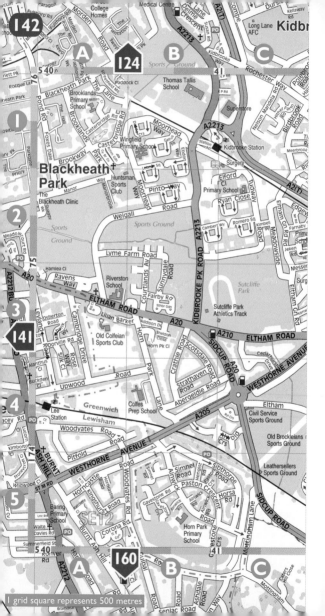

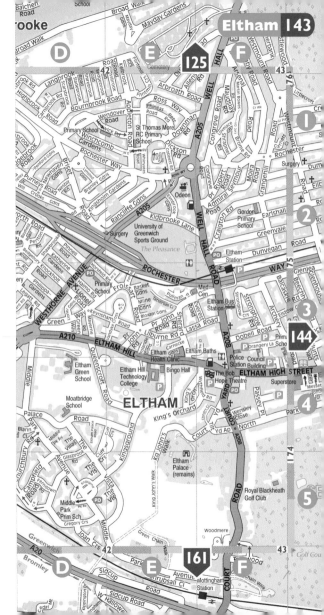

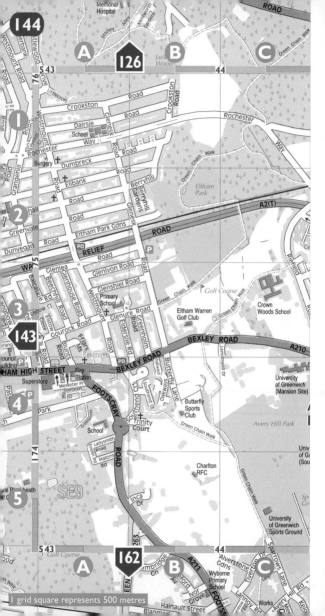

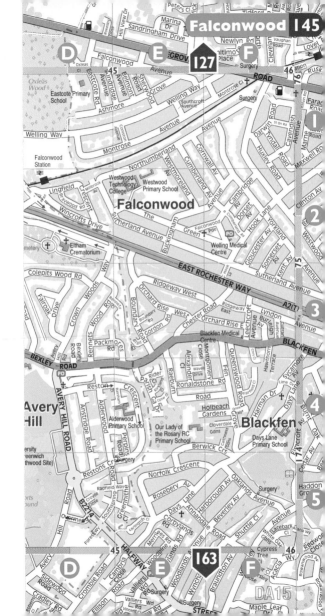

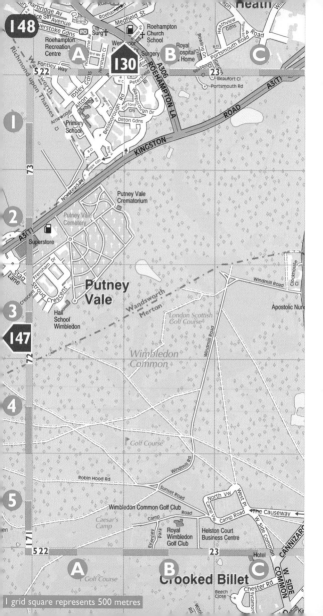

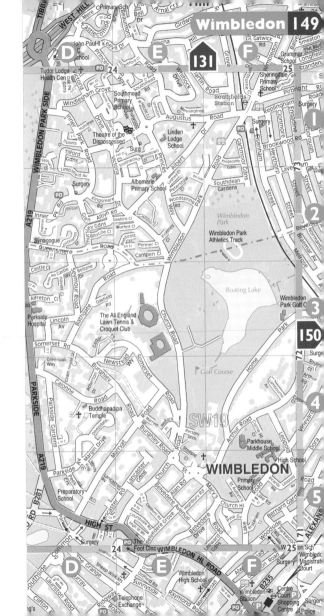

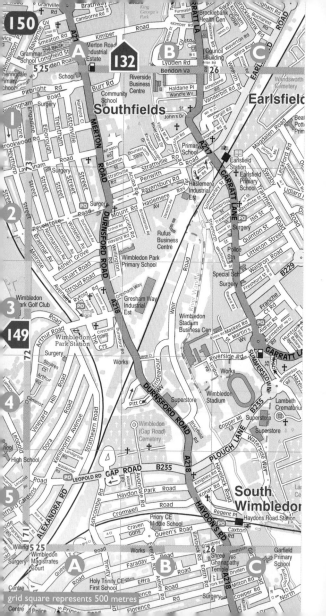

grid square represents 500 metres

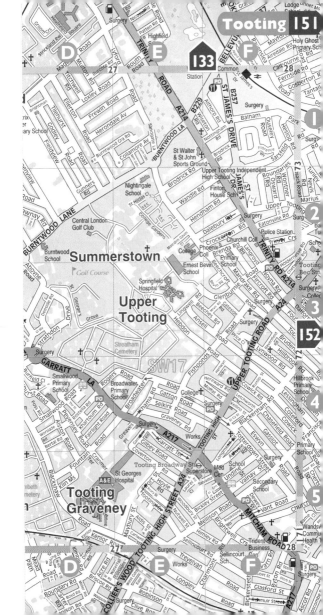

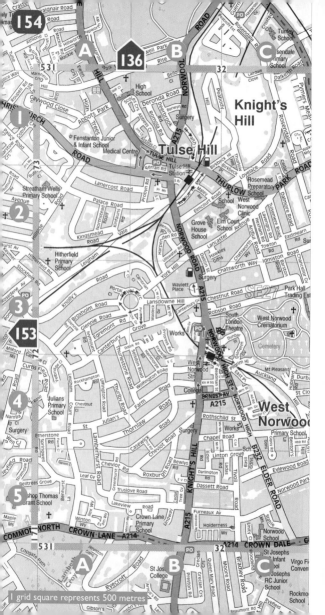

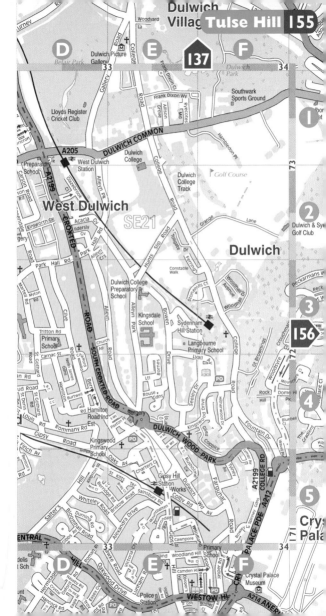

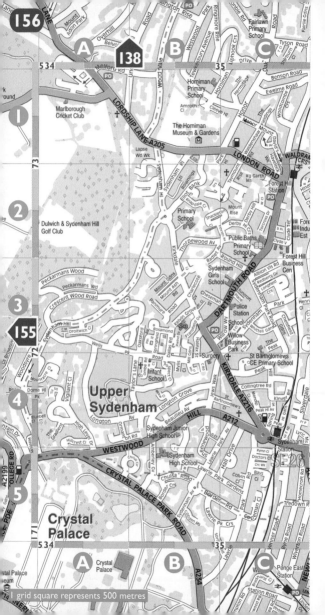

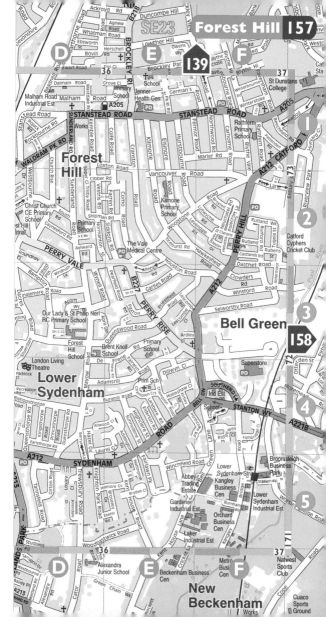

1 grid square represents 500 metres

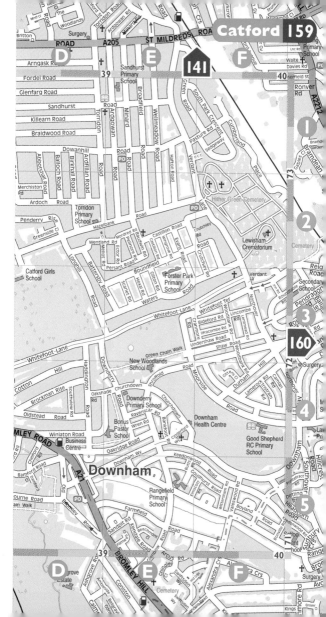

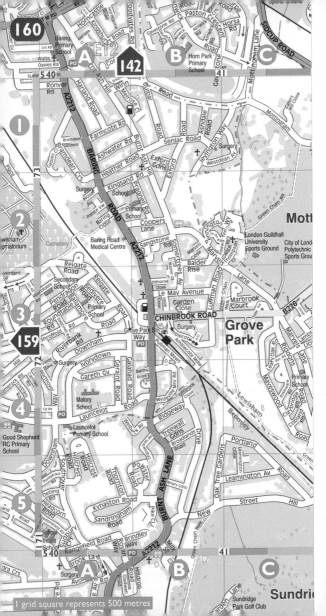

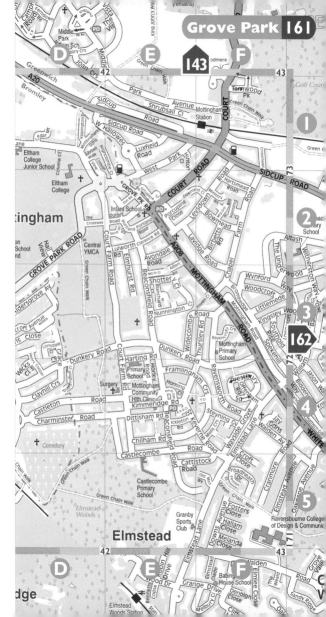

143

162

Elmstead

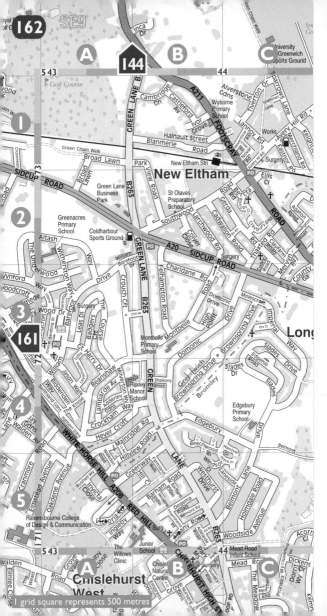

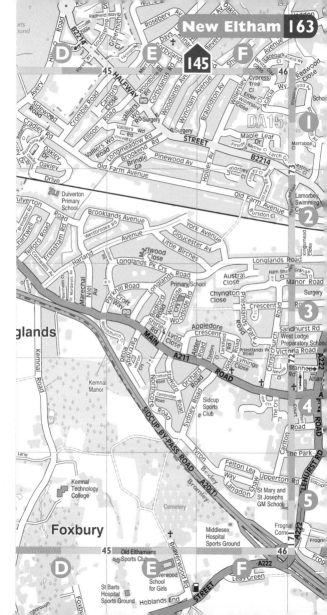

Acton	98 C2
Acton Green	99 D5
Aldersbrook	64 C3
Avery Hill	144 C4
Balham	133 F5
Barking	85 D4
Barnes	112 B4
Barnsbury	75 E4
Battersea	115 F3
Bayswater	27 D1
Beckton	95 F5
Bedford Park	99 F4
Belgravia	42 A4
Bell Green	157 F3
Bellingham	158 A4
Bermondsey	102 A3
Bethnal Green	90 B2
Blackfen	145 F4
Blackheath	123 F5
Blackheath Park	142 A2
Blackwall	105 D1
Bloomsbury	20 B2
The Borough	47 F1
Bow	92 A1
Bow Common	92 A4
Brixton	136 A2
Brockley	139 F3
Bromley	92 B2
Brompton	40 C3
Brondesbury	71 E3
Brondesbury Park	71 D5
Brook Green	100 C4
Camberwell	119 F4
Camden Town	74 A4
Canary Wharf	104 B2
Canonbury	76 C3
Catford	158 C1
Charlton	125 D1
Chelsea	116 A1
Child's Hill	53 E4
Chiswick	99 F5
Church End	69 F4
City of London	35 D1
Clapham	116 B5
Clapham Park	135 D4
Clapton Park	79 F1
Clerkenwell	10 A5
College Park	88 A2
Cranbrook	66 A2
Creekmouth	97 E4
Cricklewood	71 D1
Crouch End	56 C1
Crystal Palace	156 A5
Cubitt Town	104 C5
Custom House	107 E1
Dalston	77 F4
Dartmouth Park	56 A4
De Beauvoir Town	77 E5
Deptford	121 F2
Dollis Hill	52 B5
Downham	159 D5
Dudden Hill	70 A2
Dulwich	155 F2
Dulwich Village	137 E5
Earl's Court	38 A5
Earlsfield	150 C1
East Acton	99 E1
East Dulwich	138 A3
East Ham	95 E1
East Sheen	129 D3
Elmstead	161 E5
Eltham	143 E4
Fair Cross	85 F2
Falconwood	145 E2
Finsbury	10 A3

Finsbury Park	57 F4
Forest Gate	82 A2
Forest Hill	157 D1
Foxbury	163 D5
Fulham	113 D3
Furzedown	152 B4
Gants Hill	65 F1
Globe Town	91 D2
Golders Green	53 E1
Gospel Oak	74 A2
Greenwich	123 D1
Grove Park	111 D4
Grove Park	160 C3
Hackney	78 C3
Hackney Wick	80 A3
Haggerston	13 F1
Hammersmith	100 B5
Hampstead	73 D1
Harlesden	87 E1
Herne Hill	136 C4
Highbury	76 B1
Highgate	55 F2
Hither Green	141 E4
Holborn	21 E3
Homerton	79 D3
Honor Oak	139 D4
Honor Oak Park	139 E4
Hoxton	12 C2
Ilford	66 A5
Isle of Dogs	104 C5
Islington	76 A5
Kennington	117 E2
Kensal Green	88 C2
Kensal Rise	89 D1
Kensal Town	89 E3
Kensington	38 C3
Kentish Town	74 C3
Kidbrooke	124 C5
Kilburn	71 E5
Kingsbury	50 B1
Kingsland	77 E4
Kingston Vale	147 D5
Knightsbridge	29 D5
Knight's Hill	154 C1
Ladywell	140 A2
Lambeth	46 A2
Lea Bridge	61 D5
Lee	141 F4
Lewisham	140 C2
Leyton	63 D5
Leytonstone	63 F3
Limehouse	91 F5
Lisson Grove	17 F2
Little Ilford	84 A2
Longlands	162 C3
Lower Clapton	78 C1
Lower Holloway	75 F2
Lower Place	86 C1
Lower Sydenham	157 D4
Loxford	84 C2
Maida Vale	2 C3
Maitland Park	73 F3
Manor Park	83 E1
Marylebone	18 A3
Mayfair	30 C2
Mile End	91 E3
Mill Meads	93 D1
Millwall	104 A4
Mortlake	110 C5
Mottingham	160 C2
Neasden	69 D1
Newbury Park	67 D1
New Charlton	107 D5
New Cross	121 E5
New Cross Gate	121 E4

New Eltham 162 B2
Newington 46 B3
Nine Elms 117 D3
North Acton 86 C3
North End 54 C3
North Kensington 89 D4
North Sheen 110 B5
North Woolwich 107 E3
Notting Hill 101 E1
Nunhead 138 C2
Old Ford 79 E5
Old Oak Common 87 F3
Paddington 16 A3
Park Royal 86 A2
Parsons Green 114 A4
Peckham 120 B5
Pentonville 9 F1
Pimlico 116 C1
Plaistow 93 F2
Plashet 83 D3
Plumstead 126 C1
Plumstead Common 127 F2
Poplar 104 A1
Primrose Hill 73 F5
Putney 131 D3
Putney Heath 130 C5
Putney Vale 148 A3
Queens Park 89 E1
Ratcliff 103 E1
Regent's Park 7 D2
Roehampton 129 F3
Rotherhithe 103 D4
St George in the East 102 A1
St Giles 20 B4
St James 32 A4
St Johns 122 A5
St Luke's 11 F5
St Pancras 9 D4
Sands End 114 C5
Sandy Heath 54 C4
Seven Kings 67 E3
Shacklewell 78 A1
Shadwell 102 C1
Shepherd's Bush 100 B2
Shooters Hill 126 C4
Shoreditch 12 B4
Silvertown 106 C3
Soho 20 A5
Somers Town 8 A2
South Bromley 93 D5
Southend 158 C4
Southfields 150 A1
South Hackney 78 C5
South Hampstead 72 C4
South Kensington 39 E5

South Lambeth 117 E3
South Wimbledon 150 C5
Spitalfields 25 E2
Stamford Hill 59 F2
Stepney 90 C4
Stockwell 135 C1
Stoke Newington 59 F4
Strand 33 D1
Stratford 80 C4
Stratford Marsh 80 B5
Stratford New Town 80 C3
Streatham 153 E5
Streatham Hill 153 E1
Streatham Park 152 B4
Stroud Green 58 A1
Summerstown 151 D2
Temple Mills 80 B2
Thamesmead 109 F2
Tokyngton 68 B3
Tooting Graveney 151 D5
Tufnell Park 74 C1
Tulse Hill 154 B1
Upper Clapton 60 A3
Upper Holloway 56 C4
Upper Sydenham 156 A4
Upper Tooting 151 E3
Upton 82 B4
Upton Park 82 C5
Vale of Health 55 D5
Vauxhall 117 E1
Walham Green 113 F2
Wallend 84 A5
Walworth 118 C1
Wandsworth 132 A2
Wanstead 64 B2
Wapping 102 B2
Welsh Harp 51 D3
Wembley Park 50 A5
West Acton 86 A5
West Brompton 114 B2
West Dulwich 155 D2
West Hampstead 72 A2
West Heath 54 B4
West Hendon 52 A2
West Hill 131 E5
West Kensington 113 D1
West Kilburn 89 E2
Westminster 43 F3
West Norwood 154 C4
Whitechapel 37 F1
Willesden 70 A3
Willesden Green 70 B4
Wimbledon 149 E5
Woolwich 126 A2

USING THE STREET INDEX

Street names are listed alphabetically. Each street name is followed by its postal town or area locality, the Postcode District, the page number, and the reference to the square in which the name is found.

Standard index entries are shown as follows:

Aaron Hill Rd *EHAM* E6 ....**96** A4

Street names and selected addresses not shown on the map due to scale restrictions are shown in the index with an asterisk:

Abbeville Ms *CLAP* * SW4 ....**135** D3

GENERAL ABBREVIATIONS

ACC	ACCESS
ALY	ALLEY
AP	APPROACH
AR	ARCADE
ASS	ASSOCIATION
AV	AVENUE
BCH	BEACH
BLDS	BUILDINGS
BND	BEND
BNK	BANK
BR	BRIDGE
BRK	BROOK
BTM	BOTTOM
BUS	BUSINESS
BVD	BOULEVARD
BY	BYPASS
CATH	CATHEDRAL
CEM	CEMETERY
CEN	CENTRE
CFT	CROFT
CH	CHURCH
CHA	CHASE
CHYD	CHURCHYARD
CIR	CIRCLE
CIRC	CIRCUS
CL	CLOSE
CLFS	CLIFFS
CMP	CAMP
CNR	CORNER
CO	COUNTY
COLL	COLLEGE
COM	COMMON
COMM	COMMISSION
CON	CONVENT
COT	COTTAGE
COTS	COTTAGES
CP	CAPE
CPS	COPSE
CR	CREEK
CREM	CREMATORIUM
CRS	CRESCENT
CSWY	CAUSEWAY
CT	COURT
CTRL	CENTRAL
CTS	COURTS
CTYD	COURTYARD
CUTT	CUTTINGS
CV	COVE
CYN	CANYON
DEPT	DEPARTMENT
DL	DALE
DM	DAM
DR	DRIVE
DRO	DROVE
DRY	DRIVEWAY
DWGS	DWELLINGS
E	EAST
EMB	EMBANKMENT
EMBY	EMBASSY
ESP	ESPLANADE
EST	ESTATE
EX	EXCHANGE
EXPY	EXPRESSWAY
EXT	EXTENSION
F/O	FLYOVER
FC	FOOTBALL CLUB
FK	FORK
FLD	FIELD
FLDS	FIELDS
FLS	FALLS
FLS	FLATS
FM	FARM
FT	FORT
FWY	FREEWAY
FY	FERRY
GA	GATE
GAL	GALLERY
GDN	GARDEN
GDNS	GARDENS
GLD	GLADE
GLN	GLEN
GN	GREEN
GND	GROUND
GRA	GRANGE
GRG	GARAGE
GT	GREAT
GTWY	GATEWAY
GV	GROVE
HGR	HIGHER
HL	HILL
HLS	HILLS
HO	HOUSE
HOL	HOLLOW
HOSP	HOSPITAL
HRB	HARBOUR
HTH	HEATH
HTS	HEIGHTS
HVN	HAVEN
HWY	HIGHWAY
IMP	IMPERIAL
IN	INLET
IND EST	INDUSTRIAL ESTATE
INF	INFIRMARY
INFO	INFORMATION
INT	INTERCHANGE
IS	ISLAND
JCT	JUNCTION
JTY	JETTY
KG	KING
KNL	KNOLL
L	LAKE
LA	LANE
LDG	LODGE
LGT	LIGHT
LK	LOCK
LKS	LAKES
LNDG	LANDING
LTL	LITTLE
LWR	LOWER
MAG	MAGISTRATE
MAN	MANSIONS
MD	MEAD
MDW	MEADOWS
MEM	MEMORIAL
MKT	MARKET
MKTS	MARKETS
ML	MALL
ML	MILL
MNR	MANOR
MS	MEWS
MSN	MISSION
MT	MOUNT
MTN	MOUNTAIN
MTS	MOUNTAINS
MUS	MUSEUM
MWY	MOTORWAY
N	NORTH
NE	NORTH EAST
NW	NORTH WEST
O/P	OVERPASS
OFF	OFFICE
ORCH	ORCHARD

OV	OVAL
PAL	PALACE
PAS	PASSAGE
PAV	PAVILION
PDE	PARADE
PH	PUBLIC HOUSE
PK	PARK
PKWY	PARKWAY
PL	PLACE
PLN	PLAIN
PLNS	PLAINS
PLZ	PLAZA
POL	POLICE STATION
PR	PRINCE
PREC	PRECINCT
PREP	PREPARATORY
PRIM	PRIMARY
PROM	PROMENADE
PRS	PRINCESS
PRT	PORT
PT	POINT
PTH	PATH
PZ	PIAZZA
QD	QUADRANT
QU	QUEEN
QY	QUAY
R	RIVER
RBT	ROUNDABOUT
RD	ROAD
RDG	RIDGE
REP	REPUBLIC
RES	RESERVOIR
RFC	RUGBY FOOTBALL CLUB
RI	RISE
RP	RAMP
RW	ROW
S	SOUTH
SCH	SCHOOL
SE	SOUTH EAST
SER	SERVICE AREA
SH	SHORE

SHOP	SHOPPING
SKWY	SKYWAY
SMT	SUMMIT
SOC	SOCIETY
SP	SPUR
SPR	SPRING
SQ	SQUARE
ST	STREET
STN	STATION
STR	STREAM
STRD	STRAND
SW	SOUTH WEST
TDG	TRADING
TER	TERRACE
THWY	THROUGHWAY
TNL	TUNNEL
TOLL	TOLLWAY
TPK	TURNPIKE
TR	TRACK
TRL	TRAIL
TWR	TOWER
U/P	UNDERPASS
UNI	UNIVERSITY
UPR	UPPER
V	VALE
VA	VALLEY
VIAD	VIADUCT
VIL	VILLA
VIS	VISTA
VLG	VILLAGE
VLS	VILLAS
VW	VIEW
W	WEST
WD	WOOD
WHF	WHARF
WK	WALK
WKS	WALKS
WLS	WELLS
WY	WAY
YD	YARD
YHA	YOUTH HOSTEL

POSTCODE TOWNS AND AREA ABBREVIATIONS

ABYW	Abbey Wood
ACT	Acton
ALP/SUD	Alperton/Sudbury
ARCH	Archway
BAL	Balham
BANK	Bank
BARB	Barbican
BARK	Barking
BARN	Barnes
BAY/PAD	Bayswater/Paddington
BECK	Beckenham
BERM/RHTH	Bermondsey/Rotherhithe
BETH	Bethnal Green
BFN/LL	Blackfen/Longlands
BGVA	Belgravia
BKHTH/KID	Blackheath/Kidbrooke
BLKFR	Blackfriars
BMLY	Bromley
BMSBY	Bloomsbury
BOW	Bow
BROCKY	Brockley
BRXN/ST	Brixton north/Stockwell
BRXS/STRHMM	Brixton south/Streatham Hill
BTFD	Brentford
BTSEA	Battersea

CAMTN	Camden Town
CAN/RD	Canning Town/Royal Docks
CANST	Cannon Street station
CAT	Catford
CAVSQ/HST	Cavendish Square/Harley Street
CDALE/KGS	Colindale/Kingsbury
CEND/HSY/T	Crouch End/Hornsey/Turnpike Lane
CHARL	Charlton
CHCR	Charing Cross
CHEL	Chelsea
CHST	Chislehurst
CHSWK	Chiswick
CITYW	City of London west
CLAP	Clapham
CLKNW	Clerkenwell
CLPT	Clapton
CMBW	Camberwell
CONDST	Conduit Street
COVGDN	Covent Garden
CRICK	Cricklewood
DEPT	Deptford
DUL	Dulwich
EA	Ealing
ECT	Earl's Court

EDUL	East Dulwich
EFNCH	East Finchley
EHAM	East Ham
ELTH/MOT	Eltham/Mottingham
EMB	Embankment
FARR	Farringdon
FENCHST	Fenchurch Street
FITZ	Fitzrovia
FLST/FETLN	Fleet Street/Fetter Lane
FSBYE	Finsbury east
FSBYPK	Finsbury Park
FSBYW	Finsbury west
FSTGT	Forest Gate
FSTH	Forest Hill
FUL/PGN	Fulham/Parsons Green
GDMY/SEVK	Goodmayes/Seven Kings
GINN	Gray's Inn
GLDGN	Golders Green
GNTH/NBYPK	Gants Hill/Newbury Park
GNWCH	Greenwich
GTPST	Great Portland Street
GWRST	Gower Street
HACK	Hackney
HAMP	Hampstead
HBRY	Highbury
HCIRC	Holborn Circus
HDN	Hendon
HDTCH	Houndsditch
HGT	Highgate
HHOL	High Holborn
HMSMTH	Hammersmith
HNHL	Herne Hill
HOL/ALD	Holborn/Aldwych
HOLWY	Holloway
HOM	Homerton
IL	Ilford
IS	Islington
KENS	Kensington
KIL/WHAMP	Kilburn/West Hampstead
KTBR	Knightsbridge
KTN/HRWW/WS	Kenton/Harrow Weald/Wealdstone
KTTN	Kentish Town
KUTN/CMB	Kingston upon Thames north/Coombe
LBTH	Lambeth
LEE/GVPK	Lee/Grove Park
LEW	Lewisham
LEY	Leyton
LINN	Lincoln's Inn
LOTH	Lothbury
LSQ/SEVD	Leicester Square/Seven Dials
LVPST	Liverpool Street
MANHO	Mansion House
MBLAR	Marble Arch
MHST	Marylebone High Street
MNPK	Manor Park
MON	Monument
MORT/ESHN	Mortlake/East Sheen
MUSWH	Muswell Hill
MV/WKIL	Maida Vale/West Kilburn
MYFR/PICC	Mayfair/Piccadilly

MYFR/PKLN	Mayfair/Park Lane
NKENS	North Kensington
NOXST/BSQ	New Oxford Street/Bloomsbury Square
NRWD	Norwood
NTGHL	Notting Hill
NWCR	New Cross
OBST	Old Broad Street
OXSTW	Oxford Street west
PECK	Peckham
PIM	Pimlico
PLSTW	Plaistow
POP/IOD	Poplar/Isle of Dogs
PUT/ROE	Putney/Roehampton
RCH/KEW	Richmond/Kew
RCHPK/HAM	Richmond Park/Ham
REDBR	Redbridge
REGST	Regent Street
RSQ	Russell Square
RYNPK	Raynes Park
SCUP	Sidcup
SDTCH	Shoreditch
SEVS/STOTM	Seven Sisters/South Tottenham
SHB	Shepherd's Bush
SKENS	South Kensington
SOHO/CST	Soho/Carnaby Street
SOHO/SHAV	Soho/Shaftesbury Avenue
SRTFD	Stratford
STBT	St Bart's
STHWK	Southwark
STJS	St James's
STJSPK	St James's Park
STJWD	St John's Wood
STLK	St Luke's
STNW/STAM	Stoke Newington/Stamford Hill
STP	St Paul's
STPAN	St Pancras
STRHM/NOR	Streatham/Norbury
SYD	Sydenham
THMD	Thamesmead
TOOT	Tooting
TPL/STR	Temple/Strand
TWRH	Tower Hill
VX/NE	Vauxhall/Nine Elms
WALTH	Walthamstow
WALW	Walworth
WAN	Wanstead
WAND/EARL	Wandsworth/Earlsfield
WAP	Wapping
WBLY	Wembley
WBPTN	West Brompton
WCHPL	Whitechapel
WELL	Welling
WEST	Westminster
WESTW	Westminster west
WHALL	Whitehall
WIM/MER	Wimbledon/Merton
WKENS	West Kensington
WLSDN	Willesden
WNWD	West Norwood
WOOL/PLUM	Woolwich/Plumstead

1

1 Av *WOOL/PLUM* SE18 ....**108** B4

A

Aaron Hill Rd *EHAM* E6 ....**96** A4
Abbess Cl *BRXS/STRHM* SW2 ......**154** B1
Abbeville Ms *CLAP* * SW4 ....**135** D3
Abbeville Rd *CLAP* SW4 ....**134** C4
Abbey Dr *TOOT* SW17 ....**152** A5
Abbeyfield Est *BERM/RHTH* SE16 ...**102** C5
Abbeyfield Rd *BERM/RHTH* SE16 ...**102** C5
Abbeyfields Cl *WLSDN* NW10 ....**86** A2
Abbey Gdns *BERM/RHTH* SE16 ....**102** A5
  HMSMTH W6 ....**113** E2
  STJWD NW8 ....**3** E2
Abbey La *SRTFD* E15 ....**92** C1
Abbey Orchard St *WEST* SW1P **44** B2
Abbey Rd *BARK* IG11 ....**84** B4
  KIL/WHAMP NW6 ....**72** B5
  SRTFD E15 ....**93** D1
  WLSDN NW10 ....**68** B5
Abbey St *PLSTW* E13 ....**94** A3
  STHWK SE1 ....**49** E2
Abbotsbury Cl *SRTFD* E15 ....**92** C1
  WKENS * W14 ....**101** F3
Abbotsbury Ms *PECK* SE15 ....**138** C1
Abbotsbury Rd *WKENS* W14 ....**101** E3
Abbotshade Rd
  BERM/RHTH * SE16 ....**103** D2
Abbotshall Rd *CAT* SE6 ....**159** E1
Abbots La *STHWK* SE1 ....**37** D4
Abbotsleigh Rd
  STRHM/NOR SW16 ....**152** C4
Abbots Mnr *PIM* * SW1V **116** B1
Abbots Pk *BRXS/STRHM* SW2 ......**154** A1
Abbot's Pl *KIL/WHAMP* NW6 ....**72** B5
Abbots Rd *EHAM* E6 ....**83** D5
Abbots Ter *CEND/HSY/T* N8 ....**57** E1
Abbotstone Rd *PUT/ROE* SW15 ...**130** C1
Abbot St *HACK* E8 ....**77** F3
Abbots Wk *KENS* * W8 ....**38** C5
Abbotswell Rd *BROCKY* SE4 ....**139** F3
Abbotswood Rd *EDUL* SE22 ....**137** E2
  STRHM/NOR SW16 ....**153** D3
Abbott Rd *POP/IOD* E14 ....**92** C4
Abbotts Cl *IS* * N1 ....**76** C4
Abbotts Park Rd *LEY* E10 ....**62** C2
Abchurch La *MANHO* EC4N **36** B1
Abdale Rd *SHB* W12 ....**100** B2
Aberavon Rd *BOW* E3 ....**91** E2
Abercorn Cl *STJWD* NW8 ....**3** E2
Abercorn Pl *STJWD* NW8 ....**3** E3
Abercorn Wy *STHWK* SE1 ....**120** A1
Abercrombie St *BTSEA* SW11 ......**115** D3
Aberdare Gdns *KIL/WHAMP* NW6 ...**72** B4
Aberdeen La *HBRY* N5 ....**76** B2
Aberdeen Pk *HBRY* N5 ....**76** C1
Aberdeen Pl *STJWD* NW8 ....**16** A1
Aberdeen Rd *HBRY* N5 ....**76** C1
  WLSDN NW10 ....**69** F2
Aberdeen Ter *BKHTH/KID* SE3 .....**123** D5
Aberdour St *STHWK* SE1 ....**48** C4
Aberfeldy St *POP/IOD* E14 ....**92** C3
Aberford Gdns *WOOL/PLUM* SE18 ...**125** E4
Abergeldie Rd *LEE/GVPK* SE12 ....**142** B4
Abernethy Rd *LEW* SE13 ....**141** E2
Abersham Rd *HACK* E8 ....**77** F2

Abery St *WOOL/PLUM* SE18 ....**109** E5
Abingdon Cl *STHWK* * SE1 ....**49** F5
Abingdon Rd *KENS* W8 ....**38** B3
Abingdon St *WEST* SW1P **44** C1
Abingdon Vls *KENS* W8 ....**38** A3
Abinger Gv *DEPT* SE8 ....**121** F2
Abinger Ms *MV/WKIL* W9 ....**2** A5
Abinger Rd *CHSWK* W4 ....**99** F4
Ablett St *BERM/RHTH* SE16 ....**120** C1
Abney Park Ter *STNW/STAM* * N16 ...**59** F4
Aboyne Rd *TOOT* SW17 ....**151** D3
  WLSDN NW10 ....**51** E5
Abyssinia Cl *BTSEA* SW11 ....**133** E2
Abyssinia Rd *BTSEA* * SW11 ....**133** E2
Acacia Cl *DEPT* SE8 ....**103** E5
Acacia Gdns *STJWD* NW8 ....**4** B1
Acacia Gv *DUL* SE21 ....**155** D2
Acacia Pl *STJWD* NW8 ....**4** B1
Acacia Rd *ACT* W3 ....**98** C1
  STJWD NW8 ....**4** B1
  WALTH E17 ....**61** E1
  WAN E11 ....**63** E4
Acacia Wy *BFN/LL* DA15 ....**145** F5
Academy Pl *WOOL/PLUM* SE18 ....**125** F4
Academy Rd *WOOL/PLUM* SE18 ...**125** F3
Acanthus Dr *STHWK* SE1 ....**120** A1
Acanthus Rd *BTSEA* SW11 ....**134** A1
Accommodation Rd *GLDGN* NW11 ...**53** F2
Acfold Rd *FUL/PGN* SW6 ....**114** B4
Achilles Cl *STHWK* SE1 ....**120** A1
Achilles Rd *KIL/WHAMP* NW6 ....**72** A2
Achilles St *NWCR* SE14 ....**121** E3
Acklam Rd *NKENS* W10 ....**89** F4
Ackmar Rd *FUL/PGN* SW6 ....**114** A4
Ackroyd Dr *BOW* E3 ....**91** F4
Ackroyd Rd *FSTH* SE23 ....**139** D5
Acland Cl *WOOL/PLUM* SE18 ......**127** D3
Acland Crs *CMBW* SE5 ....**137** D2
Acland Rd *CRICK* NW2 ....**70** B3
Acol Rd *KIL/WHAMP* NW6 ....**72** A4
Acorn Cl *CHST* BR7 ....**162** C5
Acorn Gdns *ACT* W3 ....**87** D4
Acorn Pde *PECK* * SE15 ....**120** B3
Acorn Wy *FSTH* SE23 ....**157** D3
Acre Dr *EDUL* SE22 ....**138** A2
Acre La *BRXS/STRHM* SW2 ....**135** F2
Acris St *WAND/EARL* SW18 ....**132** C3
Acton Hill Ms *ACT* * W3 ....**98** B2
Acton La *ACT* W3 ....**98** C2
  WLSDN NW10 ....**86** C2
Acton Ms *HACK* E8 ....**77** F5
Acton St *FSBYW* WC1X **9** E4
Acuba Rd *WAND/EARL* SW18 ......**150** B2
Ada Ct *MV/WKIL* W9 ....**3** F4
Ada Gdns *POP/IOD* E14 ....**93** D5
  SRTFD E15 ....**81** F5
Adair Rd *NKENS* W10 ....**89** E3
Adam & Eve Ms *KENS* * W8 ....**38** B3
Adams Cl *WBLY* HA9 ....**50** B4
Adamson Rd *CAN/RD* E16 ....**94** A5
  HAMP NW3 ....**73** D4
Adams Pl *HOLWY* N7 ....**75** F2
Adamsrill Rd *SYD* SE26 ....**157** D4
Adam's Rw *MYFR/PKLN* W1K **30** C1
Adam St *TPL/STR* WC2R **33** D2
Adam Wk *FUL/PGN* * SW6 ....**112** C3
Ada Pl *BETH* E2 ....**78** A5
Adare Wk *STRHM/NOR* SW16 ......**153** E2
Ada Rd *CMBW* SE5 ....**119** E3
Ada St *HACK* E8 ....**78** B5
Adderley Gdns *ELTH/MOT* SE9 ....**162** A4
Adderley Gv *BTSEA* SW11 ....**134** A3
Adderley St *POP/IOD* E14 ....**92** C5

Addington Gv *SYD* SE26 ....**157** E4
Addington Rd *BOW* E3 ....**92** A2
   CAN/RD E16 ....**93** E3
   FSBYPK N4 ....**58** A2
Addington Sq *CMBW* SE5 ....**118** C3
Addison Av *NTGHL* W11 ....**101** E2
Addison Bridge Pl *WKENS* W14 ....**101** E3
Addison Crs *WKENS* W14 ....**101** E4
Addison Dr *LEE/GVPK* SE12 ....**142** B3
Addison Gdns *WKENS* W14 ....**101** D4
Addison Gv *CHSWK* W4 ....**99** C4
Addison Pl *NTGHL* W11 ....**101** E2
Addison Rd *NTGHL* W11 ....**101** E3
   WAN E11 ....**64** A1
Addison Ter *CHSWK* * W4 ....**98** C5
Addle Hl *BLKFR* EC4V **35** D1
Addle St *CITYW* * EC2V **23** F4
Adelaide Av *BROCKY* SE4 ....**140** A2
Adelaide Gv *SHB* W12 ....**100** A2
Adelaide Rd *CHST* BR7 ....**162** B5
   HAMP NW3 ....**73** F4
   IL IG1 ....**66** B4
   LEY E10 ....**62** C5
   WAND/EARL SW18 ....**132** A3
Adelaide St *CHCR* * WC2N **32** C2
Adela St *NKENS* W10 ....**89** E3
Adelina Gv *WCHPL* E1 ....**90** C4
Adelina Ms *BAL* SW12 ....**153** D1
Adeline Pl *RSQ* WC1B **20** B3
Adeliza Cl *BARK* IG11 ....**84** C4
Adelphi Ter *CHCR* WC2N **33** D2
Adeney Cl *HMSMTH* W6 ....**113** D2
Aden Gv *STNW/STAM* N16 ....**77** D1
Adenmore Rd *CAT* SE6 ....**140** A5
Aden Rd *IL* IG1 ....**66** B2
Adie Rd *HMSMTH* W6 ....**100** C4
Adine Rd *PLSTW* E13 ....**94** A3
Adler St *WCHPL* E1 ....**90** A4
Adley St *CLPT* E5 ....**79** E2
Admaston Rd *WOOL/PLUM* SE18 ...**126** C3
Admiral Ms *NKENS* W10 ....**89** D3
Admiral Seymour Rd
   ELTH/MOT SE9 ....**143** F2
Admiral's Ga *GNWCH* SE10 ....**122** B4
Admiral Sq *WBPTN* * SW10 ....**114** C4
Admiral St *DEPT* SE8 ....**122** A4
Admiral's Wk *HAMP* NW3 ....**54** C5
Admirals Wy *POP/IOD* E14 ....**104** B3
Admiral Wk *MV/WKIL* W9 ....**14** B2
Adolf St *CAT* SE6 ....**158** A4
Adolphus Rd *FSBYPK* N4 ....**58** B4
Adolphus St *DEPT* SE8 ....**121** F3
Adpar St *BAY/PAD* W2 ....**16** A2
Adrian Ms *WBPTN* SW10 ....**114** B2
Advance Rd *WNWD* SE27 ....**154** C4
Adys Lawn *CRICK* * NW2 ....**70** B3
Adys Rd *PECK* SE15 ....**137** F1
Affleck St *IS* * N1 ....**9** F2
Afghan Rd *BTSEA* SW11 ....**115** E5
Aftab Ter *WCHPL* * E1 ....**90** B3
Agamemnon Rd *KIL/WHAMP* NW6 ...**71** F2
Agar Gv *CAMTN* NW1 ....**75** D4
Agar St *CHCR* WC2N **32** C2
Agate Cl *CAN/RD* E16 ....**95** D5
Agate Rd *HMSMTH* W6 ....**100** C4
Agatha Cl *WAP* E1W **102** C3
Agaton Rd *ELTH/MOT* SE9 ....**162** C2
Agave Rd *CRICK* NW2 ....**70** C1
Agdon St *FSBYE* EC1V **10** C1
Agincourt Rd *HAMP* NW3 ....**73** F1
Agnes Av *IL* IG1 ....**84** A1
Agnes Cl *EHAM* E6 ....**108** A1
Agnes Riley Gdns *CLAP* * SW4 .....**134** C5
Agnes Rd *ACT* W3 ....**99** F3
Agnes St *POP/IOD* E14 ....**91** F5
Agnew Rd *FSTH* SE23 ....**139** E5
Ailsa St *POP/IOD* E14 ....**92** C4
Ainger Rd *HAMP* NW3 ....**73** F4
Ainsdale Dr *STHWK* SE1 ....**120** A1
Ainsley St *BETH* E2 ....**90** B2
Ainsty St *BERM/RHTH* * SE16 ......**102** C3
Ainsworth Cl *CMBW* * SE5 ....**119** E5
   CRICK NW2 ....**52** A5
Ainsworth Rd *HOM* E9 ....**78** C4
Ainsworth Wy *STJWD* NW8 ....**72** C5
Aintree Av *EHAM* E6 ....**83** E5
Aintree St *FUL/PGN* SW6 ....**113** E3
Airdrie Cl *IS* * N1 ....**75** F4
Airedale Av *CHSWK* W4 ....**111** F1
Airedale Av South *CHSWK* * W4 ...**111** F1
Airedale Rd *BAL* SW12 ....**133** F5
Airlie Gdns *IL* IG1 ....**66** B3
   KENS W8 ....**26** A4
Air St *REGST* W1B **31** F2
Aisgill Av *ECT* SW5 ....**113** F1
Aislibie Rd *LEW* SE13 ....**141** E2
Aiten Pl *HMSMTH* W6 ....**100** A5
Aitken Cl *HACK* E8 ....**78** A5
Aitken Rd *CAT* SE6 ....**158** B2
Aitman Dr *CHSWK* * W4 ....**110** A1
Ajax Rd *KIL/WHAMP* NW6 ....**71** F1
Akehurst St *PUT/ROE* SW15 ....**130** A4
Akenside Rd *HAMP* NW3 ....**73** D2
Akerman Rd *CMBW* SE5 ....**118** B4
Alabama St *WOOL/PLUM* SE18 ....**127** D3
Alan Hocken Wy *SRTFD* E15 ....**93** E1
Alan Rd *WIM/MER* SW19 ....**149** E5
Alanthus Cl *LEE/GVPK* SE12 ....**141** F4
Alaska St *STHWK* SE1 ....**34** A4
Albacore Crs *LEW* SE13 ....**140** B4
Alba Gdns *GLDGN* NW11 ....**53** E1
Albany *MYFR/PICC* W1J **31** E2
Albany Cl *MORT/ESHN* SW14 ....**128** B2
Albany Ctyd *MYFR/PICC* * W1J **31** F2
Albany Ms *IS* * N1 ....**76** A4
   WALW SE17 ....**118** C2
Albany Pl *HOLWY* N7 ....**76** A1
Albany Rd *CHST* BR7 ....**162** B5
   CMBW SE5 ....**119** D2
   FSBYPK N4 ....**57** F1
   MNPK E12 ....**83** D1
   WALTH E17 ....**61** E1
   WIM/MER SW19 ....**150** B5
Albany St *CAMTN* NW1 ....**7** D3
Alba Pl *NTGHL* W11 ....**89** F5
Albatross St *WOOL/PLUM* SE18 ...**127** E3
Albemarle Ap *GNTH/NBYPK* IG2 ....**66** B1
Albemarle Gdns *GNTH/NBYPK* IG2 ..**66** B1
Albemarle St *CONDST* W1S **31** E2
Albemarle Wy *FARR* EC1M **22** C1
Alberta Est *WALW* SE17 ....**118** B1
Alberta St *WALW* SE17 ....**118** B1
Albert Av *VX/NE* SW8 ....**117** F3
Albert Br *BTSEA* SW11 ....**115** E3
Albert Bridge Ga *BTSEA* SW11 ....**115** F3
Albert Bridge Rd *CHEL* SW3 ....**115** E2
Albert Carr Gdns
   STRHM/NOR SW16 ....**153** E5
Albert Cl *HOM* E9 ....**78** B5
Albert Cottages *WCHPL* * E1 ....**90** A4
Albert Dr *WIM/MER* SW19 ....**149** E2
Albert Emb *LBTH* SE11 ....**117** E1
Albert Gdns *WCHPL* E1 ....**91** D5
Albert Ga *KTBR* SW1X **29** F5
Albert Ms *BROCKY* * SE4 ....**139** F2
   FSBYPK * N4 ....**57** F3

KENS W8 ....**39** E2
POP/IOD * E14 ....**103** E1
Albert Pl *KENS* W8 ....**39** D1
Albert Rd *CAN/RD* E16 ....**107** E2
ELTH/MOT SE9 ....**161** E3
FSBYPK N4 ....**57** F3
IL IG1 ....**66** C5
KIL/WHAMP NW6 ....**89** F1
SEVS/STOTM N15 ....**59** E1
WAN E11 ....**62** C4
Albert Sq *SRTFD* E15 ....**81** E2
VX/NE SW8 ....**117** F3
Albert St *CAMTN* NW1 ....**74** B5
WLSDN * NW10 ....**69** D5
Albert Ter *CAMTN* NW1 ....**74** A5
WLSDN * NW10 ....**69** D5
Albert Terrace Ms *CAMTN* NW1 ....**74** A5
Albery Wy *PECK* SE15 ....**120** B3
Albion Av *VX/NE* SW8 ....**117** F3
Albion Cl *BAY/PAD* W2 ....**29** D1
Albion Dr *HACK* E8 ....**77** F4
Albion Est *BERM/RHTH* * SE16 ....**102** C3
Albion Gdns *HMSMTH* W6 ....**100** B5
Albion Ga *BAY/PAD* W2 ....**29** D1
Albion Gv *STNW/STAM* N16 ....**77** E1
Albion Ms *BAY/PAD* W2 ....**17** D5
IS * N1 ....**76** A4
Albion Pl *FARR* EC1M **22** C2
HMSMTH W6 ....**100** B5
Albion Rd *STNW/STAM* N16 ....**77** D2
Albion Sq *HACK* E8 ....**77** F4
Albion St *BAY/PAD* W2 ....**17** D5
BERM/RHTH SE16 ....**102** C3
Albion Ter *HACK* E8 ....**77** F4
Albion Villas Rd *FSTH* SE23 ....**156** C3
Albion Wy *LEW* SE13 ....**140** C2
STBT EC1A **23** E3
WBLY HA9 ....**50** A5
Albion Yd *IS* N1 ....**9** D2
Albrighton Rd *CMBW* SE5 ....**137** E1
Albury Ms *PLSTW* E12 ....**64** C3
Albury St *DEPT* SE8 ....**122** A4
Albyn Rd *DEPT* SE8 ....**122** A4
Alcester Crs *CLPT* E5 ....**60** B4
Alconbury Rd *CLPT* E5 ....**60** A4
Aldborough Rd South
GDMY/SEVK IG3 ....**67** E3
Aldbourne Rd *ACT* W3 ....**99** F2
Aldbridge St *WALW* SE17 ....**119** E1
Aldburgh Ms *MHST* W1U **18** B4
Aldbury Av *WBLY* HA9 ....**68** B4
Aldebert Ter *VX/NE* SW8 ....**117** F3
Aldeburgh St *GNWCH* SE10 ....**124** A1
Alden Av *SRTFD* E15 ....**93** F2
Aldenham St *CAMTN* NW1 ....**7** F2
Aldensley Rd *HMSMTH* W6 ....**100** B4
Alderbrook Rd *BAL* SW12 ....**134** B4
Alderbury Rd *BARN* SW13 ....**112** A2
Alder Cl *PECK* SE15 ....**119** F2
Alder Gv *CRICK* NW2 ....**52** A4
Alderholt Wy *PECK* * SE15 ....**119** E3
Aldermanbury *CITYW* EC2V **23** F4
Aldermanbury Sq *CITYW* EC2V **23** F3
Aldermoor Rd *CAT* SE6 ....**157** F1
Alderney Ms *STHWK* SE1 ....**48** A2
Alderney Rd *WCHPL* E1 ....**91** D3
Alderney St *PIM* SW1V **42** C5
Alder Rd *MORT/ESHN* SW14 ....**129** D1
SCUP DA14 ....**163** E3
Aldersbrook La *MNPK* E12 ....**65** F5
Aldersbrook Rd *MNPK* E12 ....**64** C4
Alders Cl *WAN* E11 ....**64** B4
Aldersey Gdns *BARK* IG11 ....**85** D3
Aldersford Cl *BROCKY* SE4 ....**139** D2

Aldersgate St *STBT* EC1A **23** E4
Aldersgrove Av *LEE/GVPK* SE12 ....**160** C3
Aldershot Rd *KIL/WHAMP* NW6 ....**71** F5
Aldershot Ter *WOOL/PLUM* * SE18 ....**126** A3
Alderson St *NKENS* W10 ....**89** E3
The Alders *STRHM/NOR* * SW16 ....**152** C4
Alderton Cl *WLSDN* NW10 ....**51** D4
Alderton Rd *HNHL* SE24 ....**136** C1
Alderville Rd *FUL/PGN* SW6 ....**113** F5
Alderwood Rd *ELTH/MOT* SE9 ....**145** D4
Aldford St *MYFR/PKLN* W1K **30** A3
Aldgate *FENCHST* EC3M **25** D5
Aldgate Barrs *WCHPL* * E1 ....**25** F4
Aldgate High St *TWRH* EC3N **25** E5
Aldine St *SHB* W12 ....**100** C3
Aldington Rd *WOOL/PLUM* SE18 ....**107** D4
Aldis Ms *TOOT* SW17 ....**151** E5
Aldis St *TOOT* SW17 ....**151** E5
Aldred Rd *KIL/WHAMP* NW6 ....**72** A2
Aldren Rd *TOOT* SW17 ....**150** C3
Aldrich Ter *WAND/EARL* SW18 ....**150** C2
Aldridge Road Vls *NTGHL* W11 ....**89** F4
Aldrington Rd *STRHM/NOR* SW16 ....**152** C5
Aidsworth Cl *MV/WKIL* W9 ....**14** C1
Aldwick Cl *CHST* BR7 ....**163** D3
Aldworth Gv *LEW* SE13 ....**140** C4
Aldworth Rd *SRTFD* E15 ....**81** E4
Aldwych *TPL/STR* WC2R **33** E1
Alestan Beck Rd *CAN/RD* E16 ....**95** D5
Alexander Av *WLSDN* NW10 ....**70** B4
Alexander Cl *BFN/LL* DA15 ....**145** E3
Alexander Evans Ms *FSTH* SE23 ....**157** D2
Alexander Ms *BAY/PAD* W2 ....**14** C1
Alexander Pl *SKENS* SW7 ....**40** C4
Alexander Rd *ARCH* N19 ....**57** E5
Alexander Sq *CHEL* SW3 ....**40** C4
Alexander St *BAY/PAD* W2 ....**14** B4
Alexandra Av *BTSEA* * SW11 ....**116** A4
Alexandra Cottages *NWCR* * SE14 ....**121** F4
Alexandra Dr *NRWD* SE19 ....**155** E5
Alexandra Ga *SKENS* SW7 ....**28** A5
Alexandra Gv *FSBYPK* N4 ....**58** B3
Alexandra Pl *STJWD* NW8 ....**72** C5
Alexandra Rd *CHSWK* W4 ....**99** D3
EHAM E6 ....**96** A2
MORT/ESHN SW14 ....**129** D1
STJWD NW8 ....**72** C5
WALTH E17 ....**61** F1
WIM/MER SW19 ....**150** A5
Alexandra Sq *CAN/RD* E16 ....**94** A4
NWCR SE14 ....**121** E3
Alexis St *BERM/RHTH* SE16 ....**102** A5
Alfearn Rd *CLPT* E5 ....**78** C1
Alford Pl *IS* * N1 ....**11** F2
Alfreda St *BTSEA* SW11 ....**116** B4
Alfriston Rd *BTSEA* SW11 ....**133** F3
Algarve Rd *WAND/EARL* SW18 ....**150** B1
Algernon Rd *HDN* NW4 ....**52** A1
KIL/WHAMP NW6 ....**72** A5
LEW SE13 ....**140** B2
Algiers Rd *LEW* SE13 ....**140** A2

Alice La *BOW* E3...............................79 F5
Alice St *STHWK* SE1.......................48 C3
Alice Thompson Cl *LEE/GVPK* SE12...160 C2
Alice Walker Cl *HNHL* * SE24 ....136 B2
Alie St *WCHPL* E1............................25 F5
Alington Crs *CDALE/KGS* NW9 ....50 C3
Alison Cl *EHAM* E6 ....96 A5
Aliwal Ms *BTSEA* * SW11 ....133 E2
Aliwal Rd *BTSEA* SW11 ....133 E2
Alkerden Rd *CHSWK* W4 ....111 E1
Alkham Rd *STNW/STAM* N16 ....59 F4
Allan Barclay Cl *STNW/STAM* N16.....59 F1
Allan Wy *ACT* W3 ....86 C4
Allardyce St *CLAP* SW4 ....135 F2
Allcroft Rd *KTTN* NW5....................74 A2
Allenby Rd *FSTH* SE23...................157 E3
Allendale Cl *CMBW* SE5.................119 D5
  SYD SE26 ....157 D5
Allen Edwards Dr *VX/NE* SW8 ....117 E4
Allen Rd *BOW* E3 ....91 F1
  STNW/STAM N16 ....77 E1
Allensbury Pl *HOLWY* N7 ....75 D4
Allen St *KENS* W8.............................38 B2
Allenswood Rd *ELTH/MOT* SE9 .....143 E1
Allerford Rd *CAT* SE6.....................158 B4
Allerton Rd *STNW/STAM* N16............58 C4
Allestree Rd *FUL/PGN* SW6 ....113 E3
Alleyn Crs *DUL* SE21 ....155 D2
Alleyn Pk *DUL* SE21 ....155 D2
Alleyn Rd *DUL* SE21.......................155 D3
Allfarthing La *WAND/EARL* SW18 ...132 C4
Allgood St *BETH* E2...........................13 F2
Alihallows La *CANST* EC4R...............36 A2
Alihallows Rd *EHAM* E6.....................95 E5
Alliance Rd *ACT* W3..........................86 B3
  PLSTW E13 ....94 C3
Allied Wy *ACT* * W3..........................99 E3
Allington Crs *WIM/MER* SW19 ....149 D5
Allington Rd *NKENS* W10..................89 E5
Allington St *WESTW* SW1E 43 D3
Allison Cl *GNWCH* SE10.................122 C4
Allison Gv *DUL* SE21 ....155 E1
Allison Rd *ACT* W3 ....86 C5
Allitsen Rd *STJWD* NW8......................4 C3
Allitson Rd *STJWD* NW8.....................4 C2
Allnutt Wy *CLAP* SW4 ....135 D3
Alloa Rd *DEPT* SE8 ....121 D1
Alloway Rd *BOW* E3..........................91 E2
Allport Rd *WCHPL* * E1 ....90 C4
All Saints Dr *BKHTH/KID* SE3 ....123 F5
All Saints Pas *WAND/EARL* * SW18 ...132 A3
All Saints' Rd *ACT* W3 ....98 C3
  NTCHL W11 ....89 F4
Allsop Pl *CAMTN* NW1 ....17 F1
All Souls' Av *WLSDN* NW10 ....88 B1
All Souls' Pl *REGST* W1B...................19 D3
Allwood Cl *SYD* SE26......................157 D4
Almack Rd *CLPT* E5...........................78 C1
Alma Gv *STHWK* SE1..........................49 F5
Alma Pl *WLSDN* NW10......................88 B2
Alma Rd *WAND/EARL* SW18 ....132 C3
Alma Sq *STJWD* NW8...........................3 F3
Alma St *KTTN* NW5 ....74 B3
  SRTFD E15.....................................81 D3
Alma Ter *BOW* E3..............................79 F5
  KENS W8.......................................38 B3
  WAND/EARL SW18 ....133 D5
Almeida St *IS* N1...............................76 B5
Almeric Rd *BTSEA* SW11...............133 F2
Almington St *FSBYPK* * N4...............57 F4
Almond Rd *BERM/RHTH* SE16 ....102 B5
Almorah Rd *IS* N1..............................77 D4

Alnwick Rd *CAN/RD* E16..................94 C5
  LEE/GVPK SE12 ....142 B5
Alperton St *NKENS* W10...................89 E3
Alpha Cl *CAMTN* NW1..........................5 D5
Alpha Gv *POP/IOD* E14 ....104 A3
Alpha Pl *CHEL* SW3..........................115 E2
  KIL/WHAMP NW6..............................2 B1
Alpha Rd *NWCR* SE14 ....121 F4
Alpha St *PECK* SE15 ....120 A5
Alpine Gv *HOM* * E9..........................78 C4
Alpine Rd *BERM/RHTH* SE16 ....102 C5
Alpine Wy *EHAM* E6 ....96 A4
Alric Av *WLSDN* NW10 ....69 D4
Alroy Rd *FSBYPK* N4 ....58 A2
Alsace Rd *WALW* SE17....................119 E1
Alscot Rd *BERM/RHTH* SE16 ....49 F3
Alscot Wy *STHWK* SE1.......................49 E4
Alston Rd *TOOT* SW17 ....151 D4
Altash Wy *ELTH/MOT* SE9..............161 F2
Altenburg Gdns *BTSEA* SW11 ....133 F2
Althea St *FUL/PGN* SW6 ....114 B5
Althorp Rd *TOOT* SW17 ....151 F1
Altmore Av *EHAM* E6 ....83 F4
Alton Rd *PUT/ROE* SW15 ....148 A1
Alton St *POP/IOD* E14......................92 B4
Alvanley Gdns *KIL/WHAMP* NW6.......72 B2
Alverstone Av *WAND/EARL* SW18 ...150 A2
Alverstone Gdns *ELTH/MOT* SE9....162 B1
Alverstone Rd *CRICK* NW2................70 C4
  MNPK E12 ....84 A1
Alverton St *DEPT* SE8....................121 F1
Alvey St *WALW* SE17 ....119 E1
Alvington Crs *HACK* E8 ....77 F2
Alwold Crs *LEE/GVPK* SE12...........142 C4
Alwyn Av *CHSWK* W4 ....111 D1
Alwyne La *IS* * N1 ....76 B4
Alwyne Pl *IS* * N1..............................76 C3
Alwyne Rd *IS* N1...............................76 C4
Alwyne Sq *IS* N1 ....76 C3
Alwyne Vls *IS* N1 ....76 B4
Alwyn Gdns *ACT* W3.........................86 B4
Alyn Bank *CEND/HSY/T* * N8 ....57 D1
Alyth Gdns *GLDGN* NW11 ....53 F1
Amar Ct *WOOL/PLUM* SE18 ....109 F5
Amardeep Ct *WOOL/PLUM* SE18.....127 F1
Amazon St *WCHPL* E1........................90 B5
Ambassador Gdns *EHAM* E6..............95 F4
Ambassador Sq *POP/IOD* E14 ....104 B5
Ambergate St *WALW* SE17 ....118 B1
Amber Gv *CRICK* NW2 ....53 D3
Amberley Gv *SYD* SE26 ....156 B4
Amberley Rd *LEY* E10 ....62 A2
  MV/WKIL W9 ....14 B2
Amber St *SRTFD* * E15......................81 D3
Amblecote Cl *LEE/GVPK* SE12 ....160 B3
Amblecote Mdw
  LEE/GVPK SE12 ....160 B3
Amblecote Rd *LEE/GVPK* SE12 ......160 B3
Ambler Rd *FSBYPK* N4 ....58 B5
Ambleside Av *STRHM/NOR* SW16 ...153 D4
Ambleside Cl *LEY* E10 ....62 B2
Ambleside Rd *WLSDN* NW10 ....69 F4
Ambrosden Av *WEST* SW1P 43 E4
Ambrose Av *GLDGN* NW11 ....53 F1
Ambrose St *BERM/RHTH* SE16 ....102 B3
Amelia St *WALW* SE17 ....118 B1
Amen Cnr *STP* EC4M 23 D5
Amen Ct *STP* EC4M 23 D5
America Sq *TWRH* * EC3N..................37 E1
America St *STHWK* SE1 ....35 E4
Amerland Rd *WAND/EARL* SW18 .....131 F4
Amersham Gv *NWCR* SE14..............121 F3
Amersham Rd *NWCR* SE14..............121 F4

Amersham V *NWCR* SE14 ....121 F3
Amery Gdns *WLSDN* NW10.................70 B5
Amesbury Av *BRXS/STRHM* SW2.........153 E2
Ames Cottages *POP/IOD* * E14 ....91 E4
Amethyst Rd *WAN* E11.........................81 D1
Amhurst Pde *STNW/STAM* * N16 ......59 F2
Amhurst Pk *STNW/STAM* N16.............59 E2
Amhurst Rd *CLPT* E5..........................78 B2
Amhurst Ter *HACK* E8..........................78 A1
Amiel St *WCHPL* E1............................90 C3
Amies St *BTSEA* SW11.......................133 F1
Amina Wy *BERM/RHTH* SE16.............102 A4
Amity Rd *SRTFD* E15...........................81 F4
Ammanford Gn *CDALE/KGS* * NW9.....51 E1
Amner Rd *BTSEA* SW11......................134 A4
Amor Rd *HMSMTH* W6.......................100 C4
Amott Rd *PECK* SE15.........................138 A1
Ampthill Est *CAMTN* NW1....................7 E2
Ampthill Sq *CAMTN* NW1.....................7 F2
Ampton St *FSBYW* WC1X.....................9 E4
Amroth Cl *FSTH* SE23........................156 B1
Amroth Gn *CDALE/KGS* * NW9............51 E1
Amsterdam Rd *POP/IOD* E14.............104 C4
Amwell St *CLKNW* EC1R......................10 A3
Amyruth Rd *BROCKY* SE4...................140 A3
Amy Warne Cl *EHAM* E6.......................95 E4
Ancaster St *WOOL/PLUM* SE18..........127 E3
Anchorage Cl *WIM/MER* SW19 ....150 A5
Anchor & Hope La *CHARL* SE7...........106 B4
Anchor St *BERM/RHTH* SE16.............102 B5
Anchor Ter *WCHPL* * E1.......................90 C3
Anchor Yd *FSBYE* * EC1V....................11 F5
Ancill Cl *HMSMTH* W6.......................113 E3
Ancona Rd *WLSDN* NW10.....................88 A1
    WOOL/PLUM SE18 ....127 D1
Andalus Rd *BRXN/ST* SW9 ....135 E1
Anderson Cl *ACT* W3...........................87 D5
Anderson Rd *HOM* E9.........................79 D3
Anderson Sq *IS* * N1...........................76 B5
Anderson St *CHEL* SW3.....................115 F1
Andover Av *CAN/RD* E16.......................95 D5
Andover Pl *KIL/WHAMP* NW6 ....2 C2
Andover Rd *HOLWY* N7........................57 F4
Andover Ter *HMSMTH* * W6................100 B5
Andre St *HACK* E8..............................78 A2
Andrew Borde St
    LSQ/SEVD * WC2H........................20 B4
Andrewes Gdns *EHAM* E6....................95 E5
Andrew Pl *VX/NE* SW8.......................117 D4
Andrews Rd *HACK* E8...........................78 B5
Andrew St *POP/IOD* E14......................92 C5
Andrews Wk *WALW* SE17...................118 B5
Anfield Cl *BAL* SW12.........................134 C5
Angel Ct *LOTH* EC2R............................24 B4
Angelica Dr *EHAM* E6...........................96 A4
Angel La *SRTFD* E15............................81 D3
Angell Park Gdns *BRXN/ST* SW9........136 A1
Angell Rd *BRXN/ST* SW9....................136 B1
Angell Town Est *BRXN/ST* * SW9........118 A5
Angel Ms *MYPL* E1............................102 B1
Angel Pas *CANST* EC4R.......................36 A2
Angel Sq *FSBYE* * EC1V.......................10 C2
Angel St *STBT* EC1A............................23 E4
Angel Wk *HMSMTH* W6......................100 C5
Angerstein La *BKHTH/KID* SE3...........123 F3
Anglers La *KTTN* NW5..........................74 B3
Anglesea Av *WOOL/PLUM* SE18..........108 B5
Anglesea Rd *WOOL/PLUM* SE18 ....108 B5
Angles Rd *STRHM/NOR* SW16.............153 E4
Anglian Rd *WAN* E11............................63 D5
Anglo Rd *BOW* E3................................91 F1
Angus Rd *PLSTW* E13...........................94 C2
Angus St *NWCR* SE14........................121 E3

Anhalt Rd *BTSEA* SW11......................115 E3
Ankerdine Crs *WOOL/PLUM* SE18.......126 B4
Anley Rd *HMSMTH* W6.......................101 D3
Annabel Cl *POP/IOD* E14......................92 B5
Anna Cl *HACK* E8................................77 F5
Annandale Rd *BFN/LL* DA15 ....145 E5
    CHSWK W4..................................99 E5
    GNWCH SE10.............................123 F1
Anna Neagle Cl *FSTGT* E7....................82 A1
Annesley Cl *WLSDN* NW10....................51 E5
Annesley Rd *BKHTH/KID* SE3.............124 B4
Anne St *PLSTW* E13.............................94 A3
Annette Rd *HOLWY* N7.........................75 F1
Annexe Market *WCHPL* * E1.................25 E2
Annie Besant Cl *BOW* * E3....................79 F5
Anning St *SDTCH* EC2A.......................13 D5
Annis Rd *HOM* * E9.............................79 E3
Ann La *WBPTN* SW10.........................115 D3
Ann Moss Wy *BERM/RHTH* SE16........102 C4
Ann's Cl *KTBR* SW1X...........................41 F1
Ann St *WOOL/PLUM* SE18..................109 D5
Ansdell Rd *PECK* SE15.......................120 C5
Ansdell St *KENS* W8.............................39 D2
Ansdell Ter *KENS* W8...........................39 D2
Ansell Rd *TOOT* SW17.......................151 E3
Anselm Rd *FUL/PGN* SW6..................114 A2
Ansford Rd *BMLY* BR1.......................158 C5
Ansleigh Pl *NTGHL* W11.....................101 D1
Anson Rd *CRICK* NW2..........................70 B2
    HOLWY N7..................................74 C1
Anstey Rd *PECK* SE15........................138 A1
Anstice Cl *CHSWK* W4.......................111 E3
Anstridge Rd *ELTH/MOT* SE9.............145 D4
Antelope Rd *WOOL/PLUM* SE18 ....107 F4
Anthony's Cl *WAP* E1W......................102 A2
Anthony St *WCHPL* E1..........................90 B5
Antill Rd *BOW* E3................................91 E2
Antill Ter *WCHPL* E1............................91 D5
Anton St *HACK* E8...............................78 A2
Antrim Rd *HAMP* NW3.........................73 F3
Antrobus Rd *CHSWK* W4......................98 C5
Apollo Pl *WAN* E11..............................63 E5
    WBPTN * SW10...........................115 D3
Apollo Wy *WOOL/PLUM* SE18.............109 D4
Apothecary St *BLKFR* * EC4V...............22 C5
Appach Rd *BRXS/STRHM* SW2...........136 A3
Apple Blossom Ct *VX/NE* * SW8.........117 D3
Appleby Rd *CAN/RD* E16......................94 A5
    HACK E8.....................................78 A4
Appleby St *BETH* E2............................13 E1
Appledore Cl *TOOT* SW17.................151 F2
Appledore Crs *BFN/LL* DA15..............163 E3
Appleford Rd *NKENS* W10....................89 E3
Applegarth Rd *WKENS* * W14.............101 D4
Apple Rd *WAN* E11.............................63 E5
Appleton Rd *ELTH/MOT* SE9..............143 E1
Apple Tree Yd *STJS* * SW1Y................31 F3
Applewood Cl *CRICK* NW2....................52 B5
Appold St *SDTCH* EC2A.......................24 C2
Apprentice Wy *CLPT* E5.......................78 B1
Approach Rd *BETH* E2.........................90 C1
The Approach *ACT* W3.........................87 D5
April Gln *FSTH* SE23..........................157 D3
April St *STNW/STAM* N16.....................77 F1
Apsley Wy *CRICK* NW2.........................52 A4
    MYFR/PICC * W1J.........................30 A3
Aquila St *STJWD* NW8...........................4 B1
Aquinas St *STHWK* SE1........................34 B4
Arabella Dr *PUT/ROE* SW15................129 E2
Arabin Rd *BROCKY* SE4.....................139 E2
Arbery Rd *BOW* E3..............................91 E2
Arborfield Cl *BRXS/STRHM* SW2........153 F1
Arbour Sq *WCHPL* E1...........................90 C5

Arbroath Rd *ELTH/MOT* SE9 ....143 E1
Arbuthnot Rd *NWCR* SE14 ....121 D5
Arbutus St *HACK* E8 ....77 F5
Arcade Chambers *ELTH/MOT* * SE9...144 A4
The Arcade *ELTH/MOT* * SE9 ....144 A4
    LVPST * EC2M 24 C3
Arcadia St *POP/IOD* E14 ....92 A5
Archangel St *BERM/RHTH* SE16 ....103 D3
Archbishop's Pl *BRXS/STRHM* SW2...135 F4
Archdale Ct *SHB* W12 ....100 B2
Archdale Rd *EDUL* SE22 ....137 F5
Archel Rd *WKENS* W14 ....113 F2
Archer Sq *DEPT* SE8 ....121 E2
Archer St *SOHO/SHAV* W1D 32 A1
Archery Cl *BAY/PAD* W2 ....17 D5
Archery Rd *ELTH/MOT* SE9.................143 F5
The Arches *CHCR* * WC2N 33 D3
Archibald Ms *MYFR/PICC* W1J 30 B2
Archibald St *HOLWY* N7 ....75 D1
Arch St *STHWK* SE1 ....47 E3
Archway Cl *ARCH* * N19 ....56 C4
    NKENS W10 ....89 D4
    WIM/MER SW19 ....150 B4
Archway Rd *ARCH* N19 ....56 C3
Archway St *BARN* SW13 ....129 E1
Arcola St *HACK* E8 ....77 F2
Arctic St *KTTN* NW5 ....74 B2
Ardbeg Rd *HNHL* SE24 ....137 D4
Arden Court Gdns *EFNCH* N2 ....55 D1
Arden Crs *POP/IOD* E14 ....104 A5
Arden Est *IS* N1 ....12 C2
Ardfillan Rd *CAT* SE6 ....159 D1
Ardgowan Rd *CAT* SE6 ....141 E5
Ardilaun Rd *HBRY* N5 ....76 C1
Ardleigh Rd *IS* N1 ....77 E3
Ardley Cl *FSTH* SE23 ....157 E3
    WLSDN NW10 ....51 E5
Ardlui Rd *WNWD* SE27 ....154 C2
Ardmere Rd *LEW* SE13 ....141 D4
Ardoch Rd *CAT* SE6 ....159 D2
Ardshiel Cl *PUT/ROE* SW15................131 D1
Ardwell Rd *BRXS/STRHM* SW2............153 E2
Ardwick Rd *CRICK* NW2 ....72 A1
Arena Est *FSBYPK* * N4 ....58 B1
Argall Av *LEY* E10....................................61 D2
Argall Wy *LEY* E10 ....61 D3
Argenta Wy *WLSDN* NW10 ....68 B4
Argon Ms *FUL/PGN* SW6 ....114 A3
Argyle Pl *HMSMTH* W6 ....100 B5
Argyle Rd *CAN/RD* E16 ....94 B5
    IL IG1..66 A4
    SRTFD E15 ....81 E1
    WCHPL E1 ....91 D3
Argyle Sq *STPAN* WC1H 9 D3
Argyle St *CAMTN* NW1 ....8 C3
Argyle Wk *STPAN* * WC1H 8 C4
Argyle Wy *STHWK* SE1 ....120 A1
Argyll Cl *BRXN/ST* SW9 ....135 F1
Argyll Rd *KENS* W8 ....38 A1
    WOOL/PLUM SE18 ....108 C4
Argyll St *REGST* W1B 19 E5
Arica Rd *BROCKY* SE4 ....139 E2
Ariel Rd *KIL/WHAMP* NW6 ....72 A3
Ariel Wy *SHB* W12 ....100 C2
Aristotle Rd *CLAP* SW4 ....135 D1
Arkindale Rd *CAT* SE6 ....158 C3
Arklow Rd *NWCR* SE14 ....121 F3
Arkwright Rd *HAMP* NW3 ....72 C2
Arlesford Rd *BRXN/ST* SW9 ....135 E1
Arlingford Rd *BRXS/STRHM* SW2 ....136 A4
Arlington Cl *BFN/LL* DA15 ....145 E5
    LEW * SE13 ....141 D3
Arlington Gdns *CHSWK* W4 ....110 C1

IL IG1..65 F2
Arlington Pde *BRXS/STRHM* * SW2 ...135 F2
Arlington Rd *CAMTN* NW1 ....74 B5
Arlington Sq *IS* N1 ....76 C5
Arlington St *MYFR/PICC* W1J 31 E3
Arlington Wy *CLKNW* EC1R 10 B3
Armadale Rd *FUL/PGN* SW6 ....114 A3
Armada St *DEPT* SE8 ....122 A2
Armada Wy *EHAM* E6 ....96 C5
Armagh Rd *BOW* E3 ....79 F5
Arminger Rd *SHB* W12 ....100 B2
Armitage Rd *GLDGN* NW11 ....53 E3
    GNWCH SE10 ....105 F5
Armour Cl *HOLWY* N7 ....75 F3
Armoury Rd *DEPT* SE8 ....122 B5
Armoury Wy *WAND/EARL* SW18 ....132 A3
Armstrong Cl *EHAM* E6 ....95 F5
Armstrong Rd *ACT* W3 ....99 F2
Arnal Crs *WAND/EARL* SW18...............131 E5
Arne St *LSQ/SEVD* WC2H 21 D5
Arne Wk *BKHTH/KID* SE3 ....141 F2
Arneway St *WEST* SW1P 44 B3
Arnewood Cl *PUT/ROE* SW15 ....148 A1
Arngask Rd *CAT* SE6 ....141 D5
Arnheim Pl *POP/IOD* E14 ....104 A4
Arnold Est *STHWK* SE1 ....49 F1
Arnold Rd *BOW* E3 ....92 A2
Arnott Cl *CHSWK* W4 ....99 D5
Arnould Av *CMBW* SE5 ....137 D2
Arnside St *WALW* SE17 ....118 C2
Arnulf St *CAT* SE6 ....158 B4
Arodene Rd *BRXS/STRHM* SW2 ....135 F4
Arragon Rd *EHAM* E6 ....83 D5
    WAND/EARL SW18 ....150 A1
Arran Dr *MNPK* E12 ....65 D3
Arran Rd *CAT* SE6 ....158 B2
Arran Wk *IS* N1 ....76 C4
Arrow Rd *BOW* E3 ....92 B2
Arsenal Rd *ELTH/MOT* SE9 ....125 F5
Artesian Cl *WLSDN* NW10 ....69 D4
Artesian Houses *NTGHL* * W11 ....14 A5
Artesian Rd *NTGHL* W11 ....14 A5
Arthingworth St *SRTFD* E15 ....81 E5
Arthurdon Rd *LEW* SE13 ....140 A3
Arthur Gv *WOOL/PLUM* SE18 ....108 C5
Arthur Rd *EHAM* E6 ....95 F1
    HOLWY N7 ....75 F1
    WIM/MER SW19 ....149 F4
Arthur St *CANST* EC4R 36 B2
Artichoke Hl *WAP* E1W 102 B1
Artichoke Pl *CMBW* * SE5 ....119 D4
Artillery Cl *GNTH/NBYPK* IG2 ....66 C1
Artillery La *LVPST* EC2M 25 D3
    SHB W12 ....88 A5
Artillery Pas *WCHPL* * E1 ....25 D3
Artillery Pl *WOOL/PLUM* SE18 ....125 F1
Artizan St *WCHPL* E1 ....25 D4
Arundel Gdns *NTGHL* W11 ....101 F1
    SRTFD E15 ....81 E1
Arundel Gv *STNW/STAM* N16 ....77 E2
Arundel Pl *IS* N1 ....76 A3
Arundel Sq *HOLWY* N7 ....76 A3
Arundel St *TPL/STR* WC2R 33 F1
Arundel Ter *BARN* SW13 ....112 B2
Arvon Rd *HBRY* N5 ....76 A2
Asbaston Ter *IL* IG1.................................84 C2
Ascalon St *VX/NE* SW8 ....116 C3
Ascham St *KTTN* NW5 ....74 C2
Ascot Pde *CLAP* * SW4 ....135 E2
Ascot Rd *EHAM* E6 ....95 F2
Ashanti Ms *HACK* * E8 ....78 B3

Ashbourne Gv *CHSWK* W4 ....**111** E1
  EDUL SE22 ....**137** F3
Ashbridge Rd *WAN* E11 ....**63** E2
Ashbridge St *STJWD* NW8 ....**16** C1
Ashbrook Rd *ARCH* N19 ....**57** D3
Ashburn Gdns *SKENS* SW7 ....**39** E4
Ashburnham Gv *GNWCH* SE10 ....**122** B3
Ashburnham Pl *GNWCH* SE10 ....**122** B3
Ashburnham Retreat
  GNWCH SE10 ....**122** B3
Ashburnham Rd *WBPTN* * SW10 ....**114** C3
  WLSDN NW10 ....**88** C2
Ashburn Pl *SKENS* SW7 ....**39** E4
Ashburton Av *GDMY/SEVK* IG3 ....**85** F1
Ashburton Gv *HOLWY* N7 ....**76** A1
Ashburton Rd *CAN/RD* E16 ....**94** A5
Ashbury Rd *BTSEA* SW11 ....**133** F1
Ashby Gv *IS* N1 ....**76** C4
Ashby Ms *BROCKY* SE4 ....**139** F1
Ashby Rd *BROCKY* SE4 ....**121** F5
Ashby St *FSBYE* EC1V **11** D4
Aschurch Gv *SHB* W12 ....**100** A3
Aschurch Park Vls *SHB* W12 ....**100** A4
Aschurch Ter *SHB* W12 ....**99** F4
Ashcombe Pk *CRICK* NW2 ....**51** E5
Ashcombe Rd *WIM/MER* SW19 ....**150** A5
Ashcombe St *FUL/PGN* * SW6 ....**114** B5
Ashcroft Rd *BOW* E3 ....**91** E2
Ashdale Rd *LEE/GVPK* SE12 ....**160** C5
Ashdown Crs *KTTN* * NW5 ....**74** A2
Ashdown Rd *WLSDN* NW10 ....**69** E5
Ashdown Wy *TOOT* SW17 ....**152** A2
Ashenden Rd *CLPT* E5 ....**79** E2
Ashen Gv *WIM/MER* SW19 ....**150** A3
Asher Wy *WAP* E1W **102** A3
Ashfield Rd *ACT* W3 ....**99** F2
  FSBYPK N4 ....**58** C1
Ashfield St *WCHPL* E1 ....**90** B4
Ashfield Yd *WCHPL* * E1 ....**90** C4
Ashford Cl *WALTH* E17 ....**61** F1
Ashford Rd *CRICK* NW2 ....**71** D1
  EHAM E6 ....**83** F3
Ashford St *IS* N1 ....**12** C3
Ash Gv *CRICK* NW2 ....**71** D1
  HACK E8 ....**78** B5
Ashgrove Rd *GDMY/SEVK* IG3 ....**67** F3
Ashington Rd *FUL/PGN* * SW6 ....**113** F5
Ashlake Rd *STRHM/NOR* SW16 ....**153** E4
Ashland Pl *MHST* W1U **18** A2
Ashlar Pl *WOOL/PLUM* SE18 ....**108** B5
Ashleigh Rd *MORT/ESHN* SW14 ....**129** E1
Ashley Crs *BTSEA* SW11 ....**134** A1
Ashley Pl *WEST* SW1P **43** E3
Ashley Rd *ARCH* N19 ....**57** E3
  FSTGT E7 ....**82** C4
Ashlin Rd *SRTFD* E15 ....**81** D1
Ashlone Rd *PUT/ROE* SW15 ....**130** C1
Ashmead Ms *DEPT* * SE8 ....**122** A4
Ashmead Rd *DEPT* SE8 ....**122** A5
Ashmere Gv *BRXS/STRHM* SW2 ....**135** E2
Ash Ms *KTTN* * NW5 ....**74** C2
Ashmill St *CAMTN* NW1 ....**16** C2
Ashmole Pl *VX/NE* SW8 ....**117** F2
Ashmore Cl *PECK* SE15 ....**119** F3
Ashmore Rd *WELL* DA16 ....**145** D1
Ashmore Rd *MV/WKIL* W9 ....**89** F2
Ashmount Rd *HGT* N6 ....**56** C2
Ashness Rd *BTSEA* SW11 ....**133** F3
Ashridge Crs *WOOL/PLUM* SE18 ....**126** C3
Ash Rd *SRTFD* E15 ....**81** E2
Ashtead Rd *CLPT* E5 ....**60** A2
Ashton Rd *SRTFD* E15 ....**81** D2
Ashton St *POP/IOD* E14 ....**104** C1

Ashurst Dr *GNTH/NBYPK* IG2 ....**66** B1
Ashurst Gdns *BRXS/STRHM* * SW2 ....**154** A1
Ashvale Rd *TOOT* SW17 ....**151** F5
Ashville Rd *WAN* E11 ....**63** D4
Ashwater Rd *LEE/GVPK* SE12 ....**160** A1
Ashwin St *HACK* E8 ....**77** F3
Ashworth Cl *CMBW* SE5 ....**119** D5
Ashworth Rd *MV/WKIL* W9 ....**3** D3
Aske St *IS* N1 ....**12** C3
Askew Crs *SHB* W12 ....**99** F3
Askew Rd *SHB* W12 ....**99** F3
Askham Rd *SHB* W12 ....**100** A2
Askill Dr *PUT/ROE* SW15 ....**131** E3
Asland Rd *SRTFD* E15 ....**81** D5
Aslett St *WAND/EARL* SW18 ....**132** B5
Asmara Rd *CRICK* NW2 ....**71** E2
Aspenlea Rd *HMSMTH* W6 ....**113** D2
Aspen Wy *POP/IOD* E14 ....**104** B1
Aspern Gv *HAMP* NW3 ....**73** E2
Aspinall Rd *BROCKY* SE4 ....**139** D1
Aspinden Rd *BERM/RHTH* SE16 ....**102** B5
Aspley Rd *WAND/EARL* SW18 ....**132** B3
Assam St *WCHPL* E1 ....**90** A5
Assata Ms *IS* N1 ....**76** B3
Assembly Pas *WCHPL* E1 ....**90** C4
Astbury Rd *PECK* SE15 ....**120** C4
Astell St *CHEL* SW3 ....**115** E1
Asteys Rw *IS* N1 ....**76** B4
Astle St *BTSEA* SW11 ....**116** A5
Astley Av *CRICK* NW2 ....**70** C2
Aston Gv *WCHPL* E1 ....**91** E5
Aston Ter *BAL* * SW12 ....**134** B4
Astonville St *WAND/EARL* SW18 ....**150** A1
Astoria Pde *STRHM/NOR*
  * SW16 ....**153** E3
Astoria Wk *BRXN/ST* SW9 ....**136** A1
Astrop Ms *HMSMTH* W6 ....**100** C4
Astrop Ter *HMSMTH* W6 ....**100** C4
Astwood Ms *SKENS* SW7 ....**39** D4
Asylum Rd *PECK* SE15 ....**120** B3
Atalanta St *FUL/PGN* SW6 ....**113** D4
Atheldene Rd *WAND/EARL* SW18 .....**150** B1
Athelney St *CAT* SE6 ....**158** A3
Athelstane Gv *BOW* E3 ....**91** F1
Athelstane Ms *FSBYPK* N4 ....**58** A3
Athelstan Gdns *KIL/WHAMP* * NW6 ....**71** E4
Athenlay Rd *PECK* SE15 ....**139** D3
Athens Gdns *MV/WKIL* * W9 ....**14** A1
Atherden Rd *CLPT* E5 ....**78** C1
Atherfold Rd *BRXN/ST* SW9 ....**135** E1
Atherstone Ms *SKENS* SW7 ....**39** F4
Atherton Dr *WIM/MER* SW19 ....**149** D4
Atherton Ms *FSTGT* E7 ....**82** A3
Atherton Rd *BARN* SW13 ....**112** A3
  FSTGT E7 ....**81** F2
Atherton St *BTSEA* SW11 ....**115** E5
Athlone Cl *CLPT* E5 ....**78** B2
Athlone Rd *BRXS/STRHM* SW2 ....**135** F5
Athlone St *KTTN* NW5 ....**74** A3
Athol Sq *POP/IOD* E14 ....**92** C5
Atkinson Rd *CAN/RD* E16 ....**94** C4
Atkins Rd *BAL* SW12 ....**134** C5
  LEY E10 ....**62** B1
Atlantic Rd *BRXN/ST* SW9 ....**136** A2
Atlas Gdns *CHARL* SE7 ....**106** C5
Atlas Ms *HACK* E8 ....**77** F3
Atlas Rd *PLSTW* E13 ....**94** A1
  WBLY HA9 ....**68** C1
  WLSDN NW10 ....**87** E2
Atley Rd *BOW* E3 ....**80** A5
Atney Rd *PUT/ROE* SW15 ....**131** E2
Atterbury Rd *FSBYPK* N4 ....**58** A1
Atterbury St *WEST* SW1P **44** B5

Attewood Av CRICK NW2 ....51 E5
Attneave St FSBYW WC1X 10 A5
Atwell Rd PECK * SE15 ....120 A5
Atwood Av RCH/KEW TW9 ....110 A5
Atwood Rd HMSMTH W6 ....100 B5
Aubert Pk HBRY N5 ....76 A1
Aubert Rd HBRY N5 ....76 B1
Aubrey Pl STJWD NW8 ....3 E2
Aubrey Rd KENS W8 ....101 F2
Aubrey Wk KENS W8 ....101 F2
Auburn Cl NWCR SE14 ....121 E3
Aubyn Hl WNWD SE27 ....154 C4
Aubyn Sq PUT/ROE SW15 ....130 A2
Auckland Hl WNWD SE27 ....154 C4
Auckland Rd BTSEA SW11 ....133 E2
   IL IG1 ....66 B3
   LEY E10 ....62 B5
Auckland St LBTH SE11 ....117 F1
Auden Pl CAMTN NW1 ....74 A5
Audley Dr CAN/RD E16 ....106 B2
Audley Gdns GDMY/SEVK IG3 ....67 F4
Audley Rd HDN NW4 ....52 A1
Audley Sq MYFR/PKLN * W1K 30 B3
Audrey Pl IL IG1 ....66 B5
Audrey St BETH E2 ....90 A1
Augurs La PLSTW E13 ....94 B2
Augustine Rd HMSMTH W6 ....101 D4
Augustus Cl SHB W12 ....100 B3
Augustus Rd WIM/MER SW19 ....149 E1
Augustus St CAMTN NW1 ....7 D2
Aulton Pl LBTH SE11 ....118 A1
Auriga Ms N1 ....77 D2
Auriol Rd WKENS W14 ....101 E5
Austin Cl CAT SE6 ....139 E5
Austin Friars OBST EC2N 24 B4
Austin Friars Sq OBST * EC2N 24 B4
Austin Rd BTSEA SW11 ....116 A4
Austin St BETH E2 ....13 E4
Austral Cl BFN/LL DA15 ....163 F3
Australia Rd SHB W12 ....100 B1
Austral St LBTH SE11 ....46 C4
Autumn St BOW E3 ....80 A5
Avalon Rd FUL/PGN SW6 ....114 B4
Avebury Rd WAN E11 ....63 D3
Avebury St IS N1 ....77 D5
Aveline St LBTH SE11 ....117 F1
Avenell Rd FSBYPK N4 ....58 B5
Avening Rd WAND/EARL SW18 ....132 A4
Avening Ter WAND/EARL SW18 ....132 A4
Avenue Crs ACT W3 ....98 B3
Avenue Gdns ACT W3 ....98 B3
   MORT/ESHN SW14 ....129 E1
Avenue Park Rd WNWD SE27 ....154 B2
Avenue Rd ACT W3 ....98 B3
   FSTGT E7 ....82 B2
   HGT N6 ....56 C2
   STJWD NW8 ....73 D5
   WLSDN NW10 ....87 F1
The Avenue BTSEA SW11 ....134 A3
   CHSWK W4 ....99 E4
   GNWCH SE10 ....123 D3
   KIL/WHAMP NW6 ....71 D5
   WAN E11 ....64 B3
Averill St HMSMTH W6 ....113 D2
Avernons Rd PLSTW E13 ....94 A4
Avery Farm Rw BGVA * SW1W 42 C5
Avery Hill Rd ELTH/MOT SE9 ....145 D4
   ELTH/MOT SE9 ....162 C1
Avery Rw MYFR/PKLN W1K 30 C1
Aviary Cl CAN/RD E16 ....93 F4
Avignon Rd BROCKY SE4 ....139 D1
Avington Wy PECK * SE15 ....119 F3
Avis Sq WCHPL E1 ....91 D5

Avoca Rd TOOT SW17 ....152 A4
Avocet Cl STHWK SE1 ....120 A1
Avocet Ms THMD SE28 ....109 D4
Avondale Av CRICK NW2 ....51 E5
Avondale Park Gdns NTGHL * W11 ....101 E1
Avondale Park Rd NTGHL W11 ....101 E1
Avondale Pavement STHWK * SE1 ....120 A1
Avondale Ri PECK SE15 ....137 F1
Avondale Rd CAN/RD E16 ....93 E4
   ELTH/MOT SE9 ....161 E2
   MORT/ESHN SW14 ....129 D1
   WALTH E17 ....62 A2
   WIM/MER SW19 ....150 B5
Avondale Sq STHWK SE1 ....120 A1
Avonley Rd NWCR SE14 ....120 C3
Avonmore Gdns WKENS * W14 ....101 F5
Avonmore Pl WKENS W14 ....101 E5
Avonmore Rd WKENS * W14 ....101 E5
Avonmouth St STHWK SE1 ....47 D2
Avon Rd BROCKY SE4 ....140 A1
Awliscombe Rd WELL DA16 ....127 F5
Axe St BARK IG11 ....84 C5
Axminster Rd HOLWY N7 ....57 E5
Aybrook St MHST W1U 18 A3
Aycliffe Rd SHB W12 ....99 F2
Aylesbury Cl FSTGT E7 ....81 F3
Aylesbury Rd WALW SE17 ....119 D3
Aylesbury St CLKNW EC1R 22 C1
   WLSDN NW10 ....51 D5
Aylesford St PIM SW1V 117 D1
Aylestone Av KIL/WHAMP NW6 ....71 D4
Aylmer Rd SHB W12 ....99 E3
   WAN E11 ....63 F2
Aylton Est BERM/RHTH * SE16 ....102 C3
Aylward Rd FSTH SE23 ....157 D2
Aylward St WCHPL * E1 ....90 C5
Aynhoe Rd HMSMTH * W6 ....101 D5
Ayres Cl PLSTW E13 ....94 A2
Ayres Crs WLSDN NW10 ....69 D4
Ayres St STHWK SE1 ....35 F5
Ayrsome Rd STNW/STAM N16 ....59 E5
Ayrton Rd SKENS SW7 ....40 A2
Aysgarth Rd DUL SE21 ....137 D3
Aytoun Pl BRXN/ST SW9 ....117 F5
Aytoun Rd BRXN/ST SW9 ....117 F5
Azalea Cl IL IG1 ....84 B2
Azania Ms KTTN NW5 ....74 B2
Azenby Rd PECK SE15 ....119 F5
Azof St GNWCH SE10 ....105 E5

B

Baalbec Rd HBRY N5 ....76 B2
Babington Ri WBLY HA9 ....68 A3
Babington Rd STRHM/NOR SW16 ....153 D5
Babmaes St STJS SW1Y 32 A5
Bache's St IS N1 ....12 B4
Back Church La WCHPL E1 ....90 A5
Back Hl CLKNW EC1R 22 B1
Back La HAMP NW3 ....72 C1
Bacon Gv STHWK SE1 ....49 E4
Bacon's La HGT N6 ....56 A3
Bacon St BETH E2 ....13 F5
Bacton St BETH E2 ....90 C2
Baden Pl STHWK SE1 ....36 A5
Baden Rd IL IG1 ....84 B2
Badgers Cft ELTH/MOT SE9 ....162 A3
Badminton Ms CAN/RD E16 ....106 A2
Badminton Rd BAL SW12 ....134 A4
Badsworth Rd CMBW SE5 ....118 C3
Bagley's La FUL/PGN SW6 ....114 B4

Bagshot Ct *WOOL/PLUM* * SE18 ....126 A4
Bagshot St *WALW* SE17......................119 E1
Baildon St *DEPT* SE8 ....121 F3
Bailey Cottages *POP/IOD* * E14 ....91 E4
Bainbridge St *NOXST/BSQ* WC1A 20 B4
Baird Cl *CDALE/KGS* NW9 ....50 C1
   LEY E10...62 A3
Baird Gdns *NRWD* SE19 ....155 E5
Baird St *STLK* EC1Y............................11 F5
Baizdon Rd *BKHTH/KID* SE3 ....123 E5
Baker Rd *WLSDN* NW10 ....69 E5
   WOOL/PLUM SE18 ....125 E4
Bakers Av *LEY* E10..............................62 B1
Bakers Hl *CLPT* E5..............................60 B3
Baker's Ms *MHST* W1U........................18 A4
Bakers Rents *BETH* E2.........................13 E4
Baker's Rw *CLKNW* EC1R 22 A1
   SRTFD E15.....................................93 E1
Baker St *CAMTN* NW1 ....17 F1
Baker's Yd *CLKNW* EC1R.......................22 A1
Bakery Cl *BRXN/ST* * SW9..................117 F3
Balaam St *PLSTW* E13..........................94 A2
Balaclava Rd *STHWK* SE1 ....49 F5
Bala Gn *CDALE/KGS* * NW9 ....51 E1
Balcaskie Rd *ELTH/MOT* SE9 ....143 F3
Balchen Rd *BKHTH/KID* SE3 ....125 D5
Balchier Rd *EDUL* SE22 ....138 C1
Balcombe St *CAMTN* NW1 ....5 E1
Balcorne St *HOM* E9 ....78 C4
Balder Ri *LEE/GVPK* SE12 ....160 B2
Balderton St *MYFR/PKLN* W1K 18 B5
Baldock St *BOW* E3..............................92 B1
Baldwin Crs *CMBW* SE5 ....118 C4
Baldwin's Gdns *FSBYW* WC1X 22 A2
Baldwin St *FSBYE* EC1V 12 A4
Baldwin Ter *IS* N1 ....11 D1
Baldwyn Gdns *ACT* W3 ....98 C1
Balfern Gv *CHSWK* W4 ....111 E1
Balfern St *BTSEA* SW11 ....115 E5
Balfe St *IS* N1 ....9 D2
Balfour Ms *MYFR/PKLN* W1K 30 B3
Balfour Pl *MYFR/PKLN* W1K................30 B2
Balfour Rd *ACT* W3 ....86 C4
   HBRY N5...76 C1
   IL IG1..66 B4
Balfour St *STHWK* SE1........................48 A4
Balgowan St *WOOL/PLUM* SE18 ....109 F5
Balham Gv *BAL* SW12.........................134 A5
Balham High Rd *BAL* SW12................152 B1
Balham Hl *BAL* SW12.........................134 B5
Balham New Rd *BAL* SW12.................134 B5
Balham Park Rd *TOOT* SW17 ....151 F1
Balham Station Rd *BAL* SW12 ....152 A1
Balkan Wk *WAP* * E1W........................102 B1
Balladier Wk *POP/IOD* E14....................92 B4
Ballamore Rd *BMLY* BR1.....................160 A3
Ballance Rd *HOM* E9 ....79 D3
Ballantine St *WAND/EARL* SW18 ......132 C2
Ballards Rd *CRICK* NW2.......................52 A4
Ballast Quay *GNWCH* SE10.................123 D1
Ballater Rd *CLAP* SW4 ....135 E2
Ballina St *FSTH* SE23 ....139 D5
Ballingdon Rd *BTSEA* SW11 ....134 A4
Balliol Rd *NKENS* W10 ....88 C3
Balloch Rd *CAT* SE6 ....159 D1
Ballogie Av *WLSDN* NW10......................69 E1
Ballow Cl *CMBW* * SE5 ....119 D3
Ball's Pond Pl *IS* * N1 ....77 D3
Balls Pond Rd *IS* N1 ....77 D3
Balmer Rd *BOW* E3..............................91 F1
Balmes Rd *IS* N1 ....77 D5
Balmoral Cl *PUT/ROE* * SW15............131 D4
Balmoral Gv *HOLWY* N7 ....75 F3

Balmoral Ms *SHB* W12 ....99 F4
Balmoral Rd *CRICK* NW2.....................70 B3
   FSTGT E7..82 C1
   LEY E10...62 B4
Balmore St *KTTN* NW5 ....56 B4
Balmuir Gdns *PUT/ROE* SW15 ....130 C2
Balnacraig Av *WLSDN* NW10 ....69 E1
Balniel Ga *PIM* SW1V..........................117 D1
Baltic Pl *IS* N1 ....77 E5
Baltic St East *STLK* EC1Y 23 E1
Baltic St West *FARR* EC1M 23 E1
Baltimore Pl *WELL* DA16....................127 F5
Balvaird Pl *PIM* SW1V.........................117 D1
Balvernie Gv *WAND/EARL* SW18 ....131 F5
Bamborough Gdns *SHB* W12 ....100 C3
Bamford Rd *BMLY* BR1.......................159 D5
Bampton Rd *FSTH* SE23 ....157 D3
Banbury Ct *COVGDN* * WC2E 32 C1
Banbury Rd *HOM* E9 ....79 D4
Banbury St *BTSEA* * SW11 ....115 E5
Banchory Rd *BKHTH/KID* SE3 ....124 B3
Bancroft Rd *WCHPL* E1.........................91 D2
Banfield Rd *PECK* SE15 ....138 B1
Bangalore St *PUT/ROE* SW15 ....130 C1
Banim St *HMSMTH* W6 ....100 B4
Banister Rd *WLSDN* NW10 ....89 D2
Bank End *STHWK* SE1 ....35 F3
Bankfoot Rd *BMLY* BR1.......................159 E4
Bankhurst Rd *CAT* SE6 ....139 F5
Bank La *PUT/ROE* SW15 ....129 E3
Bankside *STHWK* SE1 ....35 E2
Bankside Rd *IL* IG1..............................84 C2
The Bank *HGT* N6.................................56 B3
Bankton Rd *BRXS/STRHM* SW2 ....136 B3
Bankwell Rd *LEW* SE13 ....141 E2
Banner St *STLK* EC1Y 23 F1
Banning St *GNWCH* SE10 ....123 E1
Bannister Cl *BRXS/STRHM* SW2..........154 A1
Bannockburn Rd
   WOOL/PLUM SE18 ....109 E5
Banstead St *PECK* SE15 ....138 C1
Bantry St *CMBW* SE5 ....119 D3
Banyard Rd *BERM/RHTH* SE16 ....102 B4
Baptist Gdns *HAMP* NW3 ....74 A3
Barandon Wk *NTGHL* * W11 ....101 D1
Barbauld Rd *STNW/STAM* N16 ....59 E1
Barbers Rd *SRTFD* E15.........................92 B1
Barbican *BARB* EC2Y 23 F2
Barb Ms *HMSMTH* W6 ....100 C4
Barbon Cl *BMSBY* WC1N......................21 D2
Barchard St *WAND/EARL* SW18 ....132 B3
Barchester St *POP/IOD* E14 ....92 B4
Barclay Cl *FUL/PGN* * SW6 ....114 A3
Barclay Rd *FUL/PGN* SW6 ....114 A3
   PLSTW E13......................................94 C3
   WAN E11...63 F3
Barcombe Av *BRXS/STRHM* SW2 ....153 E2
Barden St *WOOL/PLUM* SE18..............127 E3
Bardolph Rd *HOLWY* N7 ....75 E1
Bard Rd *NKENS* W10 ....101 D1
Bardsey Pl *WCHPL* E1 ....90 C4
Bardsey Wk *IS* * N1 ....76 C3
Bardsley La *BRXS/STRHM* SW2 ....136 A2
   GNWCH SE10.................................122 C2
Barfett St *NKENS* W10 ....89 F3
Barfield Rd *WAN* * E11 ....63 F3
Barford St *IS* N1 ....76 A5
Barforth Rd *PECK* SE15 ....138 B1
Bargate Cl *WOOL/PLUM* SE18 ....127 F1
Barge House Rd *CAN/RD* E16 ....108 B3
Barge House St *STHWK* SE1 ....34 B3
Bargery Rd *CAT* SE6 ....158 B1
Bargrove Crs *CAT* SE6 ....157 F2

Barham Cl *CHST* BR7 ....162 B5
Barham Rd *CHST* BR7 ....162 B5
Baring Cl *LEE/GVPK* SE12 ....160 A2
Baring Rd *BMLY* BR1 ....160 B4
Baring St *IS* N1 ....77 D5
Barker Dr *CAMTN* NW1 ....74 C4
Barking Rd *EHAM* E6 ....83 F5
   POP/IOD E14 ....93 E5
Bark Pl *BAY/PAD* W2 ....26 C1
Barkston Gdns *ECT* SW5 ....38 C5
Barkworth Rd *BERM/RHTH* SE16 ......120 B1
Barlborough St *NWCR* SE14 ....121 D3
Barlby Gdns *NKENS* W10 ....89 D3
Barlby Rd *NKENS* W10 ....88 C4
Barley Mow Pas *CHSWK* W4 ....111 D1
Barlow Pl *MYFR/PICC* W1J 31 D2
Barlow Rd *ACT* W3 ....98 B2
   CRICK NW2 ....71 F3
Barlow St *WALW* SE17 ....48 B4
Barmeston Rd *CAT* SE6 ....158 B2
Barmouth Rd *WAND/EARL* SW18 ......132 C4
Barnabas Rd *HOM* E9 ....79 D3
Barnaby Pl *SKENS* SW7 ....40 A5
Barnard Ms *BTSEA* SW11 ....133 E2
Barnardo Gdns *WCHPL* * E1 ....91 D5
Barnardo St *WCHPL* E1 ....91 D5
Barnard Rd *BTSEA* SW11 ....133 E2
Barnby St *CAMTN* NW1 ....7 F2
   SRTFD E15 ....81 E5
Barn Cl *KTTN* * NW5 ....75 D2
Barnes Av *BARN* SW13 ....112 A3
Barnes Br *CHSWK* W4 ....111 E5
Barnes High St *BARN* SW13 ....111 F5
Barnes Rd *IL* IG1 ....84 C2
Barnes St *POP/IOD* E14 ....91 E5
Barnes Ter *DEPT* SE8 ....121 F1
Barnet Gv *BETH* E2 ....90 A2
Barnett St *WCHPL* E1 ....90 B5
Barney Cl *CHARL* SE7 ....124 C1
Barn Fld *HAMP* * NW3 ....73 F2
Barnfield Gdns *WOOL/PLUM* * SE18 ..126 B2
Barnfield Rd *WOOL/PLUM* SE18 ....126 B2
Barnham St *STHWK* SE1 ....37 D5
Barn Hl *WBLY* HA9 ....50 B4
Barnhill Rd *WBLY* HA9 ....50 C5
Barningham Wy *CDALE/KGS* NW9 ......50 C1
Barn Ri *WBLY* HA9 ....50 A3
Barnsbury Est *IS* N1 ....75 F5
Barnsbury Gv *HOLWY* N7 ....75 F4
Barnsbury Pk *IS* N1 ....10 A1
Barnsbury Rd *IS* N1 ....10 A1
Barnsbury Sq *IS* N1 ....76 A4
Barnsbury St *IS* N1 ....76 A4
Barnsbury Ter *IS* N1 ....75 F4
Barnsdale Av *POP/IOD* E14 ....104 B5
Barnsdale Rd *MV/WKIL* W9 ....89 F3
Barnsley St *WCHPL* E1 ....90 B3
Barnstaple La *LEW* SE13 ....140 C3
Barnston Wk *IS* * N1 ....76 C5
Barn Wy *WBLY* HA9 ....50 A3
Barnwell Rd *BRXS/STRHM* SW2 ....136 A3
Barnwood Rd *MV/WKIL* W9 ....14 C1
Baroness Rd *BETH* E2 ....13 F3
Barons Cl *IS* * N1 ....10 A1
Barons Court Rd *WKENS* * W14 ....113 F1
Barons Keep *WKENS* * W14 ....113 E1
Baronsmead Rd *BARN* SW13 ....112 A4
Baron's Pl *STHWK* SE1 ....46 B1
Baron St *IS* N1 ....10 A2
Barque Ms *DEPT* SE8 ....122 A2
Barrett's Green Rd *WLSDN* NW10 ....86 C1

Barrett's Gv *STNW/STAM* N16 ....77 E2
Barrett St *MBLAR* W1H 18 B5
Barrhill Rd *BRXS/STRHM* SW2 ....153 E2
Barriedale *NWCR* SE14 ....121 E4
Barrier Point Rd *CAN/RD* E16 ....106 C3
Barringer Sq *TOOT* SW17 ....152 A4
Barrington Cl *KTTN* NW5 ....74 A2
Barrington Rd *BRXN/ST* SW9 ....136 B1
   MNPK E12 ....84 A3
Barrington Vls *WOOL/PLUM* SE18 .....126 A4
Barrowgate Rd *CHSWK* W4 ....110 C3
Barrow Hill Est *STJWD* NW8 ....4 C2
Barrow Hill Rd *STJWD* NW8 ....4 C2
Barrs Rd *WLSDN* NW10 ....69 D4
Barry Av *SEVS/STOTM* N15 ....59 F1
Barry Pde *EDUL* * SE22 ....138 A2
Barry Rd *EDUL* SE22 ....138 A4
   EHAM E6 ....95 E5
   WLSDN NW10 ....68 C4
Barset Rd *PECK* SE15 ....138 C1
Barston Rd *WNWD* SE27 ....154 C2
Barstow Crs *BRXS/STRHM* SW2 ....153 E1
Barter St *NOXST/BSQ* WC1A 21 D3
Bartholomew Cl *STBT* EC1A 23 E3
   WAND/EARL SW18 ....132 C2
Bartholomew La *OBST* EC2N 24 B5
Bartholomew Rd *KTTN* NW5 ....74 C3
Bartholomew Sq *FSBYE* EC1V 11 F5
Bartholomew St *STHWK* SE1 ....48 B3
Bartholomew Vls *KTTN* NW5 ....74 C3
Barth Rd *WOOL/PLUM* SE18 ....109 E5
Bartle Av *EHAM* E6 ....95 E1
Bartle Rd *NTGHL* W11 ....89 E1
Bartlett Cl *POP/IOD* E14 ....92 A5
Bartlett Ct *FLST/FETLN* * EC4A 22 B4
Barton Cl *PECK* SE15 ....138 B1
Barton Rd *WKENS* W14 ....113 E1
Barton St *WEST* SW1P 44 C3
Bartram Rd *BROCKY* SE4 ....139 E3
Bartrip St *HOM* E9 ....79 E3
Barward Cl *WOOL/PLUM* SE18 ....108 A5
Barwick Rd *FSTGT* E7 ....82 B1
Baseing Cl *EHAM* E6 ....108 A1
Basevi Wy *DEPT* SE8 ....122 A2
Bashley Rd *WLSDN* NW10 ....87 D3
Basil Av *EHAM* E6 ....95 E2
Basil Gdns *WNWD* SE27 ....154 C5
Basil St *CHEL* SW3 ....41 E1
Basin Ap *POP/IOD* E14 ....91 E5
Basingdon Wy *CMBW* SE5 ....137 D2
Basinghall Av *CITYW* EC2V 24 A4
Basinghall St *CITYW* EC2V 24 A4
Basing Hl *GLDGN* NW11 ....53 F3
Basing Pl *BETH* E2 ....13 F3
Basing St *NTGHL* W11 ....89 F1
Basire St *IS* N1 ....76 C5
Baskerville Gdns *WLSDN* NW10 ....69 E1
Baskerville Rd *WAND/EARL* SW18 .....133 E5
Basket Gdns *ELTH/MOT* SE9 ....143 E3
Baslow Wk *CLPT* E5 ....79 D1
Basnett Rd *BTSEA* * SW11 ....134 A1
Bassano St *EDUL* SE22 ....137 F3
Bassant Rd *WOOL/PLUM* SE18 ....127 F2
Bassein Park Rd *SHB* W12 ....99 F3
Bassett Rd *NKENS* W10 ....89 D5
Bassett St *KTTN* NW5 ....74 A3
Bassingham Rd *WAND/EARL* SW18 ...132 C5
Basswood Cl *PECK* SE15 ....138 B1
Bastwick St *FSBYE* EC1V 11 D5
Basuto Rd *FUL/PGN* SW6 ....114 A4
Batavia Rd *NWCR* SE14 ....121 E3
Batchelor St *IS* N1 ....10 B1
Bateman Cl *BARK* IG11 ....84 C3

Batemans Cnr *CHSWK* * W4 ....99 D5
Bateman's Rw *SDTCH* EC2A..................13 C5
Bateman St *SOHO/SHAV* W1D 20 A5
Bate St *POP/IOD* E14 ....103 F1
Bath Cl *PECK* SE15 ....120 B3
Bathgate Rd *WIM/MER* SW19 ....149 D3
Bath Gv *BETH* E2 ....90 A1
Bath Pl *IS* N1 ....12 C4
Bath Rd *CHSWK* W4 ....99 E5
 FSTGT E7 ....83 D3
Baths Ap *FUL/PGN* * SW6 ....113 F3
Bath St *FSBYE* EC1V 11 F4
Bath Ter *STHWK* SE1 ....47 E3
Bathurst Gdns *WLSDN* NW10................88 B1
Bathurst Ms *BAY/PAD* W2 ....28 B1
Bathurst Rd *IL* IG1 ....66 B3
Bathurst St *BAY/PAD* W2 ....28 B1
Bathway *WOOL/PLUM* SE18 ....108 A5
Batley Pl *STNW/STAM* N16 ....59 F5
Batley Rd *STNW/STAM* N16 ....59 F5
Batman Cl *SHB* W12 ....100 B2
Batoum Gdns *HMSMTH* W6 ....100 C4
Batson St *SHB* W12 ....100 A3
Batten Cottages *POP/IOD* * E14........91 E4
Batten St *BTSEA* SW11 ....133 E1
Battersby Rd *CAT* SE6 ....159 D2
Battersea Br *BTSEA* SW11 ....115 D2
Battersea Bridge Rd *BTSEA* SW11 ....115 D3
Battersea Church Rd *BTSEA* SW11 ....115 D4
Battersea High St *BTSEA* SW11 ....115 D4
Battersea Park Rd *BTSEA* SW11 ....116 A4
Battersea Ri *BTSEA* SW11 ....133 E3
Battersea Sq *BTSEA* * SW11 ....115 E3
Battery Rd *THMD* SE28 ....109 E3
Battishill St *IS* N1 ....76 B4
Battle Bridge La *STHWK* SE1 ....36 C4
Battle Bridge Rd *CAMTN* NW1................8 C2
Battledean Rd *HBRY* N5........................76 B3
Batty St *WCHPL* E1 ....90 A5
Baudwin Rd *CAT* SE6 ....159 A5
The Baulk *WAND/EARL* SW18 ....132 A5
Bavaria Rd *ARCH* N19 ....57 E4
Bavent Rd *CMBW* SE5 ....118 C5
Bawdale Rd *EDUL* SE22........................137 F3
Bawtree Rd *NWCR* SE14 ....121 E3
Baxendale St *BETH* E2 ....90 A2
Baxter Rd *CAN/RD* E16........................94 C5
 IL IG1..84 B2
 IS N1 ....77 D3
Bayfield Rd *ELTH/MOT* SE9 ....143 D5
Bayford Ms *HACK* * E8 ....78 B4
Bayford Rd *WLSDN* NW10 ....89 D2
Bayford St *HACK* E8................................78 B4
Bayham Pl *CAMTN* NW1 ....74 C5
Bayham Rd *CHSWK* W4 ....99 D4
Bayham St *CAMTN* NW1 ....74 C5
Bayley St *FITZ* W1T................................20 A3
Baylis Rd *STHWK* SE1 ....46 A2
Bayne Cl *EHAM* E6................................95 F5
Baynes Ms *HAMP* NW3 ....73 D3
Baynes St *CAMTN* NW1 ....74 C4
Bayonne Rd *FUL/PGN* SW6 ....113 E5
Bays Cl *SYD* SE26 ....156 C5
Bayston Rd *STNW/STAM* N16 ....59 F5
Bayswater Rd *BAY/PAD* W2....................27 D2
Baythorne St *BOW* E3 ....91 F4
Baytree Cl *BFN/LL* DA15......................163 F1
Baytree Rd *BRXS/STRHM* SW2 ....135 E2
Bazely St *POP/IOD* E14 ....104 C1
Beacham Cl *CHARL* SE7 ....125 D2
Beachborough Rd *BMLY* BR1 ....158 C4
Beachcroft Rd *WAN* E11........................63 E5
Beachy Rd *BOW* E3................................80 A5

Beacon Hl *HOLWY* N7 ....75 E2
Beacon Rd *LEW* SE13..........................141 D4
Beaconsfield Cl *BKHTH/KID* SE3 ......124 C1
 CHSWK W4..110 C1
Beaconsfield Rd *BKHTH/KID* SE3 ......124 A2
 CAN/RD E16..93 F3
 CHSWK W4..99 D4
 ELTH/MOT SE9 ....161 E3
 LEY * E10..62 C5
 WALTH E17..61 F1
 WALW SE17..119 D2
 WLSDN NW10 ....69 F3
Beaconsfield Terrace Rd
 WKENS W14..101 E4
Beaconsfield Wk *FUL/PGN* SW6 ....113 F4
Beacontree Rd *WAN* E11........................63 F2
Beadman Pl *WNWD* * SE27................154 B4
Beadman St *WNWD* SE27....................154 B4
Beadnell Rd *FSTH* SE23 ....157 D1
Beadon Rd *HMSMTH* W6 ....100 C5
Beak St *REGST* W1B................................31 E1
Beale Pl *BOW* E3 ....91 F1
Beale Rd *BOW* E3..................................79 F5
Beal Rd *IL* IG1 ....66 A4
Beanacre Cl *HOM* * E9 ....79 E3
Beanshaw *ELTH/MOT* SE9 ....162 A4
Beardsfield *PLSTW* E13..........................82 A5
Beardsley Wy *ACT* W3 ....99 D3
Bear Gdns *STHWK* SE1 ....35 E3
Bear La *STHWK* SE1 ....35 D3
Bearstead Ri *BROCKY* SE4 ....139 E3
Bear St *LSQ/SEVD* WC2H 32 B1
Beatrice Cl *PLSTW* E13 ....94 A3
Beatrice Pl *KENS* W8..............................38 C3
Beatrice Rd *FSBYPK* N4 ....58 A2
 STHWK SE1 ....102 A5
Beatty Rd *STNW/STAM* N16 ....77 E1
Beatty St *CAMTN* * NW1 ....7 E1
Beauchamp Pl *CHEL* SW3......................41 D2
Beauchamp Rd *BTSEA* SW11 ....133 E2
 FSTGT E7..82 B4
Beauchamp St *HCIRC* EC1N 22 A3
Beauchamp Ter *PUT/ROE* SW15 ....130 B1
Beauclerc Rd *HMSMTH* W6 ....100 B4
Beaufort *EHAM* E6................................96 A4
Beaufort Cl *PUT/ROE* SW15 ....148 C5
Beaufort Gdns *CHEL* SW3 ....41 D2
 HDN NW4..52 C1
 IL IG1 ....66 A3
Beaufort St *CHEL* SW3 ....115 D2
Beaufoy Wk *LBTH* SE11 ....45 F5
Beaulieu Av *CAN/RD* E16 ....106 B2
 SYD SE26 ....156 B4
Beaulieu Pl *CHSWK* W4 ....98 C4
Beaumaris Gn *CDALE/KGS* * NW9 ....51 E1
Beaumont Av *WKENS* W14..................113 F1
Beaumont Crs *WKENS* W14 ....113 F1
Beaumont Gdns *HAMP* NW3................54 A5
Beaumont Gv *WCHPL* E1........................91 D3
Beaumont Ms *MHST* * W1U 18 B2
Beaumont Pl *FITZ* W1T............................7 F5
Beaumont Ri *ARCH* N19 ....57 D3
Beaumont Rd *CHSWK* W4 ....98 C4
 LEY E10..62 B2
 PLSTW E13..94 B2
 WIM/MER SW19 ....131 E5
Beaumont Sq *WCHPL* E1........................91 D4
Beaumont St *MHST* W1U 18 B2
Beaumont Ter *LEW* * SE13 ....141 E5
Beaumont Wk *HAMP* NW3 ....73 F4
Beauval Rd *EDUL* SE22........................137 F4
Beaverbank Rd *ELTH/MOT* SE9..........163 D1
Beaverwood Rd *CHST* BR7 ....163 E5

Beavor La *HMSMTH* W6 ....100 A5
Bebbington Rd
   WOOL/PLUM SE18 ....109 E5
Beccles St *POP/IOD* E14 ....91 F5
Beck Cl *LEW* SE13.........................122 B4
Becket Av *EHAM* E6 ....96 A2
Becket St *STHWK* SE1 ....48 A2
Beckett Cl *STRHM/NOR* SW16 ......153 D2
   WLSDN NW10 ....69 D3
Beckford Cl *WKENS* W14 ....101 F5
Beckford Pl *WALW* * SE17.............118 C1
Becklow Rd *SHB* W12 ....100 A3
Beck Rd *HACK* E8............................78 B5
Beckton Rd *CAN/RD* E16 ....93 F4
Beckway St *WALW* SE17 ....48 B5
Beckwith Rd *HNHL* SE24................137 D4
Becmead Av *STRHM/NOR* SW16 ....153 D4
Becondale Rd *NRWD* SE19..............155 E5
Bective Rd *FSTGT* E7 ....82 A1
   PUT/ROE SW15 ....131 F2
Bedale St *STHWK* * SE1 ....36 A4
Beddington Rd *GDMY/SEVK* IG3 .....67 F2
Bedford Av *RSQ* WC1B 20 B3
Bedfordbury *CHCR* WC2N 32 C1
Bedford Cl *CHSWK* W4...................111 E2
Bedford Cnr *CHSWK* * W4 ....99 E5
Bedford Ct *CHCR* WC2N 32 C2
Bedford Gdns *KENS* W8 ....26 A4
Bedford Hl *BAL* SW12 ....152 B2
Bedford Pl *RSQ* WC1B.....................20 C2
Bedford Rd *BFN/LL* DA15 ....163 E3
   CEND/HSY/T N8 ....57 D1
   CHSWK W4...................................99 D4
   CLAP SW4..................................135 E2
   EHAM E6 ....84 A5
   IL IG1...66 B5
Bedford Rw *FSBYW* WC1X 21 F2
Bedford Sq *RSQ* WC1B 20 B3
Bedford St *COVGDN* WC2E 32 C1
Bedford Wy *STPAN* WC1H 20 B1
Bedgebury Gdns *WIM/MER* SW19 ...149 E2
Bedgebury Rd *ELTH/MOT* SE9.......143 D2
Bedivere Rd *BMLY* BR1..................160 A3
Bedser Cl *VX/NE* SW8 ....117 F2
Beeby Rd *CAN/RD* E16 ....94 B4
Beech Av *ACT* W3...........................99 E2
Beech Cl *DEPT* SE8 ....121 F2
   PUT/ROE SW15 ....130 A5
Beech Ct *ELTH/MOT* * SE9 ....143 E4
Beechcroft Av *GLDGN* NW11 ....53 F2
Beechcroft Cl *STRHM/NOR* SW16 ..153 F5
Beechcroft Rd
   MORT/ESHN * SW14 ....128 C1
   TOOT SW17 ....151 F3
Beechdale Rd *BRXS/STRHM* SW2 ...135 F4
Beechen Pl *FSTH* SE23 ....156 C2
Beeches Rd *TOOT* SW17 ....151 E3
Beechfield Rd *CAT* SE6 ....157 F1
   FSBYPK N4...................................58 C1
Beechhill Rd *ELTH/MOT* SE9 ....144 A3
Beechmont Cl *BMLY* BR1...............159 E5
Beechmore Rd *BTSEA* SW11 ....115 F4
Beecholme Est *CLPT* * E5................60 C5
Beech St (Below) *BARB* EC2Y...........23 E2
Beech Tree Cl *IS* N1 ....76 A4
Beech Wy *WLSDN* NW10..................69 D4
Beechwood Av *RCH/KEW* TW9 ......110 A4
Beechwood Gv *ACT* W3 ....99 E1
Beechwood Rd *CHST* BR7 ....162 B4
Beechwood Rd *HACK* E8 ....77 F3
Beechworth Cl *HAMP* NW3 ....54 B4
Beecroft Rd *BROCKY* SE4...............139 E3
Beehive Cl *HACK* E8 ....77 F4

Beehive Pl *BRXN/ST* SW9 ....136 A1
Beeston Cl *HACK* E8 ....78 A2
Beeston Pl *BGVA* SW1W 43 D3
Beethoven St *NKENS* W10 ....89 E2
Begbie Rd *BKHTH/KID* SE3 ....124 C4
Begonia Cl *EHAM* E6 ....95 E4
Beira St *BAL* SW12.........................134 B5
Bekesbourne St *POP/IOD* * E14 ......91 E5
Belfast Rd *STNW/STAM* N16 ....59 F4
Belford Gv *WOOL/PLUM* SE18 ......108 A5
Belfort Rd *PECK* SE15 ....120 C5
Belfry Cl *BERM/RHTH* * SE16 ....120 B1
Belgrade Rd *STNW/STAM* N16.........77 E1
Belgrave Cl *ACT* W3.........................98 C3
Belgrave Gdns *ST/WD* NW8 ....72 B5
Belgrave Ms South *KTBR* SW1X 42 B3
Belgrave Ms West *KTBR* SW1X 42 A2
Belgrave Pl *KTBR* SW1X 42 B3
Belgrave Rd *BARN* SW13 ....111 F3
   IL IG1...66 A4
   PIM SW1V 43 E5
   PLSTW E13.................................94 C3
   WALTH E17.................................62 A1
   WAN E11 ....64 A3
Belgrave Sq *KTBR* SW1X 42 A2
Belgrave St *WCHPL* E1 ....91 D4
Belgrove St *CAMTN* NW1 ....8 C3
Belinda Rd *BRXN/ST* SW9 ....136 B1
Belitha Vls *IS* N1 ....76 A4
Bellamy Cl *ECT* SW5.......................113 F1
Bellamy St *BAL* SW12 ....134 B5
Bellasis Av *BRXS/STRHM* SW2 ......153 E1
Bell Dr *WAND/EARL* SW18 ....131 E5
Bellefields Rd *BRXN/ST* SW9 ....135 F1
Bellegrove Cl *WELL* DA16 ....127 E5
Bellegrove Rd *WELL* DA16 ....127 E5
Bellenden Rd *PECK* SE15 ....119 F5
Belleville Rd *BTSEA* SW11 ....133 E3
Bellevue Pl *WCHPL* * E1 ....90 C3
Bellevue Rd *BARN* SW13................112 A5
   TOOT SW17 ....133 F5
Bellew St *TOOT* SW17 ....150 C3
Bell Gdns *LEY* * E10 ....62 A3
Bellgate Ms *KTTN* NW5 ....74 B1
Bell Gn *SYD* SE26 ....157 E4
Bell Green La *SYD* SE26.................157 F5
Bellina Ms *KTTN* NW5 ....74 B1
Bellingham Gn *CAT* SE6 ....158 C3
Bellingham Rd *CAT* SE6 ....158 C3
Bell La *CAN/RD* E16 ....106 A2
   WCHPL E1 ....25 E3
Bell Meadow *NRWD* SE19..............155 E4
Bello Cl *BRXS/STRHM* SW2 ....154 B1
Bellot St *GNWCH* SE10...................123 E1
Bell St *BAY/PAD* W2 ....16 C2
   WOOL/PLUM SE18 ....125 E4
Belltrees Gv *STRHM/NOR* SW16 ....153 F5
Bell Water Ga *WOOL/PLUM* SE18 ..108 A4
Bell Wharf La *CANST* EC4R 35 F2
Bellwood Rd *PECK* SE15 ....139 D2
Bell Yd *LINN* WC2A 22 A5
Belmont Av *WELL* DA16 ....127 E5
Belmont Cl *CLAP* SW4 ....134 C1
Belmont Gv *CHSWK* W4 ....99 D5
   LEW SE13...................................141 D1
Belmont Hl *LEW* SE13 ....141 D1
Belmont La *CHST* BR7 ....162 C4
Belmont Pde *CHST* * BR7 ....162 B5
Belmont Pk *LEW* SE13 ....141 D2
Belmont Park Cl *LEW* SE13 ....141 E2
Belmont Park Rd *LEY* E10 ....62 A5
Belmont Rd *CHST* BR7 ....162 B5
   CLAP SW4..................................134 C1

IL IG1...66 C5
Belmont St *CAMTN* NW1..................74 A4
Belmont Ter *CHSWK* W4..................99 D5
Belmore La *HOLWY* * N7...................75 D2
Belmore St *VX/NE* SW8..................117 D4
Beloe Rd *BARN* SW13......................130 A2
Belsham St *HOM* E9..........................78 C3
Belsize Av *HAMP* NW3.....................73 E2
Belsize Court Garages *HAMP* NW3...73 D2
Belsize Crs *HAMP* NW3....................73 D2
Belsize Gv *HAMP* NW3......................73 E3
Belsize La *HAMP* NW3......................73 D3
Belsize Ms *HAMP* * NW3...................73 D3
Belsize Pk *HAMP* NW3......................73 D3
Belsize Park Gdns *HAMP* NW3..........73 D3
Belsize Park Ms *HAMP* NW3.............73 D3
Belsize Pl *HAMP* NW3.......................73 D2
Belsize Rd *KIL/WHAMP* NW6.............72 B5
Belsize Sq *HAMP* NW3......................73 D3
Belsize Ter *HAMP* NW3.....................73 D3
Belson Rd *WOOL/PLUM* SE18..........107 F5
Beltane Dr *WIM/MER* SW19.............149 E5
Belthorn Crs *BAL* SW12..................134 C5
Belton Rd *FSTGT* E7..........................82 B4
    WLSDN NW10................................70 A3
Belton Wy *BOW* E3..........................92 A4
Beltran Rd *FUL/PGN* SW6................114 B5
Belvedere Av *WIM/MER* SW19.........149 E5
Belvedere Buildings *STHWK* SE1.......47 D1
Belvedere Dr *WIM/MER* SW19..........149 E5
Belvedere Gv *WIM/MER* SW19.........149 E5
Belvedere Ms *PECK* SE15................138 C1
Belvedere Rd *LEY* E10.......................61 E3
    STHWK SE1..................................33 E3
Belvedere Sq *WIM/MER* SW19.........149 E5
The Belvedere *WBPTN* * SW10.........114 C4
Belvoir Rd *EDUL* SE22.....................138 A5
Bembridge Cl *KIL/WHAMP* NW6.........71 E4
Bemerton Est *IS* N1...........................75 F4
Bemerton St *IS* N1.............................75 F5
Bemish Rd *PUT/ROE* SW15.............131 D1
Benares Rd *WOOL/PLUM* SE18.......109 F5
Benbow Rd *HMSMTH* W6................100 B4
Benbow St *DEPT* SE8......................122 A2
Benbury Cl *BMLY* BR1......................158 C5
Bendall Ms *CAMTN* NW1...................17 D2
Bendemeer Rd *PUT/ROE* SW15.......131 D1
Bendish Rd *EHAM* E6.........................85 E4
Bendon Va *WAND/EARL* SW18........132 B5
Benedict Rd *BRXN/ST* SW9.............135 F1
Bengal Rd *IL* IG1................................84 B1
Benham Cl *BTSEA* SW11.................133 D1
Benhill Rd *CMBW* SE5.....................119 D4
Benhurst La *STRHM/NOR* SW16.....154 A5
Benin St *LEW* SE13..........................141 D5
Benjamin Cl *HACK* E8........................78 A5
Benjamin St *FARR* EC1M....................22 C2
Ben Jonson Rd *WCHPL* E1.................91 D4
Benledi St *POP/IOD* E14....................93 D5
Bennelong Cl *SHB* W12.....................100 B1
Bennerley Rd *BTSEA* SW11.............133 E3
Bennet's Hl *BLKFR* * EC4V................35 F1
Bennett Gv *LEW* SE13.....................122 B4
Bennett Pk *BKTHW/KID* SE3............141 F1
Bennett Rd *PLSTW* E13......................94 C3
Bennett St *CHSWK* W4....................111 E2
    WHALL SW1A...............................31 F3
Benn St *HOM* E9................................79 E3
Bensbury Cl *PUT/ROE* SW15...........130 B5
Ben Smith Wy *BERM/RHTH* SE16...102 A4
Benson Av *PLSTW* E13.......................94 C1
Benson Quay *WAP* E1W...................102 C1
Benson Rd *FSTH* SE23.....................156 C1

Benthal Rd *STNW/STAM* N16...........59 F4
Bentham Rd *HOM* E9.........................79 D3
Ben Tillet Cl *CAN/RD* * E16.............107 F2
Bentinck Ms *MHST* W1U....................18 A4
Bentinck St *MHST* W1U......................18 A4
Bentley Dr *GNTH/NBYPK* IG2............66 C1
Bentley Rd *IS* N1...............................77 E3
Benton Rd *IL* IG1................................67 D3
Benton's La *WNWD* SE27................154 C4
Benton's Ri *WNWD* SE27.................155 D5
Bentworth Rd *SHB* W12......................88 B5
Benwell Rd *HOLWY* N7.......................76 A1
Benwick Cl *BERM/RHTH* SE16.........102 B5
Benworth St *BOW* E3........................91 F2
Benyon Rd *IS* N1................................77 D5
Berber Rd *BTSEA* * SW11.................133 F3
Bercta Rd *ELTH/MOT* SE9................162 C2
Berenger Wk *WBPTN* * SW10...........115 D3
Berens Rd *WLSDN* NW10...................89 D2
Beresford Av *ALP/SUD* HA0................68 A5
Beresford Rd *HBRY* N5......................77 D2
Beresford Rd *WOOL/PLUM* SE18.....108 B4
Beresford Ter *HBRY* N5......................76 C2
Berestede Rd *HMSMTH* W6.............111 F1
Bere St *WAP* E1W.............................103 D1
Berger Rd *HOM* E9.............................79 D3
Berghem Ms *WKENS* W14................101 D4
Bergholt Crs *STNW/STAM* N16..........59 E2
Bergholt Ms *CAMTN* NW1..................74 C4
Bering Wk *CAN/RD* E16......................95 D5
Berisford Ms *WAND/EARL* SW18.....132 C4
Berkeley Ms *MBLAR* W1H...................17 F4
Berkeley Rd *BARN* SW13.................112 A4
    MNPK E12....................................83 E2
    SEVS/STOTM N15..........................59 D1
Berkeley Sq *MYFR/PICC* W1J............31 D2
Berkeley St *MYFR/PICC* W1J.............31 D2
Berkley Rd *CAMTN* NW1....................73 F4
Berkshire Rd *HOM* E9........................79 F3
Bermans Wy *WLSDN* NW10................69 C1
Bermondsey Wall East
    BERM/RHTH SE16.........................102 A3
Bermondsey Wall West
    BERM/RHTH SE16.........................102 A3
Bernard Ashley Dr *CHARL* SE7.........124 B1
Bernard Cassidy St *CAN/RD* * E16....93 D4
Bernard Gdns *WIM/MER* SW19........149 F5
Bernard St *BMSBY* WC1N...................20 C1
Bernay's Gv *BRXN/ST* SW9.............135 F2
Berners Ms *FITZ* W1T........................19 F3
Berners Pl *FITZ* W1T..........................19 F4
Berners Rd *IS* N1...............................76 A5
Berners St *FITZ* W1T..........................19 F3
Berner Ter *WCHPL* * E1.....................90 A5
Berridge Ms *KIL/WHAMP* NW6..........72 A2
Berridge Rd *NRWD* SE19.................155 D5
Berriman Rd *HOLWY* N7....................57 F5
Berry Cl *WLSDN* NW10.......................69 C4
Berry Cottages *POP/IOD* * E14..........91 E5
Berryfield Rd *WALW* SE17...............118 B3
Berryhill *ELTH/MOT* SE9..................144 B2
Berryhill Gdns *ELTH/MOT* SE9.........144 B2
Berry La *DUL* SE21...........................155 D4
Berryman's La *SYD* SE26.................157 D4
Berrymead Gdns *ACT* W3...................98 C2
Berrymede Rd *CHSWK* W4.................99 D4
Berry Pl *FSBYE* EC1V.........................11 D4
Berry St *FSBYE* EC1V.........................23 D1
Bertal Rd *TOOT* SW17......................151 D4
Berthon St *DEPT* SE8.......................122 A4
Bertie Rd *WLSDN* NW10.....................70 A3
Bertram Rd *HDN* NW4.........................52 A1

Bertram St *KTTN* NW5 ....56 B5
Bertrand St *LEW* SE13 ....140 B1
Berwick Crs *BFN/LL* DA15 ....145 E4
Berwick Rd *CAN/RD* E16 ....94 B5
Berwick St *SOHO/CST* W1F 19 F5
Berwyn Rd *HNHL* SE24 ....154 B1
   RCHPK/HAM TW10 ....128 B2
Beryl Av *EHAM* E6 ....95 E4
Beryl Rd *HMSMTH* W6 ....113 D1
Besant CI *CRICK* * NW2 ....53 E5
Besant Rd *CRICK* NW2 ....71 E1
Besant Wy *WLSDN* NW10 ....68 C2
Bessant Dr *RCH/KEW* TW9 ....110 B4
Bessborough PI *PIM* SW1V 117 D1
Bessborough Rd *PUT/ROE* SW15 .....148 A1
Bessborough St *PIM* SW1V 117 D1
Bessemer Rd *CMBW* SE5 ....118 C5
Bessie Lansbury CI *EHAM* E6 ....96 A5
Besson St *NWCR* SE14 ....121 D4
Bessy St *BETH* * E2 ....90 C2
Bestwood St *DEPT* SE8 ....103 D5
Beswick Ms *KIL/WHAMP* NW6 ....72 B2
Betchworth Rd *GDMY/SEVK* IG3 ....67 E4
Bethell Av *CAN/RD* E16 ....93 F3
   IL IG1 ....66 A2
Bethnal Green Rd *BETH* E2 ....13 F5
Bethune Rd *STNW/STAM* N16 ....59 D2
   WLSDN NW10 ....87 D3
Bethwin Rd *CMBW* SE5 ....118 B3
Betterton St *LSQ/SEVD* WC2H 20 C5
Bettons Pk *SRTFD* E15 ....81 E5
Bettridge Rd *FUL/PGN* SW6 ....113 F5
Betts Rd *CAN/RD* E16 ....94 B5
Betts St *WCHPL* * E1 ....102 B1
Bevan St *IS* N1 ....76 C5
Bev Callender CI *VX/NE* SW8 ....134 B1
Bevenden St *IS* N1 ....12 B3
Beveridge Rd *WLSDN* NW10 ....69 E4
Beverley Av *BFN/LL* DA15 ....145 E4
Beverley CI *BARN* SW13 ....112 A5
   BTSEA SW11 ....133 D2
Beverley Ct *BROCKY* SE4 ....139 F1
Beverley Gdns *BARN* SW13 ....129 F1
   GLDGN NW11 ....53 E2
   WBLY HA9 ....50 A3
Beverley Rd *BARN* SW13 ....129 F1
   CHSWK W4 ....111 F1
   EHAM E6 ....95 D2
Beversbrook Rd *ARCH* N19 ....57 D5
Beverstone Rd *BRXS/STRHM* SW2 ...135 F3
Beverston Ms *MBLAR* W1H 17 E3
Bevin CI *BERM/RHTH* SE16 ....103 E2
Bevington Rd *NKENS* * W10 ....89 E4
Bevington St *BERM/RHTH* SE16 ....102 A3
Bevin Sq *TOOT* SW17 ....151 F3
Bevin Wy *FSBYW* WC1X 10 A2
Bevis Marks *EC3A* 25 D4
Bewdley St *IS* N1 ....76 A4
Bewick Ms *PECK* SE15 ....120 B3
Bewick St *VX/NE* SW8 ....116 B5
Bewley St *WCHPL* * E1 ....102 B1
Bewlys Rd *WNWD* SE27 ....154 B5
Bexhill Rd *BROCKY* SE4 ....139 F4
   MORT/ESHN SW14 ....128 C1
Bexley Rd *ELTH/MOT* SE9 ....144 A4
Bianca Rd *PECK* SE15 ....119 F2
Bibury CI *PECK* SE15 ....119 E2
Bicester Rd *RCH/KEW* TW9 ....128 A1
Bickenhall St *MHST* W1U 17 F2
Bickerton Rd *KTTN* NW5 ....56 B4
Bickley Rd *LEY* E10 ....62 B2
Bickley St *TOOT* SW17 ....151 E5
Bicknell Rd *CMBW* SE5 ....136 C1

Bidborough St *STPAN* WC1H 8 C4
Biddenden Wy *ELTH/MOT* SE9 ....162 A4
Bidder St *CAN/RD* E16 ....93 E4
Biddestone Rd *HOLWY* N7 ....75 F1
Biddulph Rd *MV/WKIL* W9 ....3 D4
Bideford Rd *BMLY* BR1 ....159 F3
Bidwell St *PECK* SE15 ....120 B4
Biggerstaff Rd *SRTFD* E15 ....80 C5
Biggerstaff St *FSBYPK* N4 ....58 A4
Bigg's Rw *PUT/ROE* SW15 ....131 D1
Bigland St *WCHPL* E1 ....90 B5
Bignell Rd *WOOL/PLUM* SE18 ....126 B1
Bignold Rd *FSTGT* E7 ....82 A1
Bigwood Rd *GLDGN* NW11 ....54 B1
Bill Hamling CI *ELTH/MOT* SE9 ....161 F2
Billingford CI *BROCKY* SE4 ....139 D2
Billing Pl *WBPTN* * SW10 ....114 B3
Billing Rd *WBPTN* SW10 ....114 B3
Billing St *WBPTN* * SW10 ....114 B3
Billington Rd *NWCR* SE14 ....121 D3
Billiter Sq *FENCHST* * EC3M 25 D5
Billiter St *FENCHST* EC3M 25 D5
Billson St *POP/IOD* E14 ....104 C5
Bina Gdns *ECT* SW5 ....39 E5
Binden Rd *SHB* W12 ....99 F4
Binfield Rd *VX/NE* SW8 ....117 E4
Bingfield St *IS* N1 ....75 E5
Bingham Ct *IS* * N1 ....76 B4
Bingham Pl *MHST* W1U 18 A1
Bingham St *IS* N1 ....77 D3
Bingley Rd *CAN/RD* E16 ....94 C5
Binney St *MYFR/PKLN* W1K 30 B1
Binns Rd *CHSWK* W4 ....111 E1
Birbetts Rd *ELTH/MOT* SE9 ....161 F2
Birch CI *CAN/RD* E16 ....93 E4
Birchdale Rd *FSTGT* E7 ....82 C2
Birchen CI *CDALE/KGS* NW9 ....51 D4
Birchen Gv *CDALE/KGS* NW9 ....51 D4
Birchen La *BANK* EC3V 24 B5
The Birches *CHARL* SE7 ....124 B2
   CMBW * SE5 ....137 E1
Birchfield St *POP/IOD* E14 ....104 A1
Birch Gv *ACT* W3 ....98 A2
   LEE/GVPK SE12 ....141 F5
   WAN E11 ....63 E5
Birchington Rd *CEND/HSY/T* N8 ....57 D1
   KIL/WHAMP NW6 ....72 A5
Birchlands Av *BAL* SW12 ....133 F5
Birchmore Wk *HBRY* N5 ....58 C5
Birchwood Dr *HAMP* NW3 ....54 B5
Birchwood Rd *TOOT* SW17 ....152 B5
Birdbrook Rd *BKHTH/KID* SE3 ....142 C1
Birdcage Wk *STJSPK* SW1H 43 F1
Birdhurst Rd *WAND/EARL* SW18 ......132 C2
Bird in Bush Rd *PECK* SE15 ....120 A3
Bird-in-Hand Pas *FSTH* * SE23 ....156 C2
Birdlip CI *PECK* SE15 ....119 E2
Birdsfield La *HOM* E9 ....79 F5
Bird St *MHST* W1U 18 B5
Birkbeck Av *ACT* W3 ....98 C1
Birkbeck Gv *ACT* W3 ....99 D2
Birkbeck Hl *DUL* SE21 ....154 B2
Birkbeck Ms *ACT* * W3 ....99 D1
   HACK E8 ....77 F2
Birkbeck Pl *DUL* SE21 ....154 B1
Birkbeck Rd *ACT* W3 ....99 D2
   HACK E8 ....77 F2
   WIM/MER SW19 ....150 B5
Birkbeck St *BETH* E2 ....90 B2
Birkdale CI *BERM/RHTH* * SE16 ....120 B1
Birkenhead St *IS* N1 ....9 D1
Birkhall Rd *CAT* SE6 ....159 D1

Birkwood Cl *BAL* SW12 ....**135** D5
Birley St *BTSEA* SW11 ....**116** A5
Birnam Rd *HOLWY* N7.........................**57** F4
Birse Crs *WLSDN* NW10......................**69** E1
Biscay Rd *HMSMTH* W6 ....**113** D1
Biscoe Wy *LEW* * SE13 ....**141** D2
Bisham Gdns *HGT* N6...........................**56** A3
Bishop King's Rd *WKENS* W14........**101** E5
   WKENS * W14 ....**101** E5
Bishop's Av *FUL/PGN* SW6 ....**113** D5
   PLSTW E13...**82** B5
The Bishops Av *EFNCH* N2 ....**55** D1
Bishop's Bridge Rd *BAY/PAD* W2 ....**15** D4
Bishops Cl *CHSWK* W4.....................**110** C1
   ELTH/MOT SE9 ....**162** C2
Bishop's Ct *STP* EC4M **22** C4
Bishopsgate *LVPST* EC2M **24** C3
Bishopsgate Ar *LVPST* EC2M **24** C3
Bishops Gv *EFNCH* N2 ....**55** D1
Bishops Md *CMBW* * SE5 ....**118** C3
Bishop's Park Rd *FUL/PGN* SW6 .....**113** D5
Bishop's Rd *FUL/PGN* SW6 ....**113** F4
   HGT N6..**56** A1
Bishops Ter *LBTH* * SE11 ....**46** B4
   LBTH SE11 ....**46** B4
Bishopsthorpe Rd *SYD* SE26 ....**156** C4
Bishop St *IS* N1 ....**76** C5
Bishop's Wy *BETH* E2 ....**90** C1
Bishopswood Rd *HGT* N6....................**55** F2
Bishop Wy *WLSDN* NW10....................**69** E4
Bisson Rd *SRTFD* E15 ....**92** C1
Bittern St *STHWK* SE1 ....**47** E1
Blackall St *SDTCH* EC2A **12** C5
Blackbird Hl *CDALE/KGS* NW9 ....**50** C4
Blackbird Yd *BETH* E2...........................**13** F3
Blackburne's Ms *MYFR/PKLN* W1K ...**30** A1
Blackburn Rd *KIL/WHAMP* NW6 ....**72** B3
Blackdown Ter *WOOL/PLUM* * SE18...**125** F4
Blackenham Rd *TOOT* SW17 ....**151** F4
Blackett St *PUT/ROE* SW15 ....**131** D1
Blackfen Rd *BFN/LL* DA15 ....**145** F3
Blackfriars Br *EMB* EC4Y **22** C5
Black Friars La *BLKFR* EC4V **22** C5
Blackfriars Pas *BLKFR* EC4V **34** C3
Blackfriars Rd *STHWK* SE1 ....**34** C3
Blackfriars U/P *BLKFR* EC4V **35** D1
Blackheath Gv *GNWCH* SE10 ....**123** D3
Blackheath Gv *BKHTH/KID* SE3 ....**123** F5
Blackheath Hl *GNWCH* SE10............**122** C4
Blackheath Pk *BKHTH/KID* SE3 ....**124** A5
   BKHTH/KID SE3 ....**141** F1
Blackheath Ri *LEW* SE13...................**122** C4
Blackheath Rd *GNWCH* SE10 ....**122** B4
Blackheath V *BKHTH/KID* SE3 ....**123** E5
Black Horse Ct *STHWK* * SE1 ....**48** B3
Blackhorse Rd *DEPT* SE8 ....**121** E2
Blacklands Rd *CAT* SE6 ....**158** C4
Blacklands Ter *CHEL* SW3...................**41** E5
Black Lion Ga *KENS* W8.......................**27** D2
Black Lion La *HMSMTH* W6 ....**100** A5
Blackmans Yd *BETH* * E2 ....**13** F5
Blackpool Rd *PECK* SE15 ....**120** B5
Black Prince Rd *LBTH* SE11 ....**45** E4
Blackshaw Rd *TOOT* SW17 ....**151** D5
Black's Rd *HMSMTH* W6 ....**112** C1
Blackstock Rd *FSBYPK* N4 ....**58** B4
Blackstone Est *HACK* E8......................**78** A4
Blackstone Rd *CRICK* NW2 ....**70** C2
Black Swan Yd *STHWK* SE1.................**36** C5
Blackthorn St *BOW* E3 ....**92** A3
Blacktree Ms *BRXN/ST* * SW9 ....**136** A1
Blackwall La *GNWCH* SE10 ....**123** E1

Blackwall Tunnel Northern Ap
   BOW E3 ....**92** B2
Blackwall Wy *POP/IOD* E14 ....**104** C1
Blackwater St *EDUL* SE22 ....**137** D3
Blackwell Cl *CLPT* E5...........................**79** E1
Blackwood St *WALW* SE17 ....**119** D1
Blagdon Rd *LEW* SE13.......................**140** B4
Blagrove Rd *NKENS* W10 ....**89** E4
Blair Av *CDALE/KGS* NW9 ....**51** E2
Blair Cl *BFN/LL* DA15 ....**145** E3
   IS N1..**76** C3
Blairderry Rd *BRXS/STRHM* SW2.....**153** E2
Blair St *POP/IOD* E14..........................**92** C5
Blake Av *BARK* IG11 ....**85** E5
Blake Cl *WELL* DA16..........................**127** E4
Blake Gdns *FUL/PGN* SW6 ....**114** A4
Blake Hall Rd *WAN* E11........................**64** A3
Blakemore Rd *STRHM/NOR* SW16 ...**153** E3
Blakeney Cl *CAMTN* NW1 ....**8** A1
   HACK E8..**78** A2
Blaker Ct *CHARL* * SE7.....................**124** C3
Blake Rd *CAN/RD* E16 ....**93** F3
Blaker Rd *SRTFD* E15 ....**80** C5
Blakes Cl *NKENS* W10 ....**88** C4
Blake's Rd *PECK* SE15 ....**119** E3
   PECK * SE15.....................................**119** E3
Blanchard Cl *ELTH/MOT* SE9 ....**161** E3
Blanchard Wy *HACK* * E8 ....**78** A3
Blanch Cl *PECK* SE15 ....**120** C3
Blanchedowne *CMBW* SE5 ....**137** D2
Blanche St *CAN/RD* E16 ....**93** F3
Blandfield Rd *BAL* SW12 ....**134** A4
Blandford Rd *CHSWK* W4.....................**99** E4
Blandford Sq *CAMTN* NW1 ....**17** D1
Blandford St *MHST* W1U **17** F4
Bland St *ELTH/MOT* SE9 ....**143** D2
Blaney Crs *EHAM* E6 ....**96** B2
Blanmerle Rd *ELTH/MOT* SE9 ....**162** B1
Blann Cl *ELTH/MOT* SE9 ....**143** D4
Blantyre St *WBPTN* SW10..................**115** D3
Blantyre Wk *WBPTN* * SW10 ....**115** D3
Blashford St *LEW* SE13......................**141** D5
Bleak Hill La *WOOL/PLUM* SE18.......**127** F4
Blechynden St *NKENS* * W10 ....**101** D1
Bleeding Heart Yd *HCIRC* * EC1N **22** B3
Blendon Ter *WOOL/PLUM* SE18........**126** C1
Blendworth Wy *PECK* SE15 ....**119** E3
Blenheim Av *GNTH/NBYPK* IG2 ....**66** A1
Blenheim Ct *BFN/LL* DA15 ....**163** D3
Blenheim Crs *NTGHL* W11 ....**89** E5
Blenheim Dr *WELL* DA16....................**127** F4
Blenheim Gdns *BRXS/STRHM* SW2 ...**135** D3
   CRICK NW2..**70** C2
Blenheim Gv *PECK* SE15 ....**119** F5
Blenheim Pas *STJWD* * NW8 ....**3** E1
Blenheim Rd *BTSEA* SW11 ....**133** F4
Blenheim Rd *CHSWK* W4.....................**99** E4
   EHAM E6 ....**95** D2
   FSTGT E7 ....**81** E1
   STJWD NW8 ....**3** F1
Blenheim St *MYFR/PKLN* W1K **18** C5
Blenheim Ter *STJWD* NW8 ....**3** E1
Blenkarne Rd *BTSEA* SW11...............**133** F4
Blessington Rd *LEW* SE13 ....**141** D2
Bletchley St *IS* N1 ....**11** F1
Bletsoe Wk *IS* N1 ....**11** F1
Blincoe Cl *WIM/MER* SW19...............**149** D2
Blissett St *GNWCH* SE10 ....**122** C4
Bliss Ms *NKENS* W10 ....**89** E2
Blithfield St *KENS* W8...........................**38** C3
Bloemfontein Av *SHB* W12 ....**100** B2
Bloemfontein Rd *SHB* W12 ....**100** B1
Blomfield Rd *BAY/PAD* W2...................**15** D2
Blomfield St *LVPST* EC2M **24** B3

Blomfield Vls *BAY/PAD* W2 ....15 D3
Blondel St *BTSEA* SW11..........................116 A5
Blondin St *BOW* E3 ....92 A1
Bloomfield Crs *GNTH/NBYPK* IG2 ......66 B1
Bloomfield Pl *MYFR/PKLN* W1K 31 D1
Bloomfield Rd *HGT* N6 ....56 A1
  WOOL/PLUM SE18 ....126 B1
Bloomfield Ter *BGVA* SW1W 116 A1
Bloom Gv *WNWD* SE27 ....154 B3
Bloomhall Rd *NRWD* SE19 ....155 D5
Bloom Park Rd *FUL/PGN* SW6 ....113 F3
Bloomsbury Pl *NOXST/BSQ* WC1A 21 D3
Bloomsbury Sq *NOXST/BSQ* WC1A 21 D3
Bloomsbury St *RSQ* WC1B 20 B3
Bloomsbury Wy *NOXST/BSQ* WC1A 20 C3
Blore Cl *VX/NE* SW8 ....117 D4
Blossom St *WCHPL* E1 ....25 D2
Blount St *POP/IOD* E14...........................91 E5
Bloxam Gdns *ELTH/MOT* SE9 ....143 E3
Bloxhall Rd *LEY* E10 ....61 F3
Blucher Rd *CMBW* SE5 ....118 C3
Blue Anchor La *BERM/RHTH* SE16 ....102 A5
Blue Anchor Yd *WCHPL* E1 ....102 A1
Blue Ball Yd *WHALL* SW1A 31 E4
Bluebell Av *FSTGT* E7 ....83 D2
Bluebell Cl *HOM* E9 ....78 C5
  SYD SE26 ....155 F4
Bluebell Wy *IL* IG1 ....84 B3
Bluebird Wy *THMD* SE28 ....109 D3
Blundell St *HOLWY* N7 ....75 F4
Blunts Rd *ELTH/MOT* SE9 ....144 A3
Blurton Rd *CLPT* E5 ....79 D1
Blythe Cl *FSTH* SE23 ....139 F5
Blythe Hl *FSTH* SE23 ....139 F5
Blythe Hill La *FSTH* SE23 ....139 F5
Blythe Hill Pl *FSTH* SE23 ....139 G5
Blythe Ms *WKENS* W14..........................101 D4
Blythe Rd *WKENS* W14 ....101 D4
Blythe V *FSTH* SE23 ....157 F1
Blyth Rd *WALTH* E17 ....61 F2
Blyth's Whf *POP/IOD* E14 ....103 E3
Blythwood Rd *FSBYPK* N4 ....57 E2
Boadicea St *IS* N1 ....75 F5
Boardwalk Pl *POP/IOD* E14 ....104 C2
Boathouse Wk *PECK* SE15 ....119 F3
Boat Lifter Wy *BERM/RHTH* SE16 ....103 E5
Bob Anker Cl *PLSTW* E13 ....94 A2
Bobbin Cl *CLAP* SW4 ....134 C1
Bob Marley Wy *HNHL* SE24 ....136 A2
Bocking St *HACK* E8 ....78 B5
Boddicott Cl *WIM/MER* SW19 ....149 E2
Bodmin St *WAND/EARL* SW18 ....150 A1
Bodney Rd *CLPT* E5 ....78 B2
Bohemia Pl *HACK* E8 ....78 C3
Boileau Rd *BARN* SW13 ....112 A3
Bolden St *DEPT* SE8 ....122 B5
Boldero Pl *STJWD* * NW8 ....16 C1
Boleyn Rd *EHAM* E6 ....95 D1
  FSTGT E7 ....82 A4
  STNW/STAM N16 ....77 E2
Bolina Rd *BERM/RHTH* SE16 ....120 C1
Bolingbroke Gv *BTSEA* SW11 ....133 E3
Bolingbroke Rd *WKENS* W14 ....101 D4
Bolingbroke Wk *BTSEA* * SW11 ....115 D3
Bollo Bridge Rd *ACT* W3 ....98 B4
Bollo La *ACT* W3 ....98 B4
Bolney Ga *SKENS* SW7.............................40 C1
Bolney St *VX/NE* SW8 ....117 F3
Bolsover St *GTPST* W1W 19 D1
Bolt Ct *FLST/FETLN* * EC4A 22 B5
Bolton Crs *CMBW* SE5 ....118 A2
Bolton Gdns *ECT* SW5 ....114 B1
  WLSDN NW10 ....89 D1

Bolton Gardens Ms *WBPTN* SW10......114 B1
Bolton Rd *CHSWK* W4 ....110 C3
  FSTGT E7 ....81 F3
  KIL/WHAMP NW6 ....72 B5
  WLSDN NW10 ....69 E5
Boltons Pl *WBPTN* SW10.......................114 C1
The Boltons *WBPTN* * SW10 ....114 C1
Bolton St *MYFR/PICC* W1J 31 D3
Bombay St *BERM/RHTH* SE16 ....102 B5
Bomore Rd *NTGHL* W11 ....101 D1
Bonar Rd *PECK* SE15 ....120 A3
Bonchurch Rd *NKENS* W10 ....89 E4
Bond St *SRTFD* E15 ....81 E2
Bondway *VX/NE* SW8 ....117 E2
Boneta Rd *WOOL/PLUM* SE18 ....107 F4
Bonfield Rd *LEW* SE13 ....140 C2
Bonham Rd *BRXS/STRHM* SW2 ....135 F3
Bonheur Rd *CHSWK* W4 ....99 D3
Bonhill St *SDTCH* EC2A 24 B1
Bonita Ms *PECK* SE15 ....139 D1
Bonner Rd *BETH* E2 ....90 C1
Bonner St *BETH* * E2 ....90 C1
Bonneville Gdns *CLAP* SW4 ....134 C4
Bonnington Sq *VX/NE* SW8 ....117 F2
Bonny St *CAMTN* NW1 ....74 C4
Bonsor St *CMBW* SE5 ....119 E3
Bonville Rd *BMLY* BR1 ....159 F5
Boones Rd *LEW* SE13 ....141 E2
Boone St *LEW* SE13 ....141 E2
Boord St *GNWCH* SE10 ....105 E4
Boothby Rd *ARCH* N19 ....57 D4
Booth La *BLKFR* EC4V 35 E1
Boot St *IS* N1 ....12 C4
Border Crs *SYD* SE26 ....156 B5
Border Rd *SYD* SE26 ....156 B5
Bordon Wk *PUT/ROE* SW15 ....130 A5
Boreas Wk *IS* N1 ....11 D2
Boreham Av *CAN/RD* E16 ....94 A5
Borgard Rd *WOOL/PLUM* SE18 ....107 F5
Borland Rd *PECK* SE15 ....138 C2
Borneo St *PUT/ROE* SW15 ....130 C1
Borough High St *STHWK* SE1..................36 A4
  STHWK SE1 ....47 F1
Borough Rd *STHWK* SE1 ....46 C2
Borough Sq *STHWK* SE1 ....47 E1
Borrett Cl *WALW* SE17 ....118 C1
Borrodaile Rd *WAND/EARL* SW18 ....132 B4
Borthwick Ms *SRTFD* * E15 ....81 E1
Borthwick Rd *CDALE/KGS* NW9 ....51 F1
  SRTFD E15 ....81 E1
Borthwick St *DEPT* SE8 ....122 A1
Bosbury Rd *CAT* SE6 ....158 C3
Boscastle Rd *KTTN* NW5 ....56 B5
Boscobel Pl *BGVA* SW1W 42 B4
Boscobel St *BAY/PAD* W2 ....16 B2
Boscombe Av *LEY* E10 ....63 D2
Boscombe Cl *CLPT* E5 ....79 E2
Boscombe Rd *SHB* W12 ....100 A3
Boss St *STHWK* * SE1 ....37 E5
Boston Gdns *CHSWK* W4 ....111 E2
Boston Pl *CAMTN* NW1 ....17 E1
Boston Rd *EHAM* E6 ....95 D2
Boswell Ct *BMSBY* WC1N 21 D2
Boswell St *BMSBY* WC1N 21 D2
Bosworth Rd *NKENS* W10 ....89 E3
Botha Rd *PLSTW* E13 ....94 B4
Bothwell Cl *CAN/RD* E16 ....94 A4
Bothwell St *HMSMTH* W6 ....113 D2
Botolph Aly *MON* EC3R 36 C2
Botolph La *MON* EC3R 36 C2
Bott's Ms *BAY/PAD* W2 ....14 B5
Boughton Rd *THMD* SE28 ....109 E4
Boulcott St *WCHPL* E1 ....91 D5

Boultwood Rd *EHAM* E6 ....95 F5
Boundaries Rd *BAL* SW12 ....151 F2
Boundary Av *WALTH* E17 ....61 F2
Boundary Cl *GDMY/SEVK* IG3 ....85 E1
Boundary La *PLSTW* E13 ....95 D2
   WALW SE17 ....118 C2
Boundary Ms *STJWD* NW8 ....72 C5
Boundary Rd *BARK* IG11 ....96 C1
   BFN/LL DA15 ....145 E3
   PLSTW E13 ....94 C1
   STJWD NW8 ....72 C5
   WALTH E17 ....61 F2
Boundary Rw *STHWK* SE1 ....34 C5
Boundary St *BETH* E2 ....13 E4
Boundfield Rd *CAT* SE6 ....159 E3
Bourchier St *SOHO/CST* W1F 32 A1
Bourdon Pl *MYFR/PKLN* W1K 31 D1
Bourdon St *MYFR/PKLN* W1K 30 C2
Bourke Cl *CLAP* SW4 ....135 E4
   WLSDN NW10 ....69 E3
Bourlet Cl *FITZ* W1T 19 E3
Bournbrook Rd *BKHTH/KID* SE3 ....143 D1
Bourne Est *HCIRC* * EC1N 22 A2
Bournemouth Cl *PECK* SE15 ....120 A5
Bournemouth Rd *PECK* SE15 ....120 A5
Bourne Rd *CEND/HSY/T* N8 ....57 E1
   FSTGT E7 ....63 F5
Bourneside Gdns *CAT* SE6 ....158 C5
Bourne St *BCVA* SW1W 42 A5
Bourne Ter *BAY/PAD* W2 ....14 C2
Bournevale Rd *STRHM/NOR* SW16 ..153 E4
Bournville Rd *CAT* SE6 ....140 A5
Bousfield Rd *NWCR* SE14 ....121 D5
Boutflower Rd *BTSEA* SW11 ....133 E2
Boutique Hall *LEW* * SE13 ....140 C2
Bouverie Ms *STNW/STAM* N16 ....59 E4
Bouverie Pl *BAY/PAD* W2 ....16 B4
Bouverie Rd *STNW/STAM* N16 ....59 E4
Bouverie St *EMB* EC4Y 22 B5
Boveney Rd *FSTH* SE23 ....139 D5
Bovill Rd *FSTH* SE23 ....139 D5
Bovingdon Av *WBLY* HA9 ....68 A3
Bovingdon Rd *FUL/PGN* SW6 ....114 B4
Bowater Cl *CLAP* SW4 ....135 E4
Bowater Pl *BKHTH/KID* SE3 ....124 B3
Bowater Rd *WOOL/PLUM* SE18 ......107 D4
Bow Bridge Est *BOW* E3 ....92 B2
Bow Churchyard *STP* * EC4M 23 F5
Bow Common La *BOW* E3 ....91 F3
Bowden St *LBTH* SE11 ....118 A1
Bowditch *DEPT* SE8 ....121 F1
Bowdon Rd *LEY* E10 ....62 A2
Bowen Dr *DUL* SE21 ....155 E3
Bowen St *POP/IOD* E14 ....92 B5
Bower Av *GNWCH* SE10 ....123 E4
Bowerdean St *FUL/PGN* SW6 ....114 B4
Bowerman Av *NWCR* SE14 ....121 E2
Bower St *WCHPL* * E1 ....91 D5
Bowes Rd *ACT* W3 ....99 E1
Bowfell Rd *HMSMTH* W6 ....112 C2
Bowhill Cl *BRXN/ST* SW9 ....118 A3
Bowie Cl *CLAP* SW4 ....135 D5
Bowland Rd *CLAP* SW4 ....135 D5
Bowland Yd *KTBR* * SW1X 41 F1
Bow La *STP* EC4M 23 F5
Bowley La *NRWD* SE19 ....155 F5
Bowley St *POP/IOD* E14 ....103 F1
Bowling Green Cl *PUT/ROE* SW15 ..130 B5
Bowling Green La *CLKNW* EC1R 22 B1
Bowling Green Pl *STHWK* * SE1 ......36 A5
Bowling Green Rw
   WOOL/PLUM * SE18 ....107 F5
Bowling Green St *LBTH* SE11 ....118 A2

Bowling Green Wk *IS* N1 ....12 C3
Bow Locks *BOW* * E3 ....92 C3
Bowman Av *CAN/RD* E16 ....93 F5
Bowman Ms *WAND/EARL* SW18 ....149 F1
Bowmans Lea *FSTH* SE23 ....138 C5
Bowman's Ms *HOLWY* N7 ....57 E5
   WCHPL E1 ....102 A1
Bowman's Pl *HOLWY* N7 ....57 E5
Bowmead *ELTH/MOT* SE9 ....161 F2
Bowmore Wk *CAMTN* NW1 ....75 D4
Bowness Cl *HACK* * E8 ....77 F3
Bowness Crs *PUT/ROE* SW15 ....147 E5
Bowness Rd *CAT* SE6 ....140 B5
Bowood Rd *BTSEA* SW11 ....134 A2
Bow Rd *BOW* E3 ....92 A2
Bow St *COVGDN* WC2E 21 D5
   SRTFD E15 ....81 E2
Bowyer Cl *EHAM* E6 ....95 F4
Bowyer Pl *CMBW* SE5 ....118 C3
Bowyer St *CMBW* SE5 ....118 C3
Boxall Rd *DUL* SE21 ....137 E4
Boxley St *CAN/RD* E16 ....106 B2
Boxworth Gv *IS* N1 ....75 F5
Boyard Rd *WOOL/PLUM* SE18 ......126 B1
Boyce Wy *PLSTW* E13 ....94 A3
Boycroft Av *CDALE/KGS* NW9 ....50 C1
Boydell Ct *STJWD* NW8 ....73 D4
Boyd St *WCHPL* E1 ....90 A5
Boyfield St *STHWK* SE1 ....47 D1
Boyland Rd *BMLY* BR1 ....159 F5
Boyne Rd *LEW* SE13 ....141 D1
Boyne Terrace Ms *NTGHL* * W11 ....101 F2
Boyson Rd *WALW* SE17 ....118 C2
Boyton Cl *WCHPL* E1 ....91 D3
Brabazon St *POP/IOD* E14 ....92 B3
Brabourne Cl *NRWD* SE19 ....155 E5
Brabourn Gv *PECK* SE15 ....120 C5
Bracewell Rd *NKENS* W10 ....88 C4
Bracey St *FSBYPK* * N4 ....57 E4
Bracken Av *BAL* SW12 ....134 A4
Brackenbury Gdns *HMSMTH* W6 ...100 B4
Brackenbury Rd *HMSMTH* W6 ......100 B4
Bracken Cl *EHAM* E6 ....95 F4
Bracken Gdns *BARN* SW13 ....112 A5
Brackley Rd *CHSWK* W4 ....99 E5
Brackley St *BARB* EC2Y 23 F2
Brackley Ter *CHSWK* W4 ....111 E1
Bracklyn St *IS* N1 ....12 A1
Bracknell Gdns *HAMP* NW3 ....72 B2
Bracknell Wy *HAMP* NW3 ....72 B2
Bradbourne St *FUL/PGN* SW6 ......114 A5
Bradbury St *STNW/STAM* N16 ....77 E2
Braddyll St *GNWCH* SE10 ....123 E1
Bradenham Cl *WALW* SE17 ....119 D2
Braden St *MV/WKIL* * W9 ....14 C1
Bradfield Rd *CAN/RD* E16 ....106 A3
Bradford Cl *SYD* SE26 ....156 B4
Bradford Rd *ACT* W3 ....99 E3
   IL IG1 ....67 D3
Bradgate Rd *CAT* SE6 ....140 B4
Brading Crs *WAN* E11 ....64 B4
Brading Rd *BRXS/STRHM* SW2 .....135 F5
Brading Ter *SHB* W12 ....100 A4
Bradiston Rd *MV/WKIL* W9 ....89 F2
Bradley Cl *HOLWY* N7 ....75 E4
Bradley's Cl *IS* N1 ....10 A1
Bradley Stone Rd *EHAM* E6 ....95 F5
Bradmead *VX/NE* * SW8 ....116 B4
Bradmore Park Rd *HMSMTH* W6 ...100 B4
Bradshaw Cottages *POP/IOD* * E14 ..91 E5
Bradstock Rd *HOM* E9 ....79 D3
Brad St *STHWK* SE1 ....34 B4
Bradymead *EHAM* E6 ....96 A5

Brady St *WCHPL* E1 .... 90 B3
Braemar Av *WIM/MER* SW19 ... 150 A2
  WLSDN NW10 .... 51 D5
Braemar Gdns *BFN/LL* DA15 ... 163 D3
Braemar Rd *PLSTW* E13 .... 94 A3
Braeside *BECK* BR3 .... 158 A5
Braes St *IS* N1 .... 76 B4
Braganza St *WALW* SE17 .... 118 B3
Braham St *WCHPL* E1 .... 25 F5
Braid Av *ACT* W3 .... 87 E5
Braidwood Rd *CAT* SE6 .... 159 F4
Brailsford Rd *BRXS/STRHM* SW2 ... 136 A4
Braintree St *BETH* * E2 .... 90 C2
Bramall Cl *FSTGT* E7 .... 81 F2
Bramber Rd *FUL/PGN* SW6 ..... 113 F2
Bramblebury Rd
  WOOL/PLUM SE18 .... 127 D1
Bramble Gdns *SHB* W12 .... 99 F1
The Brambles *WIM/MER* * SW19 ... 149 F5
Bramcote Gv *BERM/RHTH* SE16 ... 120 C1
Bramcote Rd *PUT/ROE* SW15 ... 130 B2
Bramdean Crs *LEE/GVPK* SE12 ... 160 A1
Bramdean Gdns *LEE/GVPK* SE12 ... 160 A1
Bramerton St *CHEL* SW3 .... 115 E2
Bramfield Rd *BTSEA* SW11 .... 133 E4
Bramford Rd *WAND/EARL* SW18 ... 132 C2
Bramham Gdns *ECT* SW5 .... 114 B1
Bramhope La *CHARL* SE7 .... 124 B2
Bramlands Cl *BTSEA* SW11 .... 133 E1
Bramley Crs *GNTH/NBYPK* IG2 ... 66 A1
  VX/NE SW8 .... 117 D3
Bramley Rd *NKENS* W10 .... 101 D1
Brampton Cl *CLPT* E5 .... 60 B4
Brampton Gv *WBLY* HA9 .... 50 A3
Brampton Rd *EHAM* E6 .... 95 D3
Bramshaw Rd *HOM* E9 .... 79 D3
Bramshill Gdns *KTTN* NW5 .... 56 B5
Bramshill Rd *WLSDN* NW10 .... 87 E1
Bramshot Av *CHARL* SE7 .... 124 B2
Bramston Rd *WLSDN* NW10 .... 88 A1
Bramwell Ms *IS* N1 .... 75 F5
Brancaster Rd *GNTH/NBYPK* IG2 ... 67 D1
  STRHM/NOR SW16 .... 153 E3
Branch Hl *HAMP* NW3 .... 54 C5
Branch Pl *IS* N1 .... 77 D5
Branch Rd *POP/IOD* E14 .... 91 E5
Branch St *CMBW* SE5 .... 119 E3
Brand Cl *FSBYPK* N4 .... 58 B3
Brandlehow Rd *PUT/ROE* SW15 ... 131 F2
Brandon Ms *BARB* * EC2Y 24 A2
Brandon Rd *HOLWY* N7 .... 75 E4
Brandon St *WALW* SE17 .... 47 F5
Brandram Ms *LEW* * SE13 .... 141 E2
Brandram Rd *LEW* SE13 .... 141 E1
Brandreth Rd *EHAM* E6 .... 95 F5
  TOOT SW17 .... 152 B2
Brand St *GNWCH* SE10 .... 122 C3
Brangbourne Rd *BMLY* BR1 .... 158 C5
Brangton Rd *LBTH* SE11 .... 117 F1
Branksea St *FUL/PGN* SW6 .... 113 E3
Branksome Rd *BRXS/STRHM* SW2 ... 135 E3
Branscombe St *LEW* SE13 .... 140 B1
Bransdale Cl *KIL/WHAMP* NW6 ... 72 A5
Brantwood Rd *HNHL* SE24 .... 136 C3
Brasenose Dr *BARN* SW13 .... 112 C2
Brassey Rd *KIL/WHAMP* NW6 ... 71 F3
Brassey Sq *BTSEA* SW11 .... 134 A1
Brassie Av *ACT* W3 .... 87 E5
Brasted Cl *SYD* SE26 .... 156 C4
Brathway Rd *WAND/EARL* SW18 ... 132 A5
Bratley St *WCHPL* E1 .... 90 A3
Braundton Av *BFN/LL* DA15 ... 163 F4

Bravington Pl *MV/WKIL* W9 ...... 89 F3
Bravington Rd *MV/WKIL* W9 ...... 89 F2
Braxfield Rd *BROCKY* SE4 .... 139 E2
Brayard's Rd *PECK* SE15 .... 120 B5
Braybrook St *SHB* W12 .... 87 F4
Brayburne Av *VX/NE* SW8 .... 116 C5
Bray Crs *BERM/RHTH* SE16 ..... 103 D3
Braydon Rd *STNW/STAM* N16 ... 59 F3
Bray Dr *CAN/RD* E16 .... 105 F1
Brayfield Ter *IS* N1 .... 76 A4
Brayford Sq *WCHPL* * E1 .... 90 C5
Bray Pl *CHEL* SW3 .... 115 F1
Braywood Rd *ELTH/MOT* SE9 ... 145 D2
Bread St *BLKFR* EC4V 35 F1
  STP EC4M 23 F5
Breakspears Ms *BROCKY* SE4 ... 122 A5
Breakspears Rd *BROCKY* SE4 ... 139 F1
Bream Gdns *EHAM* E6 .... 96 A2
Breamore Cl *PUT/ROE* SW15 ... 148 A1
Breamore Rd *GDMY/SEVK* IG3 ... 67 F4
Bream's Buildings *LINN* WC2A ... 22 A4
Bream St *BOW* E3 .... 80 A4
Breasley Cl *PUT/ROE* SW15 ... 130 B2
Brechin Pl *SKENS* SW7 .... 114 C1
Brecknock Rd *ARCH* N19 .... 74 C1
Brecknock Road Est *ARCH* * N19 ... 75 D2
Brecon Gn *CDALE/KGS* * NW9 ... 51 E1
Brecon Ms *KTTN* NW5 .... 75 D3
Brecon Rd *HMSMTH* W6 .... 113 E2
Brede Cl *EHAM* E6 .... 96 A2
Bredgar Rd *ARCH* N19 .... 56 C4
Breer St *FUL/PGN* SW6 .... 132 B1
Breezer's Hl *WAP* * E1W 102 A1
Bremner Rd *SKENS* SW7 .... 39 F2
Brenchley Gdns *FSTH* SE23 ..... 138 C4
Brenda Rd *TOOT* SW17 .... 151 F2
Brendon Av *WLSDN* NW10 .... 69 E1
Brendon Rd *CHST* BR7 .... 163 D2
Brendon St *MBLAR* W1H 17 D4
Brenley Gdns *ELTH/RHTH* SE9 ... 143 D2
Brent Cross F/O *HDN* NW4 .... 52 C1
Brentfield *WLSDN* NW10 .... 68 B4
Brentfield Cl *WLSDN* NW10 .... 69 D3
Brentfield Gdns *CRICK* * NW2 ... 53 D2
Brentfield Rd *WLSDN* NW10 .... 69 D3
Brenthouse Rd *HACK* E8 .... 78 B4
Brenthurst Rd *WLSDN* NW10 ... 69 F3
Brenton St *POP/IOD* E14 .... 91 E5
Brent Park Rd *CDALE/KGS* NW9 ... 52 A3
Brent Rd *CAN/RD* E16 .... 94 A5
  WOOL/PLUM SE18 .... 126 B3
Brent Ter *CRICK* NW2 .... 52 C3
Brent View Rd *CDALE/KGS* NW9 ... 52 A1
Brent Wy *WBLY* HA9 .... 68 B3
Brentwood Cl *ELTH/MOT* SE9 ... 162 C1
Bressenden Pl *WESTW* SW1E ... 43 D2
Brett Cl *STNW/STAM* N16 .... 59 E4
Brett Crs *WLSDN* NW10 .... 69 D4
Brettell St *WALW* SE17 .... 119 D1
Brett Pas *HACK* E8 .... 78 B2
Brett Rd *HACK* E8 .... 78 B2
Brett Vls *ACT* * W3 .... 87 D4
Brewer St *REGST* W1B 31 F1
Brewery Rd *HOLWY* N7 .... 75 E4
  WOOL/PLUM SE18 .... 127 D1
Brewery Sq *STHWK* SE1 .... 37 E4
Brewhouse La *WAP* E1W 102 B2
Brewhouse Rd *WOOL/PLUM* SE18 ... 107 F5
Brewhouse St *PUT/ROE* SW15 ... 131 E2
Brewhouse Wk *BERM/RHTH* SE16 ... 103 E2
Brewhouse Yd *FSBYE* EC1V 10 C1
Brewster Gdns *NKENS* W10 .... 88 C4
Brewster Rd *LEY* E10 .... 62 B3

Briant St *NWCR* SE14...............................121 D4
Briardale Gdns *HAMP* NW3 ....54 A5
Briar Rd *CRICK* NW2 ....70 C1
Briar Wk *NKENS* * W10 ....89 E3
    PUT/ROE SW15........................130 B2
Briarwood Cl *CDALE/KGS* * NW9 ......50 C1
Briarwood Rd *CLAP* SW4 ....135 D3
Briary Cl *HAMP* * NW3.....................73 E4
Briary Gdns *BMLY* BR1..................160 B5
Brickbarn Cl *WBPTN* * SW10 ....114 C3
Brick Ct *EMB* * EC4Y 22 C4
Brick Farm Cl *RCH/KEW* TW9........110 B4
Brickfield Cottages
    WOOL/PLUM SE18 ....127 F3
Brickfield Rd *BOW* E3......................92 B3
    WIM/MER SW19 ....150 B4
Brick La *BETH* E2...............................13 F4
    WCHPL E1..................................25 F1
Brick St *MYFR/PICC* W1J................30 C4
Brickwood Cl *SYD* SE26 ....156 B3
Brideale Cl *PECK* * SE15 ....119 F2
Bride Ct *BLKFR* * EC4V 22 C5
Bride La *EMB* EC4Y 22 C5
Bridel Ms *FSBYE* EC1V 10 C2
Bride St *HOLWY* N7 ....75 F3
Bridewain St *STHWK* SE1 ....49 E2
Bridewell Pl *BLKFR* EC4V 22 C5
    WAP E1W...............................102 B2
Bridford Ms *REGST* W1B 19 D2
Bridge Av *HMSMTH* W6 ....112 C1
Bridge Cl *NKENS* W10 ....89 D5
Bridge House Quay *POP/IOD* E14...104 C3
Bridgeland Rd *CAN/RD* E16..........106 A1
Bridge La *BTSEA* SW11..................115 E4
Bridgeman Rd *IS* N1 ....75 F4
Bridgeman St *STJWD* NW8.................4 C2
Bridge Mdw *NWCR* SE14................121 D2
Bridge Pde *STRHM/NOR* * SW16 ....153 E5
Bridge Pl *PIM* SW1V 43 D4
Bridgeport Pl *WAP* * E1W...............102 A2
Bridge Rd *EHAM* E6 ....83 F4
    LEY E10.....................................61 F2
    SRTFD E15 ....81 D5
    WBLY HA9 ....50 A5
    WLSDN NW10 ....69 E3
Bridges Ct *BTSEA* SW11................133 D1
Bridge St *CHSWK* W4 ....99 D5
    WEST SW1P 44 C1
Bridge Ter *LEW* * SE13 ....141 D2
    SRTFD E15 ....81 D4
Bridgetown Cl *NRWD* SE19 ....155 E5
Bridgeview *HMSMTH* W6................112 C1
Bridge Vis *WIM/MER* * SW19 ....150 A5
Bridgewater Rd *SRTFD* E15..............80 C5
Bridgewater Sq *BARB* * EC2Y 23 E2
Bridgewater St *BARB* EC2Y 23 E2
Bridgeway *BARK* IG11 ....85 F4
Bridgeway St *CAMTN* NW1 ....7 F2
Bridgford St *WAND/EARL* SW18 ....150 C3
Bridgman Rd *CHSWK* W4 ....98 C4
Bridle La *SOHO/CST* W1F 31 F1
Bridport Pl *IS* N1 ....12 B1
Bridstow Pl *BAY/PAD* W2 ....14 B4
Brief St *CMBW* SE5 ....118 B4
Brierley Rd *BAL* SW12....................152 C2
    WAN E11....................................81 D1
Brierly Gdns *BETH* * E2....................90 C1
Brigade St *BKHTH/KID* * SE3 ....123 F5
Briggeford Cl *CLPT* E5......................60 A4
Brightfield Rd *LEW* SE13 ....141 E3
Brightling Rd *BROCKY* SE4............139 F4
Brightlingsea Pl *POP/IOD* E14.......103 F1
Brightman Rd *WAND/EARL* SW18 ...151 D1

Brighton Rd *EHAM* E6 ....96 A2
    STNW/STAM N16 ....77 E1
Brighton Ter *BRXN/ST* SW9 ....135 F2
Brightside Rd *LEW* SE13 ....141 D4
Bright St *POP/IOD* E14 ....92 B5
Brightwell Crs *TOOT* SW17 ....151 F5
Brig Ms *DEPT* SE8 ....122 A2
Brill Pl *CAMTN* NW1 ....5 E3
Brindle Ga *BFN/LL* DA15 ....163 E1
Brindley St *NWCR* SE14..................121 F4
Brindley Wy *BMLY* BR1...................160 A5
Brinklow Crs *WOOL/PLUM* SE18 ....126 B3
Brinkworth Wy *HOM* * E9 ....79 F3
Brinsley St *WCHPL* * E1....................90 B5
Brinton Wk *STHWK* SE1 ....34 C4
Brion Pl *POP/IOD* E14 ....92 C4
Brisbane Rd *IL* IG1 ....66 C2
    LEY E10......................................62 B4
Brisbane St *CMBW* SE5..................119 D3
Briscoe Cl *WAN* E11 ....63 F4
Briset Rd *ELTH/MOT* SE9...............143 D1
Briset St *FARR* EC1M 22 C2
Briset Wy *HOLWY* N7 ....57 F4
Bristol Gdns *MV/WKIL* W9 ....15 D1
Bristol Ms *MV/WKIL* W9 ....15 D1
Bristol Rd *FSTGT* E7..........................82 C3
Briston Gv *CEND/HSY/T* N8 ....57 E1
Bristow Rd *NRWD* SE19 ....155 E5
Britannia Cl *CLAP* SW4 ....135 D2
Britannia Ga *CAN/RD* E16..............106 A2
Britannia Rd *FUL/PGN* SW6 ....114 B3
    IL IG1..66 B5
    POP/IOD E14...........................104 A5
Britannia Rw *IS* N1 ....76 B5
Britannia St *FSBYW* WC1X 9 E3
Britannia Wk *IS* N1 ....12 A2
Britannia Wy *FUL/PGN* SW6...........114 B3
    WLSDN NW10 ....86 B3
British Est *BOW* E3............................91 F2
British Gv *CHSWK* W4 ....111 F1
British Grove Pas *CHSWK* * W4 ......111 F1
British St *BOW* E3..............................91 F2
Britten Cl *GLDGN* NW11 ....54 B3
Britten St *CHEL* SW3 ....115 E1
Britton Cl *CAT* SE6 ....141 D5
Britton St *FARR* EC1M 22 C2
Brixham Gdns *GDMY/SEVK* IG3 ......85 E2
Brixham St *CAN/RD* E16..................107 F2
Brixton HI *BRXS/STRHM* SW2 ....135 F4
Brixton Hill Pl *BRXS/STRHM* SW2 ...135 E5
Brixton Ov *BRXN/ST* SW9 ....136 A2
Brixton Rd *LBTH* SE11.....................118 A2
Brixton Station Rd *BRXN/ST* SW9 ...136 A1
Brixton Water La
    BRXS/STRHM SW2 ....135 F3
Broadbent St *MYFR/PKLN* * W1K 30 C1
Broad Bridge Cl *BKHTH/KID* SE3 ...124 A3
Broad Common Est
    STNW/STAM * N16 ....60 B4
Broad Ct *COVGDN* * WC2E 21 D5
Broadfield Cl *CRICK* NW2 ....52 C5
Broadfield La *HOLWY* N7 ....75 E4
Broadfield Rd *CAT* SE6...................159 E1
Broadfields Wy *WLSDN* NW10..........69 F1
Broadgates Rd *WAND/EARL* SW18 ...151 D1
Broadheath Dr *CHST* BR7...............161 F5
Broadhinton Rd *CLAP* SW4 ....134 B1
Broadhurst Av *GDMY/SEVK* IG3......85 F1
Broadhurst Cl *KIL/WHAMP* NW6......72 C3
Broadhurst Gdns *KIL/WHAMP* NW6 ...72 B3
Broadlands Av *STRHM/NOR* SE16 ..153 E2
Broadlands Cl *HGT* N6 ....56 A2
    STRHM/NOR SW16 ....153 E2

Broadlands Rd *BMLY* BR1 ....160 B4
　HGT N6 ....55 F2
Broad Lawn *ELTH/MOT* SE9 ....162 A1
Broadley St *STJWD* NW8 ....16 C2
Broadley Ter *CAMTN* NW1 ....17 D1
Broadmead *CAT* SE6 ....158 A3
Broadstone Pl *MHST* W1U 18 A3
Broad Street Av *LVPST* EC2M 24 C3
Broad Street Pl *LVPST* EC2M 24 B3
Broadview *CDALE/KGS* NW9 ....50 A1
Broad Wk *BKHTH/KID* SE3 ....124 C5
Broadwalk La *GLDGN* NW11 ....53 F2
The Broad Wk *KENS* W8 ....27 D3
Broadwall *STHWK* SE1 ....34 B3
Broadwater Rd *TOOT* SW17 ....151 E4
　WOOL/PLUM* SE18 ....109 D4
Broadway *BARK* IG11 ....84 C5
　SRTFD E15 ....81 D4
　STJSPK SW1H 44 A1
Broadway Market *HACK* E8 ....78 B5
Broadway Market Ms *HACK* * E8 ....78 A5
Broadway Ms *STNW/STAM* N16 ....59 F2
The Broadway *ACT* * W3 ....98 A3
　CDALE/KGS* NW9 ....51 F1
　CEND/HSY/T N8 ....57 E1
　PLSTW E13 ....94 A1
Broadwell Pde *KIL/WHAMP* * NW6 ....72 C3
Broadwick St *SOHO/CST* W1F 19 F5
Broadwood Ter *WKENS* * W14 ....101 F5
Broad Yd *FARR* EC1M 22 C1
Brocas Cl *HAMP* NW3 ....73 E4
Brockdish Av *BARK* IG11 ....85 F2
Brockenhurst Gdns *IL* IG1 ....84 C2
Brockham Cl *WIM/MER* SW19 ....149 F5
Brockham Dr *BRXS/STRHM* SW2 ....135 F5
　GNTH/NBYPK IG2 ....66 C1
Brockham St *STHWK* SE1 ....47 F2
Brockill Crs *BROCKY* SE4 ....139 E2
Brocklebank Rd *CHARL* SE7 ....106 B5
　WAND/EARL SW18 ....132 C5
Brocklehurst St *NWCR* SE14 ....121 D3
Brockley Cross *BROCKY* SE4 ....139 E1
Brockley Gdns *BROCKY* SE4 ....139 F3
Brockley Hall Rd *BROCKY* SE4 ....139 E4
Brockley Ms *BROCKY* SE4 ....139 E3
Brockley Pk *FSTH* SE23 ....139 E5
Brockley Ri *FSTH* SE23 ....139 F4
Brockley Rd *BROCKY* SE4 ....139 E4
Brockley Vw *FSTH* SE23 ....139 E5
Brockley Wy *FSTH* SE23 ....139 D3
Brockman Ri *BMLY* BR1 ....159 D4
Brock Pl *BOW* E3 ....92 B3
Brock Rd *PLSTW* E13 ....94 B4
Brock St *PECK* * SE15 ....138 C1
Brockway Cl *WAN* E11 ....63 E4
Brockwell Park Gdns *HNHL* SE24 ....136 B5
Brockworth Cl *PECK* SE15 ....119 E2
Brodia Rd *STNW/STAM* N16 ....59 E5
Brodie St *STHWK* SE1 ....119 F1
Brodlove La *WAP* E1W 103 D1
Brodrick Rd *TOOT* SW17 ....151 F1
　TOOT SW17 ....151 E2
Brokesley St *BOW* E3 ....91 F3
Broke Wk *HACK* * E8 ....78 A5
Bromar Rd *CMBW* SE5 ....137 E1
Bromehead St *WCHPL* E1 ....90 C5
Bromell's Rd *CLAP* SW4 ....134 C2
Brome Rd *ELTH/MOT* SE9 ....143 F1
Bromfelde Rd *CLAP* SW4 ....135 D1
Bromfield St *IS* N1 ....10 B1
Bromhedge *ELTH/MOT* SE9 ....161 F3
Bromley Hall Rd *POP/IOD* E14 ....92 C4
Bromley High St *BOW* E3 ....92 B2

Bromley Rd *CAT* SE6 ....158 B2
　LEY E10 ....62 B1
Bromley St *WCHPL* E1 ....91 D4
Brompton Ar *KTBR* * SW1X 41 E1
Brompton Cottages
　WBPTN * SW10 ....114 C2
Brompton Park Crs *FUL/PGN* SW6 .....114 B2
Brompton Pl *CHEL* SW3 ....41 D2
Brompton Rd *CHEL* SW3 ....40 C4
Brompton Sq *CHEL* SW3 ....40 C2
Brompton Ter *WOOL/PLUM* * SE18 ....126 A4
Bromwich Av *HGT* N6 ....56 A4
Bromyard Av *ACT* W3 ....99 E2
Brondesbury Ms *KIL/WHAMP* * NW6 ...72 A4
Brondesbury Pk *CRICK* NW2 ....70 C4
Brondesbury Rd *KIL/WHAMP* NW6 ....89 F1
Brondesbury Vls *KIL/WHAMP* NW6 ....89 F1
Bronsart Rd *FUL/PGN* SW6 ....113 E3
Bronte Cl *FSTGT* * E7 ....82 A1
Bronti Cl *WALW* SE17 ....118 C5
Bronze St *DEPT* SE8 ....122 A3
Brook Av *WBLY* HA9 ....50 A5
Brookbank Rd *LEW* SE13 ....140 A1
Brook Cl *ACT* W3 ....98 A2
　TOOT SW17 ....152 A2
Brookdale Rd *CAT* SE6 ....140 B5
Brookdene Rd *WOOL/PLUM* SE18 ......109 F3
Brook Dr *STHWK* SE1 ....46 B3
Brookehowse Rd *CAT* SE6 ....158 B3
Brookend Rd *BFN/LL* DA15 ....163 E1
Brooke Rd *CLPT* E5 ....60 A5
Brooke's Market *HCIRC* * EC1N 22 C1
Brooke St *HCIRC* EC1N 22 A3
Brookfield *KTTN* NW5 ....56 B5
Brookfield Rd *CHSWK* W4 ....99 D3
　HOM E9 ....79 E3
Brook Gdns *BARN* SW13 ....129 F1
Brook Ga *BAY/PAD* W2 ....29 F2
Brook Gn *HMSMTH* W6 ....100 C4
Brook Hill Cl *WOOL/PLUM* SE18 ....126 B1
Brookhill Rd *WOOL/PLUM* SE18 ....126 B1
Brooking Rd *FSTGT* E7 ....82 A2
Brooklands Av *BFN/LL* DA15 ....163 D2
　WAND/EARL SW18 ....150 B2
Brooklands Ct *KIL/WHAMP* * NW6 ....71 F4
Brooklands Pk *BKHTH/KID* SE3 ....142 A1
Brook La *BKHTH/KID* SE3 ....124 B5
Brook Ms North *BAY/PAD* W2 ....27 F1
Brookmill Rd *DEPT* SE8 ....122 A4
Brook Rd *CRICK* NW2 ....52 A4
　GNTH/NBYPK IG2 ....67 E1
Brooks Av *EHAM* E6 ....95 F3
Brooksbank St *HOM* * E9 ....79 D3
Brooksby Ms *IS* N1 ....76 A4
Brooksby St *IS* N1 ....76 A4
Brooksby's Wk *HOM* E9 ....79 D2
Brookside Rd *GLDGN* NW11 ....53 E1
Brooks La *CHSWK* W4 ....110 A3
Brook's Ms *MYFR/PKLN* W1K 30 C1
Brooks Rd *CHSWK* W4 ....110 A1
　PLSTW E13 ....82 A5
Brook St *BAY/PAD* W2 ....28 B1
　MYFR/PKLN W1K 30 C1
Brooksville Av *KIL/WHAMP* NW6 ....71 E5
Brookview Rd *STRHM/NOR* SW16 ....152 C5
Brookville Rd *FUL/PGN* SW6 ....113 F3
Brookway *BKHTH/KID* SE3 ....142 A1
Brookwood Av *BARN* SW13 ....129 F1
Brookwood Rd *WAND/EARL* SW18 .....149 F1
Broome Wy *CMBW* SE5 ....119 D3
Broomfield *WALTH* E17 ....61 F2
Broomfield St *POP/IOD* E14 ....92 A4
Broomgrove Rd *BRXN/ST* SW9 ....117 F5

Broomhill Rd *WAND/EARL* SW18 ....132 A3
Broomhouse La *FUL/PGN* SW6 ....114 A5
Broomhouse Rd *FUL/PGN* SW6.......114 A5
Broomsleigh St *KIL/WHAMP* * NW6 ...72 A2
Broomwood Rd *BTSEA* SW11 ....133 E4
Broseley Gv *SYD* SE26.......157 E5
Brougham Rd *ACT* W3.......86 C5
    HACK E8 ....78 A5
Brougham St *BTSEA* SW11.......115 F5
Brough Cl *VX/NE* SW8.......117 E3
Broughton Dr *HNHL* SE24 ....136 A2
Broughton Gdns *HGT* N6 ....56 C1
Broughton Rd *FUL/PGN* SW6 ....114 B5
Broughton Road Ap
    FUL/PGN * SW6.......114 B5
Broughton St *VX/NE* SW8 ....116 A5
Brouncker Rd *ACT* W3.......98 C3
Brownfield St *POP/IOD* E14.......92 C5
Brown Hart Gdns *MYFR/PKLN* W1K ...30 B1
Brownhill Rd *CAT* SE6.......140 C5
Browning Cl *MV/WKIL* * W9.......15 F1
    WELL DA16.......127 E4
Browning Ms *CAVSQ/HST* * W1G ...18 B3
Browning Rd *MNPK* E12 ....83 F3
    WAN E11 ....63 F2
Browning St *WALW* SE17 ....118 C1
Brownlow Ms *FSBYW* WC1X 9 F5
Brownlow Rd *FSTGT* E/.......82 A1
    HACK E8 ....77 F5
    WLSDN NW10.......69 E4
Brownlow St *GINN* WC1R 21 F3
Brownspring Dr *ELTH/MOT* SE9 ....162 B3
Brown St *MBLAR* W1H 17 E4
Brownswood Rd *FSBYPK* N4.......58 C4
Broxash Rd *BTSEA* SW11 ....134 A4
Broxbourne House *BOW* E3 ....92 B3
Broxbourne Rd *FSTGT* E7.......64 A5
Broxholm Rd *WNWD* SE27 ....154 A3
Broxted Rd *FSTH* SE23.......157 F2
Broxwood Wy *STJWD* NW8 ....73 E5
Bruce Cl *NKENS* W10.......89 D4
Bruce Rd *BOW* E3 ....92 B2
    WLSDN NW10.......69 D4
Bruckner St *NKENS* W10.......89 E2
Brudenell Rd *TOOT* SW17.......151 F3
Bruges Pl *CAMTN* NW1 ....74 C4
Brunel Ct *WLSDN* NW10.......88 A2
Brunel Est *BAY/PAD* W2.......14 A3
Brunel Rd *ACT* W3.......87 E4
    BERM/RHTH SE16.......102 C2
    WALTH E17.......61 E1
Brunel St *CAN/RD* E16.......93 F5
Brune St *WCHPL* E1.......25 E3
Bruno Pl *WBLY* HA9.......50 C4
Brunswick Ct *STHWK* SE1.......49 D1
Brunswick Gdns *KENS* W8 ....26 B4
Brunswick Ms *MBLAR* W1H 17 F4
Brunswick Pk *CMBW* SE5.......119 D4
Brunswick Pl *CAMTN* NW1 ....18 B1
    IS N1.......12 B4
Brunswick Quay
    BERM/RHTH SE16.......103 D4
Brunswick Rd *LEY* E10 ....62 C3
Brunswick Sq *BMSBY* WC1N 9 D5
Brunswick Vls *CMBW* SE5 ....119 E4
Brunton Pl *POP/IOD* E14 ....91 E5
Brushfield St *WCHPL* E1.......25 D3
Brussels Rd *BTSEA* SW11 ....133 D2
Bruton La *MYFR/PICC* W1J.......31 D2
Bruton Pl *MYFR/PKLN* W1K 31 D2
Bruton St *MYFR/PICC* W1J.......31 D2
Bryan Av *WLSDN* NW10 ....70 B4
Bryan Rd *BERM/RHTH* SE16.......103 F3

Bryanston Ms East *MBLAR* W1H 17 E3
Bryanston Ms West *MBLAR* W1H 17 E3
Bryanston Pl *MBLAR* W1H 17 E3
Bryanston Sq *MBLAR* W1H.......17 E4
Bryanston St *MBLAR* W1H.......17 E5
Bryant St *SRTFD* E15.......81 D4
Bryantwood Rd *HOLWY* N7 ....76 A2
Bryden Cl *SYD* SE26.......157 E5
Brydges Pl *CHCR* WC2N 32 C2
Brydges Rd *SRTFD* E15.......81 D2
Brydon Wk *IS* N1.......75 E5
Bryett Rd *HOLWY* N7 ....57 E5
Brymay Cl *BOW* E3 ....92 A1
Brynmaer Rd *BTSEA* SW11 ....115 F4
Bryony Rd *SHB* W12.......100 A3
Buchanan Gdns *WLSDN* NW10 ....88 B1
Buchan Rd *PECK* SE15.......138 C1
Bucharest Rd *WAND/EARL* SW18 ...132 C5
Buckden Cl *LEE/GVPK* SE12.......141 F4
Buckfast St *BETH* E2.......90 A2
Buckhold Rd *WAND/EARL* SW18 ...132 A4
Buckhurst St *WCHPL* E1.......90 B3
Buckingham Av *WELL* DA16.......145 E2
Buckingham Dr *CHST* BR7.......162 B5
Buckingham Ga *WESTW* SW1E.......43 E2
Buckingham La *FSTH* SE23 ....139 E5
Buckingham Ms *WESTW* * SW1E.......43 E2
    WLSDN NW10.......87 F1
Buckingham Palace Rd *PIM* SW1V...42 C4
Buckingham Pl *WESTW* SW1E.......43 E2
Buckingham Rd *FSTGT* E7.......81 F2
    IL IG1.......67 D4
    IS N1.......77 E3
    LEY E10.......62 B5
    WLSDN NW10.......87 F1
Buckingham St *CHCR* WC2N 33 D2
Buckland Crs *HAMP* NW3.......73 D3
Buckland Rd *LEY* E10.......62 C4
Buckland St *IS* N1.......12 B2
Bucklersbury *MANHO* * EC4N 24 A5
Buckle St *WCHPL* E1.......25 F4
Buckley Rd *KIL/WHAMP* NW6 ....71 F4
Buckmaster Rd *BTSEA* SW11.......133 E2
Bucknall St *NOXST/BSQ* WC1A.......20 C4
Buckner Rd *BRXS/STRHM* SW2 ....135 E2
Buckstone Cl *FSTH* SE23.......138 C4
Buck St *CAMTN* NW1.......74 B5
Buckters Rents
    BERM/RHTH SE16.......103 E2
Buckthorne Rd *BROCKY* SE4 ....139 E4
Buddings Cir *WBLY* HA9.......50 C5
Budge Rw *MANHO* EC4N 36 A1
Buer Rd *FUL/PGN* SW6 ....113 E5
Bugsby's Wy *GNWCH* SE10.......105 F5
Bulinca St *WEST* * SW1P.......44 C5
Bullace Rw *CMBW* SE5 ....119 D4
Bullar Cl *PECK* SE15.......120 A3
Bullards Pl *BETH* E2.......91 D4
Bulleid Wy *PIM* SW1V.......43 D5
Bullen St *BTSEA* SW11.......115 E5
Buller Rd *BARK* IG11 ....85 E4
    WLSDN NW10.......89 D2
Bullivant St *POP/IOD* E14.......104 C1
Bull Rd *SRTFD* E15.......93 F5
Bulls Aly *MORT/ESHN* * SW14 ....129 D1
Bull Yd *PECK* SE15.......120 A4
Bulmer Ms *NTGHL* W11.......26 A3
Bulstrode Pl *MHST* W1U.......18 B3
Bulstrode St *MHST* W1U.......18 B4
Bulwer Court Rd *WAN* E11.......63 D3
Bulwer Rd *WAN* E11.......63 D3
Bulwer St *SHB* W12.......100 C2
Bunhill Rw *STLK* EC1Y.......12 A5

Bunhouse Pl *BGVA* SW1W....................116 A1
Bunning Wy *HOLWY* * N7..................75 E4
Bunsen St *BOW* E3..............................91 E1
Bunton St *WOOL/PLUM* SE18........108 A4
Buonaparte Ms *PIM* SW1V................117 D1
Burbage Cl *STHWK* SE1......................48 A3
Burbage Rd *HNHL* SE24....................137 D4
Burcham St *POP/IOD* E14................92 B5
Burchell Rd *LEY* E10...........................62 B3
   PECK SE15.......................................120 B4
Burcote Rd *WAND/EARL* SW18....151 D1
Burdenshott Av
   RCHPK/HAM TW10.........................128 B2
Burden Wy *WAN* E11..........................64 B4
Burder Cl *IS* N1...................................77 E3
Burder Rd *IS* N1...................................77 E3
Burdett Rd *BOW* E3............................91 F3
Burfield Cl *TOOT* SW17....................150 C4
Burford Rd *CAT* SE6..........................157 F2
   EHAM E6...95 E2
   SRTFD E15..81 D4
Burford Wk *FUL/PGN* * SW6............114 B3
Burges Gv *BARN* SW13......................112 B3
Burges Rd *EHAM* E6...........................84 A4
Burgess Av *CDALE/KGS* NW9............51 D1
Burgess Hl *CRICK* NW2......................72 A1
Burgess Rd *SRTFD* E15........................81 E1
Burgess St *POP/IOD* E14....................92 A4
Burge St *STHWK* SE1...........................48 B3
Burghill Rd *SYD* SE26.......................157 D4
Burghley Hall Cl *WIM/MER* * SW19...149 E1
Burghley Rd *KTTN* NW5.....................74 B1
   WAN * E11..63 E3
   WIM/MER SW19...............................149 D4
Burgh St *IS* N1......................................11 D1
Burgon St *BLKFR* EC4V.....................23 D5
Burgos Gv *GNWCH* SE10.................122 B4
Burgoyne Rd *BRXN/ST* SW9...........135 F1
   FSBYPK N4..58 B1
Burke Cl *PUT/ROE* SW15.................129 E2
Burke St *CAN/RD* E16.........................93 F4
Burland Rd *BTSEA* SW11..................133 F3
Burleigh Av *BFN/LL* DA15...............145 E3
Burleigh Pl *PUT/ROE* SW15............131 D3
Burleigh St *COVGDN* WC2E.............33 D1
Burleigh Wk *CAT* SE6.......................158 C1
Burley Rd *CAN/RD* E16.......................94 C5
Burlington Ar *CONDST* W1S..............31 E2
Burlington Av *RCH/KEW* TW9.........110 A4
Burlington Cl *EHAM* E6......................95 E5
   MV/WKIL W9..2 A5
Burlington Gdns *ACT* W3..................98 C2
   CHSWK W4...110 C1
   CONDST W1S......................................31 E2
Burlington La *CHSWK* W4................110 C3
Burlington Ms *ACT* W3.......................98 C2
Burlington Pde *CRICK* * NW2............53 D5
Burlington Pl *FUL/PGN* SW6...........113 E5
Burlington Rd *CHSWK* * W4.............110 C1
   FUL/PGN SW6..................................113 E5
Burma Rd *STNW/STAM* N16.............77 D1
Burma Ter *NRWD* * SE19.................155 D4
Burmester Rd *TOOT* SW17..............150 C3
Burnaby Crs *CHSWK* W4..................110 B3
Burnaby Gdns *CHSWK* W4................110 B2
Burnaby St *WBPTN* SW10................114 C3
Burnbury Rd *BAL* SW12...................152 C1
Burnell Wk *STHWK* * SE1................119 F1
Burnels Av *EHAM* E6...........................96 A2
Burness Cl *HOLWY* N7........................75 F3
Burne St *CAMTN* NW1.........................16 C2
Burney St *GNWCH* SE10...................122 C3
Burnfoot Av *FUL/PGN* SW6.............113 E4

Burnham Cl *STHWK* SE1.....................49 F5
Burnham St *BETH* E2..........................90 C2
Burnham Wy *SYD* SE26....................157 F5
Burnley Rd *BRXN/ST* SW9...............117 F5
   WLSDN NW10....................................69 F2
Burnsall St *CHEL* SW3.......................115 E1
Burns Cl *WELL* DA16........................127 F4
Burnside Cl *BERM/RHTH* SE16........103 D2
Burns Rd *BTSEA* SW11......................115 F5
   WLSDN NW10....................................69 F5
Burnt Ash Hl *LEE/GVPK* SE12........141 F4
Burnt Ash La *BMLY* BR1...................160 B5
Burnt Ash Rd *LEE/GVPK* SE12.......141 F3
Burnthwaite Rd *FUL/PGN* SW6......113 F3
Burntwood Grange Rd
   WAND/EARL SW18............................151 D1
Burntwood La *TOOT* SW17..............150 C3
Burntwood Vw *NRWD* * SE19..........155 F5
Buross St *WCHPL* E1...........................90 B5
Burrage Gv *WOOL/PLUM* SE18.......108 B5
Burrage Pl *WOOL/PLUM* SE18........126 B1
Burrage Rd *WOOL/PLUM* SE18.......108 C5
Burrard Rd *CAN/RD* E16.....................94 A5
   KIL/WHAMP NW6...............................72 A2
Burr Cl *WAP* * E1W...........................102 A2
Burrell St *STHWK* SE1.........................34 C3
Burroughs Cottages *POP/IOD* * E14 .91 E4
Burrow Rd *CMBW* SE5......................137 D2
Burrows Ms *STHWK* SE1.....................34 C5
Burrows Rd *WLSDN* NW10.................88 C2
Burr Rd *WAND/EARL* SW18.............150 A1
Bursar St *STHWK* * SE1.......................36 C4
Bursdon Cl *BFN/LL* DA15.................163 F2
Burslem St *WCHPL* * E1.......................90 B5
Burstock Rd *PUT/ROE* SW15...........131 E2
Burston Rd *PUT/ROE* SW15.............131 D3
Burtley Cl *FSBYPK* N4..........................58 C3
Burton Bank *IS* * N1...........................77 D4
Burton Gv *WALW* SE17......................119 D1
Burton La *BRXN/ST* * SW9...............118 A5
Burton Ms *BGVA* SW1W......................42 B5
Burton Pl *STPAN* WC1H........................8 B5
Burton Rd *BRXN/ST* SW9..................118 A5
   KIL/WHAMP NW6...............................71 F4
Burtons Ct *SRTFD* E15.........................81 D4
Burton St *STPAN* WC1H.........................8 B5
Burt Rd *CAN/RD* E16........................106 C2
Burtwell La *WNWD* SE27...................155 D4
Burwash Rd *WOOL/PLUM* SE18......127 D1
Burwell Cl *WCHPL* * E1........................90 B5
Burwell Rd *LEY* E10.............................61 E3
Burwood Pl *BAY/PAD* W2....................17 D4
Bury Cl *BERM/RHTH* SE16...............103 D2
Bury Ct *HDTCH* EC3A..........................25 D4
Bury Pl *NOXST/BSQ* WC1A...............20 C3
Bury St *HDTCH* EC3A..........................25 D5
   STJS SW1Y..31 E3
Bury Wk *CHEL* SW3............................40 C5
Busby Pl *KTTN* NW5...........................75 D3
Bushbaby Cl *STHWK* SE1.....................48 C3
Bushberry Rd *HOM* E9........................79 E3
Bush Cottages *WAND/EARL* SW18 ..132 A3
Bushell Cl *BRXS/STRHM* SW2........153 F2
Bushell St *WAP* E1W.........................102 A2
Bushell Wy *CHST* BR7......................162 A5
Bushey Hill Rd *CMBW* SE5...............119 F4
Bushey Lees *BFN/LL* * DA15............145 F4
Bushey Rd *PLSTW* E13..........................94 C1
   SEVS/STOTM N15...............................59 E1
Bush Gv *CDALE/KGS* NW9..................50 C2
Bush La *CANST* EC4R............................36 A1
Bushmoor Crs *WOOL/PLUM* SE18...126 B3

Bushnell Rd *TOOT* SW17 ....**152** B2
Bush Rd *BERM/RHTH* SE16 ....**103** D5
   HACK E8 ....**78** B5
   WAN E11 ....**63** F2
Bushwood *WAN* E11 ....**63** F2
Bushwood Dr *STHWK* SE1 ....**49** F5
Bushwood Rd *RCH/KEW* TW9 ....**110** A2
Butcher Rw *POP/IOD* E14 ....**91** D5
Butchers Rd *CAN/RD* E16 ....**94** A5
Bute Gdns *HMSMTH* W6 ....**101** D5
Bute St *SKENS* SW7 ....**40** A4
Bute Wk *IS* * N1 ....**77** D3
Butler Rd *WLSDN* NW10 ....**69** F4
Butlers & Colonial Whf *STHWK* SE1 ...**37** F5
Butler St *BETH* * E2 ....**90** C2
Butterfield Cl *BERM/RHTH* * SE16 ...**102** A3
Butterfield Sq *EHAM* E6 ....**95** F5
Butterfly La *ELTH/MOT* SE9 ....**144** B4
Butterfly Wk *CMBW* * SE5 ....**119** D4
Buttermere Cl *STHWK* SE1 ....**49** E4
   WAN E11 ....**81** D1
Buttermere Dr *PUT/ROE* SW15 ....**131** F3
Buttermere Wk *HACK* * E8 ....**77** F3
Butterwick *HMSMTH* W6 ....**100** C5
Butterworth Ter *WALW* * SE17 ....**118** C1
Buttesland St *IS* N1 ....**12** B3
Buttmarsh Cl *WOOL/PLUM* SE18 .....**126** B1
Buttsbury Rd *IL* IG1 ....**84** C2
Butts Rd *BMLY* BR1 ....**159** E5
Buxhall Crs *HOM* E9 ....**79** F3
Buxted Rd *EDUL* SE22 ....**137** E2
   HACK E8 ....**77** F4
Buxton Gdns *ACT* W3 ....**98** B3
Buxton Rd *ARCH* N19 ....**57** D3
   CRICK NW2 ....**70** B3
   EHAM E6 ....**95** E2
   GNTH/NBYPK IG2 ....**67** E1
   MORT/ESHN SW14 ....**129** E1
   SRTFD E15 ....**81** E2
Buxton St *WCHPL* E1 ....**25** F1
Byam St *FUL/PGN* SW6 ....**114** C5
Byefield Cl *BERM/RHTH* SE16 ....**103** E3
Byelands Cl *BERM/RHTH* SE16 ....**103** D2
The Bye *ACT* W3 ....**87** E5
The Byeway *MORT/ESHN* SW14 ......**128** C1
Byfeld Gdns *BARN* SW13 ....**112** A4
Byfield Cl *BERM/RHTH* SE16 ....**103** E3
Byford Cl *SRTFD* E15 ....**81** E3
Bygrove St *POP/IOD* E14 ....**92** B5
Byng Pl *GWRST* WC1E **20** B1
Byng St *POP/IOD* E14 ....**104** A3
Byrne Rd *BAL* SW12 ....**152** B1
Byron Av *MNPK* E12 ....**83** E3
Byron Cl *HACK* E8 ....**78** A5
   SYD * SE26 ....**157** E4
Byron Dr *EFNCH* N2 ....**55** D1
Byron Ms *HAMP* NW3 ....**73** E2
Byron Rd *CRICK* NW2 ....**52** B4
   LEY E10 ....**62** B3
Bythorn St *BRXN/ST* SW9 ....**135** F1
Byward St *MON* EC3R **37** D2
Bywater Pl *BERM/RHTH* SE16 ....**103** E5
Bywater St *CHEL* SW3 ....**115** F1
Bywell Pl *GTPST* * W1W **19** E3

C

Cabbell St *CAMTN* NW1 ....**16** B1
Cable Pl *GNWCH* SE10 ....**122** C4
Cable St *WCHPL* E1 ....**102** A1

Cable Trade Pk *CHARL* * SE7 ....**124** A1
Cabot Sq *POP/IOD* E14 ....**104** A2
Cabot Wy *EHAM* E6 ....**83** D5
Cabul Rd *BTSEA* SW11 ....**115** E5
Cactus Cl *CMBW* * SE5 ....**119** E5
Cadbury Wy *BERM/RHTH* SE16 ....**49** F3
Caddington Rd *CRICK* NW2 ....**53** E5
Cadell Cl *BETH* E2 ....**13** F2
Cade Rd *GNWCH* SE10 ....**123** D4
Cader Rd *WAND/EARL* SW18 ....**132** C4
Cadet Dr *STHWK* SE1 ....**119** F1
Cadet Pl *GNWCH* SE10 ....**123** E1
Cadiz St *WALW* SE17 ....**118** C1
Cadman Cl *BRXN/ST* SW9 ....**118** B3
Cadogan Cl *HOM* * E9 ....**79** F4
Cadogan Gdns *CHEL* SW3 ....**41** F4
Cadogan Ga *KTBR* SW1X **41** F4
Cadogan La *KTBR* SW1X **42** A3
Cadogan Pl *KTBR* SW1X **41** F3
Cadogan Rd *WOOL/PLUM* SE18 ......**108** C4
Cadogan Sq *KTBR* SW1X **41** E3
Cadogan St *CHEL* SW3 ....**41** E5
Cadogan Ter *HOM* E9 ....**79** F3
Cadoxton Av *SEVS/STOTM* N15 ....**59** F1
Cadwallon Rd *ELTH/MOT* SE9 ....**162** B2
Caedmon Rd *HOLWY* N7 ....**75** F1
Cahill St *STLK* * EC1Y **23** F1
Cahir St *POP/IOD* E14 ....**104** B5
Cairnfield Av *CRICK* NW2 ....**51** E2
Cairns Rd *BTSEA* SW11 ....**133** E3
Caistor Park Rd *SRTFD* E15 ....**81** F5
Caistor Rd *BAL* SW12 ....**134** B5
Caithness Gdns *BFN/LL* DA15 ....**145** F4
Caithness Rd *HMSMTH* W6 ....**101** D4
Calabria Rd *HBRY* N5 ....**76** B3
Calais St *CMBW* SE5 ....**118** B4
Calbourne Rd *BAL* SW12 ....**133** F5
Caldecot Rd *CMBW* SE5 ....**118** C5
Caldecott Wy *CLPT* E5 ....**61** D5
Calderon Rd *WAN* E11 ....**80** C1
Caldervale Rd *CLAP* SW4 ....**135** D3
Calderwood St
   WOOL/PLUM SE18 ....**108** A5
Caldicote Gn *CDALE/KGS* * NW9 ....**51** E1
Caldwell St *BRXN/ST* SW9 ....**117** F3
Caldy Wk *IS* * N1 ....**76** B1
Caledonian Rd *HOLWY* N7 ....**75** F2
Caledonian Wharf Rd
   POP/IOD E14 ....**105** D5
Caledonia St *IS* N1 ....**9** D2
Caledon Rd *EHAM* E6 ....**83** D5
Cale St *CHEL* SW3 ....**115** E1
Calidore Cl *BRXS/STRHM* * SW2 .....**135** F4
Callaby Ter *IS* * N1 ....**77** D3
Callaghan Cottages *WCHPL* * E1 ....**90** C4
Callander Rd *CAT* SE6 ....**158** B2
Callcott Rd *KIL/WHAMP* NW6 ....**71** F4
Callcott St *KENS* W8 ....**26** A3
Callendar Rd *SKENS* SW7 ....**40** A5
Callingham Cl *POP/IOD* E14 ....**91** F4
Callis Rd *WALTH* E17 ....**61** F1
Callow St *CHEL* SW3 ....**114** C2
Calmington Rd *CMBW* SE5 ....**119** E2
Calonne Rd *WIM/MER* SW19 ....**149** D4
Calshot St *IS* N1 ....**9** E1
Calthorpe St *FSBYW* WC1X **9** F5
Calton Av *DUL* SE21 ....**137** E4
Calverley Gv *ARCH* N19 ....**57** D3
Calvert Av *BETH* E2 ....**13** D4
Calverton Rd *EHAM* E6 ....**84** A5
Calvert Rd *GNWCH* SE10 ....**123** F1
Calvert St *CAMTN* NW1 ....**74** A5

Calvin St *WCHPL* E1 ....25 E1
Calydon Rd *CHARL* SE7 ....124 B1
Calypso Wy *BERM/RHTH* SE16 ....103 F4
Camarthen Gn *CDALE/KGS* * NW9....51 E1
Cambalt Rd *PUT/ROE* SW15 ....131 D3
Cambert Wy *ELTH/MOT* SE9 ....142 B2
Camberwell Church St *CMBW* SE5 ...119 D4
Camberwell Glebe *CMBW* SE5 ....119 D4
Camberwell Gn *CMBW* SE5 ....119 D4
Camberwell Gv *CMBW* SE5 ....119 D4
Camberwell New Rd *CMBW* SE5.......118 B3
Camberwell Rd *CMBW* SE5 ....118 C2
Camberwell Station Rd
  CMBW SE5 ....118 C4
Camborne Rd *WAND/EARL* SW18 ....132 A5
  WELL DA16 ....127 E5
Cambourne Ms *NTGHL* W11 ....89 E5
Cambray Rd *BAL* SW12 ....152 C1
Cambria Cl *BFN/LL* DA15 ....163 D3
Cambria Cl *WNWD* SE27 ....154 B3
Cambrian Rd *LEY* E10 ....62 A2
Cambria Rd *CMBW* SE5 ....136 C1
Cambria St *FUL/PGN* SW6 ....114 B3
Cambridge Av *KIL/WHAMP* NW6..........2 B1
  WELL DA16 ....145 F2
Cambridge Barracks Rd
  WOOL/PLUM SE18 ....107 F5
Cambridge Cl *WALTH* E17 ....61 F1
  WLSDN NW10 ....50 C5
Cambridge Crs *BETH* E2 ....90 B1
Cambridge Dr *LEE/GVPK* SE12 ....142 A3
Cambridge Gdns *KIL/WHAMP* NW6 ......2 B1
  NKENS W10 ....89 D5
Cambridge Ga *CAMTN* NW1 ....6 C4
Cambridge Gate Ms *CAMTN* NW1 ....7 D4
Cambridge Gn *ELTH/MOT* SE9 ....162 B1
Cambridge Gv *HMSMTH* W6 ....100 B5
Cambridge Heath Rd *BETH* E2 ....90 B2
Cambridge Pk *WAN* E11 ....64 A1
Cambridge Park Rd *WAN* E11 ....63 F2
Cambridge Pas *HOM* E9 ....78 C4
Cambridge Pl *KENS* * W8 ....39 D1
Cambridge Rd *BARK* IG11 ....84 C1
  BARN SW13 ....111 F5
  BTSEA SW11 ....115 F4
  GDMY/SEVK IG3 ....67 E3
  KIL/WHAMP NW6 ....2 B2
  RCH/KEW TW9 ....110 A3
  SCUP DA14 ....163 E4
  WAN E11 ....64 A1
Cambridge Rd North *CHSWK* W4 .....110 B1
Cambridge Rd South *CHSWK* W4 .....110 B1
Cambridge Rw *WOOL/PLUM* SE18 ...126 B1
Cambridge Sq *BAY/PAD* W2 ....16 C4
Cambridge St *PIM* SW1V 116 B1
Cambridge Ter *CAMTN* NW1 ....6 C4
Cambridge Terrace Ms
  CAMTN * NW1 ....7 D4
Cambus Rd *CAN/RD* E16 ....94 A4
Camdale Rd *WOOL/PLUM* SE18 ....127 F3
Camden Gdns *CAMTN* * NW1 ....74 B4
Camden High St *CAMTN* NW1 ....74 B4
Camdenhurst St *POP/IOD* E14 ....91 E5
Camden Lock Pl *CAMTN* NW1 ....74 B4
Camden Ms *CAMTN* NW1 ....74 C4
Camden Park Rd *CAMTN* NW1 ....75 D3
Camden Pas *IS* N1 ....10 C1
Camden Rd *CAMTN* NW1 ....74 B5
  WALTH E17 ....61 F1
  WAN E11 ....64 B1
Camden Rd Permanent Wy
  CAMTN * NW1 ....75 D5
Camden Rw *BKHTH/KID* SE3 ....123 E5

Camden Sq *CAMTN* NW1 ....75 D3
Camden St *CAMTN* NW1 ....74 B4
Camden Ter *CAMTN* NW1 ....75 D3
Camden Wk *IS* N1 ....76 B5
Camelford Wk *NTGHL* * W11 ....89 E5
Camelot Cl *WIM/MER* SW19 ....149 F4
  WOOL/PLUM SE18 ....109 D3
Camel Rd *CAN/RD* E16 ....107 D2
Camera Pl *WBPTN* SW10 ....115 D2
Cameron Rd *CAT* * SE6 ....157 F2
  GDMY/SEVK IG3 ....67 E3
Cameron Ter *LEE/GVPK* * SE12 ....160 B3
Camerton Cl *HACK* E8 ....77 F3
Camilla Rd *BERM/RHTH* SE16 ....102 B5
Camlan Rd *BMLY* BR1 ....159 F4
Camlet St *BETH* E2 ....13 E5
Camley St *CAMTN* NW1 ....75 D4
Camomile St *LVPST* EC2M 24 C4
Campana Rd *FUL/PGN* SW6 ....114 A4
Campbell Cl *STRHM/NOR* * SW16 ...153 D5
  WOOL/PLUM SE18 ....126 A4
Campbell Gordon Wy *CRICK* NW2 .....70 B1
Campbell Rd *BOW* E3 ....92 A2
  EHAM E6 ....83 E5
  FSTGT E7 ....81 E1
Campbell Wk *IS* N1 ....75 E5
Campdale Rd *ARCH* N19 ....57 D5
Campden Gv *KENS* W8 ....26 B5
Campden Hl *KENS* W8 ....26 A5
Campden Hill Gdns *KENS* W8 ....26 A3
Campden Hill Pl *KENS* * W8 ....101 F2
Campden Hill Rd *KENS* W8 ....26 A3
Campden Hill Sq *KENS* W8 ....101 F2
Campden House Cl *KENS* W8 ....26 A5
Campden House Ter *KENS* * W8 ....26 B4
Campden St *KENS* W8 ....26 A4
Campen Ter *CHSWK* * W4 ....111 E1
Campen Cl *WIM/MER* SW19 ....149 E2
Camperdown St *WCHPL* E1 ....25 F5
Campfield Rd *ELTH/MOT* SE9 ....143 D5
Campion Cl *EHAM* E6 ....107 F1
Campion Rd *PUT/ROE* SW15 ....130 C2
Camplin St *NWCR* SE14 ....121 D5
Camp Rd *WIM/MER* SW19 ....148 B5
Campshill Pl *LEW* SE13 ....140 C3
Campshill Rd *LEW* SE13 ....140 C3
Campus Rd *WALTH* E17 ....61 F1
Camp Vw *WIM/MER* SW19 ....148 B5
Cam Rd *SRTFD* E15 ....81 D5
Canada Crs *ACT* W3 ....86 C4
Canada Rd *ACT* W3 ....86 C4
Canada St *BERM/RHTH* SE16 ....103 D3
Canada Wy *SHB* W12 ....100 B1
Canadian Av *CAT* SE6 ....158 B1
Canal Ap *DEPT* SE8 ....121 E2
Canal Cl *NKENS* W10 ....89 D3
  WCHPL E1 ....91 E3
Canal Gv *PECK* SE15 ....120 A2
Canal Pth *HACK* E8 ....77 F5
Canal Rd *WCHPL* E1 ....91 E3
Canal St *CMBW* SE5 ....119 D2
Canal Wk *IS* N1 ....77 D5
  WLSDN * NW10 ....68 C4
Canal Wy *NKENS* W10 ....89 D3
Canberra Rd *CHARL* SE7 ....124 C2
  EHAM E6 ....83 F5
Canbury Ms *SYD* SE26 ....156 A3
Cancell Rd *BRXN/ST* SW9 ....118 A4
Candahar Rd *BTSEA* SW11 ....115 E5
Candler St *SEVS/STOTM* * N15 ....59 D1
Candover St *GTPST* * W1W 19 E3
Candy St *BOW* E3 ....79 F5
Caney Ms *CRICK* NW2 ....53 D4

Canfield Gdns KIL/WHAMP NW6 ....72 B4
Canfield Pl HAMP NW3 ....72 C3
Canford Rd BTSEA SW11 ....134 A2
Canham Rd CHSWK W4 ....99 E3
Cann Hall Rd FSTGT E7 ....81 F1
Canning Cross CMBW SE5 ....119 E5
Canning Pl KENS W8 ....39 E2
Canning Rd FSBYPK N4 ....58 B5
  SRTFD E15 ....93 E1
Cannon Dr POP/IOD E14 ....104 A1
Cannon HI KIL/WHAMP NW6 ....72 B2
Cannon La HAMP NW3 ....55 D5
Cannon Pl CHARL SE7 ....125 E1
  HAMP NW3 ....54 C5
Cannon St STP EC4M 23 E5
Cannon Street Rd WCHPL E1 ....90 B5
Canon Beck Rd BERM/RHTH SE16 ....102 C3
Canonbie Rd FSTH SE23 ....138 C5
Canonbury Crs IS N1 ....76 C4
Canonbury Gv IS N1 ....76 C4
Canonbury La IS N1 ....76 B4
Canonbury Pk North IS N1 ....76 C3
Canonbury Pk South IS N1 ....76 C3
Canonbury Rd IS N1 ....76 B3
Canonbury Sq IS N1 ....76 B4
Canonbury St IS N1 ....76 C4
Canonbury Vls IS N1 ....76 B4
Canon Murnane Rd STHWK SE1 ....49 E3
Canon Rw WHALL SW1A 44 C1
Canons Cl EFNCH N2 ....55 D2
Canon St IS N1 ....76 C5
Canrobert St BETH E2 ....90 B1
Cantelowes Rd CAMTN NW1 ....75 D3
Canterbury Av IL IG1 ....65 E2
Canterbury Cl CMBW * SE5 ....118 C5
  EHAM E6 ....95 F5
Canterbury Crs BRXN/ST SW9 ....136 A1
Canterbury Gv WNWD SE27 ....154 A3
Canterbury Pl WALW SE17 ....47 D5
Canterbury Ter KIL/WHAMP NW6 ....2 A2
  LEY E10 ....62 C2
Canterbury Ter KIL/WHAMP NW6 ....2 A2
Cantley Gdns GNTH/NBYPK IG2 ....66 C1
Canton St POP/IOD E14 ....92 A5
Cantrell Rd BOW E3 ....92 A3
Cantwell Rd WOOL/PLUM SE18 ....126 B3
Canvey St STHWK SE1 ....35 E3
Cape Cl BARK IG11 ....84 B4
Capel Gdns GDMY/SEVK IG3 ....85 F1
Capel Rd FSTGT E7 ....82 B1
Capeners Cl KTBR SW1X 41 F1
  KTBR * SW1X 42 A1
Capern Rd WAND/EARL SW18 ....150 C1
Cape Yd WAP E1W 102 A2
Capital Interchange Wy
  CHSWK W4 ....110 A1
Capland St STJWD NW8 ....4 B5
Caple Pde WLSDN * NW10 ....87 F1
Caple Rd WLSDN NW10 ....87 F1
Capstan Rd DEPT SE8 ....103 F5
Capstan Sq POP/IOD E14 ....104 C3
Capstan Wy BERM/RHTH SE16 ....103 E2
Capstone Rd BMLY BR1 ....160 A4
Capulet Ms CAN/RD E16 ....106 A3
Capworth St LEY E10 ....62 A3
Caradoc St GNWCH SE10 ....123 E1
Caradon Ct WAN * E11 ....63 E3
Caravel Ms DEPT * SE8 ....122 A2
Caraway Cl PLSTW E13 ....94 B4
Carbis Rd POP/IOD E14 ....91 F5
Carburton St GTPST W1W 19 D2
Cardale St POP/IOD E14 ....104 C4
Carden Rd PECK SE15 ....138 B1

Cardiff St WOOL/PLUM SE18 ....127 E3
Cardigan Pl BKHTH/KID * SE3 ....123 D5
Cardigan Rd BARN SW13 ....112 A5
  BOW E3 ....91 F1
Cardigan St LBTH SE11 ....118 A1
Cardigan Wk IS * N1 ....76 C4
Cardinal Bourne St STHWK * SE1 ....48 B3
Cardinal Pl PUT/ROE SW15 ....131 D2
Cardinals Wy ARCH N19 ....57 D3
Cardine Ms PECK SE15 ....120 B3
Cardington St CAMTN NW1 ....7 F3
Cardozo Rd HOLWY N7 ....75 E2
Cardross St HMSMTH W6 ....100 B4
Cardwell Rd HOLWY * N7 ....75 E1
Cardwell Ter HOLWY * N7 ....75 E1
Carew Cl HOLWY N7 ....57 F4
Carew St CMBW SE5 ....118 C5
Carey Gdns VX/NE SW8 ....116 C3
Carey La CITYW EC2V 23 E4
Carey Pl WEST SW1P 44 A5
Carey St LINN WC2A 21 F5
Carey Wy WBLY HA9 ....68 B1
Carfax Pl CLAP SW4 ....135 D2
The Carfax SYD * SE26 ....156 C3
Carffree Cl IS N1 ....76 A4
Cargill Rd WAND/EARL SW18 ....150 C1
Carholme Rd FSTH SE23 ....157 F1
Carisbrooke Gdns PECK * SE15 ....119 F5
Carleton Gdns ARCH * N19 ....74 C2
Carleton Rd HOLWY N7 ....75 D1
Carleton Vls KTTN * NW5 ....74 C2
Carlile Cl BOW E3 ....91 F1
Carlingford Rd HAMP NW3 ....73 D1
Carlisle Av ACT W3 ....87 E5
  TWRH EC3N 25 D5
Carlisle Gdns IL IG1 ....65 E1
Carlisle La STHWK SE1 ....45 F2
Carlisle Pl WEST SW1P 43 E3
Carlisle Rd FSBYPK N4 ....58 A3
  KIL/WHAMP NW6 ....71 E5
  LEY E10 ....62 A3
Carlisle St SOHO/CST W1F 20 A5
Carlisle Wk HACK E8 ....77 F3
Carlisle Wy TOOT SW17 ....152 A5
Carlos Pl MYFR/PKLN W1K 30 B2
Carlow St CAMTN NW1 ....7 E1
Carlton Dr PUT/ROE SW15 ....131 D3
Carlton Gdns STJS SW1Y 32 A4
Carlton Gn SCUP * DA14 ....163 F4
Carlton Gv PECK SE15 ....120 B4
Carlton HI STJWD NW8 ....3 D1
Carlton House Ter STJS SW1Y 32 A4
Carlton Ms KIL/WHAMP * NW6 ....72 A2
Carlton Rd CHSWK W4 ....99 D3
  FSBYPK N4 ....58 A2
  MNPK E12 ....83 D1
  MORT/ESHN SW14 ....128 C1
  SCUP DA14 ....163 F5
  WAN E11 ....63 D3
Carlton Sq WCHPL * E1 ....91 D3
Carlton St STJS SW1Y 32 A3
Carlton Ter SYD SE26 ....156 C3
Carlton Tower Pl KTBR SW1X 41 F2
Carlton V KIL/WHAMP NW6 ....2 A3
Carlwell St TOOT SW17 ....151 E5
Carlyle Cl EFNCH N2 ....54 C1
  WLSDN NW10 ....69 D5
Carlyle Ct WBPTN * SW10 ....114 C4
Carlyle Rd MNPK E12 ....83 E1
Carlyle Sq CHEL SW3 ....115 D1
Carmalt Gdns PUT/ROE SW15 ....130 C2
Carmel Ct KENS W8 ....26 C5

Carmelite St *EMB* EC4Y **34** B1
Carmen St *POP/IOD* E14..............**92** B5
Carmichael Cl *BTSEA* * SW11 ......**133** D1
Carminia Rd *TOOT* SW17..............**152** B2
Carnaby St *REGST* W1B..............**31** E1
Carnac St *WNWD* SE27 ....**155** D4
Carnarvon Rd *LEY* E10 ....**62** C1
   SRTFD E15 ....**81** F3
Carnbrook Rd *BKHTH/KID* SE3 ......**143** D1
Carnecke Gdns *ELTH/MOT* SE9 ......**143** E3
Carnegie Pl *WIM/MER* SW19 ....**149** D5
Carnegie St *IS* N1 ....**75** F5
Carnoustie Dr *IS* N1 ....**75** F4
Carnwath Rd *FUL/PGN* SW6 ....**132** A1
Carolina Cl *SRTFD* E15..............**81** E2
Caroline Cl *BAY/PAD* W2 ....**27** D2
   STRHM/NOR SW16 ....**153** F4
Caroline Gdns *BETH* E2 ....**13** D3
   PECK * SE15..............**120** B3
Caroline Pl *BAY/PAD* W2 ....**27** D1
   VX/NE SW8 ....**116** A5
Caroline Place Ms *BAY/PAD* * W2 ....**27** D2
Caroline St *WCHPL* E1 ....**91** D5
Caroline Ter *BGVA* SW1W **42** A5
Caroline Wk *HMSMTH* W6 ....**113** E2
Carol St *CAMTN* NW1..............**74** C5
Carpenters Ms *HOLWY* * N7 ....**75** E2
Carpenter's Pl *CLAP* SW4 ....**135** D2
Carpenters Rd *SRTFD* E15 ....**80** B4
Carpenter St *MYFR/PKLN* W1K **30** C2
Carrara Ms *HACK* E8 ....**78** A2
Carr Gv *WOOL/PLUM* SE18 ....**107** F3
Carriage Dr East *BTSEA* SW11 ......**116** A2
Carriage Dr North *BTSEA* SW11......**115** F3
Carriage Dr South *BTSEA* SW11......**115** F4
Carriage Dr West *BTSEA* SW11 ......**115** F3
Carriage Ms *IL* IG1 ....**66** C4
Carrick Ms *DEPT* SE8..............**122** A2
Carrington Gdns *FSTGT* E7..............**82** A1
Carrington Rd *RCHPK/HAM* TW10 ....**128** A2
Carrington St *MYFR/PICC* W1J **30** C2
Carrol Cl *KTTN* NW5 ....**74** B1
Carroll Cl *SRTFD* E15 ....**81** E2
Carronade Pl *WOOL/PLUM* SE18 ....**109** D4
Carron Cl *POP/IOD* E14..............**92** B5
Carroun Rd *VX/NE* SW8 ....**117** F3
Carr St *POP/IOD* E14..............**91** E4
Carslake Rd *PUT/ROE* SW15 ....**130** C4
Carson Rd *CAN/RD* E16..............**94** A4
   DUL SE21 ....**154** C2
Carstairs Rd *CAT* SE6 ....**158** C3
Carston Cl *LEE/GVPK* SE12 ....**141** F3
Carswell Rd *CAT* SE6 ....**140** C5
Carteret St *STJSPK* SW1H **44** A1
Carteret Wy *DEPT* SE8 ....**103** E5
Carter La *BLKFR* EC4V **23** D5
Carter Pl *WALW* SE17..............**118** C1
Carter Rd *PLSTW* E13 ....**82** B5
Carters Cl *KTTN* * NW5 ....**75** D3
Carters Hill Cl *ELTH/MOT* SE9........**160** C1
Carter St *WALW* SE17 ....**118** C2
Carters Yd *WAND/EARL* * SW18 ......**132** A3
Carthew Rd *HMSMTH* W6 ....**100** B4
Carthew Vls *HMSMTH* W6 ....**100** B3
Carthusian St *FARR* EC1M **23** E2
Carting La *TPL/STR* WC2R **33** D2
Cartwright Gdns *STPAN* WC1H **8** B4
Cartwright St *TWRH* EC3N **37** F1
Cartwright Wy *BARN* SW13 ....**112** B3
Carver Rd *HNHL* SE24 ....**136** C4
Cary Rd *WAN* E11..............**81** E1
Carysfort Rd *STNW/STAM* N16 ......**59** D5
Casella Rd *NWCR* SE14 ....**121** D3

Casewick Rd *WNWD* SE27 ....**154** B5
Casey Cl *CAMTN* NW1 ....**17** D1
Casimir Rd *CLPT* E5..............**60** C3
Casino Av *HNHL* SE24 ....**136** C3
Caspian St *CMBW* SE5..............**119** D3
Caspian Wk *CAN/RD* E16 ....**95** D5
Casselden Rd *WLSDN* NW10..............**69** D4
Cassidy Rd *FUL/PGN* SW6 ....**114** A3
Cassland Rd *HOM* E9 ....**79** D4
Casslee Rd *CAT* SE6 ....**139** F5
Casson St *WCHPL* E1 ....**90** A4
Castellain Rd *MV/WKIL* W9 ....**2** C5
Castello Av *PUT/ROE* SW15 ....**130** C3
Castelnau *BARN* SW13 ....**112** B3
Casterbridge Rd *BKHTH/KID* SE3 ......**142** A1
Casterton St *HACK* E8..............**78** B3
Castile Rd *WOOL/PLUM* SE18..............**108** A5
Castillon Rd *CAT* SE6 ....**159** E2
Castlands Rd *CAT* SE6 ....**157** F2
Castle Baynard St *BLKFR* EC4V **35** D1
Castlebrook Cl *LBTH* SE11 ....**46** C4
Castle Cl *ACT* W3 ....**98** B3
   WIM/MER SW19 ....**149** D3
Castlecombe Dr *WIM/MER* SW19 ....**131** D5
Castlecombe Rd *ELTH/MOT* SE9 ......**161** D5
Castle Ct *BANK* * EC3V..............**24** B5
   SYD SE26 ....**157** E4
Castle Dr *REDBR* IG4..............**65** E1
Castleford Av *ELTH/MOT* SE9 ....**162** B1
Castlehaven Rd *CAMTN* NW1 ....**74** B4
Castle La *WESTW* SW1E **43** E2
Castle Md *CMBW* * SE5..............**118** C3
Castle Ms *CAMTN* NW1 ....**74** B3
Castle Pl *CAMTN* NW1..............**74** B3
Castlereagh St *MBLAR* W1H............**17** E4
Castle Rd *CAMTN* NW1 ....**74** B3
Castle Rw *CHSWK* * W4..............**111** F1
Castle St *EHAM* E6..............**94** C1
Castleton Rd *LEE/GVPK* SE12..............**161** D4
Castletown Rd *WKENS* W14..............**113** E1
Castleview Cl *FSBYPK* N4..............**58** C3
Castle View Gdns *IL* IG1 ....**65** E1
Castle Vls *CRICK* * NW2 ....**70** A3
Castle Wy *WIM/MER* SW19 ....**149** D3
Castlewood Dr *ELTH/MOT* SE9 ....**125** F5
Castlewood Rd *SEVS/STOTM* N15..........**60** A1
Castle Yd *HGT* N6 ....**56** A2
   STHWK * SE1 ....**35** D3
Castor La *POP/IOD* E14..............**104** B1
Caterham Rd *LEW* SE13 ....**140** C1
Catesby St *WALW* SE17 ....**48** B5
Catford Broadway *CAT* SE6 ....**140** B5
Catford HI *CAT* SE6 ....**157** F1
Catford Island *CAT* * SE6 ....**140** B5
Catford Rd *CAT* SE6 ....**158** A1
Cathall Rd *WAN* E11 ....**63** D4
Cathay Rd *BERM/RHTH* SE16 ....**102** B3
Cathcart HI *KTTN* NW5 ....**56** C5
Cathcart Rd *WBPTN* * SW10..............**114** B2
Cathcart St *KTTN* NW5..............**74** B3
Cathedral St *STHWK* SE1 ....**36** A3
Catherall Rd *HBRY* N5..............**58** C5
Catherine Griffiths Ct
   CLKNW * EC1R..............**10** B5
Catherine Gv *GNWCH* SE10 ....**122** B4
Catherine Pl *WESTW* SW1E **43** E2
Catherine St *HOL/ALD* * WC2B..............**33** E1
Catherine Wheel Aly *LVPST* EC2M........**25** D3
Catherine Wheel Yd *WHALL* SW1A **31** E4
Cathles Rd *BAL* SW12 ....**134** B4
Cathnor Rd *SHB* W12 ....**100** B3
Catling Cl *FSTH* SE23..............**156** C3
Catlin St *BERM/RHTH* SE16 ....**120** A1

Cato Rd *CLAP* SW4 ....**135** D1
Cator St *PECK* SE15 ....**119** F2
Cato St *MBLAR* W1H **17** D3
Cattistock Rd *ELTH/MOT* SE9 ......**161** E5
Catton St *RSQ* WC1B **21** E3
Caudwell Ter *WAND/EARL* * SW18 ...**133** D4
PECK SE15 ....**120** B5
Caulfield Rd *EHAM* E6 ....**83** F4
PECK SE15 ....**120** B5
The Causeway *WAND/EARL* SW18 ...**132** B2
WIM/MER SW19 ....**148** C5
Causton Cottages *POP/IOD* * E14 ...**91** E4
Causton Rd *HGT* * N6 ....**56** B2
Causton St *WEST* SW1P **44** B5
Cautley Av *CLAP* SW4 ....**134** C3
Cavalry Gdns *PUT/ROE* SW15 ......**131** E3
Cavaye Pl *WBPTN* SW10 ....**114** C1
Cavell St *WCHPL* E1 ....**90** B4
Cavendish Av *STJWD* NW8 ....**4** B2
WELL DA16 ....**145** F1
Cavendish Cl *KIL/WHAMP* NW6 ......**71** F3
STJWD NW8 ....**4** B3
Cavendish Dr *WAN* E11 ....**63** D3
Cavendish Gdns *BARK* IG11 ....**85** F2
CLAP * SW4 ....**134** C4
IL IG1 ....**66** A3
Cavendish Ms North *REGST* W1B **19** D2
Cavendish Ms South
GTPST * W1W **19** D3
Cavendish Pde *CLAP* * SW4 ....**134** C2
Cavendish Pl *KIL/WHAMP* NW6 ......**71** D4
MHST W1U **18** C4
Cavendish Rd *CHSWK* W4 ....**110** C4
CLAP * SW4 ....**134** C4
FSBYPK N4 ....**58** B1
KIL/WHAMP NW6 ....**71** E4
Cavendish Sq *CAVSQ/HST* * W1G ...**18** C4
Cavendish St *IS* N1 ....**12** A3
Cavendish Ter *BOW* * E3 ....**91** F2
Cavenham Gdns *IL* IG1 ....**67** D5
Cave Rd *PLSTW* E13 ....**94** B1
Caversham Flats *CHEL* * SW3 ....**115** F3
Caversham Rd *KTTN* * NW5 ....**74** C3
Caversham St *CHEL* SW3 ....**115** F2
Caverswall St *SHB* W12 ....**88** C5
Cawnpore St *NRWD* SE19 ....**155** E5
Caxton Gv *BOW* E3 ....**92** A2
Caxton Rd *SHB* W12 ....**101** D2
WIM/MER SW19 ....**150** E5
The Caxtons *CMBW* * SE5 ....**118** B3
Caxton St *STJSPK* SW1H **43** F1
Caxton St North *CAN/RD* E16 ....**93** F5
Cayenne Ct *STHWK* SE1 ....**37** D5
Cayton St *FSBYE* EC1V **12** A4
Cazenove St *STNW/STAM* N16 ....**59** F4
Cecil Av *BARK* IG11 ....**85** D4
Cecil Ct *LSO/SEVD* WC2H **32** B2
Cecile Pk *CEND/HSY/T* N8 ....**57** E1
Cecilia Rd *HACK* E8 ....**77** F2
Cecil Rd *ACT* W3 ....**86** C4
IL IG1 ....**84** B1
PLSTW E13 ....**82** A5
WAN E11 ....**63** E4
WLSDN NW10 ....**69** E5
Cedar Cl *DUL* SE21 ....**154** C1
KUTN/CMB KT2 ....**147** D4
Cedar Ct *CHARL* * SE7 ....**124** C2
ELTH/MOT * SE9 ....**143** E4
WIM/MER SW19 ....**149** D3
Cedarhurst Dr *ELTH/MOT* SE9 ......**142** C3
Cedar Mt *ELTH/MOT* SE9 ....**161** D1
Cedarne Rd *FUL/PGN* SW6 ....**114** A3
Cedar Pl *CHARL* SE7 ....**124** C1
Cedar Rd *CRICK* NW2 ....**70** C1

Cedars Cl *LEW* SE13 ....**141** D1
Cedars Cottages *PUT/ROE* * SW15 ...**130** A4
Cedars Ms *CLAP* * SW4 ....**134** B2
Cedars Rd *BARN* SW13 ....**111** F5
CLAP SW4 ....**134** B1
SRTFD E15 ....**81** E3
The Cedars *HOM* * E9 ....**79** D4
SRTFD * E15 ....**81** F5
The Cedar Tree Gv *WNWD* SE27 ....**154** B5
Cedar Wy *CAMTN* NW1 ....**75** D4
Cedric Rd *ELTH/MOT* SE9 ....**162** C3
Celandine Cl *POP/IOD* * E14 ....**92** A4
Celandine Dr *HACK* E8 ....**77** F4
Celandine Wy *SRTFD* E15 ....**93** E2
Celbridge Ms *BAY/PAD* W2 ....**15** D4
Celestial Gdns *LEW* SE13 ....**141** D2
Celia Rd *ARCH* N19 ....**74** C1
Celtic St *POP/IOD* E14 ....**92** B4
Cemetery La *CHARL* SE7 ....**125** E2
Cemetery Rd *FSTGT* E7 ....**81** F2
Cenacle Cl *HAMP* NW3 ....**54** A5
Centaur St *STHWK* SE1 ....**45** F2
Centenary Wk *WAN* E11 ....**64** A3
Central Av *WAN* E11 ....**63** D4
Central Hl *NRWD* SE19 ....**154** C5
Central Pde *ACT* * W3 ....**98** A3
STRHM/NOR * SW16 ....**153** E4
Central Park Rd *EHAM* E6 ....**95** D1
Central Sq *GLDGN* NW11 ....**54** A1
Central St *FSBYE* EC1V **11** E3
Central Wy *WLSDN* NW10 ....**86** C3
Centre Av *ACT* W3 ....**99** D2
Centre Rd *WAN* E11 ....**64** A4
Centre St *BETH* E2 ....**90** B1
Centric Cl *CAMTN* * NW1 ....**74** B5
Centurion La *HOLWY* N7 ....**75** F4
Centurion La *BOW* E3 ....**91** F1
Century Ms *CLPT* * E5 ....**78** C1
Cephas Av *WCHPL* E1 ....**90** C3
Cephas St *WCHPL* E1 ....**90** C3
Ceres Rd *WOOL/PLUM* SE18 ....**109** F5
Cerise Rd *PECK* SE15 ....**120** A4
Cervantes Ct *BAY/PAD* W2 ....**15** D5
Ceylon Rd *WKENS* W14 ....**101** D4
Chadbourn St *POP/IOD* E14 ....**92** B4
Chadwell St *CLKNW* EC1R **10** B3
Chadwick Rd *CMBW* SE5 ....**119** F5
IL IG1 ....**66** B5
WAN E11 ....**63** E2
WLSDN NW10 ....**69** F5
Chadwick St *WEST* SW1P **44** B3
Chadwin Rd *PLSTW* E13 ....**94** B4
Chagford St *CAMTN* NW1 ....**17** E1
Chailey St *CLPT* E5 ....**60** C1
Chalbury Wk *IS* N1 ....**9** F1
Chalcot Crs *CAMTN* NW1 ....**73** E3
Chalcot Gdns *HAMP* NW3 ....**73** F3
Chalcot Ms *STRHM/NOR* SW16 ....**153** E2
Chalcot Rd *CAMTN* NW1 ....**74** A5
Chalcot Sq *CAMTN* NW1 ....**74** A4
Chalcroft Rd *LEW* SE13 ....**141** E3
Chaldon Rd *FUL/PGN* SW6 ....**113** E3
Chale Rd *BRXS/STRHM* SW2 ....**135** E4
Chalfont Av *WBLY* HA9 ....**68** B3
Chalford Rd *DUL* SE21 ....**155** D4
Chalgrove Rd *HOM* E9 ....**78** C3
Chalk Farm Pde *HAMP* * NW3 ....**74** A4
Chalk Hill Rd *HMSMTH* W6 ....**101** D5
Chalkhill Rd *WBLY* HA9 ....**50** A5
Chalklands *WBLY* HA9 ....**50** C5
Chalk Rd *PLSTW* E13 ....**94** B4
Challenge Cl *WLSDN* NW10 ....**69** E5
Challice Wy *BRXS/STRHM* SW2 ....**153** F1

Challoner Crs WKENS * W14................113 E1
Challoner St WKENS W14.....................113 E1
Chalmers Wk WALW * SE17.................118 B2
Chalsey Rd BROCKY SE4.......................139 F2
Chalton Dr EFNCH N2............................54 D1
Chalton St CAMTN NW1.........................8 A1
Chamberlain Cl WOOL/PLUM SE18 .....109 D4
Chamberlain Cottages
CMBW * SE5...............................119 D4
Chamberlain St HAMP * NW3.................73 F4
Chamberlayne Rd WLSDN NW10 ....70 C5
Chamberlens Garages
HMSMTH * W6............................100 B5
Chambers La WLSDN NW10.....................70 B4
Chambers Rd HOLWY N7.......................75 E1
Chambers St BERM/RHTH SE16 ....102 A3
Chamber St WCHPL E1..........................37 F1
Chambon Pl HMSMTH W6.....................100 A5
Chambord St BETH E2...........................13 F4
Champion Crs SYD SE26........................157 E4
Champion Gv CMBW SE5.......................137 D1
Champion Hl CMBW SE5........................137 D1
Champion Pk CMBW SE5.......................137 D1
Champion Rd SYD SE26.........................157 E4
Champness Cl WNWD SE27..................155 D4
Champness Rd BARK IG11.......................85 F3
Chancellor Gv DUL SE21.......................154 C2
Chancellor's Rd HMSMTH W6..............112 C1
Chancellors St HMSMTH W6................112 C1
Chancellors Whf HMSMTH * W6..........112 C1
Chancel St STHWK SE1...........................34 C3
Chancery La LINN WC2A.........................21 F3
Chance St BETH E2................................13 E5
Chanctonbury Cl ELTH/MOT SE9 ....162 B3
Chandler Av CAN/RD E16.......................94 A4
Chandlers Ct LEE/GVPK * SE12 ....160 B2
Chandlers Ms POP/IOD E14...................104 C3
Chandler St WAP E1W..........................102 B2
Chandler Wy PECK SE15.......................119 E3
Chandos Pl CHCR WC2N.........................32 C2
Chandos Rd CRICK NW2..........................70 C2
   SRTFD E15....................................81 D2
   WLSDN NW10.................................87 E3
Chandos Wy CAVSO/HST W1G...............19 D3
Chandos Wy GLDGN NW11......................54 B3
Channel Islands Est IS N1......................76 C3
Channelsea Rd SRTFD E15......................81 D5
Chantrey Rd BRXN/ST SW9...................135 F1
Chantry Cl MV/WKIL * W9.......................89 F3
Chantry Sq KENS W8..............................38 C5
Chantry St IS * N1..................................76 B5
Chant Sq SRTFD * E15.............................81 D4
Chant St SRTFD E15................................81 D4
Chapel Ct STHWK SE1............................36 A5
Chapel Farm Rd ELTH/MOT SE9.............161 F3
Chapel House St POP/IOD E14..............122 B1
Chapel Market IS N1..............................10 A1
Chapel Pl CAVSO/HST W1G....................18 C4
   IS N1..10 B1
Chapel Rd IL IG1....................................66 A5
   WNWD SE27................................154 B4
Chapel Side BAY/PAD W2.......................26 C1
Chapel St BAY/PAD W2...........................16 A3
   KTBR SW1X...................................42 B2
Chaplin Cl STHWK SE1............................34 B5
Chaplin Rd CRICK NW2............................70 A3
   SRTFD E15....................................93 E1
Chapman Rd HOM E9.............................79 F3
Chapman Sq WIM/MER SW19...............149 E3
Chapman St WCHPL E1.........................102 B1
Chapter Rd CRICK NW2..........................70 A2
   WALW SE17.................................118 B1
Chapter St WEST SW1P...........................44 B1

Chara Pl CHSWK W4..............................111 D2
Chardin Rd CHSWK * W4.........................99 E5
Chardmore Rd STNW/STAM N16..........60 A3
Chardwell Cl EHAM E6.............................95 E5
Charecroft Wy WKENS W14...................101 D3
Charford Rd CAN/RD E16.........................94 A4
Chargeable La PLSTW E13........................94 A3
Chargeable St CAN/RD E16.......................93 F3
Charing Cross CHCR WC2N.......................32 B3
Charing Cross Rd SOHO/SHAV W1D ...20 B5
Charlbert St STJWD NW8..........................4 C1
Charlbury Gdns GDMY/SEVK IG3...........67 F4
Charlecote Gv SYD SE26........................156 B5
Charldane Rd ELTH/MOT SE9................162 B3
Charlemont Rd EHAM E6.........................95 F2
Charles Barry Cl CLAP * SW4.................134 C1
Charles Coveney Rd PECK * SE15..........119 F4
Charlesfield LEE/GVPK SE12..................160 C3
Charles Flemwell Ms
CAN/RD * E16.............................106 C2
Charles Grinling Wk
WOOL/PLUM SE18......................108 A5
Charles II Pl CHEL * SW3.......................115 F1
Charles II St STJS SW1Y..........................32 A3
Charles La STJWD NW8............................4 C1
Charles Pl CAMTN * NW1..........................7 F4
Charles Rd FSTGT E7...............................82 C4
Charles Sq IS N1....................................12 B4
Charles Square Est IS N1........................12 B4
Charles St BARN SW13..........................129 E1
   CAN/RD E16.................................106 C2
   MYFR/PICC W1J.............................30 C3
Charleston St WALW SE17.......................47 F5
Charleville Circ SYD SE26......................156 A5
Charleville Rd WKENS W14....................113 E1
Charlotte Despard Av
BTSEA SW11................................116 B4
Charlotte Ms FITZ W1T...........................19 F2
   NKENS W10..................................89 D5
Charlotte Pde FSTH * SE23....................157 E2
Charlotte Pl FITZ W1T.............................19 F3
Charlotte Rd BARN SW13.......................111 F4
   IS N1..12 C4
Charlotte Rw CLAP SW4........................134 C1
Charlotte St FITZ W1T.............................19 F2
Charlotte Ter IS * N1...............................75 F5
Charlow Cl FUL/PGN SW6.....................114 C5
Charlton Church La CHARL SE7.............124 C1
Charlton Crs BARK IG11...........................97 F1
Charlton Dene CHARL SE7.....................124 C3
Charlton King's Rd KTTN NW5.................75 D2
Charlton La CHARL SE7..........................125 D1
Charlton Park La CHARL SE7..................125 D3
Charlton Park Rd CHARL SE7.................125 D2
Charlton Pl IS N1....................................10 C1
Charlton Rd BKHTH/KID SE3.................124 A3
   WLSDN NW10.................................69 E5
Charlton Wy BKHTH/KID SE3................123 E4
Charlwood Pl PIM SW1V..........................43 F5
Charlwood Rd PUT/ROE SW15..............131 D2
Charlwood St PIM SW1V..........................43 F5
Charlwood Ter PUT/ROE SW15..............131 D2
Charminster Rd LEE/GVPK SE12............161 D4
Charnock Rd CLPT E5.............................60 B5
Charnwood Gdns POP/IOD E14.............104 A5
Charnwood St CLPT * E5..........................60 A4
Charrington Rd CAMTN NW1....................8 A1
Charsley Rd CAT SE6.............................158 B2
Charter Av GNTH/NBYPK IG2..................67 D3
Charterhouse Buildings
FARR EC1M..................................23 E1
Charterhouse Ms FARR EC1M.................23 D2
Charterhouse Rd HACK E8......................78 A2

Charterhouse St *HCIRC* EC1N **22** B3
The Charterhouse *FARR* EC1M **23** D1
Charteris Rd *FSBYPK* N4.....................**57** F3
  KIL/WHAMP NW6 ....**71** F5
Charters Cl *NRWD* SE19 ....**155** E5
Chartfield Av *PUT/ROE* SW15 ....**130** B3
Chartfield Sq *PUT/ROE* SW15 ....**131** D3
Chartham Gv *WNWD* SE27 ....**154** A3
Chartley Av *CRICK* NW2 ....**51** E5
Chartley Pde *WLSDN* * NW10 ....**51** E5
Chart St *IS* N1 ....**12** B3
Chartwell Cl *CHST* BR7 ....**163** D2
Charwood *STRHM/NOR* * SW16 ....**154** A4
Chasefield Rd *TOOT* SW17 ....**151** F4
Chaseley Ct *CHSWK* W4 ....**110** B1
Chaseley St *POP/IOD* * E14 ....**91** E5
Chase Rd *ACT* W3 ....**87** D3
The Chase *CLAP* SW4............................**134** B3
  MNPK E12 ....**83** D1
Chatfield Rd *BTSEA* SW11.....................**132** C1
Chatham Pl *HOM* E9 ....**78** C3
Chatham Rd *BTSEA* SW11......................**133** D3
Chatham St *WALW* SE17 ....**48** A4
  WOOL/PLUM SE18 ....**108** B4
Chatsworth Av *BMLY* BR1 ....**160** B5
Chatsworth Cl *CHSWK* * W4..................**110** C2
Chatsworth Est *CLPT* * E5......................**79** D1
Chatsworth Gdns *ACT* W3 ....**98** B1
Chatsworth Rd *CHSWK* W4 ....**110** C2
  CLPT E5 ....**60** C5
  CRICK NW2...**71** D3
  FSTGT E7 ....**81** F2
Chatsworth Wy *WNWD* SE27 ....**154** D3
Chatterton Ms *FSBYPK* * N4 ....**58** B5
Chatterton Rd *FSBYPK* N4.....................**58** B5
Chatto Rd *BTSEA* SW11.........................**133** F3
Chaucer Av *RCH/KEW* TW9 ....**110** B4
Chaucer Dr *STHWK* SE1..........................**49** F5
Chaucer Rd *ACT* W3 ....**98** C2
  FSTGT E7 ....**82** A3
  HNHL SE24..**136** A3
  WAN E11 ....**64** A1
  WELL DA16..**127** F4
Chaundrye Cl *ELTH/MOT* SE9...............**143** F4
Chauntler Rd *CAN/RD* E16 ....**106** D1
Cheam St *PECK* * SE15 ....**138** B1
Cheapside *CITYW* EC2V **23** F5
Cheesemans Ter *WKENS* * W14 ....**113** F1
Chelford Rd *BMLY* BR1 ....**159** D5
Chelmer Rd *HOM* E9 ....**79** D2
Chelmsford Gdns *IL* IG1.........................**65** E2
Chelmsford Rd *EHAM* E6 ....**95** F5
  HMSMTH W6 ....**113** D1
Chelmsford Gdns *IL* IG1.........................**65** E2
Chelmsford Rd *WALTH* E17 ....**62** A1
Chelmsford Sq *WLSDN* NW10 ....**70** C5
Chelsea Br *VX/NE* SW8 ....**116** A1
Chelsea Bridge Ga *BTSEA* SW11.........**116** A2
Chelsea Bridge Rd *CHEL* SW3 ....**116** A1
Chelsea Cl *WLSDN* NW10 ....**69** D5
Chelsea Crs *CRICK* * NW2 ....**71** F3
  WBPTN * SW10 ....**114** C4
Chelsea Emb *CHEL* SW3 ....**115** F2
Chelsea Gdns *BGVA* * SW1W................**116** A1
Chelsea Harbour Dr *WBPTN* SW10 ......**114** C4
Chelsea Manor Gdns *CHEL* * SW3 ......**115** F1
Chelsea Manor St *CHEL* SW3 ....**115** E1
Chelsea Park Gdns *WBPTN* SW10 ....**115** D1
Chelsea Sq *CHEL* SW3 ....**115** D1
Chelsea Towers *CHEL* * SW3 ....**115** E2
Chelsea Village *FUL/PGN* * SW6 ....**114** B3
Chelsfield Gdns *SYD* SE26 ....**156** C3
Chelsham Rd *CLAP* SW4........................**135** D1
Chelsworth Dr *WOOL/PLUM* SE18 ......**127** D4

Cheltenham Gdns *EHAM* E6 ....**95** E1
Cheltenham Pl *ACT* W3..........................**98** C3
Cheltenham Rd *LEY* E10 ....**62** C1
  PECK SE15 ....**138** C2
Cheltenham Ter *CHEL* SW3 ....**115** F1
Chelverton Rd *PUT/ROE* SW15 ....**131** D2
Chelwood Gdns *RCH/KEW* TW9 ....**110** A5
Chenappa Cl *PLSTW* E13.......................**94** A2
Cheney Rd *CAMTN* NW1 ....**8** C2
Cheneys Rd *WAN* E11 ....**63** E5
Chenies Ms *GWRST* WC1E **20** A1
Chenies Pl *CAMTN* NW1 ....**8** B1
Chenies St *FITZ* W1T **20** A2
Cheniston Gdns *KENS* W8 ....**38** B2
Chepstow Cl *PUT/ROE* SW15 ....**131** E3
Chepstow Cnr *BAY/PAD* * W2 ....**14** B5
Chepstow Crs *GDMY/SEVK* IG3 ....**67** E1
  NTGHL W11.......................................**26** A1
Chepstow Pl *BAY/PAD* W2 ....**14** B5
Chepstow Rd *BAY/PAD* W2 ....**14** B4
Chepstow Vls *NTGHL* W11 ....**101** F1
Chepstow Wy *PECK* SE15......................**119** F4
Chequer St *STLK* EC1Y **23** F1
Cherbury St *IS* N1 ....**12** B2
Cheriton Dr *WOOL/PLUM* SE18 ....**127** D3
Cheriton Sq *TOOT* SW17 ....**152** A2
Cherry Cl *BRXS/STRHM* * SW2 ....**136** A5
Cherry Garden St
  BERM/RHTH SE16..............................**102** B3
Cherrylands Cl *CDALE/KGS* * NW9......**50** C4
Cherry Orch *CHARL* SE7 ....**124** C3
Cherry Tree Ct *CHARL* * SE7 ....**124** C3
Cherry Tree Dr
  STRHM/NOR * SW16........................**153** E3
Cherry Tree Rd *SRTFD* E15 ....**81** E2
Cherry Tree Wk *STLK* EC1Y **23** F1
Cherrywood Dr *PUT/ROE* SW15 ....**131** D3
Chertsey Rd *IL* IG1 ....**85** D1
  WAN E11 ....**63** D4
Chertsey St *TOOT* SW17 ....**152** A5
Cheryls Cl *FUL/PGN* SW6.....................**114** B4
Cheseman St *SYD* SE26 ....**156** B3
Chesham Cl *KTBR* * SW1X **42** A3
Chesham Ms *KTBR* SW1X **42** A2
Chesham Pl *KTBR* SW1X........................**42** A2
Chesham St *KTBR* SW1X **42** A3
  WLSDN NW10 ....**51** D5
Cheshire St *BETH* E2 ....**90** A3
Chesholm Rd *STNW/STAM* N16 ....**59** E5
Chesil Ct *STHWK* SE26...........................**156** B3
Chesney Rd *WKENS* W14 ....**113** F1
Chesson Rd *WKENS* W14 ....**113** F2
Chester Cl *BARN* * SW13 ....**130** B1
  KTBR SW1X **42** B1
Chester Cl North *CAMTN* NW1 ....**7** D3
Chester Cl South *CAMTN* NW1..............**7** D4
Chester Crs *HACK* E8 ....**77** F2
Chesterfield Gdns *GNWCH* * SE10 ......**123** D3
  MYFR/PICC * W1J **30** C3
Chesterfield Gv *EDUL* SE22 ....**137** F3
Chesterfield Hl *MYFR/PICC* W1J **30** C2
Chesterfield Rd *CHSWK* W4 ....**110** C3
  LEY E10 ....**62** C3
Chesterfield St *MYFR/PICC* W1J **30** C3
Chesterfield Wy *PECK* SE15................**120** C3
Chesterford Gdns *HAMP* NW3 ....**72** B1
Chesterford Rd *MNPK* E12 ....**83** F2
Chester Ga *CAMTN* NW1 ....**6** C4
Chester Ms *KTBR* SW1X **42** C2
Chester Pl *CAMTN* NW1 ....**6** C3

Chester Rd *BFN/LL* DA15 ....**145** E3
  CAMTN NW1 ....**6** B4
  CAN/RD E16 ....**93** E3
  FSTGT E7 ....**83** D4
  GDMY/SEVK IG3 ....**67** F3
  KTTN NW5 ....**56** B4
  WAN E11 ....**64** B1
Chester Rw *BGVA* SW1W **42** A5
Chester Sq *BGVA* SW1W **42** B4
Chester Square Ms *BGVA* * SW1W **42** C3
Chester St *BETH* * E2 ....**78** A5
  BETH E2 ....**90** A3
  KTBR SW1X **42** B2
Chester Ter *CAMTN* NW1 ....**6** C3
Chesterton Cl *WAND/EARL* SW18 .....**132** A3
Chesterton Rd *NKENS* W10 ....**89** D4
  PLSTW E13 ....**94** A2
Chesterton Sq *WKENS* W14 ....**101** F5
Chesterton Ter *PLSTW* E13 ....**94** A2
Chester Wy *LBTH* SE11 ....**46** B5
Chestnut Aly *FUL/PGN* * SW6 ....**113** F2
Chestnut Av *FSTGT* E7 ....**82** B1
  MORT/ESHN * SW14 ....**129** D1
Chestnut Cl *CAT* SE6 ....**158** C4
  NWCR SE14 ....**121** F4
  STRHM/NOR SW16 ....**154** A4
Chestnut Dr *WAN* E11 ....**64** A1
Chestnut Gv *BAL* SW12 ....**134** A5
Chestnut Ri *WOOL/PLUM* SE18 ....**127** E1
Chestnut Rd *WNWD* SE27 ....**154** B3
Chettle Cl *STHWK* SE1 ....**48** A2
Chetwode Rd *TOOT* SW17 ....**151** F3
Chetwynd Rd *KTTN* NW5 ....**74** B3
Chetwynd Vls *KTTN* * NW5 ....**74** B3
Cheval Pl *SKENS* SW7 ....**41** D2
Cheval St *POP/IOD* E14 ....**104** A4
Chevening Rd *GNWCH* SE10 ....**123** F1
  KIL/WHAMP NW6 ....**89** D1
Cheverton Rd *ARCH* N19 ....**57** D3
Chevet St *HOM* E9 ....**79** E2
Chevington *CRICK* * NW2 ....**71** F3
Cheviot Gdns *GLDGN* NW11 ....**53** D4
Cheviot Rd *WNWD* SE27 ....**154** A5
Chevron Cl *CAN/RD* E16 ....**94** A5
Cheyne Gdns *CHEL* SW3 ....**115** E3
Cheyne Ms *CHEL* SW3 ....**115** E3
Cheyne Pl *CHEL* * SW3 ....**115** F3
Cheyne Rw *CHEL* SW3 ....**115** E3
Cheyne Wk *CHEL* SW3 ....**115** E3
  HDN NW4 ....**52** C1
Chichele Rd *CRICK* NW2 ....**71** D2
Chicheley Rd *STHWK* SE1 ....**33** F5
Chichester Cl *BKHTH/KID* SE3 ....**124** C3
  EHAM E6 ....**95** E5
Chichester Gdns *IL* IG1 ....**65** E2
Chichester Rd *BAY/PAD* W2 ....**15** D2
  KIL/WHAMP NW6 ....**2** A2
  WAN E11 ....**63** E5
Chichester St *PIM* SW1V **116** C1
Chichester Wy *POP/IOD* E14 ....**105** D5
Chicksand St *WCHPL* E1 ....**25** F3
Chiddingstone St *FUL/PGN* SW6 ....**114** A5
Chigwell Hl *WAP* E1W **102** B1
Childebert Rd *TOOT* SW17 ....**152** B2
Childeric Rd *NWCR* SE14 ....**121** E3
Childerley St *FUL/PGN* SW6 ....**113** E4
Childers St *DEPT* SE8 ....**121** E2
Child's Pl *ECT* SW5 ....**38** B5
Child's St *ECT* SW5 ....**38** B4
Child's Wk *ECT* * SW5 ....**38** B4
Chilham Rd *ELTH/MOT* SE9 ....**161** E4
Chillerton Rd *TOOT* SW17 ....**152** A5
Chillingworth Rd *HOLWY* N7 ....**75** F2
Chiltern Gdns *CRICK* NW2 ....**53** D5
Chiltern Rd *BOW* E3 ....**92** A3
Chiltern St *MHST* W1U **18** A2
Chilthorne Cl *CAT* SE6 ....**139** F5
Chilton Gv *DEPT* SE8 ....**103** D5
Chilton Rd *RCH/KEW* TW9 ....**128** A1
Chilton St *BETH* E2 ....**13** F5
Chilver St *GNWCH* SE10 ....**123** F1
Chilworth Ms *BAY/PAD* W2 ....**15** F5
Chilworth St *BAY/PAD* W2 ....**15** F5
Chinbrook Crs *LEE/GVPK* SE12 ....**160** B3
Chinbrook Rd *LEE/GVPK* SE12 ....**160** B3
Chipka St *POP/IOD* E14 ....**104** C3
Chipley St *NWCR* SE14 ....**121** E2
Chippendale St *CLPT* E5 ....**61** D5
Chippenham Ms *MV/WKIL* W9 ....**14** A1
Chippenham Rd *MV/WKIL* W9 ....**2** A5
Chipstead Gdns *CRICK* NW2 ....**52** B4
Chipstead St *FUL/PGN* SW6 ....**114** A4
Chisenhale Rd *BOW* E3 ....**91** E1
Chisley Rd *SEVS/STOTM* N15 ....**59** E1
Chiswell Sq *BKHTH/KID* SE3 ....**124** B5
Chiswell St *STLK* EC1Y **24** A2
Chiswick Br *MORT/ESHN* SW14 ....**110** C5
Chiswick Common Rd *CHSWK* W4 .....**99** D5
Chiswick High Rd *CHSWK* W4 ....**98** C5
Chiswick House Grounds
  CHSWK * W4 ....**111** D2
Chiswick La *CHSWK* W4 ....**111** E1
Chiswick La South *CHSWK* W4 ....**111** F2
Chiswick Ml *CHSWK* W4 ....**111** F2
Chiswick Pk *CHSWK* * W4 ....**98** C4
Chiswick Pier *CHSWK* * W4 ....**111** F3
Chiswick Quay *CHSWK* W4 ....**110** C4
Chiswick Rd *CHSWK* W4 ....**98** C5
Chiswick Sq *CHSWK* W4 ....**111** E2
Chiswick Staithe *CHSWK* W4 ....**110** B4
Chiswick Village *CHSWK* W4 ....**110** A2
Chitty St *FITZ* W1T **19** F2
Chivalry Rd *BTSEA* SW11 ....**133** E3
Chobham Gdns *WIM/MER* SW19 ....**149** D2
Chobham Rd *SRTFD* E15 ....**81** D2
Cholmeley Cl *HGT* * N6 ....**56** B2
Cholmeley Crs *HGT* N6 ....**56** B2
Cholmeley Pk *HGT* N6 ....**56** B3
Cholmley Gdns *KIL/WHAMP* NW6 ....**72** A2
Cholmondeley Av *WLSDN* NW10 ....**88** A1
Chopwell Cl *SRTFD* * E15 ....**81** D4
Choumert Gv *PECK* SE15 ....**120** A5
Choumert Rd *PECK* SE15 ....**137** F1
Chow Sq *HACK* * E8 ....**77** F2
Chrisp St *POP/IOD* E14 ....**92** B4
Christchurch Av *KIL/WHAMP* NW6 ....**71** D5
Christchurch Hl *HAMP* NW3 ....**55** D5
Christchurch Pas *HAMP* NW3 ....**55** D5
Christchurch Rd *BFN/LL* DA15 ....**163** F4
  BRXS/STRHM SW2 ....**153** F1
Christ Church Rd *CEND/HSY/T* N8 ......**57** E1
Christchurch Rd *IL* IG1 ....**66** B3
  MORT/ESHN SW14 ....**128** B3
Christchurch Sq *HOM* E9 ....**78** C5
Christchurch St *CHEL* SW3 ....**115** F2
Christchurch Ter *CHEL* * SW3 ....**115** F2
Christchurch Wy *GNWCH* SE10 ....**123** E1
Christian St *WCHPL* E1 ....**90** A5
Christie Rd *HOM* E9 ....**79** E3
Christina Sq *FSBYPK* N4 ....**58** B3
Christina St *SDTCH* EC2A **12** C5
Christopher Cl *BFN/LL* DA15 ....**145** F3
Christopher Pl *CAMTN* * NW1 ....**8** B3
Christophers Ms *NTGHL* * W11 ....**101** E2
Christopher St *SDTCH* EC2A **24** B1
Chryssell Rd *BRXN/ST* SW9 ....**118** A3

Chubworthy St *NWCR* SE14..............**121** E2
Chudleigh Crs *GDMY/SEVK* IG3 ....**85** E1
Chudleigh Rd *BROCKY* SE4...............**139** F3
   KIL/WHAMP NW6 ....**70** C4
Chudleigh St *WCHPL* E1..................**91** D5
Chulsa Rd *SYD* SE26 ....**156** B5
Chumleigh Gdns *CMBW* * SE5 ....**119** C2
Chumleigh St *CMBW* SE5 ....**119** C2
Church Ap *DUL* SE21 ....**155** D3
Church Av *CAMTN* NW1 ....**74** B3
   MORT/ESHN SW14 ....**129** D2
Churchbury Rd *ELTH/MOT* SE9 ....**143** D5
Church Crs *HOM* E9.........................**79** D4
Churchcroft Cl *BAL* * SW12 ....**134** A5
Churchdown *BMLY* BR1....................**159** E4
Church Dr *CDALE/KGS* NW9 ....**51** D3
Churchfield Rd *ACT* W3 ....**98** C2
Churchfields *GNWCH* SE10 ....**122** C2
Church Garth *ARCH* * N19 ....**57** D4
Church Ga *FUL/PGN* SW6 ....**131** E1
Church Gn *BRXN/ST* * SW9 ....**118** A5
Church Gv *LEW* SE13........................**140** B2
Church HI *WIM/MER* SW19 ....**149** F5
   WOOL/PLUM SE18 ....**107** F4
Church Hyde *WOOL/PLUM* SE18 ....**127** E2
Churchill Gdns *ACT* W3 ....**86** A5
Churchill Gardens Rd *PIM* SW1V......**116** B1
Churchill Pl *POP/IOD* E14...............**104** B2
Churchill Rd *CAN/RD* E16 ....**94** C5
   CRICK NW2.....................................**70** B3
   KTTN NW5 ....**74** B3
Churchill Wk *HOM* E9 ....**78** C2
Church La *CDALE/KGS* NW9 ....**50** C3
   TOOT SW17 ....**151** F5
   WAN E11 ....**63** E5
Churchley Rd *SYD* SE26 ....**156** B4
Church Md *CMBW* * SE5 ....**118** C3
Churchmead Rd *WLSDN* NW10 ....**70** A3
Church Pth *CHSWK* W4.....................**98** C4
Church Ri *FSTH* SE23 ....**157** D1
Church Rd *ACT* W3 ....**98** C3
   BARN SW13 ....**112** A5
   CNTH/NBYPK IG2 ....**67** E1
   LEY E10 ....**62** A3
   MNPK E12 ....**83** F2
   WIM/MER SW19 ....**149** E4
   WLSDN NW10 ....**69** E3
Church Rw *FUL/PGN* * SW6 ....**114** B3
   HAMP NW3 ....**72** C1
   WAND/EARL * SW18 ....**132** A3
Church St *BAY/PAD* W2 ....**16** B2
   CHSWK W4 ....**111** E2
   SRTFD E15 ....**81** E5
Church Street Est *STJWD* NW8 ....**16** B1
Church St North *SRTFD* E15.............**81** E5
Church Ter *FUL/PGN* * SW6 ....**114** B5
   LEW SE13 ....**141** E1
Church V *FSTH* SE23 ....**156** C2
Church Wk *CDALE/KGS* NW9 ....**51** D4
   CRICK NW2.....................................**53** F5
   STNW/STAM N16 ....**59** D5
Churchway *CAMTN* NW1 ....**8** B3
Churchyard Rw *LBTH* SE11 ....**47** D4
Churston Av *PLSTW* E13...................**82** B5
Churston Cl *BRXS/STRHM* * SW2 .....**154** B1
Churton Pl *CHSWK* * W4 ....**110** B2
   PIM SW1V **43** F5
Churton St *PIM* SW1V **43** F5
Chyngton Cl *BFN/LL* DA15 ....**163** F3
Cibber Rd *FSTH* SE23......................**157** D2
Cicada Rd *WAND/EARL* SW18 ....**132** C4
Cicely Rd *PECK* SE15 ....**120** A4
Cinderford Wy *BMLY* BR1 ....**159** E4

Cinnamon St *WAP* E1W....................**102** B2
Circle *POP/IOD* E14 ....**104** B2
The Circle *CRICK* NW2.....................**51** E5
Circular Wy *WOOL/PLUM* SE18 ....**125** F2
Circus Ms *MBLAR* * W1H **17** E2
Circus Pl *LVPST* * EC2M **24** B3
Circus Rd *STJWD* NW8.....................**4** A3
Circus St *GNWCH* SE10 ....**122** C3
Cirencester St *BAY/PAD* W2.............**14** C2
Citadel Pl *LBTH* SE11......................**117** F1
Citizen Rd *HOLWY* N7.....................**58** A5
Citron Ter *PECK* * SE15 ....**138** B1
City Barracks *SHB* * W12 ....**100** C2
City Garden Rw *IS* N1.....................**11** D2
City Rd *FSBYE* EC1V.........................**10** C2
   SDTCH EC2A...................................**24** B2
Clabon Ms *KTBR* SW1X **41** E3
Clack St *BERM/RHTH* SE16 ....**102** C3
Clacton Rd *WALTH* E17 ....**61** E1
Claire Pl *POP/IOD* E14....................**104** A4
Clairview Rd *TOOT* SW17 ....**152** B5
Clancarty Rd *FUL/PGN* SW6 ....**114** A5
Clandon Cl *ACT* W3 ....**98** B3
Clandon Rd *GDMY/SEVK* IG3 ....**67** E4
Clandon St *DEPT* SE8 ....**122** A5
Clanricarde Gdns *BAY/PAD* W2 ....**26** B2
Clapham Common North Side
   CLAP SW4......................................**134** A2
Clapham Common South Side
   CLAP SW4......................................**134** B4
Clapham Common West Side
   BTSEA SW11...................................**133** F2
Clapham Court Ter *CLAP* * SW4 ....**135** E3
Clapham Crs *CLAP* SW4...................**135** D2
Clapham High St *CLAP* SW4.............**135** D2
Clapham Manor St *CLAP* * SW4 ....**134** C1
Clapham Park Est *CLAP* * SW4 ....**135** D5
Clapham Park Rd *CLAP* SW4............**134** C2
Clapham Park Ter *CLAP* * SW4 ....**135** E3
Clapham Rd *BRXN/ST* SW9...............**117** E5
Clapham Rd South *IS* N1 ....**77** D3
Claps Gate La *EHAM* E6...................**96** B3
Clapton Common *CLPT* E5................**60** A2
Clapton Sq *CLPT* E5........................**78** C2
Clapton Ter *STNW/STAM* N16 ....**60** A2
Clapton Wy *CLPT* E5........................**78** A1
Clara Pl *WOOL/PLUM* SE18.............**108** A5
Clare Cnr *ELTH/MOT* SE9.................**144** B5
Claredale St *BETH* E2 ....**90** A1
Clare Gdns *BARK* IG11.....................**85** F3
   FSTGT E7 ....**82** A1
   NTGHL * W11 ....**89** E5
Clare La *IS* N1 ....**76** C4
Clare Lawn Av *MORT/ESHN* SW14....**129** D3
Clare Ms *FUL/PGN* * SW6 ....**114** B3
Claremont Cl *BRXS/STRHM* SW2 ......**153** F1
   CAN/RD E16...................................**108** A2
   IS N1 ....**10** A2
Claremont Gdns *GDMY/SEVK* IG3 ....**67** E4
Claremont Gv *CHSWK* W4 ....**111** E3
Claremont Rd *CRICK* NW2................**52** C2
   CRICK NW2.....................................**53** D3
   FSTGT E7 ....**82** B2
   HGT N6..**56** B2
   MV/WKIL W9 ....**89** E1
   WAN E11 ....**63** D5
Claremont Sq *IS* N1........................**10** A2
Claremont St *GNWCH* SE10 ....**122** B2
Claremont Vls *CMBW* * SE5 ....**119** D3
Claremont Wy *CRICK* NW2...............**52** C3
Clarence Av *CLAP* SW4....................**135** D5
   IL IG1 ....**65** F1
Clarence Crs *CLAP* SW4...................**135** D4

Clarence Gdns CAMTN NW1 .... 7 D4
Clarence Ga CAMTN NW1 .... 5 F5
Clarence La PUT/ROE SW15 .... 129 F4
Clarence Ms CLPT E5 .... 78 B2
Clarence Pas CAMTN * NW1 .... 8 C2
Clarence Pl CLPT E5 .... 78 B2
Clarence Rd CAN/RD E16 .... 93 E3
   CHSWK W4 .... 110 A1
   CLPT E5 .... 78 B1
   ELTH/MOT SE9 .... 161 E2
   FSTGT E7 .... 82 C1
   KIL/WHAMP NW6 .... 71 F4
Clarence Ter CAMTN NW1 .... 5 F5
Clarence Wk CLAP SW4 .... 117 E5
Clarence Wy CAMTN NW1 .... 74 B4
Clarendon Cl BAY/PAD * W2 .... 28 C1
Clarendon Cross NTGHL W11 .... 101 E1
Clarendon Dr PUT/ROE SW15 .... 130 C1
Clarendon Gdns IL IG1 .... 65 F3
   MV/WKIL W9 .... 15 F1
Clarendon Ga BAY/PAD W2 .... 28 C1
Clarendon Ms BAY/PAD W2 .... 28 C1
Clarendon Pl BAY/PAD W2 .... 28 C1
Clarendon Ri LEW SE13 .... 140 C1
Clarendon Rd LEY E10 .... 62 B1
   NTGHL W11 .... 101 E1
Clarendon St PIM SW1V 116 B1
Clarendon Ter MV/WKIL W9 .... 3 D1
Clarens St CAT SE6 .... 157 F2
Clare Rd NWCR SE14 .... 121 F5
   WAN E11 .... 63 D1
   WLSDN NW10 .... 70 A4
Clare St BETH E2 .... 90 B1
Clareville Gv SKENS SW7 .... 39 F5
Clareville St SKENS SW7 .... 39 F5
Clarges Ms MYFR/PICC W1J 30 C3
Clarges St MYFR/PICC W1J 31 D3
Claribel Rd BRXN/ST SW9 .... 118 B5
Clarissa St HACK E8 .... 77 F5
Clarkes Ms CAVSQ/HST W1G 18 A2
Clarkson Rd CAN/RD E16 .... 93 F5
Clarkson Rw CAMTN NW1 .... 7 D2
Clarkson St BETH * E2 .... 90 B2
Clark's Rd IL IG1 .... 67 D4
Clark St WCHPL E1 .... 90 C5
Claude Rd LEY E10 .... 62 C3
   PECK SE15 .... 120 B5
   PLSTW E13 .... 82 B5
Claude St POP/IOD E14 .... 104 A5
Claudia Pl WIM/MER SW19 .... 149 E1
Claughton Rd PLSTW E13 .... 94 C1
Clavell St GNWCH SE10 .... 122 C1
Claverdale Rd BRXS/STRHM SW2 .... 135 F5
Clavering Av BARN SW13 .... 112 B1
Clavering Rd MNPK E12 .... 65 D3
Claverton St PIM SW1V 116 C1
Clave St WAP E1W 102 C2
Claxton Gv HMSMTH W6 .... 113 D1
Claybank Gv LEW SE13 .... 140 B1
Claybridge Rd LEE/GVPK SE12 .... 160 C4
Claybrook Rd HMSMTH W6 .... 113 D2
Claydown Ms WOOL/PLUM SE18 .... 126 A1
Clayfarm Rd ELTH/MOT SE9 .... 162 C2
Clayhill Crs LEE/GVPK SE12 .... 161 D4
Claylands Pl BRXN/ST SW9 .... 118 A3
Claylands Rd VX/NE SW8 .... 117 F2
Claypole Rd SRTFD * E15 .... 92 C1
Clays La SRTFD E15 .... 80 B2
Clays Lane Cl SRTFD E15 .... 80 B2
Clay St MHST W1U 17 F3
Clayton Cl EHAM E6 .... 95 F5
Clayton Ms GNWCH SE10 .... 123 D4
Clayton Rd PECK SE15 .... 120 A4
Clayton St LBTH SE11 .... 118 A2
Cleanthus Cl WOOL/PLUM SE18 .... 126 B4
Cleanthus Rd WOOL/PLUM SE18 .... 126 B4
Clearbrook Wy WCHPL E1 .... 90 C5
Clearwater Ter WKENS W14 .... 101 D3
Clearwell Dr MV/WKIL W9 .... 14 C1
Cleaver Sq LBTH SE11 .... 118 A1
Cleaver St LBTH SE11 .... 118 A1
Cleeve Hl FSTH SE23 .... 156 B1
Clegg St PLSTW E13 .... 94 A1
   WAP E1W 102 B2
Clematis Cottages SHB * W12 .... 100 A1
Clematis St SHB W12 .... 99 F1
Clem Attlee Ct FUL/PGN * SW6 .... 113 F1
Clem Attlee Pde
   FUL/PGN * SW6 .... 113 F2
Clemence St POP/IOD E14 .... 91 F4
Clement Av CLAP SW4 .... 135 D2
Clement Cl CHSWK W4 .... 99 D5
   KIL/WHAMP NW6 .... 70 C4
Clementina Rd LEY E10 .... 61 F3
Clement Rd WIM/MER SW19 .... 149 E5
Clements Av CAN/RD E16 .... 106 A1
Clements Inn LINN WC2A 21 F5
Clements La IL IG1 .... 66 B5
   MANHO EC4N 36 B1
Clements Rd BERM/RHTH SE16 .... 102 B4
   BERM/RHTH SE16 .... 102 A4
   EHAM E6 .... 83 F4
   IL IG1 .... 66 B5
Clendon Wy WOOL/PLUM SE18 .... 109 D5
Clennam St STHWK * SE1 .... 35 F5
Clenston Ms MBLAR W1H 17 E4
Clephane Rd IS N1 .... 76 C3
Clere Pl SDTCH EC2A 12 B5
Clere St SDTCH EC2A 12 B5
Clerkenwell Cl CLKNW EC1R 10 B1
Clerkenwell Gn CLKNW EC1R 22 C1
Clerkenwell Rd CLKNW EC1R 22 A1
Clermont Rd HOM E9 .... 78 C5
Cleveland Av CHSWK W4 .... 99 F5
Cleveland Gdns BARN SW13 .... 111 F5
   BAY/PAD W2 .... 15 E5
   CRICK NW2 .... 53 D4
Cleveland Gv WCHPL E1 .... 90 C3
Cleveland Ms FITZ W1T 19 E2
Cleveland Pl STJS SW1Y 31 F3
Cleveland Rd BARN SW13 .... 111 F5
   CHSWK W4 .... 98 C4
   IL IG1 .... 66 B5
   IS N1 .... 77 D4
   WELL DA16 .... 127 F5
Cleveland Rw WHALL SW1A 31 F4
Cleveland Sq BAY/PAD W2 .... 15 E5
Cleveland St CAMTN NW1 .... 19 D1
Cleveland Ter BAY/PAD W2 .... 15 E5
Cleveland Wy WCHPL E1 .... 90 C3
Cleveleys Rd CLPT E5 .... 60 B5
Clevely Cl CHARL SE7 .... 107 D5
Clevely Est SHB * W12 .... 100 A2
Cleve Rd KIL/WHAMP NW6 .... 72 A4
Cleves Rd EHAM E6 .... 83 D5
Clifden Rd CLPT E5 .... 78 C2
Clifford Av MORT/ESHN SW14 .... 110 C5
   RCH/KEW TW9 .... 128 B1
Clifford Cl PLSTW * E13 .... 94 B2
Clifford Dr BRXN/ST SW9 .... 136 B2
Clifford Gdns WLSDN NW10 .... 88 C1
Clifford Rd CAN/RD E16 .... 93 F3
Clifford St CONDST W1S 31 E2
Clifford Wy WLSDN NW10 .... 69 F1
Cliff Rd HOLWY N7 .... 75 D3
Cliff Ter DEPT SE8 .... 122 A5

Cliffview Rd LEW SE13 ....140 A1
Cliff Vls HOLWY N7 ....75 D3
Cliff Wk CAN/RD E16 ....93 F4
Clifton Av SHB W12 ....99 F3
Clifton Crs PECK SE15 ....120 B3
Clifton Gdns CHSWK W4 ....99 D5
   GLDGN NW11 ....53 F1
   MV/WKIL W9 ....15 E1
   SEVS/STOTM N15 ....59 F1
Clifton Ga WBPTN * SW10 ....114 C2
Clifton Gv HACK E8 ....78 A3
Clifton Hl KIL/WHAMP NW6 ....3 D1
Clifton Pl BAY/PAD W2 ....28 B1
   BERM/RHTH SE16 ....102 C3
   WBPTN * SW10 ....114 C2
Clifton Ri NWCR SE14 ....121 E3
Clifton Rd CAN/RD E16 ....93 F4
   CEND/HSY/T N8 ....57 D1
   FSTGT E7 ....83 D3
   GNTH/NBYPK IG2 ....67 D1
   MV/WKIL W9 ....3 F5
   SCUP DA14 ....163 E4
   WLSDN NW10 ....88 A1
Clifton St SDTCH EC2A 24 C1
Clifton Ter FSBYPK N4 ....58 A4
Clifton Vls MV/WKIL W9 ....15 D2
Clifton Wy PECK SE15 ....120 C3
Clink St STHWK SE1 ....36 A3
Clinton Rd BOW E3 ....91 E2
   FSTGT E7 ....82 A1
Clinton Ter DEPT * SE8 ....122 A2
Clipper Cl BERM/RHTH SE16 ....103 D3
Clipper Wy LEW SE13 ....140 C3
Clipstone Ms GTPST W1W 19 E2
Clipstone St GTPST W1W 19 D2
Clissold Crs STNW/STAM N16 ....77 D1
Clissold Rd STNW/STAM N16 ....59 D5
Clitheroe Rd BRXN/ST SW9 ....117 E5
Clitterhouse Crs CRICK NW2 ....52 C3
Clitterhouse Rd CRICK NW2 ....52 C3
Clive Ct WLSDN * NW10 ....69 F4
Cliveden Pl BGVA SW1W 42 A3
Clive Rd DUL SE21 ....155 D3
Cloak La BLKFR EC4V 35 F1
Clockhouse Av BARK IG11 ....84 C5
Clockhouse Cl WIM/MER SW19 ....148 C3
Clockhouse Pl PUT/ROE SW15 ....131 E3
Clock Tower Ms IS N1 ....76 C5
Clock Tower Pl HOLWY * N7 ....75 D3
Cloister Rd ACT W3 ....86 C4
   CRICK NW2 ....53 F5
Clonbrock Rd STNW/STAM N16 ....77 E1
Cloncurry St FUL/PGN SW6 ....113 D5
Clonmel Rd FUL/PGN SW6 ....113 F3
Clonmore St WAND/EARL SW18 ....149 F3
Clorane Gdns HAMP NW3 ....54 A5
The Close GNTH/NBYPK IG2 ....67 E1
   RCH/KEW TW9 ....128 B1
   WBLY HA9 ....50 C5
Cloth Ct STBT EC1A 23 D3
Cloth Fair STBT EC1A 23 D3
Clothier St HDTCH * EC3A 25 D4
Cloth St STBT * EC1A 23 E2
Clothworkers Rd
   WOOL/PLUM SE18 ....127 D3
Cloudesdale Rd TOOT SW17 ....152 B2
Cloudesley Pl IS N1 ....76 A5
Cloudesley Rd IS N1 ....76 A5
Cloudesley Sq IS N1 ....76 A5
Cloudesley St IS N1 ....76 A5
Clova Rd FSTGT E7 ....82 A3
Clove Crs POP/IOD E14 ....104 C1
Clovelly Rd CHSWK * W4 ....99 D5

Clovelly Wy WCHPL E1 ....90 C5
Clover Cl WAN * E11 ....63 D4
Cloverdale Gdns BFN/LL DA15 ....145 E3
Clover Ms CHEL SW3 ....115 F2
Clove St PLSTW E13 ....94 A3
Clowders Rd CAT SE6 ....157 F3
Cloysters Gn WAP * E1W 102 A2
Club Rw BETH E2 ....13 E4
Cluny Est STHWK SE1 ....48 C3
Cluny Ms ECT SW5 ....38 A5
Cluny Pl STHWK SE1 ....48 C2
Clutton St POP/IOD E14 ....92 B4
Clyde Ct CAMTN NW1 ....8 B1
Clyde Flats FUL/PGN * SW6 ....113 F3
Clyde Pl LEY E10 ....62 B2
Clydesdale Gdns
   RCHPK/HAM TW10 ....128 B2
Clydesdale Rd NTGHL W11 ....89 F5
Clyde St DEPT SE8 ....121 F2
Clyde Ter FSTH SE23 ....156 C2
Clyde V FSTH SE23 ....156 C2
Clyston St VX/NE SW8 ....116 C5
Coach & Horses Yd CONDST * W1S 31 E1
Coach House La HBRY * N5 ....76 B1
   WIM/MER SW19 ....149 D4
Coach House Ms NWCR * SE14 ....121 D4
Coach House Yd
   WAND/EARL * SW18 ....132 B2
Coalecroft Rd PUT/ROE SW15 ....130 C2
Coates Av WAND/EARL SW18 ....133 E4
Coate St BETH E2 ....90 A1
Cobbett Rd ELTH/MOT SE9 ....143 E1
Cobbett St VX/NE SW8 ....117 F3
Cobble La IS N1 ....76 B4
Cobble Ms FSBYPK N4 ....58 C5
Cobbold Ms SHB * W12 ....99 E3
Cobbold Rd SHB W12 ....99 E3
   WAN E11 ....63 F5
   WLSDN NW10 ....69 F3
Cobb St WCHPL E1 ....25 E4
Cobden Ms SYD SE26 ....156 B5
Cobden Rd WAN E11 ....63 E5
Cobham Cl BTSEA * SW11 ....133 E4
Cobham Ms CAMTN NW1 ....75 D4
Cobham Rd GDMY/SEVK IG3 ....67 E4
Cobland Rd LEE/GVPK SE12 ....160 C4
Coborn Rd BOW E3 ....91 F2
Coborn St BOW E3 ....91 F2
Cobourg Rd CMBW SE5 ....119 F2
Cobourg St CAMTN NW1 ....7 F4
Coburg Cl WEST SW1P 43 F4
Coburg Crs BRXS/STRHM SW2 ....153 F1
Coburg Dwellings WCHPL * E1 ....102 C1
Cochrane Ms STJWD NW8 ....4 B2
Cochrane St STJWD NW8 ....4 B2
Cockerell Rd WALTH E17 ....61 E2
Cock La STBT EC1A 22 C3
Cockspur Ct STJS SW1Y 32 B3
Cockspur St STJS * SW1Y 32 B3
Code St WCHPL E1 ....25 F1
Codling Cl WAP E1W 102 A2
Codrington Hl FSTH SE23 ....139 E5
Codrington Ms NTGHL W11 ....89 E5
Cody Rd CAN/RD E16 ....93 D3
Cofers Cir WBLY HA9 ....50 B5
Coffey St DEPT SE8 ....122 A3
Coin St STHWK SE1 ....34 A3
Coity Rd KTTN NW5 ....74 A3
Cokers La DUL SE21 ....154 C1
Coke St WCHPL E1 ....90 A5
Colbeck Ms ECT SW5 ....39 D5
Colberg Pl STNW/STAM * N16 ....59 F2
Colby Rd NRWD SE19 ....155 E5

Colchester Rd *WALTH* E17 ....62 A1
Colchester St *WCHPL* E1 ....25 F4
Coldbath Sq *CLKNW* * EC1R 10 A5
Coldbath St *LEW* SE13 ....122 B4
Coldblow La *NWCR* SE14 ....121 D3
Coldharbour *POP/IOD* E14 ....104 C2
Coldharbour Crest *ELTH/MOT* * SE9 ...162 A3
Coldharbour La *BRXN/ST* SW9 ...136 A2
Coldharbour PI *CMBW* SE5 ....118 C5
Coldstream Gdns
    WAND/EARL SW18 ....131 F4
Colebeck Ms *IS* N1 ....76 B3
Colebert Av *WCHPL* E1 ....90 C3
Colebrooke Dr *WAN* E11 ....64 B2
Colebrooke PI *IS* N1 ....76 B5
Colebrooke Rw *IS* N1 ....10 C1
Coleby Pth *CMBW* * SE5 ....119 D3
Coleford Rd *WAND/EARL* SW18 ...132 C4
Colegrave Rd *SRTFD* E15 ....81 D2
Colegrove Rd *PECK* SE15 ....119 F2
Coleherne Ms *WBPTN* SW10 ...114 B1
Coleherne Rd *WBPTN* SW10 ...114 B1
Colehill Gdns *FUL/PGN* * SW6 ...113 E4
Colehill La *FUL/PGN* SW6 ....113 E4
Coleman Flds *IS* N1 ....76 C5
Coleman Rd *CMBW* SE5 ....119 E3
Colemans Heath *ELTH/MOT* SE9 ...162 A3
Coleman St *LOTH* EC2R 24 A4
Colenso Rd *CLPT* E5 ....78 C1
    GNTH/NBYPK IG2
Colepits Wood Rd *ELTH/MOT* SE9 ...145 D3
Coleraine Rd *BKHTH/KID* SE3 ...123 F2
Coleridge Av *MNPK* E12 ....83 E3
Coleridge CI *VX/NE* SW8 ....116 B5
Coleridge Rd *KIL/WHAMP* NW6 ...72 C4
Coleridge Rd *CEND/HSY/T* N8 ...57 D1
    FSBYPK N4.
Coles Green Rd *CRICK* NW2 ....52 A3
Colestown St *BTSEA* SW11 ....115 E5
Cole St *STHWK* SE1 ....47 F1
Colet Gdns *WKENS* W14 ....113 D1
Coley St *FSBYW* WC1X 21 F1
Colfe & Hatcliffe Glebe *LEW* * SE13 ...140 B3
Colfe Rd *FSTH* SE23 ....157 E1
Colinette Rd *PUT/ROE* SW15 ...130 C2
Colin Rd *WLSDN* NW10 ....70 A3
Coliston Rd *WAND/EARL* SW18 ...132 A5
Collamore Av *WAND/EARL* SW18...151 E1
Collard PI *CAMTN* NW1 ....74 B4
College Ap *GNWCH* SE10 ....122 C2
College Crs *KIL/WHAMP* NW6 ...72 C3
College Cross *IS* N1 ....76 A4
College East *WCHPL* * E1 ....25 F3
College Gdns *TOOT* SW17 ....151 E2
College Gv *CAMTN* NW1 ....74 C5
College HI *CANST* * EC4R 35 F1
College Ms *IS* N1 ....76 A4
    WEST SW1P 44 C2
College Pde *KIL/WHAMP* * NW6 ...71 E5
College Park CI *LEW* SE13 ....141 D2
College PI *CAMTN* NW1 ....74 C5
    WBPTN SW10 ....114 C3
College Rd *DUL* SE21 ....137 E5
    NRWD SE19 ....155 F5
    WLSDN NW10 ....88 C1
College St *CANST* * EC4R 35 F1
College Vw *ELTH/MOT* SE9 ....161 D1
College Yd *KIL/WHAMP* * NW6 ...71 E5
    KTTN * N5 ....74 B2
Collent St *HOM* E9 ....78 C3
Collett Rd *BERM/RHTH* SE16 ...102 A4
Collier CI *EHAM* E6 ....108 B1
Collier St *IS* N1 ....9 E1

Collingbourne Rd *SHB* W12 ....100 B2
Collingham Gdns *ECT* SW5 ....39 D5
Collingham PI *ECT* SW5 ....38 C5
Collingham Rd *ECT* SW5 ....39 D4
Collington St *GNWCH* * SE10 ...123 D1
Collingtree Rd *SYD* SE26 ....156 C4
Collingwood St *WCHPL* E1 ....90 B3
Collinson St *STHWK* SE1 ....47 E1
Collinson Wk *STHWK* SE1 ....47 E1
Collins Rd *HBRY* N5 ....76 C1
Collins St *BKHTH/KID* SE3 ....123 E5
Coll's Rd *PECK* SE15 ....120 A4
Collyer PI *PECK* SE15 ....120 A4
Colman Rd *CAN/RD* E16 ....94 C4
Colmar CI *WCHPL* E1 ....91 D3
Colmore Ms *PECK* SE15 ....120 B4
Colnbrook St *STHWK* SE1 ....46 C3
Colne Rd *CLPT* E5 ....79 D1
Colne St *PLSTW* E13 ....94 A2
Cologne Rd *BTSEA* SW11 ....133 D2
Colombo Rd *IL* IG1 ....66 C3
Colombo St *STHWK* SE1 ....34 C4
Colomb St *GNWCH* SE10 ....123 E1
Colonial Dr *CHSWK* W4 ....98 C5
Colonnade *BMSBY* WC1N 20 C1
The Colonnade *DEPT* * SE8 ...103 F5
Colosseum Ter *CAMTN* NW1 ....7 D5
Colson Wy *STRHM/NOR* SW16 ...152 C4
Colston Rd *FSTGT* E7 ....83 D3
    MORT/ESHN SW14 ....128 C2
Colthurst Crs *FSBYPK* N4 ....58 B4
Columbas Dr *HAMP* * NW3 ....55 D3
Columbia Rd *BETH* E2 ....13 E3
    PLSTW E13 ....93 F3
Columbine Av *EHAM* E6 ....95 E4
Columbine Wy *LEW* * SE13 ...122 C5
Colview Ct *ELTH/MOT* SE9 ....161 D2
Colvestone Crs *HACK* E8 ....77 F2
Colville Est *IS* N1 ....77 D5
Colville Gdns *NTGHL* * W11 ...89 F5
Colville Houses *NTGHL* * W11 ...89 F5
Colville Ms *NTGHL* W11 ....89 F5
Colville PI *FITZ* W1T 19 F3
Colville Rd *ACT* W3 ....98 B4
    NTGHL W11 ....89 F5
    WAN E11 ....62 C5
Colville Sq *NTGHL* * W11 ....89 F5
Colville Square Ms *NTGHL* * W11...89 F5
Colville Ter *NTGHL* W11 ....89 F5
Colvin CI *SYD* SE26 ....156 C5
Colvin Rd *EHAM* E6 ....83 E4
Colwell Rd *EDUL* SE22 ....137 E3
Colwick CI *HGT* N6 ....57 D2
Colwith Rd *HMSMTH* W6 ....112 C2
Colworth Gv *WALW* SE17 ....47 F5
Colworth Rd *WAN* E11 ....63 E1
Colwyn CI *STRHM/NOR* SW16 ...152 C5
Colwyn Gn *CDALE/KGS* * NW9 ...51 E1
Colwyn Rd *CRICK* NW2 ....52 B5
Colyer CI *ELTH/MOT* SE9 ....162 B2
Colyton Rd *EDUL* SE22 ....138 B3
Combe Av *BKHTH/KID* SE3 ....123 F3
Combedale Rd *GNWCH* SE10 ...124 A1
Combemartin Rd
    WAND/EARL SW18 ....131 E5
Comber CI *CRICK* NW2 ....52 A5
Comber Gv *CMBW* SE5 ....118 C3
Combermere Rd *BRXN/ST* SW9...135 F1
Comberton Rd *CLPT* E5 ....60 B4
Combeside *WOOL/PLUM* SE18...127 F3
Comeragh Ms *WKENS* * W14 ...113 E1
Comeragh Rd *WKENS* W14 ....113 E1
Comerford Rd *BROCKY* SE4 ...139 E2

Comet Cl *MNPK* E12 ....**83** D1
Comet Pl *DEPT* SE8 ....**122** A3
Comet St *DEPT* SE8 ....**122** A3
Commercial Rd *POP/IOD* E14 ....**91** E5
   WCHPL E1 ....**25** F4
Commercial St *WCHPL* E1 ....**25** E1
Commercial Wy *PECK* SE15 ....**119** F4
   WLSDN NW10 ....**86** B3
Commerell Pl *GNWCH* SE10 ....**123** F1
Commerell St *GNWCH* SE10 ....**123** E1
Commodore St *WCHPL* E1 ....**91** D4
Commondale *PUT/ROE* SW15 ......**112** C5
Common Rd *BARN* SW13 ....**130** A1
Commonwealth Av *SHB* W12 ......**100** B1
Community Rd *SRTFD* E15 ....**81** D2
Como Rd *FSTH* SE23 ....**157** E2
Compayne Gdns *KIL/WHAMP* NW6 ...**72** B4
Compton Av *EHAM* E6 ....**95** D1
   HGT N6 ....**55** E2
   IS N1 ....**76** B3
Compton Cl *CAMTN* NW1 ....**7** D4
   CRICK NW2 ....**53** D5
Compton Crs *CHSWK* W4 ....**110** C2
Compton Pas *FSBYE* EC1V **11** D5
Compton Pl *STPAN* WC1H **8** C5
Compton Rd *IS* N1 ....**76** B3
   WLSDN NW10 ....**89** D2
Compton St *FSBYE* EC1V **10** C5
Compton Ter *IS* N1 ....**76** B3
Comus Pl *WALW* SE17 ....**48** C5
Comyn Rd *BTSEA* SW11 ....**133** E2
Comyns Cl *CAN/RD* E16 ....**93** F4
Conant Ms *WCHPL* E1 ....**102** A1
Concanon Rd *BRXS/STRHM* SW2 ...**135** F3
Concert Hall Ap *STHWK* SE1 ....**33** F4
Concorde Dr *EHAM* E6 ....**95** F4
Concord Rd *ACT* W3 ....**86** B3
Condell Rd *VX/NE* SW8 ....**116** C4
Conder St *POP/IOD* E14 ....**91** E5
Condray Pl *BTSEA* SW11 ....**115** E3
Conduit Ct *COVGDN* * WC2E **32** C1
Conduit Ms *BAY/PAD* W2 ....**16** A5
Conduit Pas *BAY/PAD* W2 ....**16** A5
Conduit Pl *BAY/PAD* W2 ....**16** A5
Conduit Rd *WOOL/PLUM* SE18 ....**126** B1
Conduit St *CONDST* W1S **31** D1
Conduit Wy *WLSDN* NW10 ....**68** C4
Conewood St *HBRY* N5 ....**58** B5
Coney Acre *DUL* SE21 ....**154** C1
Coney Wy *VX/NE* SW8 ....**117** F2
Congleton Gv *WOOL/PLUM* SE18 ...**126** C1
Congo Rd *WOOL/PLUM* SE18 ......**127** D1
Congreve Rd *ELTH/MOT* SE9 ....**143** F1
Congreve St *WALW* SE17 ....**48** C5
Conifer Gdns *STRHM/NOR* SW16 ...**153** F3
Coniger Rd *FUL/PGN* SW6 ....**114** A5
Coningham Ms *SHB* W12 ....**100** A2
Coningham Rd *SHB* W12 ....**100** B3
Coningsby Rd *FSBYPK* N4 ....**58** B2
Conington Rd *LEW* SE13 ....**122** B5
Conisborough Crs *CAT* SE6 ....**158** C3
Coniston Av *BARK* IG11 ....**85** E4
   WELL DA16 ....**145** E1
Coniston Cl *BARN* SW13 ....**111** F3
Coniston Ct *BAY/PAD* * W2 ....**17** D5
Conistone Wy *HOLWY* N7 ....**75** E4
Conlan St *NKENS* W10 ....**89** E3
Conley Rd *WLSDN* NW10 ....**69** E3
Conley St *GNWCH* * SE10 ....**123** E1
Connaught Br *CAN/RD* E16 ....**107** D2
Connaught Cl *BAY/PAD* W2 ....**16** A1

LEY * E10 ....**61** E4
Connaught La *IL* IG1 ....**66** C4
Connaught Ms *FUL/PGN* * SW6 ...**113** E4
   HAMP * NW3 ....**73** E2
   WOOL/PLUM SE18 ....**126** A1
Connaught Pl *BAY/PAD* W2 ....**29** E1
Connaught Rd *CAN/RD* E16 ....**107** D1
   FSBYPK N4 ....**58** A2
   IL IG1 ....**67** D4
   WAN E11 ....**63** D3
   WLSDN NW10 ....**87** E1
   WOOL/PLUM SE18 ....**126** A1
Connaught Sq *BAY/PAD* W2 ....**17** D5
Connaught St *BAY/PAD* W2 ....**17** D5
Connor St *HOM* * E9 ....**79** D5
Consort Rd *PECK* SE15 ....**120** B5
Cons St *STHWK* * SE1 ....**34** B5
Constable Av *CAN/RD* E16 ....**106** B2
Constable Cl *GLDGN* NW11 ....**54** B1
Constable Wk *DUL* SE21 ....**155** E3
Constance St *CAN/RD* E16 ....**107** E2
Constantine Rd *HAMP* NW3 ....**73** E2
Constitution Hl *WHALL* SW1A **30** C5
Constitution Ri *WOOL/PLUM* SE18 ...**126** A4
Content St *WALW* SE17 ....**47** F5
Convent Gdns *NTGHL* W11 ....**89** F5
Conway Gv *ACT* W3 ....**87** D4
Conway Ms *FITZ* W1T **19** E2
Conway Rd *CRICK* NW2 ....**52** C4
   WOOL/PLUM SE18 ....**109** D5
Conway St *FITZ* W1T **19** E1
Conybeare *HAMP* NW3 ....**73** E4
Conyer's Rd *STRHM/NOR* SW16 ...**153** D5
Conyer St *BOW* * E3 ....**91** E1
Cookes Cl *WAN* E11 ....**63** F4
Cook's Rd *SRTFD* E15 ....**92** B1
   WALW * SE17 ....**118** B2
Coolfin Rd *CAN/RD* E16 ....**94** A5
Coolhurst Rd *CEND/HSY/T* N8 ....**57** F3
Cool Oak Br *CDALE/KGS* NW9 ....**51** F2
Cool Oak La *CDALE/KGS* NW9 ....**51** F2
Coomassie Rd *MV/WKIL* W9 ....**89** F3
Coombe Ldg *CHARL* SE7 ....**124** C2
Coombe Pk *KUTN/CMB* KT2 ....**146** C5
Coombe Ridings *KUTN/CMB* KT2 ...**146** C5
Coombe Rd *CHSWK* W4 ....**111** E1
   SYD SE26 ....**156** B4
   WLSDN NW10 ....**51** D5
Coombe Vls *WAND/EARL* * SW18 ...**132** A5
Coombe Wood Rd *KUTN/CMB* KT2 ...**146** C5
Coombs St *IS* N1 ....**11** D2
Coomer Ms *FUL/PGN* * SW6 ....**113** E4
Coomer Pl *FUL/PGN* SW6 ....**113** F2
Cooper Cl *STHWK* SE1 ....**46** B1
Cooper Rd *CRICK* NW2 ....**70** A2
   HDN NW4 ....**53** D1
Coopersale Rd *HOM* E9 ....**79** D2
Coopers Cl *WCHPL* E1 ....**90** C3
Coopers La *CAMTN* NW1 ....**8** B2
   LEE/GVPK SE12 ....**160** B2
   LEY E10 ....**62** B3
Cooper's Rd *STHWK* SE1 ....**119** F1
Cooper's Rw *TWRH* EC3N **37** E1
Cooper St *CAN/RD* E16 ....**93** F4
Copeland Rd *PECK* SE15 ....**120** A5
Copeman Cl *SYD* SE26 ....**156** C5
Copenhagen Pl *POP/IOD* E14 ....**91** F5
Copenhagen St *IS* N1 ....**75** E5
Cope Pl *KENS* W8 ....**38** A3
Cope St *BERM/RHTH* SE16 ....**103** D5
Copford Wk *IS* * N1 ....**76** C5
Copleston Rd *PECK* SE15 ....**137** F1
Copley Cl *WALW* SE17 ....**118** B2

Coppelia Rd *BKHTH/KID* SE3 ....141 F2
Copperas St *DEPT* SE8 ....122 B2
Copperfield Rd *BOW* E3 ....91 E3
Copperfield St *STHWK* SE1 ....35 D5
Coppermead Cl *CRICK* NW2 ....52 C5
Copper Mill La *TOOT* SW17 ....150 C4
Coppermill La *WALTH* E17 ....60 C1
Copper Rw *STHWK* SE1 ....37 E4
Coppice Dr *PUT/ROE* SW15 ....130 A4
Coppock Cl *BTSEA* SW11 ....115 E5
Copse Cl *CHARL* SE7 ....124 B2
Copsewood Cl *BFN/LL* DA15 ....145 E4
Copthall Av *LOTH* EC2R 24 B4
Copthorne Av *BAL* SW12 ....135 D5
Coptic St *NOXST/BSQ* WC1A 20 C3
Copton Cl *BOW* E3 ....92 A4
Coral St *STHWK* SE1 ....46 B1
Coram St *STPAN* WC1H 20 C1
Corbet Pl *WCHPL* E1 ....25 E2
Corbett Rd *WAN* E11 ....64 C1
Corbett's La *BERM/RHTH* SE16 ....102 C5
Corbicum *WAN* E11 ....63 E2
Corbridge Crs *BETH* E2 ....90 B1
Corbylands Rd *BFN/LL* DA15 ....145 E5
  BFN/LL DA15 ....163 E1
Corbyn St *FSBYPK* N4 ....57 E3
Corby Rd *WLSDN* NW10 ....86 C1
Cordelia Cl *HNHL* SE24 ....136 B2
Cordelia St *POP/IOD* E14 ....92 B5
Cording St *POP/IOD* E14 ....92 B4
Cordova Rd *BOW* E3 ....91 E2
Cordwell Rd *LEW* SE13 ....141 D3
Corelli Rd *BKHTH/KID* SE3 ....125 E4
Corfield St *BETH* E2 ....90 B3
Coriander Av *POP/IOD* E14 ....93 D5
Corinne Rd *ARCH* N19 ....74 C1
Cork St Ms *CONDST* W1S 31 E2
Cork Sq *WAP* E1W 102 A2
Cork St *CONDST* W1S 31 E2
Corlett St *CAMTN* NW1 ....16 C2
Cormont Rd *CMBW* SE5 ....118 B4
Cormorant Rd *FSTGT* E7 ....81 F2
Cornelia St *HOLWY* N7 ....75 F3
Corner Fielde *BRXS/STRHM* * SW2 ....153 F1
Corner Gn *BKHTH/KID* SE3 ....124 A5
Corney Reach Wy *CHSWK* W4 ....111 E3
Corney Rd *CHSWK* W4 ....111 E2
Cornflower Ter *EDUL* SE22 ....138 B4
Cornford Gv *BAL* SW12 ....152 B2
Cornhill *BANK* EC3V 24 B5
Cornmill La *LEW* SE13 ....140 B1
Cornmow Dr *WLSDN* NW10 ....69 F2
Cornthwaite Rd *CLPT* E5 ....60 C5
Cornwall Av *BETH* E2 ....90 C2
  WELL DA16 ....145 E1
Cornwall Cl *BARK* IG11 ....85 F3
Cornwall Crs *NTGHL* W11 ....101 E1
Cornwall Gdns *SKENS* SW7 ....39 E3
  WLSDN NW10 ....70 B3
Cornwall Gv *CHSWK* W4 ....111 E1
Cornwallis Av *BFN/LL* DA15 ....163 D2
Cornwallis Rd *ARCH* N19 ....57 E4
  WOOL/PLUM SE18 ....108 B4
Cornwallis Sq *ARCH* N19 ....57 E4
Cornwallis Wk *ELTH/MOT* SE9 ....143 F1
Cornwall Ms South *SKENS* SW7 ....39 E3
Cornwall Ms West *SKENS* * SW7 ....39 D3
Cornwall Rd *FSBYPK* N4 ....58 A2
  STHWK SE1 ....34 A3
Cornwall Sq *LBTH* * SE11 ....118 A1
Cornwall St *WCHPL* * E1 ....102 B1
Cornwall Ter *CAMTN* NW1 ....17 F1
Cornwall Terrace Ms *CAMTN* NW1 ....17 F1
Corn Wy *WAN* E11 ....63 D5
Cornwood Dr *WCHPL* E1 ....90 C5
Corona Rd *LEE/GVPK* SE12 ....142 A5
Coronation Rd *PLSTW* E13 ....94 C2
  WLSDN NW10 ....86 B2
Coronation Vls *WLSDN* * NW10 ....86 B3
Coronet St *IS* N1 ....12 C4
Corporation Rw *CLKNW* EC1R 10 B5
Corporation St *HOLWY* N7 ....75 D2
  SRTFD E15 ....93 E1
Corrance Rd *BRXS/STRHM* SW2 ....135 E2
Corringham Rd *GLDGN* NW11 ....54 A2
  WBLY HA9 ....50 A4
Corringway *GLDGN* NW11 ....54 B2
Corris Gn *CDALE/KGS* * NW9 ....51 E1
Corscombe Cl *KUTN/CMB* KT2 ....146 C1
Corsham St *IS* N1 ....12 B4
Corsica St *HBRY* N5 ....76 B3
Cortayne Rd *FUL/PGN* * SW6 ....113 F5
Cortis Rd *PUT/ROE* SW15 ....130 B4
Cortis Ter *PUT/ROE* SW15 ....130 B3
Corunna Rd *VX/NE* SW8 ....116 C4
Corunna Ter *VX/NE* SW8 ....116 C4
Coryton Pth *MV/WKIL* W9 ....89 F3
Cosbycote Av *HNHL* SE24 ....136 C3
Cosmo Pl *RSQ* WC1B 21 D2
Cosmur Cl *SHB* W12 ....99 F4
Cossall Wk *PECK* SE15 ....120 B4
Cosser St *STHWK* SE1 ....46 A2
Costa St *PECK* SE15 ....120 A5
Cosway St *CAMTN* NW1 ....17 D2
Cotall St *POP/IOD* E14 ....92 A5
Coteford St *TOOT* SW17 ....151 F4
Cotesbach Rd *CLPT* E5 ....60 C5
Cotham St *WALW* SE17 ....47 F5
Cotherstone Rd *BRXS/STRHM* SW2 ....153 F1
Cotleigh Rd *KIL/WHAMP* NW6 ....72 A1
Cotman Cl *EFNCH* N2 ....54 C1
Cotswold Gdns *CRICK* NW2 ....53 D4
  GNTH/NBYPK IG2 ....67 D2
Cotswold Ga *CRICK* NW2 ....53 E3
Cotswold St *WNWD* SE27 ....154 B4
Cottage Gn *CMBW* SE5 ....119 D3
Cottage Gv *BRXN/ST* SW9 ....135 E1
Cottage Pl *SKENS* SW7 ....40 C2
Cottage St *POP/IOD* E14 ....104 B1
Cottesbrook St *NWCR* SE14 ....121 E3
Cottesloe Ms *STHWK* SE1 ....46 B2
Cottesmore Gdns *KENS* W8 ....39 D2
Cottingham Rd *VX/NE* SW8 ....117 F3
Cottington St *LBTH* SE11 ....118 A1
Cotton Av *ACT* W3 ....87 D5
Cotton Gardens Est *LBTH* SE11 ....46 C5
Cotton HI *BMLY* BR1 ....159 D4
Cotton Rw *BTSEA* SW11 ....132 C1
Cottons Centre *STHWK* * SE1 ....36 C3
Cotton's Gdns *BETH* E2 ....13 D3
Cotton St *POP/IOD* E14 ....104 C1
Coulgate St *BROCKY* SE4 ....139 E1
Coulson St *CHEL* SW3 ....115 F1
Coulter Rd *HMSMTH* W6 ....100 B4
Councillor St *CMBW* SE5 ....118 C3
Counter St *STHWK* SE1 ....36 C3
Countess Rd *KTTN* NW5 ....74 C2
County Ga *CHST* BR7 ....162 C3
County Gv *CMBW* SE5 ....118 C4
County Rd *EHAM* E6 ....96 B4
County St *STHWK* SE1 ....47 F3
Coupland Pl *WOOL/PLUM* SE18 ....126 C1
Courland Gv *VX/NE* SW8 ....117 D4
Courland Rd *VX/NE* SW8 ....117 D4
The Course *ELTH/MOT* SE9 ....162 A3
Courtauld Rd *ARCH* N19 ....57 D3

Court Cl *HAMP* * NW3 ....**73** D4
Courtenay Av *HGT* N6 ....**55** E2
Courtenay Rd *WAN* * E11 ....**63** F5
Courtenay Sq *LBTH* * SE11 ....**118** A1
Court Farm Rd *ELTH/MOT* SE9 ....**161** D2
Courtfield Gdns *ECT* SW5 ....**39** D5
Courtfield Ms *SKENS* * SW7 ....**39** E5
Courtfield Rd *SKENS* SW7 ....**39** E5
Court Gdns *HOLWY* N7 ....**76** A3
Courthill Rd *LEW* SE13 ....**140** C2
Courthope Rd *HAMP* NW3 ....**73** F1
    WIM/MER SW19 ....**149** E5
Courtland Av *IL* IG1 ....**65** F4
Courtland Rd *EHAM* E6 ....**83** E5
Courtlands *RCHPK/HAM* TW10 ....**128** A3
Courtlands Av *LEE/GVPK* SE12 ....**142** B3
    RCH/KEW TW9 ....**110** B5
Court La *DUL* SE21 ....**137** F5
Court Lane Gdns *DUL* SE21 ....**137** F5
Courtmead Cl *HNHL* SE24 ....**136** C4
Courtnell St *BAY/PAD* W2 ....**14** A4
Courtney Rd *HOLWY* N7 ....**76** A2
Courtrai Rd *BROCKY* SE4 ....**139** E4
Court Rd *ELTH/MOT* SE9 ....**161** F1
Courtside *CEND/HSY/T* N8 ....**57** D1
    SYD * SE26 ....**156** C3
Court St *WCHPL* E1 ....**90** B4
Court Vw *HGT* * N6 ....**56** B4
Court Wy *ACT* W3 ....**86** C4
Court Yd *ELTH/MOT* SE9 ....**143** E4
The Courtyard *IS* N1 ....**75** F4
Cousin La *CANST* EC4R **36** A2
Couthurst Rd *BKHTH/KID* SE3 ....**124** B2
Coutts Crs *KTTN* * NW5 ....**56** B2
Coval Gdns *MORT/ESHN* SW14 ....**128** B2
Coval La *MORT/ESHN* SW14 ....**128** B2
Coval Rd *MORT/ESHN* SW14 ....**128** C2
Covelees Wall *EHAM* E6 ....**96** A5
Covent Gdn *COVGDN* WC2E **33** D1
Covent Garden Piazza
    COVGDN WC2E **33** D1
Coventry Cl *EHAM* E6 ....**95** F5
    KIL/WHAMP NW6 ....**2** B1
Coventry Cross Est *BOW* E3 ....**92** C3
Coventry Rd *IL* IG1 ....**66** B3
    WCHPL E1 ....**90** B3
Coventry St *MYFR/PICC* W1J **32** A2
Coverdale Rd *KIL/WHAMP* NW6 ....**71** E4
    SHB W12 ....**100** B3
The Coverdales *BARK* IG11 ....**97** D1
Coverley Cl *WCHPL* * E1 ....**90** A4
Coverton Rd *TOOT* SW17 ....**151** E4
Cowbridge La *BARK* IG11 ....**84** D4
Cowcross St *FARR* EC1M **22** C2
Cowdenbeath Pth *IS* N1 ....**75** E5
Cowden St *CAT* SE6 ....**158** A4
Cowick Rd *TOOT* SW17 ....**151** F4
Cow Leaze *EHAM* E6 ....**96** A5
Cowley La *WAN* * E11 ....**63** E5
Cowley Rd *ACT* W3 ....**99** F2
    BRXN/ST SW9 ....**118** A4
    IL IG1 ....**65** F2
    MORT/ESHN SW14 ....**129** E1
Cowley St *WEST* SW1P **44** C3
Cowling Cl *NTGHL* W11 ....**101** E1
Cowper Av *EHAM* E6 ....**83** E4
Cowper Rd *ACT* W3 ....**99** D2
    STNW/STAM N16 ....**77** D1
Cowper St *STLK* EC1Y **12** B5
Cowper Ter *NKENS* * W10 ....**89** E4
Cowthorpe Rd *VX/NE* SW8 ....**117** D4
Coxmount Rd *CHARL* SE7 ....**125** D1

Coxson Wy *STHWK* SE1.........................**49** E1
Coxwell Rd *WOOL/PLUM* SE18 ....**127** E1
Crabtree Cl *BETH* E2 ....**13** E2
Crabtree La *FUL/PGN* SW6 ....**113** D3
Craddock St *CAMTN* * NW1 ....**74** A3
Cradley Rd *ELTH/MOT* SE9 ....**163** D1
Craigerne Rd *BKHTH/KID* SE3 ....**124** B3
Craigholm *WOOL/PLUM* SE18 ....**126** A5
Craignair Rd *BRXS/STRHM* SW2 ....**135** F5
Craig's Ct *WHALL* SW1A **32** C3
Craigton Rd *ELTH/MOT* SE9 ....**143** F2
Crail Rw *WALW* SE17 ....**48** B5
Cramer St *MHST* W1U **18** B3
Crammond Cl *HMSMTH* W6 ....**113** E2
Cranberry La *CAN/RD* E16 ....**93** E3
Cranberry Rd *MNPK* E12 ....**83** E2
Cranbourne Rd *MNPK* E12 ....**83** E2
    SRTFD E15 ....**80** C1
Cranbourn St *LSQ/SEVD* WC2H **32** B1
Cranbrook Ri *IL* IG1 ....**65** F1
Cranbrook Rd *CHSWK* W4 ....**111** E1
    DEPT SE8 ....**122** A4
    IL IG1 ....**66** A2
Cranbrook St *BETH* E2 ....**91** D1
Cranbury Rd *FUL/PGN* SW6 ....**114** B3
Crane Av *ACT* W3 ....**98** C1
Crane Ct *FLST/FETLN* EC4A **22** B5
    MORT/ESHN * SW14 ....**128** C2
Crane Gv *HOLWY* N7 ....**76** A3
Crane Md *BERM/RHTH* SE16 ....**103** D5
Crane St *PECK* SE15 ....**119** F4
Cranfield Rd *BROCKY* SE4 ....**139** F1
Cranford Cottages *WAP* * E1W **103** D1
Cranford St *WAP* E1W **103** D1
Cranhurst Rd *CRICK* NW2 ....**70** C2
Cranleigh Gdns *BARK* IG11 ....**85** D4
Cranleigh Ms *BTSEA* SW11 ....**115** E5
Cranleigh St *CAMTN* NW1 ....**7** F2
Cranley Dr *GNTH/NBYPK* IG2 ....**66** C2
Cranley Gdns *SKENS* SW7 ....**114** C1
Cranley Ms *SKENS* SW7 ....**114** C1
Cranley Pl *SKENS* SW7 ....**40** A5
Cranley Rd *GNTH/NBYPK* IG2 ....**66** C1
    PLSTW E13 ....**94** B4
Cranmer Rd *BRXN/ST* SW9 ....**118** A3
    FSTGT E7 ....**82** B1
Cranmer Ter *TOOT* SW17 ....**151** D5
Cranmore Rd *BMLY* BR1 ....**159** E3
    CHST BR7 ....**161** F5
Cranston Est *IS* N1 ....**12** B1
Cranston Rd *FSTH* SE23 ....**157** E1
Cranswick Rd *BERM/RHTH* SE16 ....**120** B1
Crantock Rd *CAT* SE6 ....**158** C2
Cranwell Cl *BOW* E3 ....**92** B3
Cranwich Rd *STNW/STAM* N16 ....**59** F1
Cranwood St *FSBYE* EC1V **12** B4
Cranworth Gdns *BRXN/ST* SW9 ....**118** A4
Craster Rd *BRXS/STRHM* SW2 ....**135** F5
Crathie Rd *LEE/GVPK* SE12 ....**142** B4
Craven Cl *CLPT* * E5 ....**60** A2
Craven Gdns *BARK* IG11 ....**97** E1
    WIM/MER SW19 ....**150** B5
Craven Hl *BAY/PAD* W2 ....**27** E1
Craven Hill Gdns *BAY/PAD* W2 ....**27** E1
Craven Hill Ms *BAY/PAD* W2 ....**27** F1
Craven Pk *WLSDN* NW10 ....**69** D4
Craven Park Ms *WLSDN* NW10 ....**69** E4
Craven Park Rd *STNW/STAM* N16.........**59** F1
    WLSDN NW10 ....**69** E5
Craven Rd *BAY/PAD* W2 ....**27** E1
    WLSDN NW10 ....**69** D5
Craven St *CHCR* * WC2N **32** C3

Craven Ter *BAY/PAD* W2 ....27 F1
Craven Wk *CLPT* E5 ....60 A2
Crawford Pas *CLKNW* EC1R 22 A1
Crawford Pl *BAY/PAD* W2 ....17 D4
Crawford St *CMBW* SE5 ....118 C3
Crawford St *MBLAR* W1H 17 E3
Crawley Rd *LEY* E10 ....62 B3
Crawthew Gv *EDUL* SE22 ....137 F2
Craybury End *ELTH/MOT* SE9 ....162 C2
Crayford Rd *HOLWY* N7 ....75 E1
Crealock St *WAND/EARL* SW18 ....132 B4
Crebor St *EDUL* SE22 ....138 A4
Crediton HI *KIL/WHAMP* NW6 ....72 B2
Crediton Rd *WLSDN* NW10 ....71 D5
Credon Rd *BERM/RHTH* SE16 ....120 B1
   PLSTW E13 ....94 C1
Creechurch La *HDTCH* EC3A 25 D4
Creechurch Pl *HDTCH* EC3A 25 D5
Creed La *BLKFR* EC4V 23 D5
Creek Rd *BARK* IG11 ....97 F2
   DEPT SE8 ....122 A2
Creekside *DEPT* SE8 ....122 A3
Creeland Gv *CAT* SE6 ....157 F1
Crefeld Cl *FUL/PGN* SW6 ....113 D2
Creffield Rd *ACT* W3 ....98 A1
Creighton Av *EHAM* E6 ....95 D1
Creighton Cl *SHB* W12 ....100 B1
Creighton Rd *KIL/WHAMP* NW6 ....89 D1
Cremer St *BETH* E2 ....13 E2
Cremorne Est *WBPTN* SW10 ....115 D2
Cremorne Rd *WBPTN* SW10 ....114 C3
Crescent *TWRH* EC3N 37 F1
Crescent Gdns *WIM/MER* SW19 ....150 A3
Crescent Gv *CLAP* SW4 ....134 C2
Crescent La *CLAP* SW4 ....135 D3
Crescent Pl *CHEL* SW3 ....40 C4
Crescent Rd *BFN/LL* DA15 ....163 F3
   CEND/HSY/T N8 ....57 D1
   LEY E10 ....62 B4
   PLSTW E13 ....82 A5
   WOOL/PLUM SE18 ....126 B1
Crescent Rw *STLK* EC1Y 23 E1
Crescent St *IS* N1 ....75 F4
The Crescent *ACT* W3 ....87 E5
   BARN SW13 ....111 F3
   CRICK NW2 ....52 B5
   GNTH/NBYPK IG2 ....66 A1
   SCUP DA14 ....163 F4
   WIM/MER SW19 ....150 A3
Crescent Wy *BROCKY* SE4 ....140 C4
Crescent Wood Rd *DUL* SE21 ....156 A3
Cresford Rd *FUL/PGN* SW6 ....114 B4
Crespigny Rd *HDN* NW4 ....52 B1
Cresset Rd *HOM* E9 ....78 C3
Cresset St *CLAP* SW4 ....135 D1
Cressfield Cl *KTTN* NW5 ....74 A2
Cressida Rd *ARCH* N19 ....56 C3
Cressingham Rd *LEW* SE13 ....140 C1
Cressington Cl *STNW/STAM* N16 ....77 E2
Cresswell Pk *BKHTH/KID* SE3 ....141 F1
Cresswell Pl *WBPTN* SW10 ....114 C1
Cressy Ct *HMSMTH* W6 ....100 B4
Cressy Houses *WCHPL* * E1 ....90 C4
Cressy Pl *WCHPL* E1 ....90 C4
Cressy Rd *HAMP* NW3 ....73 F1
Crestfield St *CAMTN* NW1 ....9 D3
Crest Rd *CRICK* NW2 ....52 A4
The Crest *KTTN* * NW5 ....75 D2
Crestway *PUT/ROE* SW15 ....130 A4
Creswick Rd *ACT* W3 ....98 A1
Crewdson Rd *BRXN/ST* SW9 ....117 F3
Crewe Pl *WLSDN* NW10 ....87 F2
Crews St *POP/IOD* * E14 ....104 B3

Crewys Rd *CRICK* NW2 ....53 F4
   PECK SE15 ....120 B5
Crichton St *VX/NE* * SW8 ....116 C5
Cricketers Wk *SYD* SE26 ....156 C5
Cricketfield Rd *CLPT* E5 ....78 B1
Cricklade Av *BRXS/STRHM* SW2 ....153 E2
Cricklewood Broadway
   CRICK NW2 ....52 C5
Cricklewood La *CRICK* NW2 ....71 E3
Cridland St *SRTFD* E15 ....81 F5
Crieff Rd *WAND/EARL* SW18 ....132 C4
Criffel Av *BRXS/STRHM* SW2 ....153 D2
Crimscott St *STHWK* SE1 ....49 D5
Crimsworth Rd *VX/NE* SW8 ....117 D4
Crinan St *IS* N1 ....9 D1
Cringle St *VX/NE* SW8 ....116 C3
Cripplegate St *BARB* * EC2Y 23 E2
Crispian Cl *WLSDN* NW10 ....69 E1
Crispin St *WCHPL* E1 ....25 E3
Crisp Rd *HMSMTH* W6 ....112 C1
Cristowe Rd *FUL/PGN* * SW6 ....113 F5
Criterion Ms *ARCH* N19 ....57 D4
Cricketers Ms *WAND/EARL* SW18 .....132 B3
Crockerton Rd *TOOT* SW17 ....151 F2
Crockham Wy *ELTH/MOT* SE9 ....162 A4
Croft Cl *CHST* BR7 ....161 F5
Croftdown Rd *KTTN* NW5 ....56 A5
Crofters Ct *DEPT* SE8 ....103 E5
Crofters Wy *CAMTN* NW1 ....75 D5
Crofton Av *CHSWK* W4 ....110 C3
Crofton Gate Wy *BROCKY* SE4 ....139 E3
Crofton Park Rd *BROCKY* SE4 ....139 F4
Crofton Rd *CMBW* SE5 ....119 E4
   PLSTW E13 ....94 B3
Crofts St *WCHPL* E1 ....102 A1
Croft St *DEPT* SE8 ....103 E5
   WCHPL E1 ....102 A1
The Croft *WLSDN* NW10 ....87 F1
Croft Wy *BFN/LL* DA15 ....163 E3
Crogsland Rd *CAMTN* NW1 ....74 A4
Cromartie Rd *ARCH* N19 ....57 D2
Cromarty Vls *BAY/PAD* * W2 ....27 E1
Crombie Ms *BTSEA* * SW11 ....115 E5
Crombie Rd *BFN/LL* DA15 ....163 D1
Cromer Rd *LEY* E10 ....63 D2
Cromer St *STPAN* WC1H 9 D4
Cromer Ter *HACK* E8 ....78 A2
Cromer Villas Rd
   WAND/EARL SW18 ....131 F4
Cromford Rd *PUT/ROE* SW15 ....131 F3
Crompton St *BAY/PAD* W2 ....16 A1
Cromwell Av *HGT* N6 ....56 B5
   HMSMTH W6 ....112 B1
Cromwell Cl *CHSWK* * W4 ....110 B4
Cromwell Crs *ECT* SW5 ....38 A4
Cromwell Gv *HMSMTH* W6 ....100 C4
Cromwell Ms *SKENS* * SW7 ....40 A4
Cromwell Pl *ACT* W3 ....98 C2
   HGT * N6 ....56 B3
   MORT/ESHN SW14 ....128 C1
   SKENS SW7 ....40 B4
Cromwell Rd *BRXN/ST* SW9 ....118 B4
   FSTGT E7 ....82 C4
   SKENS SW7 ....40 B4
   WIM/MER SW19 ....150 A5
Crondace Rd *FUL/PGN* SW6 ....114 A4
Crondall St *IS* N1 ....12 B2
Cronin St *PECK* SE15 ....119 F3
Crooke Rd *DEPT* SE8 ....121 D4
Crookham Rd *FUL/PGN* SW6 ....113 F4
Crookston Rd *ELTH/MOT* SE9 ....144 A1
Croombs Rd *CAN/RD* E16 ....94 C4
Croom's HI *GNWCH* SE10 ....123 D3

Croom's Hill Gv GNWCH SE10............**122** C3
Cropley St IS N1..............................**12** A1
Cropthorne Ct MV/WKIL W9..................**3** F4
Crosby Rd FSTGT E7........................**82** A3
Crosby Rw STHWK SE1......................**48** A1
Crosby Wk HACK E8..........................**77** F3
Crosier Cl WOOL/PLUM SE18...........**125** D4
Crossbrook Rd BKHTH/KID SE3.........**125** C5
Crossfield Est DEPT SE8..................**122** A3
Crossfield Rd HAMP NW3...................**73** D3
Crossfield St DEPT SE8.....................**122** A3
Crossford St BRXN/ST SW9...............**117** F5
Cross Keys Cl MHST W1U...................**18** B3
Crosslet St WALW SE17.....................**48** B4
Crosslet V GNWCH SE10..................**122** B4
Crossley St HOLWY N7.......................**76** A3
Crossmead ELTH/MOT SE9...............**161** F1
Crossness Rd BARK IG11....................**97** F2
Cross Rd SIDC DA14
Cross St BARN SW13........................**111** E5
  IS N1..**76** B3
Crossthwaite Av HNHL SE24...........**137** D2
Crosswall TWRH EC3N.......................**37** E1
Crossway STNW/STAM N16..................**77** E2
Crossways Ter CLPT * E5...................**78** C1
The Crossways WBLY HA9...................**50** A4
The Crossway ELTH/MOT SE9...........**161** D2
Croston St HACK E8..........................**78** A5
Crouch Cft ELTH/MOT SE9...............**162** A3
Crouch End Hl ARCH N19....................**57** D2
Crouch Hall Rd CEND/HSY/T N8..........**57** D1
Crouch Hl ARCH N19..........................**57** E2
Crouchmans Cl DUL SE21.................**155** F3
Crouch Rd WLSDN NW10.....................**69** D4
Crowborough Rd TOOT SW17............**152** A5
Crowder St WCHPL E1......................**102** B1
Crowfoot Cl HOM E9..........................**79** F2
Crowhurst Cl BRXN/ST SW9.............**118** A5
Crowland Ter IS N1............................**77** D4
Crowline Wk IS * N1...........................**76** C3
Crown Cl BOW E3.............................**80** A5
  KIL/WHAMP NW6...........................**72** B3
Crown Ct HOL/ALD WC2B...................**21** D5
Crowndale Rd CAMTN NW1...................**7** F1
Crownfield Rd SRTFD E15..................**81** D2
Crownhill Rd WLSDN NW10..................**69** F5
Crown La STRHM/NOR SW16.............**154** A5
Crown Lane Gdns WNWD * SE27.......**154** A5
Crown Office Rw EMB EC4Y...............**34** A1
Crown Pas STJS SW1Y.......................**31** F1
Crown Pl KTTN NW5............................**74** B3
  SDTCH EC2A.................................**24** C1
Crownstone Rd
  BRXS/STRHM SW2.......................**136** A3
Crown St ACT W3.............................**98** B2
  CMBW SE5..................................**118** C3
Crown Ter CRICK * NW2......................**71** D1
Crown Vis ACT * W3..........................**98** C3
Crown Woods Wy ELTH/MOT SE9......**145** D3
Crows Rd BARK IG11..........................**84** B3
  SRTFD E15...................................**93** D2
Crowthorne Cl
  WAND/EARL SW18........................**131** E3
Crowthorne Rd NKENS W10................**89** D5
Croxley Rd MV/WKIL W9......................**89** D5
Croxted Cl DUL SE21........................**136** C5
Croxted Rd DUL SE21.......................**155** D2
Croyde Cl ELTH/MOT SE9.................**145** D5
Croydon Rd PLSTW E13.......................**94** A3
Crozier Ter HOM E9............................**79** D2
Crucifix La STHWK SE1.......................**36** C5
Cruden St IS N1................................**76** B5
Cruickshank Rd FSBYW WC1X............**10** A3

Cruikshank Rd SRTFD E15...................**81** E1
Crusoe Ms STNW/STAM N16................**59** D4
Crutched Friars TWRH EC3N................**37** D1
Crutchley Rd CAT SE6.......................**159** E2
Crystal Palace Park Rd
  NRWD SE19.................................**156** A5
Crystal Palace Rd EDUL SE22............**137** F4
Cuba St POP/IOD E14.......................**104** A3
Cubitt St FSBYW WC1X.......................**9** F4
Cubitt Ter CLAP SW4........................**134** C1
Cudham St CAT SE6..........................**140** B5
Cudworth St WCHPL E1.......................**90** B3
Cuff Crs ELTH/MOT SE9....................**143** D5
Culford Gdns CHEL SW3.....................**41** F5
Culford Gv IS N1...............................**77** E3
Culford Ms IS N1..............................**77** E3
Culford Rd IS N1...............................**77** E4
Cullen Wy WLSDN NW10.....................**86** C5
Culling Rd BERM/RHTH SE16...........**102** C4
Cullingworth Rd WLSDN NW10............**70** A2
Culloden Cl STHWK SE1....................**120** A1
Culloden St POP/IOD E14....................**92** C5
Cullum St FENCHST EC3M...................**36** C1
Culmore Rd PECK SE15....................**120** B3
Culmstock Rd BTSEA SW11...............**134** A3
Culross St MYFR/PKLN W1K................**30** A2
Culverden Rd BAL SW12...................**152** C3
Culverhouse Gdns
  STRHM/NOR SW16.......................**153** F4
Culverley Rd CAT SE6......................**158** B1
Culvert Pl BTSEA SW11....................**116** A5
Culvert Rd BTSEA SW11...................**115** F5
Culworth St STJWD NW8.....................**4** C2
Cumberland Av WELL DA16...............**145** E1
  WLSDN NW10...............................**86** B2
Cumberland Cl HACK E8.....................**77** F3
Cumberland Gdns FSBYW WC1X...........**9** F3
Cumberland Ga BAY/PAD W2...............**29** E1
  CAMTN NW1...................................**6** C3
Cumberland Market CAMTN NW1...........**7** D3
Cumberland Pk ACT W3.....................**98** C1
Cumberland Pl CAMTN NW1..................**6** C3
  CAT SE6....................................**159** F1
Cumberland Rd ACT W3.....................**98** C1
  BARN SW13................................**111** F4
  MNPK E12...................................**83** D1
  PLSTW E13.................................**94** B4
  RCH/KEW TW9.............................**110** A4
Cumberland St PIM SW1V.................**116** B1
Cumberland Ter CAMTN NW1................**6** C2
Cumberland Terrace Ms
  CAMTN NW1...................................**6** C2
Cumbrian Gdns CRICK NW2.................**53** D4
Cumming St IS N1..............................**9** F2
Cumnor Cl BRXN/ST * SW9...............**117** F5
Cunard Rd WLSDN NW10......................**87** D2
Cundy Rd CAN/RD E16........................**94** C5
Cundy St BGVA SW1W.........................**42** B5
Cunningham Pl STJWD NW8..................**4** A5
Cunnington St CHSWK W4...................**98** C4
Cupar Rd BTSEA SW11......................**116** A4
Cupola Cl BMLY BR1.........................**160** B5
Cureton St WEST * SW1P...................**117** D1
Curlew St STHWK SE1.........................**37** E5
Curnick's La WNWD SE27..................**154** C4
Curran Av BFN/LL DA15....................**145** F3
Curricle St ACT W3............................**99** E2
Currie Hill Cl WIM/MER SW19...........**149** F4
Cursitor St FLST/FETLN EC4A..............**22** A4
Curtain Pl SDTCH EC2A.....................**13** D5
Curtain Rd IS N1...............................**13** D4
  SDTCH EC2A................................**24** C1

Curtis Dr *ACT* W3 ....**87** D5
Curtis Field Rd *STRHM/NOR* SW16 ...**153** F4
Curtis St *STHWK* SE1 ....**49** E4
Curtis Wy *STHWK* SE1 ....**49** E4
The Curve *SHB* W12 ....**100** A1
Curwen Av *FSTGT* E7 ....**82** B1
Curwen Rd *SHB* W12.....................**100** A3
Curzon Crs *BARK* IG11 ....**97** F2
　　　　　WLSDN NW10 ....**69** E4
Curzon Pl *MYFR/PKLN* W1K **30** D4
Curzon St *MYFR/PICC* W1J **31** D3
Custom House Reach
　　　　　BERM/RHTH * SE16 ....**103** F4
Cutcombe Rd *CMBW* SE5 ....**118** C5
Cuthberga Cl *BARK* IG11 ....**84** C4
Cuthbert St *BAY/PAD* W2 ....**16** A2
Cutlers Gardens Ar *LVPST* EC2M **25** D4
Cutler St *HDTCH* EC3A....................**25** D4
The Cut *STHWK* SE1 ....**34** B5
Cygnet Cl *WLSDN* NW10 ....**69** D2
Cygnet St *WCHPL* E1 ....**13** F5
Cynthia St *IS* N1............................**9** F2
Cypress Gdns *BROCKY* SE4 ....**139** E3
Cypress Tree Cl *BFN/LL* DA15.........**163** F1
Cyprus Cl *FSBYPK* N4 ....**58** A1
Cyprus Pl *BETH* E2.........................**90** C1
　　　　　EHAM E6 ....**108** A1
Cyprus St *BETH* E2 ....**90** C1
Cyrena Rd *EDUL* SE22 ....**137** E4
Cyrus St *FSBYE* EC1V **11** D5
Czar St *DEPT* SE8 ....**122** A2

D

Dabin Crs *GNWCH* SE10 ....**122** C4
Dacca St *DEPT* SE8 ....**121** F2
Dace Rd *BOW* E3 ....**80** A5
Dacre Gdns *LEW* * SE13 ....**141** E2
Dacre Pk *LEW* SE13 ....**141** E1
Dacre Pl *LEW* SE13........................**141** E1
Dacre Rd *PLSTW* E13.......................**82** B5
　　　　　WAN E11 ....**63** F3
Dacres Est *FSTH* * SE23 ....**157** D1
Dacres Rd *FSTH* SE23 ....**157** D1
Dacre St *STJSPK* SW1H **44** A2
Daffodil Gdns *IL* IG1 ....**84** B2
Daffodil St *SHB* W12 ....**99** F1
Dafforne Rd *TOOT* SW17 ....**151** E1
Dagenham Rd *LEY* E10 ....**61** F3
Dagmar Gdns *WLSDN* NW10 ....**89** D1
Dagmar Pas *IS* * N1........................**76** B5
Dagmar Rd *CMBW* SE5 ....**119** E4
　　　　　FSBYPK N4.......................**58** A2
Dagmar Ter *IS* * N1.........................**76** B5
Dagnall St *BTSEA* SW11 ....**115** F4
Dagnan Rd *BAL* SW12 ....**134** B5
Dagonet Rd *BMLY* BR1 ....**160** A3
Dahlia Gdns *IL* IG1 ....**84** B3
Daines Cl *MNPK* E12 ....**65** F5
Dainford St *BMLY* BR1 ....**159** D5
Dairsie Rd *ELTH/MOT* SE9 ....**144** A4
Dairy La *WOOL/PLUM* SE18 ....**107** F5
Dairyman Cl *CRICK* * NW2 ....**53** D5
Daisy La *FUL/PGN* SW6 ....**132** A1
Dakota Gdns *EHAM* E6 ....**95** E3
Dalberg Rd *BRXS/STRHM* SW2 ....**136** A3
Dalby Rd *WAND/EARL* SW18...........**132** C2
Dalby St *KTTN* NW5 ....**74** B3
Dalebury Rd *TOOT* SW17 ....**151** F2
Dale Cl *BKHTH/KID* SE3 ....**142** A1
Daleham Gdns *HAMP* NW3 ....**73** D2

Daleham Ms *HAMP* * NW3 ....**73** D3
Dale Rd *KTTN* NW5 ....**74** A2
　　　　　WALW SE17 ....**118** B2
Dale Rw *NTGHL* W11 ....**89** E5
Daleside Rd *TOOT* SW17 ....**152** B5
Dale St *CHSWK* W4.........................**111** E1
Daleview Rd *SEVS/STOTM* N15 ....**59** E1
Daley St *HOM* E9 ....**79** D3
Daley Thompson Wy *VX/NE* SW8 ...**116** B5
Dalgarno Gdns *NKENS* W10 ....**88** C4
Dalgarno Wy *NKENS* W10 ....**88** C3
Dalkeith Rd *DUL* SE21 ....**154** C1
　　　　　IL IG1 ....**66** C5
Dallas Rd *HDN* NW4.........................**52** A2
　　　　　SYD SE26 ....**156** B4
Dallinger Rd *LEE/GVPK* SE12 ....**141** F4
Dalling Rd *HMSMTH* W6 ....**100** B4
Dallington Sq *FSBYE* EC1V **11** D5
Dallington St *FSBYE* EC1V **11** D5
Dallin Rd *WOOL/PLUM* SE18 ....**126** B3
Dalmain Rd *FSTH* SE23 ....**157** D1
Dalmeny Av *HOLWY* N7 ....**75** D1
Dalmeny Rd *HOLWY* N7 ....**75** D1
Dalmeyer Rd *WLSDN* NW10 ....**69** F3
Dalmore Rd *DUL* SE21 ....**154** C2
Dalrymple Rd *BROCKY* SE4 ....**139** E2
Dalston La *HACK* E8.........................**77** F3
Dalton St *WNWD* SE27 ....**154** B2
Dalwood St *CMBW* SE5..................**119** E4
Dalyell Rd *BRXN/ST* SW9 ....**135** F1
Damask Crs *CAN/RD* E16 ....**93** E3
Damer Ter *WBPTN* SW10 ....**114** C3
Dames Rd *FSTGT* E7 ....**82** A1
Dame St *IS* N1 ....**11** E1
Damien Ct *WCHPL* E1 ....**90** B4
Damien St *WCHPL* E1 ....**90** B4
Damsel Ct *BERM/RHTH* * SE16 ....**102** A3
Danbury St *IS* N1............................**11** D1
Danby St *PECK* SE15 ....**137** F1
Dancer Rd *FUL/PGN* SW6 ....**113** F4
　　　　　RCH/KEW TW9....................**128** A1
Dando Crs *BKHTH/KID* SE3 ....**142** B1
Dandridge Cl *GNWCH* SE10 ....**123** F1
Danebury Av *PUT/ROE* SW15 ....**129** F5
Daneby Rd *CAT* SE6.......................**158** A3
Danecroft Rd *HNHL* SE24 ....**136** C3
Danehurst St *FUL/PGN* SW6 ....**113** E4
Danemere St *PUT/ROE* SW15 ....**130** C1
Dane Pl *BOW* E3.............................**91** E1
Dane Rd *IL* IG1 ....**84** C2
Danescombe *LEE/GVPK* SE12 ....**160** C3
Danesdale Rd *HOM* E9 ....**79** E3
Danes Ct *GINN* WC1R......................**21** E3
Daneswood Av *CAT* SE6 ....**158** C3
Daneville Rd *CMBW* SE5 ....**119** D4
Dangan Rd *WAN* E11.......................**64** C1
Daniel Bolt Cl *POP/IOD* E14 ....**92** B4
Daniel Gdns *PECK* SE15 ....**119** F3
Daniel Pl *HDN* NW4 ....**52** B1
Daniel's Rd *PECK* SE15 ....**138** C1
Dan Leno Wk *FUL/PGN* * SW6 ....**114** B3
Dansey Pl *SOHO/SHAV* W1D **32** A1
Dante Rd *LBTH* SE11 ....**46** C4
Danube St *CHEL* SW3 ....**115** E1
Danvers St *CHEL* SW3 ....**115** D2
Daphne St *WAND/EARL* SW18 ....**132** C1
Daplyn St *WCHPL* E1 ....**90** A4
D'arblay St *SOHO/CST* W1F **19** F5
Darell Rd *RCH/KEW* TW9.................**128** A1
Darenth Rd *STNW/STAM* N16 ....**59** F2
Darfield Rd *BROCKY* SE4................**139** E3
Darfield Wy *NKENS* W10 ....**101** D1
Darfur St *PUT/ROE* SW15 ....**131** D1
Darien Rd *BTSEA* SW11 ....**133** D1

Darlan Rd *FUL/PGN* SW6 ....**113** F3
Darley Rd *BTSEA* SW11 ....**133** F4
Darling Rd *BROCKY* SE4 ....**140** A1
Darling Rw *WCHPL* E1 ....**90** B3
Darlington Rd *WNWD* SE27 ....**154** B5
Darnley Rd *HACK* E8 ....**78** B3
Darnley Ter *NTGHL* W11 ....**101** D2
Darrell Rd *EDUL* SE22 ....**138** A3
Darren Cl *FSBYPK* N4 ....**57** F2
Darsley Dr *VX/NE* SW8 ....**117** D4
Dartford St *WALW* SE17 ....**118** C2
Dartmoor Wk *POP/IOD* * E14 ....**104** A5
Dartmouth Cl *NTGHL* W11 ....**89** F5
Dartmouth Gv *GNWCH* SE10 ......**122** C4
Dartmouth Hl *GNWCH* SE10 ....**122** C4
Dartmouth Park Av *KTTN* NW5 ......**56** B5
Dartmouth Park Hl *ARCH* N19 ......**56** B5
Dartmouth Park Rd *KTTN* NW5 ......**56** B5
Dartmouth Pl *CHSWK* W4 ....**111** E2
  FSTH SE23 ....**156** C2
Dartmouth Rd *CRICK* NW2 ....**71** D3
  HDN NW4 ....**52** A1
  SYD SE26 ....**156** B3
Dartmouth Rw *LEW* SE13 ....**122** C5
Dartmouth St *STJSPK* SW1H **44** A1
Dartmouth Ter *GNWCH* SE10 ....**123** D4
Dartrey Wk *WBPTN* * SW10 ....**114** C3
Dart St *MV/WKIL* W9 ....**89** F2
Darville Rd *STNW/STAM* N16 ....**59** F5
Darwell Cl *EHAM* E6 ....**96** A1
Darwin Rd *WELL* DA16 ....**145** F1
Darwin St *WALW* SE17 ....**48** B1
Dashwood Rd *CEND/HSY/T* N8 .....**57** D2
Dassett Rd *WNWD* SE27 ....**154** B5
Datchelor Pl *CMBW* * SE5 ....**119** D4
Datchet Rd *CAT* SE6 ....**157** F3
Date St *WALW* SE17 ....**118** C1
Daubeney Rd *CLPT* E5 ....**79** E2
Dault Rd *WAND/EARL* SW18 ....**132** C4
Davenant Rd *ARCH* N19 ....**57** D4
Davenant St *WCHPL* E1 ....**90** A4
Davenport Rd *LEW* SE13 ....**140** B4
Daventry Av *WALTH* E17 ....**62** A1
Daventry St *CAMTN* NW1 ....**16** C2
Davern Cl *GNWCH* SE10 ....**105** F5
Davey Cl *HOLWY* N7 ....**75** F3
Davey Rd *HOM* E9 ....**80** A4
Davey St *PECK* SE15 ....**119** F2
Davidge St *STHWK* SE1 ....**46** C1
David Ms *MHST* W1U **17** F2
David Gdns *VX/NE* SW8 ....**117** D4
Davidson Gdns *VX/NE* SW8 ....**117** D4
David's Rd *FSTH* SE23 ....**156** C1
David St *SRTFD* E15 ....**81** D3
Davies La *WAN* E11 ....**63** E4
Davies Ms *MYFR/PKLN* W1K **30** C1
Davies St *MYFR/PKLN* W1K **30** C1
Davis Rd *ACT* W3 ....**99** F2
Davis St *PLSTW* E13 ....**94** B1
Davisville Rd *SHB* W12 ....**100** A3
Dawes Rd *FUL/PGN* SW6 ....**113** F3
Dawes St *WALW* SE17 ....**119** D1
Dawlish Av *WAND/EARL* SW18 .....**150** B2
Dawlish Dr *GDMY/SEVK* IG3 ....**85** F1
Dawlish Rd *CRICK* NW2 ....**71** D3
  LEY E10 ....**62** C4
Dawnay Gdns *WAND/EARL* SW18 **151** D2
Dawnay Rd *WAND/EARL* SW18 ...**150** C2
Dawn Crs *SRTFD* E15 ....**81** D5
Dawpool Rd *CRICK* NW2 ....**51** F4
Dawson Av *BARK* IG11 ....**85** F4
Dawson Cl *WOOL/PLUM* SE18 ....**108** C5
Dawson Gdns *BARK* IG11 ....**85** F4
Dawson Pl *BAY/PAD* W2 ....**26** A1

Dawson Rd *CRICK* NW2 ....**70** C2
Dawson St *BETH* E2 ....**13** F2
Daylesford Av *PUT/ROE* SW15 ....**130** A2
Daysbrook Rd *BRXS/STRHM* SW2 **153** F1
Days La *BFN/LL* DA15 ....**145** E5
Dayton Gv *PECK* SE15 ....**120** C4
Deacon Ms *IS* N1 ....**77** D4
Deacon Rd *CRICK* NW2 ....**70** A3
Deacons Ter *IS* * N1 ....**76** C3
Deacon Wy *WALW* SE17 ....**47** E4
Deal Porters Wy
  BERM/RHTH SE16 ....**102** C4
Deal St *WCHPL* E1 ....**90** A4
Dealtry Rd *PUT/ROE* SW15 ....**130** C2
Deal Wk *BRXN/ST* SW9 ....**118** A3
Dean Bradley St *WEST* SW1P **44** C3
Deancross St *WCHPL* E1 ....**90** C5
Deanery Ms *MYFR/PKLN* * W1K **30** B3
Deanery Rd *SRTFD* E15 ....**81** E3
Deanery St *MYFR/PKLN* W1K **30** B3
Dean Farrar St *STJSPK* SW1H **44** B2
Deanhill Ct *MORT/ESHN* * SW14 ..**128** B2
Deanhill Rd *MORT/ESHN* SW14 ...**128** B2
Dean Rd *CRICK* NW2 ....**70** C3
Dean Ryle St *WEST* SW1P **44** C4
Dean's Buildings *WALW* SE17 ....**48** B5
Deans Cl *CHSWK* W4 ....**110** B2
Dean's Ct *BLKFR* EC4V **23** D5
Deanscroft Av *CDALE/KGS* NW9 ...**50** C4
Deans Gate Cl *FSTH* SE23 ....**157** D3
Dean's Ms *CAVSO/HST* * W1G **19** D4
Dean Stanley St *WEST* * SW1P **44** C3
Dean St *FSTGT* E7 ....**82** A2
  SOHO/CST W1F **20** A4
Deans Yd *WEST* SW1P **44** B2
Dean Trench St *WEST* * SW1P **44** C3
Deason St *SRTFD* E15 ....**80** C5
De Barowe Ms *HBRY* * N5 ....**76** B1
De Beauvoir Crs *IS* N1 ....**77** E5
De Beauvoir Est *IS* * N1 ....**77** E5
De Beauvoir Rd *IS* N1 ....**77** E4
De Beauvoir Sq *IS* N1 ....**77** E4
Debnams Rd *BERM/RHTH* SE16 ...**102** C5
Decima St *STHWK* SE1 ....**48** C2
Deck Cl *BERM/RHTH* SE16 ....**103** D2
De Crespigny Pk *CMBW* SE5 ....**119** D5
Deeley Rd *VX/NE* SW8 ....**117** D4
Deepdale *WIM/MER* SW19 ....**149** D4
Deepdene Gdns
  BRXS/STRHM SW2 ....**135** F5
Deepdene Rd *HNHL* SE24 ....**136** C2
Deerbrook Rd *BRXS/STRHM* SW2 **154** B1
Deerdale Rd *HNHL* SE24 ....**136** C2
Deerhurst Rd *KIL/WHAMP* NW6 .....**71** D4
  STRHM/NOR SW16 ....**153** F5
Deeside Rd *TOOT* SW17 ....**151** D3
Dee St *POP/IOD* E14 ....**92** C5
Defoe Av *RCH/KEW* TW9 ....**110** A3
Defoe Rd *BERM/RHTH* SE16 ....**103** F3
  STNW/STAM N16 ....**59** E4
De Frene Rd *SYD* SE26 ....**157** D4
Degema Rd *CHST* BR7 ....**162** B5
Dehar Crs *CDALE/KGS* NW9 ....**51** F2
Dekker Rd *DUL* SE21 ....**137** E4
Delacourt Rd *BKHTH/KID* SE3 .....**124** B3
Delafield Rd *CHARL* SE7 ....**124** B1
Delaford Rd *BERM/RHTH* SE16 ....**120** B1
Delaford St *FUL/PGN* SW6 ....**113** E3
Delamere St *BAY/PAD* W2 ....**15** E3
Delamere Ter *BAY/PAD* W2 ....**15** D2
Delancey Pas *CAMTN* NW1 ....**74** B5
Delancey St *CAMTN* NW1 ....**74** B5
De Laune St *WALW* SE17 ....**118** B2

Delaware Rd *MV/WKIL* W9 ....2 C5
Delawyk Crs *HNHL* SE24 ....137 D2
Delhi St *IS* N1 ....75 E5
Delia St *WAND/EARL* SW18 ....132 B5
Delisle Rd *THMD* SE28 ....109 E2
Dell Cl *SRTFD* E15 ....81 D5
Dellow Cl *GNTH/NBYPK* IG2 ....67 D2
Dellow St *WCHPL* E1 ....102 B1
Dell's Ms *PIM* * SW1V 43 F5
Delme Crs *BKHTH/KID* SE3 ....124 B5
Deloraine St *DEPT* SE8 ....122 A4
Delorme St *HMSMTH* W6 ....113 D2
Delta Est *BETH* * E2 ....90 A2
Delta St *BETH* * E2 ....90 A2
Delverton Rd *WALW* SE17 ....118 B1
Delvino Rd *FUL/PGN* SW6 ....114 A4
Demeta Cl *WBLY* HA9 ....50 C5
De Montfort Pde
    STRHM/NOR * SW16 ....153 E3
De Montfort Rd
    STRHM/NOR SW16 ....153 D2
De Morgan Rd *FUL/PGN* SW6 ....132 B1
Dempster Rd *WAND/EARL* SW18 ...132 C3
Denbigh Cl *NTGHL* W11 ....101 F1
    WLSDN NW10 ....69 E4
Denbigh Dr *PIM* * SW1V 116 C1
Denbigh Rd *EHAM* E6 ....95 D2
    NTGHL W11 ....101 F1
Denbigh St *PIM* SW1V 43 E5
Denbigh Ter *NTGHL* W11 ....101 F1
Dendy St *BAL* SW12 ....152 A1
Dene Cl *BROCKY* SE4 ....139 E1
Denehurst Gdns *ACT* W3 ....98 B2
    HDN NW4 ....52 C1
    RCHPK/HAM TW10 ....128 A2
Denewood Rd *HGT* N6 ....55 E1
Dengie Wk *IS* * N1 ....76 C3
Dengil Crs *KTTN* NW5 ....74 A2
Denham Dr *GNTH/NBYPK* IG2 ....66 C1
Denham Wy *BARK* IG11 ....85 E5
Denholme Rd *MV/WKIL* W9 ....89 F2
Denman Rd *PECK* SE15 ....119 F4
Denman St *REGST* W1B 31 F2
Denmark Gv *IS* N1 ....10 A1
Denmark Hl *CMBW* SE5 ....119 D4
    HNHL SE24 ....137 D2
Denmark Hl *CMBW* SE5 ....118 C4
    KIL/WHAMP NW6 ....89 F1
Denmark St *LSQ/SEVD* WC2H 20 B5
    PLSTW E13 ....94 B4
    WAN E11 ....63 E5
Denne Ter *HACK* E8 ....77 F5
Dennett's Gv *NWCR* SE14 ....121 D5
Dennett's Rd *NWCR* SE14 ....120 C4
Denning Cl *STJWD* NW8 ....3 F3
Denning Rd *HAMP* NW3 ....73 D1
Dennington Park Rd
    KIL/WHAMP NW6 ....72 A3
Dennis Wy *CLAP* SW4 ....135 D2
Denny Crs *LBTH* SE11 ....118 A1
Denny St *LBTH* SE11 ....118 A1
Densham Rd *SRTFD* E15 ....81 E5
Denton St *WAND/EARL* SW18 ....132 B4
Denton Wy *CLPT* E5 ....61 D5
Dents Rd *BTSEA* SW11 ....133 F4
Denver Rd *STNW/STAM* N16 ....59 E2
Denyer St *CHEL* SW3 ....41 D4
Denzil Rd *WLSDN* NW10 ....69 F2
Deodar Rd *PUT/ROE* SW15 ....131 E2
Depot Ap *CRICK* NW2 ....71 D1
Depot St *CMBW* SE5 ....119 D2
Deptford Br *GNWCH* SE10 ....122 A4
Deptford Broadway *DEPT* SE8 .....122 A4

Deptford Church St *DEPT* SE8 .....122 A2
Deptford Gn *DEPT* SE8 ....122 A2
Deptford High St *DEPT* SE8 ....122 A3
Deptford Market *DEPT* * SE8 ....122 A3
Deptford Whf *DEPT* SE8 ....103 F5
Derby Ga *WHALL* SW1A 32 C5
Derby Hl *FSTH* SE23 ....156 C2
Derby Hill Crs *FSTH* SE23 ....156 C2
Derby Rd *FSTGT* E7 ....83 D4
    HOM E9 ....79 D5
    MORT/ESHN SW14 ....128 B2
Derbyshire St *BETH* E2 ....90 A2
Derby St *MYFR/PICC* W1J 30 B4
Dereham Pl *SDTCH* EC2A 13 D5
Dereham Rd *BARK* IG11 ....85 F3
Derek Av *WBLY* HA9 ....68 B4
Derek Walcott Cl *HNHL* * SE24 .....136 B3
Dericote St *HACK* E8 ....78 A5
Derifall Cl *EHAM* E6 ....95 F4
Dering St *CONDST* W1S 18 C5
Derinton Rd *TOOT* SW17 ....152 A4
Dermody Gdns *LEW* * SE13 ....141 D3
Dermody Rd *LEW* SE13 ....141 D3
Deronda Rd *BRXS/STRHM* SW2 ....154 B1
Derrick Gdns *CHARL* SE7 ....106 C4
Derry St *KENS* W8 ....38 C1
Dersingham Av *MNPK* E12 ....83 F1
Dersingham Rd *CRICK* NW2 ....53 E5
Derwent Av *PUT/ROE* SW15 ....147 E4
Derwent Gv *EDUL* SE22 ....137 F2
Derwent Ri *CDALE/KGS* NW9 ....51 E1
Derwent St *GNWCH* SE10 ....123 E1
Derwentwater Rd *ACT* W3 ....98 C2
Desborough Cl *BAY/PAD* W2 ....15 D2
Desenfans Rd *DUL* SE21 ....137 E4
Desford Rd *CAN/RD* E16 ....93 E3
Desmond St *NWCR* SE14 ....121 E2
Despard Rd *ARCH* N19 ....56 C3
Detling Rd *BMLY* BR1 ....160 A5
Detmold Rd *CLPT* E5 ....60 B4
Devalls Cl *EHAM* E6 ....108 A1
Devas St *BOW* E3 ....92 B3
Devenay Rd *SRTFD* E15 ....81 F4
De Vere Gdns *IL* IG1 ....65 F4
    KENS W8 ....39 E1
Deverell St *STHWK* SE1 ....48 A3
De Vere Ms *KENS* W8 ....39 E2
Devereux Ct *TPL/STR* WC2R 22 A5
Devereux La *BARN* SW13 ....112 B3
Devereux Rd *BTSEA* SW11 ....133 E4
Devizes St *IS* N1 ....77 D5
Devon Gdns *FSBYPK* N4 ....58 B3
Devonhurst Pl *CHSWK* * W4 ....111 D1
Devonia Rd *IS* N1 ....11 D1
Devonport Gdns *IL* IG1 ....65 F3
Devonport Ms *SHB* * W12 ....100 B2
Devonport Rd *SHB* W12 ....100 B2
Devonport St *WCHPL* E1 ....90 C5
Devon Rd *BARK* IG11 ....85 E5
Devons Est *BOW* E3 ....92 B2
Devonshire Cl *CAVSQ/HST* W1G 18 C2
    SRTFD E15 ....81 E1
Devonshire Dr *GNWCH* SE10 ....122 B4
Devonshire Gdns *CHSWK* W4 ....110 C3
Devonshire Gv *PECK* SE15 ....120 B2
Devonshire Ms South
    CAVSQ/HST W1G 18 C2
Devonshire Ms West
    CAVSQ/HST W1G 18 B1
Devonshire Pl *CAVSQ/HST* W1G 18 B1
    CRICK NW2 ....54 A3
    KENS * W8 ....38 C3
Devonshire Place Ms *MHST* W1U 18 B1

Devonshire Rd *CAN/RD* E16 ....**94** B5
  CHSWK W4 ....**111** E1
  ELTH/MOT SE9 ....**161** E2
  FSTH SE23 ....**139** D5
  GNTH/NBYPK IG2 ....**67** D2
  WALTH E17 ....**62** A1
Devonshire Rw *LVPST* EC2M **25** D3
Devonshire Sq *LVPST* EC2M **25** D4
Devonshire St *CAVSQ/HST* W1G **18** B3
  CHSWK W4 ....**111** E1
Devonshire Ter *BAY/PAD* W2 ....**15** F5
  EDUL * SE22 ....**138** A2
Devons Rd *BOW* E3 ....**92** A4
Devon St *PECK* SE15 ....**120** B2
De Walden St *CAVSQ/HST* W1G **18** B3
Dewar St *PECK* SE15 ....**138** A3
Dewberry Gdns *EHAM* E6 ....**95** E4
Dewberry St *POP/IOD* E14 ....**92** C5
Dewey Rd *IS* N1 ....**10** A1
Dewey St *TOOT* SW17 ....**151** F5
Dewhurst Rd *HMSMTH* W6 ....**101** D4
Dewsbury Rd *WLSDN* NW10 ....**70** A2
D'Eynsford Rd *CMBW* SE5 ....**119** D4
Diadem Ct *SOHO/SHAV* * W1D **20** A4
Diamond St *PECK* SE15 ....**119** E3
  WLSDN NW10 ....**68** C2
Diana Cl *DEPT* SE8 ....**121** F2
Diana Pl *CAMTN* NW1 ....**7** D5
Dibden St *IS* N1 ....**76** C5
Dicey Av *CRICK* NW2 ....**70** C2
Dickens Est *BERM/RHTH* * SE16 ....**102** A4
Dickens Ms *FARR* EC1M **22** C1
Dickenson Rd *CEND/HSY/T* N8 ....**57** E2
Dickens Rd *EHAM* E6 ....**95** D1
Dickens Sq *STHWK* SE1 ....**47** F5
Dickens St *VX/NE* SW8 ....**116** B5
Dickson Rd *ELTH/MOT* SE9 ....**143** E1
Didsbury Cl *EHAM* E6 ....**83** F5
Digby Crs *FSBYPK* N4 ....**58** C4
Digby Rd *BARK* IG11 ....**85** F4
  HOM E9 ....**79** D3
Digby St *BETH* E2 ....**90** D2
Diggon St *WCHPL* E1 ....**91** D4
Dighton Rd *WAND/EARL* SW18 ....**132** C3
Dignum St *IS* * N1 ....**10** A1
Digswell St *HOLWY* * N7 ....**76** A3
Dilhorne Cl *LEE/GVPK* SE12 ....**160** B3
Dilke St *CHEL* SW3 ....**115** F2
Dillwyn Cl *SYD* SE26 ....**157** E4
Dilton Gdns *PUT/ROE* SW15 ....**148** A3
Dimes Pl *HMSMTH* W6 ....**100** B5
Dimond Cl *FSTGT* E7 ....**82** A1
Dimsdale Dr *CDALE/KGS* NW9 ....**50** C3
Dimson Crs *BOW* E3 ....**92** A3
Dingle Gdns *POP/IOD* * E14 ....**104** A1
Dingley La *STRHM/NOR* SW16 ....**153** D2
Dingley Pl *FSBYE* EC1V **11** F4
Dingley Rd *FSBYE* EC1V **11** E4
Dingwall Gdns *GLDGN* NW11 ....**54** C3
Dingwall Rd *WAND/EARL* SW18 ....**132** C5
Dinmont St *BETH* E2 ....**90** C2
Dinsdale Rd *BKHTH/KID* SE3 ....**123** F2
Dinsmore Rd *BAL* SW12 ....**134** B5
Dirleton Rd *SRTFD* E15 ....**81** F5
Disbrowe Rd *HMSMTH* W6 ....**113** E2
Discovery Wk *WAP* E1W **102** B1
Disney Pl *STHWK* SE1 ....**35** F5
Disney St *STHWK* SE1 ....**35** F5
Disraeli Rd *FSTGT* E7 ....**82** A3
  PUT/ROE SW15 ....**131** D2
  WLSDN NW10 ....**86** C1
Diss St *BETH* E2 ....**13** D4
Distaff La *BLKFR* EC4V **35** E1

Distillery La *HMSMTH* W6 ....**112** C1
Distillery Rd *HMSMTH* W6 ....**112** C1
Distin St *LBTH* SE11 ....**46** A5
Ditchburn St *POP/IOD* E14 ....**104** C1
Dittisham Rd *ELTH/MOT* SE9 ....**161** E2
Dixon Cl *EHAM* E6 ....**95** F5
Dixon Rd *NWCR* SE14 ....**121** E4
Dobell Rd *ELTH/MOT* SE9 ....**143** F3
Dobree Av *WLSDN* NW10 ....**70** B4
Dobson Cl *KIL/WHAMP* NW6 ....**73** C1
Dockers Tanner Rd
  POP/IOD E14 ....**104** A5
Dockhead *STHWK* SE1 ....**49** F1
Dock Hill Av *BERM/RHTH* SE16 ....**103** D3
Dockland St *CAN/RD* E16 ....**108** A2
Dockley Rd *BERM/RHTH* SE16 ....**102** A4
Dock Rd *CAN/RD* E16 ....**105** F1
Dockside Rd *CAN/RD* E16 ....**107** D1
Dock St *WCHPL* E1 ....**102** A1
Doctors Cl *SYD* SE26 ....**156** C5
Dodbrooke Rd *WNWD* SE27 ....**154** A3
Doddington Gv *WALW* SE17 ....**118** B2
Doddington Pl *WALW* SE17 ....**118** B2
Dodson St *STHWK* SE1 ....**46** B1
Dod St *POP/IOD* E14 ....**91** F5
Doggett Rd *CAT* SE6 ....**140** A5
Dog Kennel Hl *CMBW* SC5 ....**137** E1
Dog La *WLSDN* NW10 ....**69** E1
Doherty Rd *PLSTW* E13 ....**94** A3
Dolben Ct *DEPT* * SE8 ....**103** F5
Dolben St *STHWK* * SE1 ....**35** D4
Dolby Rd *FUL/PGN* SW6 ....**113** F5
Dolland St *LBTH* SE11 ....**117** F1
Dollis Hill Av *CRICK* NW2 ....**52** B5
Dollis Hill Est *CRICK* * NW2 ....**52** A5
Dollis Hill La *CRICK* NW2 ....**69** F1
Dolman Rd *CHSWK* W4 ....**99** D5
Dolman St *CLAP* SW4 ....**135** F2
Dolphin La *POP/IOD* E14 ....**104** B1
Dolphin Sq *CHSWK* * W4 ....**111** E3
  PIM SW1V **116** C1
Dombey St *BMSBY* WC1N **21** E2
Dome Hill Pk *SYD* SE26 ....**155** F4
Domett Cl *CMBW* SE5 ....**137** D2
Domingo St *FSBYE* EC1V **11** E5
Dominica Cl *PLSTW* E13 ....**95** D2
Dominion St *LVPST* EC2M **24** B2
Domonic Dr *ELTH/MOT* SE9 ....**162** B3
Donald Rd *PLSTW* E13 ....**82** B5
Donaldson Rd *KIL/WHAMP* NW6 ....**71** F5
  WOOL/PLUM SE18 ....**126** A4
Doncaster Gdns *FSBYPK* * N4 ....**58** C1
Donegal St *IS* N1 ....**9** F2
Doneraile St *FUL/PGN* SW6 ....**113** D5
Dongola Rd *PLSTW* E13 ....**94** B2
Dongola Rd West *PLSTW* E13 ....**94** B2
Donkey Aly *EDUL* SE22 ....**138** A5
Donne Pl *CHEL* SW3 ....**41** D4
Donnington Rd *WLSDN* NW10 ....**70** B5
Donoghue Cottages *POP/IOD* * E14 ....**91** E4
Don Phelan Cl *CMBW* SE5 ....**119** D4
Doon St *STHWK* SE1 ....**34** A4
Dorando Cl *SHB* * W12 ....**100** B1
Doran Gv *WOOL/PLUM* SE18 ....**127** E3
Dora Rd *WIM/MER* SW19 ....**150** A5
Dora St *POP/IOD* E14 ....**91** F5
Dorchester Ct *CRICK* NW2 ....**53** D5
  HNHL SE24 ....**136** C3
Dorchester Dr *HNHL* SE24 ....**136** C3
Dorchester Gv *CHSWK* W4 ....**111** E2
Dorchester Pde
  STRHM/NOR * SW16 ....**153** E2
Dordrecht Rd *ACT* W3 ....**99** E2

Dore Av MNPK E12 ....84 A2
Doreen Av CDALE/KGS NW9 ....51 D3
Doria Rd FUL/PGN SW6 ....113 F5
Doric Wy CAMTN NW1 ....8 A3
Doris Rd FSTGT E7 ....82 A4
Dorking Cl DEPT SE8 ....121 F2
Dorlcote Rd WAND/EARL SW18 ....133 E3
Dorman Wy STJWD NW8 ....73 D5
Dormay St WAND/EARL SW18 ....132 B3
Dormer Cl SRTFD E15 ....81 F3
Dornberg Cl BKHTH/KID SE3 ....124 A3
Dornberg Rd BKHTH/KID * SE3 ......124 B3
Dorncliffe Rd FUL/PGN SW6 ....113 E5
Dornfell St KIL/WHAMP NW6 ....71 F2
Dornton Rd BAL SW12 ....152 B2
Dorothy Rd BTSEA SW11 ....133 F1
Dorrington St HCIRC EC1N 22 A2
Dorrit St STHWK * SE1 ....35 F5
Dors Cl CDALE/KGS NW9 ....51 D3
Dorset Av WELL DA16 ....145 F2
Dorset Buildings EMB * EC4Y 22 C5
Dorset Cl CAMTN NW1 ....17 E2
Dorset Ms KTBR SW1X 42 C2
Dorset Pl SRTFD E15 ....81 D3
Dorset Ri EMB EC4Y 22 C5
Dorset Rd ELTH/MOT SE9 ....161 E2
    VX/NE SW8 ....117 F3
Dorset Sq CAMTN NW1 ....17 E1
Dorset St MHST W1U 17 F3
Dorton Cl PECK * SE15 ....119 E3
Dorville Crs HMSMTH W6 ....100 A5
Dorville Rd LEE/GVPK SE12 ....142 A3
Dothill Rd WOOL/PLUM SE18 ....126 C3
Doughty Ms BMSBY WC1N 21 E1
Doughty St BMSBY WC1N 9 E5
Douglas Est IS * N1 ....76 C3
Douglas Ms CRICK NW2 ....53 E5
Douglas Pl POP/IOD * E14 ....122 C1
Douglas Rd CAN/RD E16 ....94 A4
    IS N1 ....76 C4
    KIL/WHAMP NW6 ....71 F5
Douglas Rd North IS * N1 ....76 C3
Douglas Rd South IS * N1 ....76 C3
Douglas St WEST SW1P 44 A5
Douglas Wy NWCR SE14 ....121 F3
Doulton Ms HAMP NW3 ....72 B3
Dounesforth Gdns
    WAND/EARL SW18 ....150 B1
Douro Pl KENS W8 ....39 D2
Douro St BOW E3 ....92 A1
Douthwaite Sq WAP E1W 102 A2
Dove Ap EHAM E6 ....95 E4
Dove Ct LOTH * EC2R 24 A5
Dovedale Rd EDUL SE22 ....138 B3
Dovehouse Md BARK IG11 ....97 D1
Dovehouse St CHEL SW3 ....115 E1
Dove Ms ECT SW5 ....39 E5
Dover Cl CRICK NW2 ....53 D4
Dovercourt Est IS N1 ....77 D3
Dovercourt Rd DUL SE21 ....137 E4
Doverfield Rd BRXS/STRHM SW2 ....135 E4
Dover House Rd PUT/ROE SW15 ....130 A2
Dove Rd IS N1 ....77 D3
Dove Rw BETH E2 ....90 A1
Dover Park Dr PUT/ROE SW15 ....130 B4
Dover Patrol BKHTH/KID SE3 ....124 B5
Dover Rd MNPK E12 ....64 C5
    WOOL/PLUM SE18 ....126 B5
Dover St MYFR/PICC W1J 31 D2
Dover Ter RCH/KEW * TW9 ....110 A5
Doves Cl IS N1 ....76 A5
Doveton St WCHPL E1 ....90 C3
Dowanhill Rd CAT SE6 ....159 D3

Dowdeswell Cl PUT/ROE SW15 ....129 E2
Dowgate HI CANST EC4R 36 A1
Dowlas St CMBW SE5 ....119 E3
Downderry Rd BMLY BR1 ....159 D3
Downend WOOL/PLUM SE18 ....126 B3
Downer's Cottages CLAP SW4 ....134 C2
Downfield Cl MV/WKIL W9 ....14 C1
Downham Rd IS N1 ....77 D4
Downham Wy BMLY BR1 ....159 E5
Downings EHAM E6 ....96 A5
Downing St WHALL SW1A 32 C5
Downland Cl MV/WKIL W9 ....89 E1
Downleys Cl ELTH/MOT SE9 ....161 E2
Downman Rd ELTH/MOT SE9 ....143 E1
Down Pl HMSMTH W6 ....100 B5
Downs Av CHST BR7 ....161 F5
Downs Court Pde CLPT * E5 ....78 B2
Downsell Rd WAN E11 ....81 D1
Downsfield Rd WALTH E17 ....61 E1
Downshall Av GDMY/SEVK IG3 ....67 E1
Downshire HI HAMP NW3 ....73 D1
Downside Crs HAMP NW3 ....73 E2
Downs La CLPT E5 ....78 B1
Downs Park Rd HACK E8 ....78 A2
Downs Rd CLPT E5 ....78 A1
Down St MYFR/PICC W1J 30 C4
Down Street Ms MYFR/PICC W1J 30 C5
Downton Av BRXS/STRHM SW2 ......153 F2
Downtown Rd BERM/RHTH SE16 ....103 E3
Dowrey St IS N1 ....76 A5
Dowson Cl CMBW * SE5 ....137 D2
Doyce St STHWK * SE1 ....35 E5
Doyle Gdns WLSDN NW10 ....70 B5
D'Oyley St KTBR SW1X 42 A4
Doynton St KTTN * NW5 ....56 B4
Draco Ga PUT/ROE * SW15 ....130 C1
Draco St WALW SE17 ....118 C2
Dragonfly Cl PLSTW E13 ....94 B2
Dragon Rd PECK * SE15 ....119 E2
Dragoon Rd DEPT SE8 ....121 F1
Dragor Rd WLSDN NW10 ....86 C2
Drake Cl BERM/RHTH SE16 ....103 D3
Drakefell Rd NWCR SE14 ....121 D5
Drakefield Rd TOOT SW17 ....152 A3
Drake Rd BROCKY SE4 ....140 A1
Drakes Ctyd KIL/WHAMP NW6 ....71 F4
Drake St BMSBY WC1N 21 E3
Draper Est WALW SE17 ....47 D4
Draper Pl IS N1 ....76 B5
Drapers Rd SRTFD E15 ....80 C1
Drappers Wy BERM/RHTH SE16 ......102 A5
Drawell Cl WOOL/PLUM SE18 ....127 E1
Draycot Rd WAN E11 ....64 B1
Draycott Av CHEL SW3 ....41 D5
Draycott Cl CRICK NW2 ....53 D5
Draycott Pl CHEL SW3 ....41 E5
Draycott Ter CHEL SW3 ....41 E4
Drayford Cl MV/WKIL * W9 ....89 F3
Drayson Ms KENS W8 ....38 B1
Drayton Cl IL IG1 ....67 D3
Drayton Gdns WBPTN SW10 ....114 C1
Drayton Pk HBRY N5 ....58 A5
Drayton Park Ms HOLWY * N7 ....76 A2
Drayton Rd WAN E11 ....63 D3
    WLSDN NW10 ....69 F5
Dreadnought St GNWCH SE10 ....105 E4
Dresden Cl HAMP NW3 ....72 B3
Dresden Rd ARCH N19 ....56 C3
Dressington Av BROCKY SE4 ....140 A4
Drewery Ct BKHTH/KID * SE3 ....141 E1
Drew Rd CAN/RD E16 ....107 E2
Drews Cottages BAL * SW12 ....153 D2
Drewstead Rd STRHM/NOR SW16 ...153 D2

Driffield Rd BOW E3 ....91 E1
The Drive ACT W3 ....86 C5
  BARK IG11 ....85 F4
  GLDGN NW11 ....53 E2
  HOLWY N7 ....75 F3
  IL IG1 ....65 E1
  WBLY HA9 ....50 C4
Dr Johnson Av TOOT SW17 ....152 B3
Droitwich Cl SYD SE26 ....156 A3
Dromore Rd PUT/ROE SW15 ....131 E4
Droop St NKENS W10 ....89 E3
Drovers Pl PECK SE15 ....120 B3
Druce Rd DUL SE21 ....137 E4
Druid St STHWK SE1 ....37 E5
Drummond Crs CAMTN NW1 ....8 A3
Drummond Ga PIM SW1V 117 D1
Drummond Rd BERM/RHTH SE16 ....102 B4
  WAN E11 ....64 B1
Drummond St CAMTN NW1 ....7 E5
Drum St WCHPL E1 ....25 E2
Drury La HOL/ALD WC2B 21 D4
Drury Wy WLSDN NW10 ....69 D2
Dryad St PUT/ROE SW15 ....131 D1
Dryden Rd WIM/MER SW19 ....147 E5
Dryden Rd WOOL/PLUM SE18 ....127 F4
Dryden St COVGDN WC2E 21 D5
Dryfield Cl WLSDN NW10 ....68 C3
Drylands Rd CEND/HSY/T N8 ....57 E1
Drysdale Dwellings HACK * E8 ....77 F2
Drysdale Pl IS N1 ....13 D3
Drysdale St IS N1 ....13 D4
Dublin Av HACK E8 ....78 A5
Ducal St BETH E2 ....13 F4
Du Cane Cl SHB * W12 ....88 C5
Du Cane Rd SHB W12 ....88 B5
Duchess Ms CAVSO/HST W1G 19 D3
Duchess of Bedford's Wk
  KENS W8 ....101 F3
Duchess St REGST W1B 19 C3
Duchy St STHWK SE1 ....34 B3
Ducie St CLAP SW4 ....135 E2
Duckett Rd FSBYPK N4 ....58 B1
Duckett St WCHPL E1 ....91 D4
Duck La SOHO/CST W1F 20 A5
Du Cros Rd ACT W3 ....99 E2
Dudden Hill La WLSDN NW10 ....69 F1
Dudden Hill Pde WLSDN * NW10 ....69 F1
Duddington Cl ELTH/MOT SE9 ....161 D4
Dudley Rd IL IG1 ....84 B1
  KIL/WHAMP NW6 ....89 E1
Dudley St BAY/PAD * W2 ....16 A3
Dudlington Rd CLPT E5 ....60 C4
Dudmaston Ms CHEL SW3 ....115 D1
Dufferin Av STLK EC1Y 24 A1
Dufferin St STLK EC1Y 23 F1
Duff St POP/IOD E14 ....92 B5
Dufour's Pl SOHO/CST W1F 19 F5
Duke Humphrey Rd
  BKHTH/KID SE3 ....123 E4
Duke of Wellington Pl
  WHALL SW1A 42 B1
Duke of York St STJS SW1Y 31 F3
Duke Rd CHSWK W4 ....111 D1
Duke's Av CHSWK W4 ....111 D1
Dukes Ga CHSWK * W4 ....98 C5
Dukes La KENS W8 ....26 C5
Duke's Ms MHST W1U 18 B4
Duke's Pl HDTCH EC3A 25 E5
Dukes Rd ACT W3 ....86 A3
  CAMTN NW1 ....8 B4
  EHAM E6 ....84 A5
Dukesthorpe Rd SYD SE26 ....157 D4
Duke St MBLAR W1H 18 B4

Duke Street Hl STHWK SE1 ....36 B3
Duke Street St James's
  MYFR/PICC W1J 31 F3
Duke's Yd MYFR/PKLN W1K 30 B1
Dulas St FSBYPK N4 ....57 F3
Dulford St NTGHL W11 ....101 E1
Dulka Rd BTSEA SW11 ....133 F3
Dulverton Rd ELTH/MOT SE9 ....162 C2
Dulwich Common DUL SE21 ....155 D1
The Dulwich Oaks DUL * SE21 ....155 F3
Dulwich Rd HNHL SE24 ....136 A3
Dulwich Village DUL SE21 ....137 D4
Dulwich Wood Av NRWD SE19 ....155 E5
Dulwich Wood Pk NRWD SE19 ....155 E4
Dumbarton Rd
  BRXS/STRHM SW2 ....135 E4
Dumbreck Rd ELTH/MOT SE9 ....144 A2
Dumont Rd STNW/STAM N16 ....59 E5
Dumpton Pl CAMTN NW1 ....74 A4
Dunbar Rd FSTGT E7 ....82 A3
Dunbar St WNWD SE27 ....154 C3
Dunblane Rd ELTH/MOT SE9 ....143 E1
Dunboyne Rd HAMP NW3 ....73 F2
Dunbridge St BETH E2 ....90 A3
Duncan Gv ACT W3 ....87 E5
Duncannon St CHCR WC2N 32 C2
Duncan Rd HACK E8 ....78 B5
Duncan St IS N1 ....10 C1
Duncan Ter IS * N1 ....10 C2
Dunch St WCHPL * E1 ....90 B5
Duncombe Hl FSTH SE23 ....139 E5
Duncombe Rd ARCH N19 ....57 D3
Duncrievie Rd LEW SE13 ....141 D4
Duncroft WOOL/PLUM SE18 ....127 E3
Dundalk Rd BROCKY SE4 ....139 E1
Dundas Rd PECK SE15 ....120 C5
Dundee Rd PLSTW E13 ....94 B1
Dundee St WAP E1W 102 B2
Dundonald Cl EHAM E6 ....95 E5
Dundonald Rd WLSDN NW10 ....71 D5
Dunedin Rd IL IG1 ....66 C3
  LEY E10 ....62 B5
Dunelm Gv WNWD SE27 ....154 C4
Dunelm St WCHPL E1 ....91 D5
Dunfield Rd CAT SE6 ....158 B5
Dunford Rd HOLWY N7 ....75 F1
Dungarvan Av PUT/ROE SW15 ....130 A2
Dunkery Rd ELTH/MOT SE9 ....161 D4
Dunkirk St WNWD * SE27 ....154 C4
Dunlace Rd CLPT E5 ....78 C2
Dunloe St BETH E2 ....13 E2
Dunlop Pl BERM/RHTH SE16 ....49 F3
Dunmore Rd KIL/WHAMP NW6 ....71 F5
Dunmow Rd SRTFD E15 ....81 D1
Dunmow Wk IS * N1 ....76 C3
Dunnock Rd EHAM E6 ....95 E5
Dunn St HACK E8 ....77 F2
Dunollie Pl KTTN NW5 ....74 C2
Dunollie Rd KTTN NW5 ....74 C2
Dunoon Gdns FSTH * SE23 ....139 D5
Dunoon Rd FSTH SE23 ....138 C5
Dunraven Rd SHB W12 ....100 A2
Dunraven St MYFR/PKLN W1K 29 F1
Dunsany Rd HMSMTH W6 ....101 D4
Dunsmure Rd STNW/STAM N16 ....59 E3
Dunstable Ms CAVSO/HST W1G 18 B2
Dunstan Houses WCHPL * E1 ....90 C4
Dunstan Rd GLDGN NW11 ....53 F3
Dunstan's Gv EDUL SE22 ....138 B4
Dunstan's Rd EDUL SE22 ....138 A5
Dunster Ct FENCHST EC3M 36 C1
Dunster Dr CDALE/KGS NW9 ....50 C3
Dunster Gdns KIL/WHAMP NW6 ....71 F4

Dunsterville Wy STHWK SE1	48	B1
Dunston Rd BTSEA SW11	116	A5
HACK E8	77	F5
Dunston St HACK E8	77	F5
Dunton Rd LEY E10	62	B2
STHWK SE1	49	E5
Duntshill Rd WAND/EARL SW18	150	B1
Dunvegan Rd ELTH/MOT SE9	143	F2
Dunworth Ms NTGHL * W11	89	F5
Duplex Ride KTBR SW1X	41	F1
Dupont St POP/IOD E14	91	E5
Dupree Rd CHARL SE7	124	B1
Durand Gdns BRXN/ST SW9	117	F1
Durand Wy WLSDN NW10	68	C4
Durant St BETH E2	90	A1
Durban Gdns GNTH/NBYPK IG2	67	E3
SRTFD E15	93	E2
WNWD SE27	154	C4
Durford Crs PUT/ROE SW15	148	A1
Durham HI BMLY BR1	159	F4
Durham House St CHCR * WC2N	33	D2
Durham PI CHEL * SW3	115	F1
Durham Ri WOOL/PLUM SE18	126	C1
Durham Rd CAN/RD E16	93	E3
HOLWY N7	57	F4
MNPK E12	83	D1
Durham Rw WCHPL E1	91	D4
Durham St LBTH SE11	117	F1
Durham Ter BAY/PAD W2	14	C4
Durham Yd BETH * E2	90	B2
Durley Rd STNW/STAM N16	59	E2
Durlston Rd CLPT E5	60	A4
Durning Rd NRWD SE19	155	D5
Durnsford Av WAND/EARL SW18	150	A2
Durnsford Rd WAND/EARL SW18	150	A2
Durrell Rd FUL/PGN SW6	113	E4
Durrington Av CLPT E5	79	E1
Dursley Cl BKHTH/KID SE3	124	C5
Dursley Gdns BKHTH/KID SE3	125	D4
Dursley Rd BKHTH/KID SE3	124	C5
Durward St WCHPL E1	90	B4
Durweston Ms MHST * W1U	17	F2
Dutch Yd WAND/EARL SW18	132	A3
Duthie St POP/IOD E14	104	C1
Dutton St GNWCH SE10	122	C4
Dye House La BOW E3	80	A5
Dyer's Buildings FLST/FETLN EC4A	22	A3
Dyers Hall Rd WAN E11	63	E3
Dyer's La PUT/ROE SW15	130	B3
Dylways CMBW SE5	137	D2
Dymock St FUL/PGN SW6	132	B1
Dyneley Rd LEE/GVPK SE12	160	C4
Dyne Rd KIL/WHAMP NW6	71	F4
Dynevor Rd STNW/STAM N16	59	E5
Dynham Rd KIL/WHAMP NW6	72	A4
Dyott St NOXST/BSQ WC1A	20	C4
Dysart St SDTCH EC2A	24	B1
Dyson Rd FSTGT E7	81	F3
WAN E11	63	E1

E

Eade Rd FSBYPK N4	58	C2
Eagle Ct FARR EC1M	22	C2
Eagle Ms IS N1	77	E3
Eagle PI WBPTN SW10	114	C1
Eaglesfield Rd WOOL/PLUM SE18	126	B4
Eagle St GINN WC1R	21	E3
Eagle Wharf Rd IS N1	11	F1
Ealdham Sq ELTH/MOT SE9	142	C2
Eamont St STJWD NW8	4	C1

Eardley Crs ECT SW5	114	A1
Earldom Rd PUT/ROE SW15	130	C2
Earlham Gv FSTGT E7	81	F2
Earlham St LSQ/SEVD WC2H	20	B5
Earl Ri WOOL/PLUM SE18	127	D1
Earl Rd MORT/ESHN SW14	128	C2
Earls Court Gdns ECT SW5	38	C5
Earl's Court Rd KENS W8	38	A3
Earl's Court Sq ECT SW5	114	B1
Earlsferry Wy IS N1	75	E4
Earlsfield Rd WAND/EARL SW18	150	C1
Earlshall Rd ELTH/MOT SE9	143	F2
Earlsmead Rd WLSDN NW10	88	B2
Earls Ter KENS W8	101	F4
Earlsthorpe Ms BAL SW12	134	A4
Earlsthorpe Rd SYD SE26	157	D4
Earlstoke Est FSBYE EC1V	10	C3
Earlstoke St FSBYE EC1V	10	C3
Earlston Gv HOM E9	78	B5
Earl St SDTCH EC2A	24	C2
Earls Wk KENS W8	38	A3
Earlswood St GNWCH SE10	123	E1
Early Ms CAMTN NW1	74	B5
Earnshaw St NOXST/BSQ WC1A	20	B4
Earsby St WKENS W14	101	E5
East Acton Ar ACT * W3	87	F5
East Acton La ACT W3	99	D2
East Arbour St WCHPL E1	91	D5
East Av MNPK E12	83	E4
East Bank STNW/STAM N16	59	E2
Eastbourne Av ACT W3	87	D5
Eastbourne Gdns MORT/ESHN SW14	128	C1
Eastbourne Ms BAY/PAD W2	15	F4
Eastbourne Rd CHSWK W4	110	C2
EHAM E6	96	A2
SEVS/STOTM N15	59	E1
SRTFD E15	81	E5
Eastbourne Ter BAY/PAD W2	15	F4
Eastbrook Rd BKHTH/KID SE3	124	B4
Eastbury Av BARK IG11	85	E5
Eastbury Gv CHSWK W4	111	E1
Eastbury Rd EHAM E6	96	A3
Eastbury Sq BARK IG11	85	F5
Eastbury Ter WCHPL E1	91	D3
Eastcastle St GTPST W1W	19	E4
Eastcheap FENCHST EC3M	36	B1
East Churchfield Rd ACT W3	99	D2
East Cl EA W5	86	A3
Eastcombe Av CHARL SE7	124	C2
Eastcote Rd WELL DA16	127	D5
Eastcote St BRXN/ST SW9	117	F5
East Cross Route HOM E9	79	F3
Eastdown Pk LEW SE13	141	D2
East Dulwich Gv EDUL SE22	137	E3
East Dulwich Rd EDUL SE22	137	F2
Eastern Av WAN E11	64	C1
Eastern Rd BROCKY SE4	140	A2
PLSTW E13	94	B1
Easternville Gdns GNTH/NBYPK IG2	66	C1
East Ferry Rd POP/IOD E14	104	B4
Eastfields Rd ACT W3	86	C4
East Ham Manor Wy EHAM E6	96	A5
East Harding St FLST/FETLN EC4A	22	B4
East Heath Rd HAMP NW3	55	D5
East HI WAND/EARL SW18	132	C3
WBLY HA9	50	A4
East India Dock Rd POP/IOD E14	92	A3
Eastlake Rd CMBW SE5	118	B5
Eastlands Crs EDUL SE22	137	F4
East La BERM/RHTH SE16	102	A3
Eastlea Ms CAN/RD E16	93	E3

Eastleigh Cl *CRICK* NW2 ....51 E5
Eastman Rd *ACT* W3 ....99 D3
Eastmearn Rd *DUL* SE21 ....154 C2
Eastmoor Pl *WOOL/PLUM* SE18 ...107 D4
Eastmoor St *CHARL* SE7 ....107 D4
East Mount St *WCHPL* E1 ....90 B4
Eastnor Rd *ELTH/MOT* SE9 ....162 C1
Easton St *FSBYW* WC1X 10 A5
East Parkside *GNWCH* SE10 ....105 E3
East Pl *WNWD* SE27 ....154 C4
East Poultry Av *FARR* EC1M 22 C3
East Rd *IS* N1 ....12 A4
   SRTFD E15 ....82 A5
East Rochester Wy *BFN/LL* DA15 ...145 E3
East Rw *NKENS* W10 ....89 E3
   WAN E11 ....64 A1
East Sheen Av *MORT/ESHN* SW14 ...129 D3
East Side *SHB* * W12 ....100 C3
East Smithfield *WAP* E1W 37 F2
East St *BARK* IG11 ....84 C4
   WALW SE17 ....118 C1
East Surrey Gv *PECK* SE15 ....119 F3
East Tenter St *WCHPL* E1 ....25 F5
East Ter *BFN/LL* * DA15 ....163 E1
East V *ACT* * W3 ....99 F2
Eastview Av *WOOL/PLUM* SE18 ....107 E2
Eastway *HOM* E9 ....79 E5
Eaton Cl *BGVA* SW1W 42 A4
Eaton Dr *BRXN/ST* SW9 ....136 B2
Eaton Ga *BGVA* SW1W 42 A4
Eaton La *BGVA* SW1W 43 D3
Eaton Ms North *KTBR* SW1X 42 B3
Eaton Ms South *BGVA* SW1W 42 B4
Eaton Ms West *BGVA* SW1W 42 B4
Eaton Pl *BGVA* SW1X 42 A3
Eaton Rw *BGVA* SW1W 42 C2
Eaton Sq *BGVA* SW1W 42 B3
Eaton Ter *BGVA* SW1W 42 A4
   BOW * E3 ....91 E2
Eaton Terrace Ms *KTBR* SW1X 42 A4
Eatonville Rd *TOOT* SW17 ....151 F2
Eatonville Vls *TOOT* SW17 ....151 F2
Ebbisham Dr *VX/NE* SW8 ....117 F2
Ebbsfleet Rd *CRICK* NW2 ....71 E2
Ebdon Wy *BKHTH/KID* SE3 ....142 B1
Ebenezer St *IS* N1 ....12 A3
Ebley Cl *PECK* SE15 ....119 F2
Ebner St *WAND/EARL* SW18 ....132 B3
Ebor St *BETH* E2 ....13 E5
Ebsworth St *FSTH* SE23 ....139 D5
Eburne Rd *HOLWY* N7 ....57 E5
Ebury Bridge Rd *BGVA* SW1W 116 A1
Ebury Ms *BGVA* SW1W 42 B4
Ebury Ms East *BGVA* SW1W 42 C4
Ebury Sq *BGVA* SW1W 42 C5
Ebury St *BGVA* SW1W 42 B5
Ecclesbourne Rd *IS* N1 ....76 C4
Eccles Rd *BTSEA* SW11 ....133 F2
Eccleston Ms *KTBR* SW1X 42 B3
Eccleston Pl *BGVA* SW1W 42 C4
Eccleston Sq *PIM* SW1V 43 D5
Eccleston Square Ms *PIM* SW1V 43 D5
Eccleston St *BGVA* SW1W 42 B3
Eckford St *IS* N1 ....10 A1
Eckstein Rd *BTSEA* SW11 ....133 E2
Eclipse Rd *PLSTW* E13 ....94 B4
Ector Rd *CAT* SE6 ....159 E2
Edans Ct *SHB* W12 ....99 F3
Edbrooke Rd *MV/WKIL* W9 ....14 A5
Eddiscombe Rd *FUL/PGN* SW6 ....113 F5
Eddystone Rd *BROCKY* SE4 ....139 E3
Edenbridge Cl *BERM/RHTH* * SE16 ...120 B1

Edenbridge Rd *HOM* * E9 ....79 D4
Eden Cl *HAMP* NW3 ....54 A4
   KENS W8 ....38 B2
Eden Gv *HOLWY* N7 ....75 F2
Edenham Wy *NKENS* W10 ....89 F3
Edenhurst Av *FUL/PGN* SW6 ....131 F1
Eden Rd *WNWD* SE27 ....154 B5
Edensor Rd *CHSWK* W4 ....111 E3
Edenvale St *FUL/PGN* SW6 ....114 B5
Edgar Kail Wy *CMBW* SE5 ....137 E1
Edgarley Ter *FUL/PGN* * SW6 ....113 E4
Edgar Rd *BOW* E3 ....92 B2
Edgbury *CHST* BR7 ....162 B4
Edgecote Cl *ACT* W3 ....98 C2
Edgefield Av *BARK* IG11 ....85 F4
Edge Hl *WOOL/PLUM* SE18 ....126 B2
Edgehill Rd *CHST* BR7 ....162 C3
Edgeley La *CLAP* SW4 ....135 D1
Edgeley Rd *CLAP* SW4 ....135 D1
Edgel St *WAND/EARL* SW18 ....132 B2
Edgepoint Cl *WNWD* * SE27 ....154 B5
Edge St *KENS* W8 ....26 B3
Edgeworth Rd *ELTH/MOT* SE9 ....142 C2
Edgware Rd *BAY/PAD* W2 ....16 A1
   CDALE/KGS NW9 ....52 A3
Edinburgh Cl *BETH* E2 ....90 C1
Edinburgh Ga *BAY/PAD* W2 ....29 E5
Edinburgh Rd *PLSTW* E13 ....94 D1
Edison Gv *WOOL/PLUM* SE18 ....127 F3
Edison Rd *CEND/HSY/T* N8 ....57 D1
   WELL DA16 ....127 F4
Edis St *CAMTN* NW1 ....74 A5
Edith Gv *WBPTN* SW10 ....114 C2
Edithna St *BRXN/ST* SW9 ....135 E1
Edith Rd *EHAM* E6 ....83 D4
   SRTFD E15 ....81 D2
   WKENS W14 ....101 E5
Edith Rw *FUL/PGN* SW6 ....114 B4
Edith St *BETH* E2 ....13 F1
Edith Ter *WBPTN* * SW10 ....114 C3
Edith Vls *WKENS* W14 ....101 F5
Edmeston Cl *HOM* E9 ....79 E3
Edmund Halley Wy *GNWCH* SE10 ....105 E3
Edmund Hurst Dr *EHAM* E6 ....96 B4
Edmund St *CMBW* SE5 ....119 D3
Edna St *BTSEA* SW11 ....115 E4
Edric Rd *NWCR* SE14 ....121 D3
Edward Ct *CAN/RD* E16 ....94 A4
Edwardes Pl *WKENS* W14 ....101 F4
Edwardes Sq *KENS* W8 ....38 A3
Edward Mann Cl East *WCHPL* * E1 ....91 D5
Edward Mann Cl West *WCHPL* * E1 ....91 D5
Edward Ms *CAMTN* * NW1 ....7 D3
Edward Pl *DEPT* SE8 ....121 F2
Edward Rd *CHST* BR7 ....162 B5
Edward's Cottages *IS* * N1 ....76 B4
Edward's La *STNW/STAM* N16 ....59 D4
Edwards Ms *IS* N1 ....76 B4
   MBLAR W1H 18 A5
Edward Sq *IS* N1 ....75 F5
Edward St *CAN/RD* E16 ....94 A3
   NWCR SE14 ....121 E3
Edward Temme Av *SRTFD* E15 ....81 F4
Edward Tyler Rd *LEE/GVPK* SE12 ....160 B3
Edwin Av *EHAM* E6 ....96 A1
Edwin's Md *HOM* E9 ....79 E1
Edwin St *CAN/RD* E16 ....94 A4
   WCHPL E1 ....90 C3
Effie Pl *FUL/PGN* SW6 ....114 A3
Effie Rd *FUL/PGN* SW6 ....114 A3
Effingham Rd *LEW* SE13 ....141 E3
Effort St *TOOT* SW17 ....151 E5
Effra Pde *HNHL* SE24 ....136 A3

Effra Rd *BRXS/STRHM* SW2 ....135 F2
Egbert St *CAMTN* NW1 ....74 A5
Egerton Crs *CHEL* SW3 ....40 C4
Egerton Dr *GNWCH* SE10 ....122 B4
Egerton Gdns *CHEL* SW3 ....40 C3
  GDMY/SEVK IG3 ....67 F5
  WLSDN * NW10 ....70 C5
Egerton Gardens Ms *CHEL* SW3 ....41 D3
Egerton Pl *CHEL* * SW3 ....41 D3
Egerton Rd *STNW/STAM* * N16 ....59 F2
Egerton Ter *CHEL* SW3 ....41 D3
Egham Rd *PLSTW* E13...........................94 B4
Eglantine Rd *WAND/EARL* SW18 ......132 C3
Eglinton Hl *WOOL/PLUM* SE18..........126 B2
Eglinton Rd *WOOL/PLUM* SE18 ....126 A2
Egliston Ms *PUT/ROE* SW15 ....130 C1
Egliston Rd *PUT/ROE* SW15 ....130 C1
Eglon Ms *CAMTN* NW1 ....73 F4
Egmont St *NWCR* SE14 ....121 D3
Egremont Rd *WNWD* SE27 ....154 A3
Eider Cl *FSTGT* E7..............................81 F2
Eighth Av *MNPK* E12.............................83 F1
Eisenhower Dr *EHAM* E6 ....95 E4
Elaine Gv *KTTN* NW5 ....74 A2
Elam Cl *CMBW* SE5 ....118 B5
Elam St *CMBW* SE5 ....118 B5
Eland Rd *BTSEA* SW11.......................133 F1
Elba Pl *WALW* * SE17 ....47 F4
Elbe St *FUL/PGN* SW6 ....114 C5
Elborough St *WAND/EARL* SW18........150 A1
Elbury Dr *CAN/RD* E16 ....94 A5
Elcho St *BTSEA* SW11 ....115 E3
Elcot Av *PECK* SE15 ....120 B3
Elder Cl *BFN/LL* DA15 ....163 F1
Elderfield Rd *CLPT* E5 ....79 D1
Elderflower Wy *SRTFD* E15 ....81 E4
Elder Rd *WNWD* SE27 ....154 C5
Elderslie Rd *ELTH/MOT* SE9 ....144 A3
Elder St *WCHPL* E1 ....25 E2
Elderton Rd *SYD* SE26.......................157 E4
Elder Wk *IS* N1 ....76 B5
Eldon Gv *HAMP* NW3 ....73 D2
Eldon Rd *KENS* W8 ....39 D3
Eldon St *LVPST* EC2M 24 B3
Eldon Wy *WLSDN* NW10 ....86 B1
Eleanor Gv *BARN* SW13.....................129 E1
Eleanor Rd *HACK* E8 ....78 B3
  SRTFD E15 ....81 F3
Eleanor St *BOW* E3 ....92 A2
Electric Av *BRXN/ST* SW9 ....136 B1
Electric La *BRXN/ST* * SW9 ....136 A2
Elephant & Castle *STHWK* SE1 ....47 D4
Elephant La *BERM/RHTH* SE16 ....102 C3
Elephant Rd *WALW* SE17 ....47 E4
Elfindale Rd *HNHL* SE24 ....136 C3
Elford Cl *ELTH/MOT* SE9 ....142 C2
Elfort Rd *HBRY* N5 ....76 A1
Elf Rw *WAP* E1W 102 C1
Elgar Av *WLSDN* NW10 ....69 D3
Elgar Cl *DEPT* SE8 ....122 A3
  PLSTW E13...94 C1
Elgar St *BERM/RHTH* SE16 ....103 E3
Elgin Av *MV/WKIL* W9 ....14 A1
  SHB W12 ....100 A3
Elgin Crs *NTGHL* W11 ....101 E1
Elgin Est *MV/WKIL* W9 ....14 A1
Elginmeads South *MV/WKIL* W9 ....3 D1
Elgin Ms *NTGHL* W11 ....89 E5
Elgin Ms North *MV/WKIL* W9 ....3 D1
Elgin Rd *GDMY/SEVK* IG3 ....67 E3
Elgood Cl *NTGHL* W11 ....101 E1
Elia Ms *IS* N1 ....10 C1

Elias Pl *LBTH* SE11 ....118 A2
Elia St *IS* N1 ....10 C2
Elibank Rd *ELTH/MOT* SE9 ....144 A2
Elim St *STHWK* SE1 ....48 B2
Elim Wy *PLSTW* E13..............................93 F3
Eliot Bank *FSTH* SE23 ....156 B2
Eliot Gdns *PUT/ROE* SW15 ....130 A2
Eliot Hl *BKHTH/KID* SE3 ....122 C5
Eliot Pk *LEW* SE13 ....122 C5
Eliot Pl *BKHTH/KID* SE3 ....123 E5
Eliot V *BKHTH/KID* SE3 ....123 D5
Elizabeth Av *IL* IG1 ....67 D4
  IS N1..76 C4
Elizabeth Barnes Ct
  FUL/PGN SW6 ....114 B5
Elizabeth Br *BCVA* SW1W 42 C5
Elizabeth Cl *MV/WKIL* * W9 ....15 F1
Elizabeth Gdns *ACT* W3 ....99 F2
Elizabeth Ms *HAMP* NW3 ....73 E3
Elizabeth Rd *EHAM* E6 ....83 D5
Elizabeth Sq *BERM/RHTH* SE16 ....103 E1
Elizabeth St *BGVA* SW1W 42 B4
Elkington Rd *PLSTW* E13 ....94 B3
Elkstone Rd *NKENS* W10 ....89 F4
Ellaline Rd *HMSMTH* W6 ....113 D2
Ella Ms *HAMP* NW3 ....73 F1
Elland Rd *PECK* SE15 ....138 C2
Ella Rd *CEND/HSY/T* N8 ....57 E2
Ellenborough Pl *PUT/ROE* SW15 ......130 A2
Ellen St *WCHPL* E1 ....90 A5
Ellerby St *FUL/PGN* SW6 ....113 D4
Ellerdale Rd *HAMP* NW3 ....72 C2
Ellerdale St *LEW* SE13 ....140 B2
Ellerslie Rd *SHB* W12 ....100 B2
Ellerton Rd *BARN* * SW13 ....112 A4
  WAND/EARL SW18 ....151 D1
Ellery St *PECK* SE15 ....120 B5
Ellesmere Rd *BOW* E3 ....91 E1
  WLSDN NW10 ....70 B3
Ellesmere St *POP/IOD* E14 ....92 B5
Ellingfort Rd *HACK* E8 ....78 B4
Ellingham Rd *SHB* W12 ....100 A3
  WAN E11 ....81 D1
Ellington St *HOLWY* N7 ....76 A3
Elliot Cl *SRTFD* E15 ....81 E4
Elliot Rd *HDN* NW4 ....52 B1
Elliott Rd *BRXN/ST* SW9 ....118 B3
  CHSWK W4 ....99 E5
Elliott's Pl *IS* N1 ....76 B5
Elliott Sq *HAMP* NW3 ....73 E4
Elliott's Rw *LBTH* SE11 ....47 D4
Ellis Cl *CRICK* NW2 ....70 C3
  ELTH/MOT SE9 ....162 C2
Elliscombe Mt *CHARL* * SE7 ....124 C2
Elliscombe Rd *CHARL* SE7 ....124 C1
Ellisfield Dr *PUT/ROE* SW15 ....129 F5
Ellison Rd *BARN* SW13.......................111 F5
  BFN/LL DA15 ....163 D1
Ellis St *KTBR* SW1X 41 F4
Ellora Rd *STRHM/NOR* SW16 ....153 D5
Ellsworth St *BETH* * E2 ....90 B2
Elm Bank Gdns *BARN* SW13 ....111 E5
Elmbourne Rd *TOOT* SW17.................152 B3
Elmbridge Wk *HACK* * E8 ....78 A4
Elmbrook Gdns *ELTH/MOT* SE9 ....143 E2
Elm Cl *WAN* E11 ....64 B1
Elmcourt Rd *WNWD* SE27 ....154 B2
Elmcroft Av *BFN/LL* DA15 ....145 F5
  GLDGN NW11 ....53 F2
Elmcroft Crs *GLDGN* NW11................53 D2
Elmcroft St *CLPT* E5 ....78 C1
Elmdene Rd *WOOL/PLUM* SE18.........126 B1
Elmer Rd *CAT* SE6 ....140 C5

Elmfield Rd *TOOT* SW17 ....152 B2
   WALTH E17 ....61 D1
Elmfield Wy *MV/WKIL* W9 ....14 A2
Elm Friars Wk *HOLWY* N7 ....75 D4
Elm Gn *ACT* W3 ....87 E5
Elmgreen Cl *SRTFD* E15 ....81 E5
Elm Gv *CEND/HSY/T* N8 ....57 E1
   CRICK NW2 ....71 D1
   PECK SE15 ....120 A5
Elm Grove Rd *BARN* SW13 ....112 A4
Elm Hall Gdns *WAN* E11 ....64 B1
Elmhurst Rd *ELTH/MOT* SE9 ....161 E2
   FSTGT E7 ....82 B4
Elmhurst St *CLAP* SW4 ....135 D1
Elmington Est *CMBW* SE5 ....118 C3
Elmington Rd *CMBW* SE5 ....119 D4
Elmira St *LEW* SE13 ....140 B1
Elm La *CAT* SE6 ....157 F2
Elmley St *WOOL/PLUM* SE18 ....109 D5
Elmore Rd *LEY* E10 ....62 C5
Elmore St *IS* N1 ....77 D4
Elm Pk *BRXS/STRHM* SW2 ....135 F4
Elm Park Gdns *WBPTN* SW10 ....115 D1
Elm Park La *CHEL* SW3 ....115 D2
Elm Park Rd *CHEL* SW3 ....115 D2
   LEY E10 ....61 E1
Elm Pl *SKENS* SW7 ....115 D1
Elm Rd *FSTGT* E7 ....81 F3
   MORT/ESHN SW14 ....128 C1
   WAN E11 ....63 D4
Elm Rw *HAMP* NW3 ....54 C5
Elmscott Rd *BMLY* BR1 ....159 E5
Elms Crs *CLAP* SW4 ....134 C4
Elmshaw Rd *PUT/ROE* SW15 ....130 A3
Elmside Rd *WBLY* HA9 ....50 A5
Elms Ms *BAY/PAD* W2 ....28 A1
Elms Rd *CLAP* SW4 ....134 C3
Elmstead Av *CHST* BR7 ....161 F5
Elmstead Rd *GDMY/SEVK* IG3 ....67 E4
The Elms *BARN* SW13 ....129 F1
   TOOT SW17 ....152 A3
Elmstone Rd *FUL/PGN* SW6 ....114 A4
Elm St *FSBYW* WC1X 21 F1
Elm Ter *CRICK* NW2 ....54 A5
   ELTH/MOT SE9 ....144 A5
Elmton Wy *STNW/STAM* N16 ....60 A5
Elm Tree Cl *STJWD* NW8 ....4 A5
Elm Tree Ct *CHARL* * SE7 ....124 C2
Elm Tree Rd *STJWD* NW8 ....4 A5
Elm Wk *HAMP* NW3 ....54 A4
Elm Wy *WLSDN* NW10 ....69 E1
Elmwood Rd *CHSWK* W4 ....110 C2
   HNHL SE24 ....137 D3
Elmworth Gv *DUL* SE21 ....155 D2
Elnathan Ms *MV/WKIL* W9 ....15 D1
Elphinstone St *HBRY* N5 ....76 B1
Elrington Rd *HACK* E8 ....78 A3
Elsa Cottages *POP/IOD* * E14 ....91 E4
Elsa St *WCHPL* * E1 ....91 E4
Elsdale St *HOM* E9 ....78 C3
Elsden Rd *BETH* * E2 ....90 C1
Elsenham Rd *MNPK* E12 ....83 F2
Elsenham St *WIM/MER* SW19 ....149 F1
Elsham Rd *WAN* E11 ....63 E5
   WKENS W14 ....101 E3
Elsham Ter *WKENS* * W14 ....101 E3
Elsie Lane Ct *BAY/PAD* W2 ....14 B3
Elsiemaud Rd *BROCKY* SE4 ....139 F3
Elsie Rd *EDUL* SE22 ....137 F2
Elsinore Gdns *CRICK* * NW2 ....53 E5
Elsinore Rd *FSTH* SE23 ....157 E1
Elsinore Wy *RCH/KEW* TW9 ....128 C3
Elsley Rd *BTSEA* SW11 ....133 F1

Elspeth Rd *BTSEA* SW11 ....133 F2
Elsted St *WALW* SE17 ....48 B5
Elstow Cl *ELTH/MOT* SE9 ....143 F3
Elstree Gdns *IL* IG1 ....84 C2
Elswick Rd *LEW* SE13 ....140 B1
Elswick St *FUL/PGN* SW6 ....114 C5
Elsworthy Ri *HAMP* NW3 ....73 E4
Elsworthy Rd *HAMP* NW3 ....73 E5
Elsworthy Ter *HAMP* NW3 ....73 E4
Elsynge Rd *WAND/EARL* SW18 ....133 D3
Eltham Green Rd *ELTH/MOT* SE9 ....142 C3
Eltham High St *ELTH/MOT* SE9 ....143 F4
Eltham Hl *ELTH/MOT* SE9 ....143 D3
Eltham Palace Rd *ELTH/MOT* SE9 ....142 C4
Eltham Park Gdns *ELTH/MOT* SE9 ....144 A2
Eltham Rd *ELTH/MOT* SE9 ....142 C3
Elthiron Rd *FUL/PGN* SW6 ....114 A4
Elthorne Rd *ARCH* N19 ....57 D4
   CDALE/KCS NW9 ....51 D2
Elthorne Wy *CDALE/KCS* NW9 ....51 D1
Elthruda Rd *LEW* SE13 ....141 D4
Eltisley Rd *IL* IG1 ....84 B1
Elton Pl *STNW/STAM* N16 ....77 E2
Eltringham St *WAND/EARL* SW18 ....132 C2
Elvaston Ms *SKENS* SW7 ....39 F3
Elvaston Pl *SKENS* SW7 ....39 E3
Elveden Pl *WLSDN* NW10 ....86 A1
Elveden Rd *WLSDN* NW10 ....86 A1
Elver Gdns *BETH* E2 ....90 A2
Elverson Ms *DEPT* * SE8 ....121 F3
Elverson Rd *DEPT* SE8 ....122 B5
Elverton St *WEST* SW1P 44 A4
Elvino Rd *SYD* SE26 ....157 D5
Elvis Rd *CRICK* NW2 ....70 C3
Elwin St *BETH* E2 ....90 A2
Elwood St *HBRY* N5 ....58 B5
Elwyn Gdns *LEE/GVPK* SE12 ....142 A5
Ely Cottages *VX/NE* * SW8 ....117 F3
Elyne Rd *FSBYPK* N4 ....58 A1
Ely Pl *HCIRC* EC1N 22 B3
Ely Rd *LEY* E10 ....62 C1
Elysium Pl *FUL/PGN* SW6 ....113 F5
Elysium St *FUL/PGN* SW6 ....113 F5
Elystan Pl *CHEL* SW3 ....115 E1
Elystan St *CHEL* SW3 ....40 C5
Elystan Wk *IS* N1 ....76 A5
Emanuel Av *ACT* W3 ....86 A5
Embankment *PUT/ROE* SW15 ....131 D1
Embankment Gdns *CHEL* SW3 ....115 F2
Embankment Pl *CHCR* WC2N 33 D3
Emba St *BERM/RHTH* SE16 ....102 A3
Embleton Rd *LEW* SE13 ....140 B2
Emden St *FUL/PGN* SW6 ....114 B4
Emerald Cl *CAN/RD* E16 ....95 E5
Emerald St *BMSBY* WC1N 21 E2
Emerson Rd *STHWK* SE1 ....35 E2
Emerson St *STHWK* SE1 ....46 B2
Emery Hill St *WEST* SW1P 43 F3
Emery St *STHWK* SE1 ....46 B2
Emily Pl *HOLWY* N7 ....76 A1
Emily St *CAN/RD* E16 ....93 F5
Emlyn Rd *SHB* W12 ....99 E3
Emmanuel Rd *BAL* SW12 ....152 C1
Emma Rd *PLSTW* E13 ....93 F2
Emma St *BETH* E2 ....90 B1
Emmott Cl *EFNCH* N2 ....54 C1
   WCHPL E1 ....91 E3
Emperor's Ga *SKENS* SW7 ....39 E4
Empire Pde *WBLY* * HA9 ....50 A5
Empire Way *WBLY* HA9 ....68 A3
Empire Wharf Rd *POP/IOD* E14 ....105 D5
Empress Av *IL* IG1 ....65 F4
   MNPK E12 ....64 C4
Empress Pl *ECT* SW5 ....114 A1

Empress St *WALW* SE17 ....118 C2
Empson St *BOW* E3 ....92 B3
Emsworth St *BRXS/STRHM* SW2 ....153 F2
Emu Rd *VX/NE* SW8 ....116 B5
Enbrook St *NKENS* W10 ....89 E2
Enclave St *FSBYE* EC1V 11 D5
Endeavour Wy *WIM/MER* SW19 ....150 B4
Endell St *LSQ/SEVD* WC2H 20 C4
Enderby St *GNWCH* SE10 ....123 E1
Endlesham Rd *BAL* SW12 ....134 A5
Endsleigh Gdns *IL* IG1 ....65 F3
　STPAN WC1H 8 A5
Endsleigh Pl *STPAN* WC1H 8 B5
Endsleigh St *STPAN* WC1H 8 B5
Endwell Rd *BROCKY* SE4 ....121 D5
Endymion Rd *BRXS/STRHM* SW2 ....135 F5
　FSBYPK N4 ....58 A2
Energen Cl *WLSDN* NW10 ....69 E3
Enfield Rd *ACT* W3 ....98 B3
　IS N1 ....77 E4
Enford St *MBLAR* W1H 17 E2
Engadine St *WAND/EARL* SW18 .....149 F1
Engate St *LEW* SE13 ....140 C2
Engineer Cl *WOOL/PLUM* SE18 .....126 A2
Engineers Wy *WBLY* HA9 ....68 A1
England's La *HAMP* NW3 ....73 F4
Englefield Rd *IS* N1 ....77 D4
Engleheart Rd *CAT* SE6 ....140 B5
Englewood Rd *CLAP* SW4 ....134 B4
English St *BOW* E3 ....91 F3
Enid St *STHWK* SE1 ....49 F2
Enmore Gdns *MORT/ESHN* SW14 ...129 D3
Enmore Rd *PUT/ROE* SW15 ....130 C2
Ennersdale Rd *LEW* SE13 ....141 D3
Ennismore Av *CHSWK* W4 ....99 F5
Ennismore Gdns *SKENS* SW7 ....40 B2
Ennismore Gardens Ms *SKENS* SW7 ..40 B2
Ennismore Ms *SKENS* SW7 ....40 C1
Ennismore St *SKENS* SW7 ....40 C2
Ennis Rd *FSBYPK* N4 ....58 A3
　WOOL/PLUM SE18 ....127 D2
Ensign St *WCHPL* E1 ....102 A1
Enslin Rd *ELTH/MOT* SE9 ....144 A4
Ensor Ms *SKENS* SW7 ....115 D1
Enterprise Wy *WAND/EARL* SW18 ..132 A2
　WLSDN NW10 ....87 F2
Enterprize Wy *DEPT* SE8 ....103 F5
Epcot Ms *WLSDN* NW10 ....89 D2
Epirus Ms *FUL/PGN* SW6 ....114 A3
Epirus Rd *FUL/PGN* SW6 ....113 F3
Epping Cl *POP/IOD* E14 ....104 A5
Epping Pl *HOLWY* N7 ....76 A3
Epple Rd *FUL/PGN* SW6 ....113 F4
Epsom Rd *GDMY/SEVK* IG3 ....67 F1
　LEY E10 ....62 C1
Epworth St *SDTCH* EC2A 24 B1
Equity Sq *BETH* E2 ....13 F4
Erasmus St *WEST* SW1P 44 B5
Erconwald St *ACT* W3 ....87 F5
Eresby Pl *KIL/WHAMP* NW6 ....72 A4
Erica St *SHB* W12 ....100 A1
Eric Clarke La *BARK* IG11 ....96 B3
Ericcson Cl *WAND/EARL* SW18 ......132 A3
Eric Est *BOW* E3 ....91 F3
Eric Rd *FSTGT* E7 ....82 A1
　WLSDN NW10 ....69 E3
Eric St *BOW* E3 ....91 F3
Eridge Rd *CHSWK* W4 ....99 D4
Erindale *WOOL/PLUM* SE18 ....127 D2
Erindale Ter *WOOL/PLUM* SE18 .....127 D2
Erlanger Rd *NWCR* SE14 ....121 D4
Erlich Cottages *WCHPL* E1 ....90 C4
Ermine Rd *LEW* SE13 ....140 B2

SEVS/STOTM* N15 ....59 F1
Ermington Rd *ELTH/MOT* SE9 ....162 C2
Ernald Av *EHAM* E6 ....95 E1
Ernest Av *WNWD* SE27 ....154 B4
Ernest Gdns *CHSWK* W4 ....110 B2
Ernest St *WCHPL* E1 ....91 D3
Ernshaw Pl *PUT/ROE* SW15 ....131 E3
Erpingham Rd *PUT/ROE* SW15 ......130 C1
Errington Rd *MV/WKIL* W9 ....89 F3
Errol St *STLK* EC1Y 23 F1
Erskine Ms *HAMP* * NW3 ....73 F4
Erskine Rd *HAMP* NW3 ....73 F4
Erwood Rd *CHARL* SE7 ....125 E1
Esam Wy *STRHM/NOR* SW16 ....154 A5
Escreet Gv *WOOL/PLUM* SE18 ....108 A5
Esher Rd *GDMY/SEVK* IG3 ....67 E5
Esk Rd *PLSTW* E13 ....94 B3
Esmar Crs *CDALE/KGS* NW9 ....52 A2
Esmeralda Rd *STHWK* SE1 ....102 A5
Esmond Gdns *CHSWK* * W4 ....99 D5
Esmond Rd *CHSWK* W4 ....99 D4
　KIL/WHAMP NW6 ....71 F5
Esmond St *PUT/ROE* SW15 ....131 E2
Esparto St *WAND/EARL* SW18 ....132 B5
Essendine Rd *MV/WKIL* W9 ....2 B5
Essex Ct *BARN* SW13 ....111 F5
　TPL/STR * WC2R 22 A5
Essex Gdns *FSBYPK* N4 ....58 B1
Essex Park Ms *ACT* W3 ....99 E2
Essex Pl *CHSWK* W4 ....98 C5
Essex Place Sq *CHSWK* * W4 ....99 D5
Essex Rd *ACT* W3 ....98 C1
　BARK IG11 ....85 D4
　CHSWK W4 ....99 D5
　IS N1 ....76 B5
　LEY E10 ....62 C1
　WALTH E17 ....61 E1
　WLSDN NW10 ....69 E4
Essex Rd South *WAN* E11 ....63 D2
Essex St *FSTGT* E7 ....82 A2
　TPL/STR WC2R 22 A5
　WOOL/PLUM SE18 ....108 C5
Essex Vls *KENS* W8 ....38 A1
Essex Whf *CLPT* * E5 ....61 D4
Essian St *WCHPL* E1 ....91 E4
Estate Wy *LEY* E10 ....61 F3
Estcourt Rd *FUL/PGN* SW6 ....113 F3
Estelle Rd *HAMP* NW3 ....73 F1
Esterbrooke St *WEST* SW1P 44 A5
Este Rd *BTSEA* SW11 ....133 E1
Esther Rd *WAN* E11 ....63 E2
Estoria Cl *BRXS/STRHM* SW2 ....136 A5
Eswyn Rd *TOOT* SW17 ....151 F4
Etchingham Rd *SRTFD* E15 ....80 C1
Ethelbert St *BAL* SW12 ....152 B1
Ethelburga St *BTSEA* * SW11 ....115 E4
Ethelden Rd *SHB* W12 ....100 B2
Ethelred Est *LBTH* SE11 ....46 A5
Ethel Rd *CAN/RD* E16 ....106 D1
Ethel St *WALW* * SE17 ....47 F5
Etheridge Rd *CRICK* NW2 ....52 C2
Etherow St *EDUL* SE22 ....138 A4
Etherstone Rd *STRHM/NOR* SW16 ..153 F4
Ethnard Rd *PECK* SE15 ....120 B2
Etloe Rd *LEY* E10 ....62 A4
Eton Av *HAMP* NW3 ....73 E4
Eton Cl *WAND/EARL* SW18 ....132 B5
Eton College Rd *HAMP* NW3 ....73 F3
Eton Garages *HAMP* NW3 ....73 E3
Eton Gv *LEW* SE13 ....141 E1
Eton Pl *HAMP* * NW3 ....74 A4
Eton Ri *HAMP* * NW3 ....73 F3
Eton Rd *HAMP* NW3 ....73 F4

Eton Vls *HAMP* NW3 ....73 F3
Etta St *DEPT* SE8 ....121 E2
Ettrick St *POP/IOD* E14 ....92 C5
Eugenia Rd *BERM/RHTH* SE16 ....120 C1
Europa Pl *FSBYE* EC1V 11 E4
Europe Rd *WOOL/PLUM* SE18 ....107 F4
Eustace Pl *WOOL/PLUM* SE18 ....107 F5
Eustace Rd *EHAM* E6 ....95 E2
  FUL/PGN SW6 ....114 A3
Euston Rd *CAMTN* NW1 ....7 E5
Euston Sq *CAMTN* NW1 ....8 A4
Euston St *CAMTN* NW1 ....7 F5
Evandale Rd *BRXN/ST* SW9 ....118 A5
Evangelist Rd *KTTN* NW5 ....74 B1
Evans Cl *HACK* E8 ....77 F3
Evans Rd *CAT* SE6 ....159 E2
Evanston Gdns *REDBR* IG4 ....65 E1
Evelina Rd *PECK* SE15 ....138 C1
Eveline Lowe Est
  BERM/RHTH SE16 ....102 A4
Evelyn Denington Rd *EHAM* E6 ....95 E3
Evelyn Est *DEPT* SE8 ....121 E2
Evelyn Gdns *WBPTN* SW10 ....114 C1
Evelyn Rd *CAN/RD* E16 ....106 A2
  CHSWK W4 ....99 D4
  WIM/MER SW19 ....150 B5
Evelyn St *DEPT* SE8 ....121 F2
Evelyn Wk *IS* N1 ....12 A1
Evenwood Cl *PUT/ROE* SW15 ....131 E3
Everatt Cl *WAND/EARL* SW18 ....131 H4
Everdon Rd *BARN* SW13 ....112 A2
Everest Pl *POP/IOD* E14 ....92 C4
Everest Rd *ELTH/MOT* SE9 ....143 E3
Evergreen Sq *HACK* E8 ....77 E4
Everilda St *IS* N1 ....75 F5
Evering Rd *STNW/STAM* N16 ....59 F5
Everington St *HMSMTH* W6 ....113 D2
Everitt Rd *WLSDN* NW10 ....87 D2
Everleigh St *FSBYPK* N4 ....57 F3
Eve Rd *SRTFD* E15 ....81 E1
  SRTFD E15 ....93 E1
Eversholt St *CAMTN* NW1 ....7 E1
Evershot Rd *FSBYPK* N4 ....57 E1
Eversleigh Rd *BTSEA* SW11 ....133 F1
  EHAM E6 ....83 D5
Eversley Av *WBLY* HA9 ....50 A4
Eversley Pk *WIM/MER* SW19 ....148 B5
Eversley Rd *CHARL* SE7 ....124 B2
Everthorpe Rd *PECK* SE15 ....137 F1
Everton Buildings *CAMTN* NW1 ....7 E4
Evesham Rd *SRTFD* E15 ....81 F4
Evesham St *NTGHL* W11 ....101 D1
Evesham Wk *BRXN/ST* SW9 ....118 A5
Evesham Wy *BTSEA* SW11 ....134 A1
Ewald Rd *FUL/PGN* SW6 ....113 F5
Ewart Pl *BOW* E3 ....91 F1
Ewart Rd *FSTH* SE23 ....139 D5
Ewe Cl *HOLWY* N7 ....75 E3
Ewelme Rd *FSTH* SE23 ....156 C1
Ewen Crs *BRXS/STRHM* SW2 ....136 A5
Ewer St *STHWK* SE1 ....35 E4
Ewhurst Cl *WCHPL* E1 ....90 C5
Ewhurst Rd *BROCKY* SE4 ....139 F4
Exbury Rd *CAT* SE6 ....158 A2
Excel Ct *LSQ/SEVD* WC2H 32 B2
Exchange Ar *LVPST* EC2M 24 C3
Exchange Ct *COVGDN* WC2E 33 D2
Exchange Sq *SDTCH* EC2A 25 D2
Exeter Cl *EHAM* E6 ....95 F5
Exeter Gdns *IL* IG1 ....65 F3
Exeter Ms *FUL/PGN* SW6 ....114 A4
Exeter Pde *CRICK* NW2 ....71 E3
Exeter Rd *CAN/RD* E16 ....94 A4

CRICK NW2 ....71 E2
  WELL DA16 ....127 F5
Exeter St *COVGDN* WC2E 33 D1
Exeter Wy *NWCR* SE14 ....121 F1
Exford Gdns *LEE/GVPK* SE12 ....160 B1
Exford Rd *LEE/GVPK* SE12 ....160 B2
Exhibition Rd *SKENS* SW7 ....40 B1
Exmoor St *NKENS* W10 ....89 D3
Exmouth Market *CLKNW* EC1R 10 A5
Exmouth Ms *CAMTN* NW1 ....7 F4
Exmouth Pl *HACK* E8 ....78 B5
Exmouth St *WCHPL* E1 ....90 C5
Exning Rd *CAN/RD* E16 ....93 F3
Exon St *WALW* SE17 ....48 C5
Exton Crs *WLSDN* NW10 ....68 C4
Exton St *STHWK* SE1 ....34 A4
Eyhurst Cl *CRICK* NW2 ....52 A4
Eylewood Rd *WNWD* SE27 ....154 C5
Eynella Rd *DUL* SE21 ....137 F5
Eynham Rd *SHB* W12 ....88 C5
Eynsford Rd *GDMY/SEVK* IG3 ....67 E4
Eyot Gdns *HMSMTH* W6 ....111 F1
Eyre Street HI *CLKNW* EC1R 22 A1
Eythorne Rd *BRXN/ST* SW9 ....118 A4
Ezra St *BETH* E2 ....13 F3

F

Fabian Rd *FUL/PGN* SW6 ....113 F3
Fabian St *EHAM* E6 ....95 F3
The Facade *FSTH* SE23 ....156 C2
Factory Pl *POP/IOD* E14 ....122 C1
Factory Rd *CAN/RD* E16 ....107 D2
Fairbank St *IS* N1 ....12 A2
Fairbridge Rd *ARCH* N19 ....57 D4
Fairby Rd *LEE/GVPK* SE12 ....142 B3
Fairchild Cl *BTSEA* SW11 ....115 D5
Fairchild Pl *SDTCH* EC2A 25 D1
Fairchild St *SDTCH* EC2A 25 D1
Fairclough St *WCHPL* E1 ....90 A5
Faircross Av *BARK* IG11 ....84 C3
Fairdale Gdns *PUT/ROE* SW15 ....130 B2
Fairfax Gdns *BKHTH/KID* SE3 ....124 C4
Fairfax Ms *PUT/ROE* SW15 ....130 C2
Fairfax Pl *KIL/WHAMP* NW6 ....72 C4
Fairfax Rd *CHSWK* W4 ....99 E4
  KIL/WHAMP NW6 ....72 C4
Fairfield Av *HDN* NW4 ....52 B1
Fairfield Cl *BFN/LL* DA15 ....145 F4
Fairfield Dr *WAND/EARL* SW18 ....132 B3
Fairfield Gv *CHARL* SE7 ....125 D2
Fairfield Rd *BOW* E3 ....92 A1
  IL IG1 ....84 B3
Fairfield St *WAND/EARL* SW18 ....132 B3
Fairfoot Rd *BOW* E3 ....92 A3
Fairhazel Gdns *KIL/WHAMP* NW6 ....72 B3
Fairholme Rd *IL* IG1 ....65 F2
  WKENS W14 ....113 E1
Fairholt Rd *STNW/STAM* N16 ....59 D3
Fairholt St *SKENS* SW7 ....41 D2
Fairland Rd *SRTFD* E15 ....81 F3
Fairlawn *CHARL* SE7 ....124 C3
Fairlawn Av *CHSWK* W4 ....98 C5
Fairlawn Cl *CHARL* SE7 ....124 C3
Fairlawn Gv *CHSWK* W4 ....98 C5
Fairlawn Pk *SYD* SE26 ....157 E5
Fairlie Gdns *FSTH* SE23 ....138 C5
Fairlight Av *WLSDN* NW10 ....87 E1
Fairlight Rd *TOOT* SW17 ....151 D4
Fairlop Rd *WAN* E11 ....63 D2
Fairmead Rd *HOLWY* N7 ....57 E5

Fairmile Av STRHM/NOR SW16 ....153 D5
Fairmount Rd BRXS/STRHM SW2 ......135 F4
Fairoak Dr ELTH/MOT SE9 ....145 D3
Fairstead Wk IS * N1 ....76 C5
Fair St STHWK SE1 ....37 D5
Fairthorn Rd CHARL SE7 ....124 A1
Fairview CI SYD * SE26 ....157 E4
Fairview PI BRXS/STRHM SW2 ....135 F5
Fairview Rd SEVS/STOTM N15 ....59 F4
Fairway CI GLDGN NW11 ....54 C2
Fairway Gdns IL IG1 ....84 C3
The Fairway ACT W3 ....87 E5
Fairweather Rd STNW/STAM N16........60 A1
Fairwyn Rd SYD SE26 ....157 E3
Fakruddin St WCHPL E1 ....90 A3
Falaize Av IL IG1 ....84 B1
Falconberg Ct SOHO/SHAV * W1D 20 A4
Falcon CI CHSWK W4 ....110 B2
                STHWK SE1 ....35 D3
Falcon Ct IS N1 ....11 D2
Falcon La BTSEA SW11 ....133 E1
Falcon Rd BTSEA SW11 ....133 E1
Falcon St PLSTW E13 ....94 B3
Falcon Ter BTSEA * SW11 ....133 E1
Falconwood Av WELL DA16 ....127 D5
Falconwood Pde WELL DA16 ....145 E2
Falkirk St IS N1 ....13 D3
Falkland PI KTTN NW5 ....74 C2
Falkland Rd KTTN NW5 ....74 C2
Fallow Ct STHWK * SE1 ....120 A1
Falmouth CI LEE/GVPK SE12 ....141 E3
Falmouth Rd STHWK SE1 ....47 E3
Falmouth St SRTFD E15 ....81 D2
Fambridge CI SYD SE26 ....157 F4
Fane St WKENS W14 ....113 F2
Fann St FARR EC1M 23 E1
Fanshawe Av BARK IG11 ....84 C3
Fanshaw St IS N1 ....12 C3
Fanthorpe St PUT/ROE SW15 ....130 C1
Faraday CI HOLWY N7 ....75 F3
Faraday Rd ACT W3 ....98 C1
                NKENS W10 ....89 E4
                SRTFD E15 ....81 F3
Faraday Wy WOOL/PLUM SE18 ....107 D4
Fareham St SOHO/CST * W1F 20 A4
Faringford Rd SRTFD E15 ....81 E4
Farjeon Rd BKHTH/KID SE3 ....125 D4
Farleigh PI STNW/STAM N16 ....77 F1
Farleigh Rd STNW/STAM N16 ....77 F1
Farley Dr GDMY/SEVK IG3 ....67 E3
Farley Rd CAT SE6 ....140 C5
Farlington PI PUT/ROE SW15 ....130 B5
Farlow Rd PUT/ROE SW15 ....131 D1
Farlton Rd WAND/EARL SW18 ....132 B5
Farm Av CRICK NW2 ....53 E5
                STRHM/NOR SW16 ....153 E4
Farm CI FUL/PGN * SW6 ....114 A3
Farmcote Rd LEE/GVPK SE12 ....160 A1
Farmdale Rd GNWCH SE10 ....124 A1
Farmer Rd LEY E10 ....62 B3
Farmers Rd CMBW SE5 ....118 B3
Farmer St KENS W8 ....26 A3
Farmfield Rd BMLY BR1 ....159 E5
Farmilo Rd WALTH E17 ....62 A2
Farmland Wk CHST BR7 ....162 B5
Farm La FUL/PGN SW6 ....114 A2
Farm PI KENS W8 ....26 A3
Farm Rd WLSDN NW10 ....69 D5
Farmstead Rd CAT SE6 ....158 B4
Farm St MYFR/PICC W1J 30 C2
The Farm WIM/MER * SW19 ....131 D5
Farnaby Rd ELTH/MOT SE9 ....142 C2

Farnan Rd STRHM/NOR SW16 ....153 E5
Farnborough CI WBLY HA9 ....50 B4
Farnborough Wy PECK * SE15 ....119 E3
Farncombe St BERM/RHTH SE16 ....102 A3
Farnell Ms ECT SW5 ....114 B1
Farnham PI STHWK SE1 ....35 D4
Farnham Rd GDMY/SEVK IG3 ....67 F1
Farnham Royal LBTH SE11 ....117 E1
Faroe Rd WKENS W14 ....101 D4
Farquhar Rd NRWD SE19 ....155 F5
                WIM/MER SW19 ....150 A3
Farrance St POP/IOD E14 ....92 A5
Farren Rd FSTH SE23 ....157 E2
Farrier St CAMTN NW1 ....74 B4
Farrier Wk WBPTN * SW10 ....114 C2
Farringdon La CLKNW EC1R 22 B1
Farringdon Rd FARR EC1M 22 C3
                FSBYW WC1X 10 A5
Farringdon St FLST/FETLN EC4A 22 C4
Farrins Rents BERM/RHTH SE16 ....103 E2
Farrow La PECK SE15 ....120 C3
Farrow PI BERM/RHTH SE16 ....103 E4
Farthing Aly STHWK * SE1 ....102 A3
Farthing Flds WAP E1W 102 B2
Fashion St WCHPL E1 ....25 E3
Fassett Rd HACK E8 ....78 A3
Fassett Sq HACK E8 ....78 A3
Fauconberg Rd CHSWK W4 ....110 C2
Faulkner St NWCR SE14 ....120 C4
Faunce St WALW SE17 ....118 B2
Favart Rd FUL/PGN SW6 ....114 A4
Faversham Rd CAT SE6 ....139 F5
Fawcett CI BTSEA SW11 ....115 D5
                STRHM/NOR SW16 ....154 A4
Fawcett Est CLPT * E5 ....60 A3
Fawcett Rd WLSDN NW10 ....69 F4
Fawcett St WBPTN SW10 ....114 C2
Fawe Park Rd PUT/ROE SW15 ....131 F2
Fawe St POP/IOD E14 ....92 B4
Fawley Rd KIL/WHAMP NW6 ....72 B2
Fawnbrake Av HNHL SE24 ....136 B3
Fawn Rd PLSTW E13 ....94 C1
Fawood Av WLSDN NW10 ....69 D4
Faygate Rd BRXS/STRHM SW2 ....153 F2
Fayland Av STRHM/NOR SW16 ....152 C5
Fearon St GNWCH SE10 ....124 A1
Feathers PI GNWCH SE10 ....123 D2
Featherstone Av FSTH SE23 ....156 B2
Featherstone St STLK EC1Y 12 A5
Featley Rd BRXN/ST SW9 ....136 B1
Felbridge CI STRHM/NOR SW16 ....154 A4
Felday Rd LEW SE13 ....140 B4
Felden St FUL/PGN SW6 ....113 F4
Feldman CI STNW/STAM N16 ....60 A3
Felgate Ms HMSMTH W6 ....100 B5
Felhampton Rd ELTH/MOT SE9 ....162 B3
Felix Av CEND/HSY/T N8 ....57 E1
Felixstowe Rd WLSDN * NW10 ....88 B2
Felix St BETH * E2 ....90 B1
Fellbrigg Rd EDUL SE22 ....137 E3
Fellbrigg St WCHPL E1 ....90 B3
Fellows Rd HAMP NW3 ....73 D4
Feltram Wy CHARL SE7 ....124 A1
Felmersham CI CLAP SW4 ....135 E2
Felsberg Rd BRXS/STRHM SW2 ....135 E4
Felsham Rd PUT/ROE SW15 ....130 C1
Felspar CI WOOL/PLUM SE18 ....127 F1
Felstead Rd HOM E9 ....80 A3
                WAN E11 ....64 A2
Felstead St HOM E9 ....79 F3
Felsted Rd CAN/RD E16 ....95 D3
Felton Lea SCUP DA14 ....163 F5

Felton Rd *BARK* IG11 ....**97** E1
Felton St *IS* N1 ....**77** D5
Fenchurch Av *FENCHST* EC3M **24** C5
Fenchurch Buildings
  FENCHST EC3M **25** D5
Fenchurch Pl *FENCHST* * EC3M **37** D1
Fenchurch St *FENCHST* EC3M **36** C1
Fendall St *STHWK* SE1 ....**49** D3
Fendt Cl *CAN/RD* E16 ....**93** F5
Fenelon Pl *WKENS* W14 ....**101** F5
Fen Gv *BFN/LL* DA15 ....**145** F4
Fenham Rd *PECK* SE15 ....**120** A3
Fennel Cl *CAN/RD* E16 ....**93** E3
Fennell St *WOOL/PLUM* SE18 ....**126** A2
Fenner Cl *BERM/RHTH* SE16 ....**102** B5
Fenner Sq *BTSEA* * SW11 ....**133** D1
Fenning St *STHWK* SE1 ....**36** C5
Fenn St *HOM* E9 ....**79** D2
Fen St *CAN/RD* E16 ....**105** F1
Fentiman Rd *VX/NE* SW8 ....**117** E2
Fenton Cl *BRXN/ST* * SW9 ....**117** F5
  CHST BR7 ....**161** F5
  HACK E8 ....**77** F3
Fenton's Av *PLSTW* E13 ....**94** B2
Fenwick Gv *PECK* SE15 ....**138** A1
Fenwick Pl *BRXN/ST* SW9 ....**135** E1
Fenwick Rd *PECK* SE15 ....**138** A1
Ferdinand Pl *CAMTN* NW1 ....**74** A4
Ferdinand St *CAMTN* NW1 ....**74** A4
Ferguson Dr *ACT* W3 ....**87** D5
Ferguson's Cl *POP/IOD* E14 ....**104** A5
Fergus Rd *HBRY* N5 ....**76** B2
Fermor Rd *FSTH* SE23 ....**157** E1
Fermoy Rd *MV/WKIL* W9 ....**89** F3
Fernbank Ms *CLAP* SW4 ....**134** B4
Fernbrook Rd *LEW* SE13 ....**141** E4
Ferncliff Rd *HACK* E8 ....**78** A3
Fern Cl * N1 ....**12** C1
Ferncroft Av *HAMP* NW3 ....**54** A5
Ferndale Rd *CLAP* SW4 ....**135** E2
  FSTGT E7 ....**82** B4
  SEVS/STOTM N15 ....**59** F1
  WAN E11 ....**63** F4
Ferndale St *EHAM* E6 ....**108** B1
Ferndene Rd *HNHL* SE24 ....**136** C2
Ferndown Rd *ELTH/MOT* SE9 ....**143** D5
Fernhead Rd *MV/WKIL* W9 ....**89** F2
Fernhill St *CAN/RD* E16 ....**107** F2
Fernholme Rd *PECK* SE15 ....**139** D3
Fernhurst Rd *FUL/PGN* SW6 ....**113** E4
Fernlea Rd *BAL* SW12 ....**152** B1
Fernleigh Cl *MV/WKIL* W9 ....**89** F2
Fernsbury St *FSBYW* WC1X **10** A4
Fernshaw Cl *WBPTN* * SW10 ....**114** C2
Fernshaw Rd *WBPTN* SW10 ....**114** C2
Fernside Rd *BAL* SW12 ....**151** F1
Ferns Rd *SRTFD* E15 ....**81** E3
Fern St *BOW* E3 ....**92** A3
Ferntower Rd *HBRY* N5 ....**77** D2
Fern Wk *STHWK* SE1 ....**120** A1
Fernways *IL* IG1 ....**66** B5
Fernwood Av *STRHM/NOR* SW16 ....**153** D4
Ferranti Cl *WOOL/PLUM* SE18 ....**107** D4
Ferrers Rd *STRHM/NOR* SW16 ....**153** D5
Ferriby Rd *IS* N1 ....**76** A4
Ferrier St *WAND/EARL* SW18 ....**132** B2
Ferrings *DUL* SE21 ....**155** E2
Ferris Rd *EDUL* SE22 ....**138** A2
Ferron Rd *CLPT* * E5 ....**60** B5
Ferry La *BARN* SW13 ....**111** F2
Ferry Rd *BARN* SW13 ....**112** A3
Ferry St *POP/IOD* E14 ....**122** C1
Festing Rd *PUT/ROE* SW15 ....**131** D1

Fetter La *FLST/FETLN* EC4A **22** B4
Ffinch St *DEPT* SE8 ....**122** A3
Field Cottages *FUL/PGN* * SW6 ....**113** F5
Field Ct *GINN* WC1R **21** F3
Fieldgate St *WCHPL* E1 ....**90** A4
Fieldhouse Rd *BAL* SW12 ....**152** C1
Fielding Rd *CHSWK* W4 ....**99** D4
  WKENS W14 ....**101** D4
The Fieldings *FSTH* SE23 ....**156** C1
Fielding St *WALW* SE17 ....**118** C2
Field Rd *FSTGT* E7 ....**82** A1
  HMSMTH W6 ....**113** E1
Fields Est *HACK* * E8 ....**78** A4
Field St *FSBYW* WC1X **9** E3
Fieldview *WAND/EARL* SW18 ....**151** D1
Field Wy *WLSDN* NW10 ....**68** C4
Fieldway Crs *HOLWY* N7 ....**76** A2
Fife Rd *CAN/RD* E16 ....**94** A4
  MORT/ESHN SW14 ....**128** C3
Fife Ter *IS* N1 ....**9** F1
Fifield Pth *FSTH* SE23 ....**157** D3
Fifth Av *MNPK* E12 ....**83** F1
  NKENS W10 ....**89** E3
Fifth Wy *WBLY* HA9 ....**68** B1
Filey Av *STNW/STAM* N16 ....**60** A3
Fillebrook Rd *WAN* E11 ....**63** D3
Filmer Chambers *FUL/PGN* * SW6 ....**113** F4
Filmer Rd *FUL/PGN* SW6 ....**113** F4
Finborough Rd *WBPTN* SW10 ....**114** B2
Finch Av *WNWD* SE27 ....**155** D4
Finch La *BANK* EC3V **24** B5
Finchley Pl *STJWD* NW8 ....**4** A1
Finchley Rd *GLDGN* NW11 ....**54** A4
  KIL/WHAMP NW6 ....**72** A1
Finch Ms *PECK* * SE15 ....**119** F4
Finden Rd *FSTGT* E7 ....**82** B2
Findhorn St *POP/IOD* E14 ....**92** C5
Findon Cl *WAND/EARL* SW18 ....**132** A4
Findon Rd *SHB* W12 ....**100** A3
Fingal St *GNWCH* SE10 ....**123** F1
Finland Rd *BROCKY* SE4 ....**139** E1
Finland St *BERM/RHTH* SE16 ....**103** E4
Finlay St *FUL/PGN* SW6 ....**113** D4
Finnis St *BETH* E2 ....**90** B2
Finsbury Av *LVPST* * EC2M **24** B3
Finsbury Circ *LVPST* EC2M **24** B3
Finsbury Est *CLKNW* EC1R **10** B4
Finsbury Market *SDTCH* EC2A **24** C1
Finsbury Park Av *FSBYPK* N4 ....**58** C1
Finsbury Park Rd *FSBYPK* N4 ....**58** B4
Finsbury Pavement *SDTCH* EC2A **24** B2
Finsbury Sq *SDTCH* EC2A **24** B1
Finsbury St *STLK* EC1Y **24** A2
Finsen Rd *HNHL* SE24 ....**136** C2
Finstock Rd *NKENS* W10 ....**89** D5
Firbank Cl *CAN/RD* E16 ....**95** D4
Firbank Rd *PECK* SE15 ....**120** B5
Fircroft Rd *TOOT* SW17 ....**151** F3
Firecrest Dr *HAMP* NW3 ....**54** B5
Firefly Gdns *EHAM* E6 ....**95** E3
Firhill Rd *CAT* SE6 ....**158** A3
Firs Av *MORT/ESHN* SW14 ....**128** C2
Firsby Rd *STNW/STAM* N16 ....**59** F3
Firs Cl *FSTH* SE23 ....**139** D5
Firside Gv *BFN/LL* DA15 ....**163** F1
First Av *ACT* W3 ....**99** F2
  MNPK E12 ....**83** E1
  MORT/ESHN SW14 ....**111** E5
  NKENS W10 ....**89** F3
  PLSTW E13 ....**94** A2
First Dr *WLSDN* NW10 ....**68** C4
First St *CHEL* SW3 ....**41** D4
First Wy *WBLY* HA9 ....**68** B1

Firth Gdns *FUL/PGN* SW6 ....**113** E4
Fir Tree La *STRHM/NOR* SW16 ....**152** C5
Fir Trees Cl *BERM/RHTH* SE16 ....**103** E2
Fishermans Dr *BERM/RHTH* SE16.....**103** D3
Fishers Ct *NWCR* SE14 ....**121** D4
Fisher's La *CHSWK* W4 ....**99** D5
Fisher St *CAN/RD* E16 ....**94** A4
  RSQ WC1B **21** E3
Fisherton St *STJWD* NW8 ....**16** A1
Fishguard Wy *CAN/RD* E16 ....**108** B2
Fishponds Rd *TOOT* SW17 ....**151** E1
Fish Street Hl *MON* * EC3R................**36** B1
Fisons Rd *CAN/RD* E16 ....**106** A2
Fitzalan St *LBTH* SE11 ....**45** F4
Fitz-george Av *WKENS* W14 ....**101** E5
Fitzgerald Av *MORT/ESHN* SW14 ....**129** E1
Fitzgerald Rd *MORT/ESHN* SW14 ....**129** D1
Fitzhardinge St *MBLAR* W1H **18** A4
Fitzhugh Gv *WAND/EARL* SW18.......**133** D4
Fitzjames Av *WKENS* W14 ....**101** E5
Fitzjohn's Av *HAMP* NW3 ....**73** D2
Fitzmaurice Pl *MYFR/PICC* W1J **31** D1
Fitzneal St *ACT* W3 ....**87** F5
Fitzroy Cl *HGT* N6 ....**55** F3
Fitzroy Crs *CHSWK* * W4 ....**111** D3
Fitzroy Ms *GTPST* W1W **19** E5
Fitzroy Pk *HGT* N6 ....**55** F3
Fitzroy Rd *CAMTN* NW1 ....**74** A5
Fitzroy Sq *FITZ* W1T **19** E1
Fitzroy St *CAMTN* NW1 ....**19** E1
Fitzwarren Gdns *ARCH* N19 ....**56** C3
Fitzwilliam Ms *CAN/RD* E16 ....**106** A2
Fitzwilliam Rd *CLAP* SW4 ....**134** C1
Fiveways Rd *BRXN/ST* SW9 ....**118** A5
Fladbury Rd *SEVS/STOTM* N15 ....**59** D3
Fladgate Rd *WAN* E11 ....**63** E1
Flamborough St *POP/IOD* E14 ....**91** E5
Flamsted Av *WBLY* HA9 ....**68** A3
Flamsteed St *CHARL* SE7 ....**125** E1
Flanchford Rd *SHB* W12 ....**99** F4
Flanders Rd *CHSWK* W4 ....**99** E5
  EHAM E6 ....**95** F1
Flanders Wy *HOM* E9 ....**79** D3
Flank St *WCHPL* E1 ....**102** A1
Flask Wk *HAMP* NW3 ....**72** C1
Flavell Ms *GNWCH* SE10 ....**123** E1
Flaxman Rd *CMBW* SE5 ....**118** B5
Flaxman Ter *STPAN* WC1H **8** B4
Flaxton Rd *WOOL/PLUM* SE18............**127** D4
Fleece Wk *HOLWY* * N7 ....**75** D3
Fleet Pl *STP* EC4M **22** C4
Fleet Rd *HAMP* NW3 ....**73** E2
Fleet Sq *FSBYW* WC1X **9** E4
Fleet St *EMB* EC4Y **22** B5
Fleet Street Hl *BETH* * E2 ....**90** A3
Fleet Ter *CAT* * SE6 ....**140** C5
Fleetwood Cl *CAN/RD* E16 ....**95** D4
Fleetwood Rd *WLSDN* NW10 ....**70** A2
Fleetwood St *STNW/STAM* N16...........**59** E4
Fleming Cl *MV/WKIL* W9 ....**14** A1
  WBPTN * SW10 ....**114** C2
Fleming Rd *WALW* SE17 ....**118** B2
Flempton Rd *LEY* E10 ....**61** E3
Fletcher Cl *EHAM* E6 ....**108** D1
Fletcher La *LEY* E10 ....**62** C2
Fletcher Rd *CHSWK* W4 ....**98** C4
Fletcher St *WCHPL* E1 ....**102** A1
Fletching Rd *CHARL* SE7 ....**125** D2
  CLPT E5 ....**60** C5
Fleur De Lis St *WCHPL* E1 ....**25** E1
Flimwell Cl *BMLY* BR1 ....**159** E5
Flintmill Crs *BKHTH/KID* SE3 ....**125** E5
  ELTH/MOT SE9 ....**143** E1

Flinton St *WALW* SE17 ....**119** E1
Flint St *WALW* SE17 ....**48** B5
Flitcroft St *LSQ/SEVD* WC2H **20** B5
Flock Mill Pl *WAND/EARL* SW18 ....**150** B1
Flockton St *BERM/RHTH* SE16 ....**102** A3
Flodden Rd *CMBW* SE5 ....**118** C4
Flood St *CHEL* SW3 ....**115** E1
Flood Wk *CHEL* SW3 ....**115** E2
Flora Cl *POP/IOD* E14 ....**92** B5
Floral Pl *IS* N1 ....**77** D2
Floral St *COVGDN* WC2E **33** D1
Florence Gdns *CHSWK* W4 ....**110** C2
Florence Rd *CHSWK* W4 ....**99** D4
  EHAM E6 ....**82** C5
  FSBYPK N4 ....**57** F2
  NWCR SE14 ....**121** F4
  PLSTW E13 ....**94** A1
Florence St *CAN/RD* E16 ....**93** F3
  IS N1 ....**76** B4
Florence Ter *NWCR* SE14 ....**121** F4
Florence Vls *HGT* * N6 ....**56** B2
Florence Wy *BAL* SW12 ....**151** F1
Florfield Rd *HACK* E8 ....**78** B3
Florian Rd *PUT/ROE* SW15 ....**131** E2
Florida St *BETH* E2 ....**90** A2
Floss St *PUT/ROE* SW15 ....**112** C5
Flower & Dean Wk *WCHPL* E1 ....**25** F3
Flowers Cl *CRICK* NW2 ....**52** A5
Flowers Ms *ARCH* N19 ....**56** C4
Floyd Rd *CHARL* SE7 ....**124** C1
Fludyer St *LEW* SE13 ....**141** E2
Foley St *GTPST* W1W **19** E3
Folgate St *WCHPL* E1 ....**25** D2
Foliot St *ACT* W3 ....**87** F5
Folkestone Rd *EHAM* E6 ....**96** A1
Follett St *POP/IOD* E14 ....**92** C5
Folly Wall *POP/IOD* E14 ....**104** C3
Fontarabia Rd *BTSEA* SW11 ....**134** A2
Fontenoy Rd *TOOT* SW17 ....**152** B2
Fonthill Ms *FSBYPK* N4 ....**57** F4
Fonthill Rd *FSBYPK* N4 ....**57** F4
Fontley Wy *PUT/ROE* SW15 ....**130** A5
The Footpath *PUT/ROE* * SW15 ....**130** A3
Footscray Rd *ELTH/MOT* SE9 ....**144** A4
Forbes Cl *CRICK* NW2 ....**52** A5
Forbes St *WCHPL* E1 ....**90** A5
Forburg Rd *STNW/STAM* N16 ....**60** A3
Fordel Rd *CAT* SE6 ....**159** D1
Fordham St *WCHPL* E1 ....**90** A5
Fordingley Rd *MV/WKIL* W9 ....**89** F2
Fordmill Rd *CAT* SE6 ....**158** A2
Ford Rd *BOW* E3 ....**91** E1
Fords Park Rd *CAN/RD* E16 ....**94** A5
Ford Sq *WCHPL* E1 ....**90** B4
Ford St *BOW* E3 ....**79** E5
  CAN/RD E16 ....**93** F5
Fordwych Rd *CRICK* NW2 ....**71** E2
Fordyce Rd *LEW* SE13 ....**140** C4
Foreland St *WOOL/PLUM* SE18 ....**109** D5
Foreshore *DEPT* SE8 ....**103** F5
Forest Dr *MNPK* E12 ....**65** D5
Forest Dr East *WAN* E11 ....**63** D2
Forest Dr West *WAN* E11 ....**62** C2
Forester Rd *PECK* SE15..........................**138** B2
Forest Gld *WAN* E11 ....**63** E1
Forest Gv *HACK* E8 ....**77** F3
Forest Hill Rd *EDUL* SE22 ....**138** B4
Forestholme Cl *FSTH* * SE23 ....**156** C2
Forest La *FSTGT* E7 ....**82** A2
Fore St *BARB* EC2Y **24** A3
Forest Rd *FSTGT* E7 ....**82** A1
  HACK E8 ....**77** F3
  RCH/KEW TW9 ....**110** A3

WAN E11 ....**63** D2
Forest Side *FSTGT* E7 ....**82** B1
Forest St *FSTGT* E7 ....**82** A2
Forest Vw *WAN* E11 ....**63** F2
Forest View Rd *MNPK* E12..............**83** E1
Forest Wy *BFN/LL* DA15 ....**145** D5
Forfar Rd *BTSEA* SW11 ....**116** A4
Forge Pl *CAMTN* NW1 ....**74** A3
Forman Pl *STNW/STAM* N16 ....**77** F1
Formosa St *MV/WKIL* W9 ....**15** D1
Formunt Cl *CAN/RD* E16..................**93** F4
Forres Gdns *GLDGN* NW11 ....**54** C1
Forrester Pth *SYD* SE26 ....**156** C4
Forset St *MBLAR* W1H....................**17** D4
Forster Rd *BRXS/STRHM* SW2 ....**135** E5
WALTH E17......................................**61** E1
Forston St *IS* N1 ....**11** F1
Forsyth Gdns *WALW* SE17 ....**118** B2
Forsythia Cl *IL* IG1 ....**84** B2
Fortess Gv *KTTN* NW5 ....**74** C2
Fortess Rd *KTTN* NW5 ....**74** B2
Fortess Wk *KTTN* NW5 ....**74** B2
Forthbridge Rd *BTSEA* SW11 ....**134** A2
Fortis Cl *CAN/RD* E16 ....**94** C5
Fortnam Rd *ARCH* N19 ....**57** D5
Fort Rd *STHWK* SE1 ....**49** F5
Fortrose Gdns *BRXS/STRHM* SW2...**153** E1
Fort St *CAN/RD* E16.......................**106** B2
WCHPL * E1 ....**25** D3
Fortuna Cl *HOLWY* N7 ....**75** F3
Fortunegate Rd *WLSDN* NW10 ....**69** E5
Fortune Green Rd
KIL/WHAMP NW6 ....**72** A1
Fortune St *STLK* EC1Y **23** F1
Fortune Wy *WLSDN* NW10 ....**88** A2
Forty Acre La *CAN/RD* E16..............**94** A4
Forty La *WBLY* HA9 ....**50** B4
Forum Magnum Sq *STHWK* SE1 ......**33** E5
Fosbury Rd *BAY/PAD* W2 ....**27** D2
Foscote Ms *MV/WKIL* W9 ....**14** B1
Foscote Rd *HDN* NW4 ....**52** B1
Foskett Rd *FUL/PGN* SW6 ....**113** F5
Fossdene Rd *CHARL* SE7 ....**124** B1
Fossil Rd *LEW* SE13 ....**140** A1
Foss Rd *TOOT* SW17 ....**151** D4
Foster La *CITYW* EC2V **23** E4
Foster Rd *ACT* W3 ....**99** E1
CHSWK W4.....................................**111** D1
PLSTW E13 ....**94** A3
Fosters Cl *CHST* BR7 ....**161** F5
Fothergill Cl *PLSTW* E13 ....**82** A5
Foulden Rd *STNW/STAM* N16 ....**77** F1
Foulden Ter *STNW/STAM* N16 ....**77** F1
Foulis Ter *SKENS* SW7 ....**40** A5
Foulser Rd *TOOT* SW17 ....**151** F4
Foundry Cl *BERM/RHTH* SE16 ....**103** E2
Foundry Ms *CAMTN* NW1 ....**7** F5
Foundry Pl *WAND/EARL* SW18 ....**132** B5
Fountain Dr *NRWD* SE19 ....**155** F4
Fountain Green Sq
BERM/RHTH SE16 ....**102** A3
Fountain Ms *HAMP* * NW3 ....**73** F3
Fountain Pl *BRXN/ST* SW9 ....**118** A4
Fountain Rd *TOOT* SW17 ....**151** D5
Fountayne Rd *STNW/STAM* N16 ....**60** A3
Fount St *VX/NE* SW8 ....**117** D3
Fournier St *WCHPL* E1 ....**25** F2
Four Seasons Cl *BOW* E3 ....**92** A1
Fourth Av *MNPK* E12 ....**83** F1
NKENS W10 ....**89** E3
Fourth Wy *WBLY* HA9 ....**68** B1
Fowey Cl *WAP* E1W **102** B2
Fowler Cl *BTSEA* SW11 ....**133** D1

Fowler Rd *FSTGT* E7 ....**82** A1
IS N1 ....**76** B5
Fownes St *BTSEA* SW11 ....**133** E1
Fox and Knot St *FARR* * EC1M.......**23** D2
Foxberry Rd *BROCKY* SE4 ....**139** E2
Foxborough Gdns *BROCKY* SE4 ....**140** A4
Foxbourne Rd *TOOT* SW17 ....**152** A2
Fox Cl *CAN/RD* E16 ....**94** A4
WCHPL E1 ....**90** C3
Foxcroft Rd *WOOL/PLUM* SE18......**126** B4
Foxes Dl *BKHTH/KID* SE3 ....**142** A1
Foxglove St *ACT* W3 ....**99** F1
Foxham Rd *ARCH* N19 ....**57** D5
Foxhole Rd *ELTH/MOT* SE9 ....**143** E3
Fox Hollow Cl *WOOL/PLUM* SE18 ...**127** E1
Foxholt Gdns *WLSDN* NW10 ....**68** C4
Foxley Cl *HACK* E8 ....**78** A2
Foxley Rd *CMBW* SE5 ....**118** A3
Foxley Sq *BRXN/ST* * SW9 ....**118** B3
Foxmore St *BTSEA* SW11 ....**115** F4
Fox Rd *CAN/RD* E16 ....**93** F4
Foxwell St *BROCKY* SE4 ....**139** E1
Foxwood Rd *BKHTH/KID* SE3 ....**141** F2
Foyle Rd *BKHTH/KID* SE3 ....**123** F2
Framfield Rd *HBRY* N5 ....**76** B2
Framlingham Crs *ELTH/MOT* SE9 ...**161** E4
Frampton Park Rd *HOM* E9.............**78** C3
Frampton St *STJWD* NW8 ....**16** B1
Francemary Rd *LEW* SE13 ....**140** A3
Frances St *WOOL/PLUM* SE18 ......**107** F5
Franche Court Rd *TOOT* SW17.......**150** B3
Francis Av *IL* IG1 ....**67** D4
Francis Barber Cl
STRHM/NOR * SW16 ....**153** F4
Franciscan Rd *TOOT* SW17 ....**152** A4
Francis Chichester Wy
BTSEA * SW11 ....**116** A4
Francis Ms *LEE/GVPK* * SE12 ....**141** F4
Francis Rd *LEY* E10 ....**62** C4
Francis St *SRTFD* E15 ....**81** E2
WEST SW1P **43** F4
Francis Ter *ARCH* N19 ....**56** C5
Francis Wk *IS* N1 ....**75** F5
Franconia Rd *CLAP* SW4 ....**134** C3
Frank Burton Cl *CHARL* SE7 ....**124** B1
Frank Dixon Cl *DUL* SE21 ....**137** E5
Frank Dixon Wy *DUL* SE21 ....**155** E1
Frankfurt Rd *HNHL* SE24 ....**136** C3
Frankham St *DEPT* SE8 ....**122** A3
Frankland Cl *BERM/RHTH* SE16 ....**102** B4
Frankland Rd *SKENS* SW7 ....**40** A3
Franklin Cl *LEW* SE13 ....**122** B4
WNWD SE27 ....**154** B3
Franklin Sq *WKENS* W14 ....**113** F1
Franklin's Rw *CHEL* SW3 ....**115** F1
CHEL * SW3 ....**115** F1
Franklin St *BOW* E3......................**92** B2
SEVS/STOTM N15 ....**59** E1
Franklyn Rd *WLSDN* NW10............**69** F4
Fransfield Gv *SYD* SE26 ....**156** B3
Franthorne Wy *CAT* SE6 ....**158** B2
Fraser St *CHSWK* W4 ....**111** E1
Frazier St *STHWK* SE1 ....**46** A1
Frean St *BERM/RHTH* SE16 ....**102** A4
Freda Corbett Cl *PECK* SE15 ....**120** A3
Frederica St *HOLWY* N7 ....**75** F4
Frederick Cl *BAY/PAD* W2 ....**29** D1
Frederick Crs *BRXN/ST* SW9 ....**118** B3
Frederick Pl *WOOL/PLUM* SE18.....**126** B1
Frederick Rd *WALW* SE17 ....**118** B2
Frederick's Pl *LOTH* * EC2R **24** A5
Frederick Sq *BERM/RHTH* SE16 ....**103** E1
Frederick's Rw *FSBYE* EC1V **10** C3

Frederick St *FSBYW* WC1X 9 E4
Frederick Ter *HACK* * E8..........................77 F4
Frederic Ms *KTBR* * SW1X 42 A1
Freedom St *BTSEA* SW11 ....115 F5
Freegrove Rd *HOLWY* N7 ....75 E2
Freeling St *IS* N1 ....75 F4
Freemantle St *WALW* SE17 ....119 E1
Freemasons Rd *CAN/RD* E16 ....94 B5
Freke Rd *BTSEA* SW11 ....134 A1
Fremont St *HOM* E9 ....78 B5
French Pl *SDTCH* EC2A 13 D4
Frendsbury Rd *BROCKY* SE4 ....139 E2
Frensham Dr *PUT/ROE* SW15 ....148 A3
Frensham Rd *BFN/LL* DA15 ....163 D2
Frensham St *PECK* SE15 ....120 A2
Frere St *BTSEA* SW11 ....115 E5
Freshfield Av *HACK* E8 ....77 F4
Freshfield Cl *LEW* SE13 ....141 D2
Freshford St *TOOT* SW17 ....150 C3
Fresh Wharf Rd *BARK* IG11 ....84 B5
Freston Rd *NKENS* W10 ....101 D1
Frewin Rd *WAND/EARL* SW18 ....151 D1
Friar Ms *WNWD* SE27 ....154 B3
Friars Av *PUT/ROE* SW15 ....147 F5
Friars Cl *STHWK* * SE1 ....35 D3
Friars Gdns *ACT* W3................................87 D5
Friars Md *POP/IOD* E14 ....104 C4
Friars Ms *ELTH/MOT* SE9 ....144 A3
Friars Place La *ACT* W3 ....99 D1
Friar's Rd *EHAM* E6 ....83 D5
Friars Wy *ACT* W3 ....87 D5
Friary Est *PECK* * SE15 ....120 A3
Friary Park ct *ACT* * W3 ....86 C5
Friary Rd *ACT* W3....................................86 C5
  PECK SE15 ....120 A3
Friday St *BLKFR* EC4V 35 E1
Frideswide Pl *KTTN* NW5 ....74 C2
Friendly Pl *LEW* SE13 ....122 B4
Friendly St *DEPT* SE8 ....122 A4
Friendly Street Ms *DEPT* SE8................122 A5
Friend St *FSBYE* EC1V 10 C3
Friern Rd *EDUL* SE22 ....138 A4
Frigate Ms *DEPT* SE8..............................122 A2
Frimley Cl *WIM/MER* SW19 ....149 E2
Frimley Rd *GDMY/SEVK* IG3 ....67 E5
Frimley Wy *WCHPL* * E1 ....91 D3
Frinton Ms *IL* IG1 ....66 A1
Frinton Rd *EHAM* E6 ....95 D2
  SEVS/STOTM N15 ....59 E1
Friston St *FUL/PGN* SW6........................114 B5
Frith Rd *WAN* E11 ....80 C1
Frith St *SOHO/SHAV* W1D........................20 A5
Frithville Gdns *SHB* W12 ....100 C2
Frobisher Crs *BARB* * EC2Y 23 F2
Frobisher Gdns *LEY* * E10 ....62 B1
Frobisher Rd *EHAM* E6 ....95 F5
Frogley Rd *EDUL* SE22 ....137 F2
Frogmore *WAND/EARL* SW18 ....132 A3
Frogmore Est *HBRY* * N5 ....76 C1
Frognal *HAMP* NW3 ....72 C1
Frognal Cl *HAMP* NW3 ....72 C2
Frognal Gdns *HAMP* NW3 ....72 C1
Frognal La *HAMP* NW3 ....72 B2
Frognal Man *HAMP* * NW3......................72 C1
Frognal Pde *HAMP* NW3 ....72 C3
Frognal Ri *HAMP* NW3 ....54 C5
Frognal Wy *HAMP* NW3 ....72 C1
Froissart Rd *ELTH/MOT* SE9..................143 E3
Frome St *IS* N1 ....11 E1
Fromows Cnr *CHSWK* * W4 ....110 C1
Frostic Wk *WCHPL* E1 ....25 F3
Froude St *VX/NE* SW8 ....116 B5
Fryent Cl *KTN/HRWW/W* HA3 ....50 A1

Fryent Crs *CDALE/KGS* NW9..................51 E1
Fryent Flds *CDALE/KGS* NW9 ....51 E1
Fryent Gv *CDALE/KGS* NW9 ....51 E1
Fryent Wy *CDALE/KGS* NW9....................50 A1
Frying Pan Aly *WCHPL* E1 ....25 D3
Fry Rd *EHAM* E6......................................83 D4
  WLSDN NW10 ....69 F5
Fulbourne St *WCHPL* E1 ....90 B4
Fulbrook Rd *ARCH* N19 ....74 C1
Fulford St *BERM/RHTH* SE16 ....102 B3
Fulham Broadway *FUL/PGN* SW6.........114 A3
Fulham Est *FUL/PGN* SW6 ....114 A2
Fulham High St *FUL/PGN* SW6 ....113 E5
Fulham Palace Rd *FUL/PGN* SW6 ....113 D3
Fulham Park Gdns *FUL/PGN* SW6........113 F5
Fulham Park Rd *FUL/PGN* SW6 ....113 F5
Fulham Rd *FUL/PGN* SW6......................113 E5
Fuller Cl *BETH* * E2 ....90 A3
Fullerton Rd *WAND/EARL* SW18 ....132 C3
Fullwood's Ms *IS* * N1..............................12 B3
Fulmead St *FUL/PGN* SW6 ....114 B4
Fulmer Rd *CAN/RD* E16 ....95 D4
Fulthorp Rd *BKHTH/KID* SE3 ....123 F5
Fulton Ms *BAY/PAD* W2 ....27 E1
Fulton Rd *WBLY* HA9 ....50 A5
Fulwood Pl *GINN* WC1R 21 F3
Fulwood Wk *WIM/MER* SW19 ....149 E1
Furber St *HMSMTH* W6 ....100 B4
Furley Rd *PECK* SE15..............................120 A3
Furlong Rd *HOLWY* N7 ....76 A3
Furmage St *WAND/EARL* SW18 ....132 B5
Furneaux Av *WNWD* SE27 ....154 B5
Furness Rd *FUL/PGN* SW6 ....114 B5
  WLSDN NW10 ....88 A1
Furnival St *FLST/FETLN* EC4A 22 A4
Furrow La *HOM* E9 ....78 C2
Further Green Rd *CAT* SE6 ....141 E5
Furzedown Dr *TOOT* SW17 ....152 B5
Furzedown Rd *TOOT* SW17 ....152 B5
Furzefield Rd *BKHTH/KID* SE3 ....124 B2
Furze St *BOW* * E3 ....92 A4
Fye Foot La *BLKFR* * EC4V 35 E1
Fyfield Rd *BRXN/ST* SW9 ....136 A1
Fynes St *WEST* SW1P 44 A4

G

Gable Ct *SYD* SE26 ....156 B4
Gables Cl *CMBW* SE5 ....119 E4
  LEE/GVPK SE12 ....160 A1
Gabriel St *FSTH* SE23 ....139 D5
Gad Cl *PLSTW* E13 ....94 B2
Gadsbury Cl *CDALE/KGS* NW9 ....51 F1
Gadwall Cl *CAN/RD* E16 ....94 B5
Gage Rd *CAN/RD* E16 ....93 E4
Gainford St *IS* N1 ....76 A5
Gainsborough Av *MNPK* E12 ....84 A2
Gainsborough Ct *SHB* W12 ....100 C3
Gainsborough Gdns *GLDGN* NW11 ....53 F2
  HAMP NW3 ....55 D5
Gainsborough Rd *CHSWK* W4 ....99 F5
  SRTFD E15 ....93 E2
  WAN E11 ....63 E2
Gainsford St *STHWK* SE1 ....37 E4
Gairloch Rd *CMBW* SE5..........................119 E5
Gaisford St *KTTN* NW5 ....74 C3
Gaitskell Rd *ELTH/MOT* SE9 ....162 C1
Galahad Rd *BMLY* BR1 ....160 A3
Galata Rd *BARN* SW13 ....112 A3
Galatea Sq *PECK* SE15 ....138 B1
Galbraith St *POP/IOD* E14 ....104 C4

Galena Rd *HMSMTH* W6 ....**100** B5
Galen Pl *NOXST/BSQ* WC1A **20** C3
Galesbury Rd *WAND/EARL* SW18 .....**132** C4
Gales Gdns *BETH* E2 ....**90** B2
Gale St *BOW* E3 ....**92** A4
  CHEL SW3 ....**115** E1
Galgate Cl *WIM/MER* SW19 ....**149** D1
Galleon Cl *BERM/RHTH* SE16 ....**102** C3
The Galleries *IS* * N1 ....**10** C1
Gallery Rd *DUL* SE21 ....**155** D1
Galleywall Rd *BERM/RHTH* SE16 ......**102** B5
Gallia Rd *HBRY* N5 ....**76** B2
Gallions Rd *CAN/RD* E16 ....**108** B1
  CHARL SE7 ....**106** B5
Gallions View Rd *THMD* SE28 ....**109** E3
Gallon Cl *CHARL* SE7 ....**106** C5
Gallosson Rd *WOOL/PLUM* SE18 ......**109** E5
Galloway Rd *SHB* W12 ....**100** A3
Gallus Sq *BKHTH/KID* SE3 ....**142** B1
Galsworthy Crs *BKHTH/KID* * SE3 ....**124** C4
Galsworthy Rd *CRICK* NW2 ....**71** E1
Galton St *NKENS* W10 ....**89** E3
Galveston Rd *PUT/ROE* SW15 ....**131** F3
Galway Cl *BERM/RHTH* * SE16 ....**120** B1
Galway St *FSBYE* EC1V **11** F4
Gambetta St *VX/NE* SW8 ....**116** B5
Gambia St *STHWK* SE1 ....**35** D4
Gambole Rd *TOOT* SW17 ....**151** E4
Gamlen Rd *PUT/ROE* SW15 ....**131** D2
Gamuel Cl *WALTH* E17 ....**62** A1
Gandhi Cl *WALTH* E17 ....**62** A1
Ganton St *SOHO/CST* * W1F **19** F5
Gap Rd *WIM/MER* SW19 ....**150** A5
Garage Rd *ACT* W3 ....**86** A5
Garbutt Pl *MHST* * W1U **18** B2
Garden Cl *LEE/GVPK* SE12 ....**160** B3
  PUT/ROE SW15 ....**130** B5
Garden Ct *TPL/STR* * WC2R **34** A1
Garden Flats *HMSMTH* * W6 ....**113** D3
Garden La *BRXS/STRHM* SW2 ....**153** F1
Garden Pl *HACK* E8 ....**77** F5
Garden Rd *RCH/KEW* TW9 ....**128** A1
  STJWD NW8 ....**3** F3
Garden Rw *STHWK* SE1 ....**46** C3
The Gardens *EDUL* SE22 ....**138** A2
  STNW/STAM * N16 ....**59** F2
Garden St *WCHPL* E1 ....**91** D4
Garden Studios *BAY/PAD* * W2 ....**15** E3
Garden Ter *PIM* * SW1V **117** D1
Garden Wk *SDTCH* EC2A **12** C5
Garden Wy *WLSDN* NW10 ....**68** C3
Gardiner Av *CRICK* * NW2 ....**70** C2
Gardner Cl *WAN* E11 ....**64** B1
Gardner Rd *PLSTW* E13 ....**94** B3
Gardners La *BLKFR* EC4V **35** E1
Gardnor Rd *HAMP* NW3 ....**73** D1
Gard St *FSBYE* EC1V **11** D3
Gareth Gv *BMLY* BR1 ....**160** A4
Garfield Rd *BTSEA* SW11 ....**134** A1
  PLSTW E13 ....**93** F3
Garford St *POP/IOD* E14 ....**104** A1
Garibaldi St *WOOL/PLUM* SE18 ....**109** E5
Garland Rd *WOOL/PLUM* SE18 ....**127** D3
Garlick Hl *BLKFR* EC4V **35** F1
Garlies Rd *FSTH* SE23 ....**157** E3
Garlinge Rd *CRICK* NW2 ....**71** F3
Garnault Ms *CLKNW* EC1R **10** B4
Garnault Pl *CLKNW* EC1R **10** B4
Garner St *BETH* E2 ....**90** A1
Garnet Rd *WLSDN* NW10 ....**69** E3
Garnet St *WAP* E1W **102** C1
Garnett Cl *ELTH/MOT* SE9 ....**143** F1
Garnett Rd *HAMP* NW3 ....**73** E2

Garnham St *STNW/STAM* N16 ....**59** F4
Garnies Cl *PECK* SE15 ....**119** F3
Garrad's Rd *STRHM/NOR* SW16 ....**153** D3
Garrard Cl *CHST* BR7 ....**162** B5
Garrard Wk *WLSDN* * NW10 ....**69** E3
Garratt La *TOOT* SW17 ....**150** C3
  WAND/EARL SW18 ....**132** B5
Garratt Ter *TOOT* SW17 ....**151** E4
Garrett Cl *ACT* W3 ....**87** D4
Garrett St *STLK* EC1Y **23** E1
Garrick Av *GLDGN* NW11 ....**53** E1
Garrick Cl *BTSEA* SW11 ....**132** C2
Garrick Dr *WOOL/PLUM* SE18 ....**109** D4
Garrick Rd *CDALE/KGS* NW9 ....**51** F1
  RCH/KEW TW9 ....**110** A5
Garrick St *COVGDN* WC2E **32** C1
Garrick Yd *CHCR* WC2N **32** C1
Garrison Cl *WOOL/PLUM* SE18 ....**126** A3
Garsdale Ter *WKENS* * W14 ....**113** F1
Garside Cl *WOOL/PLUM* SE18 ....**109** D4
Garthorne Rd *FSTH* SE23 ....**139** D5
Garth Rd *CHSWK* W4 ....**111** D1
  CRICK NW2 ....**53** F4
Gartmoor Gdns *WIM/MER* SW19 ....**149** F1
Gartmore Rd *GDMY/SEVK* IG3 ....**67** F3
Garton Pl *WAND/EARL* SW18 ....**132** C4
Gartons Wy *BTSEA* SW11 ....**132** C1
Garvary Rd *CAN/RD* E16 ....**94** B5
Garway Rd *BAY/PAD* W2 ....**14** C3
Gascoigne Pl *BETH* E2 ....**13** E3
Gascoigne Rd *BARK* IG11 ....**84** C5
Gascony Av *KIL/WHAMP* NW6 ....**72** A4
Gascoyne Rd *HOM* E9 ....**79** D4
Gaselee St *POP/IOD* E14 ....**104** C1
Gasholder Pl *LBTH* SE11 ....**117** F1
Gaskarth Rd *BAL* SW12 ....**134** B4
Gaskell Rd *HGT* N6 ....**55** F1
Gaskell St *CLAP* SW4 ....**117** E5
Gaskin St *IS* N1 ....**76** B5
Gaspar Cl *ECT* * SW5 ....**39** D4
Gaspar Ms *ECT* SW5 ....**39** D4
Gassiot Rd *TOOT* SW17 ....**151** F4
Gastein Rd *HMSMTH* W6 ....**113** D2
Gataker St *BERM/RHTH* SE16 ....**102** B4
Gatcombe Rd *ARCH* N19 ....**57** D5
Gateforth St *STJWD* NW8 ....**16** C1
Gatehouse Sq *STHWK* SE1 ....**35** F3
Gateley Rd *BRXN/ST* SW9 ....**135** F1
Gate Ms *SKENS* SW7 ....**41** D1
Gates Ct *WALW* * SE17 ....**118** C5
Gateside Rd *TOOT* SW17 ....**151** F3
Gate St *HHOL* WC1V **21** E4
Gateway *WALW* SE17 ....**118** C2
Gateway Ar *IS* * N1 ....**10** C1
Gateway Ms *HACK* * E8 ....**77** F2
Gathorne St *BETH* E2 ....**91** D1
Gatliff Cl *BGVA* * SW1W **116** A1
Gatliff Rd *BGVA* SW1W **116** B1
Gatonby St *PECK* SE15 ....**119** E4
Gatton Rd *TOOT* SW17 ....**151** E4
Gatwick Rd *WAND/EARL* SW18 ....**131** F5
Gauden Cl *CLAP* SW4 ....**135** D1
Gauden Rd *CLAP* SW4 ....**135** D1
Gaumont Ter *SHB* * W12 ....**100** C3
Gaunt St *STHWK* SE1 ....**47** D2
Gautrey Rd *PECK* SE15 ....**120** C5
Gavel St *WALW* * SE17 ....**48** B4
Gaverick St *POP/IOD* E14 ....**104** A5
Gavestone Crs *LEE/GVPK* SE12 ....**142** B5
Gavestone Rd *LEE/GVPK* SE12 ....**142** B5
Gawber St *BETH* E2 ....**90** C2
Gawsworth Cl *SRTFD* E15 ....**81** F2
Gay Cl *CRICK* NW2 ....**70** B2

Gayfere St *WEST* SW1P **44** C3
Gayford Rd *SHB* W12 ....**99** F3
Gayhurst Rd *HACK* E8 ....**78** A4
Gaynesford Rd *FSTH* SE23 ....**157** D2
Gay Rd *SRTFD* E15 ....**93** D1
Gayton Crs *HAMP* NW3 ....**73** D1
Gayton Rd *HAMP* NW3 ....**73** D1
Gayville Rd *BTSEA* SW11 ....**133** F4
Gaywood Cl *BRXS/STRHM* SW2 ..**155** F1
Gaywood St *STHWK* SE1 ....**47** D3
Gaza St *WALW* SE17 ....**118** B1
Geary Rd *WLSDN* NW10 ....**70** A3
Geary St *HOLWY* N7 ....**75** F2
Gedling Pl *STHWK* SE1 ....**49** E2
Geere Rd *SRTFD* E15 ....**81** F5
Gees Ct *MHST* W1U **18** B5
Gee St *FSBYE* EC1V **11** E5
Geffrye Est *IS* N1 ....**13** D2
Geffrye St *BETH* E2 ....**13** E1
Geldart Rd *PECK* SE15 ....**120** B3
Geldeston Rd *CLPT* E5 ....**60** A4
Gellatly Rd *PECK* SE15 ....**120** C5
General Wolfe Rd *GNWCH* SE10 ..**123** D4
Genesta Rd *WOOL/PLUM* SE18 ..**126** B2
Geneva Dr *HNHL* SE24 ....**136** A2
Genoa Av *PUT/ROE* SW15 ......**130** C3
Geoffrey Cl *CMBW* SE5 ....**118** C5
Geoffrey Gdns *EHAM* E6 ....**95** F4
Geoffrey Rd *BROCKY* SE4 ......**139** F1
George Beard Rd *DEPT* SE8 ....**103** F5
George Downing Est
    STNW/STAM N16 ....**59** F4
George La *LEW* SE13 ....**140** C4
George Mathers Rd *LBTH* SE11 ..**46** C4
George Ms *CAMTN* NW1 ....**7** F4
George Rw *BERM/RHTH* SE16 ..**102** A3
Georges Rd *HOLWY* N7 ....**75** F3
    HOLWY N7 ....**75** F2
George St *BARK* IG11 ....**84** C4
    CAN/RD E16 ....**93** F5
    MBLAR W1H **17** F4
Georgetown Cl *NRWD* SE19 ....**155** D5
Georgette Pl *GNWCH* SE10 ....**122** C3
George Wyver Cl *WIM/MER* SW19 ..**131** E5
George Yd *BANK* EC3V **24** B5
    MYFR/PKLN W1K **30** B1
Georgiana St *CAMTN* NW1 ......**74** C5
Georgian Ct *WBLY* HA9 ....**68** A3
Georgina Gdns *BETH* * E2 ......**13** F3
Geraint Rd *BMLY* BR1 ....**160** A3
Geraldine Rd *CHSWK* W4 ......**110** A2
    WAND/EARL SW18 ....**132** C3
Geraldine St *LBTH* SE11 ....**46** C3
Gerald Rd *BGVA* SW1W **42** B4
    CAN/RD E16 ....**93** F3
Gerard Rd *BARN* SW13 ....**111** F4
Gerards Cl *BERM/RHTH* SE16 ..**120** C2
Gerda Rd *ELTH/MOT* SE9 ......**162** B3
Germander Wy *SRTFD* E15 ......**93** D2
Gernon Rd *BOW* E3 ....**91** E1
Geron Wy *CRICK* NW2 ....**52** C3
Gerrard Pl *SOHO/SHAV* * W1D ..**32** B1
Gerrard St *IS* N1 ....**10** C1
Gerrard St *SOHO/SHAV* W1D ..**32** B1
Gerridge St *STHWK* SE1 ....**46** B1
Gertrude St *WBPTN* SW10 ......**114** C2
Gervase Cl *WBLY* HA9 ....**50** C5
Gervase St *PECK* SE15 ....**120** B3
Ghent St *CAT* SE6 ....**158** A2
Ghent Wy *HACK* E8 ....**77** F3
Giant Arches Rd *HNHL* SE24 ....**136** C5
Gibbins Rd *SRTFD* E15 ....**80** C3
Gibbon Rd *ACT* W3 ....**99** E1

PECK SE15 ....**120** C5
Gibbons Rd *WLSDN* NW10 ......**69** D3
Gibbon Wk *PUT/ROE* * SW15 ..**130** A2
Gibbs Cl *NRWD* * SE19 ....**155** D5
Gibbs Gn *WKENS* * W14 ....**113** F1
Gibbs Sq *NRWD* * SE19 ....**155** D5
Gibraltar Wk *BETH* E2 ....**13** F1
Gibson Cl *WCHPL* E1 ....**90** C3
Gibson Gdns *STNW/STAM* * N16 ..**59** F3
Gibson Rd *LBTH* SE11 ....**45** F5
Gibson Sq *IS* N1 ....**76** A5
Gibson St *GNWCH* SE10 ....**123** E1
Gideon Rd *BTSEA* SW11 ....**134** A1
Giesbach Rd *ARCH* N19 ....**56** C4
Giffin St *DEPT* SE8 ....**122** A3
Gifford St *IS* N1 ....**75** E4
Gift La *SRTFD* E15 ....**81** E5
Gilbert Cl *WOOL/PLUM* SE18 ..**125** F4
Gilbert Pl *NOXST/BSQ* WC1A ..**20** C3
Gilbert Rd *LBTH* SE11 ....**46** B4
Gilbert St *MYFR/PKLN* W1K **18** B5
    SRTFD E15 ....**81** E1
Gilbey Rd *TOOT* SW17 ....**151** E4
Gilbeys Yd *CAMTN* NW1 ....**74** A4
Gilbourne Rd *WOOL/PLUM* SE18 ..**127** F2
Gilda Crs *STNW/STAM* N16 ....**60** A3
Gildea St *REGST* W1B **19** D3
Gildersome St *WOOL/PLUM* SE18 ..**126** A2
Giles Coppice *NRWD* SE19 ....**155** F4
Gilkes Crs *EDUL* SE22 ....**137** E4
Gilkes Pl *DUL* SE21 ....**137** E4
Gill Av *CAN/RD* E16 ....**94** A5
Gillender St *BOW* E3 ....**92** C5
Gillespie Rd *FSBYPK* N4 ....**58** A5
Gillett Av *EHAM* E6 ....**95** E1
Gillett Pl *HACK* E8 ....**77** F2
Gillett St *STNW/STAM* N16 ....**77** F2
Gillian St *LEW* SE13 ....**140** B3
Gillingham Ms *PIM* SW1V **43** D4
Gillingham Rd *CRICK* NW2 ....**53** E5
Gillingham Rw *PIM* SW1V **43** E4
Gillingham St *PIM* SW1V **43** D5
Gillison Wk *BERM/RHTH* * SE16 ..**102** A4
Gilman Dr *SRTFD* E15 ....**81** E5
Gill St *POP/IOD* E14 ....**91** F5
Gilmore Rd *LEW* SE13 ....**141** D2
Gilpin Av *MORT/ESHN* SW14 ..**129** D2
Gilpin Cl *BAY/PAD* W2 ....**15** F3
Gilpin Rd *CLPT* E5 ....**79** E1
Gilstead Rd *FUL/PGN* SW6 ....**114** B5
Gilston Rd *WBPTN* SW10 ......**114** C1
Gilton Rd *CAT* SE6 ....**159** E3
Giltspur St *STBT* EC1A **23** D4
Gipsy Hl *NRWD* SE19 ....**155** F4
Gipsy La *BARN* SW13 ....**130** A1
Gipsy Rd *WNWD* SE27 ....**155** D4
Gipsy Road Gdns *WNWD* SE27 ..**154** C4
Giralda Cl *CAN/RD* E16 ....**95** D4
Giraud St *POP/IOD* E14 ....**92** B5
Girdlers Rd *HMSMTH* W6 ......**101** D5
Girdwood Rd *WAND/EARL* SW18 ..**131** E5
Gironde Rd *FUL/PGN* SW6 ....**113** F3
Girton Rd *SYD* SE26 ....**157** D5
Gissing St *IS* * N1 ....**76** A4
Gittens Cl *BMLY* BR1 ....**159** F4
Gladding Rd *MNPK* E12 ....**83** D1
Gladesmore Rd *SEVS/STOTM* N15 ..**59** F1
The Glade *CHARL* SE7 ....**124** C3
    HACK * E8 ....**77** F3
    SHB * W12 ....**100** B3
Gladiator St *FSTH* SE23 ....**139** E4
Glading Ter *STNW/STAM* N16 ..**59** F5
Gladsmuir Rd *ARCH* N19 ......**56** C3

Gladstone Av *MNPK* E12 ....**83** E4
Gladstone Ms *KIL/WHAMP* NW6 ....**71** F3
Gladstone Pde *CRICK* * NW2 ....**52** C5
Gladstone Park Gdns *CRICK* NW2 .....**52** B5
Gladstone Rd *CHSWK* * W4 ....**99** D4
Gladstone St *STHWK* SE1 ....**46** C2
Gladstone Ter *VX/NE* * SW8 ....**116** A1
    WNWD * SE27 ....**154** C4
Gladwell Rd *CEND/HSY/T* N8 ....**57** F1
Gladwyn Rd *PUT/ROE* SW15 ....**131** D1
Gladys Rd *KIL/WHAMP* NW6 ....**72** A4
Glaisher St *DEPT* SE8...............**122** B2
Glamis Pl *WAP* E1W **102** C1
Glamis Rd *WAP* E1W **102** C1
Glanville Rd *BRXS/STRHM* SW2 ......**135** E3
Glasbrook Rd *ELTH/MOT* SE9 ....**143** D5
Glaserton Rd *STNW/STAM* N16 ....**59** E2
Glasgow Rd *PLSTW* E13 ....**94** B1
Glasgow Ter *PIM* SW1V **116** C1
Glasshill St *STHWK* SE1 ....**35** D5
Glasshouse Flds *WAP* E1W **103** D1
Glasshouse St *REGST* W1B **31** F2
Glasshouse Wk *LBTH* SE11 ....**117** E1
Glasshouse Yd *STBT* EC1A **23** E1
Glass St * E2 ....**90** B3
Glass Yd *WOOL/PLUM* SE18 ....**108** C4
Glastonbury Pl *WCHPL* E1 ....**90** C5
Glastonbury St *KIL/WHAMP* NW6 ......**71** F3
Glaucus St *BOW* E3 ....**92** B4
Glazbury Rd *WKENS* W14 ....**101** E3
Glazebrook Cl *DUL* SE21 ....**155** D2
Glebe Cl *CHSWK* * W4 ....**111** D1
Glebe Ct *BKHTH/KID* * SE3 ....**141** E1
Glebelands Av *GNTH/NBYPK* IG2 ....**67** D2
Glebelands Cl *CMBW* * SE5...........**137** E1
Glebe Pl *CHEL* SW3 ....**115** E2
Glebe Rd *BARN* SW13 ....**112** A5
    HACK * E8 ....**77** F4
    WLSDN NW10 ....**70** A3
Glebe St *CHSWK* W4 ....**111** D1
Glebe Ter *BOW* E3 ....**92** B2
The Glebe *BKHTH/KID* * SE3 ....**141** E1
    STRHM/NOR * SW16 ....**153** D4
Gledhow Gdns *ECT* SW5 ....**39** E5
Gledstanes Rd *WKENS* W14 ....**113** E1
Glegg Pl *PUT/ROE* * SW15 ....**131** D2
Glenaffric Av *POP/IOD* E14 ....**104** C5
Glen Albyn Rd *WIM/MER* SW19 ......**149** D2
Glenalvon Wy *CHARL* SE7 ....**107** E5
Glenarm Rd *CLPT* E5 ....**78** C3
Glenavon Rd *SRTFD* E15 ....**81** E4
Glenbarr Cl *ELTH/MOT* SE9 ....**144** B1
Glenbrook Rd *KIL/WHAMP* NW6 ....**72** A2
Glenburnie Rd *TOOT* SW17 ....**151** F3
Glencairne Cl *CAN/RD* E16 ....**95** D4
Glencoe Av *GNTH/NBYPK* IG2 ....**67** D4
Glendale Cl *ELTH/MOT* SE9 ....**144** A1
Glendall St *CLAP* SW4 ....**135** F1
Glendarvon St *PUT/ROE* SW15 ....**131** D1
Glendower Gdns
    MORT/ESHN SW14 ....**129** D1
Glendower Rd *MORT/ESHN* SW14 .....**129** D1
Glendun Rd *ACT* W3 ....**99** E1
Gleneagle Ms *STRHM/NOR* SW16 ....**153** D5
Gleneagle Rd *STRHM/NOR* SW16 .....**153** D5
Gleneagles Cl *BERM/RHTH* * SE16...**120** B1
Gleneldon Ms *STRHM/NOR* SW16 ....**153** E4
Gleneldon Rd *STRHM/NOR* SW16 ....**153** E4
Glenelg Rd *BRXS/STRHM* SW2 ....**135** E3
Glenesk Rd *ELTH/MOT* SE9 ....**144** A1
Glenfarg Rd *CAT* SE6 ....**159** D1
Glenfield Rd *BAL* SW12 ....**152** C1
Glenfinlas Wy *CMBW* SE5 ....**118** B3

Glenforth St *GNWCH* SE10 ....**105** F5
Glengall Br *POP/IOD* E14 ....**104** B4
Glengall Gv *POP/IOD* E14 ....**104** B4
Glengall Rd *KIL/WHAMP* NW6 ....**71** F2
    PECK SE15 ....**119** F2
Glengall Ter *PECK* SE15 ....**119** F2
Glengarnock Av *POP/IOD* E14........**104** C5
Glengarry Rd *EDUL* SE22 ....**137** E2
Glenhead Cl *ELTH/MOT* SE9 ....**144** B1
Glenhouse Rd *ELTH/MOT* SE9 ....**144** A3
Glenhurst Av *KTTN* NW5 ....**74** A1
Glenilla Rd *HAMP* NW3 ....**73** E3
Glenister Rd *GNWCH* SE10 ....**123** F1
Glenlea Rd *ELTH/MOT* SE9 ....**144** A3
Glenloch Rd *HAMP* NW3 ....**73** E3
Glenluge Rd *BKHTH/KID* SE3 ....**124** A2
Glenlyon Rd *ELTH/MOT* SE9 ....**144** A3
Glenmore Rd *HAMP* NW3 ....**73** E3
    WELL DA16........................**127** F4
Glennie Rd *WNWD* SE27 ....**154** A3
Glenny Rd *BARK* IG11 ....**84** C3
Glenparke Rd *FSTGT* E7 ....**82** B3
Glen Rd *PLSTW* E13 ....**94** C3
Glenrosa St *FUL/PGN* SW6 ....**114** C5
Glenroy St *SHB* W12 ....**88** C5
Glensdale Rd *BROCKY* SE4 ....**139** F1
Glenshiel Rd *ELTH/MOT* SE9.........**144** A3
Glentanner Wy *TOOT* SW17 ....**151** D3
Glen Ter *POP/IOD* E14..............**104** C3
Glentham Cottages *BARN* * SW13 ...**112** A2
Glentham Gdns *BARN* SW13 ....**112** B1
Glentham Rd *BARN* SW13............**112** A2
Glenthorne Rd *HMSMTH* W6 ....**100** B5
Glenton Rd *LEW* SE13 ....**141** E1
Glentworth St *CAMTN* NW1 ....**17** F1
Glenure Rd *ELTH/MOT* SE9..........**144** A3
Glenville Gv *DEPT* SE8..............**121** F3
Glenwood Av *CDALE/KGS* NW9 ....**51** E3
Glenwood Gv *CDALE/KGS* NW9 ....**50** C3
Glenwood Rd *CAT* SE6 ....**157** F1
Glenworth Av *POP/IOD* E14.........**105** D5
Gliddon Rd *WKENS* W14 ....**101** E5
Globe Pond Rd *BERM/RHTH* SE16 ...**103** E2
Globe Rd *BETH* E2 ....**90** C2
    FSTGT E7 ....**81** F2
Globe St *STHWK* SE1 ....**48** A1
Globe Ter *BETH* E2..................**90** C2
Gloucester Av *BFN/LL* DA15 ....**163** E2
    CAMTN NW1 ....**74** A4
    WELL DA16.......................**145** F3
Gloucester Circ *GNWCH* SE10 ......**122** C3
Gloucester Crs *CAMTN* * NW1 ....**74** B5
Gloucester Ct *MON* EC3R **37** D2
    RCH/KEW * TW9 ....**110** A3
Gloucester Dr *FSBYPK* N4 ....**58** A4
Gloucester Gdns *BAY/PAD* W2 ......**15** D4
    GLDGN NW11.....................**53** F2
    IL IG1 ....**65** E2
Gloucester Ga *CAMTN* NW1 ....**6** B1
Gloucester Gate Br *CAMTN* * NW1 ...**74** B5
Gloucester Gate Ms *CAMTN* NW1 ....**6** C1
Gloucester Ms *BAY/PAD* W2 ....**15** E5
Gloucester Ms West *BAY/PAD* W2 ...**15** E5
Gloucester Pl *CAMTN* NW1.............**17** E1
Gloucester Place Ms *MBLAR* W1H.....**17** F3
Gloucester Rd *ACT* W3 ....**98** C3
    LEY E10 ....**62** A2
    MNPK E12 ....**65** F5
    RCH/KEW TW9.....................**110** A3
    SKENS SW7 ....**39** C1
Gloucester Sq *BAY/PAD* W2 ....**16** B5
    BETH E2 ....**78** A5

Gloucester St *PIM* SW1V	116	C1
Gloucester Ter *BAY/PAD* W2	15	D4
Gloucester Wk *KENS* W8	26	B5
Gloucester Wy *CLKNW* EC1R	10	A4
Glycena Rd *BTSEA* SW11	133	F1
Glynde Ms *CHEL* SW3	41	D3
Glynde St *BROCKY* SE4	139	F4
Glyndon Rd *WOOL/PLUM* SE18	108	C5
Glynfield Rd *WLSDN* NW10	69	G4
Glyn Rd *CLPT* E5	79	D1
Glyn St *LBTH* SE11	117	F1
Godalming Rd *POP/IOD* E14	92	B4
Godbold Rd *SRTFD* E15	93	E3
Goddard Pl *ARCH* N19	56	C5
Goddards Wy *IL* IG1	67	D3
Godfrey Hl *WOOL/PLUM* SE18	107	E5
Godfrey Rd *WOOL/PLUM* SE18	107	F5
Godfrey St *CHEL* SW3	115	E1
SRTFD E15	92	C1
Goding St *LBTH* SE11	117	E1
Godley Rd *WAND/EARL* SW18	151	D1
Godliman St *BLKFR* * EC4V	23	D5
Godman Rd *PECK* * SE15	120	B5
Godolphin Pl *ACT* W3	99	D1
Godolphin Rd *SHB* W12	100	B2
Godwin Cl *IS* N1	11	F1
Godwin Rd *FSTGT* E7	82	B1
Goffers Rd *BKHTH/KID* SE3	123	E4
Golborne Gdns *NKENS* * W10	89	E3
Golborne Ms *NKENS* W10	89	E4
Golborne Rd *NKENS* W10	89	E4
Goldcrest Cl *CAN/RD* E16	95	D4
Golden Cross Ms *NTCHL* * W11	89	F5
Golden Hind Pl *DEPT* * SE8	103	F5
Golden La *STLK* EC1Y	11	E5
Golden Lane Est *STLK* EC1Y	23	E1
Golden Plover Cl *CAN/RD* E16	94	A5
Golden Sq *SOHO/CST* W1F	31	F1
Golden Yd *HAMP* * NW3	72	C1
Golders Gdns *GLDGN* NW11	53	E2
Golders Green Crs *GLDGN* NW11	53	F2
Golders Green Rd *GLDGN* NW11	53	E1
Golders Hl *GLDGN* * NW11	54	B4
Golderslea *GLDGN* * NW11	54	A3
Golders Manor Dr *GLDGN* NW11	53	D1
Golders Park Cl *GLDGN* NW11	54	A3
Golders Wy *GLDGN* NW11	53	F2
Goldfinch Rd *THMD* SE28	109	D4
Goldhawk Ms *SHB* W12	100	B3
Goldhawk Rd *HMSMTH* W6	99	F5
Goldhurst Ter *KIL/WHAMP* NW6	72	B4
Golding St *WCHPL* E1	90	A5
Goldington Crs *CAMTN* NW1	8	A1
Goldington St *CAMTN* NW1	8	A1
Goldman Cl *BETH* E2	90	A3
Goldney Rd *MV/WKIL* W9	14	A1
Goldsboro Rd *VX/NE* SW8	117	D4
Goldsmid St *WOOL/PLUM* SE18	127	E1
Goldsmith Av *ACT* W3	99	D1
CDALE/KGS NW9	51	E1
MNPK E12	83	E3
Goldsmith Pl *KIL/WHAMP* *) NW6	72	B5
Goldsmith Rd *ACT* W3	99	D2
LEY E10	62	B3
PECK SE15	120	A4
Goldsmiths Cl *ACT* * W3	99	D2
Goldsmith's Rw *BETH* E2	78	A5
Goldsmith St *CITYW* EC2V	23	F4
Goldsworthy Gdns		
BERM/RHTH SE16	102	C5
Goldwing Cl *CAN/RD* E16	94	A5
Golfe Rd *IL* IG1	67	D5
Gollogly Ter *CHARL* SE7	124	C1

Gomm Rd *BERM/RHTH* SE16	102	C4
Gondar Gdns *CRICK* NW2	71	F2
Gonson St *DEPT* SE8	122	B2
Gonston Cl *WIM/MER* SW19	149	E2
Gonville St *FUL/PGN* SW6	131	E1
Goodall Rd *WAN* E11	62	C5
Goodey Rd *BARK* IG11	85	F4
Goodge Pl *FITZ* W1T	19	F3
Goodge St *FITZ* W1T	19	F3
Goodhall St *WLSDN* NW10	87	F2
Gooding Cl *HOLWY* N7	75	E2
Goodinge Rd *HOLWY* N7	75	E3
Goodman Crs *BRXS/STRHM* SW2	153	D2
Goodman Rd *LEY* E10	62	C2
Goodman's Stile *WCHPL* E1	90	A5
Goodman's Yd *TWRH* EC3N	37	E1
Goodrich Rd *EDUL* SE22	137	F4
Goodson Rd *WLSDN* NW10	69	E4
Goods Wy *CAMTN* NW1	8	C1
Goodway Gdns *POP/IOD* E14	93	D5
Goodwin Cl *BERM/RHTH* SE16	49	F3
Goodwin Rd *SHB* W12	100	A3
Goodwins Ct *CHCR* WC2N	32	C1
Goodwin St *FSBYPK* N4	58	A4
Goodwood Rd *NWCR* SE14	121	E3
Goosander Wy *WOOL/PLUM* SE18	109	D4
Gooseley La *EHAM* E6	96	A2
Gophir La *CANST* * EC4R	36	A1
Gopsall St *IS* N1	77	D5
Gordon Av *MORT/ESHN* SW14	129	E2
Gordonbrock Rd *BROCKY* SE4	140	A3
Gordon Cl *WALTH* E17	62	A1
Gordondale Rd *WIM/MER* SW19	150	A2
Gordon Gv *CMBW* SE5	118	B5
Gordon House Rd *KTTN* NW5	74	A1
Gordon Pl *KENS* W8	26	B5
Gordon Rd *BARK* IG11	85	E5
BFN/LL DA15	145	E3
CHSWK W4	110	B2
IL IG1	67	D5
PECK SE15	120	B5
SRTFD E15	80	C1
WAN E11	64	A1
Gordon Sq *STPAN* WC1H	8	B5
Gordon St *PLSTW* E13	94	A2
STPAN WC1H	8	A5
Gorefield Pl *KIL/WHAMP* NW6	2	A1
Gore Rd *HOM* E9	78	C5
Gore St *SKENS* SW7	39	F2
Gorham Pl *NTCHL* W11	101	E1
Goring St *HDTCH* EC3A	25	D4
Gorleston St *WKENS* W14	101	E1
Gorman Rd *WOOL/PLUM* SE18	107	F5
Gorse Ri *TOOT* SW17	152	A5
Gorst Rd *BTSEA* SW11	133	F4
WLSDN NW10	86	C3
Gorsuch Pl *BETH* E2	13	E3
Gorsuch St *BETH* E2	13	E3
Gosberton Rd *BAL* SW12	151	F1
Gosfield St *GTPST* W1W	19	D2
Goslett Yd *SOHO/SHAV* W1D	20	B4
Gosling Wy *BRXN/ST* SW9	118	A4
Gosport Rd *WALTH* E17	62	B1
Gossage Rd *WOOL/PLUM* SE18	127	D1
Gosset St *BETH* E2	90	A2
Gossington Cl *CHST* BR7	162	B4
Gosterwood St *DEPT* SE8	121	E2
Goswell Pl *FSBYE* EC1V	11	D4
Goswell Rd *FSBYE* EC1V	11	D3
Gottfried Ms *KTTN* NW5	74	C1
Goudhurst Rd *BMLY* BR1	159	F5
Gough Rd *FSTGT* E7	81	F1
Gough Sq *FLST/FETLN* EC4A	22	B4

Gough St *FSBYW* WC1X 9 F5
Gould Ter *HACK* E8 ....78 B2
Goulston St *WCHPL* E1 ....25 E4
Goulton Rd *CLPT* E5 ....78 B2
Gourock Rd *ELTH/MOT* SE9 ....144 A3
Govan St *BETH* E2 ....78 A5
Govier Cl *SRTFD* E15 ....81 E4
Gowan Av *FUL/PGN* SW6 ....113 F4
Gowan Rd *WLSDN* NW10 ....70 B4
Gower Cl *BAL* SW12 ....134 C4
Gower Ms *GWRST* WC1E 20 B3
Gower Pl *STPAN* WC1H 7 F1
Gower Rd *FSTGT* E7 ....82 A3
Gower St *GWRST* WC1E 7 F5
Gower's Wk *WCHPL* E1 ....90 A5
Gowlett Rd *PECK* SE15 ....138 A1
Gowrie Rd *BTSEA* SW11 ....134 A1
Gracechurch St *BANK* EC3V 36 B1
Grace Cl *ELTH/MOT* SE9 ....161 D3
Gracedale Rd *TOOT* SW17 ....152 B5
Gracefield Gdns
    STRHM/NOR SW16 ....153 E3
Grace Jones Cl *HACK* * E8 ....77 F3
Grace Pl *BOW* E3 ....92 B2
Grace's Ms *CMBW* SE5 ....119 D5
    STJWD * NW8 ....3 F2
Grace's Rd *CMBW* SE5 ....119 E5
Grace St *BOW* E3 ....92 B2
The Gradient *SYD* SE26 ....156 A4
Graemesdyke Av
    MORT/ESHN SW14 ....128 B1
Grafton Crs *CAMTN* NW1 ....74 B3
Grafton Gdns *FSBYPK* N4 ....58 C3
Grafton Ms *FITZ* W1T 19 E1
Grafton Pl *CAMTN* NW1 ....8 A4
Grafton Rd *ACT* W3 ....98 C1
    KTTN NW5 ....74 A2
Grafton Sq *CLAP* SW4 ....134 C1
Grafton St *MYFR/PICC* W1J 31 D2
Grafton Ter *KTTN* NW5 ....73 F2
Grafton Wy *GTPST* W1W 19 E2
Grafton Yd *KTTN* NW5 ....74 B3
Graham Rd *CHSWK* W4 ....99 D4
    HACK E8 ....78 A3
    HDN NW2 ....52 B1
    PLSTW E13 ....94 A3
Graham St *IS* N1 ....11 D2
Graham Ter *BGVA* SW1W 42 B5
Gramer Cl *WAN* E11 ....63 D4
Grampian Gdns *CRICK* NW2 ....53 E3
Granada St *TOOT* SW17 ....151 F5
Granard Av *PUT/ROE* SW15 ....130 B3
Granard Rd *BAL* SW12 ....133 F5
Granary Rd *WCHPL* E1 ....90 B3
Granary Sq *IS* * N1 ....76 A3
Granary St *CAMTN* NW1 ....75 D5
Granby Rd *ELTH/MOT* SE9 ....125 F5
    WOOL/PLUM SE18 ....108 B4
Granby St *BETH* E2 ....13 F5
Granby Ter *CAMTN* NW1 ....7 E2
Grand Av *FARR* EC1M 23 D2
    WBLY HA9 ....68 A2
Grand Av East *WBLY* HA9 ....68 B2
Grand Depot Rd
    WOOL/PLUM SE18 ....126 A1
Grandison Rd *BTSEA* SW11 ....133 F3
Grand Junction Whf *IS* * N1 ....11 E2
Grand Pde *FSBYPK* * N4 ....58 B1
    MORT/ESHN * SW14 ....128 C2
    WBLY * HA9 ....50 B4
Grand Union Canal Wk
    BAY/PAD W2 ....14 B2
    WLSDN NW10 ....86 B1

Grand Union Cl *MV/WKIL* W9 ....89 F4
Grand Union Crs *HACK* * E8 ....78 A5
Grand Union Wk *CAMTN* * NW1 ....74 B4
Grand Wk *WCHPL* * E1 ....91 E3
Granfield St *BTSEA* * SW11 ....115 D4
Grangecourt Rd *STNW/STAM* N16 ....59 E3
Grange Gdns *HAMP* NW3 ....54 B5
Grange Gv *IS* N1 ....76 C3
Grangehill Pl *ELTH/MOT* SE9 ....143 F1
Grangehill Rd *ELTH/MOT* SE9 ....143 F1
Grange Houses *HBRY* * N5 ....76 C1
Grange La *DUL* SE21 ....155 F2
Grangemill Rd *CAT* SE6 ....158 A3
Grangemill Wy *CAT* SE6 ....158 A2
Grange Park Rd *LEY* E10 ....62 B3
Grange Pl *KIL/WHAMP* NW6 ....72 A4
Grange Rd *BARN* SW13 ....112 A4
    CHSWK W4 ....110 B1
    HGT N6 ....56 A1
    IL IG1 ....84 C1
    LEY E10 ....62 A3
    PLSTW E13 ....93 F2
    STHWK SE1 ....49 D3
    WLSDN NW10 ....70 B3
Grange St *IS* * N1 ....77 D5
The Grange *ALP/SUD* HA0 ....68 A4
    STHWK SE1 ....49 E2
    WKENS * W14 ....101 F5
Grange Wk *STHWK* SE1 ....49 D2
Grange Walk Ms *STHWK* SE1 ....49 D3
Grangeway *KIL/WHAMP* NW6 ....72 A4
Grange Yd *STHWK* SE1 ....49 E3
Granite St *WOOL/PLUM* SE18 ....127 F1
Granleigh Rd *WAN* E11 ....63 E4
Gransden Av *HACK* E8 ....78 B4
Gransden Rd *SHB* W12 ....99 F3
Grantbridge St *IS* N1 ....11 D1
Grantham Pl *MYFR/PICC* W1J 30 C4
Grantham Rd *BRXN/ST* SW9 ....135 E1
    CHSWK W4 ....111 E3
    MNPK E12 ....66 A5
Grantley St *WCHPL* E1 ....91 D2
Grant Rd *BTSEA* SW11 ....133 D1
Grant St *IS* N1 ....10 A1
    PLSTW E13 ....94 A2
Grant Ter *CLPT* * E5 ....60 A2
Grantully Rd *MV/WKIL* W9 ....2 C4
Granville Ar *BRXN/ST* * SW9 ....136 A2
Granville Gv *LEW* SE13 ....140 C1
Granville Pk *LEW* SE13 ....140 C1
Granville Pl *FUL/PGN* * SW6 ....114 B3
    MBLAR W1H 18 A5
Granville Rd *CRICK* NW2 ....53 F4
    FSBYPK N4 ....57 F1
    IL IG1 ....66 B3
    KIL/WHAMP NW6 ....2 A2
    LEY E10 ....62 B1
    WAND/EARL SW18 ....131 F5
Granville Sq *PECK* * SE15 ....119 E3
Granville St *FSBYW* WC1X 9 F4
Grape St *LSQ/SEVD* WC2H 20 C4
Graphite Sq *LBTH* * SE11 ....117 F1
Grasmere Av *ACT* W3 ....98 C1
    PUT/ROE SW15 ....147 D4
Grasmere Rd *PLSTW* E13 ....94 A1
    STRHM/NOR SW16 ....153 F5
Grassmount *FSTH* SE23 ....156 B2
Grately Wy *PECK* * SE15 ....119 E3
Gratton Rd *WKENS* W14 ....101 E4
Gravel La *WCHPL* E1 ....25 E4
Gravelwood Cl *CHST* BR7 ....162 C3
Gravenel Gdns *TOOT* * SW17 ....151 E5
Graveney Rd *TOOT* SW17 ....151 E4

Gravesend Rd *SHB* W12 ....100 A1
Grayling Cl *CAN/RD* E16 ....93 E3
Grayling Rd *STNW/STAM* N16 ......59 D4
Grayling Sq *BETH* * E2 ....90 A2
Grayshott Rd *BTSEA* SW11 ....134 A1
Gray's Inn Rd *FSBYW* WC1X 9 D3
Gray's Inn Sq *GINN* WC1R 22 A2
Gray St *STHWK* SE1 ....34 C5
Gray's Yd *MHST* * W1U 18 B5
Grazebrook Rd *STNW/STAM* N16 ...59 D4
Great Brownings *DUL* SE21 ......155 F4
Great Castle St *REGST* W1B 19 E4
Great Central St *CAMTN* NW1 ......17 E2
Great Central Wy *WBLY* HA9 ....68 C2
Great Chapel St *SOHO/CST* W1F 20 A4
Great Chertsey Rd *CHSWK* W4 ....111 D4
Great Church La *HMSMTH* W6 ....113 D1
Great College St *WEST* SW1P 44 C2
Great Cross Av *GNWCH* SE10 ......123 E3
Great Cumberland Ms *MBLAR* W1H ...17 E5
Great Cumberland Pl *MBLAR* W1H ...17 E4
Great Dover St *STHWK* SE1 ....48 A2
Great Eastern Rd *SRTFD* E15 ....81 D4
Great Eastern St *SDTCH* EC2A 12 C4
Great Eastern Whf *BTSEA* * SW11...115 E3
Greatfield Av *EHAM* E6 ....95 F3
Greatfield Cl *LEW* SE13 ....140 A2
Greatfields Rd *BARK* IG11 ....85 D5
Great George St *STJSPK* SW1H 44 B1
Great Guildford St *STHWK* SE1 ....35 E4
Great Harry Dr *ELTH/MOT* SE9 ....162 A3
Great James St *BMSBY* WC1N 21 E2
Great Marlborough St
      SOHO/SHAV * W1F 19 E5
Great Maze Pond *STHWK* SE1 ....36 B1
Great New St *FLST/FETLN* * EC4A ...22 B4
Greatorex St *WCHPL* E1 ....90 A4
Great Ormond St *BMSBY* WC1N 21 D2
Great Percy St *FSBYW* WC1X 9 F3
Great Peter St *WEST* SW1P 44 A3
Great Portland St *GTPST* * W1W ...19 D1
Great Pulteney St *SOHO/CST* W1F ...31 F1
Great Queen St *HOL/ALD* WC2B 21 D4
Great Russell St *FITZ* W1T 20 B3
Great St Helen's *HDTCH* EC3A 24 C5
Great St Thomas Apostle
      BLKFR EC4V 35 F1
Great Scotland Yd *WHALL* SW1A 32 C4
Great Smith St *WEST* SW1P 44 B2
Great Spilmans *EDUL* SE22 ....137 D3
Great Suffolk St *STHWK* SE1 ....35 D4
Great Sutton St *FSBYE* EC1V 23 D1
Great Swan Aly *LOTH* EC2R 24 A4
Great Titchfield St *GTPST* W1W 19 D1
Great Tower St *MON* EC3R 36 C1
Great Trinity La *BLKFR* EC4V 35 F1
Great Turnstile *HHOL* WC1V 21 F3
Great Western Rd *MV/WKIL* W9 .....89 F4
Great West Rd *CHSWK* W4 ....110 C2
      HMSMTH W6 ....112 B1
Great West Road Chiswick
      CHSWK W4 ....111 F2
Great West Road Ellesmere Rd
      CHSWK W4 ....110 C2
Great West Road Hogarth La
      CHSWK W4 ....111 D3
Great Winchester St *OBST* EC2N 24 B4
Great Windmill St *SOHO/SHAV* W1D ...32 A2
Greaves Cl *BARK* IG11 ....85 D4
Greaves Cottages *POP/IOD* * E14 ...91 E4
Greaves Pl *TOOT* SW17 ....151 E4
Grebe Cl *FSTGT* E7 ....81 F2
Greek St *SOHO/SHAV* W1D 20 A4

Greenacres *ELTH/MOT* SE9 ....144 A4
Green Acres *SCUP* * DA14 ....163 F4
Greenacre Sq *BERM/RHTH* * SE16 ...103 D3
Green Arbour Ct *STP* * EC4M 22 C4
Greenaway Gdns *HAMP* NW3 ....72 B1
Green Bank *WAP* E1W 102 B2
Greenbay Rd *CHARL* SE7 ....125 D3
Greenberry St *STJWD* NW8 ....4 C2
Green Chain Wk *CHARL* SE7 ....107 D5
      ELTH/MOT SE9 ....144 B3
Green Cl *CDALE/KGS* NW9 ....50 C1
      EFNCH N2 ....54 C2
Greencoat Pl *WEST* SW1P 43 F4
Greencoat Rw *WEST* SW1P 43 F3
Greencroft Gdns *KIL/WHAMP* NW6 ...72 B4
Green Dl *EDUL* SE22 ....137 D3
Green Dragon Yd *WCHPL* E1 ....90 A4
Greenend Rd *CHSWK* W4 ....99 E3
Greenfell Man *DEPT* * SE8 ....121 F1
Greenfield Gdns *CRICK* NW2 ....53 E4
Greenfield Rd *WCHPL* E1 ....90 A4
Greengate *PLSTW* E13 ....94 B1
Greenham Cl *STHWK* SE1 ....46 A1
Greenhill *HAMP* NW3 ....73 D1
      WBLY HA9 ....50 B4
Green Hl *WOOL/PLUM* SE18 ....125 F1
Greenhill Gv *MNPK* E12 ....83 E1
Greenhill Pk *WLSDN* NW10 ....69 E5
Greenhill Rd *WLSDN* NW10 ....69 E5
Greenhill's Rents *FARR* * EC1M 22 C2
Greenhills Ter *IS* N1 ....77 D3
Greenhill Wy *WBLY* HA9 ....50 B4
Greenhithe Cl *ELTH/MOT* SE9 .....145 E3
Greenholm Rd *ELTH/MOT* SE9 ....144 B3
Green Hundred Rd *PECK* SE15 ....120 A2
Greenhurst Rd *WNWD* SE27 ......154 A5
Greenland Ms *DEPT* SE8 ....121 D1
Greenland Pl *CAMTN* * NW1 ....74 B5
Greenland Quay
      BERM/RHTH SE16 ....103 D5
Greenland Rd *CAMTN* NW1 ....74 B5
Greenland St *CAMTN* * NW1 ....74 B5
Green La *ELTH/MOT* SE9 ....162 A1
      IL IG1 ....67 D4
      FSBYPK N4 ....58 B1
Greenlaw St *WOOL/PLUM* SE18...108 A4
Greenleaf Cl *BRXS/STRHM* * SW2 ...136 A5
Greenleaf Rd *EHAM* E6 ....82 C5
Greenman St *IS* N1 ....76 C4
Greenoak Wy *WIM/MER* SW19 ....149 E4
Greenock Rd *ACT* W3 ....98 B4
Greens Ct *NTGHL* * W11 ....101 F2
      SOHO/CST W1F 32 A1
Greens End *WOOL/PLUM* SE18 ....108 B5
Greenside *IS* CAT* SE6 ....159 D2
Greenside Rd *SHB* W12 ....100 A4
Greenslade Rd *BARK* IG11 ....85 D5
Greenstead Gdns *PUT/ROE* SW15...130 A3
Greenstone Ms *WAN* E11 ....64 A1
Green St *FSTGT* E7 ....82 B2
      MYFR/PKLN W1K 29 F1
Greenstreet Hl *NWCR* * SE14 .....139 D1
Green Ter *CLKNW* EC1R 10 B4
The Green *ACT* W3 ....87 E5
      SRTFD E15 ....81 F3
      WAN E11 ....64 B1
      WELL DA16 ....145 E2
Greenvale Rd *ELTH/MOT* SE9.....143 F2
Greenview Cl *ACT* W3 ....99 E2
Green Wk *STHWK* SE1 ....48 C3
Greenway *CHST* BR7 ....162 A5
Green Wy *ELTH/MOT* SE9 ....143 D3
Greenway Cl *FSBYPK* N4 ....58 C4

Greenway Ct *IL* IG1 ....**66** A3
Greenwell St *GTPST* W1W...................**19** D1
Greenwich Church St
  GNWCH * SE10................................**122** C2
Greenwich Crs *EHAM* E6 ....**95** E4
Greenwich Foot Tnl *POP/IOD* E14 ...**122** C1
Greenwich High Rd *GNWCH* SE10....**122** B3
Greenwich Park St *GNWCH* * SE10 ..**123** D2
Greenwich Quay *DEPT* * SE8................**122** A2
Greenwich South St *GNWCH* SE10 ...**122** B4
Greenwich Vw *POP/IOD* E14 ....**104** B4
Greenwood Pl *KTTN* NW5 ....**74** B2
Greenwood Rd *HACK* E8 ....**78** A2
  PLSTW E13.......................................**93** F1
Greenwood Ter *WLSDN* * NW10 ....**69** D5
Green Yd *FSBYW* WC1X.........................**9** F5
Greet St *STHWK* SE1 ....**34** B4
Greg Cl *LEY* E10 ....**62** C1
Gregor Ms *BKHTH/KID* SE3 ....**124** A3
Gregory Crs *ELTH/MOT* SE9 ....**143** D5
Gregory Pl *KENS* W8 ....**26** C5
Greig Ter *WALW* SE17 ....**118** B2
Grenada Rd *CHARL* SE7......................**124** C3
Grenade St *POP/IOD* E14 ....**103** F1
Grenadier St *CAN/RD* E16 ....**108** A2
Grendon Gdns *WBLY* HA9.....................**50** A4
Grendon St *STJWD* NW8...........................**4** C5
Grenfell Rd *NTGHL* W11 ....**101** D1
Grenfell Wk *NTGHL* W11 ....**101** D1
Grenville Pl *SKENS* SW7 ....**39** E4
Grenville Rd *ARCH* N19.........................**57** E3
Grenville St *BMSBY* WC1N **21** D1
Gresham Gdns *CRICK* NW2....................**53** E3
Gresham Rd *BRXN/ST* SW9 ....**136** A1
  CAN/RD E16.....................................**94** B5
  EHAM E6 ....**95** F1
  WLSDN NW10 ....**69** D2
Gresham St *CITYW* EC2V **23** E4
Gresham Wy *WIM/MER* SW19 ....**150** A3
Gresley Cl *WALTH* E17 ....**61** E1
Gresley Rd *ARCH* N19 ....**56** C3
Gressenhall Rd *WAND/EARL* SW18 ..**131** F4
Gresse St *FITZ* W1T **20** A3
Greswell St *FUL/PGN* SW6 ....**113** D4
Greville Ms *KIL/WHAMP* NW6............**72** B5
Greville St *HCIRC* EC1N **22** B3
Grey Cl *ENCH* N2 ....**54** C1
Greycoat Pl *WEST* SW1P **44** A3
Greycoat St *WEST* SW1P **44** A3
Greycot Rd *BECK* BR3 ....**158** A5
Grey Eagle St *WCHPL* E1 ....**25** F2
Greyhound Rd *HMSMTH* W6 ....**113** D2
  WLSDN * NW10 ....**88** B2
Greyladies Gdns *GNWCH* * SE10 ......**122** C5
Greystead Rd *FSTH* SE23 ....**138** C5
Grierson Rd *FSTH* SE23 ....**139** D5
Griffin Cl *WLSDN* NW10 ....**70** B2
Griffin Manor Wy *THMD* SE28 ....**109** D4
Griffin Rd *WOOL/PLUM* SE18...........**127** D1
Griggs Ap *IL* IG1 ....**66** C4
Grigg's Pl *STHWK* SE1 ....**49** D3
Griggs Rd *LEY* E10 ....**62** C1
Grimsby Gv *CAN/RD* E16 ....**108** B2
Grimsby St *WCHPL* E1 ....**25** F1
Grimsel Pth *CMBW* SE5.......................**118** B3
Grimshaw Cl *HGT* * N6 ....**56** A2
Grimston Rd *FUL/PGN* SW6 ....**113** F5
Grindal St *STHWK* SE1 ....**46** A1
Grinling Pl *DEPT* SE8 ....**122** A2
Grinstead Rd *DEPT* SE8 ....**121** E1
Grittleton Av *WBLY* HA9.......................**68** B3
Grittleton Rd *MV/WKIL* W9 ....**2** A5
Grocers' Hall Ct *LOTH* * EC2R...............**24** C1

Groombridge Rd *HOM* E9 ....**79** D4
Groom Crs *WAND/EARL* SW18 ....**133** D2
Groomfield Cl *TOOT* SW17 ....**152** A4
Groom Pl *KTBR* SW1X **42** B2
Grosmont Rd *WOOL/PLUM* SE18.......**127** F1
Grosse Wy *PUT/ROE* SW15.................**130** B4
Grosvenor Av *HBRY* N5 ....**76** C3
  MORT/ESHN SW14 ....**129** E1
Grosvenor Br *VX/NE* SW8....................**116** B1
Grosvenor Cottages *KTBR* SW1X **42** A4
Grosvenor Crs *KTBR* SW1X **42** A3
Grosvenor Crescent Ms *KTBR* SW1X **42** A3
Grosvenor Gdns *BGVA* SW1W..............**42** C3
  CRICK NW2..**70** C3
  EHAM E6 ....**95** D2
  GLDGN NW11.....................................**53** F1
  MORT/ESHN SW14 ....**129** E1
Grosvenor Gardens Ms East
  BGVA * SW1W **43** D2
Grosvenor Gardens Ms North
  BGVA SW1W......................................**42** C3
Grosvenor Ga *BAY/PAD* W2 ....**29** F2
Grosvenor Hl *MYFR/PKLN* W1K **30** C1
Grosvenor Pde *ACT* * W3 ....**98** A2
Grosvenor Pk *CMBW* SE5 ....**118** C3
Grosvenor Pl *KTBR* SW1X **30** B5
Grosvenor Rd *CHSWK* W4 ....**110** C1
  EHAM E6 ....**83** D3
  FSTGT E7 ....**82** B3
  IL IG1 ....**66** C5
  LEY E10 ....**62** C3
  PIM SW1V **116** C2
Grosvenor Sq *MYFR/PKLN* W1K **30** B1
Grosvenor St *MYFR/PKLN* W1K **30** B1
Grosvenor Ter *CMBW* SE5 ....**118** C3
Grosvenor Wy *CLPT* E5 ....**60** C2
Grosvernor Wharf Rd
  POP/IOD E14....................................**105** D5
Grote's Buildings *BKHTH/KID* SE3....**123** E5
Grote's Pl *BKHTH/KID* SE3 ....**123** E5
Groton Rd *WAND/EARL* SW18 ....**150** B2
Grotto Ct *STHWK* * SE1 ....**35** E5
Grotto Pas *MHST* W1U **18** A2
Grove Cl *FSTH* SE23 ....**157** D1
Grove Cottages *CHSWK* * W4 ....**111** E3
Grove Crescent Rd *SRTFD* E15 ....**81** D3
Grovedale Rd *ARCH* N19 ....**57** D4
Grove Dwellings *WCHPL* * E1 ....**90** C4
Grove End *KTTN* NW5 ....**74** B1
Grove End Rd *STJWD* NW8.......................**4** B1
Grove Gdns *STJWD* NW8 ....**5** D4
Grove Green Rd *LEY* E10 ....**62** C5
Grove Hill Rd *CMBW* SE5 ....**137** E1
Groveland Ct *STP* EC4M **23** F5
Grovelands Cl *CMBW* SE5 ....**119** E5
Grovelands Rd *SEVS/STOTM* N15 ......**60** A1
Grove La *CMBW* SE5 ....**119** D4
Grove Market Pl *ELTH/MOT* * SE9.....**143** F4
Grove Ms *HMSMTH* W6 ....**100** C4
Grove Pk *CMBW* SE5 ....**119** E5
Grove Park Br *CHSWK* W4 ....**110** C3
Grove Park Gdns *CHSWK* W4 ....**110** B3
Grove Park Rd *CHSWK* W4 ....**110** B3
  ELTH/MOT SE9 ....**161** E2
Grove Park Ter *CHSWK* W4 ....**110** B3
Grove Pl *ACT* W3 ....**98** C2
  BAL SW12...**134** B4
  HAMP NW3 ....**55** D5
Grove Rd *ACT* W3...................................**98** C2
  BARN SW13 ....**111** F5
  BOW E3 ....**91** E1
  CRICK NW2 ....**70** C3
  HOM E9 ....**79** D5

WAN E11 ....**63** F2
Groveside Cl *ACT* W3.........................**86** A5
Grove St *BERM/RHTH* SE16 ....**103** F5
Grove Ter *KTTN* NW5...........................**56** A5
The Grove *FSBYPK* N4.........................**57** F2
   GLDGN NW11.......................................**53** D2
   HGT N6...**56** A3
   SRTFD E15..**81** E3
Grove V *EDUL* SE22 ....**137** E2
Groveway *BRXN/ST* SW9 ....**117** F4
Grove Wy *WBLY* HA9............................**68** C2
Grummant Rd *PECK* SE15 ....**119** F4
Grundy St *POP/IOD* E14.....................**92** B5
Gubyon Av *HNHL* SE24....................**136** B3
Guernsey Gv *HNHL* SE24..................**136** C5
Guernsey Rd *IS* N1...............................**76** C3
   WAN E11 ....**63** D3
Guibal Rd *LEE/GVPK* SE12.............**160** B1
Guildford Gv *GNWCH* SE10............**122** B4
Guildford Rd *EHAM* E6......................**95** E5
   GDMY/SEVK IG3..................................**67** E4
   VX/NE SW8...**117** E1
Guildhall Buildings *CITYW* EC2V **23** F4
Guildhall Yd *CITYW* EC2V **23** F4
Guildhouse St *PIM* SW1V **43** E5
Guild Rd *CHARL* SE7.........................**125** D1
Guilford Pl *BMSBY* WC1N **21** E1
Guilford St *BMSBY* WC1N **21** E1
Guilsborough Cl *WLSDN* NW10.......**69** E4
Guinness Cl *HOM* E9...........................**79** E4
Guinness Sq *STHWK* SE1 ....**48** C3
Guinness Trust *STNW/STAM* * N16 ...**59** F3
Guinness Trust Est *CHEL* SW3..........**41** E5
   SRTFD * E15...**81** F5
Guion Rd *FUL/PGN* SW6 ....**113** F5
Gulland Wk *IS* * N1 ....**76** C3
Gulliver Rd *BFN/LL* DA15.................**163** D2
Gulliver St *BERM/RHTH* SE16.........**103** F4
Gunmakers La *HOM* E9 ....**79** E3
Gunnell Cl *SYD* * SE26......................**156** A4
Gunner La *WOOL/PLUM* SE18.......**126** A1
Gunnersbury Av
   (North Circular Rd) *ACT* W3..........**98** A4
Gunnersbury Cl *CHSWK* * W4.........**110** B1
Gunnersbury Crs *ACT* W3.................**98** A3
Gunnersbury Gdns *ACT* W3.............**98** A3
Gunnersbury La *ACT* W3...................**98** A3
Gunners Rd *WAND/EARL* SW18 ....**151** D2
Gunning St *WOOL/PLUM* SE18.....**109** E5
Gunstor Rd *STNW/STAM* * N16 ....**77** E1
Gun St *WCHPL* E1.................................**25** E5
Gunter Gv *WBPTN* SW10..................**114** C2
Gunterstone Rd *WKENS* W14...........**113** E5
Gunthorpe St *WCHPL* E1....................**25** F5
Gunton Rd *CLPT* E5...............................**60** B5
Gunwhale Cl *BERM/RHTH* SE16.....**103** D2
Gurdon Rd *CHARL* SE7.....................**124** A1
Gurney Cl *BARK* IG11..........................**84** B3
   SRTFD E15..**81** E2
Gurney Rd *FUL/PGN* SW6 ....**132** C1
   SRTFD E15..**81** E2
Guthrie St *CHEL* SW3.......................**115** E1
Gutter La *CITYW* EC2V.........................**23** E4
Guy Barnett Gv *BKHTH/KID* SE3 ...**142** A1
Guyscliff Rd *LEW* SE13......................**140** C3
Guy St *STHWK* SE1...............................**36** B5
Gwalior Rd *PUT/ROE* SW15............**131** D2
Gwendolen Av *PUT/ROE* SW15......**131** D3
Gwendoline Av *PLSTW* E13................**82** B5
Gwendwr Rd *WKENS* W14................**113** E1
Gwyn Cl *FUL/PGN* SW6 ....**114** C3
Gwynne Rd *BTSEA* SW11.................**115** D5

Gwynne Whf *CHSWK* W4 ....**111** F2
Gylcote Cl *HNHL* SE24.....................**137** D2
Gyllyngdune Gdns *GDMY/SEVK* IG3 ...**67** F5

H

Haarlem Rd *HMSMTH* W6.................**101** D4
Haberdasher Pl *IS* N1...........................**12** B3
Haberdasher St *IS* N1...........................**12** B3
Hackford Rd *BRXN/ST* SW9 ....**117** F4
Hackford Wk *BRXN/ST* SW9...........**117** F4
Hackney Gv *HACK* E8............................**78** B3
Hackney Rd *BETH* E2............................**13** E5
Hadden Rd *THMD* SE28 ....**109** E4
Haddington Rd *BMLY* BR1................**159** D3
Haddo St *GNWCH* SE10....................**122** B2
Hadleigh Cl *WCHPL* E1.........................**90** C3
Hadleigh St *BETH* E2.............................**90** C3
Hadley Gdns *CHSWK* W4..................**111** D1
Hadley St *KTTN* NW5............................**74** B3
Hadrian Est * *BETH* * E2...........................**90** A1
Hadrian St *GNWCH* SE10..................**123** F1
Hafer Rd *BTSEA* SW11........................**133** E3
Hafton Rd *CAT* SE6.............................**159** E1
Haggerston Rd *HACK* E8.....................**77** F4
Hague St *BETH* E2..................................**90** A2
Ha-Ha Rd *WOOL/PLUM* SE18.........**125** F2
Haig Rd East *PLSTW* E13.....................**94** C2
Haig Rd West *PLSTW* E13....................**94** C2
Hailsham Av *BRXS/STRHM* SW2 .....**153** F2
Haimo Rd *ELTH/MOT* SE9.................**143** D3
Hainault Buildings *LEY* * E10...............**62** C3
Hainault Rd *WAN* E11...........................**62** C3
Hainault St *ELTH/MOT* SE9...............**162** B1
   IL IG1...**66** B4
Hainford Cl *PECK* SE15.....................**139** D2
Haining Cl *CHSWK* W4......................**110** A1
Hainthorpe Rd *WNWD* SE27............**154** B3
Hainton Cl *WCHPL* E1...........................**90** B5
Halcomb St *IS* N1..................................**77** E3
Halcrow St *WCHPL* * E1........................**90** B4
Haldane Pl *WAND/EARL* SW18 ....**150** B1
Haldane Rd *EHAM* E6...........................**95** D2
   FUL/PGN SW6.....................................**113** F3
Haldon Rd *WAND/EARL* SW18 ....**131** F4
Hale Gdns *ACT* W3................................**98** A2
Hale Rd *EHAM* E6...................................**95** E3
Hales St *DEPT* SE8..............................**122** A3
Hale St *POP/IOD* E14.........................**104** B1
Halesworth Rd *LEW* SE13.................**140** B1
Haley Rd *HDN* NW4................................**52** C1
Half Moon Crs *IS* * N1.............................**9** F1
Half Moon La *HNHL* SE24.................**136** C4
Halfmoon Pas *WCHPL* * E1...................**25** F5
Half Moon Pas *WCHPL* E1...................**25** F5
Half Moon St *MYFR/PICC* W1J..........**31** D3
Halford Rd *FUL/PGN* SW6................**114** A2
Halfway St *BFN/LL* DA15...................**163** E1
Haliday Wk *IS* N1...................................**77** D3
Halifax St *SYD* SE26............................**156** B3
Halkin Ar *KTBR* SW1X...........................**42** A2
Halkin Ms *KTBR* * SW1X........................**42** A2
Halkin Pl *KTBR* SW1X............................**42** A2
Halkin St *KTBR* SW1X............................**42** B1
Hallam Cl *CHST* BR7...........................**161** F5
Hallam Ms *REGST* W1B........................**19** D2
Hallam St *GTPST* W1W.........................**19** D2
Hall Dr *SYD* SE26...............................**156** C5
Halley Rd *FSTGT* E7..............................**82** C3
Halley St *POP/IOD* E14........................**91** E4

Hallfield Est *BAY/PAD* W2 ....**15** D5
Hall Ga *STJWD* NW8......................**3** F4
Halliford St *IS* N1......................**76** C4
Halliwell Rd *BRXS/STRHM* SW2 ......**135** F4
Hall Oak Wk *KIL/WHAMP* NW6......**71** F3
Hall Pl *BAY/PAD* W2......................**16** A1
Hall Rd *EHAM* E6......................**83** F5
  MV/WKIL W9 ....**3** F4
  WAN E11......................**81** D1
Hall St *FSBYE* EC1V......................**11** D3
Hallsville Rd *CAN/RD* E16......................**93** F5
The Hall *BKHTH/KID* SE3 ....**142** A1
Hall Vw *ELTH/MOT* SE9......................**161** D2
Hallywell Crs *EHAM* E6......................**95** F4
Halons Rd *ELTH/MOT* SE9......................**148** A5
Halpin Pl *WALW* SE17......................**48** B5
Halsbrook Rd *BKHTH/KID* SE3 ......**142** C1
Halsbury Rd *SHB* W12......................**100** B2
Halsey St *CHEL* SW3......................**41** E4
Halsham Crs *BARK* IG11......................**85** F3
Halsmere Rd *CMBW* SE5......................**118** B4
Halstow Rd *GNWCH* SE10......................**124** A1
  WLSDN NW10......................**89** D2
Halton Cross St *IS* * N1......................**76** B5
Halton Rd *IS* N1......................**76** B4
Hambalt Rd *CLAP* SW4......................**134** C3
Hambledon Av * *SF17*......................**119** D2
Hambledon Pl *DUL* SE21......................**155** F1
Hambledon Rd *WAND/EARL* SW18 ......**131** F5
Hambledown Rd *ELTH/MOT* * SE9 ......**145** D5
Hamble St *FUL/PGN* SW6......................**132** B1
Hameway *EHAM* E6......................**96** A3
Hamfrith Rd *SRTFD* E15......................**81** F3
Hamilton Cl *BERM/RHTH* SE16 ......**103** E3
  STJWD NW8......................**4** A4
Hamilton Gdns *STJWD* NW8......................**3** F3
Hamilton Pk *HBRY* N5......................**76** B1
Hamilton Pk West *HBRY* N5......................**76** B1
Hamilton Pl *MYFR/PKLN* W1K......................**30** B4
Hamilton Rd *CHSWK* W4......................**99** E4
  GLDGN NW11......................**53** D2
  IL IG1......................**84** B1
  SRTFD E15......................**93** E2
  WLSDN NW10......................**70** A2
  WNWD SE27......................**155** D4
Hamilton St *DEPT* SE8......................**122** A2
Hamilton Ter *STJWD* NW8......................**3** E2
Hamlea Cl *BKHTH/KID* SE3......................**142** A3
Hamlet Cl *LEW* SE13......................**141** E2
Hamlet Gdns *HMSMTH* W6......................**100** A5
Hamlet Sq *CRICK* NW2......................**53** E5
Hamlets Wy *BOW* E3......................**91** F3
The Hamlet *CMBW* * SE5......................**137** D1
Hamlet Wy *STHWK* SE1......................**48** B1
Hammersmith Br *HMSMTH* W6 ......**112** B1
Hammersmith Bridge Rd
  BARN SW13......................**112** B2
Hammersmith Broadway
  HMSMTH W6......................**100** C5
Hammersmith Emb *BARN* * SW13 ......**112** C1
Hammersmith F/O *HMSMTH* W6 ......**112** C1
Hammersmith Gv *HMSMTH* W6 ......**100** C4
Hammersmith Rd *HMSMTH* W6 ......**100** C5
Hammersmith Ter *HMSMTH* * W6 ......**112** A1
Hammett St *TWRH* EC3N......................**37** E1
Hammond St *KTTN* NW5......................**74** C3
Hamond Sq *IS* N1......................**12** C1
Ham Park Rd *FSTGT* E7......................**82** A4
Hampden Cl *CAMTN* NW1......................**8** B2
Hampden Gurney St *MBLAR* W1H **17** E5
Hampden Rd *ARCH* N19......................**57** D4
Hampshire Hog La *HMSMTH* * W6 ......**100** B5
Hampshire St *KTTN* * NW5......................**75** D3

Hampson Wy *VX/NE* SW8......................**117** F4
Hampstead Gdns *GLDGN* NW11 ......**54** A1
Hampstead Ga *HAMP* NW3......................**72** C2
Hampstead Gn *HAMP* NW3......................**73** E2
Hampstead Gv *HAMP* NW3......................**72** C1
Hampstead Hill Gdns *HAMP* NW3 ......**73** E1
Hampstead La *HGT* N6......................**55** F2
Hampstead Rd *CAMTN* NW1......................**7** E2
Hampstead Sq *HAMP* NW3......................**54** C5
Hampstead Wy *GLDGN* NW11......................**54** B2
Hampton Cl *KIL/WHAMP* NW6......................**2** A4
Hampton Ct *IS* N1......................**76** B3
Hampton Rd *FSTGT* E7......................**82** B2
  IL IG1......................**84** C1
  WAN E11......................**63** D3
Hampton St *WALW* SE17......................**47** D5
Ham Shades Cl *BFN/LL* DA15......................**163** F3
Ham Yd *SOHO/SHAV* * W1D......................**32** A1
Hanameel St *CAN/RD* E16......................**106** A2
Hanbury Rd *ACT* W3......................**98** B3
Hanbury St *WCHPL* E1......................**90** A4
Hancock Rd *BOW* E3......................**92** C2
Handa Wk *IS* N1......................**76** C3
Hand Ct *HHOL* WC1V......................**21** F3
Handel Pl *WLSDN* NW10......................**69** D3
Handel St *BMSBY* WC1N......................**8** C5
Handen Rd *LEW* SE13......................**141** E3
Handforth Rd *BRXN/ST* SW9......................**118** A3
  IL IG1......................**66** B5
Handley Gv *CRICK* NW2......................**53** D5
Handley Rd *HOM* E9......................**78** C4
Handtrough Wy *BARK* IG11......................**96** B1
Hanford Cl *WAND/EARL* SW18......................**150** A1
Hangar View Wy *ACT* W3......................**86** A5
Hanger Gn *EA* W5......................**86** A5
Hankey Pl *STHWK* SE1......................**48** B1
Hanley Gdns *FSBYPK* N4......................**57** F3
Hanley Rd *FSBYPK* N4......................**57** E3
Hannah Cl *WLSDN* * NW10......................**68** C1
Hannah Mary Wy *STHWK* * SE1......................**102** A5
Hannan Cl *WLSDN* NW10......................**68** C1
Hannay La *ARCH* N19......................**57** D2
Hannell Rd *FUL/PGN* SW6......................**113** E3
Hannen Rd *WNWD* SE27......................**154** B3
Hannibal Rd *WCHPL* E1......................**90** C4
Hannington Rd *CLAP* SW4......................**134** B1
Hanover Av *CAN/RD* E16......................**106** A2
Hanover Cl *RCH/KEW* TW9......................**110** A3
Hanover Dr *CHST* BR7......................**162** C4
Hanover Gdns *LBTH* SE11......................**118** A2
Hanover Pk *PECK* SE15......................**120** A4
Hanover Pl *COVGDN* WC2E......................**21** D5
Hanover Rd *WLSDN* NW10......................**70** C4
Hanover Sq *CONDST* W1S......................**19** D5
Hanover Steps *BAY/PAD* * W2......................**17** D5
Hanover St *CONDST* W1S......................**19** D5
Hanover Ter *CAMTN* NW1......................**5** D4
Hanover Terrace Ms *CAMTN* NW1......................**5** D4
Hanover Yd *IS* * N1......................**11** D1
Hansard Ms *WKENS* W14......................**101** D3
Hans Crs *CHEL* SW3......................**41** E2
Hansler Rd *EDUL* SE22......................**137** F3
Hanson Cl *BAL* SW12......................**134** B5
  MORT/ESHN SW14......................**128** C1
Hanson St *GTPST* W1W......................**19** E2
Hans Pl *KTBR* SW1X......................**41** E2
Hans Rd *CHEL* SW3......................**41** E2
Hans St *KTBR* SW1X......................**41** F3
Hanway Pl *FITZ* W1T......................**20** A4
Hanway St *FITZ* W1T......................**20** A4
Harben Pde *KIL/WHAMP* * NW6 ......**73** D5
Harben Rd *KIL/WHAMP* NW6......................**72** C4

Harberson Rd *BAL* SW12 ....152 B1
  SRTFD E15 ....81 F5
Harberton Rd *ARCH* N19 ....56 C3
Harbet Rd *BAY/PAD* W2 ....16 B3
Harbinger Rd *POP/IOD* E14 ....104 B5
Harbledown Rd *FUL/PGN* SW6 .....114 A4
Harbord Cl *CMBW* SE5 ....119 D5
Harbord St *FUL/PGN* SW6 ....113 D4
Harborough Av *BFN/LL* DA15 ......145 E5
Harborough Rd
  STRHM/NOR SW16 ....153 F4
Harbour Av *WBPTN* SW10 ....114 C4
Harbour Rd *CMBW* SE5 ....136 C1
Harbour Yd *WBPTN* * SW10 ....114 C4
Harbridge Av *PUT/ROE* SW15 .....129 F5
Harbut Rd *BTSEA* SW11 ....133 D2
Harcombe Rd *STNW/STAM* N16 ....59 E5
Harcourt Av *MNPK* E12 ....83 F1
Harcourt Buildings *EMB* * EC4Y 34 A1
Harcourt Rd *BROCKY* SE4 ....139 F2
  SRTFD E15 ....93 F1
Harcourt St *CAMTN* NW1 ....17 D3
Harcourt Ter *WBPTN* SW10 ....114 B1
Hardel Wk *BRXS/STRHM* SW2 ....136 A5
Hardens Manorway
  WOOL/PLUM SE18 ....107 D4
Harders Rd *PECK* SE15 ....120 B5
Hardess St *HNHL* SE24 ....136 C1
Hardie Cl *WLSDN* NW10 ....69 D2
Harding Cl *WALW* SE17 ....118 D2
Hardinge Rd *WLSDN* NW10 ....70 C5
Hardinge St *WCHPL* E1 ....90 C5
  WOOL/PLUM SE18 ....108 B4
Hardman Rd *CHARL* SE7 ....124 B1
Hardwicke Ms *FSBYW* * WC1X 9 F4
Hardwicke Rd *CHSWK* W4 ....98 C5
Hardwicke St *BARK* IG11 ....84 C5
Hardwick St *CLKNW* EC1R 10 B4
Hardwick's Wy *WAND/EARL* SW18 .132 A3
Hardwidge St *STHWK* SE1 ....36 C5
Hardy Av *CAN/RD* E16 ....106 A2
Hardy Cl *BERM/RHTH* SE16 ....103 D3
Hardy Cottages *GNWCH* * SE10 ....123 D2
Hardy Rd *BKHTH/KID* SE3 ....123 F2
Harebell Dr *EHAM* E6 ....96 A4
Hare & Billet Rd *BKHTH/KID* SE3 ..123 E4
Hare Ct *EMB* * EC4Y 22 A5
Harecourt Rd *IS* N1 ....76 C3
Haredale Rd *HNHL* SE24 ....136 C2
Haredon Cl *FSTH* SE23 ....138 C5
Harefield Ms *BROCKY* SE4 ....139 F1
Harefield Rd *BROCKY* SE4 ....139 F1
Hare Marsh *BETH* E2 ....90 A3
Hare Rw *BETH* E2 ....90 B1
Hare St *WOOL/PLUM* SE18 ....108 A4
Hare Wk *IS* N1 ....13 D2
Harewood Av *CAMTN* NW1 ....5 D5
Harewood Pl *CONDST* W1S 19 D5
Harewood Rw *CAMTN* NW1 ....17 D2
Harfield Gdns *CMBW* * SE5 ....137 E1
Harford St *WCHPL* E1 ....91 E3
Hargood Rd *BKHTH/KID* SE3 ....124 C4
Hargrave Pk *KTTN* NW5 ....56 C4
Hargrave Rd *ARCH* N19 ....56 C4
Hargwyne St *BRXN/ST* SW9 ....135 F1
Haringey Pk *CEND/HSY/T* N8 ....57 E1
Harland Av *BFN/LL* DA15 ....163 D3
Harland Rd *LEE/GVPK* SE12 ....160 A1
Harlescott Rd *PECK* SE15 ....139 D2
Harlesden Gdns *WLSDN* NW10 .....69 F5
Harlesden Rd *WLSDN* NW10 ....70 A3
Harleyford Rd *LBTH* SE11 ....117 F2
Harley Gdns *WBPTN* SW10 ....114 C1

Harley Gv *BOW* E3 ....91 F2
Harley Pl *CAVSQ/HST* W1G 18 C3
Harley Rd *HAMP* NW3 ....73 D4
  WLSDN NW10 ....87 E1
Harley St *CAVSQ/HST* W1G 18 C1
Harley Vls *WLSDN* * NW10 ....87 E1
Harlinger St *WOOL/PLUM* SE18 ...107 E4
Harman Cl *CRICK* NW2 ....53 E5
  STHWK * SE1 ....120 A1
Harman Dr *BFN/LL* DA15 ....145 F4
  CRICK NW2 ....53 E5
Harmood Gv *CAMTN* NW1 ....74 B4
Harmood St *CAMTN* NW1 ....74 B3
Harmsworth Ms *STHWK* SE1 ....46 B3
Harmsworth St *WALW* SE17 ....118 B1
Harold Rd *PLSTW* E13 ....82 B5
  WAN E11 ....63 E3
  WLSDN NW10 ....87 D2
Harp Cross La *MON* EC3R 36 C2
Harpenden Rd *MNPK* E12 ....64 C4
  WNWD SE27 ....154 B2
Harper Rd *EHAM* E6 ....95 F5
  STHWK SE1 ....47 F2
Harp Island Cl *WLSDN* NW10 ....51 D4
Harpley Sq *WCHPL* E1 ....90 C3
Harpour Rd *BARK* IG11 ....84 C3
Harpsden St *BTSEA* SW11 ....116 A4
Harpur St *BMSBY* WC1N 21 E2
Harraden Rd *BKHTH/KID* SE3 .....124 C4
Harrier Ms *THMD* SE28 ....109 D3
Harrier Wy *EHAM* E6 ....95 F4
Harriet Cl *BRXS/STRHM* SW2 ......136 A5
  HACK E8 ....78 A5
Harriet St *KTBR* SW1X 41 F1
Harriet Wk *KTBR* SW1X 41 F1
Harrington Cl *WLSDN* NW10 ....51 D5
Harrington Ct *MV/WKIL* * W9 ....89 F2
Harrington Gdns *SKENS* SW7 ....39 E5
Harrington Hl *CLPT* E5 ....60 B3
Harrington Rd *SKENS* SW7 ....40 A4
  WAN E11 ....63 E3
Harrington Sq *CAMTN* NW1 ....7 E1
Harrington St *CAMTN* NW1 ....7 E2
Harrington Wy *WOOL/PLUM* SE18 .107 D4
Harriott Cl *GNWCH* SE10 ....105 F3
Harrison St *STPAN* WC1H 9 D4
Harris St *CMBW* SE5 ....119 D3
  WALTH E17 ....61 F2
Harroway Rd *BTSEA* SW11 ....115 D5
Harrowby St *MBLAR* W1H 17 D4
Harrowgate Rd *HOM* E9 ....79 E3
Harrow Gn *WAN* E11 ....63 E5
Harrow La *POP/IOD* E14 ....104 C1
Harrow Pl *WCHPL* E1 ....25 D4
Harrow Rd *IL* IG1 ....84 C1
  WAN E11 ....63 F5
  WBLY HA9 ....68 B3
  WLSDN NW10 ....88 B2
Harrow Rd F/O *BAY/PAD* W2 ....16 B3
Harrow St *CAMTN* * NW1 ....17 D2
Hartfield Ter *BOW* E3 ....92 A1
Hart Gv *ACT* W3 ....98 A2
Hartham Cl *HOLWY* N7 ....75 E2
Hartham Rd *HOLWY* N7 ....75 E2
Harting Rd *ELTH/MOT* SE9 ....161 E4
Hartington Rd *CAN/RD* E16 ....94 B5
  CHSWK W4 ....110 B3
  VX/NE SW8 ....117 E4
  WALTH E17 ....61 E1
Hartismere Rd *FUL/PGN* SW6 .....113 F3
Hartlake Rd *HOM* E9 ....79 D3
Hartland Rd *CAMTN* * NW1 ....74 B4
  KIL/WHAMP NW6 ....89 F1

SRTFD E15 ....81 F4
Hartland Rd Arches CAMTN * NW1...74 A4
Hartley Av EHAM E6 ....83 E5
Hartley Rd WAN E11 ....63 F3
Hartley St BETH E2 ....90 C2
Hartmann Rd CAN/RD E16.............107 D2
Hartnoll St HOLWY N7 ....75 F2
Harton St DEPT SE8 ....122 A4
Hartshorn Gdns EHAM E6 ....96 A3
Harts La BARK IG11 ....84 B3
NWCR SE14 ....121 D4
Hartsmead Rd ELTH/MOT SE9.........161 F2
Hart St MON EC3R 37 D1
Hartswood Gdns SHB * W12 ....99 F4
Hartswood Rd SHB W12 ....99 F4
Hartsworth Cl PLSTW E13 ....93 F1
Hartville Rd WOOL/PLUM SE18 ......109 E1
Hartwell St HACK E8 ....77 F3
Harvard Hl CHSWK W4..................110 B1
Harvard Rd CHSWK W4.................110 B1
LEW SE13 ....140 C3
Harvey Gdns CHARL SE7 ....124 C1
Harvey Rd CMBW SE5 ....119 D4
IL IG1 ....84 B2
WAN E11 ....63 E3
Harvey St IS N1 ....77 D3
Harvington St HACK * E8 ....78 A4
Harvist Rd KIL/WHAMP NW6 ....89 E1
Harwood Ms FUL/PGN * SW6.........114 B3
Harwood Rd FUL/PGN SW6 ....114 A3
Harwood Ter FUL/PGN SW6...........114 B4
Hascombe Ter CMBW * SE5 ....119 D4
Haseley End FSTH * SE23 ....138 C5
Haselrigge Rd CLAP SW4 ....135 F2
Haseltine Rd SYD SE26 ....157 F4
Hasker St CHEL SW3 ....41 D4
Haslam Cl IS N1 ....76 A4
Haslam St PECK SE15 ....119 F4
Haslemere Av HDN NW4 ....53 D1
WAND/EARL SW18 ....150 B2
Haslemere Rd CEND/HSY/T N8 ....57 E2
GDMY/SEVK IG3 ....67 F4
Hassard St BETH E2 ....13 F2
Hassendean Rd BKHTH/KID SE3 .....124 B2
Hassett Rd HOM E9.......................79 D3
Hassocks Cl SYD SE26 ....156 B3
Hassop Rd CRICK NW2 ....71 D1
Hasted Rd CHARL SE7 ....125 D1
Hastings Cl PECK * SE15 ....120 A3
Hastings St STPAN WC1H 8 C1
Hatcham Park Ms NWCR SE14........121 D4
Hatcham Park Rd NWCR SE14........121 D4
Hatcham Rd PECK SE15 ....120 C2
Hatchard Rd ARCH N19 ....57 D4
Hatcliffe Cl BKHTH/KID SE3 ....141 F1
Hatcliffe St GNWCH SE10 ....123 F1
Hatfield Cl BKHTH/KID * SE3 ....124 A3
Hatfield Rd CHSWK W4...................99 D3
SRTFD E15 ....81 E2
Hatfields STHWK SE1.....................34 B3
Hathaway Crs MNPK E12 ....83 F3
Hatherley Gdns CEND/HSY/T N8 .....57 E1
EHAM E6 ....95 D2
Hatherley Gv BAY/PAD W2 ....14 C4
Hatherley St WEST SW1P 43 F5
Hathern Gdns ELTH/MOT SE9 ....162 A4
Hathorne Cl PECK SE15 ....120 B5
Hathorne Ter ARCH * N19 ....57 D3
Hathway St PECK SE15.................120 C4
Hatley Rd HOLWY N7 ....57 F4
Hat & Mitre Ct FARR EC1M 23 D1
Hatteraick St BERM/RHTH SE16......102 C3
Hatton Cl WOOL/PLUM SE18 ....127 D3

Hatton Gdn CLKNW EC1R 22 B1
Hatton Pl HCIRC EC1N 22 B1
Hatton Rw STJWD * NW8 ....16 B1
Hatton St STJWD NW8 ....16 B1
Hatton Wall HCIRC EC1N 22 A2
Haunch of Venison Yd
MYFR/PKLN W1K 18 C5
Havana Rd WIM/MER SW19............150 A2
Havannah St POP/IOD E14 ....104 A3
Havelock Cl SHB * W12 ....100 B1
Havelock Rd WIM/MER SW19 ....150 C5
Havelock St IL IG1 ....66 B4
IS N1 ....75 E5
Havelock Ter VX/NE SW8 ....116 B3
Havelock Wk FSTH SE23 ....156 C1
Haven Cl ELTH/MOT SE9 ....161 F3
WIM/MER SW19 ....149 D3
Haven St CAMTN NW1 ....74 B4
The Haven RCH/KEW TW9 ....128 A1
Havenwood WBLY HA9....................50 B5
Haverfield Gdns RCH/KEW TW9 .....110 A3
Haverfield Rd BOW E3 ....91 D2
Haverhill Rd BAL SW12 ....152 C1
Havering St WCHPL E1 ....91 D5
Haverstock Hl HAMP NW3 ....73 E3
Haverstock Pl IS N1 ....10 B2
Haverstock Rd KTTN NW5 ....74 A2
Haverstock St IS N1 ....11 D2
Havil St CMBW SE5 ....119 E4
Hawarden Gv HNHL SE24 ....136 C5
Hawarden Hl CRICK NW2 ....52 A5
Hawbridge Rd WAN E11..................63 D3
Hawes St IS N1 ....76 B4
Hawgood St BOW E3 ....92 A4
Hawke Pl BERM/RHTH * SE16 ....103 D3
Hawkesbury Rd PUT/ROE SW15 .....130 B3
Hawkesfield Rd FSTH SE23 ....157 E2
Hawkins Wy CAT SE6 ....158 A5
Hawkley Gdns WNWD SE27 ....154 B2
Hawkshead Rd CHSWK W4 ....99 E4
WLSDN * NW10 ....69 F4
Hawkslade Rd PECK SE15 ....139 D3
Hawksley Rd STNW/STAM N16 ....59 D5
Hawks Ms GNWCH * SE10 ....122 C3
Hawksmoor Cl EHAM E6 ....95 E5
WOOL/PLUM SE18 ....127 E1
Hawksmoor Ms WCHPL E1 ....102 B3
Hawksmoor St HMSMTH W6...........113 D2
Hawkstone Rd BERM/RHTH SE16....102 C5
Hawkwell Wk IS * N1 ....76 C5
Hawkwood Mt CLPT E5 ....60 B3
Hawley Crs CAMTN NW1 ....74 B4
Hawley Ms CAMTN NW1 ....74 B4
Hawley Rd CAMTN NW1 ....74 B4
Hawstead Rd LEW SE13 ....140 B4
Hawthorne Cl IS N1 ....77 E3
Hawthorne Gv CDALE/KGS NW9 ......50 C2
Hawthorne Rd WLSDN NW10 ....70 A4
Hawthorn Ter BFN/LL DA15...........145 F4
Hawthorn Wk NKENS W10...............89 F3
Hawtrey Rd HAMP NW3 ....73 F4
Hay Cl SRTFD E15..........................81 F4
Haycroft Gdns WLSDN NW10 ....70 A5
Haycroft Rd BRXS/STRHM SW2......135 E3
Hay Currie St POP/IOD E14 ....92 B5
Hayday Rd CAN/RD E16 ....94 A3
Hayden's Pl NTGHL W11 ....89 F5
Hayden Park Rd WIM/MER SW19.....150 A5
Haydon's Rd WIM/MER SW19 ....150 B5
Haydon St TWRH EC3N 37 E1
Haydon Wk WCHPL E1 ....25 E1
Haydon Wy BTSEA SW11 ....132 C2
Hayes Pl CAMTN NW1 ....17 D1

Hayfield Pas *WCHPL* E1 ....90 C3
Haygarth Pl *WIM/MER* SW19......149 D5
Hay Hl *MYFR/PICC* W1J............31 D2
Hayles St *LBTH* SE11 ....46 C4
Hayling Cl *STNW/STAM* N16.......77 E2
Haymarket *STJS* SW1Y 32 A2
Haymerle Rd *STHWK* SE1 ....120 A2
Haynes Cl *BKHTH/KID* SE3 ......141 E1
Hayne St *STBT* EC1A 23 D2
Hays La *STHWK* SE1 ....36 C3
Hay's Ms *MYFR/PICC* W1J..........30 C2
Hay St *BETH* E2 ....78 A5
Hayter Rd *BRXS/STRHM* SW2 ...135 E3
Hayton Cl *HACK* E8 ....77 F3
Hayward Gdns *PUT/ROE* SW15 ...130 C4
Hayward's Pl *CLKNW* EC1R 22 C1
Hazelbank Rd *CAT* SE6 ....159 D2
Hazelbourne Rd *BAL* SW12 ....134 B4
Hazeldean Rd *WLSDN* NW10 ....69 D2
Hazeldon Rd *BROCKY* SE4 ....139 E3
Hazel Gv *SYD* SE26....................157 D4
Hazelhurst Rd *TOOT* SW17 ....150 C4
Hazellville Rd *ARCH* N19.............57 D2
Hazelmere Rd *KIL/WHAMP* NW6....71 F5
Hazel Rd *SRTFD* * E15 ....81 E2
    WLSDN NW10...........................88 B2
Hazel Wy *STHWK* SE1 ....49 E4
Hazelwood Cl *CLPT* E5 ....61 C5
Hazlebury Rd *FUL/PGN* SW6 ......114 B5
Hazledene Rd *CHSWK* W4 ....110 C2
Hazlewell Rd *PUT/ROE* SW15 ....130 C3
Hazlewood Crs *NKENS* W10 ....89 E3
Hazlitt Ms *WKENS* * W14...........101 E4
Hazlitt Rd *WKENS* W14 ....101 E4
Headcorn Rd *BMLY* BR1 ....159 F5
Headfort Pl *KTBR* SW1X 42 B1
Headington Rd *WAND/EARL* SW18...150 C1
Headlam Rd *CLAP* SW4 ....135 D4
Headlam St *WCHPL* E1 ....90 B3
Headley Dr *GNTH/NBYPK* IG2.......66 B1
Head St *WCHPL* E1 ....91 D5
Heald St *NWCR* SE14 ....121 F4
Healey St *CAMTN* * NW1..............74 B3
Hearne Rd *CHSWK* W4 ....110 A1
Hearn's Buildings *WALW* SE17 .....48 B5
Hearn St *SDTCH* EC2A 25 D1
Hearnville Rd *BAL* SW12 ....152 A1
Heath Brow *HAMP* NW3 ....54 C5
Heath Cl *GLDGN* NW11 ....54 B2
Heathcote St *BMSBY* WC1N 9 E5
Heath Dr *HAMP* NW3 ....54 C5
Heathedge *SYD* * SE26 ....72 B1
Heatherbank *ELTH/MOT* SE9 .....125 F5
Heather Cl *EHAM* E6 ....96 A5
    LEW SE13 ....141 D5
    VX/NE SW8 ....134 B1
Heather Gdns *GLDGN* NW11 ....53 E1
Heather Park Dr *ALP/SUD* HA0.....68 A4
Heather Rd *CRICK* NW2 ....51 F4
    LEE/GVPK SE12 ....160 D2
Heather Wk *NKENS* W10 ....89 E3
Heatherwood Cl *MNPK* E12..........64 B4
Heathfield Av *WAND/EARL* SW18 ...133 D5
Heathfield Cl *CAN/RD* E16 ....95 D4
Heathfield Gdns *CHSWK* W4 ....110 C1
    GLDGN NW11 ....53 D1
    WAND/EARL SW18 ....133 D4
Heathfield Pk *CRICK* NW2 ....70 C3
Heathfield Rd *ACT* W3 ....98 B3
    WAND/EARL SW18 ....132 C4
Heathfield Sq *WAND/EARL* SW18 ...133 D4
Heathfield Ter *CHSWK* W4 ....110 C1
    WOOL/PLUM SE18 ....127 D2

Heathgate *GLDGN* NW11 ....54 B1
Heathgate Pl *HAMP* NW3 ....73 F2
Heathland Rd *STNW/STAM* N16 ....59 E3
Heath La *BKHTH/KID* SE3 ....123 D5
Heathlee Rd *BKHTH/KID* SE3 .....141 F2
Heathman's Rd *FUL/PGN* * SW6 ...113 F4
Heath Md *WIM/MER* SW19 ....149 D3
Heath Ri *PUT/ROE* SW15 ....131 D4
Heath Rd *VX/NE* SW8 ....116 B5
Heathside *HAMP* NW3 ....73 D1
Heathstan Rd *SHB* W12 ....88 A5
Heath St *HAMP* NW3 ....54 C5
Heathview Gdns *PUT/ROE* SW15 ...130 C5
Heath Vls *WAND/EARL* * SW18 ....150 C1
    WOOL/PLUM SE18 ....127 F1
Heathville Rd *ARCH* N19..............57 E2
Heathwall St *BTSEA* SW11 ....133 F1
Heathway *BKHTH/KID* SE3 ....124 A3
Heathwood Gdns *CHARL* SE7 .....107 E5
Heaton Rd *PECK* SE15 ....138 B1
Heaver Rd *BTSEA* * SW11 ....133 D1
Heavitree Cl *WOOL/PLUM* SE18 ...127 D1
Heavitree Rd *WOOL/PLUM* SE18 ...127 D1
Hebdon Rd *TOOT* SW17 ....151 E3
Heber Rd *CRICK* NW2 ....71 D2
    EDUL SE22 ....137 F4
Hebron Rd *HMSMTH* W6 ....100 B4
Heckfield Pl *FUL/PGN* SW6 ....114 A3
Heckford St *WAP* E1W 103 D1
Hector St *WOOL/PLUM* * SE18 ...109 E5
Heddington Gv *HOLWY* N7 ....75 F2
Heddon St *CONDST* W1S...............31 E2
Hedger's Gv *HOM* * E9 ....79 E5
Hedger St *LBTH* SE11 ....46 C4
Hedgley St *LEE/GVPK* SE12 ....141 F3
Hedingham Cl *IS* N1 ....76 C4
Hedley Rw *HBRY* N5 ....77 D2
Heenan Cl *BARK* IG11 ....84 C3
Heidegger Crs *BARN* SW13.........112 B3
Heigham Rd *EHAM* E6 ....83 D4
The Heights *CHARL* SE7 ....124 C1
Heiron St *WALW* SE17 ....118 B2
Helby Rd *CLAP* SW4 ....135 D4
Helder Gv *LEE/GVPK* SE12 ....141 F5
Helena Pl *HOM* E9 ....78 B5
Helena Rd *PLSTW* E13 ....93 F1
    WLSDN NW10 ....70 B2
Helena Sq *BERM/RHTH* SE16 .....103 E1
Helenslea Av *GLDGN* NW11 ....53 F3
Helen's Pl *BETH* E2 ....90 C2
Helen St *WOOL/PLUM* * SE18 ....108 B5
Helix Gdns *BRXS/STRHM* SW2 ...135 F4
Helix Rd *BRXS/STRHM* SW2 ....135 F4
Hellings St *WAP* E1W..................102 A2
Helme Cl *WIM/MER* SW19 ....149 F5
Helmet Rw *FSBYE* EC1V 11 F5
Helmore Rd *BARK* IG11 ....85 E4
Helmsley Pl *HACK* E8 ....78 B4
Helmsley St *HACK* E8 ....78 B4
Helsinki Sq *BERM/RHTH* SE16 ...103 F4
Helvetia St *CAT* SE6 ....157 F2
Hemans St *VX/NE* SW8 ....117 D3
Hemingford Rd *IS* N1 ....75 F5
Hemlock Rd *SHB* W12 ....99 F1
Hemming St *WCHPL* E1 ....90 A3
Hemmingway Cl *KTTN* NW5 ....74 A1
Hemp Wk *WALW* SE17 ....48 B4
Hemstal Rd *KIL/WHAMP* NW6 ......72 A4
Hemsworth St *IS* N1 ....12 C1
Henchman St *SHB* W12 ....87 F5
Henderson Cl *WLSDN* NW10 ....68 C3
Henderson Dr *STJWD* NW8 ....4 A5

Henderson Rd *FSTGT* E7....................82 C3
    WAND/EARL SW18....................133 E5
Hendham Rd *TOOT* SW17 ....151 E2
Hendon Park Rw *GLDGN* NW11 ......53 F1
Hendon Wy *HDN* NW4 ....52 C1
Hendre Rd *STHWK* SE1 ....49 D5
Hendrick Av *BAL* SW12 ....133 F5
Heneage La *HDTCH* EC3A 25 D5
Heneage St *WCHPL* E1 ....25 F3
Henfield Cl *ARCH* N19 ....56 C3
Hengist Rd *LEE/GVPK* SE12 ....142 C5
Hengrave Rd *FSTH* SE23 ....138 C5
Henley Cl *BERM/RHTH* * SE16 ....102 C3
Henley Dr *BERM/RHTH* SE16 ....49 F4
Henley Rd *CAN/RD* E16 ....107 F3
    IL IG1..84 C1
    WLSDN NW10..................................70 C5
Henley St *BTSEA* SW11 ....116 A5
Hennel Cl *FSTH* SE23 ....156 C3
Henniker Gdns *EHAM* E6 ....95 D2
Henniker Ms *CHEL* SW3 ....115 D2
Henniker Rd *SRTFD* E15 ....81 D2
Henning St *BTSEA* SW11 ....115 E4
Henrietta Cl *DEPT* SE8 ....122 A2
Henrietta Ms *BMSBY* WC1N 9 D3
Henrietta Pl *CAVSQ/HST* W1G 18 C4
Henrietta St *COVGDN* WC2E 33 D1
    SRTFD E15 ....80 C2
Henriques St *WCHPL* E1 ....90 A5
Henry Addlington Cl *EHAM* E6 ....96 B4
Henry Cooper Wy *LEE/GVPK* SE12 ..161 D3
Henry Dickens Ct *NTGHL* W11 ....101 D1
Henry Doulton Dr *TOOT* SW17 ....152 A4
Henry Jackson Rd *PUT/ROE* SW15 ..131 D1
Henry Rd *EHAM* E6 ....95 E1
    FSBYPK N4..58 C3
Henryson Rd *BROCKY* SE4 ....140 A3
Hensford Gdns *SYD* SE26 ....156 B4
Henshall St *IS* N1 ....77 D3
Henshaw St *WALW* SE17 ....48 A4
Henslowe Rd *EDUL* SE22 ....138 A3
Henson Av *CRICK* NW2 ....70 C2
Henstridge Pl *STJWD* NW8 ....4 C1
Henty Cl *BTSEA* SW11 ....115 E3
Henty Wk *PUT/ROE* SW15 ....130 B3
Henwick Rd *ELTH/MOT* SE9 ....143 D1
Hepscott Rd *HOM* E9 ....80 A3
Heralds Pl *LBTH* SE11 ....46 C4
Herald St *BETH* E2 ....90 B3
Herbal Hl *CLKNW* EC1R 22 B1
Herbert Crs *KTBR* SW1X 41 F2
Herbert Gdns *CHSWK* W4 ....110 B3
    WLSDN NW10..................................88 B1
Herbert Pl *WOOL/PLUM* SE18 ....126 B2
Herbert Rd *CDALE/KGS* NW9 ....52 A1
    GDMY/SEVK IG3................................67 E4
    MNPK E12..83 E1
    WALTH E17..61 F2
    WOOL/PLUM SE18 ....126 B3
Herbert St *KTTN* NW5 ....74 A3
    PLSTW E13..94 A1
Herbrand St *BMSBY* WC1N 8 C3
Hercules Pl *HOLWY* N7 ....57 E5
Hercules Rd *STHWK* SE1 ....45 F3
Hercules St *HOLWY* N7 ....57 E5
Hereford Gdns *IL* IG1 ....65 E2
Hereford Ms *BAY/PAD* W2 ....14 B4
Hereford Pl *NWCR* * SE14 ....121 F3
Hereford Retreat *PECK* SE15 ....120 A3
Hereford Rd *ACT* W3 ....98 C1
    BAY/PAD W2 ....14 B5
Hereford Sq *SKENS* SW7 ....39 F5
Hereford St *BETH* E2 ....90 A3

Hereward Rd *TOOT* SW17..................151 E4
Heritage Pl *WAND/EARL* * SW18 ......133 D4
Herlwyn Gdns *TOOT* SW17 ....151 F4
Hermes Cl *MV/WKIL* W9 ....14 A1
Hermes St *IS* N1 ....10 A2
Hermitage Gdns *HAMP* NW3 ....54 A5
Hermitage La *CRICK* NW2..................54 A5
Hermitage Rd *FSBYPK* N4 ....58 C2
Hermitage Rw *HACK* * E8 ....78 A2
Hermitage St *BAY/PAD* W2 ....16 A3
The Hermitage *BARN* * SW13............111 F4
    FSTH SE23 ....156 C1
    LEW * SE13 ....122 C5
Hermitage Wall *WAP* E1W 102 A2
Hermit Rd *CAN/RD* E16......................93 F3
Hermit St *FSBYE* EC1V 10 C3
Herndon Rd *WAND/EARL* SW18........132 C3
Herne Cl *WLSDN* NW10 ....69 D2
Herne Hl *HNHL* SE24 ....136 C3
Herne Hill Rd *HNHL* SE24................136 C1
Herne Pl *HNHL* SE24 ....136 B4
Heron Cl *WLSDN* NW10 ....69 E3
Heron Crs *SCUP* DA14 ....163 E4
Herondale Av *WAND/EARL* SW18 ....151 D1
Heron Dr *FSBYPK* N4 ....58 C4
Herongate Rd *MNPK* E12 ....64 C4
Heron Ms *IL* IG1................................66 B4
Herons Lea *HGT* * N6 ....55 F1
Herrick Rd *FSBYPK* N4 ....58 C5
Herrick St *WEST* SW1P 44 B5
Herries St *NKENS* W10 ....89 E1
Herringham Rd *CHARL* SE7 ....106 C4
Hersant Cl *WLSDN* NW10 ....70 A5
Herschell Rd *FSTH* SE23 ....139 D5
Hersham Cl *PUT/ROE* SW15 ....130 A3
Hershell Ct *MORT/ESHN* * SW14 ....128 B2
Hertford Av *MORT/ESHN* SW14........129 D3
Hertford Rd *BARK* IG11 ....84 B4
    GNTH/NBYPK IG2..............................67 E1
    IS N1..77 E4
Hertford St *MYFR/PICC* W1J 30 C3
Hertslet Rd *HOLWY* N7 ....57 F5
Hertsmere Rd *POP/IOD* E14 ....104 A1
Hesewall Cl *VX/NE* SW8 ....116 C5
Hesketh Pl *NTGHL* W11 ....101 E1
Hesketh Rd *FSTGT* E7 ....64 A5
Heslop Rd *BAL* SW12 ....151 F1
Hesper Ms *ECT* SW5..........................114 B3
Hesperus Crs *POP/IOD* E14 ....104 B5
Hessel St *WCHPL* E1 ....90 B5
Hestercombe Av *FUL/PGN* SW6 ......113 E5
Hester Rd *BTSEA* SW11 ....115 E3
Hester Ter *RCH/KEW* TW9 ....128 A1
Heston St *DEPT* SE8 ....121 F4
Hetherington Rd *CLAP* SW4 ....135 E2
Hetley Rd *SHB* W12..........................100 B2
Hevelius Cl *GNWCH* SE10 ....123 F1
Hever Cft *ELTH/MOT* SE9 ....162 A4
Heverham Rd *WOOL/PLUM* SE18 ....109 E5
Hewer St *NKENS* W10 ....89 D4
Hewett St *SDTCH* EC2A 25 D1
Hewison St *BOW* E3..........................91 F1
Hewlett Rd *BOW* E3 ....91 E1
The Hexagon *HGT* N6........................55 F3
Hexal Rd *CAT* SE6 ....159 E3
Hexham Rd *WNWD* SE27 ....154 C2
Heybridge Wy *LEY* E10......................61 E2
Heyford Av *VX/NE* SW8 ....117 E3
Heyford Ter *VX/NE* SW8 ....117 E3
Heygate Est *WALW* SE17 ....47 F4
Heygate St *WALW* SE17 ....47 E5

Heysham La *HAMP* NW3 ....**54** B5
Heysham Rd *SEVS/STOTM* N15 .....**59** D1
Heythorp St *WAND/EARL* SW18......**149** F1
Heyworth Rd *CLPT* E5 ....**78** B1
   FSTGT E7 ....**81** F2
Hibbert Rd *WALTH* E17 ....**61** F2
Hibbert St *BTSEA* SW11 ....**132** C5
Hichisson Rd *PECK* SE15 ....**138** C3
Hickin Cl *CHARL* SE7.....................**107** D5
Hickin St *POP/IOD* E14 ....**104** C4
Hickling Rd *IL* IG1 ....**84** B2
Hickman Cl *CAN/RD* E16 ....**95** D4
Hicks Cl *BTSEA* SW11 ....**133** E1
Hicks St *DEPT* SE8 ....**121** E1
Hide Pl *WEST* SW1P........................**44** A5
Highbank Pl *WAND/EARL* * SW18 ...**132** B5
Highbank Wy *CEND/HSY/T* N8.......**58** A1
Highbridge Rd *BARK* IG11..............**84** B5
Highbrook Rd *BKHTH/KID* SE3 .....**143** D1
Highbury Cnr *HBRY* N5 ....**76** B3
Highbury Crs *HBRY* N5 ....**76** B2
Highbury Est *HBRY* N5 ....**76** C2
Highbury Gdns *IL* IG1 ....**67** E4
Highbury Gra *HBRY* N5 ....**76** B1
Highbury Gv *HBRY* N5 ....**76** B2
Highbury Hl *HBRY* N5 ....**76** B3
Highbury New Pk *HBRY* N5.............**76** B3
Highbury Pk *HBRY* N5 ....**76** B1
Highbury Pl *HBRY* N5 ....**76** B3
Highbury Qd *HBRY* N5 ....**58** C5
Highbury Rd *WIM/MER* SW19 ....**149** E5
Highbury Station Pde *IS* * N1 ....**76** B3
Highbury Station Rd *IS* * N1 ....**76** A3
Highbury Ter *HBRY* N5 ....**76** B2
Highbury Terrace Ms *HBRY* N5.......**76** B2
Highclere St *SYD* SE26 ....**157** E4
Highcliffe Dr *PUT/ROE* SW15.......**129** F3
Highcombe *CHARL* SE7 ....**124** B2
Highcombe Cl *ELTH/MOT* SE9.......**161** D1
Highcroft Gdns *GLDGN* NW11 ....**53** F1
Highcroft Rd *ARCH* N19..................**57** E2
Highdown Rd *PUT/ROE* SW15 ......**130** B4
Highfield Av *GLDGN* NW11 ....**53** D2
Highfield Cl *LEW* SE13 ....**141** D4
Highfield Gdns *GLDGN* NW11 ....**53** E1
Highfield Rd *ACT* W3 ....**86** B3
   GLDGN * NW11 ....**53** E1
Highfields Gv *HGT* N6 ....**56** A3
Highgate Av *HGT* N6 ....**56** B2
Highgate Cl *HGT* N6 ....**56** A2
Highgate High St *HGT* N6 ....**56** A3
Highgate Hl *ARCH* N19 ....**56** B3
Highgate Rd *KTTN* NW5 ....**56** B4
Highgate Spinney *CEND/HSY/T* * N8 ..**57** D1
Highgate West Hl *HGT* N6 ....**56** A4
High Gv *WOOL/PLUM* SE18...........**127** D3
High Hill Ferry *CLPT* E5 ....**60** B3
High Holborn *HHOL* WC1V **21** D4
Highland Cft *BECK* BR3................**158** B5
Highlands Av *ACT* W3 ....**98** C3
Highlands Gdns *IL* IG1 ....**65** F3
Highland Ter *LEW* * SE13 ....**140** B1
High Level Dr *SYD* SE26 ....**156** A4
Highlever Rd *NKENS* W10 ....**88** C4
Highmead *WOOL/PLUM* SE18 ....**127** F3
High Meads Rd *CAN/RD* E16 ....**95** D5
Highmore Rd *BKHTH/KID* SE3 ......**123** E3
High Mt *HDN* * NW4 ....**52** A1
The High Pde *STRHM/NOR* * SW16 ..**153** E3
High Park Rd *RCH/KEW* TW9 ....**110** A4
High Point *ELTH/MOT* SE9 ....**162** B5
High Rd *IL* IG1 ....**66** B5
   LEY E10 ....**62** B1

WLSDN NW10 ....**69** E3
High Rd Leyton *LEY* E10...................**62** B4
High Rd Leytonstone *WAN* E11 ......**63** E5
Highshore Rd *PECK* SE15 ....**119** F5
Highstone Av *WAN* E11 ....**64** A1
High St *ACT* W3 ....**98** C2
   SRTFD E15 ....**81** D4
   WAN E11 ....**64** B1
   WIM/MER SW19 ....**149** D5
High St Harlesden *WLSDN* NW10 ...**87** F1
High Street Ms *WIM/MER* SW19 ...**149** D5
High St North *MNPK* E12 ....**83** E2
High St South *EHAM* E6 ....**95** F1
High Timber St *BLKFR* EC4V...........**35** E1
High Trees *BRXS/STRHM* SW2 .....**154** A1
The Highway *WAP* E1W **102** A1
Highwood Rd *ARCH* N19 ....**57** E5
Highworth St *CAMTN* * NW1 ....**17** D2
Hilary Cl *FUL/PGN* * SW6...............**114** B3
Hilary Rd *ACT* W3 ....**99** F1
   SHB * W12 ....**87** F5
Hilborough Rd *HACK* E8 ....**77** F4
Hilda Rd *CAN/RD* E16 ....**93** E3
   EHAM E6 ....**83** D4
Hilda Ter *BRXN/ST* * SW9 ....**118** A5
Hildreth St *BAL* SW12....................**152** B1
Hildyard Rd *FUL/PGN* SW6............**114** A2
Hiley Rd *WLSDN* NW10 ....**88** C2
Hilgrove Rd *KIL/WHAMP* NW6 ....**72** C4
Hillbeck Cl *PECK* SE15 ....**120** C3
Hillbrook Rd *TOOT* SW17 ....**151** F3
Hillbury Rd *TOOT* SW17 ....**152** B3
Hill Cl *CHST* BR7 ....**162** B5
   CRICK NW2 ....**52** B5
   GLDGN NW11 ....**54** A1
Hillcourt Rd *EDUL* SE22 ....**138** B4
Hillcrest *HGT* N6 ....**56** A2
   HNHL * SE24 ....**137** D2
Hillcrest Cl *SYD* SE26 ....**156** A4
Hill Crest Gdns *CRICK* NW2 ....**52** A5
Hillcrest Rd *ACT* W3.......................**98** A2
   BMLY BR1 ....**160** A4
Hillcroft *EHAM* E6 ....**96** B4
Hill Dr *CDALE/KGS* NW9................**50** C3
Hilldrop Crs *HOLWY* N7 ....**75** D2
Hilldrop Est *HOLWY* N7 ....**75** D2
   HOLWY N7 ....**75** E1
Hilldrop La *HOLWY* N7 ....**75** D2
Hilldrop Rd *HOLWY* N7 ....**75** D2
Hill End *WOOL/PLUM* SE18 ....**126** A4
Hillersdon Av *BARN* SW13............**112** A5
Hillery Cl *WALW* SE17.....................**48** B5
Hill Farm Rd *NKENS* W10 ....**88** C4
Hillfield Rd *KIL/WHAMP* NW6.........**71** F2
Hill Gdns Craven *BAY/PAD* * W2 ....**27** E1
Hillgate Pl *BAL* SW12....................**134** B1
   KENS W8 ....**26** A3
Hillgate St *KENS* W8 ....**26** A3
Hill House Rd *STRHM/NOR* SW16 ..**153** F5
Hilliard's Ct *WAP* E1W **102** C2
Hillier Rd *BTSEA* SW11 ....**133** F4
Hillingdon St *WALW* SE17 ....**118** C5
Hillman St *HACK* E8 ....**78** B3
Hillmarton Rd *HOLWY* N7 ....**75** D2
Hillmarton Ter *HOLWY* * N7 ....**75** E2
Hillmead Dr *BRXN/ST* SW9............**136** B2
Hillmore Gv *SYD* SE26 ....**157** D5
Hillreach *WOOL/PLUM* SE18.........**125** F1
Hillrise Rd *ARCH* N19.....................**57** E2
Hill Rd *STJWD* NW8 ....**3** F2
Hillsboro Rd *EDUL* SE22 ....**137** D3
Hillside *WLSDN* NW10 ....**69** D5
Hillside Cl *MV/WKIL* W9....................**3** D1

Hillside Gdns *BRXS/STRHM* * SW2 ......154 A2
  HGT N6 ....56 A1
Hillside Rd *BRXS/STRHM* SW2 ....153 F2
  SEVS/STOTM N15 ....59 E1
Hillsleigh Rd *KENS* W8 ....101 F2
Hills Pl *SOHO/CST* W1F 19 E5
Hillstowe St *CLPT* E5 ....60 C1
Hill St *MYFR/PICC* W1J 30 C3
Hilltop Cottages *SYD* * SE26 ....156 B4
Hilltop Rd *KIL/WHAMP* NW6 ....72 A4
Hill View Crs *IL* IG1 ....65 F1
Hill View Dr *WELL* DA16 ....127 E5
Hillview Rd *CHST* BR7 ....162 A5
Hillway *CDALE/KGS* NW9 ....51 E3
  HGT N6 ....56 A1
Hillworth Rd *BRXS/STRHM* SW2 ....136 A5
Hillyard St *BRXN/ST* SW9 ....118 A4
Hillyfield Cl *HOM* E9 ....79 E2
Hilly Flds *BROCKY* * SE4 ....140 A2
Hilly Fields Crs *BROCKY* SE4 ....140 A2
Hilsea St *CLPT* E5 ....78 C1
Himley Rd *TOOT* SW17 ....151 E5
Hinckley Rd *EDUL* SE22 ....138 A2
Hind Ct *FLST/FETLN* * EC4A 22 B5
Hinde Ms *MHST* * W1U 18 B4
Hinde St *MHST* W1U 18 B4
Hind Gv *POP/IOD* E14 ....92 A5
Hindmans Rd *EDUL* SE22 ....138 A3
Hindmarsh Cl *WCHPL* E1 ....102 A1
Hindrey Rd *CLPT* E5 ....78 B2
Hindsley's Pl *FSTH* SE23 ....156 C2
Hinstock Rd *WOOL/PLUM* SE18 ....126 C3
Hinton Cl *ELTH/MOT* SE9 ....161 E1
Hinton Rd *BRXN/ST* SW9 ....136 B1
Hippodrome Pl *NTGHL* W11 ....101 E1
Hitcham Rd *LEY* E10 ....61 F2
Hither Farm Rd *BKHTH/KID* SE3 ......142 C1
Hitherfield Rd *STRHM/NOR* SW16 ....153 F2
Hither Green La *LEW* SE13 ....140 C4
Hitherwood Dr *DUL* SE21 ....155 F4
Hoadly Rd *STRHM/NOR* SW16 ....153 E4
Hobart Pl *BGVA* SW1W 42 C3
Hobbes Wk *PUT/ROE* SW15 ....130 B3
Hobbs Pl *IS* * N1 ....77 E5
Hobbs Place Est *IS* N1 ....12 C1
Hobbs Rd *WNWD* SE27 ....154 C4
Hobday St *POP/IOD* E14 ....92 B5
Hobsons Pl *WCHPL* * E1 ....90 A4
Hobury St *WBPTN* SW10 ....114 C2
Hocker St *BETH* * E2 ....13 E4
Hockley Av *EHAM* E6 ....95 E1
Hockley Ms *BARK* IG11 ....97 E1
Hocroft Av *CRICK* NW2 ....53 F5
Hocroft Rd *CRICK* NW2 ....71 F1
Hocroft Wk *CRICK* NW2 ....53 F5
Hodford Rd *GLDGN* NW11 ....53 F3
Hodister Cl *CMBW* SE5 ....118 C3
Hoffman Sq *IS* * N1 ....12 B3
Hofland Rd *WKENS* W14 ....101 E4
Hogan Ms *BAY/PAD* W2 ....16 A2
Hogarth Cl *CAN/RD* E16 ....95 D4
Hogarth Pl *ECT* * SW5 ....38 C5
Hogarth Rd *ECT* SW5 ....38 C5
Hogarth Ter *CHSWK* * W4 ....111 E2
Hogshead Pas *WAP* * E1W 102 B1
Holbeach Gdns *BFN/LL* DA15 ....145 E4
Holbeach Rd *CAT* SE6 ....140 A5
Holbeck Row *PECK* SE15 ....120 A3
Holbein Ms *BGVA* SW1W 116 A1
Holbein Pl *BGVA* SW1W 42 A5
Holberton Gdns *WLSDN* NW10 ....88 B2
Holborn *HCIRC* EC1N 22 A3
Holborn Circ *HCIRC* EC1N 22 B3

Holborn Pl *HHOL* WC1V 21 E3
Holborn Rd *PLSTW* E13 ....94 B4
Holborn Viad *STBT* EC1A 22 C3
Holbrooke Ct *HOLWY* N7 ....57 E5
Holbrook Rd *SRTFD* E15 ....93 F1
Holburne Cl *BKHTH/KID* SE3 ....124 C4
Holburne Gdns *BKHTH/KID* SE3 ....125 D4
Holburne Rd *BKHTH/KID* SE3 ....124 C4
Holcombe St *HMSMTH* W6 ....112 B1
Holcroft Rd *HOM* E9 ....78 C4
Holden Av *CDALE/KGS* NW9 ....50 C3
Holdenby Rd *BROCKY* SE4 ....139 E3
Holden St *BTSEA* SW11 ....116 A5
Holdernesse Rd *TOOT* SW17 ....151 F3
Holderness Wy *WNWD* SE27 ....154 B5
Holford Ms *FSBYW* * WC1X 9 E3
Holford Rd *HAMP* NW3 ....54 C1
Holford St *FSBYW* WC1X 10 A3
Holford Yd *FSBYW* * WC1X 10 A3
Holgate Av *BTSEA* SW11 ....133 D1
Holgate St *CHARL* SE7 ....107 D4
Holland Dr *FSTH* SE23 ....157 E3
Holland Gdns *WKENS* W14 ....101 E4
Holland Gv *BRXN/ST* SW9 ....118 A3
Holland Pk *KENS* W8 ....101 E2
Holland Park Av *GDMY/SEVK* IG3 ......67 E1
  WKENS W14 ....101 E2
Holland Park Gdns *WKENS* W14 ....101 E2
Holland Park Ms *NTGHL* W11 ....101 F2
Holland Park Rd *WKENS* W14 ....101 F2
Holland Park Ter *NTGHL* * W11 ....101 E2
Holland Pas *IS* N1 ....76 C5
Holland Pl *KENS* * W8 ....26 C5
Holland Rd *EHAM* E6 ....83 F5
  SRTFD E15 ....93 E2
  WKENS W14 ....101 D3
  WLSDN NW10 ....70 A5
Holland St *KENS* W8 ....38 B1
  STHWK SE1 ....35 D3
Holland Villas Rd *WKENS* W14 ....101 E3
Hollar Rd *STNW/STAM* N16 ....59 F5
Hollen St *SOHO/CST* W1F 19 F5
Holles St *CAVSQ/HST* W1G 19 D4
Holley Rd *ACT* W3 ....99 E3
Holliday Sq *BTSEA* SW11 ....133 D1
Hollies Av *BFN/LL* DA15 ....163 F2
Hollies Wy *BAL* * SW12 ....134 A5
Hollingbourne Rd *HNHL* SE24 ....136 C3
Hollington Rd *EHAM* E6 ....95 F2
Holloway Rd *ARCH* N19 ....57 D4
  EHAM E6 ....95 F2
  HOLWY N7 ....76 A2
  WAN E11 ....63 D5
Hollybush Gdns *BETH* E2 ....90 B1
Hollybush Hl *WAN* E11 ....63 F1
Hollybush Pl *BETH* E2 ....90 B2
Hollybush St *PLSTW* E13 ....94 B2
Holly Bush V *HAMP* * NW3 ....72 C1
Holly Cl *WLSDN* NW10 ....69 E4
Hollycroft Av *HAMP* NW3 ....54 C4
Hollydale Rd *PECK* SE15 ....120 C5
Hollydown Wy *WAN* E11 ....63 D5
Holly Gv *CDALE/KGS* NW9 ....50 C2
  PECK SE15 ....119 F5
Holly Hedge Ter *LEW* SE13 ....140 C3
Holly Hl *HAMP* NW3 ....72 C1
Holly Lodge Gdns *HGT* N6 ....56 A4
Holly Ms *WBPTN* SW10 ....114 C1
Holly Mt *HAMP* * NW3 ....72 C1
Hollymount Cl *GNWCH* SE10 ....122 C4
Holly Pk *FSBYPK* N4 ....57 E2
Holly Rd *CHSWK* * W4 ....99 D5
Holly St *HACK* E8 ....77 F4

Horsa Rd *LEE/GVPK* SE12 ....**142** C5
Horseferry Pl *GNWCH* SE10 ....**122** C2
Horseferry Rd *POP/IOD* E14 ....**103** E1
  WEST SW1P **44** A3
Horse Guards Av *WHALL* SW1A **32** C4
Horse Guards Rd *WHALL* SW1A **32** B4
Horse Leaze *EHAM* E6 ....**96** B5
Horsell Rd *HBRY* N5 ....**76** A2
Horselydown La *STHWK* SE1 ....**37** E5
Horseshoe Cl *CRICK* NW2 ....**52** B4
  POP/IOD E14 ....**122** C1
Horse Yd *IS* N1 ....**76** B5
Horsfeld Gdns *ELTH/MOT* SE9 ......**143** E3
Horsfeld Rd *ELTH/MOT* SE9 ....**143** D3
Horsford Rd *BRXS/STRHM* SW2 ....**135** F3
Horsley St *WALW* SE17 ....**119** D2
Horsman St *CMBW* SE5 ....**118** C2
Horsmonden Rd *BROCKY* SE4 ......**139** F3
Hortensia Rd *WBPTN* SW10 ....**114** C2
Horticultural Pl *CHSWK* W4 ....**111** D1
Horton Av *CRICK* NW2....................**71** E1
Horton Rd *HACK* E8..........................**78** B3
Horton St *LEW* SE13 ....**140** B1
Hosack Rd *BAL* SW12 ....**151** F2
Hoser Av *LEE/GVPK* SE12 ....**160** A2
Hosier La *STBT* EC1A **22** C3
Hoskin's Cl *CAN/RD* E16 ....**94** C5
Hoskins St *GNWCH* SE10 ....**123** D1
Hospital Wy *LEW* SE13 ....**141** D4
Hotham Rd *PUT/ROE* SW15 ....**130** C1
Hotham St *SRTFD* E15 ....**81** E5
Hothfield Pl *BERM/RHTH* SE16 ....**102** C4
Houghton Cl *HACK* * E8 ....**77** F3
Houghton St *HOL/ALD* * WC2B **21** F5
Houndsditch *HDTCH* EC3A **25** D4
Houseman Wy *CMBW* SE5 ....**119** D3
Houston Rd *FSTH* SE23 ....**157** E2
Hoveden Rd *CRICK* NW2................**71** D2
Howard Cl *ACT* W3 ....**86** B5
  CRICK * NW2 ....**71** E1
Howard Rd *CRICK* NW2..................**71** D1
  EHAM E6 ....**95** F1
  IL IG1..**84** B1
  SEVS/STOTM N15 ....**59** E1
  STNW/STAM N16 ....**77** D1
  WAN E11 ....**63** E5
Howard's La *PUT/ROE* SW15 ....**130** C2
Howard's Rd *PLSTW* E13 ....**94** A2
Howbury Rd *PECK* SE15 ....**138** C1
Howden St *PECK* SE15 ....**138** A1
Howell Wk *WALW* SE17 ....**47** D5
Howgate Rd *MORT/ESHN* SW14 ....**129** D1
Howick Pl *WEST* SW1P **43** F3
Howie St *BTSEA* SW11 ....**115** E3
Howitt Cl *HAMP* NW3 ....**73** E3
Howitt Rd *HAMP* NW3 ....**73** E3
Howland Ms East *FITZ* W1T **19** F2
Howland St *FITZ* W1T **19** F2
Howland Wy *BERM/RHTH* SE16 ....**103** E3
Howletts Rd *HNHL* SE24 ....**136** C4
Howley Pl *BAY/PAD* W2 ....**15** F2
Howsman Rd *BARN* SW13 ....**112** A2
Howson Rd *BROCKY* SE4 ....**139** E2
How's St *BETH* E2 ....**13** E1
Hoxton Market *IS* N1 ....**12** C4
Hoxton Sq *IS* N1 ....**12** C4
Hoylake Rd *ACT* W3........................**87** E5
Hoyland Cl *PECK* * SE15 ....**120** B3
Hoyle Rd *TOOT* SW17 ....**151** E5
Hoy St *CAN/RD* E16 ....**94** C4
Hubbard Rd *WNWD* SE27 ....**154** C4
Hubbard St *SRTFD* E15 ....**81** E5
Hubert Gv *BRXN/ST* SW9 ....**135** E2

Hubert Rd *EHAM* E6 ....**95** D2
Huddart St *BOW* E3........................**91** F4
Huddleston Cl *BETH* * E2 ....**90** C1
Huddlestone Rd *CRICK* NW2 ....**70** B3
  FSTGT E7 ....**81** F1
Huddleston Rd *ARCH* N19 ....**56** C5
Hudson Cl *SHB* * W12....................**100** B1
Hudson Pl *WOOL/PLUM* SE18 ......**126** C1
Huggin Hl *BLKFR* EC4V **35** F1
Huggins Pl *BRXS/STRHM* SW2 ....**153** F1
Hughan Rd *SRTFD* E15 ....**81** D2
Hugh Dalton Av *FUL/PGN* SW6 ....**113** F2
Hughes Ter *CAN/RD* * E16 ....**93** F4
Hugh Gaitskell Cl *FUL/PGN* * SW6 **113** F2
Hugh Ms *PIM* SW1V **43** D5
Hugh Pl *WEST* SW1P **44** A4
Hugh St *PIM* SW1V **43** D5
Hugon Rd *FUL/PGN* SW6 ....**132** B1
Hugo Rd *ARCH* N19 ....**74** C1
Huguenot Pl *WAND/EARL* SW18 ..**132** C3
  WCHPL E1 ....**25** F2
Hullbridge Ms *IS* N1 ....**77** D5
Hull Cl *BERM/RHTH* * SE16 ....**103** D2
Hull St *FSBYE* EC1V **11** E4
Hulme Pl *STHWK* SE1....................**47** F1
Hulse Av *BARK* IG11 ....**85** D3
Humber Dr *NKENS* W10 ....**89** D3
Humber Rd *BKHTH/KID* SE3 ....**124** A2
  CRICK NW2 ....**52** B4
Humberstone Rd *PLSTW* E13 ......**94** C2
Humbolt Rd *HMSMTH* W6 ....**113** E2
Humphrey St *STHWK* SE1 ....**119** F1
Hungerford Br *STHWK* SE1 ....**33** E3
Hungerford Rd *HOLWY* N7 ....**75** D3
Hungerford St *WCHPL* * E1 ....**90** B5
Hunsdon Rd *NWCR* SE14 ....**121** D3
Hunslett St *BETH* * E2....................**90** C1
Hunt Cl *BKHTH/KID* * SE3 ....**124** A5
Hunter Cl *BAL* SW12 ....**152** A1
  STHWK SE1 ....**48** B3
Hunter Ct *CMBW* * SE5 ....**137** D2
Hunters Meadow *NRWD* SE19......**155** E4
Hunters Rd *IL* IG1 ....**84** B2
Hunter St *BMSBY* WC1N **9** D5
Huntingdon Gdns *CHSWK* * W4....**110** C3
Huntingdon St *CAN/RD* E16 ....**93** F5
  IS N1 ....**75** F4
Huntingfield Rd *PUT/ROE* SW15 ..**130** A4
Huntley St *GWRST* WC1E **19** F1
Hunton St *WCHPL* E1 ....**90** A4
Hunt's La *SRTFD* SE15 ....**92** C1
Huntsman St *WALW* SE17 ....**48** C5
Huntspill St *TOOT* SW17 ....**150** C3
Hunts Slip Rd *DUL* SE21 ....**155** E3
Huntsworth Ms *CAMTN* NW1 ......**5** E3
Hurdwick Pl *CAMTN* * NW1 ....**7** E1
Hurlingham Gdns *FUL/PGN* SW6 ..**131** F1
Hurlingham Pk *FUL/PGN* * SW6 ..**131** F1
Hurlingham Rd *FUL/PGN* SW6 ......**113** F5
Hurlingham Sq *FUL/PGN* * SW6 ..**132** A1
Hurlock St *FSBYPK* N4 ....**58** B5
Huron Rd *TOOT* SW17....................**152** A2
Hurren Cl *BKHTH/KID* SE3............**141** E1
Hurry Cl *SRTFD* E15 ....**81** E4
Hurst Av *HGT* N6 ....**56** C1
Hurstbourne Gdns *BARK* IG11 ......**85** D3
Hurstbourne Rd *FSTH* SE23 ....**157** E1
Hurst Cl *GLDGN* NW11 ....**54** B1
Hurstdene Gdns *SEVS/STOTM* N15**59** E2
Hurst St *HNHL* SE24 ....**136** B4
Hurstway Wk *NKENS* * W10 ....**101** D1
Huson Cl *HAMP* * NW3 ....**73** E4
Hutching's St *POP/IOD* E14 ....**104** A3

Hutchins Cl *SRTFD* E15 ....**80** C4
Hutton St *EMB* EC4Y **22** B5
Huxbear St *BROCKY* SE4 ....**139** F3
Huxley Rd *LEY* E10 ....**62** C4
  WELL DA16 ....**145** F1
Huxley St *NKENS* W10 ....**89** E2
Hyacinth Rd *PUT/ROE* SW15 ....**148** A1
Hyde Cl *PLSTW* E13 ....**94** A1
Hyde La *BTSEA* SW11 ....**115** E4
Hyde Park Cnr *MYFR/PICC* W1J **30** B5
Hyde Park Crs *BAY/PAD* W2 ....**16** C5
Hyde Park Gdns *BAY/PAD* W2 ....**28** B1
Hyde Park Gardens Ms
  BAY/PAD W2 ....**28** B1
Hyde Park Ga *KENS* W8 ....**39** E1
Hyde Park Gate Ms *SKENS* SW7 ......**39** E1
Hyde Park Pl *BAY/PAD* W2 ....**29** D1
Hyde Park Sq *BAY/PAD* W2 ....**16** C5
Hyde Park St *BAY/PAD* W2 ....**28** C1
Hyderabad Wy *SRTFD* E15 ....**81** E4
Hyde Rd *IS* N1 ....**77** E5
Hyde's Pl *IS* N1 ....**76** B4
Hyde St *DEPT* SE8 ....**122** A2
Hydethorpe Rd *BAL* SW12 ....**152** C2
Hyde V *GNWCH* SE10 ....**122** C3
Hylton St *WOOL/PLUM* SE18 ....**109** F5
Hyndewood *FSTH* SE23 ....**157** D3
Hyndman St *PECK* SE15 ....**120** B2
Hyson Rd *BERM/RHTH* SE16 ....**120** B1
Hythe Rd *WLSDN* NW10 ....**87** F2

Ibbotson Av *CAN/RD* E16 ....**93** F5
Ibbott St *WCHPL* E1 ....**90** C3
Ibis La *CHSWK* W4 ....**110** C4
Ibsley Gdns *PUT/ROE* SW15 ....**148** A1
Iceland Rd *BOW* E3 ....**80** A5
Ickburgh Est *CLPT* * E5 ....**60** B4
Ickburgh Rd *CLPT* E5 ....**60** B5
Ickleton Rd *ELTH/MOT* SE9 ....**161** E4
Ida St *POP/IOD* E14 ....**92** C5
Idmiston Rd *FSTGT* E7 ....**81** F2
  WNWD SE27 ....**154** C3
Idol St *MON* EC3R **36** C2
Idonia St *DEPT* SE8 ....**121** F3
Iffley Rd *HMSMTH* W6 ....**100** B4
Ifield Rd *WBPTN* SW10 ....**114** B2
Ilbert St *NKENS* W10 ....**89** E2
Ilchester Gdns *BAY/PAD* W2 ....**26** C1
Ilchester Pl *WKENS* W14 ....**101** F4
Ildersly Gv *DUL* SE21 ....**155** D3
Ilderton Rd *BERM/RHTH* SE16 ....**120** C2
Ilex Rd *WLSDN* NW10 ....**69** E4
Ilex Wy *STRHM/NOR* SW16 ....**154** A5
Ilford Hl *IL* IG1 ....**66** A5
Ilford La *IL* IG1 ....**84** B1
Ilfracombe Rd *BMLY* BR1 ....**159** F3
Iliffe St *WALW* SE17 ....**118** B1
Iliffe Yd *WALW* SE17 ....**118** B1
Ilkley Rd *CAN/RD* E16 ....**94** C4
Ilminster Gdns *BTSEA* SW11 ....**133** E2
Imber St *IS* N1 ....**77** D5
Imperial Av *STNW/STAM* * N16 ......**77** E1
Imperial College Rd *SKENS* SW7 ....**40** A3
Imperial Rd *FUL/PGN* SW6 ....**114** B4
Imperial Sq *FUL/PGN* SW6 ....**114** B4
Imperial St *BOW* E3 ....**92** C2
Imperial Wy *CHST* BR7 ....**162** C3
Imre Cl *SHB* W12 ....**100** B2
Inca Dr *ELTH/MOT* SE9 ....**144** A3

Inchmery Rd *CAT* SE6 ....**158** B2
Independent Pl *HACK* E8 ....**77** F2
Independents Rd *BKHTH/KID* SE3 ....**141** F1
Inderwick Rd *CEND/HSY/T* N8 ....**57** F1
Indescon Ct *POP/IOD* E14 ....**104** A3
India St *TWRH* EC3N **25** E5
India Wy *SHB* W12 ....**100** B3
Indigo Ms *POP/IOD* * E14 ....**104** C1
  STNW/STAM N16 ....**59** D5
Indus Rd *CHARL* SE7 ....**124** C3
Ingal Rd *PLSTW* E13 ....**94** A3
Ingate Pl *VX/NE* SW8 ....**116** B4
Ingatestone Rd *MNPK* E12 ....**64** C3
Ingelow Rd *VX/NE* SW8 ....**116** B5
Ingersoll Rd *SHB* W12 ....**100** B2
Ingestre Pl *SOHO/CST* W1F **19** F5
Ingestre Rd *FSTGT* E7 ....**82** A1
  KTTN NW5 ....**74** B1
Ingham Rd *KIL/WHAMP* NW6 ....**72** A1
Inglebert St *CLKNW* EC1R **10** A3
Ingleborough St *BRXN/ST* SW9 ......**118** A5
Ingleby Rd *HOLWY* N7 ....**57** F5
  IL IG1 ....**66** B3
Ingleby Wy *CHST* BR7 ....**162** A5
Ingledew Rd *WOOL/PLUM* SE18 ......**127** D3
Inglefield Sq *WAP* * E1W **102** B2
Inglemere Rd *FSTH* SE23 ....**157** D3
Ingleside Gv *BKHTH/KID* SE3 ....**123** F2
Inglethorpe St *FUL/PGN* SW6 ....**113** D4
Ingleton St *BRXN/ST* SW9 ....**118** A5
Inglewood Cl *POP/IOD* E14 ....**104** A5
Inglewood Rd *KIL/WHAMP* NW6......**72** A2
Inglis St *CMBW* SE5 ....**118** B5
Ingram Av *EFNCH* N2 ....**54** C2
Ingram Cl *LBTH* SE11 ....**45** F4
Ingrave St *BTSEA* SW11 ....**133** D1
Ingress St *CHSWK* W4 ....**111** E1
Inigo Jones Rd *CHARL* SE7 ....**125** D3
Inkerman Rd *KTTN* NW5 ....**74** B3
Inman Rd *WAND/EARL* SW18 ....**132** C5
  WLSDN NW10 ....**69** E5
Inner Cir *CAMTN* NW1 ....**6** A4
Inner Park Rd *WIM/MER* SW19 ......**149** D3
Innes Gdns *PUT/ROE* SW15 ....**130** B4
Inniskilling Rd *PLSTW* E13 ....**94** C1
Inskip Cl *LEY* E10 ....**62** B4
Institute Pl *HACK* E8 ....**78** B2
Integer Gdns *WAN* * E11..................**63** D2
Inver Ct *BAY/PAD* W2 ....**15** D5
Inverforth Cl *HAMP* NW3 ....**54** C4
Inverine Rd *CHARL* SE7 ....**124** B1
Invermore Pl *WOOL/PLUM* SE18......**108** C5
Inverness Gdns *KENS* W8 ....**38** C4
Inverness Ms *BAY/PAD* W2 ....**27** D1
Inverness Pl *BAY/PAD* W2 ....**27** D1
Inverness Rd *CAMTN* NW1 ....**74** B5
Inverness Ter *BAY/PAD* W2 ....**15** D5
Inverton Rd *PECK* SE15 ....**139** D2
Invicta Cl *CHST* BR7 ....**162** A5
Invicta Plaza *STHWK* SE1 ....**34** C2
Invicta Rd *BKHTH/KID* SE3 ....**124** A3
Inville Rd *WALW* SE17 ....**119** D1
Inworth St *BTSEA* SW11 ....**115** E5
Inworth Wk *IS* * N1 ....**76** C5
Iona Cl *CAT* SE6 ....**140** A5
Ion Sq *BETH* * E2 ....**90** A1
Ireland Cl *EHAM* E6 ....**95** F4
Irene Rd *FUL/PGN* SW6 ....**114** A4
Ireton St *BOW* E3 ....**92** A3
Iris Cl *EHAM* E6 ....**95** E4
Iron Bridge Cl *WLSDN* NW10 ....**69** E2
Iron Mill Pl *WAND/EARL* * SW18 ....**132** B4
Iron Mill Rd *WAND/EARL* SW18 ......**132** B4

Ironmonger La *CITYW* EC2V................24 A5
Ironmonger Rw *FSBYE* EC1V...............11 F4
Ironside Cl *BERM/RHTH* SE16.........103 D3
Irving Gv *BRXN/ST* SW9...................117 F5
Irving Ms *IS* N1...................................76 C3
Irving Rd *WKENS* W14....................101 D4
Irving Rd *LSO/SEVD* WC2H................32 B2
Irwell Est *BERM/RHTH* * SE16.........102 C3
Irwin Av *WOOL/PLUM* SE18.............127 E3
Irwin Gdns *WLSDN* NW10.................70 B5
Isabella Rd *HOM* * E9........................78 C2
Isabella St *STHWK* SE1.....................34 C4
Isabel St *BRXN/ST* SW9...................117 F4
Isambard Ms *POP/IOD* E14..............104 C4
Isambard Pl *BERM/RHTH* SE16.......102 C2
Isis Cl *WAND/EARL* SW18...............150 C2
Island Rw *POP/IOD* E14....................91 F5
Isla Rd *WOOL/PLUM* SE18...............126 C2
Islay Wk *IS* * N1.................................76 C3
Islay Whf *POP/IOD* * E14...................92 C4
Isledon Rd *HOLWY* N7.......................58 A5
Islington Gn *IS* N1.............................76 B5
Islington High St *IS* N1......................10 C1
Islington Park Ms *IS* N1.....................76 A4
Islington Park St *IS* N1......................76 A4
Islip St *KTTN* NW5.............................74 C2
Ismailia Rd *FSTGT* E7........................82 B4
Isom Cl *PLSTW* E13............................94 B2
Ivanhoe Rd *CMBW* SE5....................137 F5
Ivatt Pl *WKENS* W14........................113 F1
Iveagh Av *WLSDN* NW10....................86 A1
Iveagh Cl *HOM* E9.............................79 D5
  WLSDN NW10..................................86 A1
Ive Farm Cl *LEY* E10.........................62 A4
Ive Farm La *LEY* E10.........................62 A4
Iveley Rd *CLAP* SW4........................116 C5
Iverna Ct *KENS* W8...........................38 B2
Iverna Gdns *KENS* W8.......................38 B2
Iverson Rd *KIL/WHAMP* NW6.............71 F3
Ives Rd *CAN/RD* E16..........................93 E4
Ives St *CHEL* SW3.............................41 D4
Ivimey St *BETH* * E2..........................90 A2
Ivor Gv *ELTH/MOT* SE9...................162 B1
Ivor Pl *CAMTN* NW1............................17 E1
Ivor St *CAMTN* NW1...........................74 C4
Ivorydown *BMLY* BR1......................160 A4
Ivy Church La *STHWK* * SE1..............119 F1
Ivy Ct *STHWK* * SE1.........................120 A1
Ivy Crs *CHSWK* W4.............................98 C5
Ivydale Rd *PECK* SE15.....................139 D1
Ivyday *WLSDN/NOR* SW16..............153 F3
Ivy Gdns *CEND/HSY/T* N8..................57 E1
Ivymount Rd *WNWD* SE27...............154 A3
Ivy Rd *BROCKY* SE4..........................139 F2
  CAN/RD E16.....................................94 A5
  CRICK NW2......................................70 C1
  LEY E10..62 A1
  TOOT SW17....................................151 E5
Ivy St *IS* N1..12 C1
Ixworth Pl *CHEL* SW3........................40 C5

J

Jacaranda Gv *HACK* E8.......................77 F4
Jack Clow Rd *SRTFD* E15....................93 E1
Jack Cornwell St *MNPK* E12...............84 A1
Jackman Ms *WLSDN* NW10.................51 E5
Jackman St *HACK* E8..........................78 B5
Jackson Cl *HOM* E9............................79 D4
Jackson Rd *BARK* IG11.......................85 D5
  HOLWY N7.......................................75 F1

Jackson's La *HGT* N6...........................56 A2
Jackson St *WOOL/PLUM* SE18.........126 A2
Jack Walker Ct *HBRY* N5.....................76 B1
Jacob St *STHWK* SE1..........................37 F5
Jacob's Well Ms *MHST* W1U...............18 B4
Jacqueline Creft Ter *HGT* * N6............56 A1
Jade Cl *CAN/RD* E16...........................95 D5
  CRICK NW2......................................53 D2
Jade Ter *KIL/WHAMP* * NW6................72 C4
Jaffe Rd *IL* IG1....................................66 C3
Jaggard Wy *BAL* SW12.....................133 F5
Jago Cl *WOOL/PLUM* SE18...............126 C2
Jago Wk *CMBW* SE5...........................119 D3
Jamaica Rd *BERM/RHTH* SE16.........102 B4
  STHWK SE1......................................49 E1
Jamaica St *WCHPL* E1.........................90 C4
James Av *CRICK* NW2.........................70 C2
James Cl *GLDGN* * NW11...................53 E1
  PLSTW E13.......................................94 A1
James Collins Cl *NKENS* W10............89 F3
James Joyes Wk *HNHL* * SE24.........136 B2
James La *WAN* E11.............................62 C2
Jameson St *KENS* W8.........................26 B3
James St *BARK* IG11............................84 C4
  COVGDN WC2E.................................33 D1
  MHST W1U.......................................18 B5
Jamestown Rd *CAMTN* NW1...............74 B5
Jamestown Wy *POP/IOD* E14...........105 D1
Jane St *WCHPL* E1..............................90 B5
Janet St *POP/IOD* E14.......................104 A4
Janeway Pl *BERM/RHTH* SE16..........102 B3
Janeway St *BERM/RHTH* SE16..........102 A3
Janson Cl *SRTFD* E15..........................81 E2
  WLSDN NW10...................................51 D5
Janson Rd *SRTFD* E15.........................81 E2
Japan Crs *FSBYPK* N4..........................57 F3
Jardine Rd *WAP* E1W.........................103 D1
Jarrett Cl *BRXS/STRHM* SW2............154 B1
Jarrow Rd *BERM/RHTH* SE16...........102 C5
Jarrow Wy *HOM* E9.............................79 E1
Jarvis Rd *EDUL* SE22.........................137 E2
Jasmine Cl *IL* IG1.................................84 B2
Jasmine Ct *LEE/GVPK* SE12.............142 A4
Jason Wk *ELTH/MOT* SE9.................162 A4
Jasper Rd *CAN/RD* E16.......................95 D5
Jay Gdns *CHST* BR7...........................161 F4
Jay Ms *SKENS* SW7.............................39 F1
Jebb Av *BRXS/STRHM* SW2..............135 E4
Jebb St *BOW* E3...................................92 A1
Jedburgh Rd *PLSTW* E13.....................94 C2
Jedburgh St *BTSEA* SW11.................134 A2
Jeddo Ms *SHB* * W12...........................99 F3
Jeddo Rd *SHB* W12.............................99 F3
Jeffrey's Pl *CAMTN* NW1....................74 C4
Jeffrey's Rd *CLAP* SW4.....................117 E5
Jeffrey's St *CAMTN* NW1....................74 B4
Jeger Av *BETH* * E2.............................77 F5
Jeken Rd *ELTH/MOT* SE9.................142 C2
Jelf Rd *BRXS/STRHM* SW2................136 A3
Jenkins La *BARK* IG11.........................96 B1
Jenkins Rd *PLSTW* E13........................94 B3
Jenner Av *ACT* W3..............................87 D4
Jenner Rd *STNW/STAM* N16...............59 F4
Jennifer Rd *BMLY* BR1.......................159 F3
Jennings Rd *EDUL* SE22....................137 F3
Jenny Hammond Cl *WAN* E11.............63 F5
Jephson Rd *FSTGT* E7.........................82 C4
Jephson St *CMBW* SE5.....................119 D4
Jephtha Rd *WAND/EARL* SW18........132 A4
Jerdan Pl *FUL/PGN* SW6...................114 A3
Jeremiah St *POP/IOD* E14..................92 B5
Jermyn St *STJS* SW1Y.........................31 E3
Jerningham Rd *NWCR* SE14..............121 E5

Jerome Crs *STJWD* NW8 ....4 C5
Jerome St *WCHPL* E1 ....25 E2
Jerrard St *LEW* SE13 ....140 B1
Jerrold St *IS* * N1 ....13 D2
Jersey Rd *CAN/RD* E16 ....94 C4
  IL IG1 ....84 B1
  IS N1 ....76 C3
  WAN E11 ....63 D3
Jersey St *BETH* E2 ....90 B2
Jerusalem Pas *CLKNW* EC1R 22 C1
Jesmond Dene *HAMP* * NW3 ....72 C3
Jessam Av *STNW/STAM* N16 ....60 B3
Jesse Rd *LEY* E10 ....62 C3
Jessica Rd *WAND/EARL* SW18 ....132 C4
Jessup Cl *WOOL/PLUM* SE18 ....108 C5
Jevington Wy *LEE/GVPK* SE12 ....160 B1
Jewry St *TWRH* EC3N 25 E5
Jews Rw *WAND/EARL* SW18 ....132 A3
Jews Wk *SYD* SE26 ....156 B4
Jeymer Av *CRICK* NW2 ....70 A5
Jeypore Rd *WAND/EARL* SW18 ....132 C5
Jim Bradley Cl *WOOL/PLUM* SE18 ....108 A5
Joan Crs *PECK* SE15 ....120 A4
Joan St *STHWK* SE1 ....34 C4
Jocelyn St *PECK* SE15 ....120 B1
Jockey's Flds *FSBYW* WC1X 21 F2
Jodane Rd *DEPT* SE8 ....103 F5
Jodrell Rd *HOM* E9 ....79 F5
Johanna St *STHWK* * SE1 ....46 A1
John Adam St *CHCR* WC2N 33 D3
John Aird Ct *BAY/PAD* W2 ....15 F2
John Archer Wy
  WAND/EARL SW18 ....133 D4
John Ashby Cl *BRXS/STRHM* SW2 ....135 E4
John Burns Dr *BARK* IG11 ....85 E1
John Campbell Rd
  STNW/STAM N16 ....77 E2
John Carpenter St *EMB* EC4Y 34 C1
John Felton Rd
  BERM/RHTH * SE16 ....102 A3
John Fisher St *WCHPL* E1 ....102 A1
John Harrison Wy *GNWCH* SE10 ....105 F4
John Islip St *WEST* SW1P 44 C5
John Maurice Cl *WALW* SE17 ....48 A4
John McKenna Wk
  BERM/RHTH * SE16 ....102 A4
John Parker Sq *BTSEA* SW11 ....133 D1
John Penn St *LEW* SE13 ....122 B1
John Prince's St *CAVSQ/HST* W1G 19 D4
John Rennie Wk *WAP* E1W 102 B1
John Roll Wy *BERM/RHTH* SE16 ....102 A4
John Ruskin St *CMBW* SE5 ....118 B3
John Silkin La *DEPT* SE8 ....121 D1
John's Ms *BMSBY* WC1N 21 F1
John Smith Av *FUL/PGN* SW6 ....113 F3
Johnson Cl *HACK* E8 ....78 A5
Johnson Rd *WLSDN* NW10 ....69 D5
Johnson's Pl *PIM* SW1V 116 C1
Johnson St *WCHPL* E1 ....90 C5
Johnsons Wy *WLSDN* NW10 ....86 B3
John Spencer Sq *IS* * N1 ....76 B3
Johns Pl *WCHPL* E1 ....90 B5
Johnston Cl *BRXN/ST* SW9 ....117 F4
Johnstone Rd *EHAM* E6 ....95 F2
John St *BMSBY* WC1N 21 F1
  SRTFD E15 ....81 D5
John Trundle Highwalk *BARB* * EC2Y 23 F1
John Williams Cl *PECK* SE15 ....121 D1
John Wilson St *WOOL/PLUM* SE18 ....108 A5
John Wooley Cl *LEW* * SE13 ....141 D1
Joiners Arms Yd *CMBW* * SE5 ....119 D4
Joiner St *STHWK* SE1 ....36 A2
Jonathan St *LBTH* SE11 ....117 F1

Jones Rd *PLSTW* E13 ....94 B3
Joseph Av *ACT* W3 ....87 D5
Josephine Av *BRXS/STRHM* SW2 ....135 F3
Joseph Powell Cl *BAL* SW12 ....134 C4
Joseph Ray Rd *WAN* E11 ....63 E4
Joseph St *BOW* E3 ....91 F4
Joseph Trotter Cl *CLKNW* EC1R 10 B4
Joshua St *POP/IOD* E14 ....92 C5
Joslings Cl *SHB* W12 ....100 A1
Joubert St *BTSEA* SW11 ....115 F5
Jowett St *PECK* SE15 ....119 F3
Jubilee Bridge *STHWK* SE1 ....35 F2
Jubilee Cl *CDALE/KGS* NW9 ....51 D1
Jubilee Gdns *STHWK* * SE1 ....33 F4
Jubilee Market *COVGDN* * WC2E 33 D3
Jubilee Pl *CHEL* SE3 ....115 E1
Jubilee St *WCHPL* E1 ....90 C5
Jubilee Ter *FUL/PGN* * SW6 ....113 E5
The Jubilee *GNWCH* * SE10 ....122 B3
Judd St *STPAN* WC1H 8 C4
Jude St *CAN/RD* E16 ....93 F5
Judges' Wk *HAMP* NW3 ....54 C5
Juer St *BTSEA* SW11 ....115 E3
Julian Av *ACT* W3 ....98 B1
Julian Pl *POP/IOD* E14 ....122 B1
Julian Tayler Pth *SYD* * SE26 ....156 B2
Juliette Rd *PLSTW* E13 ....94 A1
Julius Nyerere Cl *IS* * N1 ....75 F5
Junction Ap *BTSEA* SW11 ....133 E1
  LEW SE13 ....140 C1
Junction Ms *BAY/PAD* W2 ....16 C4
Junction Pl *BAY/PAD* * W2 ....16 B4
Junction Rd *ARCH* N19 ....56 C5
  PLSTW E13 ....82 B5
Juniper Crs *CAMTN* NW1 ....74 A3
Juniper La *EHAM* E6 ....95 E4
Juniper Rd *IL* IG1 ....84 A1
Juniper St *WCHPL* * E1 ....102 C1
Juno Wy *NWCR* SE14 ....121 D2
Jupiter Wy *HOLWY* N7 ....75 F3
Jupp Rd *SRTFD* E15 ....81 D4
Jupp Rd West *SRTFD* E15 ....80 C5
Justice Wk *CHEL* SW3 ....115 E2
Jutland Rd *CAT* SE6 ....140 C1
  PLSTW E13 ....94 A3
Juxon St *LBTH* SE11 ....45 F4

K

Kambala Rd *BTSEA* SW11 ....115 D5
Kangley Bridge Rd *SYD* SE26 ....157 F5
Kashgar Rd *WOOL/PLUM* SE18 ....127 F1
Kashmir Rd *CHARL* SE7 ....125 D3
Kassala Rd *BTSEA* SW11 ....115 F4
Katherine Cl *BERM/RHTH* SE16 ....103 D2
Katherine Gdns *ELTH/MOT* SE9 ....143 D2
Katherine Rd *EHAM* E6 ....83 D4
Katherine Sq *NTGHL* * W11 ....101 E2
Kathleen Av *ACT* W3 ....86 C5
Kathleen Rd *BTSEA* SW11 ....133 F1
Kay Rd *BRXN/ST* SW9 ....117 E5
Kay St *BETH* E2 ....90 A1
  SRTFD * E15 ....81 D4
Kean St *HOL/ALD* WC2B 21 E5
Keats Av *CAN/RD* E16 ....106 B2
Keats Cl *STHWK* SE1 ....49 E5
Keats Est *STNW/STAM* * N16 ....59 F4
Keats Gv *HAMP* NW3 ....73 E1
Keats Rd *WELL* DA16 ....127 E4
Keble Pl *BARN* SW13 ....112 B1
Keble St *TOOT* SW17 ....150 C4

Kedleston Wk *BETH* E2 ....90 B2
Keeble Cl *WOOL/PLUM* * SE18 ....126 B2
Keedonwood Rd *BMLY* BR1 ....159 E4
Keel Cl *BERM/RHTH* SE16 ....103 D2
Keeley St *HOL/ALD* WC2B 21 E5
Keeling Rd *ELTH/MOT* SE9 ....143 D3
Keemor Cl *WOOL/PLUM* * SE18 ....126 A3
Keens Cl *STRHM/NOR* SW16 ....153 D5
Keen's Yd *IS* N1 ....76 B3
The Keep *BKHTH/KID* SE3 ....124 A5
Keesey St *WALW* SE17 ....119 D2
Keetons Rd *BERM/RHTH* * SE16 ....102 B4
  BERM/RHTH SE16 ....102 B4
Keevil Dr *WIM/MER* SW19 ....131 D5
Keighley Cl *HOLWY* N7 ....75 E1
Keightley Dr *ELTH/MOT* SE9 ....162 A1
Keildon Rd *BTSEA* SW11 ....133 F2
Keir Hardie Est *CLPT* * E5 ....60 B3
Keith Connor Cl *VX/NE* SW8 ....134 B1
Keith Gv *SHB* W12 ....100 A3
Keith Rd *BARK* IG11 ....97 D1
Kelbrook Rd *BKHTH/KID* SE3 ....125 E5
Kelceda Cl *CRICK* NW2 ....52 A4
Kelfield Gdns *NKENS* W10 ....89 D5
Kelfield Ms *NKENS* W10 ....89 D4
Kelland Rd *PLSTW* E13 ....94 A3
Kellaway Rd *BKHTH/KID* SE3 ....124 C5
Keller Crs *MNPK* E12 ....83 D1
Kellerton Rd *LEW* SE13 ....141 E3
Kellett Rd *BRXS/STRHM* SW2 ....136 A2
Kellino St *TOOT* SW17 ....151 F4
Kellner Rd *THMD* SE28 ....109 F1
Kell St *STHWK* SE1 ....47 D2
Kelly Av *PECK* SE15 ....119 F4
Kelly Cl *WLSDN* NW10 ....51 D5
Kelly Ms *MV/WKIL* * W9 ....89 F4
Kelly St *CAMTN* NW1 ....74 B3
Kelman Cl *CLAP* SW4 ....117 D5
Kelmore Gv *EDUL* SE22 ....138 A2
Kelmscott Gdns *SHB* W12 ....100 A4
Kelmscott Rd *BTSEA* SW11 ....133 E3
Kelross Rd *HBRY* N5 ....76 B1
Kelsall Cl *BKHTH/KID* SE3 ....124 B5
Kelsey St *BETH* E2 ....90 A3
Kelso Pl *KENS* W8 ....38 C2
Kelvedon Rd *FUL/PGN* SW6 ....113 F3
Kelvin Gv *SYD* SE26 ....156 B3
Kelvington Rd *PECK* SE15 ....139 D3
Kelvin Rd *HBRY* N5 ....76 B1
Kember St *IS* N1 ....75 F4
Kemble Rd *FSTH* SE23 ....157 D1
Kemble St *HOL/ALD* WC2B 21 E5
Kemerton Rd *CMBW* SE5 ....136 C1
Kemey's St *HOM* E9 ....79 E2
Kempe Rd *KIL/WHAMP* NW6 ....89 D1
Kemplay Rd *HAMP* NW3 ....73 D1
Kemps Dr *POP/IOD* E14 ....104 A3
Kempsford Gdns *ECT* SW5 ....114 A1
Kempsford Rd *LBTH* SE11 ....46 B5
Kempson Rd *FUL/PGN* SW6 ....114 A4
Kempthorne Rd *DEPT* SE8 ....103 E5
Kempton Rd *EHAM* E6 ....83 F5
Kempt St *WOOL/PLUM* SE18 ....126 A2
Kemsing Rd *GNWCH* SE10 ....124 A1
Kenbury St *CMBW* SE5 ....118 C5
Kenchester Cl *VX/NE* SW8 ....117 E3
Kendal Av *BARK* IG11 ....85 E5
Kendal Cl *CMBW* SE5 ....118 B3
Kendal Ct *ACT* W3 ....86 A4
Kendale Rd *BMLY* BR1 ....159 E5
Kendall Pl *MHST* W1U 18 A3
Kendall Rd *WOOL/PLUM* SE18 ....125 E4
Kendal Pl *PUT/ROE* SW15 ....131 F3

Kendal Rd *WLSDN* NW10 ....70 A1
Kendal Steps *BAY/PAD* * W2 ....17 D5
Kendal St *BAY/PAD* W2 ....17 D5
Kender St *NWCR* SE14 ....120 C3
Kendoa Rd *CLAP* SW4 ....135 D2
Kendrick Ms *SKENS* SW7 ....40 A4
Kendrick Pl *SKENS* * SW7 ....40 A5
Kenilford Rd *BAL* SW12 ....134 B5
Kenilworth Av *WIM/MER* SW19 ....150 A5
Kenilworth Gdns *GDMY/SEVK* IG3 .....67 F4
  WOOL/PLUM SE18 ....126 B5
Kenilworth Rd *BOW* E3 ....91 E1
  KIL/WHAMP NW6 ....71 F5
Kenley Wk *NTGHL* * W11 ....101 E2
Kenlor Rd *TOOT* SW17 ....151 D5
Kenmere Gdns *ALP/SUD* HA0 ....68 A5
Kenmont Gdns *WLSDN* NW10 ....88 B2
Kenmure Rd *HACK* * E8 ....78 B2
Kenmure Yd *HACK* * E8 ....78 B2
Kennard Rd *SRTFD* E15 ....81 D4
Kennard St *BTSEA* SW11 ....116 A4
  CAN/RD E16 ....107 F2
Kennedy Cl *PLSTW* E13 ....94 A1
Kennedy Rd *BARK* IG11 ....85 E5
Kennedy Wk *WALW* SE17 ....48 B5
Kennet Cl *BTSEA* SW11 ....133 D2
Kenneth Av *IL* IG1 ....84 B1
Kenneth Crs *CRICK* NW2 ....70 B2
Kenneth Moor Rd *IL* * IG1 ....66 B5
Kennet Rd *MV/WKIL* W9 ....89 F3
Kennet St *WAP* E1W 102 A2
Kennett Wharf La *BLKFR* EC4V 35 F1
Kenninghall Rd *CLPT* E5 ....60 B5
Kenning St *BERM/RHTH* SE16 ....102 C3
Kennings Wy *LBTH* SE11 ....118 A1
Kennington Gv *LBTH* SE11 ....117 F2
Kennington La *LBTH* SE11 ....117 F1
Kennington Ov *LBTH* SE11 ....117 F2
Kennington Park Gdns *LBTH* SE11 ...118 B2
Kennington Park Pl *WALW* SE17 ....118 A2
Kennington Park Rd *LBTH* SE11 ....118 A2
Kennington Rd *LBTH* SE11 ....46 A3
Kenrick Pl *MHST* W1U 18 A2
Kensal Rd *NKENS* W10 ....89 E3
Kensal Whf *NKENS* * W10 ....89 E3
Kensington Av *MNPK* E12 ....83 E3
Kensington Church Ct *KENS* W8 ....38 C1
Kensington Church St *KENS* W8 ....26 B3
Kensington Church Wk *KENS* * W8 ...26 C5
Kensington Ct *KENS* W8 ....39 D1
Kensington Court Gdns *KENS* * W8 ....39 D2
Kensington Court Ms *KENS* * W8 ....39 D2
Kensington Court Pl *KENS* W8 ....39 D2
Kensington Gdns *IL* IG1 ....65 F3
Kensington Gardens Sq
  BAY/PAD W2 ....14 C5
Kensington Ga *SKENS* SW7 ....39 E2
Kensington Gore *SKENS* SW7 ....39 F1
Kensington Hall Gdns
  WKENS * W14 ....113 F1
Kensington High St *KENS* W8 ....38 A2
  WKENS W14 ....101 F3
Kensington Palace *KENS* * W8 ....27 D4
Kensington Palace Gdns *KENS* W8 ....26 C3
Kensington Park Gdns
  NTGHL W11 ....101 F1
Kensington Park Ms *NTGHL* W11 ....89 F5
Kensington Park Rd *NTGHL* W11 ....89 F5
Kensington Pl *KENS* W8 ....26 A4
Kensington Rd *KENS* W8 ....39 D1
  SKENS SW7 ....40 A1
Kensington Sq *KENS* W8 ....38 C1
Kent Av *WELL* DA16 ....145 F3

Kentish Town Rd *CAMTN* NW1 ....74 B3
Kentlea Rd *THMD* SE28 ....109 E3
Kentmere Rd *WOOL/PLUM* SE18....109 E5
Kenton Rd *E9* 79 D3
Kenton St *STPAN* WC1H 8 C5
Kent Rd *CHSWK* W4 ....98 C4
  RCH/KEW TW9.................................110 A3
Kent St *BETH* E2 ....13 F1
  PLSTW E13....................................94 B2
Kent Ter *CAMTN* NW1 ....5 D4
Kent View Gdns *GDMY/SEVK* IG3.......67 E4
Kentwell Cl *BROCKY* * SE4 ....139 E2
Kentwode Gn *BARN* SW13 ....112 A3
Kent Yd *SKENS* SW7 ....41 D1
Kenward Rd *ELTH/MOT* SE9 ....142 C3
Ken Wy *WBLY* HA9 ....50 C4
Kenway Rd *ECT* SW5.........................38 C5
Kenwood Cl *GLDGN* NW11 ....55 D3
Kenwood Rd *HGT* N6 ....55 F1
Kenworthy Rd *HOM* E9 ....79 E3
Kenwyn Dr *CRICK* NW2.....................51 E5
Kenwyn Rd *CLAP* SW4 ....135 D2
Kenya Rd *CHARL* SE7......................125 D3
Kenyon St *FUL/PGN* SW6 ....113 D4
Keogh Rd *SRTFD* E15........................81 E3
Kepler Rd *CLAP* SW4.......................135 E2
Keppel Rd *EHAM* E6..........................83 F4
Keppel St *GWRST* WC1E 20 B2
Kerbela St *BETH* E2 ....90 A3
Kerbey St *POP/IOD* E14 ....92 B5
Kerfield Crs *CMBW* SE5 ....119 D4
Kerfield Pl *CMBW* SE5......................119 D4
Kerrison Rd *BTSEA* SW11 ....133 E1
  SRTFD E15.....................................81 D5
Kerry Cl *CAN/RD* E16........................94 B5
Kerry Pth *NWCR* SE14.....................121 F2
Kerry Rd *NWCR* SE14......................121 F2
Kersfield Rd *PUT/ROE* SW15 ....131 D4
Kersley Ms *BTSEA* SW11 ....115 F4
Kersley Rd *STNW/STAM* N16 ....59 E5
Kersley St *BTSEA* SW11 ....115 F4
Kerwick Cl *HOLWY* N7.......................75 F4
Keslake Rd *KIL/WHAMP* NW6 ....89 D1
Keston Rd *PECK* SE15 ....138 A1
Kestrel Av *EHAM* E6..........................95 E4
  HNHL SE24....................................136 B3
Kestrel Cl *WLSDN* NW10 ....69 D2
Kestrel Pl *NWCR* * SE14..................121 E2
Keswick Av *KUTN/CMB* KT2 ....147 E5
Keswick Rd *PUT/ROE* SW15 ....131 E3
Kettlebaston Rd *LEY* E10 ....61 F3
Kew Br *RCH/KEW* TW9 ....110 A2
Kew Bridge Arches *CHSWK* * W4 .....110 A2
Kew Meadow Pth *RCH/KEW* TW9 ....110 B4
Key Cl *WCHPL* E1..............................90 B3
Keyes Rd *CRICK* NW2 ....71 D2
Keymer Rd *BRXS/STRHM* SW2.......153 F2
Keynsham Gdns *ELTH/MOT* SE9 .....143 D2
Keynsham Rd *ELTH/MOT* SE9 ....143 D3
Keyse Rd *STHWK* SE1........................49 E3
Keystone Crs *IS* N1 ....9 D2
Keyworth Cl *CLPT* E5.........................79 E1
Keyworth St *STHWK* SE1 ....47 D2
Kezia St *DEPT* SE8 ....121 E1
Khama Rd *TOOT* SW17 ....151 E4
Khartoum Rd *IL* IG1............................84 B2
  PLSTW E13....................................94 B2
  TOOT SW17..................................151 D4
Khyber Rd *BTSEA* SW11 ....115 E5
Kibworth St *VX/NE* SW8 ....117 F3
Kidbrooke Gdns *BKHTH/KID* SE3.....124 A5
Kidbrooke Gv *BKHTH/KID* SE3.........124 A4
Kidbrooke La *ELTH/MOT* SE9 ....143 E2

Kidbrooke Park Cl *BKHTH/KID* SE3 ....124 B4
Kidbrooke Park Rd
  BKHTH/KID SE3 ....124 B4
Kidbrooke Wy *BKHTH/KID* SE3 ....124 B5
Kidderpore Av *HAMP* NW3................72 A1
Kidderpore Gdns *HAMP* NW3 ....72 A1
Kidd Pl *CHARL* SE7 ....125 E1
Kilburn Br *KIL/WHAMP* NW6..............72 A5
Kilburn High Rd *KIL/WHAMP* NW6 .....72 A4
Kilburn La *NKENS* W10 ....89 D2
Kilburn Park Rd *KIL/WHAMP* NW6 ....2 A4
Kilburn Pl *KIL/WHAMP* NW6 ....72 A5
Kilburn Priory *KIL/WHAMP* NW6........72 B5
Kilburn Sq *KIL/WHAMP* NW6 ....72 A5
Kilburn V *KIL/WHAMP* NW6 ....72 B5
Kildare Gdns *BAY/PAD* W2 ....14 B4
Kildare Rd *CAN/RD* E16.....................94 A4
Kildare Ter *BAY/PAD* W2 ....14 B4
Kildoran Rd *CLAP* SW4 ....135 E3
Kilgour Rd *FSTH* SE23 ....139 E4
Kilkie St *FUL/PGN* SW6 ....114 C5
Killarney Rd *WAND/EARL* SW18.......132 C4
Killearn Rd *CAT* SE6 ....159 D1
Killick St *IS* N1....................................9 E1
Killieser Av *BRXS/STRHM* SW2.......153 E2
Killip Cl *CAN/RD* E16.........................93 F5
Killowen Rd *HOM* * E9 ....79 D3
Killyon Rd *VX/NE* SW8.....................116 C5
Kilmaine Rd *FUL/PGN* SW6..............113 E3
Kilmarsh Rd *HMSMTH* W6 ....100 C5
Kilmington Rd *BARN* SW13 ....112 A2
Kilmorie Rd *FSTH* SE23 ....157 F1
Kilner St *POP/IOD* E14 ....92 A4
Kiln Ms *TOOT* SW17 ....151 D5
Kiln Pl *KTTN* NW5..............................74 A1
Kilravock St *NKENS* W10 ....89 E2
Kimball Gdns *FUL/PGN* SW6 ....113 E4
Kimball Pl *ELTH/MOT* SE9 ....142 C2
Kimberley Av *EHAM* E6 ....95 E1
  GNTH/NBYPK IG2...........................67 D2
  PECK SE15...................................120 B5
Kimberley Rd *BRXN/ST* SW9 ....117 E5
  CAN/RD E16....................................93 F3
  KIL/WHAMP NW6.............................71 E5
  WAN E11...63 D4
Kimber Rd *WAND/EARL* SW18 ....132 A5
Kimbolton Cl *LEE/GVPK* SE12 ....141 E4
Kimmeridge Gdns *ELTH/MOT* SE9 ...161 E4
Kimmeridge Rd *ELTH/MOT* SE9.......161 E4
Kimpton Rd *CMBW* SE5...................119 D4
Kinburn St *BERM/RHTH* * SE16 ....103 D3
Kincaid Rd *PECK* SE15 ....120 B3
Kincardine Gdns *MV/WKIL* * W9 ....14 A1
Kinder St *WCHPL* E1..........................90 B5
Kinfauns Rd *BRXS/STRHM* SW2.......154 A2
King Alfred Av *CAT* SE6 ....158 A5
King Arthur Cl *PECK* SE15...............120 C3
King Charles Rd *WHALL* SW1A..........32 A1
King Charles Ter *WAP* * E1W 102 B1
King Charles Wk
  WIM/MER * SW19..........................149 E1
King David La *WCHPL* E1 ....102 C1
Kingdon Rd *KIL/WHAMP* NW6 ....72 A3
King Edward Rd *LEY* E10 ....62 C3
King Edward's Gdns *ACT* W3..............98 A2
King Edward's Rd *BARK* IG11.............85 D3
  HACK E8...78 B5
King Edward St *STBT* EC1A 23 E4
King Edward the Third Ms
  BERM/RHTH SE16 ....102 B3
King Edward Wk *STHWK* SE1..............46 B3
Kingfield St *POP/IOD* E14 ....104 C5
Kingfisher St *EHAM* E6 ....95 E4

Kingfisher Wy WLSDN * NW10 ....69 D3
King Garth Ms FSTH SE23 ....156 C2
King George Av CAN/RD E16 ....95 D5
   GNTH/NBYPK IG2 ....67 D1
King George St GNWCH SE10 ....122 C3
Kingham Cl NTGHL W11 ....101 E3
   WAND/EARL SW18 ....132 C5
King Henry's Rd HAMP NW3 ....73 E4
King Henry St STNW/STAM N16 ....77 E2
King Henry's Wk IS N1 ....77 E3
King Henry Ter WAP * E1W 102 B1
Kinghorn St STBT * EC1A 23 E3
King James St STHWK SE1 ....47 D1
King John Ct SDTCH EC2A 13 D5
King John St WCHPL E1 ....91 D4
King John's Wk ELTH/MOT SE9 ......143 E5
Kinglake Est WALW * SE17 ....119 E1
Kinglake St WALW SE17 ....119 E1
Kingly Ct REGST * W1B 31 F1
Kingly St REGST W1B 19 E5
King & Queen Cl ELTH/MOT * SE9 ...161 E4
King & Queen St WALW * SE17 ....118 C1
King & Queen Whf
   BERM/RHTH * SE16 ....103 D2
Kingsand Rd LEE/GVPK SE12 ....160 A2
King's Arms Yd LOTH EC2R 24 A4
Kings Av BAL SW12 ....153 D1
   CLAP SW4 ....135 E4
King's Bench St STHWK SE1 ....35 D5
King's Bench Wk EMB * EC4Y 34 B1
Kingsbridge Ct POP/IOD E14 ....104 A5
Kingsbridge Rd BARK IG11 ....97 D1
   NKENS W10 ....88 C5
Kingsbury Rd IS N1 ....77 E3
Kingsbury Ter IS N1 ....77 E3
Kingsclere Cl PUT/ROE SW15 ....130 A5
Kingscliffe Gdns WIM/MER SW19 ....149 F1
King's Cl LEY E10 ....62 B2
King's College Rd HAMP * NW3 ....73 D4
Kingscote Rd CHSWK W4 ....99 D4
Kingscote St EMB EC4Y 34 C1
Kings Ct PLSTW E13 ....82 B5
   STHWK * SE1 ....35 D5
Kingscourt Rd STRHM/NOR SW16 ...153 D3
King's Crs FSBYPK N4 ....58 C5
Kingscroft Rd CRICK NW2 ....71 F3
King's Cross Br FSBYW * WC1X 9 E3
King's Cross Rd FSBYW WC1X 9 E3
Kingsdale Gdns NTGHL W11 ....101 D2
Kingsdale Rd WOOL/PLUM SE18 .....127 E4
Kingsdown Av ACT W3 ....86 C2
Kingsdown Cl BERM/RHTH * SE16 ...120 B1
   NTGHL W11 ....89 D5
Kingsdown Rd ARCH N19 ....57 E5
   WAN E11 ....63 E5
Kings Dr WBLY HA9 ....50 B4
Kings Farm Av RCHPK/HAM TW10 ...128 A2
Kingsford St KTTN NW5 ....73 F2
Kingsford Wy EHAM E6 ....95 F4
Kings Gdns IL IG1 ....67 D3
   KIL/WHAMP NW6 ....72 A4
Kingsgate WBLY HA9 ....50 C5
Kingsgate Est IS * N1 ....77 E3
Kingsgate Pl KIL/WHAMP NW6 ....72 A4
Kingsgate Rd KIL/WHAMP NW6 ....72 A4
Kingsground ELTH/MOT SE9 ....143 D5
King's Gv PECK SE15 ....120 B4
Kings Hall Ms LEW * SE13 ....140 C1
King's Hwy WOOL/PLUM SE18 ....127 E4
Kingshold Rd HOM E9 ....78 C4
Kingsholm Gdns ELTH/MOT SE9 .....143 D5
Kingshurst Rd LEE/GVPK SE12 ....142 A5
Kingsland Gn STNW/STAM N16 ....77 E3

Kingsland High St HACK E8 ....77 F3
Kingsland Pas HACK E8 ....77 F3
Kingsland Rd BETH E2 ....13 D2
   HACK E8 ....77 F4
   PLSTW E13 ....94 C2
Kingslawn Cl PUT/ROE SW15 ....130 B3
Kingsley Ms KENS * W8 ....39 D3
   WAP * E1W 102 B1
Kingsley Pl HGT N6 ....56 A2
Kingsley Rd FSTGT E7 ....82 A4
   KIL/WHAMP NW6 ....71 F5
   WIM/MER SW19 ....150 B5
Kingsley St BTSEA SW11 ....133 F1
Kingsley Wy EFNCH N2 ....54 C1
Kingsley Wood Dr ELTH/MOT SE9 ...161 F3
Kings Ml HMSMTH * W6 ....100 C5
Kingsman St WOOL/PLUM SE18 .....107 F5
Kingsmead Av CDALE/KGS NW9 ....51 D2
Kingsmead Rd BRXS/STRHM SW2 ...154 A2
Kingsmead Wy HOM E9 ....79 E1
Kingsmere Cl PUT/ROE SW15 ....131 D1
Kingsmere Pk CDALE/KGS NW9 ....50 C3
Kingsmere Pl STNW/STAM * N16 ......59 D3
Kingsmere Rd WIM/MER SW19 ....149 D2
King's Ms BMSBY WC1N 21 F1
Kingsmill Ter STJWD NW8 ....4 B1
King's Orch ELTH/MOT SE9 ....143 E4
Kings Pde SHB * W12 ....100 A4
   WLSDN * NW10 ....70 C5
Kings Pas WAN * E11 ....63 E2
Kings Pl CHSWK W4 ....110 C5
   STHWK SE1 ....47 E1
King Sq FSBYE EC1V 11 E4
King's Quay WBPTN * SW10 ....114 C4
Kings Reach EMB * EC4Y 34 B1
King's Rd BARK IG11 ....84 B1
   BCVA SW1W 42 B3
   CHEL * SW3 ....115 D2
   EHAM E6 ....82 C5
   FUL/PGN SW6 ....114 B4
   MORT/ESHN SW14 ....129 D1
   WAN E11 ....63 E2
King's Scholars Pas WEST * SW1P 43 E3
   WEST SW1P 43 E3
King Stairs Cl BERM/RHTH SE16 .....102 B3
King's Ter CAMTN NW1 ....74 C5
Kingsthorpe Rd SYD SE26 ....157 D4
Kingston Hl KUTN/CMB KT2 ....146 C5
Kingston Hill Pl KUTN/CMB KT2 .....146 C4
Kingston Rd IL IG1 ....84 C1
   PUT/ROE SW15 ....148 B1
Kingston Sq NRWD SE19 ....155 D5
Kingston V PUT/ROE SW15 ....147 D4
Kingstown St CAMTN NW1 ....73 F5
King St CITYW EC2V 23 F5
   COVGDN WC2E 32 C1
   HMSMTH W6 ....99 F5
   PLSTW E13 ....94 A3
   STJS SW1Y 31 F4
King St Cloisters HMSMTH * W6 .....100 B5
Kingswater Pl BTSEA * SW11 ....115 E3
Kingsway HOL/ALD WC2B 21 E4
   MORT/ESHN SW14 ....128 B1
Kingsway Pde STNW/STAM * N16 .....59 D5
Kingsway Pl CLKNW EC1R 10 B5
Kingswear Rd KTTN NW5 ....56 B5
Kingswood Av KIL/WHAMP NW6 ....71 E5
Kingswood Cl VX/NE SW8 ....117 E3
Kingswood Dr NRWD SE19 ....155 E4
Kingswood Pl LEW SE13 ....141 E2
Kingswood Rd BRXS/STRHM SW2 ...135 E4
   CHSWK W4 ....98 C4
   WAN E11 ....63 E2

Kingswood Ter *CHSWK* W4 ....98 C4
Kings Yd *PUT/ROE* * SW15 ....131 D1
  SRTFD * E15..........................80 A3
Kingthorpe Rd *WLSDN* NW10 ....69 D4
Kingthorpe Ter *WLSDN* * NW10.........69 D4
King William La *GNWCH* SE10 ....123 E1
King William St *CANST* EC4R 36 B2
King William Wk *GNWCH* SE10 ....122 C2
Kingwood Rd *FUL/PGN* SW6 ....113 C5
Kinlet Rd *WOOL/PLUM* SE18 ....126 C3
Kinloch Dr *CDALE/KGS* NW9 ....51 E2
Kinloch St *HOLWY* N7 ....57 F5
Kinnaird Av *CHSWK* W4 ....110 C3
Kinnear Rd *SHB* W12.......................99 F3
Kinnerton Pl North *KTBR* * SW1X 41 F1
Kinnerton Pl South *KTBR* * SW1X 41 F1
Kinnerton St *KTBR* SW1X 42 A1
Kinnerton Yd *KTBR* * SW1X 42 A1
Kinnoul Rd *HMSMTH* W6 ....113 E2
Kinsale Rd *PECK* SE15 ....138 C1
Kinveachy Gdns *CHARL* SE7 ....125 E1
Kinver Rd *SYD* SE26......................156 C4
Kipling Est *STHWK* SE1 ....48 B1
Kipling St *STHWK* SE1 ....48 B1
Kippington Dr *ELTH/MOT* SE9 ....161 D2
Kirby Est *BERM/RHTH* * SE16 ....102 B4
Kirby Gv *STHWK* SE1 ....36 C5
Kirby St *HCIRC* EC1N 22 B2
Kirkdale *SYD* SE26........................156 B2
Kirkdale Cnr *SYD* * SE26 ....156 C4
Kirkdale Rd *WAN* E11 ....63 E3
Kirkham Rd *EHAM* E6 ....95 E5
Kirkham St *WOOL/PLUM* SE18.........127 E2
Kirkland Cl *BFN/LL* DA15 ....145 E4
Kirkland Wk *HACK* E8 ....77 F3
Kirk La *WOOL/PLUM* SE18 ....126 C2
Kirkmichael Rd *POP/IOD* E14 ....92 C5
Kirk Rd *WALTH* E17 ....61 F1
Kirkside Rd *BKHTH/KID* SE3 ....124 A2
Kirk's Pl *POP/IOD* E14......................91 F4
Kirkstall Gdns *BRXS/STRHM* SW2 ....153 D1
Kirkstall Rd *BRXS/STRHM* SW2 ....153 E1
Kirkwall Pl *BETH* * E2 ....90 C2
Kirkwood Rd *PECK* SE15 ....120 B5
Kirtley Rd *SYD* SE26.....................157 E4
Kirtling St *VX/NE* SW8...................116 C3
Kirton Cl *CHSWK* W4......................99 D5
Kirton Gdns *BETH* E2 ....13 E1
Kirton Ldg *PLSTW* E13 ....94 C1
Kirwyn Wy *CMBW* SE5 ....118 B3
Kitcat Ter *BOW* E3 ....92 A2
Kitchener Rd *FSTGT* E7 ....82 B3
Kite Pl *BETH* * E2 ....90 C2
Kite Yd *BTSEA* * SW11 ....115 F4
Kitson Rd *BARN* SW13 ....112 A4
  CMBW SE5 ....118 C3
Kitto Rd *NWCR* SE14 ....121 D5
Kiver Rd *ARCH* N19..........................57 E4
Klea Av *BAL* SW12..........................134 C4
Knapdale Cl *FSTH* SE23.................156 B2
Knapmill Rd *CAT* SE6.....................158 A2
Knapmill Wy *CAT* SE6.....................158 A2
Knapp Cl *WLSDN* NW10...................69 E3
Knapp Rd *BOW* E3 ....92 A3
Knaresborough Dr
  WAND/EARL SW18.......................150 B1
Knaresborough Pl *ECT* SW5 ....38 C3
Knatchbull Rd *CMBW* SE5 ....118 B5
  WLSDN NW10 ....69 D5
Knebworth Rd *STNW/STAM* * N16 .....77 E1
Kneller Rd *BROCKY* SE4 ....139 E2
Knighten St *WAP* E1W 102 B2

Knighthead Point *POP/IOD* E14.......104 A3
Knightland Rd *CLPT* E5 ....60 B4
Knighton Park Rd *SYD* SE26 ....157 D5
Knighton Rd *FSTGT* E7 ....64 A5
Knightrider Ct *BLKFR* * EC4V 23 D5
Knightrider St *BLKFR* EC4V 35 D1
Knightsbridge *SKENS* SW7 ....41 D1
Knightsbridge Gn *KTBR* * SW1X 41 E1
Knight's Hl *WNWD* SE27 ....154 B3
Knight's Hill Sq *WNWD* SE27 ....154 B4
Knights Rd *CAN/RD* E16 ....106 A2
Knights Wk *LBTH* SE11 ....46 C5
Knivet Rd *FUL/PGN* SW6................114 A2
Knobs Hill Rd *SRTFD* E15 ....80 B5
Knockholt Rd *ELTH/MOT* SE9 ....143 D3
The Knole *ELTH/MOT* SE9...............162 A4
Knoll Rd *WAND/EARL* SW18 ....132 C5
Knolly's Cl *STRHM/NOR* SW16 ....154 A3
  WNWD * SE27............................154 B3
Knolly's Rd *STRHM/NOR* SW16 ....154 A3
Knottisford St *BETH* E2 ....91 D2
Knotts Green Rd *LEY* E10 ....62 B1
Knowle Cl *BRXN/ST* SW9 ....136 A1
Knowles Hill Crs *LEW* SE13 ....141 E3
Knowsley Rd *BTSEA* SW11 ....115 F5
Knox Rd *FSTGT* E7 ....82 A3
Knox St *MBLAR* W1H.......................17 E2
Knoyle St *NWCR* SE14 ....121 E2
Kohat Rd *WIM/MER* SW19 ....150 B5
Kossuth St *GNWCH* SE10 ....123 E1
Kramer Ms *ECT* * SW5 ....114 A2
Kreedman Wk *HACK* * E8 ....78 A2
Kylemore Cl *EHAM* E6......................95 D1
Kylemore Rd *KIL/WHAMP* NW6..........72 A4
Kynance Ms *KENS* W8 ....39 D3
Kynance Pl *KENS* W8 ....39 E3
Kynaston Rd *BMLY* BR1 ....160 B5
  STNW/STAM N16 ....59 E5
Kyrle Rd *BTSEA* SW11 ....134 A1
Kyverdale Rd *STNW/STAM* N16 ....59 F2

L

Laburnum Gv *CDALE/KGS* NW9 ....50 C2
Laburnum Pl *ELTH/MOT* * SE9.........144 B3
Laburnum St *BETH* E2 ....77 F5
Lacebark Cl *BFN/LL* DA15 ....145 F5
Lackington St *SDTCH* EC2A 24 B2
Lacon Rd *EDUL* SE22 ....138 A2
Lacy Rd *PUT/ROE* SW15 ....131 D2
Ladas Rd *WNWD* SE27 ....154 C5
Ladbroke Crs *NTGHL* W11 ....89 F1
Ladbroke Gdns *NTGHL* W11 ....101 F1
Ladbroke Gv *NKENS* W10 ....89 D3
  NTGHL W11 ....101 F1
Ladbroke Ms *NTGHL* W11 ....101 F2
Ladbroke Rd *NTGHL* W11 ....101 F2
Ladbroke Sq *NTGHL* W11 ....101 F1
Ladbroke Ter *NTGHL* W11 ....101 F1
Ladbroke Wk *NTGHL* W11 ....101 F2
Ladderstile Ride
  RCHPK/HAM TW10 ....146 B5
Ladycroft Rd *LEW* SE13 ....140 B1
Lady Margaret Rd *ARCH* N19 ....74 C1
Ladyship Ter *EDUL* * SE22 ....138 B3
Ladysmith Av *EHAM* E6 ....95 E1
  GNTH/NBYPK IG2 ....67 D2
Ladysmith Rd *CAN/RD* E16 ....93 F2
  ELTH/MOT SE9 ....144 A4
Lady Somerset Rd *KTTN* NW5 ....74 B1
Ladywell Rd *LEW* SE13 ....140 A3

Ladywell St *SRTFD* E15 ....81 F5
Ladywell Water Tower
  BROCKY * SE4 ....139 H1
Lafone St *STHWK* SE1 ....37 E5
Lagado Ms *BERM/RHTH* SE16 ....103 D2
Lainson St *WAND/EARL* SW18 ....132 A5
Lairdale Cl *DUL* SE21 ....154 C1
Lairs Cl *HOLWY* * N7 ....75 E3
Laitwood Rd *BAL* SW12 ....152 B1
Lakedale Rd *WOOL/PLUM* SE18...........127 E1
Lake House Rd *WAN* E11 ....64 A5
Lake Rd *WIM/MER* SW19 ....149 F5
Lakeside Rd *WKENS* W14 ....101 H1
Lakeside Wy *WBLY* HA9 ....68 A1
Lake View Est *BOW* * E3.........................91 D1
Lakeview Rd *WNWD* SE27 ....154 A5
Lakis Cl *HAMP* NW3 ....72 C1
Laleham Rd *CAT* SE6 ....140 C5
Lalor St *FUL/PGN* SW6 ....113 E5
Lambarde Av *ELTH/MOT* SE9 ....162 A4
Lamberhurst Rd *WNWD* SE27 ....154 A4
Lambert Av *RCH/KEW* TW9 ....128 C1
Lambert Jones Ms *BARB* * EC2Y 23 E2
Lambert Rd *BRXS/STRHM* SW2 ....135 E2
  CAN/RD E16...94 B5
Lambert St *IS* N1 ....76 A4
Lamb La *WEST* SW1P 45 D4
Lambeth High St *STHWK* SE1................45 E5
Lambeth HI *BLKFR* * EC4V 35 E1
Lambeth Palace Rd *STHWK* SE1 ....45 E3
Lambeth Rd *STHWK* SE1 ....46 A3
Lambeth Wk *LBTH* SE11 ....45 F4
Lamb La *HACK* E8....................................78 B4
Lamble St *KTTN* NW5 ....74 A1
Lambolle PI *HAMP* NW3 ....73 E3
Lambolle Rd *HAMP* NW3 ....73 E3
Lambourn Cl *KTTN* * NW5 ....74 C1
Lambourne Av *WIM/MER* SW19 ....149 F4
Lambourne Gdns *BARK* IG11 ....85 E4
Lambourne PI *BKHTH/KID* SE3 ....124 B4
Lambourne Rd *BARK* IG11 ....85 E4
  GDMY/SEVK IG3 ....67 E4
  WAN E11 ....62 C2
Lambourn Rd *CLAP* SW4 ....134 B1
Lambrook Ter *FUL/PGN* SW6 ....113 E4
Lamb's Conduit Pas *FSBYW* WC1X 21 E2
Lamb's Conduit St *BMSBY* WC1N 21 E1
Lambscroft Av *LEE/GVPK* SE12 ....160 C5
Lambs Ms *IS* N1 ....76 B5
Lamb's Pas *STLK* EC1Y 24 A1
Lamb St *WCHPL* E1 ....25 E2
Lambton PI *NTGHL* * W11 ....101 F1
Lambton Rd *ARCH* N19 ....57 E3
Lamb Wk *STHWK* SE1 ....48 C1
Lamerock Rd *BMLY* BR1 ....159 F4
Lamerton St *DEPT* SE8 ....122 A2
Lamington St *HMSMTH* W6 ....100 B5
Lamlash St *LBTH* SE11 ....46 C4
Lammas Rd *HOM* E9 ....79 D4
  LEY E10 ....61 E4
Lammermoor Rd *BAL* * SW12 ....134 B5
Lamont Rd *WBPTN* SW10 ....115 D2
Lamont Road Pas *WBPTN* * SW10 ....115 D2
Lamorbey Cl *BFN/LL* DA15 ....163 F2
Lampard Gv *STNW/STAM* N16 ....59 F3
Lampern Sq *BETH* * E2 ....90 A2
Lampeter Sq *HMSMTH* W6.....................113 E2
Lamplighter Cl *WCHPL* E1 ....90 C3
Lampmead Rd *LEW* SE13 ....141 D3
Lamport Cl *WOOL/PLUM* SE18..............107 F5
Lampton House Cl
  WIM/MER SW19 ....149 D4
Lanark Pl *MV/WKIL* W9 ....3 F5

Lanark Rd *MV/WKIL* W9 ....3 D2
Lanbury Rd *PECK* SE15 ....139 D2
Lancashire Ct *MYFR/PKLN* W1K 30 C1
Lancaster Av *BARK* IG11 ....85 E4
  WIM/MER SW19 ....149 D5
  WNWD SE27 ....154 B2
Lancaster Cl *IS* N1 ....77 E4
Lancaster Ct *BAY/PAD* W2 ....27 F1
Lancaster Dr *HAMP* NW3 ....73 E3
  POP/IOD E14 ....104 C2
Lancaster Gdns *WIM/MER* SW19 ....149 D5
Lancaster Gv *HAMP* NW3 ....73 D3
Lancaster Ms *BAY/PAD* W2 ....27 F1
  WAND/EARL * SW18 ....132 B3
Lancaster Pl *WIM/MER* SW19 ....149 D5
Lancaster Rd *FSBYPK* N4 ....58 A2
  FSTGT E7 ....82 A4
  NTGHL W11 ....89 E5
  WAN E11 ....63 E4
  WIM/MER SW19 ....149 D5
  WLSDN NW10 ....69 F2
Lancaster Stables *HAMP* * NW3 ....73 E3
Lancaster St *STHWK* SE1 ....46 C1
Lancaster Ter *BAY/PAD* W2 ....28 A1
Lancaster West *NTGHL* * W11 ....89 E5
Lancefield St *MV/WKIL* W9 ....89 F2
Lancell St *STNW/STAM* N16 ....59 E4
Lancelot PI *SKENS* SW7 ....41 E4
Lancer Sq *KENS* W8.................................26 C5
Lancey Cl *CHARL* SE7 ....107 D5
Lancing Rd *GNTH/NBYPK* IG2..................67 D1
Lancing St *CAMTN* NW1 ....8 A4
Landcroft Rd *EDUL* SE22 ....137 E4
Landells Rd *EDUL* SE22 ....137 F4
Landford Rd *PUT/ROE* SW15 ....130 C1
Landgrove Rd *WIM/MER* SW19 ....150 A5
Landleys Flds *KTTN* * NW5 ....75 D3
Landmann Wy *NWCR* SE14 ....121 D2
Landon Pl *KTBR* SW1X 41 E2
Landons Cl *POP/IOD* E14 ....104 C2
Landor Rd *BRXN/ST* SW9 ....135 E1
Landor Wk *SHB* W12 ....100 A3
Landridge Rd *FUL/PGN* SW6 ....113 E5
Landrock Rd *CEND/HSY/T* N8 ....57 E1
Landseer Av *MNPK* E12 ....84 A2
Landseer Rd *ARCH* N19 ....57 E5
Landstead Rd *WOOL/PLUM* SE18 ....127 D3
Lane Cl *CRICK* NW2 ....52 B1
Lanercost Rd *BRXS/STRHM* SW2...........154 A2
Laneside *CHST* BR7 ....162 B5
The Lane *BKHTH/KID* SE3 ....142 A1
  STJWD NW8 ....3 E2
Laneway *PUT/ROE* SW15 ....130 B3
Lanfranc St *BOW* E3 ....91 E1
Lanfrey PI *WKENS* W14 ....113 F1
Langbourne Av *HGT* N6 ....56 A4
Langbrook Rd *BKHTH/KID* SE3 ....143 D1
Langdale Cl *MORT/ESHN* SW14 ....128 A3
Langdale Rd *GNWCH* SE10 ....122 C3
Langdale St *WCHPL* * E1........................90 B5
Langdon Ct *WLSDN* NW10 ....69 E5
Langdon Crs *EHAM* E6 ....96 A1
Langdon Dr *CDALE/KGS* NW9 ....50 C3
Langdon Park Rd *HGT* N6 ....56 B2
Langdon Pl *MORT/ESHN* SW14 ....128 C3
Langdon Shaw *SCUP* DA14 ....163 F5
Langdon Wy *STHWK* SE1 ....102 A5
Langford Cl *HACK* E8 ....78 A2
  SEVS/STOTM N15 ....59 E1
Langford PI *STJWD* NW8 ....3 F2
Langford Rd *FUL/PGN* SW6 ....114 A5
Langham PI *CAVSQ/HST* W1G 19 D3
  CHSWK W4..111 E2

Langham St *GTPST* W1W **19** E3
Langholm Cl *BAL* SW12 ....**135** D5
Langland Gdns *HAMP* NW3 ....**72** B2
Langler Rd *WLSDN* NW10 ....**88** C1
Langley Ct *COVGDN* WC2E **32** C1
Langley Crs *WAN* E11 ....**64** B2
Langley Dr *ACT* W3 ....**98** B3
   WAN E11 ....**64** B2
Langley La *VX/NE* SW8 ....**117** E1
Langley St *LSQ/SEVD* WC2H **20** C5
Langmead St *WNWD* SE27 ....**154** B3
Langroyd Rd *TOOT* SW17 ....**151** F2
Langside Av *PUT/ROE* SW15 ....**130** A2
Langston Hughes Cl *HNHL* * SE24 ...**136** B2
Lang St *WCHPL* E1 ....**90** C3
Langthorn Ct *LOTH* * EC2R **24** B4
Langthorne Rd *WAN* E11 ....**63** D5
Langthorne St *FUL/PGN* SW6 ....**113** D4
Langton Av *EHAM* E6 ....**96** A2
Langton Cl *FSBYW* WC1X **9** F1
Langton Ri *EDUL* SE22 ....**138** B5
Langton Rd *BRXN/ST* SW9 ....**118** B3
   CRICK NW2 ....**52** C5
Langton St *WBPTN* SW10 ....**114** C2
Langton Wy *BKHTH/KID* SE3 ....**124** A3
Langtry Pl *FUL/PGN* SW6 ....**114** A2
Langtry Rd *STJWD* NW8 ....**72** B5
Langtry Wk *STJWD* NW8 ....**72** C5
Lanhill Rd *MV/WKIL* W9 ....**2** A5
Lanier Rd *LEW* SE13 ....**140** C4
Lannoy Rd *ELTH/MOT* SE9 ....**162** B1
Lanrick Rd *POP/IOD* E14 ....**93** D5
Lansbury Cl *WLSDN* NW10 ....**68** C2
Lansbury Gdns *POP/IOD* * E14 ....**93** D5
Lanscombe Wk *VX/NE* * SW8 ....**117** E1
Lansdowne Crs *NTGHL* W11 ....**101** E1
Lansdowne Dr *HACK* E8 ....**78** B5
Lansdowne Gdns *VX/NE* SW8 ......**117** E4
Lansdowne Gn *VX/NE* SW8 ....**117** E3
Lansdowne Gv *WLSDN* NW10 ....**69** E1
Lansdowne Hl *WNWD* SE27 ....**154** B3
Lansdowne La *CHARL* SE7 ....**125** D1
Lansdowne Ms *CHARL* SE7 ....**125** D1
   NTGHL W11 ....**101** F2
Lansdowne Pl *STHWK* * SE1 ....**48** B2
Lansdowne Ri *NTGHL* W11 ....**101** E1
Lansdowne Rd *CDMY/SEVK* IG3 ...**67** F3
   HACK E8 ....**78** A4
   NTGHL W11 ....**101** E1
   WALTH E17 ....**62** A1
   WAN E11 ....**63** F4
Lansdowne Ter *BMSBY* WC1N **21** D1
Lansdowne Wk *NTGHL* W11 ....**101** E2
Lansdowne Wy *VX/NE* SW8 ....**117** E4
Lansdowne Wood Cl
   WNWD SE27 ....**154** B3
Lansdown Rd *FSTGT* E7 ....**82** C4
Lantern Cl *PUT/ROE* SW15 ....**130** A2
Lanterns Ct *POP/IOD* E14...............**104** A4
Lant St *STHWK* SE1 ....**35** E5
Lanvanor Rd *PECK* SE15 ....**120** C5
Lapford Cl *MV/WKIL* * W9 ....**89** F3
Lapse Wood Wk *DUL* SE21 ....**156** B1
Lapworth Ct *BAY/PAD* W2 ....**15** D2
Lara Cl *LEW* SE13 ....**140** C4
Larch Av *ACT* W3 ....**99** E2
Larch Cl *BAL* SW12 ....**152** B2
   DEPT SE8 ....**121** F2
Larch Dr *CHSWK* * W4 ....**110** A1
Larches Av *MORT/ESHN* SW14 ....**129** D2
Larch Gv *BFN/LL* DA15 ....**163** F1
Larch Rd *CRICK* NW2 ....**70** C1
   LEY E10 ....**62** A4

Larchwood Rd *ELTH/MOT* SE9 ....**162** B2
Larcom St *WALW* SE17 ....**47** F5
Larden Rd *ACT* W3 ....**99** E3
Larissa St *WALW* * SE17 ....**48** B5
Larkbere Rd *SYD* SE26 ....**157** E4
Larkfield Rd *SCUP* DA14 ....**163** F3
Larkhall La *CLAP* SW4 ....**117** D5
Larkhall Ri *CLAP* SW4 ....**134** C1
Larkhill Ter *WOOL/PLUM* * SE18 ..**126** A3
Lark Rw *BETH* E2 ....**78** C5
Larnach Rd *HMSMTH* W6 ....**113** D2
Larpent Av *PUT/ROE* SW15 ....**130** C3
Lascelles Cl *WAN* E11........................**63** D4
Lassa Rd *ELTH/MOT* SE9 ....**143** E3
Lassell St *GNWCH* SE10 ....**123** D1
Latchmere Rd *BTSEA* SW11 ....**115** F5
Latchmere St *BTSEA* SW11 ....**115** F5
Latham Cl *EHAM* E6 ....**95** E5
Lathom Rd *EHAM* E6 ....**83** F4
Latimer Av *EHAM* E6 ....**83** F5
Latimer Pl *NKENS* W10 ....**88** C5
Latimer Rd *FSTGT* E7 ....**82** B1
   NKENS W10 ....**88** C4
   SEVS/STOTM N15 ....**59** E1
Latona Rd *PECK* SE15 ....**120** A2
Lattimer Pl *CHSWK* W4 ....**111** E3
Lauderdale Pde *MV/WKIL* * W9 ....**2** C4
Lauderdale Pl *BARB* * EC2Y **23** F3
Lauderdale Rd *MV/WKIL* W9 ....**3** D4
Laud St *LBTH* SE11 ....**117** F1
Launcelot Rd *BMLY* BR1 ....**160** A4
Launcelot St *STHWK* SE1 ....**46** A1
Launceston Pl *KENS* W8 ....**39** E2
Launch St *POP/IOD* E14 ....**104** C4
Launders Ga *ACT* * W3 ....**98** B3
Laundress La *CLPT* * E5 ....**60** A5
Laundry Rd *HMSMTH* W6 ....**113** D3
Laura Pl *CLPT* E5 ....**78** C1
Laura Ter *FSBYPK* * N4 ....**58** B4
Laurel Bank Gdns *FUL/PGN* SW6 ..**113** F5
Laurel Cl *TOOT* SW17 ....**151** E5
Laurel Gv *SYD* SE26 ....**157** D5
Laurel Rd *BARN* SW13 ....**112** A5
The Laurels *CMBW* * SE5 ....**118** B3
Laurel St *HACK* E8 ....**77** F3
Laurence Ms *SHB* W12 ....**100** A3
Laurence Pountney Hl
   CANST * EC4R **36** A1
Laurence Pountney La *CANST* EC4R ...**36** A1
Laurie Gv *NWCR* SE14 ....**121** E4
Laurier Rd *KTTN* NW5 ....**56** B5
Lauriston Rd *HOM* E9 ....**79** D4
Lausanne Rd *PECK* SE15 ....**120** C4
Lavender Av *CDALE/KGS* NW9 ....**50** C3
Lavender Cl *CHEL* SW3 ....**115** D2
Lavender Gdns *BTSEA* SW11 ....**133** F2
Lavender Gv *HACK* E8 ....**78** A4
Lavender Hl *BTSEA* SW11 ....**133** F1
Lavender Pl *IL* IG1 ....**84** B2
Lavender Rd *BERM/RHTH* SE16 ....**103** E2
   BTSEA SW11 ....**133** D1
Lavender St *SRTFD* E15 ....**81** E3
Lavender Sweep *BTSEA* SW11 ....**133** F2
Lavender Ter *BTSEA* * SW11 ....**133** E1
Lavengro Rd *WNWD* SE27 ....**154** C2
Lavenham Rd *WAND/EARL* SW18 ..**149** F2
Lavers Rd *STNW/STAM* N16 ....**59** E5
Laverstoke Gdns *PUT/ROE* SW15 ..**129** F5
Laverton Ms *ECT* * SW5 ....**39** D5
Laverton Pl *ECT* SW5 ....**39** D5
Lavidge Rd *ELTH/MOT* SE9 ....**161** E2
Lavina Gv *IS* N1 ....**9** E1
Lavington St *STHWK* SE1 ....**35** D4

Lawford Rd *CHSWK* W4 ....**110** C3
  IS N1 ....**77** E4
  KTTN NW5 ....**74** C3
Lawless St *POP/IOD* * E14 ....**104** B1
Lawley St *CLPT* E5 ....**78** C1
Lawn Crs *RCH/KEW* TW9 ....**110** A5
Lawn House Cl *POP/IOD* E14....**104** C4
Lawn La *VX/NE* SW8 ....**117** E2
Lawn Rd *HAMP* NW3 ....**73** D2
Lawns Ct *WBLY* * HA9 ....**50** A4
The Lawns *BKHTH/KID* * SE3 ...**141** E1
Lawn Ter *BKHTH/KID* SE3 ....**141** F1
Lawrence Av *MNPK* E12 ....**84** A3
Lawrence Cl *SHB* * W12 ....**100** B1
Lawrence La *CITYW* EC2V..........**23** F5
Lawrence Pl *IS* * N1 ....**75** E5
Lawrence Rd *EHAM* E6...............**83** E5
  PLSTW E13..............................**82** B5
Lawrence St *CAN/RD* E16...........**93** F4
  CHEL SW3................................**115** E2
Lawrence Wy *WLSDN* NW10 ....**50** C5
Lawrie Park Av *SYD* SE26 ....**156** B5
Lawrie Park Crs *SYD* SE26 ....**156** B5
Lawrie Park Gdns *SYD* SE26....**156** B5
Lawson Cl *CAN/RD* E16...............**94** C4
  WIM/MER SW19 ....**149** D3
Law St *STHWK* SE1 ....**48** B2
Lawton Rd *BOW* E3 ....**91** E2
  LEY E10 ....**62** C3
Laxcon Cl *WLSDN* NW10 ....**69** D2
Laxley Cl *CMBW* SE5 ....**118** B3
Laxton Pl *CAMTN* NW1 ....**7** D5
Layard Rd *BERM/RHTH* SE16 ...**102** B5
Layard Sq *BERM/RHTH* SE16 ...**102** B5
Laycock St *IS* N1 ....**76** A3
Layer Gdns *ACT* W3 ....**98** A1
Layfield Cl *HDN* NW4 ....**52** B2
Layfield Crs *HDN* NW4 ....**52** B2
Layfield Rd *HDN* NW4 ....**52** B2
Laystall St *FSBYW* WC1X **22** A1
Layton Pl *RCH/KEW* TW9 ....**110** A5
Layzell Wk *ELTH/MOT* SE9 ......**161** D1
Lazenby Ct *COVGDN* * WC2E **32** C1
Leabank Sq *HOM* E9 ....**80** C1
Leabank Vw *SEVS/STOTM* N15 ...**60** A1
Leabourne Rd *STNW/STAM* N16 ...**60** A1
Lea Bridge Rd *CLPT* E5 ....**61** D4
Leacroft Av *BAL* SW12................**133** E5
Leadale Rd *STNW/STAM* N16 ......**60** A1
Leadenhall Pl *FENCHST* EC3M ...**24** C5
Leadenhall St *BANK* EC3V...........**24** C5
Leader Av *MNPK* E12 ....**84** A2
The Leadings *WBLY* HA9 ....**50** C5
Leaf Gv *STRHM/NOR* SW16 ......**154** A5
Leafy Oak Rd *LEE/GVPK* SE12 ...**160** C4
Leagrave St *CLPT* E5 ....**60** C5
Lea Hall Gdns *LEY* * E10 ....**62** A3
Lea Hall Rd *LEY* E10....................**62** A3
Leahurst Rd *LEW* SE13 ....**141** D3
Leake St *STHWK* SE1 ....**33** F1
Lealand Rd *SEVS/STOTM* N15 ....**59** F1
Leamington Av *BMLY* BR1 ....**160** C5
Leamington Cl *BMLY* BR1..........**160** C4
Leamington Gdns *GDMY/SEVK* IG3....**67** F4
Leamington Pk *ACT* W3 ....**87** D4
Leamington Road Vls *NTGHL* W11 ...**89** F4
Leamore St *HMSMTH* W6 ....**100** B5
Leamouth Rd *EHAM* E6 ....**95** E5
  POP/IOD E14..........................**93** D5
Leander Rd *BRXS/STRHM* SW2 ...**135** F4
Learoyd Gdns *EHAM* E6 ....**108** A1
Leas Dl *ELTH/MOT* SE9 ....**162** A3
Leaside Rd *CLPT* E5 ....**60** C4

Leasowes Rd *LEY* E10..................**62** A3
Leatherdale St *WCHPL* * E1 ....**91** D2
Leatherhead Cl *STNW/STAM* N16 ...**59** E3
Leather Gdns *SRTFD* E15 ....**81** E5
Leather La *CLKNW* EC1R **22** A1
Leathermarket Ct *STHWK* SE1 ....**48** C1
Leathermarket St *STHWK* SE1 ....**48** C1
Leathwaite Rd *BTSEA* SW11......**133** F2
Leathwell Rd *DEPT* SE8 ....**122** B5
Lea Valley Wk *CLPT* E5 ....**60** B2
Leaway *CLPT* * E5 ....**60** C2
Lebanon Gdns *WAND/EARL* SW18 ...**132** A4
Lebanon Rd *WAND/EARL* SW18 ...**132** A3
Lebrun Sq *BKHTH/KID* SE3 ......**142** B2
Lechmere Rd *CRICK* NW2 ....**70** A3
Leckford Rd *WAND/EARL* SW18 ...**150** C2
Lecky St *SKENS* SW7 ....**115** D1
Leconfield Av *BARN* SW13.........**129** F1
Leconfield Rd *HBRY* N5 ....**77** D1
Leda Rd *WOOL/PLUM* SE18 ......**107** F4
Ledbury Ms North *NTGHL* W11 ....**26** A1
Ledbury Ms West *NTGHL* * W11 ...**26** A1
Ledbury Rd *NTGHL* W11 ....**89** F5
Ledbury St *PECK* SE15 ....**120** A3
Leechcroft Av *BFN/LL* DA15......**145** F3
Lee Church St *LEW* SE13...........**141** E2
Lee Conservancy Rd *HOM* E9 .....**79** F1
Leeds Rd *IL* IG1............................**67** D3
Lee High Rd *LEW* SE13 ....**141** D2
Leeke St *FSBYW* WC1X **9** E1
Leeland Wy *WLSDN* NW10 ....**69** E1
Lee Pk *BKHTH/KID* SE3 ....**141** F2
Lee Rd *BKHTH/KID* SE3 ....**141** F1
Leeside Crs *GLDGN* NW11 ....**53** E1
Leeson Rd *HNHL* * SE24 ....**136** A3
Lees Pl *MYFR/PKLN* W1K **30** A1
Lee St *HACK* E8.............................**77** F5
Lee Ter *BKHTH/KID* SE3 ....**141** E1
Leeway *DEPT* SE8 ....**121** F1
Leewood Cl *LEE/GVPK* * SE12 ...**141** F4
Lefevre Wk *BOW* E3 ....**79** E5
Leffern Rd *SHB* W12 ....**100** A3
Lefroy Rd *SHB* W12 ....**99** F3
Legard Rd *HBRY* N5 ....**58** B5
Legatt Rd *ELTH/MOT* SE9 ....**143** D3
Leggatt Rd *SRTFD* E15 ....**92** C1
Legge St *LEW* SE13 ....**140** C3
Leghorn Rd *WLSDN* NW10 ....**88** A1
  WOOL/PLUM SE18 ....**127** D1
Legion Cl *IS* N1.............................**76** A3
Legion Ter *BOW* E3 ....**80** A5
Leicester Gdns *GDMY/SEVK* IG3 ...**67** F2
Leicester Pl *LSQ/SEVD* * WC2H ...**32** B1
Leicester Rd *WLSDN* NW10 ....**69** D4
Leicester Sq *LSQ/SEVD* WC2H **32** B2
Leicester St *SOHO/SHAV* W1D ...**32** B1
Leigham Av *STRHM/NOR* SW16 ...**153** E3
Leigham Court Rd
  STRHM/NOR SW16 ....**153** F3
Leigham Hall Pde
  STRHM/NOR * SW16.............**153** E3
Leigham V *STRHM/NOR* SW16 ...**154** A3
Leigh Gdns *WLSDN* NW10...........**88** C1
Leigh Orchard Cl
  STRHM/NOR SW16 ....**153** F3
Leigh Rd *EHAM* E6........................**84** A4
  HBRY N5 ....**76** B1
  LEY E10 ....**62** C2
Leigh St *STPAN* WC1H **8** C5
Leighton Av *MNPK* E12.................**84** A2
Leighton Crs *KTTN* NW5 ....**74** C2
Leighton Gdns *WLSDN* NW10 ......**88** C1
Leighton Gv *KTTN* NW5 ....**74** C2

Leighton Pl *KTTN* NW5 ....74 C2
Leighton Rd *KTTN* NW5 ....74 C2
Leila Parnell Pl *CHARL* SE7 ....124 C2
Leinster Av *MORT/ESHN* SW14 ....128 C1
Leinster Gdns *BAY/PAD* W2 ....15 E5
Leinster Ms *BAY/PAD* W2 ....27 E2
Leinster Pl *BAY/PAD* W2 ....15 E5
Leinster Sq *BAY/PAD* W2 ....26 B1
Leinster Ter *BAY/PAD* W2 ....27 E1
Leith Cl *CDALE/KGS* NW9 ....51 D3
Leithcote Gdns *STRHM/NOR* SW16 ....153 F5
Leithcote Pth *STRHM/NOR* SW16 ....153 F3
Leith Yd *KIL/WHAMP* * NW6 ....72 A5
Lelitia Cl *HACK* E8 ....78 A5
Leman St *WCHPL* E1 ....25 E3
Le May Av *LEE/GVPK* SE12 ....160 B3
Lemmon Rd *GNWCH* SE10 ....123 E2
Lemna Rd *WAN* E11 ....63 E2
Lemonwell Dr *ELTH/MOT* SE9 ....144 B3
Lemsford Cl *SEVS/STOTM* N15 ....60 A1
Lena Gdns *HMSMTH* W6 ....100 C4
Lendal Ter *CLAP* * SW4 ....135 D1
Len Freeman Pl *FUL/PGN* SW6 ....113 F2
Lenham Rd *LEW* SE13 ....141 F2
Lennon Rd *CRICK* NW2 ....70 C2
Lennox Gdns *IL* IG1 ....65 F3
    KTBR SW1X 41 E3
    WLSDN NW10 ....69 F1
Lennox Gardens Ms *CHEL* SW3 ....41 E4
Lennox Rd *FSBYPK* N4 ....57 F4
    WALTH E17 ....61 F1
Lens Rd *FSTGT* E7 ....82 C4
Lenthall Rd *HACK* E8 ....77 F4
Lenthorp Rd *GNWCH* SE10 ....105 F5
Lentmead Rd *BMLY* BR1 ....159 F3
Lenton St *WOOL/PLUM* SE18 ....109 D5
Lenton Ter *FSBYPK* * N4 ....58 A4
Leof Crs *CAT* SE6 ....158 B5
Leonard Ct *KENS* * W8 ....38 C3
Leonard Pl *STNW/STAM* * N16 ....77 E1
Leonard Rd *FSTGT* E7 ....82 A1
Leonard St *CAN/RD* E16 ....107 E2
    SDTCH EC2A 12 B5
Leontine Cl *PECK* SE15 ....120 A3
Leopold Av *WIM/MER* SW19 ....149 E1
Leopold Ms *HOM* E9 ....78 C5
Leopold Rd *WIM/MER* SW19 ....149 E4
    WLSDN NW10 ....69 E4
Leopold St *BOW* E3 ....91 F4
Leo St *PECK* SE15 ....120 B4
Leppoc Rd *CLAP* SW4 ....135 D3
Leroy St *STHWK* SE1 ....48 C4
Lerry Cl *WKENS* W14 ....113 F2
Lescombe Cl *FSTH* SE23 ....157 E3
Lescombe Rd *FSTH* SE23 ....157 E3
Leslie Rd *CAN/RD* E16 ....94 B5
    WAN E11 ....81 D1
Lessar Av *CLAP* SW4 ....134 C3
Lessingham Av *TOOT* SW17 ....151 F4
Lessing St *FSTH* SE23 ....139 E5
Lester Av *SRTFD* E15 ....93 E3
Leswin Pl *STNW/STAM* N16 ....59 F5
Leswin Rd *STNW/STAM* N16 ....59 F5
Letchford Gdns *WLSDN* NW10 ....88 A2
Letchford Ms *WLSDN* * NW10 ....88 A2
Letchworth St *TOOT* SW17 ....151 F4
Letterstone Rd *FUL/PGN* SW6 ....113 F3
Lettice St *FUL/PGN* SW6 ....113 F5
Lett Rd *SRTFD* E15 ....81 D4
Levana Cl *WIM/MER* SW19 ....149 E1
Levehurst Wy *CLAP* SW4 ....117 E5
Levendale Rd *FSTH* SE23 ....157 E2
Leven Rd *POP/IOD* E14 ....92 C4

Leverett St *CHEL* SW3 ....41 D4
Leverholme Gdns *ELTH/MOT* SE9 ....162 A4
Lever St *FSBYE* EC1V 11 E4
Leverton Pl *KTTN* NW5 ....74 C2
Leverton St *KTTN* NW5 ....74 C2
Levett Gdns *GDMY/SEVK* IG3 ....85 F1
Levett Rd *BARK* IG11 ....85 E3
Lewesdon Cl *WIM/MER* SW19 ....149 D1
Leweston Pl *STNW/STAM* N16 ....59 F2
Lewgars Av *CDALE/KGS* NW9 ....50 C1
Lewin Rd *MORT/ESHN* SW14 ....129 D1
Lewis Crs *WLSDN* NW10 ....69 D2
Lewis Gv *LEW* SE13 ....140 C5
Lewisham High St *LEW* SE13 ....140 B4
Lewisham Hl *LEW* SE13 ....122 C5
Lewisham Pk *LEW* SE13 ....140 B4
Lewisham Rd *LEW* SE13 ....122 C5
Lewisham Wy *BROCKY* SE4 ....121 F5
Lewis Pl *HACK* E8 ....78 A2
Lewis St *CAMTN* NW1 ....74 B4
Lexden Rd *ACT* W3 ....98 B1
Lexham Gdns *KENS* W8 ....38 B4
Lexham Ms *KENS* W8 ....38 B4
Lexington St *SOHO/CST* W1F 19 F5
Lexton Gdns *BAL* SW12 ....153 D1
Leyborne Pk *RCH/KEW* TW9 ....110 A4
Leybourne Rd *CAMTN* * NW1 ....74 B4
    WAN E11 ....63 F3
Leybourne St *CAMTN* NW1 ....74 B4
Leyden St *WCHPL* E1 ....25 E3
Leyes Rd *CAN/RD* E16 ....106 C1
Leyland Rd *LEE/GVPK* SE12 ....141 F3
Leylang Rd *NWCR* SE14 ....121 D3
Leysdown Rd *ELTH/MOT* SE9 ....161 E2
Leysfield Rd *SHB* W12 ....100 A3
Leyspring Rd *WAN* E11 ....63 F3
Ley St *IL* IG1 ....66 B4
Leythe Rd *ACT* W3 ....98 C3
Leyton Gra *LEY* E10 ....62 A4
Leyton Green Rd *LEY* E10 ....62 C1
Leyton Park Rd *LEY* E10 ....62 C4
Leyton Rd *SRTFD* E15 ....80 C2
Leytonstone Rd *SRTFD* E15 ....81 E2
Leywick St *SRTFD* E15 ....93 E1
Liardet St *NWCR* SE14 ....121 E2
Liberia Rd *HBRY* N5 ....76 B3
Liberty St *BRXN/ST* SW9 ....117 F4
Libra Rd *BOW* E3 ....79 F5
    PLSTW E13 ....94 A3
Library Pde *WLSDN* * NW10 ....69 E5
Library St *STHWK* SE1 ....47 D1
Lichfield Rd *BOW* E3 ....91 E2
    CRICK NW2 ....71 E1
    EHAM E6 ....95 D2
Lidcote Gdns *BRXN/ST* * SW9 ....118 A5
Liddell Gdns *WLSDN* NW10 ....88 C1
Liddell Rd *KIL/WHAMP* NW6 ....72 A3
Liddington Rd *SRTFD* E15 ....81 F1
Liddon Rd *PLSTW* E13 ....94 B2
Liden Cl *LEY* E10 ....61 F2
Lidfield Rd *STNW/STAM* N16 ....77 D1
Lidgate Rd *PECK* * SE15 ....119 F3
Lidiard Rd *WAND/EARL* SW18 ....150 C2
Lidyard Rd *ARCH* N19 ....56 C3
Liffler Rd *WOOL/PLUM* SE18 ....127 E1
Lifford St *PUT/ROE* SW15 ....131 D2
Lighterman Ms *WCHPL* E1 ....91 D5
Lighterman's Rd *POP/IOD* E14 ....104 A3
Ligonier St *BETH* E2 ....13 E5
Lilac Pl *LBTH* SE11 ....45 E5
Lilac St *SHB* W12 ....100 A1
Lilburne Gdns *ELTH/MOT* SE9 ....143 E3
Lilburne Rd *ELTH/MOT* SE9 ....143 E3

Lilestone St *CAMTN* NW1 .... 4 C5
Lilford Rd *BRXN/ST* SW9 .... 118 B5
Lilian Barker Cl *LEE/GVPK* SE12 .... 142 A3
Lilley Cl *WAP* E1W 102 A2
Lillian Av *ACT* W3 .... 98 A3
Lillian Rd *BARN* SW13 .... 112 A2
Lillie Rd *FUL/PGN* SW6 .... 113 D2
Lillieshall Rd *CLAP* SW4 .... 134 B1
Lillie Yd *FUL/PGN* SW6 .... 114 A2
Lillington Gardens Est *PIM* SW1V 43 F5
Lily Cl *WKENS* * W14 .... 101 E5
Lily Pl *HCIRC* EC1N 22 B2
Lily Rd *LEY* E10 .... 62 A1
Lilyville Rd *FUL/PGN* SW6 .... 113 F4
Limburg Rd *BTSEA* SW11 .... 133 E4
Limeburner La *STP* EC4M 22 C4
Lime Cl *WAP* E1W 102 A2
Lime Gv *BFN/LL* DA15 .... 145 F4
   SHB W12 .... 100 C3
Limeharbour *POP/IOD* E14 .... 104 B4
Limehouse *POP/IOD* * E14 .... 104 A1
Limehouse Cswy *POP/IOD* E14 .... 103 F1
Limehouse Link *POP/IOD* E14 .... 103 E1
Lime Kiln Dr *CHARL* SE7 .... 124 B2
Limerick Cl *BAL* SW12 .... 134 C5
Limerston St *WBPTN* SW10 .... 114 C2
Limes Av *BARN* SW13 .... 111 F5
   GLDGN NW11 .... 53 F2
Limes Field Rd *BARN* SW13 .... 129 E1
Limesford Rd *PECK* SE15 .... 139 E1
Limes Gdns *WAND/EARL* SW18 .... 132 A4
Limes Gv *LEW* SE13 .... 140 C2
The Limes *CMBW* * SE5 .... 137 E1
   WAND/EARL * SW18 .... 132 A4
Lime St *FENCHST* EC3M 36 C1
Lime Street Pas *BANK* * EC3V 24 C5
Limetree La *BRXS/STRHM* SW2 .... 153 F1
Lime Tree Ter *FSTH* * SE23 .... 157 F1
Lime Wk *SRTFD* * E15 .... 81 E5
Limpsfield Av *WIM/MER* SW19 .... 149 D2
Linacre Rd *CRICK* NW2 .... 70 B3
Linchmere Rd *LEE/GVPK* SE12 .... 142 A5
Lincoln Av *WIM/MER* SW19 .... 149 D3
Lincoln Est *BOW* E3 .... 92 A3
Lincoln Gdns *IL* IG1 .... 65 E2
Lincoln Ms *KIL/WHAMP* NW6 .... 71 F5
Lincoln Rd *PLSTW* E13 .... 94 B3
Lincoln's Inn Flds *LINN* WC2A 21 E4
Lincoln St *CHEL* SW3 .... 41 E5
   WAN E11 .... 63 E4
Lincombe Rd *BMLY* BR1 .... 159 F3
Lindal Rd *BROCKY* SE4 .... 139 F3
Linden Av *WLSDN* NW10 .... 89 D1
Linden Gdns *BAY/PAD* W2 .... 26 B2
   CHSWK W4 .... 111 D1
Linden Gv *PECK* SE15 .... 138 B1
Linden Ms *BAY/PAD* W2 .... 26 B2
   IS N1 .... 77 D2
The Lindens *CHSWK* W4 .... 110 C4
Lindfield Gdns *HAMP* NW3 .... 72 C2
Lindfield St *POP/IOD* E14 .... 92 A5
Lindisfarne Md *HOM* E9 .... 79 E1
Lindley Est *PECK* * SE15 .... 120 A3
Lindley Pl *RCH/KEW* TW9 .... 110 A4
Lindley Rd *LEY* E10 .... 62 C4
Lindley St *WCHPL* E1 .... 90 C4
Lindore Rd *BTSEA* SW11 .... 133 F2
Lindo St *PECK* SE15 .... 120 C5
Lindrop St *FUL/PGN* SW6 .... 114 C5
Lindsay Sq *PIM* SW1V 117 D1
Lindsell St *GNWCH* SE10 .... 122 C4
Lindsey Ms *IS* N1 .... 76 C4

Lindsey St *STBT* EC1A 23 D2
Lind St *DEPT* SE8 .... 122 B5
Lindway *WNWD* SE27 .... 154 B5
Linford St *VX/NE* SW8 .... 116 C4
Lingards Rd *LEW* SE13 .... 140 C2
Lingey Cl *BFN/LL* DA15 .... 163 F2
Lingfield Crs *ELTH/MOT* SE9 .... 145 D2
Lingham St *BRXN/ST* SW9 .... 117 E5
Ling Rd *CAN/RD* E16 .... 94 A4
Lingwell Rd *TOOT* SW17 .... 151 E3
Lingwood Rd *CLPT* E5 .... 60 A2
Linhope St *CAMTN* NW1 .... 5 E5
Links Rd *ACT* W3 .... 86 A5
   CRICK NW2 .... 51 F4
Link St *HOM* E9 .... 78 C3
Links Yd *WCHPL* E1 .... 25 F2
The Link *ACT* W3 .... 86 B5
Linkway *FSBYPK* N4 .... 58 C2
Linkwood Wk *CAMTN* NW1 .... 75 D4
Linnell Cl *GLDGN* NW11 .... 54 B1
Linnell Dr *GLDGN* NW11 .... 54 B1
Linnell Rd *CMBW* SE5 .... 119 E5
Linnet Ms *BAL* SW12 .... 134 A5
Linom Rd *CLAP* SW4 .... 135 E2
Linscott Rd *CLPT* E5 .... 78 C1
Linsdell Rd *BARK* IG11 .... 84 C5
Linsey St *BERM/RHTH* SE16 .... 102 A4
Linstead St *KIL/WHAMP* NW6 .... 72 A4
Linstead Wy *WAND/EARL* SW18 ..... 131 E5
Lintaine Cl *FUL/PGN* * SW6 .... 113 E2
Linthorpe Rd *STNW/STAM* N16 .... 59 E2
Linton Cl *CHARL* SE7 .... 124 C1
Linton Gdns *EHAM* E6 .... 95 E5
Linton Gv *WNWD* SE27 .... 154 B5
Linton Rd *BARK* IG11 .... 84 C4
Linton St *IS* N1 .... 76 C5
Linver Rd *FUL/PGN* SW6 .... 113 F5
Linwood Cl *CMBW* SE5 .... 119 F5
Lionel Gdns *ELTH/MOT* SE9 .... 143 D3
Lionel Ms *NKENS* * W10 .... 89 E4
Lionel Rd *ELTH/MOT* SE9 .... 143 D3
Lion Mills *BETH* * E2 .... 90 A1
Lion Rd *EHAM* E6 .... 95 F4
Lions Cl *LEE/GVPK* SE12 .... 160 C3
Liphook Crs *FSTH* SE23 .... 138 C5
Lisburne Rd *HAMP* NW3 .... 73 F1
Lisford St *PECK* SE15 .... 119 F4
Lisgar Ter *WKENS* W14 .... 101 F5
Liskeard Gdns *BKHTH/KID* SE3 ...... 124 A4
Lisle Cl *TOOT* SW17 .... 152 B4
Lisle St *SOHO/SHAV* W1D 32 B1
Lismore *WIM/MER* * SW19 .... 149 F5
Lismore Circ *HAMP* NW3 .... 73 F2
Lismore Wk *IS* N1 .... 76 C3
Lissenden Gdns *KTTN* NW5 .... 74 A1
Lisson Gv *CAMTN* NW1 .... 16 C1
   STJWD NW8 .... 4 B5
Lisson St *CAMTN* NW1 .... 16 C2
Lister Cl *ACT* W3 .... 87 D4
Lister Ms *HOLWY* N7 .... 75 F1
Lister Rd *WAN* E11 .... 63 E3
Liston Rd *CLAP* SW4 .... 134 C1
Listowel Cl *BRXN/ST* SW9 .... 118 A3
Listria Pk *STNW/STAM* N16 .... 59 E4
Litchfield Av *SRTFD* * E15 .... 81 E3
Litchfield Gdns *WLSDN* NW10 .... 70 A3
Lithos Rd *HAMP* NW3 .... 72 B3
Little Albany St *CAMTN* NW1 .... 7 D5
Little Argyll St *CONDST* * W1S 19 E5
Little Birches *BFN/LL* DA15 .... 163 E2
The Little Boltons *WBPTN* SW10 ..... 114 B1
Little Bornes *DUL* SE21 .... 155 E4
Little Britain *STBT* EC1A 23 D3

Littlebury Rd CLAP * SW4 ....135 D1
Little Chester St KTBR SW1X 42 C2
Little Cloisters WEST SW1P 44 C2
Littlecombe Cl PUT/ROE * SW15 ......131 D4
Littlecote Cl WIM/MER SW19 ....131 D5
Littlecroft ELTH/MOT SE9 ....144 A1
Little Deans Yd WEST SW1P 44 B2
Little Dimocks BAL SW12 ....152 B2
Little Dorrit Ct STHWK SE1 ....35 F3
Little Edward St CAMTN * NW1 ....7 D3
Little Essex St TPL/STR * WC2R 34 A1
Littlefield Cl ARCH N19 ....74 C1
Little George St WEST SW1P 44 C1
Little Green St KTTN * NW5 ....74 B1
Little Heath CHARL SE7 ....125 E2
Little Ilford La MNPK E12 ....83 F1
Little Marlborough St REGST * W1B 19 E5
Littlemede ELTH/MOT SE9 ....161 F3
Littlemoor Rd IL IG1 ....67 D5
Little Newport St LSQ/SEVD WC2H 32 B1
Little New St FLST/FETLN EC4A 22 B4
Little Portland St REGST W1B 19 D4
Little Rownings FSTH SE23 ....156 B2
Little Russell St NOXST/BSQ WC1A 20 C3
Little St James's St WHALL SW1A 31 E4
Little St Leonards
    MORT/ESHN SW14 ....128 C1
Little Smith St WEST SW1P 44 B2
Little Titchfield St GTPST W1W 19 E3
Littleton St WAND/EARL SW18 ....150 C2
Little Trinity La BLKFR EC4V 35 F1
Little Turnstile LINN WC2A 21 E3
Littlewood LEW SE13 ....140 C3
Livermere Rd HACK E8 ....77 F5
Liverpool Gv WALW SE17 ....119 D1
Liverpool Rd CAN/RD E16 ....93 E4
    IS N1 ....76 A4
    LEY E10 ....62 C1
Liverpool St LVPST EC2M 24 C4
Livesey Pl PECK SE15 ....120 A2
Livingstone Rd BTSEA SW11 ....133 D1
    LEY E10 ....62 B1
    SRTFD E15 ....80 C5
Lizard St FSBYE EC1V 11 F4
Lizban St BKHTH/KID SE3 ....124 B3
Llanelly Rd CRICK NW2 ....53 F4
Llanover Rd WOOL/PLUM SE18 ....126 A3
Llanvanor Rd CRICK NW2 ....53 F4
Llewellyn St BERM/RHTH SE16 ....102 A3
Lloyd Baker St FSBYW WC1X 10 A4
Lloyd Rd EHAM E6 ....83 F5
Lloyd's Av TWRH EC3N 25 D5
Lloyd's Pl BKHTH/KID * SE3 ....123 E5
Lloyd Sq FSBYW WC1X 10 A3
Lloyd's Rw CLKNW EC1R 10 B4
Lloyd St FSBYW WC1X 10 A3
Lloyd Vls BROCKY SE4 ....122 A5
Loampit Hl LEW SE13 ....122 A5
Loampit V LEW SE13 ....140 B1
Loanda Cl HACK E8 ....77 F5
Loats Rd CLAP SW4 ....135 E4
Locarno Rd ACT W3 ....98 C2
Lochaber Rd LEW SE13 ....141 E2
Lochaline St HMSMTH W6 ....112 C3
Lochinvar St BAL SW12 ....134 B5
Lochnagar St POP/IOD E14 ....92 C4
Lock Cha LEW SE13 ....141 E1
Lockgate Cl HOM E9 ....79 F2
Lockhart Cl HOLWY N7 ....75 F3
Lockhart St BOW E3 ....91 F3
Lockhurst St CLPT E5 ....79 D1
Lockington Rd VX/NE SW8 ....116 B4
Lockmead Rd LEW SE13 ....140 C1

Locksley Est POP/IOD E14 ....91 F5
Locksley St POP/IOD E14 ....91 F4
Lockwood Cl SYD SE26 ....157 E5
Lockwood Sq BERM/RHTH SE16 ....102 B4
Lockyer St STHWK SE1 ....48 B1
Locton Gn BOW * E3 ....79 F5
Loddiges Rd HOM E9 ....78 C4
Loder St PECK SE15 ....120 C3
Lodge Ms HBRY * N5 ....76 C1
Lodge Rd STJWD NW8 ....4 B4
The Lodge SHB * W12 ....101 D3
Lodore St POP/IOD E14 ....92 C4
Loftie St BERM/RHTH SE16 ....102 A3
Lofting Rd IS N1 ....76 A4
Loftus Rd SHB W12 ....100 B2
Loftus Vls SHB * W12 ....100 B2
Logan Ms KENS W8 ....38 A4
Logan Pl KENS W8 ....38 A4
Lolesworth Cl WCHPL * E1 ....25 F3
Lollard St LBTH SE11 ....45 F4
Loman St STHWK SE1 ....35 D5
Lomas St WCHPL E1 ....90 A4
Lombard Av GDMY/SEVK IG3 ....67 E3
Lombard Rd BTSEA SW11 ....115 D5
Lombard St BANK EC3V 24 B5
Lombard Wall CHARL SE7 ....106 B4
Lombardy Pl BAY/PAD W2 ....26 C2
Lomond Gv CMBW SE5 ....119 D3
Loncroft Rd CMBW SE5 ....119 E2
Londesborough Rd
    STNW/STAM N16 ....77 D3
London Br CANST EC4R 36 B2
London Bridge Wk STHWK * SE1 ....36 B3
London Flds HACK * E8 ....78 B4
London Fields East Side HACK E8 ......78 B4
London Fields West Side HACK E8 ......78 A4
London La HACK E8 ....78 B4
London Ms BAY/PAD W2 ....16 B5
London Rd BARK IG11 ....84 B4
    FSTH SE23 ....156 C1
    PLSTW E13 ....94 A1
    STHWK SE1 ....46 A1
London Stile CHSWK W4 ....110 A1
London St BAY/PAD W2 ....16 A5
    FENCHST * EC3M 37 D1
London Ter BETH * E2 ....90 A1
London Wall BARB EC2Y 23 F3
London Wall Buildings LVPST EC2M 24 B3
Long Acre COVGDN WC2E 20 C5
Longbeach Rd BTSEA SW11 ....133 F1
Longbridge Rd BARK IG11 ....85 D3
Longbridge Wy LEW SE13 ....140 C3
Longcroft ELTH/MOT SE9 ....162 A3
Longdown Rd CAT SE6 ....158 A4
Long Dr ACT W3 ....87 E5
Longfellow Rd BOW * E3 ....91 E2
    WALTH * E17 ....61 F1
Longfellow Wy STHWK * SE1 ....49 F5
Longfield Crs SYD SE26 ....156 C3
Longfield Dr MORT/ESHN SW14 ....128 B3
Longfield Est STHWK SE1 ....49 F4
Longfield St WAND/EARL SW18 ....132 A5
Longford St CAMTN NW1 ....7 D5
Longhedge St BTSEA SW11 ....116 A5
Longhill Rd CAT SE6 ....159 D2
Longhope Cl PECK SE15 ....119 E2
Longhurst Rd LEW SE13 ....141 E3
Longlands Park Crs BFN/LL DA15 ......163 E3
Longlands Rd BFN/LL DA15 ....163 E3
Long La STBT EC1A 23 D2
    STHWK SE1 ....48 B1
Longley St STHWK SE1 ....102 A5

Longley Wy CRICK NW2 ....52 C5
Long Mark Rd CAN/RD E16 ....95 D5
Long Meadow KTTN * NW5 ....75 D3
Longmeadow Rd BFN/LL DA15 ....163 E1
Longmead Rd TOOT SW17 ....151 F5
Longmoore St PIM SW1V 43 E5
Longnor Rd WCHPL E1 ....91 D2
Long Pond Rd BKHTH/KID SE3 ....123 E4
Long Reach Rd BARK IG11 ....97 F3
Longridge Rd ECT SW5 ....38 A5
Long Rd CLAP SW4 ....134 C2
Longshore DEPT SE8 ....103 F5
Longstaff Crs WAND/EARL SW18 .....132 A4
Longstaff Rd WAND/EARL SW18 ......132 A4
Longstone Av WLSDN NW10 ....69 F4
Longstone Rd TOOT SW17 ....152 B5
Long St BETH E2 ....13 E2
Longton Av SYD SE26 ....156 A4
Longton Gv SYD SE26 ....156 B4
Longville Rd LBTH SE11 ....46 C4
Long Wk STHWK SE1 ....49 D2
Longwood Dr PUT/ROE SW15 ....130 A4
Long Yd BMSBY WC1N 21 E1
Lonsdale Av EHAM E6 ....95 D3
Lonsdale Cl EHAM E6 ....95 E3
    LEE/GVPK SE12 ....161 D3
Lonsdale Crs GNTH/NBYPK IG2 ....66 B1
Lonsdale Ms RCH/KEW * TW9 ....110 A4
Lonsdale Pl IS N1 ....76 A4
Lonsdale Rd BARN SW13 ....111 F3
    CHSWK W4 ....99 F5
    KIL/WHAMP NW6 ....89 F1
    NTGHL W11 ....89 E5
    WAN E11 ....63 F2
Lonsdale Sq IS * N1 ....76 A4
Loop Rd CHST BR7 ....162 B5
Loraine Cottages HOLWY * N7 ....75 F1
Loraine Rd CHSWK W4 ....110 B3
    HOLWY N7 ....75 F1
Lord Hills Rd BAY/PAD W2 ....15 D2
Lord Holland La BRXN/ST SW9 ....118 A5
Lord Napier Pl HMSMTH W6 ....112 A1
Lord North St WEST SW1P 44 C3
Lord Roberts Ms FUL/PGN * SW6 .....114 B3
Lords Cl DUL SE21 ....154 C2
Lordship Gv STNW/STAM N16 ....59 D4
Lordship La DUL SE21 ....156 A1
    EDUL SE22 ....137 F4
Lordship Pk STNW/STAM N16 ....59 D4
Lordship Park Ms
    STNW/STAM N16 ....58 C4
Lordship Pl CHEL SW3 ....115 E2
Lordship Rd STNW/STAM N16 ....59 D3
Lordship Ter STNW/STAM N16 ....59 D3
Lord St CAN/RD E16 ....107 E2
Lords Vw STJWD NW8 ....4 C4
Lord Warwick St
    WOOL/PLUM SE18 ....107 F4
Lorenzo St FSBYW WC1X 9 E3
Loris Rd HMSMTH W6 ....100 C4
Lorn Ct BRXN/ST SW9 ....118 A5
Lorne Cl STJWD NW8 ....5 D4
Lorne Gdns WKENS W14 ....101 D3
Lorne Rd FSBYPK N4 ....57 F3
    FSTGT E7 ....82 B1
Lorn Rd BRXN/ST SW9 ....117 F5
Lorrimore Rd WALW SE17 ....118 A5
Lorrimore Sq WALW SE17 ....118 B2
Lothair Rd North FSBYPK N4 ....58 B1
Lothair Rd South FSBYPK N4 ....58 A2
Lothbury LOTH EC2R 24 A4
Lothian Rd BRXN/ST SW9 ....118 B4
Lothrop St NKENS W10 ....89 E2

Lots Rd WBPTN SW10 ....114 C3
Loudoun Rd STJWD NW8 ....72 C5
Loughborough Pk HNHL SE24 ....136 B2
Loughborough Rd BRXN/ST SW9 ......118 A5
Loughborough St LBTH SE11 ....117 F1
Lough Rd HOLWY N7 ....75 F2
Louisa Cl HOM E9 ....78 C4
Louisa St WCHPL E1 ....91 D4
Louise Bennett Cl HNHL * SE24 ....136 B2
Louise Rd SRTFD E15 ....81 E3
Louisville Rd TOOT SW17 ....152 A3
Louvaine Rd BTSEA SW11 ....133 D2
Lovage Ap EHAM E6 ....95 E4
Lovat Cl CRICK NW2 ....51 F5
Lovat La FENCHST EC3M 36 C1
Lovegrove St STHWK SE1 ....120 A1
Lovegrove Wk POP/IOD E14 ....104 C2
Lovelace Gn ELTH/MOT SE9 ....143 F1
Lovelace Rd DUL SE21 ....154 C2
Love La CITYW EC2V 23 F4
    WOOL/PLUM SE18 ....108 A5
Lovelinch Cl PECK SE15 ....120 C1
Lovell Pl BERM/RHTH SE16 ....103 E4
Loveridge Ms KIL/WHAMP NW6 ....71 F3
Loveridge Rd KIL/WHAMP NW6 ....71 F3
Lovett Wy WLSDN NW10 ....68 C2
Love Wk CMBW SE5 ....119 D5
Lowbrook Rd IL IG1 ....84 B1
Lowden Rd HNHL SE24 ....136 B2
Lowe Av CAN/RD E16 ....94 A4
Lowell St POP/IOD E14 ....91 E5
Lower Addison Gdns WKENS W14 .....101 E3
Lower Belgrave St BCVA SW1W 42 C2
Lower Clapton Rd CLPT E5 ....78 B1
Lower Clarendon Wk NTGHL W11 ....89 E5
Lower Common South
    PUT/ROE SW15 ....130 B1
Lower Grosvenor Pl KTBR SW1X 42 C2
Lower James St SOHO/CST * W1F 31 F1
Lower John St SOHO/CST W1F 31 F1
Lower Lea Crossing
    POP/IOD E14 ....105 E1
Lower Marsh STHWK SE1 ....46 A1
Lower Merton Ri HAMP NW3 ....73 E4
Lower Richmond Rd
    PUT/ROE SW15 ....130 C1
    RCH/KEW TW9 ....128 A1
Lower Rd BERM/RHTH SE16 ....102 C3
Lower Sloane St BCVA SW1W 41 F5
Lower Ter HAMP NW3 ....54 C5
Lower Thames St MON EC3R 36 C2
Lowfield Rd ACT W3 ....86 C5
    KIL/WHAMP NW6 ....72 A4
Low Hall La WALTH E17 ....61 E1
Lowman Rd HOLWY N7 ....75 F1
Lowndes Cl KTBR SW1X 42 B3
Lowndes Ct REGST W1B 19 E5
Lowndes Pl KTBR * SW1X 42 A3
Lowndes Sq KTBR SW1X 41 F1
Lowndes St KTBR SW1X 41 F2
Lowood St WCHPL E1 ....102 B1
Lowther Hl FSTH SE23 ....139 E5
Lowther Man BARN * SW13 ....112 A4
Lowther Rd BARN SW13 ....111 F4
    HOLWY * N7 ....76 A2
Lowth Rd CMBW SE5 ....118 C5
Loxford Av EHAM E6 ....95 D1
Loxford La IL IG1 ....84 C2
Loxford Rd BARK IG11 ....84 B3
Loxham St STPAN * WC1H 9 D4
Loxley Cl SYD SE26 ....157 D5
Loxley Rd WAND/EARL SW18 ....151 D1
Loxton Rd FSTH SE23 ....157 D1

Lubbock St *NWCR* SE14 ....120 C3
Lucan Pl *CHEL* SW3 ....40 C5
Lucas Av *PLSTW* E13 ....82 B5
Lucas Sq *GLDGN* NW11 ....54 A1
Lucas St *DEPT* SE8 ....122 A5
Lucerne As *KENS* * W8 ....26 B3
Lucerne Rd *HBRY* N5 ....76 B1
Lucey Rd *BERM/RHTH* SE16 ....102 A4
Lucey Wy *BERM/RHTH* SE16 ....102 A4
Lucien Rd *TOOT* SW17 ....152 A4
   WAND/EARL SW18 ....150 B2
Lucknow St *WOOL/PLUM* SE18 ...127 E3
Lucorn Cl *LEE/GVPK* SE12 ....141 F4
Ludgate Broadway *BLKFR* * EC4V ..23 D5
Ludgate Circ *STP* * EC4M 22 C5
Ludgate HI *STP* EC4M 22 C5
Ludgate Sq *BLKFR* * EC4V 23 D5
Ludlow St *FSBYE* * EC1V 11 E5
Ludovick Wk *PUT/ROE* SW15 ....129 E2
Luffman Rd *LEE/GVPK* SE12 ....160 B3
Lugard Rd *PECK* SE15 ....120 B5
Lugg Ap *MNPK* E12 ....66 A5
Luke St *SDTCH* EC2A 12 C5
Lukin St *WCHPL* E1 ....102 C1
Lullingstone La *LEW* SE13 ....141 D4
Lulworth Rd *ELTH/MOT* SE9 ....161 E2
   PECK * SE15 ....120 B5
   WELL DA16 ....127 F5
Lumley Flats *BGVA* * SW1W 116 A1
Lumley St *MYFR/PKLN* W1K 18 B5
Lundy Wk *IS* * N1 ....76 C3
Lupin Cl *BRXS/STRHM* SW2 ....154 B2
Lupton Cl *LEE/GVPK* SE12 ....160 B3
Lupton St *KTTN* NW5 ....74 C1
Lupus St *PIM* SW1V 116 B1
Lurgan Av *HMSMTH* W6 ....113 D2
Lurline Gdns *BTSEA* SW11 ....116 A4
Luscombe Wy *VX/NE* SW8 ....117 E3
Lushington Rd *CAT* SE6 ....158 B5
   WLSDN NW10 ....88 B1
Lushington Ter *HACK* E8 ....78 A2
Luther King Cl *WALTH* E17 ....61 E1
Luton Pl *GNWCH* SE10 ....122 C3
Luton Rd *PLSTW* E13 ....94 A3
Luton St *STJWD* NW8 ....16 B1
Luttrell Av *PUT/ROE* SW15 ....130 B3
Lutwyche Rd *FSTH* SE23 ....157 F2
Luxborough St *MHST* W1U 18 A1
Luxemburg Gdns *HMSMTH* W6 ....101 D5
Luxfield Rd *ELTH/MOT* SE9 ....161 E1
Luxford St *BERM/RHTH* SE16 ....103 D5
Luxmore St *BROCKY* SE4 ....121 F4
Luxor St *CMBW* SE5 ....118 B5
Lyall Av *DUL* SE21 ....155 E4
Lyall Ms *KTBR* SW1X 42 A5
Lyall Ms West *KTBR* * SW1X 42 A3
Lyall St *KTBR* SW1X 42 A3
Lyal Rd *BOW* E3 ....91 E1
Lycett Pl *SHB* W12 ....100 A3
Lydd Cl *BFN/LL* DA15 ....163 E3
Lydden Gv *WAND/EARL* SW18 .....132 B5
Lydden Rd *WAND/EARL* SW18 .....132 B5
Lydeard Rd *EHAM* E6 ....83 F4
Lydford Cl *STNW/STAM* N16 ....77 E2
Lydford Rd *CRICK* NW2 ....71 D3
   MV/WKIL W9 ....89 F3
Lydhurst Av *BRXS/STRHM* SW2 ...153 F2
Lydney Cl *PECK* SE15 ....119 E3
   WIM/MER SW19 ....149 E2
Lydon Rd *CLAP* SW4 ....134 C1
Lydstep Rd *CHST* BR7 ....162 A4
Lyford Rd *WAND/EARL* SW18 ....133 D5
Lyford St *CHARL* SE7 ....107 E5

Lygon Pl *BGVA* * SW1W 42 C3
Lyham Cl *CLAP* SW4 ....135 E4
Lyham Rd *BRXS/STRHM* SW2 .....135 E3
Lyme Farm Rd *LEE/GVPK* SE12 ...142 A2
Lyme Gv *HOM* E9 ....78 C4
Lymer Av *NRWD* SE19 ....155 F5
Lyme St *CAMTN* NW1 ....74 C4
Lyme Ter *CAMTN* NW1 ....74 C4
Lyminge Cl *SCUP* DA14 ....163 F4
Lyminge Gdns *WAND/EARL* SW18 .151 E1
Lymington Rd *KIL/WHAMP* * NW6 ...72 B3
Lympstone Gdns *PECK* SE15 ......120 A3
Lynbrook Cl *PECK* SE15 ....119 E3
Lyncourt *BKHTH/KID* * SE3 ....123 D5
Lyncroft Gdns *KIL/WHAMP* NW6 ....72 A1
Lyndale *CRICK* NW2 ....53 F5
Lyndale Av *CRICK* NW2 ....53 F5
Lyndale Cl *BKHTH/KID* SE3 ....123 F2
Lyndhurst Cl *WLSDN* NW10 ....51 D5
Lyndhurst Dr *WAN* E11 ....62 C2
Lyndhurst Gdns *BARK* IG11 ....85 E3
   GNTH/NBYPK IG2 ....67 D1
   HAMP NW3 ....73 D2
Lyndhurst Gv *CMBW* SE5 ....119 E5
Lyndhurst Rd *HAMP* NW3 ....73 D2
Lyndhurst Sq *PECK* SE15 ....119 E4
Lyndhurst Ter *HAMP* NW3 ....73 D2
Lyndhurst Wy *PECK* SE15 ....119 E4
Lyndon Av *BFN/LL* DA15 ....145 F3
Lyndon Yd *TOOT* SW17 ....150 B4
Lyneham Wk *CLPT* * E5 ....79 E2
Lynette Av *CLAP* SW4 ....134 B4
Lynford Gdns *GDMY/SEVK* IG3 ......67 F4
Lyn Ms *STNW* * N16 ....77 F1
Lynmouth Rd *STNW/STAM* N16 .....59 F3
   WALTH E17 ....61 E1
Lynne Wy *WLSDN* NW10 ....69 E3
Lynn Ms *WAN* E11 ....63 E4
Lynn Rd *BAL* SW12 ....134 B5
   GNTH/NBYPK IG2 ....67 D2
   WAN E11 ....63 E4
Lynsted Gdns *ELTH/MOT* SE9 .....143 D2
Lynton Av *ACT* W3 ....86 C5
Lynton Cl *WLSDN* NW10 ....69 E2
Lynton Crs *GNTH/NBYPK* IG2 ....66 B1
Lynton Est *STHWK* SE1 ....49 F5
Lynton Rd *ACT* W3 ....98 A1
   KIL/WHAMP NW6 ....71 F5
   STHWK SE1 ....49 F5
Lynton Ter *ACT* * W3 ....86 C5
Lynwood Rd *TOOT* SW17 ....151 F3
Lyons Pl *STJWD* NW8 ....16 A1
Lyon St *IS* N1 ....75 F4
Lyons Wk *WKENS* W14 ....101 E5
Lyric Ms *SYD* SE26 ....156 C4
Lyric Rd *BARN* SW13 ....111 F4
Lysander Gv *ARCH* N19 ....57 D3
Lysander Ms *ARCH* * N19 ....57 D3
Lysias Rd *BAL* SW12 ....134 A4
Lysia St *FUL/PGN* SW6 ....113 D3
Lysons Wk *PUT/ROE* * SW15 ....130 A3
Lytcott Gv *EDUL* SE22 ....137 F3
Lytham St *WALW* SE17 ....119 D1
Lyttelton Rd *LEY* E10 ....62 B5
Lytham Cl *HAMP* NW3 ....73 E4
Lytton Gv *PUT/ROE* SW15 ....131 D3
Lytton Rd *WAN* E11 ....63 E2
Lyveden Rd *BKHTH/KID* SE3 ....124 B3

M

Mabledon Pl *CAMTN* NW1 ....8 B4
Mablethorpe Rd *FUL/PGN* SW6.......113 E3
Mabley St *HOM* E9 ....79 E2
Macarthur Cl *STJWD* E7 ....82 A3
Macarthur Ter *CHARL* SE7 ....125 D2
Macaulay Rd *CLAP* SW4 ....134 B1
 EHAM E6 ....95 D1
Macbean St *WOOL/PLUM* SE18 ......108 A4
Macbeth St *HMSMTH* W6 ....112 B1
Macclesfield Br *STJWD* NW8 ....5 D1
Macclesfield Rd *FSBYE* EC1V 11 E3
Macclesfield St *SOHO/SHAV* W1D 32 B1
Macdonald Rd *ARCH* N19 ....56 C4
 FSTGT E7 ....82 A1
Macduff Rd *BTSEA* SW11 ....116 A4
Mace Cl *WAP* E1W 102 B2
Mace Gtwy *CAN/RD* E16 ....106 A1
Mace St *BETH* E2 ....91 D1
Macfarlane Rd *SHB* W12 ....100 C2
Mac Farren Pl *CAMTN* NW1 ....18 C1
Macgregor Rd *CAN/RD* E16 ....94 C2
Machell Rd *PECK* SE15 ....138 C1
Mackay Rd *CLAP* SW4 ....134 B1
Mackennal St *STJWD* NW8 ....5 D2
Mackenzie Cl *SHB* * W12 ....100 B1
Mackenzie Rd *HOLWY* N7 ....75 F3
Mackeson Rd *HAMP* NW3 ....73 F1
Mackie Rd *BRXS/STRHM* SW2 ....136 A5
Mackintosh La *HOM* E9 ....79 D2
Macklin St *HOL/ALD* * WC2B 21 D4
Macks Rd *BERM/RHTH* SE16 ....102 A5
Mackworth St *CAMTN* NW1 ....7 E3
Maclean Rd *FSTH* SE23 ....139 E4
Macleod St *WALW* SE17 ....118 C1
Maclise Rd *WKENS* W14 ....101 E4
Macoma Rd *WOOL/PLUM* SE18 ....127 D2
Macoma Ter *WOOL/PLUM* SE18 ....127 D2
Maconochies Rd *POP/IOD* * E14......122 B1
Macquarie Wy *POP/IOD* E14 ....104 B5
Macroom St *MV/WKIL* W9 ....89 F2
Maddams St *BOW* E3 ....92 B3
Maddock Wy *WALW* SE17 ....118 B2
Maddox St *MYFR/PKLN* W1K 31 D1
Madeira Rd *STRHM/NOR* SW16 ....153 E5
 WAN E11 ....63 D3
Madeline Gv *IL* IG1 ....85 D2
Madge Gill Wy *EHAM* E6 ....83 E5
Madinah Rd *HACK* E8 ....78 A3
Madras Pl *HOLWY* N7 ....76 A3
Madras Rd *IL* IG1 ....84 B1
Madrid Rd *BARN* SW13 ....112 A4
Madron St *STHWK* SE1 ....119 E1
Mafeking Av *EHAM* E6 ....95 D1
 GNTH/NBYPK IG2 ....67 D2
Mafeking Rd *CAN/RD* E16 ....93 F3
Magazine Ga *BAY/PAD* * W2 ....29 D3
Magdala Av *KTTN* NW5 ....56 C4
Magdalene Gdns *EHAM* E6 ....96 A3
Magdalen Rd *WAND/EARL* SW18 ......150 C1
Magdalen St *STHWK* SE1 ....36 C1
Magee St *LBTH* SE11 ....118 A2
Magnin Cl *HACK* E8 ....78 A5
Magnolia Cl *LEY* E10 ....62 A4
Magnolia Pl *CLAP* * SW4 ....135 E3
Magnolia Rd *CHSWK* W4 ....110 B2
Magnolia Whf *CHSWK* * W4 ....110 B2
Magpie Pl *FSTGT* E7 ....81 F2
Magpie Pl *NWCR* * SE14 ....121 E2
Magri Wk *WCHPL* E1 ....90 C4

Maguire St *STHWK* SE1 ....37 F4
Mahogany Cl *BERM/RHTH* SE16 ....103 E2
Maida Av *BAY/PAD* W2 ....15 F2
Maida V *KIL/WHAMP* NW6 ....3 D2
Maiden La *CAMTN* NW1 ....75 D4
 STHWK SE1 ....35 F4
Maiden Rd *SRTFD* E15 ....81 E4
Maidenstone Hl *GNWCH* SE10 ....122 C4
Maidstone Buildings Ms
 STHWK SE1 ....35 F4
Main Barracks *WOOL/PLUM* * SE18 .125 F1
Mainridge Rd *CHST* BR7 ....162 A4
Main Rd *BFN/LL* DA15 ....163 E3
Maismore St *PECK* SE15 ....120 A2
Maitland Cl *GNWCH* SE10 ....122 B3
Maitland Park Rd *HAMP* NW3 ....73 F3
Maitland Park Vls *HAMP* NW3 ....73 F3
Maitland Rd *SRTFD* * E15 ....81 F3
Majendie Rd *WOOL/PLUM* SE18 ....127 D1
Major Rd *BERM/RHTH* * SE16 ....102 A4
 SRTFD E15 ....80 C2
Makepeace Av *HGT* N6 ....56 A4
Makins St *CHEL* SW3 ....41 D5
Malabar St *POP/IOD* E14 ....104 A3
Malam Gdns *POP/IOD* E14 ....104 B1
Malbrook Rd *PUT/ROE* SW15 ....130 B2
Malcolm Gavin Cl *TOOT* SW17 ....151 E2
Malcolm Pl *BETH* E2 ....90 C3
Malcolm Rd *WCHPL* E1 ....90 C3
Malden Pl *KTTN* NW5 ....74 A2
Malden Rd *KTTN* NW5 ....73 F2
Maldon Cl *CMBW* * SE5 ....137 E1
 IS N1 ....76 C5
Maldon Rd *ACT* W3 ....98 C1
Malet St *CWRST* WC1E 20 A1
Maley Av *WNWD* SE27 ....154 B2
Malfort Rd *CMBW* SE5 ....137 E1
Malham Rd *FSTH* SE23 ....157 D1
Mallams Ms *BRXN/ST* SW9 ....136 A1
Mallard Wy *CDALE/KGS* NW9 ....50 C2
Mall Chambers *KENS* * W8 ....26 B3
Mallet Rd *LEW* SE13 ....141 D4
Mallinson Rd *BTSEA* SW11 ....133 E1
Mallord St *CHEL* SW3 ....115 D2
Mallory Cl *BROCKY* SE4 ....139 E2
Mallory St *CAMTN* NW1 ....17 D1
Mallow St *FSBYE* EC1V 12 A5
Mall Rd *HMSMTH* W6 ....112 B1
The Mall *MORT/ESHN* SW14 ....128 C2
 WHALL SW1A 31 E5
Mall Vls *HMSMTH* * W6 ....112 B1
Malmesbury Rd *BOW* E3 ....91 F1
 CAN/RD E16 ....93 E4
Malmesbury Ter *CAN/RD* E16 ....93 F4
Malmesbury West Est *BOW* E3 ....91 F2
Malpas Rd *BROCKY* SE4 ....121 F5
 HACK E8 ....78 B3
Malta Rd *LEY* E10 ....62 A3
Malta St *FSBYE* EC1V 10 C5
Maltby St *STHWK* SE1 ....49 E1
Maltings Pl *FUL/PGN* SW6 ....114 B4
Malton Ms *NKENS* * W10 ....89 E5
 WOOL/PLUM SE18 ....127 E2
Malton Rd *NKENS* W10 ....89 E5
Malton St *WOOL/PLUM* SE18 ....127 E2
Maltravers St *TPL/STR* WC2R 33 F1
Malt St *STHWK* SE1 ....120 A2
Malva Cl *WAND/EARL* SW18 ....132 B3
Malvern Cl *NKENS* W10 ....89 F4
Malvern Dr *GDMY/SEVK* IG3 ....85 F1
Malvern Gdns *CRICK* NW2 ....53 E4
Malvern Ms *KIL/WHAMP* NW6 ....2 A4
Malvern Pl *MV/WKIL* * W9 ....89 F2

Malvern Rd EHAM E6 ....83 E5
   HACK E8 ....78 A4
   KIL/WHAMP NW6 ....2 A3
   MV/WKIL * W9 ....89 F2
   WAN E11 ....63 E4
Malvern Ter IS N1 ....76 A5
Malwood Rd BAL SW12 ....134 B4
Malyons Rd LEW SE13 ....140 B3
Malyons Ter BROCKY SE4 ....140 B3
Managers St POP/IOD * E14 ....104 C2
Manaton Cl PECK SE15 ....138 B1
Manbey Gv SRTFD E15 ....81 E3
Manbey Park Rd SRTFD E15 ....81 E3
Manbey Rd SRTFD * E15 ....81 E3
Manbey St SRTFD E15 ....81 E3
Manbre Rd HMSMTH W6 ....112 C2
Manbrough Av EHAM E6 ....95 F2
Manchester Dr NKENS * W10 ....89 E3
Manchester Gv POP/IOD E14 ....122 C1
Manchester Ms MHST W1U 18 A3
Manchester Rd POP/IOD E14 ....122 C1
   SEVS/STOTM N15 ....59 D1
Manchester Sq MBLAR W1H 18 B4
Manchester St MHST W1U 18 A3
Manchuria Rd BTSEA SW11 ....134 A4
Manciple St STHWK SE1 ....48 B1
Mandalay Rd CLAP SW4 ....134 C3
Mandela Cl WLSDN NW10 ....68 C4
Mandela Rd CAN/RD E16 ....94 A5
Mandela St BRXN/ST SW9 ....118 A3
   CAMTN NW1 ....74 C5
Mandela Wy STHWK SE1 ....49 D4
Mandeville Pl MHST W1U 18 B4
Mandeville St CLPT E5 ....61 E5
Mandrake Rd TOOT SW17 ....151 F3
Mandrake Wy SRTFD * E15 ....81 E4
Mandrell Rd BRXS/STRHM SW2 ....135 E3
Manette St SOHO/SHAV W1D 20 B5
Manfred Rd PUT/ROE SW15 ....131 F3
Manger Rd HOLWY N7 ....75 E3
Manilla St POP/IOD E14 ....104 A3
Manley Ct STNW/STAM N16 ....59 F5
Manley St CAMTN NW1 ....74 A5
Manningford Cl FSBYE * EC1V 10 C3
Manningtree Cl WIM/MER SW19 ....149 E5
Manningtree St WCHPL E1 ....90 A5
Manor Av BROCKY SE4 ....121 F5
Manorbrook BKHTH/KID SE3 ....142 A2
Manor Ct ACT * W3 ....98 A5
Manor Est BERM/RHTH SE16 ....102 B5
Manor Gdns ACT W3 ....98 A5
   HOLWY N7 ....57 E5
   VX/NE * SW8 ....116 C5
Manor Gv PECK SE15 ....120 C2
   RCH/KEW TW9 ....128 A2
Manor Hall Gdns LEY E10 ....62 A3
Manor House Dr KIL/WHAMP NW6 ....71 D4
Manor La LEW SE13 ....141 E3
Manor Lane Ter LEW SE13 ....141 E2
Manor Ms KIL/WHAMP NW6 ....2 B1
Manor Mt FSTH SE23 ....156 C1
Manor Pde STNW/STAM * N16 ....59 F4
Manor Pk LEW SE13 ....141 D3
Manor Park Rd MNPK E12 ....83 D1
   WLSDN NW10 ....69 D1
Manor Pl WALW SE17 ....118 B1
Manor Rd BFN/LL DA15 ....163 F3
   CAN/RD E16 ....93 E4
   LEY E10 ....62 A2
   STNW/STAM N16 ....59 E5
Manor Wy BKHTH/KID SE3 ....142 A2
Manresa Rd CHEL * SW3 ....115 D1
Mansard Beeches TOOT SW17 ....152 A5

Mansell Rd ACT W3 ....99 D2
Mansell St TWRH EC3N 37 F2
   WCHPL E1 ....25 F5
Mansergh Cl WOOL/PLUM SE18 ....125 E3
Manse Rd STNW/STAM N16 ....59 F5
Mansfield Ms CAVSQ/HST W1G 18 C3
Mansfield Rd ACT W3 ....86 B3
   HAMP NW3 ....73 F2
   IL IG1 ....66 A4
   WAN E11 ....64 B1
Mansfield St CAVSQ/HST W1G 18 C3
Mansford St BETH E2 ....90 A1
Mansion House Pl MANHO * EC4N 24 A5
The Mansions ECT * SW5 ....114 B1
Manson Ms SKENS SW7 ....39 F5
Manson Pl SKENS SW7 ....40 A5
Manstone Rd CRICK NW2 ....71 E2
Manthorpe Rd WOOL/PLUM SE18 ....126 C1
Mantilla Rd TOOT SW17 ....152 A4
Mantle Rd BROCKY SE4 ....139 E1
Mantle Wy SRTFD E15 ....81 E4
Mantua St BTSEA SW11 ....133 D1
Mantus Cl WCHPL E1 ....90 C3
Mantus Rd WCHPL E1 ....90 C3
Manville Gdns TOOT SW17 ....152 B3
Manville Rd TOOT SW17 ....152 A2
Manwood Rd BROCKY SE4 ....139 F4
Manwood St CAN/RD E16 ....107 F2
Many Gates BAL SW12 ....152 B2
Mapesbury Rd CRICK NW2 ....71 E3
Mapeshill Pl CRICK NW2 ....70 C3
Mape St BETH E2 ....90 B3
Maple Av ACT W3 ....99 E2
Maple Cl CLAP SW4 ....135 D4
   STNW/STAM N16 ....60 A1
Maplecroft Cl EHAM E6 ....95 D5
Mapledene Est HACK * E8 ....78 A4
Mapledene Rd HACK E8 ....77 F4
Maple Gv CDALE/KGS NW9 ....50 C2
Maple Leaf Dr BFN/LL DA15 ....163 F1
Maple Leaf Sq BERM/RHTH * SE16 ....103 D3
Maple Ms KIL/WHAMP * NW6 ....2 C1
   STRHM/NOR SW16 ....153 F5
Maple Pl FITZ W1T 19 F2
Maple Rd WAN E11 ....63 E1
Maples Pl WCHPL * E1 ....90 B4
Maplestead Rd BRXS/STRHM SW2 ....135 F5
Maple St FITZ W1T 19 E2
Mapleton Crs WAND/EARL SW18 ....132 B4
Mapleton Rd WAND/EARL SW18 ....132 A4
Maple Wk NKENS * W10 ....89 D3
Maplin Rd CAN/RD E16 ....94 A5
Maplin St BOW E3 ....91 F2
Marban Rd MV/WKIL W9 ....89 F1
Marble Cl ACT W3 ....98 B2
Marble Dr CRICK NW2 ....53 D3
Marble Quay WAP E1W 37 F3
Marbrook Ct LEE/GVPK SE12 ....160 C3
Marchant Rd WAN E11 ....63 D4
Marchant St NWCR SE14 ....121 E2
Marchbank Rd WKENS W14 ....113 F2
Marchmont St BMSBY WC1N 8 C5
Marchwood Cl CMBW SE5 ....119 E3
Marcia Rd STHWK SE1 ....49 D5
Marcilly Rd WAND/EARL SW18 ....133 D3
Marconi Rd LEY E10 ....62 A3
Marcon Pl HACK E8 ....78 B3
Marco Rd HMSMTH W6 ....100 B4
Marcus Garvey Ms EDUL SE22 ....138 B4
Marcus Garvey Wy HNHL SE24 ....136 A2
Marcus St SRTFD E15 ....81 E5
   WAND/EARL SW18 ....132 B4
Marcus Ter WAND/EARL SW18 ....132 B4

Marden Sq *BERM/RHTH* SE16 ....102 B4
Marechal Niel Av *BFN/LL* DA15 ....163 D3
Marechal Niel Pde *BFN/LL* * DA15 ...163 D3
Maresfield Gdns *HAMP* NW3 ....72 C2
Mare St *HACK* E8 ....78 B4
Margaret Gardner Dr
  ELTH/MOT SE9 ....161 F2
Margaret Ingram Cl
  FUL/PGN * SW6 ....113 F2
Margaret Rd *STNW/STAM* * N16 ....59 F3
Margaretta Ter *CHEL* SW3 ....115 E2
Margaretting Rd *MNPK* E12 ....64 C4
Margaret Wy *REDBR* IG4 ....65 E1
Margate Rd *CLAP* SW4 ....135 E3
Margery St *FSBYW* WC1X 10 A4
Margin Dr *WIM/MER* SW19 ....149 D5
Margravine Gdns *HMSMTH* W6 ....113 D1
Margravine Rd *HMSMTH* W6 ....113 D2
Marham Gdns *WAND/EARL* SW18 .....151 E1
Maria Cl *BERM/RHTH* SE16 ....102 A5
Marian Pl *BETH* E2 ....90 B1
Marian Sq *BETH* E2 ....90 A1
Marian St *BETH* * E2 ....90 B1
Marian Wy *WLSDN* NW10 ....69 F4
Maria Ter *WCHPL* E1 ....91 D4
Marie Curie *CMBW* * SE5 ....119 E4
Marie Lloyd Wk *HACK* * E8 ....78 A3
Marigold Aly *STHWK* SE1 ....34 C2
Marigold St *BERM/RHTH* SE16 ....102 B3
Marina Dr *WELL* DA16 ....127 E5
Marine Dr *WOOL/PLUM* SE18 ....107 F5
Marinefield Rd *FUL/PGN* SW6 ....114 B5
Mariner Rd *MNPK* E12 ....84 A1
Mariners Ms *POP/IOD* E14 ....105 D5
Marine St *BERM/RHTH* SE16 ....102 A4
Marischal Rd *LEW* SE13 ....141 D1
Maritime Quay *POP/IOD* E14 ....122 A1
Maritime St *BOW* E3 ....91 F3
Marius Rd *TOOT* SW17 ....152 A2
Marjorie Gv *BTSEA* SW11 ....133 F2
Market Est *HOLWY* N7 ....75 E3
Market Ms *MYFR/PICC* W1J 30 C4
Market Pde *LEY* * E10 ....62 B1
  STNW/STAM * N16 ....60 A3
Market Pl *ACT* W3 ....98 C2
  BERM/RHTH * SE16 ....102 A5
  SOHO/SHAV W1D 19 E4
Market Rd *HOLWY* N7 ....75 E3
  RCH/KEW TW9 ....128 A1
Market St *EHAM* E6 ....95 F1
  WOOL/PLUM SE18 ....108 A5
The Market *COVGDN* * WC2E 33 D1
  PECK * SE15 ....120 A4
Markham Rd *CHEL* SW3 ....115 F1
Markham Sq *CHEL* SW3 ....115 F1
Markham St *CHEL* SW3 ....115 F1
Markhouse Av *WALTH* E17 ....61 E1
Markhouse Rd *WALTH* E17 ....61 F1
Mark La *MON* EC3R 37 D1
Markmanor Av *WALTH* E17 ....61 E2
Marksbury Av *RCH/KEW* TW9 ....128 A1
Mark St *SDTCH* EC2A 12 C5
  SRTFD E15 ....81 E4
Markwell Cl *SYD* SE26 ....156 B4
Marlborough Av *HACK* * E8 ....78 A5
Marlborough Cl *WALW* SE17 ....47 D5
Marlborough Ct *REGST* W1B 19 E5
Marlborough Crs *CHSWK* W4 ....99 D4
Marlborough Ga *BAY/PAD* W2 ....28 A2
Marlborough Gv *STHWK* SE1 ....120 A1
Marlborough Hl *STJWD* NW8 ....72 C5
Marlborough La *CHARL* SE7 ....124 C2

Marlborough Ms
  BRXS/STRHM SW2 ....135 F2
Marlborough Pde *FSBYPK* * N4 ....58 C3
Marlborough Pl *STJWD* NW8 ....3 C2
Marlborough Rd *ARCH* N19 ....57 E4
  CHSWK W4 ....110 C3
  FSTGT E7 ....82 C4
  SRTFD * E15 ....81 E1
  WHALL SW1A 31 F4
  WOOL/PLUM SE18 ....108 B4
Marlborough St *CHEL* SW3 ....40 C5
Marlborough Yd *ARCH* N19 ....57 D4
Marler Rd *FSTH* SE23 ....157 F1
Marloes Rd *KENS* W8 ....38 C2
The Marlowes *STJWD* NW8 ....73 D5
Marlow Rd *EHAM* E6 ....95 F2
Marlow Wy *BERM/RHTH* SE16 ....103 D3
Marl Rd *WAND/EARL* SW18 ....132 B2
Marlton St *GNWCH* SE10 ....123 F1
Marlwood Cl *BFN/LL* DA15 ....163 E2
Marmadon Rd *WOOL/PLUM* SE18 ....109 F5
Marmion Ms *BTSEA* * SW11 ....134 A1
Marmion Rd *BTSEA* SW11 ....134 A2
Marmont Rd *PECK* SE15 ....120 A4
Marmora Rd *EDUL* SE22 ....138 C4
Marne St *NKENS* W10 ....89 E2
Marney Rd *BTSEA* SW11 ....134 A2
Marnfield Crs *BRXS/STRHM* SW2 .....153 F3
Marnham Av *CRICK* NW2 ....71 E1
Marnock Rd *BROCKY* SE4 ....139 F3
Maroon St *POP/IOD* E14 ....91 E4
Maroons Wy *CAT* SE6 ....158 A5
Marquess Rd *IS* N1 ....77 D3
Marquess Rd North *IS* N1 ....76 C3
Marquess Rd South *IS* * N1 ....76 C3
Marquis Rd *CAMTN* NW1 ....75 D3
  FSBYPK N4 ....57 F3
Marrick Cl *PUT/ROE* SW15 ....130 A2
Marriott Rd *FSBYPK* N4 ....57 F3
  SRTFD E15 ....81 E5
Marriotts Cl *CDALE/KGS* NW9 ....51 F1
Marryat Pl *WIM/MER* SW19 ....149 E4
Marryat Rd *WIM/MER* SW19 ....149 D5
Marryat Sq *FUL/PGN* * SW6 ....113 E4
Marsala Rd *LEW* SE13 ....140 B2
Marsden Rd *PECK* SE15 ....137 F1
Marsden St *KTTN* NW5 ....74 A3
Marshall Cl *WAND/EARL* SW18 ....132 C4
Marshalls Gv *WOOL/PLUM* SE18 ......107 E5
Marshall St *SOHO/CST* W1F 19 F5
Marshalsea Rd *STHWK* SE1 ....35 F5
Marsham Cl *CHST* * BR7 ....162 B5
Marsham St *WEST* SW1P 44 B4
Marshbrook Cl *BKHTH/KID* SE3 ....143 D1
Marsh Dr *CDALE/KGS* NW9 ....51 F1
Marshfield St *POP/IOD* E14 ....104 C4
Marshgate La *SRTFD* E15 ....80 B2
Marsh Hl *HOM* E9 ....79 E2
Marsh La *LEY* E10 ....61 F4
Marsh St *POP/IOD* * E14 ....104 B5
Marsh Wall *POP/IOD* E14 ....104 A3
Marsland Cl *WALW* SE17 ....118 B1
Marston Cl *KIL/WHAMP* NW6 ....72 C4
Martaban Rd *STNW/STAM* N16 ....59 E4
Martello St *HACK* E8 ....78 B4
Martell Rd *DUL* SE21 ....155 D3
Martel Pl *HACK* E8 ....77 F3
Martha Rd *SRTFD* E15 ....81 E1
Martha St *WCHPL* E1 ....90 C5
Martha's Buildings *FSBYE* EC1V 12 A5
Martin Bowes Rd *ELTH/MOT* SE9 .....143 D1
Martindale *MORT/ESHN* SW14 ....128 C3
Martindale Av *CAN/RD* E16 ....106 A1

Martindale Rd *BAL* SW12 ....**134** B5
Martineau Rd *HBRY* N5 ....**76** B1
Martineau St *WCHPL* E1 ....**102** C1
Martin La *CANST* EC4R **36** B1
The Martins *SYD* SE26 ....**156** B5
Martin St *THMD* SE28 ....**109** E2
Martlett Ct *HOL/ALD* WC2B **21** D5
Marton Cl *CAT* SE6 ....**158** A3
Marton Rd *STNW/STAM* N16 ....**59** E4
Martys Yd *HAMP* NW3 ....**73** D1
Marvels Cl *LEE/GVPK* SE12 ....**160** B2
Marvels La *LEE/GVPK* SE12 ....**160** B2
Marville Rd *FUL/PGN* SW6 ....**113** F5
Marvin St *HACK* E8 ....**78** B3
Mary Adelaide Cl *PUT/ROE* SW15 ...**147** E3
Mary Ann Buildings *DEPT* SE8 ....**122** A2
Marybank *WOOL/PLUM* SE18 ....**107** F5
Mary Datchelor Cl *CMBW* SE5 ....**119** D4
Mary Gn *STJWD* * NW8 ....**72** B5
Maryland Pk *SRTFD* E15 ....**81** E2
Maryland Rd *MV/WKIL* W9 ....**14** B1
  SRTFD E15 ....**81** D2
Maryland Sq *SRTFD* E15 ....**81** E2
Marylands Rd *MV/WKIL* W9 ....**14** B1
Maryland St *SRTFD* E15 ....**81** D2
Maryland Wk *IS* * N1 ....**76** C5
Mary Lawrencson Pl
  BKHTH/KID SE3 ....**123** F3
Marylebone High St *MHST* W1U **18** B2
Marylebone La *MHST* W1U **18** B4
Marylebone Ms *CAVSQ/HST* W1G **18** B3
Marylebone Pas *GTPST* W1W **19** F4
Marylebone Rd *CAMTN* NW1 ....**17** D2
Marylebone St *MHST* W1U **18** B3
Marylee Wy *LBTH* SE11 ....**45** F5
Maryon Gv *CHARL* SE7 ....**107** E5
Maryon Ms *HAMP* NW3 ....**73** E1
Maryon Rd *CHARL* SE7 ....**107** E5
Mary Pl *NTGHL* W11 ....**101** E1
Mary Seacole Cl *HACK* * E8 ....**77** F5
Mary Secole Cl *HACK* E8 ....**77** F5
Mary St *CAN/RD* E16 ....**93** F4
  IS N1 ....**76** C5
Mary Ter *CAMTN* NW1 ....**74** B3
Masbro' Rd *WKENS* W14 ....**101** D4
Mascalls Rd *CHARL* SE7 ....**124** C2
Mascotts Cl *CRICK* NW2 ....**52** B5
Mashie Rd *ACT* W3 ....**87** E5
Maskall Cl *BRXS/STRHM* * SW2 ......**154** A1
Maskell Rd *TOOT* SW17 ....**150** C3
Maskelyne Cl *BTSEA* SW11 ....**115** E4
Mason Cl *BERM/RHTH* SE16 ....**120** A1
Mason Ct *WBLY* * HA9 ....**50** A4
Mason's Arms Ms *CONDST* * W1S **19** D5
Mason's Av *CITYW* EC2V **24** A4
Masons Hl *WOOL/PLUM* SE18 ....**108** B5
Mason's Pl *FSBYE* EC1V **11** D3
Mason St *WALW* SE17 ....**48** B4
Masons Yd *FSBYE* EC1V **11** E5
  STJS SW1Y **31** F3
Massie Rd *HACK* E8 ....**78** A3
Massingberd Wy *TOOT* SW17 ....**152** B4
Massinger St *WALW* SE17 ....**48** C5
Massingham St *WCHPL* E1 ....**91** D3
Masterman Rd *EHAM* E6 ....**95** E2
Masters Dr *BERM/RHTH* SE16 ....**120** B1
Master's St *WCHPL* E1 ....**91** D4
Mast House Ter *POP/IOD* * E14 ....**104** A5
Masthouse Ter *POP/IOD* E14 ....**104** A5
Mastmaker Rd *POP/IOD* E14 ....**104** A3
Matcham Rd *WAN* E11 ....**63** E5
Matchless Dr *WOOL/PLUM* SE18 .....**126** A3

Matham Gv *EDUL* SE22 ....**137** F2
Matheson Rd *WKENS* W14 ....**101** F5
Mathews Av *EHAM* E6 ....**96** A1
Mathews Park Av *SRTFD* E15 ....**81** F3
Mathews Yd *LSQ/SEVD* * WC2H **20** C1
Mathieson Ct *STHWK* SE1 ....**47** D1
Matilda St *IS* N1 ....**75** F5
Matlock Rd *LEY* E10 ....**62** C1
Matlock St *WCHPL* E1 ....**91** E5
Matthew Cl *NKENS* * W10 ....**89** D3
Matthews St *BTSEA* * SW11 ....**115** F5
Matthias Rd *STNW/STAM* N16 ....**77** D2
Mattingley Wy *PECK* * SE15 ....**119** F3
Mattingly Wy *PECK* SE15 ....**119** F3
Mattison Rd *FSBYPK* N4 ....**58** A1
Maud Cashmore Wy
  WOOL/PLUM SE18 ....**107** F4
Maude Rd *CMBW* SE5 ....**119** E5
Maud Gdns *BARK* IG11 ....**97** F1
  PLSTW E13 ....**93** F1
Maudlins Gn *WAP* * E1W **102** A2
Maud Rd *LEY* E10 ....**62** C5
  PLSTW E13 ....**81** F5
Maudslay Rd *ELTH/MOT* SE9 ....**143** F1
Maud St *CAN/RD* E16 ....**93** F4
Maud Wilkes Cl *KTTN* NW5 ....**74** C2
Mauleverer Rd *BRXS/STRHM* SW2 ...**135** E3
Maundeby Wk *WLSDN* * NW10 ....**69** E2
Maunsel St *WEST* SW1P **44** A4
Maurice St *SHB* W12 ....**88** B5
Mauritius Rd *GNWCH* SE10 ....**105** E5
Maury Rd *STNW/STAM* N16 ....**60** A4
Maverton Rd *BOW* * E3 ....**80** A5
Mawbey Pl *STHWK* SE1 ....**119** F1
Mawbey Rd *STHWK* SE1 ....**119** F1
Mawbey St *VX/NE* SW8 ....**117** E3
Mawson La *CHSWK* W4 ....**111** F2
Maxey Rd *WOOL/PLUM* SE18 ....**108** C5
Maxted Rd *PECK* SE15 ....**137** F1
Maxwell Rd *FUL/PGN* SW6 ....**114** B3
Mayall Rd *HNHL* SE24 ....**136** B3
Maybury Gdns *WLSDN* NW10 ....**70** A4
Maybury Rd *PLSTW* E13 ....**94** C3
Maybury St *TOOT* SW17 ....**151** E5
Mayday Gdns *BKHTH/KID* SE3 ....**125** E5
Mayerne Rd *ELTH/MOT* SE9 ....**143** D3
Mayesbrook Rd *BARK* IG11 ....**85** F5
Mayeswood Rd *LEE/GVPK* SE12 ......**160** C4
Mayfair Av *IL* IG1 ....**65** F4
Mayfair Ms *HAMP* * NW3 ....**73** D1
Mayfair Pl *MYFR/PICC* W1J **31** D3
Mayfield Av *CHSWK* W4 ....**99** E5
Mayfield Cl *CLAP* SW4 ....**135** D3
  HACK E8 ....**77** F3
Mayfield Gdns *HDN* NW4 ....**53** D1
Mayfield Rd *ACT* W3 ....**98** B1
  CEND/HSY/T N8 ....**57** F1
  HACK * E8 ....**77** F4
  PLSTW E13 ....**93** F3
  SHB W12 ....**99** E3
Mayfields *WBLY* HA9 ....**50** A4
Mayfields Cl *WBLY* HA9 ....**50** A4
Mayflower Cl *BERM/RHTH* SE16 .....**103** D5
Mayflower Rd *BRXN/ST* SW9 ....**135** E1
Mayflower St *BERM/RHTH* SE16 ......**102** C3
Mayford Cl *BAL* SW12 ....**133** F5
Mayford Rd *BAL* SW12 ....**133** F5
Maygood St *IS* N1 ....**9** F1
Maygrove Rd *KIL/WHAMP* NW6 ....**71** F3
Mayhill Rd *CHARL* SE7 ....**124** B2
Maynard Cl *FUL/PGN* SW6 ....**114** B3
Maynards Quay *WAP* * E1W **102** C1
Mayola Rd *CLPT* E5 ....**78** C1

Mayo Rd *WLSDN* NW10 ....69 E3
Mayow Rd *SYD* SE26 ....157 D4
Mayplace La *WOOL/PLUM* SE18 ...126 B2
May Rd *PLSTW* E13 ....94 A1
May's Buildings Ms *GNWCH* SE10 ..123 D3
Mays Ct *CHCR* WC2N 32 C2
Maysoule Rd *BTSEA* SW11 ....133 D2
May St *WKENS* W14 ....113 F1
Maythorne Cottages *LEW* SE13 .....141 D4
Mayton St *HOLWY* N7 ....57 F5
Maytree Wk *BRXS/STRHM* SW2 ......154 A2
Mayville Est *STNW/STAM* * N16.......77 E2
Mayville Rd *IL* IG1 ....84 B2
   WAN E11 ....63 E4
Maze HI *GNWCH* SE10 ....123 E2
Mazenod Av *KIL/WHAMP* NW6 ....72 A4
Maze Rd *RCH/KEW* TW9 ....110 A3
McAuley CI *ELTH/MOT* SE9 ....144 A3
   STHWK SE1 ....46 A2
McCall CI *CLAP* SW4 ....117 E5
McCall Crs *CHARL* SE7 ....125 E1
McCoid Wy *STHWK* SE1 ....47 E1
McCrone Ms *HAMP* NW3 ....73 D3
McCullum Rd *BOW* E3 ....79 F5
McDermott CI *BTSEA* SW11 ....115 E5
McDermott Rd *PECK* SE15 ....138 A1
McDougall Ct *RCH/KEW* TW9 ....110 A5
McDowall CI *CAN/RD* E16 ....94 A4
McEwan Wy *SRTFD* * E15 ....81 D5
McGrath Rd *FSTGT* E7 ....81 F2
McGregor Rd *NTGHL* W11 ....89 F5
McKerrell Rd *PECK* SE15 ....120 A4
McLeod's Ms *SKENS* SW7 ....39 D3
McMillan St *DEPT* * SE8 ....122 A2
McNeil Rd *CMBW* SE5 ....119 E5
McNicol Dr *WLSDN* NW10 ....86 C1
Mead CI *CAMTN* * NW1 ....74 A4
Meadcroft Rd *LBTH* SE11 ....118 A2
Meade CI *CHSWK* W4 ....110 A2
Meadowbank *BKHTH/KID* SE3.........141 F1
   HAMP NW3 ....73 F4
Meadowbank CI *FUL/PGN* SW6 .....112 C3
Meadowbank Rd *CDALE/KGS* NW9...51 D2
Meadow CI *CAT* SE6.......................158 A5
   CHST BR7 ....162 B5
   HOM E9 ....79 F2
Meadowcourt Rd *BKHTH/KID* SE3 ...141 F2
Meadow Garth *WLSDN* NW10 ....68 C3
Meadow La *LEE/GVPK* * SE12 ....160 C3
Meadow Ms *VX/NE* SW8 ....117 F2
Meadow PI *CHSWK* * W4 ....111 E3
   VX/NE SW8 ....117 E3
Meadow Rd *BARK* IG11 ....85 F4
   VX/NE SW8 ....117 F2
Meadow Rw *STHWK* SE1 ....47 E3
Meadows CI *LEY* E10 ....62 A4
Meadowside *ELTH/MOT* SE9 ....142 C2
Meadowsweet CI *CAN/RD* E16 ....95 D4
Meadowview Rd *CAT* SE6 ....158 A4
Mead PI *HOM* E9 ....78 C3
Mead Plat *WLSDN* NW10 ....68 C3
Mead Rw *STHWK* SE1 ....46 A2
Meads La *GDMY/SEVK* IG3 ....67 F2
Meadway *GDMY/SEVK* IG3 ....85 E1
   GLDGN NW11..........................54 B1
Meadway CI *GLDGN* NW11 ....54 B1
The Meadway *BKHTH/KID* SE3 .....123 D5
Meanley Rd *MNPK* E12 ....83 E2
Meard St *SOHO/CST* W1F 20 A5
Meath Rd *IL* IG1 ....66 C5
   SRTFD E15 ....93 F1
Meath St *BTSEA* SW11 ....116 B4
Mecklenburgh PI *BMSBY* WC1N 9 E5

Mecklenburgh Sq *BMSBY* WC1N 9 E5
Mecklenburgh St *BMSBY* WC1N 9 E5
Medburn St *CAMTN* NW1 ....8 A1
Medcroft Gdns *MORT/ESHN* SW14 ..128 C2
Medebourne CI *BKHTH/KID* SE3 .....142 A1
Medfield St *PUT/ROE* SW15 ....130 A5
Medhurst CI *BOW* E3........................91 E1
Median Rd *CLPT* E5 ....78 C2
Medina Rd *HOLWY* N7 ....58 A5
Medlar St *CMBW* SE5 ....118 C4
Medley Rd *KIL/WHAMP* NW6 ....72 A3
Medora Rd *BRXS/STRHM* SW2.......135 F4
Medusa Rd *LEW* SE13 ....140 B4
Medway CI *IL* IG1 ....84 C2
Medway Rd *BOW* E3 ....91 E1
Medway St *WEST* SW1P 44 A3
Medwin St *BRXS/STRHM* SW2 ....135 F2
Meerbrook Rd *ELTH/MOT* SE9 ....142 C1
Meeson Rd *SRTFD* E15 ....81 F4
Meeson St *CLPT* E5 ....79 E1
Meesons Whf *SRTFD* * E15..............92 C1
Meeting Field Pth *HOM* * E9 ....78 C3
Meeting House Aly *WAP* * E1W 102 B2
Meeting House La *PECK* SE15 ....120 B4
Mehetabel Rd *HACK* E8 ....78 C3
Meister CI *IL* IG1 ....67 D3
Melanda CI *CHST* BR7 ....161 F5
Melaris Ms *KIL/WHAMP* NW6 ....72 A2
Melbourne Gv *EDUL* SE22 ....137 E2
Melbourne Ms *BRXN/ST* SW9 ....118 A4
   CAT SE6 ....140 C5
Melbourne PI *HOL/ALD* WC2B 21 F5
Melbourne Rd *EHAM* E6 ....95 F1
   IL IG1....................................66 B3
   LEY E10 ....62 B2
Melbourne Sq *BRXN/ST* SW9 ....118 A4
Melbourne Ter *EDUL* * SE22 ....137 E2
   FUL/PGN * SW6 ....114 B3
Melbury CI *WKENS* W14 ....101 F4
Melbury Dr *CMBW* SE5 ....119 E3
Melbury Rd *WKENS* W14 ....101 F4
Melbury Ter *CAMTN* NW1 ....17 D1
Melcombe PI *CAMTN* NW1 ....17 E2
Melcombe St *CAMTN* NW1 ....17 E1
Meldon CI *FUL/PGN* * SW6 ....114 B4
Melfield Gdns *CAT* SE6 ....158 B4
Melford Av *BARK* IG11 ....85 E3
Melford Rd *DUL* SE21 ....156 A1
   EHAM E6 ....95 F3
   IL IG1....................................67 D4
   WAN E11 ....63 E4
Melgund Rd *HBRY* N5 ....76 A2
Melina PI *STJWD* NW8 ....4 A4
Melina Rd *SHB* W12 ....100 B3
Melior PI *STHWK* * SE1 ....36 C5
Melior St *STHWK* SE1 ....36 B5
Meliot Rd *CAT* SE6 ....159 D2
Melling St *WOOL/PLUM* SE18.........127 E2
Mellish St *POP/IOD* E14 ....104 A4
Mellison Rd *TOOT* SW17 ....151 E5
Mellitus St *SHB* W12 ....87 F5
Mells Crs *ELTH/MOT* SE9 ....161 F4
Mell St *GNWCH* SE10 ....123 E1
Melody Rd *WAND/EARL* SW18 ....132 C3
Melon PI *KENS* * W8 ....26 B5
Melon Rd *PECK* SE15 ....120 A4
   WAN E11 ....63 E5
Melrose Av *CRICK* NW2 ....70 C2
   WIM/MER SW19 ....149 F2
Melrose CI *LEE/GVPK* SE12 ....160 A1
Melrose Gdns *HMSMTH* W6 ....100 C4
Melrose Rd *BARN* SW13 ....111 F5
   WAND/EARL SW18 ....131 F4

Melrose Ter *HMSMTH* W6.....................100 C3
Melthorpe Gdns
   WOOL/PLUM SE18.....................125 D4
Melton St *CAMTN* NW1..........................7 F4
Melville Ct *DEPT* SE8............................103 D5
Melville Pl *IS* * N1.................................76 C4
Melville Rd *BARN* SW13........................112 A4
   WLSDN NW10.....................69 D3
Melville Villas Rd *ACT* * W3.....................99 D2
Memel St *STLK* EC1Y............................23 E1
Memorial Av *SRTFD* E15.........................93 E2
Mendip Cl *SYD* SE26............................156 C4
Mendip Dr *GLDGN* NW11........................53 E4
Mendip Houses *BETH* * E2.......................90 C2
Mendip Rd *BTSEA* SW11........................132 C1
Mendora Rd *FUL/PGN* SW6....................113 E3
Menelik Rd *CRICK* NW2..........................71 E1
Menotti St *BETH* * E2............................90 A3
Mentmore Ter *HACK* E8...........................78 B4
Meon Rd *ACT* W3...................................98 C3
Mepham St *STHWK* SE1...........................34 A4
Merbury Cl *LEW* SE13...........................140 C3
Merbury Rd *THMD* SE28........................109 D2
Merbury St *WOOL/PLUM* SE18................108 B4
Mercator Pl *POP/IOD* E14......................122 A1
Mercator Rd *LEW* SE13.........................141 D2
Merceron Houses *BETH* * E2.....................90 C2
Merceron St *WCHPL* E1...........................90 B3
Mercers Cl *GNWCH* SE10.......................105 F5
Mercers Cottages *WCHPL* * E1..................91 E5
Mercers Pl *HMSMTH* W6.......................100 C5
Mercers Rd *ARCH* N19............................57 D5
Merchant St *BOW* * E3.............................91 F2
Merchiston Rd *CAT* SE6.........................159 D2
Merchland Rd *ELTH/MOT* SE9.................162 C1
Mercia Gv *LEW* SE13............................140 C1
Mercier Rd *PUT/ROE* SW15....................131 E3
Mercury Wy *NWCR* SE14........................121 D2
Mercy Ter *LEW* SE13............................140 B3
Mere Cl *WIM/MER* SW19........................131 D5
Meredith Av *CRICK* NW2..........................70 C2
Meredith Ms *BROCKY* * SE4....................139 F2
Meredith St *CLKNW* EC1R.......................10 C4
   PLSTW E13.....................94 A2
Meredyth Rd *BARN* SW13.......................112 A5
Meretone Cl *BROCKY* SE4......................139 E2
Mereworth Dr *WOOL/PLUM* SE18............126 B3
Meridian Rd *CHARL* SE7........................125 D3
Meridian Sq *SRTFD* E15..........................81 D4
Merifield Rd *ELTH/MOT* SE9...................142 C1
Merivale Rd *PUT/ROE* SW15....................131 E2
Merley Ct *CDALE/KGS* NW9......................50 C3
Merlin Rd *MNPK* E12...............................65 D4
Merlin St *FSBYW* WC1X...........................10 A4
Mermaid Ct *STHWK* SE1..........................36 A5
Merredene St *BRXS/STRHM* SW2.............135 F4
Merrick Sq *STHWK* SE1............................48 A2
Merrilees Rd *BFN/LL* DA15......................145 E5
Merriman Rd *BKHTH/KID* SE3..................124 C4
Merrington Rd *FUL/PGN* SW6...................114 A2
Merritt Rd *BROCKY* SE4.........................139 F3
Merrow St *WALW* SE17..........................119 D1
Merrow Wk *WALW* SE17..........................119 D1
Merryfield *BKHTH/KID* SE3.....................123 F5
Merthyr Ter *BARN* SW13.........................112 B2
Merton Av *CHSWK* W4.............................99 F5
Merton La *HGT* N6...................................55 F4
Merton Ri *HAMP* NW3..............................73 E4
Merton Rd *BARK* IG11..............................85 F4
   GDMY/SEVK IG3.....................67 F2
   WAND/EARL SW18.....................132 A5
Mertoun Ter *MBLAR* * W1H.......................17 E4

Merttins Rd *PECK* SE15.........................139 D2
Meru Cl *KTTN* NW5.................................74 A2
Mervan Rd *BRXS/STRHM* SW2.................136 A2
Mervyn Av *ELTH/MOT* SE9......................162 C3
Messaline Av *ACT* W3..............................86 C5
Messent Rd *ELTH/MOT* SE9.....................142 C3
Messeter Pl *ELTH/MOT* SE9....................144 A4
Messina Av *KIL/WHAMP* NW6....................72 A4
Meteor St *BTSEA* SW11..........................134 A2
Methley St *LBTH* SE11...........................118 A1
Methwold Rd *NKENS* W10..........................89 D4
Metropolitan Cl *POP/IOD* E14...................92 A4
Metropolitan Whf *WAP* * E1W...................102 C2
Mews Clare *FUL/PGN* SW6......................114 B3
Mews North *BGVA* SW1W..........................42 C3
Mews South *PIM* SW1V...........................116 C1
Mews St *WAP* E1W...................................37 F3
Mexfield Rd *PUT/ROE* SW15....................131 F3
Meymott St *STHWK* SE1...........................34 C4
Meynell Crs *HOM* E9...............................79 D4
Meynell Gdns *HOM* E9.............................79 D4
Meynell Rd *HOM* E9................................79 D4
Meyrick Rd *BTSEA* SW11........................133 D1
   WLSDN NW10.....................70 A3
Miah Ter *WAP* * E1W..............................102 A2
Micawber St *IS* N1..................................11 E3
Michael Rd *FUL/PGN* SW6......................114 B4
   WAN E11.....................63 E3
Michaels Cl *LEW* SE13...........................141 E1
Micheldever Rd *LEW* SE13.....................141 E4
Michigan Av *MNPK* E12............................83 F3
Micklethwaite Rd *FUL/PGN* SW6...............114 A2
Middle Dartrey Wk *WBPTN* * SW10...........114 C5
Middlefield *STJWD* NW8............................73 D5
Middle Park Av *ELTH/MOT* SE9.................143 D4
Middle Rd *PLSTW* E13.............................94 A1
Middle Rw *NKENS* W10.............................89 D3
Middlesex Pl *HOM* E9..............................78 C3
Middlesex St *WCHPL* E1...........................25 D3
Middle St *STBT* EC1A..............................23 E2
Middle Temple La *TPL/STR* WC2R..............22 A5
Middleton Buildings *GTPST* W1W................19 E3
Middleton Dr *BERM/RHTH* SE16...............103 D3
Middleton Gdns *GNTH/NBYPK* IG2...............66 B1
Middleton Gv *HOLWY* N7...........................75 E2
Middleton Pl *GTPST* W1W..........................19 E3
Middleton Rd *GLDGN* NW11......................54 A2
   HACK E8.....................77 F4
Middleton St *BETH* E2.............................90 B2
Middleton Wy *LEW* SE13.........................141 D2
Middle Yd *STHWK* SE1.............................36 B3
Midford Pl *FITZ* * W1T.............................19 F1
Midholm *WBLY* HA9.................................50 A3
Midhope St *STPAN* WC1H...........................9 D4
Midland Arches *CRICK* * NW2....................52 B4
Midland Crs *HAMP* NW3............................72 C3
Midland Rd *CAMTN* NW1.............................8 B2
   LEY E10.....................62 C2
Midland Ter *WLSDN* NW10.........................87 E3
Midlothian Rd *BOW* E3..............................91 F3
Midmoor Rd *BAL* SW12...........................152 A1
Midship Cl *BERM/RHTH* * SE16................103 D2
Midship Point *POP/IOD* * E14..................104 A3
Midstrath Rd *WLSDN* NW10.......................69 E1
Milborne Gv *WBPTN* SW10.....................114 C5
Milborne St *HOM* E9................................78 C3
Milborough Crs *LEE/GVPK* SE12...............141 E4
Milcote St *STHWK* SE1.............................46 C1
Mildenhall Rd *CLPT* E5.............................78 C1
Mildmay Av *IS* N1...................................77 D3
Mildmay Gv North *IS* N1...........................77 D2
Mildmay Gv South *IS* N1...........................77 D2
Mildmay Pk *IS* N1...................................77 D2

Mildmay Pl *STNW/STAM* * N16 ....**77** E2
Mildmay Rd *IL* IG1 ....**66** B5
  IS N1 ....**77** D2
Mildmay St *IS* N1 ....**77** D3
Mile End Pl *WCHPL* E1 ....**91** D3
Mile End Rd *WCHPL* E1 ....**90** C4
Miles Dr *THMD* SE28 ....**109** D2
Miles St *VX/NE* SW8 ....**117** E2
Milfoil St *SHB* W12 ....**100** A1
Milford La *TPL/STR* WC2R **34** A1
Milford Ms *STRHM/NOR* SW16 ....**153** F3
Milk St *BMLY* BR1 ....**160** B5
  CAN/RD E16 ....**108** B2
  CITYW EC2V **23** F4
Milkwell Yd *CMBW* SE5 ....**118** C4
Milkwood Rd *HNHL* SE24 ....**136** B3
Milk Yd *WAP* E1W **102** C1
Millais Av *MNPK* E12 ....**84** A2
Millais Rd *WAN* E11 ....**80** C1
Millard Cl *STNW/STAM* N16 ....**77** D1
Millbank *WEST* SW1P **44** C4
Millbank Est *WEST* SW1P **44** B5
Millbank Wy *LEE/GVPK* SE12 ....**142** A3
Millbrook Av *WELL* DA16 ....**145** D2
Millbrook Rd *BRXN/ST* SW9 ....**136** B1
Millennium Br *STHWK* SE1 ....**35** E2
Millennium Cl *CAN/RD* E16 ....**94** A5
Millennium Dr *POP/IOD* E14 ....**105** D4
Millennium Pl *BETH* * E2 ....**90** B1
Millennium Sq *STHWK* SE1 ....**37** E5
Millennium Wy *GNWCH* SE10 ....**105** D2
Millennium Whf *POP/IOD* E14 ....**105** D5
Miller's Av *HACK* E8 ....**77** F2
Miller's Ct *CHSWK* W4 ....**111** F1
Miller's Ter *HACK* E8 ....**77** F1
Miller St *CAMTN* NW1 ....**7** E1
Miller's Wy *HMSMTH* W6 ....**100** C3
Miller Wk *STHWK* SE1 ....**34** B4
Millfield La *HGT* N6 ....**55** F4
Millfields Rd *CLPT* E5 ....**78** C1
Mill Gdns *SYD* SE26 ....**156** B4
Millgrove St *BTSEA* SW11 ....**116** A4
Millharbour *POP/IOD* E14 ....**104** B4
Mill Hl *BARN* SW13 ....**130** A1
Mill Hill Gv *ACT* * W3 ....**98** B2
Mill Hill Rd *ACT* W3 ....**98** B3
  BARN SW13 ....**130** B1
Mill Hill Ter *ACT* W3 ....**98** B2
Millhouse Pl *WNWD* SE27 ....**154** B4
Millicent Rd *LEY* * E10 ....**61** F3
Milligan St *POP/IOD* E14 ....**103** F1
Mill La *CRICK* NW2 ....**71** E2
  WOOL/PLUM SE18 ....**126** A1
Millman Ms *BMSBY* WC1N **21** E1
Millman Pl *BMSBY* WC1N **21** E1
Millman St *BMSBY* WC1N **21** E1
Millmark Gv *NWCR* SE14 ....**121** E5
Mill Pl *POP/IOD* E14 ....**91** E5
Millpond Est *BERM/RHTH* * SE16 ....**102** B3
Mill Rd *CAN/RD* E16 ....**106** B2
  IL IG1 ....**66** A5
Mill Rw *IS* N1 ....**77** E5
Mills Gv *POP/IOD* E14 ....**92** C4
Millshot Cl *FUL/PGN* SW6 ....**112** C4
Mills Rw *CHSWK* W4 ....**99** D5
Millstream Rd *STHWK* SE1 ....**49** E1
Mill St *CONDST* W1S **31** D1
  STHWK SE1 ....**49** F1
Millwall Dock Rd *POP/IOD* E14 ....**104** A4
Millwood St *WLSDN* NW10 ....**89** E4
Milman Rd *KIL/WHAMP* NW6 ....**89** D1
Milman's St *WBPTN* SW10 ....**115** D2
  WBPTN * SW10 ....**115** D2

Milne Gdns *ELTH/MOT* SE9 ....**143** E3
Milner Pl *IS* N1 ....**76** A5
Milner Rd *SRTFD* E15 ....**93** E2
Milner Sq *IS* * N1 ....**76** A4
Milner St *CHEL* SW3 ....**41** E4
Milnthorpe Rd *CHSWK* W4 ....**111** D2
Milo Rd *EDUL* SE22 ....**137** E4
Milroy Wk *STHWK* SE1 ....**34** B3
Milson Rd *WKENS* W14 ....**101** E4
Milton Av *EHAM* E6 ....**83** D4
  HGT N6 ....**56** C2
  WLSDN NW10 ....**69** D5
Milton Cl *EFNCH* N2 ....**54** C1
  STHWK SE1 ....**49** E5
Milton Ct *BARB* EC2Y **24** A2
Milton Court Rd *NWCR* SE14 ....**121** E2
Milton Crs *GNTH/NBYPK* IG2 ....**66** C2
Milton Gv *STNW/STAM* N16 ....**77** D1
Milton Pk *HGT* N6 ....**56** C2
Milton Rd *ACT* W3 ....**99** D2
  CDALE/KGS * NW9 ....**52** A2
  HGT N6 ....**56** C2
  HNHL SE24 ....**136** B3
  MORT/ESHN SW14 ....**129** D1
  WELL DA16 ....**127** F4
Milton St *BARB* EC2Y **24** A2
Milverton Gdns *GDMY/SEVK* IG3 ....**67** F4
Milverton Rd *KIL/WHAMP* NW6 ....**70** C4
Milverton St *LBTH* SE11 ....**118** A1
Milverton Wy *ELTH/MOT* SE9 ....**162** A4
Milward St *WCHPL* E1 ....**90** B4
Mimosa St *FUL/PGN* SW6 ....**113** F4
Minard Rd *CAT* SE6 ....**141** E5
Mina Rd *WALW* SE17 ....**119** E1
Mincing La *MON* EC3R **36** C1
Minehead Rd *STRHM/NOR* SW16 ....**153** F5
Mineral St *WOOL/PLUM* SE18 ....**109** E5
Minera Ms *BGVA* SW1W **42** B4
Minerva Cl *BRXN/ST* SW9 ....**118** A3
  SCUP DA14 ....**163** E4
Minerva Rd *WLSDN* NW10 ....**86** C3
Minerva St *BETH* E2 ....**90** B1
Minet Av *WLSDN* NW10 ....**87** E1
Minet Gdns *WLSDN* NW10 ....**87** E1
Minet Rd *CMBW* SE5 ....**118** B5
Minford Gdns *WKENS* W14 ....**101** D3
Ming St *POP/IOD* E14 ....**104** A1
Ministry Wy *ELTH/MOT* SE9 ....**161** F2
Minnow Wk *WALW* SE17 ....**49** D5
Minories *TWRH* EC3N **25** E5
Minshull St *VX/NE* * SW8 ....**117** D2
Minson Rd *HOM* E9 ....**79** D5
Minstead Gdns *PUT/ROE* SW15 ....**129** F5
Minster Ct *MON* * EC3R **36** C1
Minster Rd *CRICK* NW2 ....**71** E2
Mintern St *IS* N1 ....**12** B1
Minton Ms *KIL/WHAMP* NW6 ....**72** B3
Mint St *STHWK* SE1 ....**35** E5
Mirabel Rd *FUL/PGN* SW6 ....**113** F3
Miranda Cl *WCHPL* E1 ....**90** C4
Miranda Rd *ARCH* N19 ....**56** C3
Mirfield St *CHARL* SE7 ....**107** D4
Miriam Rd *WOOL/PLUM* SE18 ....**127** E1
Mission Pl *PECK* SE15 ....**120** A4
Mitali Pas *WCHPL* E1 ....**90** A5
Mitcham La *STRHM/NOR* SW16 ....**152** C5
Mitcham Rd *EHAM* E6 ....**95** E2
  GDMY/SEVK IG3 ....**67** F2
  TOOT SW17 ....**151** F5
Mitchellbrook Wy *WLSDN* NW10 ....**69** D3
Mitchell St *FSBYE* EC1V **11** E5
Mitchell Wy *WLSDN* NW10 ....**68** C3
Mitchison Rd *IS* N1 ....**77** D3

Mitford Rd *ARCH* N19 ....**57** E4
Mitre Rd *SRTFD* E15 ....**93** E1
  STHWK SE1 ....**34** B5
Mitre Sq *HDTCH* EC3A **25** D5
Mitre St *HDTCH* EC3A **25** D5
The Mitre *POP/IOD* E14 ....**103** F1
Mitre Wy *WLSDN* NW10 ....**88** B4
Moat Ct *ELTH/MOT* * SE9 ....**143** F4
Moat Pl *ACT* W3 ....**86** B5
  BRXN/ST SW9 ....**135** F1
Moberly Rd *CLAP* SW4 ....**135** D5
Modbury Gdns *HAMP* NW3 ....**74** A3
Model Farm Cl *ELTH/MOT* SE9 ....**161** E3
Moffat Rd *TOOT* SW17 ....**151** E4
Mohammad Khan Rd *WAN* * E11 ....**63** F3
Moiety Rd *POP/IOD* E14 ....**104** A3
Moira Rd *ELTH/MOT* SE9 ....**143** F2
Molescroft *ELTH/MOT* SE9 ....**162** C3
Molesford Rd *FUL/PGN* * SW6 ....**114** A4
Molesworth St *LEW* SE13 ....**140** C1
Molly Huggins Cl *BAL* SW12 ....**134** C5
Molyneux Dr *TOOT* SW17 ....**152** B4
Molyneux St *MBLAR* W1H **17** D3
Monarch Dr *CAN/RD* E16 ....**95** D4
Monarch Ms *WNWD* SE27 ....**154** A5
Mona Rd *PECK* SE15 ....**120** C5
Mona St *CAN/RD* E16 ....**93** F4
Monck's Rw *WAND/EARL* * SW18 ....**131** F4
Monck St *WEST* SW1P **44** B3
Monclar Rd *CMBW* SE5 ....**137** D2
Moncorvo Cl *SKENS* SW7 ....**40** C1
Moncrieff St *PECK* SE15 ....**120** A5
Monega Rd *FSTGT* E7 ....**82** C3
Monier Rd *BOW* E3 ....**80** A4
Monk Dr *CAN/RD* E16 ....**106** A1
Monks Dr *ACT* W3 ....**86** A4
Monks Pk *WBLY* HA9 ....**68** C5
Monks Park Gdns *WBLY* HA9 ....**68** B3
Monk St *WOOL/PLUM* SE18 ....**108** A5
Monkton Rd *WELL* DA16 ....**127** F5
Monkton St *LBTH* SE11 ....**46** B4
Monkwell Sq *BARB* EC2Y **23** F3
Monmouth Cl *CHSWK* W4 ....**99** D4
Monmouth Pl *BAY/PAD* W2 ....**14** B5
Monmouth Rd *BAY/PAD* W2 ....**14** B5
  EHAM E6 ....**95** F2
Monmouth St *LSQ/SEVD* WC2H **20** C5
Monnery Rd *ARCH* N19 ....**56** C5
Monnow Rd *STHWK* SE1 ....**120** A1
Monroe Dr *MORT/ESHN* SW14 ....**128** B3
Monsell Rd *FSBYPK* N4 ....**58** B5
Monson Rd *NWCR* SE14 ....**121** D3
  WLSDN NW10 ....**88** A1
Montacute Rd *CAT* SE6 ....**139** F5
Montague Av *BROCKY* SE4 ....**139** F2
Montague Cl *STHWK* SE1 ....**36** A3
Montague Gdns *ACT* W3 ....**98** A1
Montague Pl *GWRST* WC1E **20** B2
Montague Rd *HACK* E8 ....**78** A2
  WAN E11 ....**63** F4
Montague Sq *NWCR* SE14 ....**120** C3
Montague St *RSQ* WC1B **20** C2
  STBT EC1A **23** E3
Montagu Man *MHST* W1U **17** F3
Montagu Ms North *MBLAR* W1H **17** F3
Montagu Ms South *MBLAR* W1H **17** F4
Montagu Ms West *MBLAR* W1H **17** F4
Montagu Pl *MBLAR* W1H **17** E3
Montagu Rd *HDN* NW4 ....**52** A1
Montagu Rw *MHST* W1U **17** F3
Montagu Sq *MBLAR* W1H **17** F3
Montagu St *MBLAR* W1H **17** F4
Montana Gdns *CAT* SE6 ....**157** F5
Montana Rd *TOOT* SW17 ....**152** A3
Montbelle Rd *ELTH/MOT* SE9 ....**162** B3
Montcalm Rd *CHARL* SE7 ....**125** D3
Montclare St *BETH* E2 ....**13** E4
Monteagle Av *BARK* IG11 ....**84** C3
Monteagle Wy *PECK* SE15 ....**138** B1
Montefiore St *VX/NE* SW8 ....**116** B5
Monteith Rd *BOW* E3 ....**79** F5
Montem Rd *FSTH* SE23 ....**139** F1
Montem St *FSBYPK* N4 ....**57** F3
Montesquieu Ter *CAN/RD* * E16 ....**93** F5
Montford Pl *LBTH* SE11 ....**118** A2
Montfort Pl *WIM/MER* SW19 ....**149** D1
Montgomery Cl *BFN/LL* DA15 ....**145** E3
Montgomery Rd *CHSWK* W4 ....**98** C5
Montholme Rd *BTSEA* SW11 ....**133** F4
Monthorpe Rd *WCHPL* E1 ....**90** A4
Montolieu Gdns *PUT/ROE* SW15 ....**130** B3
Montpelier Gdns *EHAM* E6 ....**95** D2
Montpelier Gv *KTTN* NW5 ....**74** C2
Montpelier Ms *SKENS* SW7 ....**41** D2
Montpelier Pl *SKENS* SW7 ....**41** D2
  WCHPL E1 ....**90** C5
Montpelier Ri *GLDGN* NW11 ....**53** E2
Montpelier Rd *PECK* SE15 ....**120** B4
Montpelier Rw *BKHTH/KID* SE3 ....**123** F5
Montpelier Sq *SKENS* SW7 ....**41** D1
Montpelier St *SKENS* SW7 ....**41** D1
Montpelier Ter *SKENS* SW7 ....**41** D1
Montpelier V *BKHTH/KID* * SE3 ....**123** F5
Montpelier Wk *SKENS* SW7 ....**41** D1
Montpelier Wy *GLDGN* NW11 ....**53** E2
Montreal Pl *HOL/ALD* WC2B **33** E1
Montreal Rd *IL* IG1 ....**66** C2
Montrell Rd *BRXS/STRHM* SW2 ....**153** E1
Montrose Av *KIL/WHAMP* NW6 ....**89** E1
  WELL DA16 ....**145** D1
Montrose Cl *WELL* DA16 ....**145** F1
Montrose Pl *KTBR* SW1X **42** B1
Montrose Vls *HMSMTH* * W6 ....**112** A1
Montrose Wy *FSTH* SE23 ....**157** D1
Montserrat Cl *NRWD* SE19 ....**155** D5
Montserrat Rd *PUT/ROE* SW15 ....**131** E2
Monument St *MON* EC3R **36** B2
Monza St *WAP* E1W **102** C1
Moodkee St *BERM/RHTH* SE16 ....**102** C4
Moody St *WCHPL* E1 ....**91** D2
Moon Ct *LEE/GVPK* * SE12 ....**142** A4
Moon St *IS* N1 ....**76** B5
Moorcroft Rd *STRHM/NOR* SW16 ....**153** E3
Moordown *WOOL/PLUM* SE18 ....**126** A4
Moore Cl *MORT/ESHN* SW14 ....**128** C1
Moore Park Rd *FUL/PGN* SW6 ....**114** B3
Moore St *CHEL* SW3 ....**41** E4
Moorey Cl *SRTFD* E15 ....**81** F5
Moorfields *LVPST* EC2M **24** A3
Moorfields Highwalk *BARB* EC2Y **24** A3
Moorgate *LOTH* EC2R **24** A4
Moorgate Pl *LOTH* * EC2R **24** A4
Moorhead Wy *BKHTH/KID* SE3 ....**142** B1
Moorhouse Rd *BAY/PAD* W2 ....**14** A4
The Moorings *CHSWK* * W4 ....**110** A2
Moorland Rd *BRXN/ST* SW9 ....**136** B2
Moor La *BARB* EC2Y **24** A3
Moorside Rd *BMLY* BR1 ....**159** E4
Moor St *SOHO/SHAV* W1D **20** B5
Morant St *POP/IOD* E14 ....**104** A1
Mora Rd *CRICK* NW2 ....**70** C1
Mora St *FSBYE* EC1V **11** F4
Morat St *BRXN/ST* SW9 ....**117** F4
Moravian Pl *WBPTN* SW10 ....**115** D2
Moravian St *BETH* E2 ....**90** C1
Moray Ms *HOLWY* N7 ....**57** F4

Moray Rd *HOLWY* N7 ....57 F4
Mordaunt Rd *WLSDN* NW10..............69 D5
Mordaunt St *BRXN/ST* SW9 ....135 F1
Morden HI *LEW* SE13 ....122 C5
Morden La *LEW* SE13 ....122 C5
Morden Rd *BKHTH/KID* SE3 ....124 A5
Morden Road Ms *BKHTH/KID* SE3 ..124 A5
Morden St *LEW* SE13 ....122 B4
Morden Wharf Rd *GNWCH* SE10 ....105 E4
Mordon Rd *GDMY/SEVK* IG3............67 F2
Mordred Rd *CAT* SE6........................159 E2
Morecambe CI *WCHPL* E1 ....91 D4
Morecambe St *WALW* SE17..............47 F5
More CI *CAN/RD* E16 ....93 F5
WKENS W14..101 D5
Moreland Cottages *BOW* E3..............92 A1
Moreland St *FSBYE* EC1V 11 D3
Morella Rd *BAL* SW12 ....133 F5
Moremead Rd *CAT* SE6 ....157 F4
Morena St *CAT* SE6 ....140 B5
Moresby Rd *CLPT* E5..........................60 B3
Mores Gdn *CHEL* * SW3 ....115 D2
Moreton CI *CLPT* E5 ....60 C4
SEVS/STOTM N15 ....59 D1
Moreton PI *SEVS/STOTM* N15..........59 D1
Moreton PI *PIM* SW1V 116 C1
Moreton St *PIM* SW1V......................116 C1
Moreton Ter *PIM* SW1V 116 C1
Moreton Terrace Ms North
PIM SW1V 116 C1
Moreton Terrace Ms South
PIM * SW1V..116 C1
Morgan Rd *HOLWY* N7 ....76 A2
NKENS NW10 ....89 F4
Morgans La *STHWK* SE1....................36 C4
Morgan St *BOW* E3 ....91 F2
CAN/RD E16..93 F2
Moriatry CI *HOLWY* N7 ....75 E1
Morie St *WAND/EARL* SW18 ....132 B2
Morieux St *LEY* E10 ....61 F3
Moring Rd *TOOT* SW17....................152 A4
Morkyns Wk *DUL* * SE21 ....155 E3
Morland CI *GLDGN* NW11..................54 B3
Morland Est *HACK* * E8......................78 A4
Morland Gdns *WLSDN* NW10............69 D4
Morland Ms *IS* N1 ....76 A4
Morland Rd *IL* IG1 ....66 B4
Morley Rd *BARK* IG11........................85 D5
LEW SE13..140 C2
LEY E10..62 C3
SRTFD E15 ....93 F1
Morley St *STHWK* SE1 ....46 B1
Morna Rd *CMBW* SE5 ....118 C5
Morning La *HOM* E9 ....78 C3
Mornington Av *IL* IG1 ....66 A2
WKENS W14 ....101 F5
Mornington Crs *CAMTN* NW1 ....7 E1
Mornington Gv *BOW* E3 ....92 A2
Mornington Ms *CMBW* SE5 ....118 C4
Mornington PI *CAMTN* NW1..............7 D1
Mornington Rd *DEPT* SE8 ....121 F3
WAN E11 ....63 F3
Mornington St *CAMTN* NW1..............7 D1
Mornington Ter *CAMTN* NW1 ....74 B1
Morocco St *STHWK* SE1 ....48 C1
Morpeth Gv *HOM* E9 ....79 D5
Morpeth Rd *HOM* E9 ....78 C5
Morpeth St *BETH* E2 ....91 D2
Morpeth Ter *WEST* SW1P 43 E3
Morrab Gdns *GDMY/SEVK* IG3..........67 F5
Morris Av *MNPK* * E12 ....83 F2
Morris Bishop Ter *HGT* * N6..............56 A1
Morris Gdns *WAND/EARL* SW18 ....132 A5

Morrish Rd *BRXS/STRHM* SW2........135 E5
Morrison St *BTSEA* SW11 ....134 A1
Morris PI *FSBYPK* N4 ....58 A4
Morris Rd *POP/IOD* E14 ....92 B4
WAN E11 ....81 E1
Morris St *WCHPL* E1............................90 B5
Morse CI *PLSTW* E13............................94 A2
Morshead Rd *MV/WKIL* W9..................2 B4
Mortham St *SRTFD* E15......................81 E5
Mortimer CI *BAL* SW12 ....153 D2
CRICK NW2..53 F5
Mortimer Crs *KIL/WHAMP* NW6 ......72 B5
Mortimer PI *KIL/WHAMP* NW6..........72 B5
Mortimer Rd *EHAM* E6........................95 F2
IS N1 ....77 E4
WLSDN NW10 ....88 C2
Mortimer Sq *NTGHL* W11 ....101 D1
Mortimer St *REGST* W1B....................19 D4
Mortimer Ter *KTTN* * NW5..................74 B1
Mortlake High St
MORT/ESHN SW14 ....129 D1
Mortlake Rd *CAN/RD* E16 ....94 B3
IL IG1 ....84 C1
MORT/ESHN SW14 ....128 B1
RCH/KEW TW9 ....110 A3
Morton Ms *ECT* * SW5 ....38 C5
Morton PI *STHWK* SE1........................46 A3
Morton Rd *IS* N1 ....76 C3
SRTFD E15 ....81 F4
Morval Rd *BRXS/STRHM* SW2 ....136 A3
Morven Rd *TOOT* SW17....................151 F3
Morville St *BOW* E3 ....92 A1
Morwell St *FITZ* W1T 20 A3
Moscow PI *BAY/PAD* W2 ....26 C1
Moscow Rd *BAY/PAD* W2 ....26 C1
Mossbury Rd *BTSEA* SW11 ....133 E1
Moss CI *WCHPL* E1..............................90 A4
Mossford St *BOW* E3............................91 F3
Mossop St *CHEL* SW3..........................41 D4
Mostyn Gdns *WLSDN* NW10 ....89 D2
Mostyn Gv *BOW* E3 ....91 F1
Mostyn Rd *BRXN/ST* SW9 ....118 A4
Motcomb St *KTBR* SW1X....................42 A1
The Mothers Sq *CLPT* * E5..............78 B1
Motley St *VX/NE* SW8 ....116 C5
Mottingham Gdns *ELTH/MOT* SE9 ..161 D1
Mottingham La *ELTH/MOT* SE9........160 C1
Mottingham Rd *ELTH/MOT* SE9 ......161 D3
Moulins Rd *HOM* E9 ....78 C4
Moundfield Rd *STNW/STAM* N16......60 A1
Mountacre CI *SYD* SE26....................155 F4
Mount Adon Pk *DUL* SE21 ....138 A5
Mountague PI *POP/IOD* E14 ....104 C1
Mount Angelus Rd
PUT/ROE SW15 ....129 F5
Mount Ash Rd *SYD* SE26..................156 B3
Mountbatten CI *NRWD* SE19 ....155 E5
WOOL/PLUM SE18 ....127 G2
Mount Dr *WBLY* HA9............................50 C4
Mountearl Gdns
STRHM/NOR SW16 ....153 F3
Mount Ephraim La
STRHM/NOR SW16 ....153 D3
Mount Ephraim Rd
STRHM/NOR SW16 ....153 D3
Mountfield CI *LEW* SE13 ....141 D5
Mountfield Rd *EHAM* E6 ....95 F1
Mountford St *WCHPL* E1 ....90 A5
Mountfort Crs *IS* N1 ....76 A4
Mountfort Ter *IS* N1............................76 A4
Mount Gdns *SYD* SE26......................156 B3
Mountgrove Rd *FSBYPK* N4 ....58 C5
Mount Mills *FSBYE* EC1V....................11 D4

Mount Nod Rd STRHM/NOR SW16 ....153 F3
Mount Pl ACT W3.................................98 B2
Mount Pleasant FSBYW WC1X.............21 F2
　WNWD SE27......................................154 C4
Mount Pleasant Crs FSBYPK * N4........57 F2
Mount Pleasant Hl CLPT E5..................60 B4
Mount Pleasant La CLPT E5...................60 B3
Mount Pleasant Pl
　WOOL/PLUM SE18.............................109 D5
Mount Pleasant Rd LEW SE13.............140 C4
　WLSDN NW10....................................70 C4
Mount Pleasant Vis FSBYPK N4 ....57 F2
Mount Ri FSTH SE23............................156 C3
Mount Rd CRICK NW2..........................52 B5
　HDN NW4...52 A1
　IL IG1...84 B2
　WAND/EARL SW18............................150 A2
Mount Rw MYFR/PKLN W1K 30 C2
Mounts Pond Rd BKHTH/KID SE3 ....123 D5
The Mount Sq HAMP * NW3.................54 C5
Mount St MYFR/PKLN W1K....................30 A2
The Mount CLPT * E5............................60 B4
Mount Ter WCHPL E1...........................90 B4
The Mount * E5....................................60 B4
　HAMP NW3.......................................72 C1
　WBLY HA9...50 B4
Mount View Rd FSBYPK N4...................57 F2
Mount Vis WNWD SE27........................154 B3
Movers La BARK IG11............................85 D5
Mowatt Cl ARCH N19............................57 D3
Mowbray Rd KIL/WHAMP NW6 ....71 E4
Mowlem St BETH E2.............................90 B1
Mowll St BRXN/ST SW9.......................118 A3
Moxon Cl HMSMTH W6........................113 D2
Moxon St MHST W1U............................18 A3
Moye Cl BETH * E2...............................90 A1
Moyers Rd WAN E11.............................62 C3
Moylan Rd HMSMTH W6......................113 D2
Moyne Pl WLSDN NW10.........................86 A2
Moyser Rd TOOT SW17........................152 B5
Mozart St NKENS W10...........................89 F2
Muir Cl WAND/EARL SW18...................133 E4
Muirdown Av MORT/ESHN SW14 ....128 C2
Muirfield ACT W3..................................87 E5
Muirfield Cl BERM/RHTH * SE16...........120 B1
Muirfield Crs POP/IOD E14...................104 B4
Muirkirk Rd CAT SE6............................158 C1
Muir Rd CLPT E5...................................78 A1
Muir St CAN/RD E16............................107 F2
Mulberry Cl CHEL * SW3.....................115 D2
　STRHM/NOR SW16...........................152 C4
Mulberry Ms NWCR SE14....................121 F4
Mulberry Pl HMSMTH W6...................112 A1
Mulberry Rd HACK E8...........................77 F4
Mulberry St WCHPL E1..........................90 A5
Mulberry Wk CHEL SW3......................115 D2
Mulgrave Rd WKENS W14....................113 F2
　WLSDN NW10....................................69 F1
　WOOL/PLUM SE18.............................107 F1
Mulkern Rd ARCH N19..........................57 D3
Mullet Gdns BETH E2............................90 A2
Mullins Pth MORT/ESHN SW14 ....129 D1
Mull Wk IS N1.......................................76 C3
Mulready St STJWD NW8.......................16 C1
Multi Wy ACT W3..................................99 E3
Multon Rd WAND/EARL SW18..............133 D5
Mumford Ct CITYW EC2V......................23 F4
Mumford Rd HNHL SE24......................136 B3
Muncaster Rd BTSEA SW11.................133 F2
Muncies Ms CAT SE6...........................158 C2
Mundania Rd EDUL SE22....................138 B4
Munday Rd CAN/RD E16........................94 A5
Munden St WKENS W14......................101 E5
Mundford Rd CLPT E5...........................60 C2

Mundon Gdns IL IG1.............................67 D3
Mund St WKENS W14...........................113 F1
Mundy St IS N1.....................................12 C3
Munro Ms NKENS W10..........................89 E4
Munster Ms FUL/PGN * SW6...............113 F3
Munster Rd FUL/PGN SW6...................113 E3
Munster Sq CAMTN NW1.........................7 D4
Munton Rd WALW SE17..........................47 F4
Murchison Rd LEY E10..........................62 C4
Murdock Cl CAN/RD E16........................93 F5
Murdock St PECK SE15........................120 B2
Murfett Cl WIM/MER SW19..................149 E2
Muriel St IS N1..9 F1
Murillo Rd LEW SE13...........................141 D2
Murphy St STHWK SE1...........................46 A1
Murray Gv IS N1....................................12 A2
Murray Ms CAMTN NW1........................75 D4
Murray Sq CAN/RD E16.........................94 A5
Murray St CAMTN NW1.........................75 D4
Murray Ter HAMP NW3..........................72 C1
Musard Rd HMSMTH W6......................113 E2
Musbury St WCHPL E1...........................90 C5
Muscatel Pl CMBW SE5.......................119 E4
Muschamp Rd PECK SE15...................137 F5
Muscovy St TWRH EC3N........................37 D2
Museum St NOXST/BSQ WC1A..............20 C3
Musgrave Crs FUL/PGN SW6...............114 A3
Musgrove Rd NWCR SE14...................121 D4
Musjid Rd BTSEA SW11.......................115 D5
Muston Rd CLPT E5...............................60 B4
Muswell Hill Rd HGT N6........................56 A1
Mutrix Rd KIL/WHAMP NW6...................72 A3
Mutton Pl CAMTN NW1..........................74 A3
Myatt Rd BRXN/ST SW9.......................118 B4
Mycenae Rd BKHTH/KID SE3..............124 A2
Myddelton Pas CLKNW EC1R.................10 B3
Myddelton Sq CLKNW EC1R...................10 B3
Myddelton St CLKNW EC1R...................10 B4
Myddleton Av FSBYPK N4.....................58 B4
Myers La NWCR SE14..........................121 D2
Mylis Cl SYD SE26...............................156 B4
Mylne Cl HMSMTH * W6.......................112 A1
Mylne St CLKNW EC1R..........................10 A2
Myrdle St WCHPL E1..............................90 A4
Myron Pl LEW SE13............................140 C1
Myrtle Aly WOOL/PLUM SE18..............108 A4
Myrtleberry Cl HACK * E8.......................77 F3
Myrtle Rd ACT W3.................................98 A3
　EHAM E6...83 E5
　WALTH E17.......................................61 E1
Myrtle St IS N1......................................12 C2
Myrtle Wk IS N1....................................12 C2
Mysore Rd BTSEA SW11.....................133 F2
Myton Rd DUL SE21............................155 D3

N

Nadine St CHARL SE7..........................124 C1
Nairne Gv HNHL SE24..........................137 D3
Nairn St POP/IOD E14............................92 C4
Namba Roy Cl STRHM/NOR SW16.......153 F4
Nankin St POP/IOD E14..........................92 A5
Nansen Rd BTSEA SW11......................134 A2
Nantes Cl WAND/EARL SW18...............132 C2
Nant Ct CRICK NW2...............................53 F4
Nant St BETH E2....................................90 B2
Naoroji St FSBYW WC1X........................10 A4
Napier Av FUL/PGN SW6......................131 F1
　POP/IOD E14....................................122 A1
Napier Cl DEPT SE8.............................121 F3
Napier Ct LEE/GVPK SE12...................160 B2

Napier Gv *IS* N1 ....**11** F2
Napier Pl *WKENS* W14 ....**101** F4
Napier Rd *EHAM* E6 ....**84** A5
   SRTFD E15 ....**93** E1
   WAN E11 ....**63** E5
   WKENS W14 ....**101** F4
   WLSDN NW10 ....**88** B2
Napier Ter *IS* N1 ....**76** B4
Napoleon St *CLPT* E5 ....**60** B5
Narbonne Av *CLAP* SW4 ....**134** C4
Narborough St *FUL/PGN* SW6 ....**114** B5
Narford Rd *CLPT* E5 ....**60** A5
Narcissus Rd *KIL/WHAMP* NW6 ......**72** A2
Narrow Boat Cl *THMD* SE28 ....**109** D3
Narrow St *ACT* W3 ....**98** B2
   POP/IOD E14 ....**103** E1
Nascot St *SHB* W12 ....**88** C5
Naseby Cl *KIL/WHAMP* * NW6 ....**72** C4
Nash Rd *BROCKY* SE4 ....**139** E2
Nash St *CAMTN* NW1 ....**7** D3
Nasmyth St *HMSMTH* W6 ....**100** B4
Nassau Rd *BARN* SW13 ....**111** F4
Nassau St *GTPST* W1W **19** E3
Nassington Rd *HAMP* NW3 ....**73** E1
Natal Rd *IL* IG1 ....**84** B1
Nathaniel Cl *WCHPL* E1 ....**25** F3
Nathan Wy *THMD* SE28 ....**109** F4
National St *BERM/RHTH* * SE16 .....**102** B3
Naval Rw *POP/IOD* E14 ....**104** C1
Navarino Gv *HACK* E8 ....**78** A3
Navarino Rd *HACK* E8 ....**78** A3
Navarre Rd *EHAM* E6 ....**95** E1
Navarre St *BETH* E2 ....**13** E5
Navy St *CLAP* SW4 ....**135** D1
Nayim Pl *HACK* E8 ....**78** B3
Naylor Rd *PECK* SE15 ....**120** B3
Nazareth Cl *PECK* SE15 ....**120** B5
Nealden St *BRXN/ST* SW9 ....**135** F1
Neal St *LSQ/SEVD* WC2H **20** C5
Neal Ter *FSTH* * SE23 ....**157** D1
Neal Yd *LSQ/SEVD* WC2H **20** C5
Neasden Cl *WLSDN* NW10 ....**69** E2
Neasden La *WLSDN* NW10 ....**51** D5
Neasden La North *WLSDN* NW10 ......**51** E4
Neate St *CMBW* SE5 ....**119** E2
Neathouse Pl *PIM* SW1V **43** E4
Neatscourt Rd *EHAM* E6 ....**95** D4
Nebraska St *STHWK* SE1 ....**48** A1
Neckinger *STHWK* SE1 ....**49** F2
Neckinger Est *BERM/RHTH* SE16 .....**49** F2
Neckinger St *STHWK* SE1 ....**49** F1
Nectarine Wy *LEW* SE13 ....**122** B5
Needham Rd *NTGHL* W11 ....**14** A4
Needleman St *BERM/RHTH* SE16 ...**103** D3
Neeld Crs *WBLY* HA9 ....**68** A3
Neils Yd *LSQ/SEVD* * WC2H **20** C5
Nelgarde Rd *CAT* SE6 ....**140** A5
Nella Rd *HMSMTH* W6 ....**113** D2
Nelldale Rd *BERM/RHTH* SE16 ....**102** B5
Nello James Gdns *WNWD* SE27 ....**155** D4
Nelson Cl *KIL/WHAMP* NW6 ....**2** A3
Nelson Gdns *BETH* E2 ....**90** A2
Nelson Mandela Rd
   BKHTH/KID SE3 ....**142** C1
Nelson Pl *IS* N1 ....**11** D1
Nelson Rd *GNWCH* SE10 ....**122** C2
Nelson Sq *STHWK* SE1 ....**34** C5
Nelsons Rw *CLAP* SW4 ....**135** D2
Nelson St *CAN/RD* E16 ....**105** F1
   EHAM E6 ....**95** F1
   WCHPL E1 ....**90** B5
Nelsons Yd *CAMTN* NW1 ....**7** E1
Nelson Ter *FSBYE* EC1V **11** D2

Nemoure Rd *ACT* W3 ....**98** C1
Nepaul Rd *BTSEA* SW11 ....**115** E5
Nepean St *PUT/ROE* SW15 ....**130** A4
Neptune St *BERM/RHTH* SE16 ....**102** C4
Nesbit Cl *BKHTH/KID* SE3 ....**141** E1
Nesbit Rd *ELTH/MOT* SE9 ....**143** D2
Nesham St *WAP* E1W **102** A2
Ness St *BERM/RHTH* SE16 ....**102** A4
Netheravon Rd *CHSWK* W4 ....**111** F1
Netheravon Rd South *CHSWK* W4 ...**111** F2
Netherby Rd *FSTH* SE23 ....**138** C5
Netherfield Gdns *BARK* IG11 ....**85** D3
Netherfield Rd *TOOT* SW17 ....**152** A3
Netherford Rd *CLAP* SW4 ....**116** C5
Netherhall Gdns *HAMP* NW3 ....**72** C3
Netherhall Wy *HAMP* NW3 ....**72** C2
Netherleigh Cl *ARCH* * N19 ....**56** D3
Netherton Gv *WBPTN* SW10 ....**114** C2
Netherton Rd *SEVS/STOTM* N15 ......**59** D1
Netherwood Pl *HMSMTH* * W6 ....**101** D4
Netherwood Rd *HMSMTH* W6 ....**101** D4
Netherwood St *KIL/WHAMP* NW6 .....**71** F4
Netley St *CAMTN* NW1 ....**7** E4
Nettleden Av *WBLY* HA9 ....**68** A3
Nettlefold Pl *WNWD* SE27 ....**154** B3
Nettleton Rd *NWCR* SE14 ....**121** D3
Neuchatel Rd *CAT* SE6 ....**157** F2
Nevada St *GNWCH* SE10 ....**122** C3
Nevern Pl *ECT* SW5 ....**38** B5
Nevern Rd *ECT* SW5 ....**38** A5
Neville Cl *ACT* W3 ....**98** C3
   BFN/LL DA15 ....**163** F4
   KIL/WHAMP NW6 ....**89** F1
   PECK SE15 ....**120** A3
   WAN E11 ....**63** F5
Neville Dr *EFNCH* N2 ....**54** C1
Neville Gill Cl *WAND/EARL* SW18 ...**132** A4
Neville Rd *FSTGT* E7 ....**82** A4
   KIL/WHAMP * NW6 ....**89** F1
Neville St *SKENS* SW7 ....**115** D1
Neville Ter *SKENS* * SW7 ....**115** D1
Nevill Rd *STNW/STAM* N16 ....**77** E1
Nevinson Cl *WAND/EARL* SW18 ....**133** D1
Nevis Rd *TOOT* SW17 ....**152** A2
New Acres Rd *THMD* SE28 ....**109** E2
Newark Crs *WLSDN* NW10 ....**87** D2
Newark Knok *EHAM* E6 ....**96** A5
Newark St *WCHPL* E1 ....**90** B4
New Barn St *PLSTW* E13 ....**94** A3
Newbold Cottages *WCHPL* * E1 ....**90** C5
New Bond St *MYFR/PICC* W1J **31** D1
   MYFR/PKLN W1K **19** D5
New Bridge St *STP* EC4M **22** C5
New Broad St *LVPST* EC2M **24** B3
Newburgh Rd *ACT* W3 ....**98** C2
Newburgh St *SOHO/CST* W1F **19** E5
New Burlington Ms *CONDST* W1S **31** E1
New Burlington Pl *CONDST* W1S........**31** E1
New Burlington St *CONDST* W1S **31** E1
Newburn St *LBTH* SE11 ....**117** F1
Newbury Ms *KTTN* NW5 ....**74** A3
Newbury Rd *GNTH/NBYPK* IG2 ....**67** D1
Newbury St *STBT* EC1A **23** E3
New Butt La *DEPT* * SE8 ....**122** A3
Newby Pl *POP/IOD* E14 ....**104** C1
Newby St *VX/NE* SW8 ....**134** B1
Newcastle Cl *STP* EC4M **22** C4
Newcastle Pl *BAY/PAD* W2 ....**16** B3
Newcastle Rw *CLKNW* EC1R **22** B1
New Cavendish St *MHST* W1U **18** B3
New Change *STP* EC4M **23** E5
New Charles St *FSBYE* EC1V **11** D3
New Church Rd *CMBW* SE5 ....**118** C3

New City Rd *PLSTW* E13 ....94 C2
New College Ms *IS* * N1 ....76 A4
New College Pde *HAMP* * NW3 ...72 C3
Newcombe St *KENS* * W8 ....26 B3
Newcome Gdns
  STRHM/NOR SW16 ....153 E4
Newcomen Rd *BTSEA* SW11 ....133 F1
  WAN * E11 ....63 F5
Newcomen St *STHWK* SE1 ....36 A5
New Compton St
  LSQ/SEVD * WC2H 20 B5
New Ct *TPL/STR* * WC2R 34 A1
Newcourt St *STJWD* NW8 ....4 C2
New Crane Pl *WAP* * E1W 102 C2
New Crescent Yd *WLSDN* * NW10 ..87 F1
New Cross Rd *NWCR* SE14 ....120 C3
Newdigate St *STRHM/NOR* * SW16 ..154 A4
Newell St *POP/IOD* E14 ....103 F1
New End *HAMP* NW3 ....72 C1
New End Sq *HAMP* NW3 ....73 D1
Newent Cl *PECK* SE15 ....119 E3
New Era Est *IS* N1 ....77 E5
New Ferry Ap *WOOL/PLUM* SE18 ..108 A4
New Fetter La *FLST/FETLN* EC4A ..22 B4
Newfield Ri *CRICK* NW2 ....52 A5
Newgate St *STBT* EC1A 23 D4
New Globe Wk *STHWK* SE1 ....35 E3
New Goulston St *WCHPL* E1 ....25 E4
Newham's Rw *STHWK* SE1 ....49 D1
Newham Wy *CAN/RD* E16 ....93 F4
Newhaven Gdns *ELTH/MOT* SE9 ..143 D2
Newhaven La *PLSTW* E13 ....93 F4
Newick Rd *CLPT* E5 ....60 B5
Newington Barrow Wy *HOLWY* N7 ..57 F5
Newington Butts *LBTH* SE11 ....47 D5
Newington Cswy *STHWK* SE1 ....47 E2
Newington Gn *STNW/STAM* N16 ...77 D2
Newington Green Rd *IS* N1 ....77 D2
New Inn Broadway *SDTCH* * EC2A ..13 D5
New Inn Sq *SDTCH* * EC2A 13 D5
New Inn St *SDTCH* * EC2A 13 D5
New Inn Yd *SDTCH* * EC2A 13 D5
New Kent Rd *STHWK* SE1 ....47 E4
New Kings Rd *FUL/PGN* SW6 ....113 F5
  FUL/PGN SW6 ....114 A5
New King St *DEPT* SE8 ....122 A2
New Lydenburg St *CHARL* SE7 ....106 C4
Newlands Ct *WBLY* HA9 ....50 A4
Newlands Quay *WAP* E1W 102 C1
Newland St *CAN/RD* E16 ....107 E2
Newling Cl *EHAM* E6 ....95 F5
Newling Est *BETH* E2 ....13 F3
New London St *MON* * EC3R 37 D1
Newlyn Rd *WELL* DA16 ....127 F5
Newman Ap *PLSTW* E13 ....94 B2
Newman's Rw *LINN* WC2A 21 F3
Newman St *FITZ* W1T 19 F3
New Mount St *SRTFD* * E15 ....81 D5
Newnham Ter *STHWK* SE1 ....46 A2
New North Pl *SDTCH* EC2A 12 C5
New North Rd *IS* N1 ....12 B2
New North St *BMSBY* WC1N 21 E2
Newnton Cl *FSBYPK* N4 ....59 D2
New Oxford St *NOXST/BSQ* WC1A ..20 B4
New Park Rd *BAL* SW12 ....153 E1
  BRXS/STRHM SW2 ....135 E5
New Place Sq *BERM/RHTH* SE16 ..102 B4
New Plaistow Rd *SRTFD* E15 ....81 E5
Newport Av *POP/IOD* E14 ....105 D1
Newport Ct *SOHO/SHAV* W1D 32 B1
Newport Pl *SOHO/SHAV* * W1D 32 B1
Newport Rd *BARN* SW13 ....112 A4
  WAN E11 ....63 D1

Newport St *LBTH* SE11 ....45 E5
Newquay Rd *CAT* SE6 ....158 B2
New Quebec St *MBLAR* W1H 17 E5
New River Wy *FSBYPK* N4 ....59 D2
New Rd *GDMY/SEVK* IG3 ....67 E4
  WCHPL E1 ....90 B4
New Rw *CHCR* WC2N 32 C1
New Spring Gardens Wk
  LBTH * SE11 ....117 E1
New Sq *LINN* WC2A 21 F4
Newstead Rd *LEE/GVPK* SE12 .....141 E5
Newstead Wy *WIM/MER* SW19 .....149 D4
New St *LVPST* EC2M 25 D3
New Street Hl *BMLY* BR1 ....160 B5
New Street Sq *FLST/FETLN* EC4A ..22 B4
Newton Av *ACT* W3 ....98 C3
Newton Cl *WALTH* E17 ....61 E1
Newton Gv *CHSWK* W4 ....99 E4
Newton Rd *BAY/PAD* W2 ....14 B5
  CRICK NW2 ....70 C1
  SRTFD * E15 ....81 D2
Newton St *HOL/ALD* WC2B 21 D4
Newton's Yd *WAND/EARL* SW18 ..132 A3
New Tower Buildings *WAP* * E1W ..102 B2
Newtown St *BTSEA* * SW11 ....116 B4
New Union Cl *POP/IOD* E14 ....104 C4
New Union St *BARB* EC2Y 24 A3
New Wanstead *WAN* E11 ....64 A1
New Wharf Rd *IS* N1 ....9 D1
Niagara Cl *IS* N1 ....11 F1
Nicholas La *MANHO* EC4N 36 B1
Nicholas Rd *WCHPL* E1 ....90 C3
Nicholay Rd *ARCH* N19 ....57 D3
Nichollsfield Wk *HOLWY* N7 ....75 E2
Nicholl St *BETH* E2 ....78 A5
Nichols Cl *FSBYPK* * N4 ....58 A3
Nicholson St *STHWK* SE1 ....34 C4
Nicoll Pl *HDN* NW4 ....52 B1
Nicoll Rd *WLSDN* NW10 ....69 E5
Nicosia Rd *WAND/EARL* SW18 ....133 E5
Niederwald Rd *SYD* SE26 ....157 F4
Nigel Ms *IL* IG1 ....84 B1
Nigel Playfair Av *HMSMTH* W6 ....112 B1
Nigel Rd *FSTGT* E7 ....82 C2
  PECK SE15 ....138 A1
Nigeria Rd *CHARL* SE7 ....124 C3
Nightingale Cl *CHSWK* W4 ....110 C2
Nightingale Gv *LEW* SE13 ....141 D3
Nightingale La *BAL* SW12 ....133 F5
Nightingale Ms *LBTH* SE11 ....46 B4
Nightingale Pl *WBPTN* SW10 ....114 C2
  WOOL/PLUM SE18 ....126 A2
Nightingale Rd *CLPT* E5 ....60 B5
  WLSDN NW10 ....87 F1
Nightingale Sq *BAL* SW12 ....134 A5
Nightingale V *WOOL/PLUM* SE18 ..126 A2
Nightingale Wk *BAL* SW12 ....134 B4
Nightingale Wy *EHAM* E6 ....95 E4
Nile Cl *STNW/STAM* N16 ....59 F5
Nile Rd *PLSTW* E13 ....94 C1
Nile St *IS* N1 ....12 A3
Nile Ter *PECK* SE15 ....119 F1
Nimrod Pas *IS* N1 ....77 E3
Nina Mackay Cl *SRTFD* * E15 ....81 E5
Nine Acres Cl *MNPK* E12 ....83 E2
Nine Elms La *VX/NE* SW8 ....116 C3
Nithdale Rd *WOOL/PLUM* SE18 ..126 B3
Niton Rd *RCH/KEW* TW9 ....128 A1
Niton St *FUL/PGN* SW6 ....113 D3
No 1 St *WOOL/PLUM* SE18 ....108 B4
No 2 St *WOOL/PLUM* SE18 ....108 B4
Noble St *CITYW* EC2V 23 E4

Noel Rd *ACT* W3 ....86 A5
  EHAM E6 ....95 E3
  IS N1 ....10 C1
Noel St *SOHO/CST* * W1F 19 F5
Nolan Wy *CLPT* E5 ....78 A1
Norbiton Rd *POP/IOD* E14 ....91 F5
Norbroke St *ACT* W3 ....99 F1
Norburn St *NKENS* W10 ....89 E4
Norcott Rd *STNW/STAM* N16 ....60 A4
Norcroft Gdns *EDUL* SE22 ....138 A5
Norfolk Av *SEVS/STOTM* N15 ....59 F1
Norfolk Crs *BAY/PAD* W2 ....16 C4
  BFN/LL DA15 ....145 E5
Norfolk House Rd
  STRHM/NOR SW16 ....153 D3
Norfolk Ms *NKENS* W10 ....89 E4
Norfolk Pl *BAY/PAD* W2 ....16 B4
Norfolk Rd *BARK* IG11 ....85 E4
  EHAM E6 ....83 F5
  GDMY/SEVK IG3 ....67 E3
  STJWD NW8 ....73 D5
  WLSDN NW10 ....69 E4
Norfolk Rw *STHWK* SE1 ....45 E4
Norfolk Sq *BAY/PAD* W2 ....16 B5
Norfolk Square Ms *BAY/PAD* W2 ......16 B5
Norfolk St *FSTGT* E7 ....82 A2
Norgrove St *BAL* SW12 ....152 A1
Norland Pl *NTGHL* W11 ....101 E2
Norland Rd *NTGHL* W11 ....101 D2
Norland Sq *NTGHL* W11 ....101 E2
Norley V *PUT/ROE* SW15 ....148 A1
Norlington Rd *LEY* E10 ....62 C3
Normanby Cl *PUT/ROE* SW15 ....131 F3
Normanby Rd *WLSDN* NW10 ....69 F2
Normand Gdns *WKENS* * W14 ....113 E2
Normand Ms *WKENS* W14 ....113 E2
Normand Rd *WKENS* W14 ....113 E2
Normandy Cl *SYD* SE26 ....157 E3
Normandy Rd *BRXN/ST* SW9 ....118 A4
Normandy Rd *CAN/RD* E16 ....94 B5
Norman Gv *BOW* E3 ....91 E1
Normanhurst Rd
  BRXS/STRHM SW2 ....153 F2
Norman Rd *EHAM* E6 ....95 F3
  GNWCH SE10 ....122 B3
  IL IG1 ....84 B2
  WAN E11 ....63 F4
Normans Cl *WLSDN* NW10 ....69 D3
Normans Md *WLSDN* NW10 ....69 D3
Norman St *FSBYE* EC1V 11 E4
Norman Ter *KIL/WHAMP* * NW6 ....71 F2
Normanton Av *WIM/MER* SW19 ....150 A2
Normanton St *FSTH* SE23 ....157 D2
Norman Wy *ACT* W3 ....86 B4
Normington Cl *STRHM/NOR* SW16 ...154 A5
Norris St *STJS* SW1Y 32 A5
Norroy Rd *PUT/ROE* SW15 ....131 D2
Norstead Pl *PUT/ROE* SW15 ....148 A3
North Access Rd *WALTH* E17 ....61 D1
North Acton Rd *WLSDN* NW10 ....87 D1
Northampton Gv *IS* N1 ....76 C2
Northampton Pk *IS* N1 ....76 C3
Northampton Rd *CLKNW* EC1R 10 B5
Northampton Rw *CLKNW* * EC1R 10 B5
Northampton Sq *FSBYE* EC1V 10 C4
Northampton St *IS* * N1 ....76 C2
North Audley St *MYFR/PKLN* W1K 18 A5
North Av *RCH/KEW* TW9 ....110 A4
North Bank *STJWD* NW8 ....4 C4
North Birkbeck Rd *WAN* E11 ....63 D5
Northbourne Rd *CLAP* SW4 ....135 D2
Northbrook Rd *IL* IG1 ....66 A4
  LEW SE13 ....141 D3
Northburgh St *FSBYE* EC1V 23 D1
North Carriage Dr *BAY/PAD* W2 ....29 D1
Northchurch Rd *IS* N1 ....76 C4
  WBLY HA9 ....68 A3
Northchurch Ter *IS* * N1 ....77 E4
North Circular Rd *CRICK* NW2 ....51 E5
  WLSDN NW10 ....69 D2
North Colonnade *POP/IOD* E14 ....104 A2
Northcote Rd *BTSEA* SW11 ....133 E3
  SCUP DA14 ....163 E4
  WLSDN NW10 ....69 E4
North Crs *CAN/RD* E16 ....93 D3
  FITZ W1T 20 A2
North Cross Rd *EDUL* SE22 ....137 F3
Northdene Gdns *SEVS/STOTM* N15 ...59 F1
Northdown St *IS* N1 ....9 E2
North Dr *STRHM/NOR* SW16 ....152 C4
North End *GLDGN* NW11 ....54 A4
North End Av *HAMP* NW3 ....54 C4
North End Crs *WKENS* W14 ....101 F5
North End Rd *FUL/PGN* SW6 ....114 A3
  GLDGN NW11 ....54 A3
  WBLY HA9 ....50 A5
North End Wy *HAMP* NW3 ....54 C4
Northern Relief Rd *BARK* IG11 ....84 C4
North Eyot Gdns *HMSMTH* * W6 .....111 F1
Northey St *POP/IOD* E14 ....103 E1
Northfield Av *EHAM* E6 ....83 F3
  STNW/STAM N16 ....59 E2
Northfields *WAND/EARL* SW18 ....132 A2
Northfields Rd *ACT* W3 ....86 C4
Northgate Dr *CDALE/KGS* NW9 ....51 E4
North Gower St *CAMTN* NW1 ....7 E4
North Gv *HGT* N6 ....56 A2
North Hl *HGT* N6 ....55 F1
North Hill Av *HGT* N6 ....55 F1
Northiam St *HACK* E8 ....78 B5
Northington St *BMSBY* WC1N 21 E2
Northlands St *CMBW* SE5 ....118 C5
North Lodge Cl *PUT/ROE* * SW15 ....131 D3
North Ms *BMSBY* WC1N 21 E1
Northolme Rd *HBRY* N5 ....76 B1
Northover *BMLY* BR1 ....159 F5
North Pk *ELTH/MOT* SE9 ....143 F4
North Pas *WAND/EARL* SW18 ....132 A3
North Pole Rd *SHB* W12 ....88 B5
Northport St *IS* N1 ....77 D5
North Ri *BAY/PAD* * W2 ....17 D5
North Rd *GDMY/SEVK* IG3 ....67 E4
  HGT N6 ....56 A2
  HOLWY N7 ....75 D5
  WOOL/PLUM SE18 ....109 E5
North Rw *MYFR/PKLN* W1K 30 A1
North Several *BKHTH/KID* * SE3 ......123 D5
North Side Wandsworth Common
  WAND/EARL SW18 ....132 C3
North Sq *GLDGN* NW11 ....54 A1
Northstead Rd *BRXS/STRHM* SW2 ...154 A1
North St *BARK* IG11 ....84 B4
  PLSTW E13 ....94 B1
  VX/NE SW8 ....134 B1
North Tenter St *WCHPL* E1 ....25 F5
North Ter *CHEL* SW3 ....40 C4
Northumberland Aly *TWRH* * EC3N 25 D5
Northumberland Av *CHCR* WC2N 32 C5
  MNPK E12 ....64 C3
  WELL DA16 ....145 E2
Northumberland Pl *BAY/PAD* W2 ....14 A5
Northumberland Rd *EHAM* E6 ....95 E5
  WALTH E17 ....62 A2
Northumbria St *POP/IOD* E14 ....92 A5
North Verbena Gdns
  HMSMTH * W6 ....112 A1

North Vw *WIM/MER* SW19................**148** B5
Northview Crs *WLSDN* NW10................**69** F1
Northview Pde *HOLWY* * N7................**57** E5
North Vls *CAMTN* NW1................**75** D3
Northway Rd *CMBW* SE5................**136** C1
Northways Pde *KIL/WHAMP* * NW6.....**73** D4
North Wharf Rd *BAY/PAD* W2................**16** A3
Northwick Cl *STJWD* NW8................**4** A5
Northwick Ter *STJWD* NW8................**4** A5
Northwold Rd *STNW/STAM* N16........**59** F4
Northwood Rd *FSTH* SE23................**157** F1
HGT N6................**56** B2
North Woolwich Rd *CAN/RD* E16.....**106** B2
North Worple Wy
MORT/ESHN SW14................**129** D1
Norton Folgate *WCHPL* E1................**25** D1
Norton Rd *LEY* E10................**61** F3
Norval Gn *BRXN/ST* * SW9................**118** A5
Norway Ga *BERM/RHTH* SE16........**103** E4
Norway Pl *POP/IOD* E14................**91** F5
Norway St *GNWCH* SE10................**122** B2
Norwich Rd *FSTGT* E7................**82** A2
Norwich St *FLST/FETLN* EC4A........**22** A4
Norwood High St *WNWD* SE27.......**154** B3
Norwood Park Rd *WNWD* SE27........**154** C5
Norwood Rd *HNHL* SE24................**154** B1
Notley St *CMBW* SE5................**119** D3
Notting Barn Rd *NKENS* W10........**89** D3
Nottingdale Sq *NTGHL* * W11........**101** E2
Nottingham Av *CAN/RD* E16........**94** C4
Nottingham Ct *LSQ/SEVD* * WC2H....**20** C5
Nottingham Pl *MHST* W1U................**18** A1
Nottingham Rd *LEY* E10................**62** C1
TOOT SW17................**151** F1
Nottingham St *MHST* W1U................**18** A1
Nottingham Ter *CAMTN* NW1........**18** A1
Notting Hill Ga *KENS* W8................**26** B3
Novar Rd *ELTH/MOT* SE9................**162** C1
Novello St *FUL/PGN* SW6................**114** A4
Nowell Rd *BARN* SW13................**112** A2
Noyna Rd *TOOT* SW17................**151** F3
Nuding Cl *LEW* SE13................**140** A1
Nugent Rd *ARCH* N19................**57** E3
Nugent Ter *STJWD* NW8................**3** F2
Nunhead Gv *PECK* SE15................**138** B1
Nunhead La *PECK* SE15................**138** B1
Nunnington Cl *ELTH/MOT* SE9......**161** E3
Nursery Cl *BROCKY* SE4................**121** F5
Nursery La *BETH* E2................**77** F5
FSTGT E7................**82** A3
NKENS W10................**88** C4
Nursery Rd *BRXN/ST* SW9................**135** F2
HACK E8................**78** C3
Nursery Rw *WALW* SE17................**48** A5
Nutbourne St *NKENS* W10................**89** E2
Nutbrook St *PECK* SE15................**137** F1
Nutcroft Rd *PECK* SE15................**120** B3
Nutfield Gdns *GDMY/SEVK* IG3........**67** F4
Nutfield Rd *CRICK* NW2................**52** A4
EDUL SE22................**137** F3
SRTFD E15................**80** C1
Nutford Pl *BAY/PAD* W2................**17** D4
Nuthatch Gdns *THMD* SE28........**109** D3
Nuthurst Av *BRXS/STRHM* SW2.....**153** F2
Nutley Ter *HAMP* NW3................**73** D3
Nutmeg Cl *CAN/RD* E16................**93** E3
Nutmeg La *POP/IOD* E14................**93** D5
Nuttall St *IS* N1................**13** D1
Nutt St *PECK* SE15................**119** F3
Nutwell St *TOOT* SW17................**151** E5
Nyanza St *WOOL/PLUM* SE18........**127** D2
Nylands Av *RCH/KEW* TW9................**110** A5
Nynehead St *NWCR* SE14................**121** D3

Nyon Gv *FSTH* SE23................**157** F2

Oakbank Gv *HNHL* SE24................**136** C2
Oakbrook Cl *BMLY* BR1................**160** B4
Oakbury Rd *FUL/PGN* SW6................**114** B5
Oak Cottage Cl *CAT* SE6................**159** E1
Oak Crs *CAN/RD* E16................**93** E4
Oakcroft Rd *BKHTH/KID* SE3........**123** D5
Oakdale Rd *FSBYPK* N4................**58** C1
FSTGT E7................**82** B4
PECK SE15................**138** C1
STRHM/NOR SW16................**153** E5
WAN E11................**63** D4
Oakdene Av *CHST* BR7................**162** A5
Oakden St *LBTH* SE11................**46** B4
Oakeshott Av *HGT* N6................**56** A4
Oakey La *STHWK* SE1................**46** A2
Oakfield Rd *EHAM* E6................**83** E5
FSBYPK N4................**58** A1
IL IG1................**66** B5
WIM/MER SW19................**149** D3
Oakfields Rd *GLDGN* NW11................**53** D2
Oakfield St *WBPTN* SW10................**114** C2
Oakford Rd *KTTN* NW5................**74** C1
Oak Gv *CRICK* NW2................**71** D1
Oak Hall Rd *WAN* E11................**64** B1
Oakham Cl *CAT* * SE6................**157** F2
Oakhill Av *HAMP* NW3................**72** B1
Oak Hill Pk *HAMP* NW3................**72** B1
Oak Hill Park Ms *HAMP* NW3........**72** C1
Oakhill Pl *PUT/ROE* SW15................**132** C3
Oakhill Rd *PUT/ROE* SW15................**131** F3
Oak Hill Wy *HAMP* NW3................**72** B1
Oakhurst Gv *EDUL* SE22................**138** A2
Oakington Manor Dr *WBLY* HA9....**68** A2
Oakington Rd *MV/WKIL* W9................**2** B5
Oakington Wy *CEND/HSY/T* N8......**57** E1
Oakland Rd *SRTFD* E15................**81** E3
Oaklands *BFN/LL* DA15................**145** E5
Oaklands Gv *SHB* W12................**100** A2
Oaklands Ms *CRICK* NW2................**71** D1
Oaklands Park Av *IL* IG1................**66** C4
Oaklands Pl *CLAP* SW4................**134** C2
Oaklands Rd *BAL* SW12................**152** B1
MORT/ESHN SW14................**129** D1
Oak La *POP/IOD* E14................**103** F1
Oakley Av *ACT* W3................**98** A1
BARK IG11................**85** F3
Oakley Crs *FSBYE* * EC1V................**11** D2
Oakley Dr *BFN/LL* DA15................**163** D1
LEW SE13................**141** D4
Oakley Gdns *CHEL* SW3................**115** E2
Oakley Pl *STHWK* SE1................**119** E1
Oakley Rd *IS* N1................**77** D4
Oakley Sq *CAMTN* NW1................**7** F1
Oakley St *CHEL* SW3................**115** E1
Oakley Yd *BETH* * E2................**13** E1
Oakmead Rd *BAL* SW12................**152** B1
Oak Park Gdns *WIM/MER* SW19......**149** D5
Oakridge Rd *BMLY* BR1................**159** E4
Oaks Av *NRWD* SE19................**155** E5
Oaksford Av *SYD* SE26................**156** B3
Oakshade Rd *BMLY* BR1................**159** D4
Oakshaw Rd *WAND/EARL* SW18.....**132** B5
The Oaks *WOOL/PLUM* SE18........**126** C1
Oak Tree Gdns *BMLY* BR1................**160** B5
Oaktree Gv *IL* IG1................**85** D2
Oak Tree Rd *STJWD* NW8................**4** B4
Oakview Rd *CAT* SE6................**158** B5

Oak Village HAMP NW3 ....74 A1
Oak Vls GLDGN * NW11 ....53 F1
Oak Wy ACT W3 ....99 E2
Oakways ELTH/MOT SE9 ....144 B4
Oakwood Ct WKENS W14 ....101 F4
Oakwood Gdns GDMY/SEVK IG3 ......67 F4
Oakwood La WKENS W14 ....101 F4
Oakworth Rd NKENS W10 ....88 C4
Oat La CITYW EC2V 23 E4
Oban Cl PLSTW E13 ....94 C3
Oban Rd PLSTW E13 ....94 C3
Oban St POP/IOD E14 ....93 D5
Oberstein Rd BTSEA SW11 ....133 D2
Oborne Cl HNHL SE24 ....136 B3
Observatory Gdns KENS W8 ....26 A5
Observatory Rd
    MORT/ESHN SW14 ....128 C2
    SKENS SW7 ....40 B2
Occupation La WOOL/PLUM SE18 ...126 B4
Occupation Rd WALW SE17 ....118 C1
Ocean Est WCHPL E1 ....91 D3
Ocean St WCHPL E1 ....91 D4
Ockendon Ms IS * N1 ....77 D3
Ockendon Rd IS N1 ....77 D3
Ockley Rd STRHM/NOR SW16 ....153 E3
Octagon Ar LVPST * EC2M 24 C3
Octavia Ms CRICK * NW2 ....70 B3
Octavia St BTSEA SW11 ....115 E4
Octavius St DEPT SE8 ....122 A3
Odeon Pde ELTH/MOT * SE9 ....143 E2
    HOLWY * N7 ....57 E5
Odessa Rd FSTGT E7 ....81 F1
    WLSDN NW10 ....88 A1
Odessa St BERM/RHTH SE16 ....103 F4
Odger St BTSEA SW11 ....115 F5
Odhams Wk LSQ/SEVD WC2H 20 C5
Offa's Md HOM E9 ....79 E1
Offenham Rd ELTH/MOT SE9 ....161 E4
Offerton Rd CLAP SW4 ....134 C1
Offley Rd BRXN/ST SW9 ....118 A3
Offord Rd IS N1 ....76 A4
Offord St IS N1 ....75 F4
Ogilby St WOOL/PLUM SE18 ....107 F5
Oglander Rd PECK SE15 ....137 F2
Ogle St GTPST W1W 19 E2
Ohio Rd PLSTW E13 ....93 F3
Oil Mill La HMSMTH W6 ....112 A1
Okeburn Rd TOOT SW17 ....152 A5
Okehampton Rd WLSDN NW10 ....70 C5
Olaf St NTGHL W11 ....101 D1
Old Bailey STP EC4M 23 D5
Old Barrack Yd KTBR SW1X 30 A3
Old Bethnal Green Rd BETH E2 ....90 B2
Old Bond St CONDST W1S 31 E2
Old Broad St LVPST EC2M 24 C4
Old Brewery Ms HAMP NW3 ....73 D1
Old Bromley Rd BMLY BR1 ....159 D5
Old Brompton Rd ECT SW5 ....114 A1
Old Buildings LINN WC2A 22 A4
Old Burlington St CONDST W1S 31 E1
Oldbury Pl MHST W1U 18 B2
Old Castle St WCHPL E1 ....25 E4
Old Cavendish St CAVSQ/HST W1G ...18 C4
Old Church La CDALE/KGS NW9 ....50 C4
Old Church Rd WCHPL * E1 ....91 D5
Old Church St CHEL SW3 ....115 D1
Old Compton St SOHO/SHAV W1D 32 A1
Old Court Pl KENS W8 ....26 C5
Old Dairy Ms BAL SW12 ....152 A1
    KTTN * NW5 ....74 B3
Old Devonshire Rd BAL SW12 ....134 B5
Old Dock Cl RCH/KEW TW9 ....110 A2

Old Dover Rd BKHTH/KID SE3 ....124 A3
Old Farm Av BFN/LL DA15 ....163 D1
Old Farm Rd West BFN/LL DA15 ......163 F2
Oldfield Gv DEPT SE8 ....103 D5
Oldfield Rd ACT W3 ....99 F3
    STNW/STAM N16 ....59 E5
    WLSDN NW10 ....69 F4
Old Fish Street HI BLKFR * EC4V 35 E1
Old Fleet La STP EC4M 22 C4
Old Ford Lock BOW * E3 ....80 A4
Old Ford Rd BETH E2 ....90 C1
    BOW E3 ....79 E5
Old Gloucester St BMSBY WC1N 21 D2
Oldham Ter ACT W3 ....98 C2
Oldhill St STNW/STAM N16 ....60 A3
Old Hospital Cl TOOT SW17 ....151 F1
Old House Cl WIM/MER SW19 ....149 E5
Old Jamaica Rd STHWK SE1 ....102 A4
Old James St PECK SE15 ....138 B1
Old Jewry LOTH * EC2R 24 A5
Old Kent Rd STHWK SE1 ....119 D3
Old Manor Wy ELTH/MOT SE9 ....161 F5
Old Manor Yd ECT SW5 ....38 C5
Old Market Sq BETH E2 ....13 E3
Old Marylebone Rd CAMTN NW1 ....17 D3
Old Mill Rd WOOL/PLUM SE18 ....127 D2
Old Mitre Ct EMB * EC4Y 22 B5
Old Montague St WCHPL E1 ....90 A4
Old Nichol St BETH E2 ....13 E5
Old North St FSBYW * WC1X 21 E2
Old Oak Common La
    WLSDN NW10 ....87 E3
Old Oak La WLSDN NW10 ....87 F2
Old Oak Rd ACT W3 ....99 F1
The Old Orch HAMP * NW3 ....73 F1
Old Paradise St LBTH SE11 ....45 E4
Old Park Av BAL SW12 ....134 A4
Old Park La MYFR/PICC W1J 30 B4
Old Pye St WEST SW1P 44 A2
Old Quebec St MBLAR W1H 17 F5
Old Queen St STJSPK SW1H 44 B1
Oldridge Rd BAL SW12 ....134 A5
Old Rd LEW SE13 ....141 E2
Old Royal Free Pl IS * N1 ....76 A5
Old Royal Free Sq IS * N1 ....76 A5
Old School Crs FSTGT E7 ....82 A3
Old Seacoal La STP * EC4M 22 C5
Old South Lambeth Rd
    VX/NE * SW8 ....117 E3
Old Sq LINN WC2A 21 F4
Old Stable Ms FSBYPK * N4 ....58 B1
Oldstead Rd BMLY BR1 ....159 D4
Old St FSBYE EC1V 11 E5
    PLSTW E13 ....94 B1
Old Town CLAP SW4 ....134 C1
Old Tramyard WOOL/PLUM SE18 ....109 E5
Old Woolwich Rd GNWCH SE10 ....123 D3
Old York Rd WAND/EARL SW18 ....132 B3
O'Leary Sq WCHPL E1 ....90 C4
Olga St BOW E3 ....91 E1
Olinda Rd STNW/STAM N16 ....59 F1
Oliphant St NKENS W10 ....89 E2
Oliver Cl CHSWK W4 ....110 B2
Oliver Gdns EHAM E6 ....95 E4
Olive Rd CRICK NW2 ....70 C1
    PLSTW E13 ....94 C2
Oliver Rd LEY E10 ....62 B4
Oliver's Yd STLK EC1Y 12 B5
Ollerton Gn BOW E3 ....79 F5
Ollgar Cl ACT W3 ....99 F2
Olliffe St POP/IOD E14 ....104 C4
Olmar St STHWK SE1 ....120 A2

Olney Rd *WALW* SE17 ....118 B2
Olven Rd *WOOL/PLUM* SE18 ......126 C3
Olympia Wy *WKENS* W14 ....101 E4
Olympic Wy *WBLY* HA9 ....68 A1
Oman Av *CRICK* NW2 ....70 C2
O'Meara St *STHWK* SE1 ....35 F4
Omega Pl *IS* N1 ....9 D2
Omega St *NWCR* SE14 ....121 F4
Ommaney Rd *NWCR* SE14 ....121 D3
Ondine Rd *EDUL* SE22 ....137 F2
Onega Ga *BERM/RHTH* SE16 ....103 E3
One Tree Cl *FSTH* SE23 ....138 C4
Ongar Rd *FUL/PGN* SW6 ....114 A2
Onra Rd *LEY* E10 ....62 A2
Onslow Gdns *SKENS* SW7 ....40 A5
Onslow Ms East *SKENS* SW7 ....40 A5
Onslow Ms West *SKENS* SW7 ....40 A5
Onslow Sq *SKENS* SW7 ....40 A5
Onslow St *FARR* EC1M 22 B1
Ontario St *STHWK* SE1 ....47 D3
Ontario Wy *POP/IOD* E14 ....104 A1
Opal Cl *CAN/RD* E16 ....95 D5
Openview *WAND/EARL* SW18 ......150 C1
Ophir Ter *PECK* SE15 ....120 A4
Oppenheim Rd *LEW* SE13 ....122 C5
Oppidans Rd *HAMP* NW3 ....73 F4
Orange Gv *WAN* E11 ....63 E5
Orange Pl *BERM/RHTH* SE16 ......102 C4
Orangery La *ELTH/MOT* SE9 ......143 F3
Orange St *LSQ/SEVD* WC2H 32 B2
Oratory La *CHEL* * SW3 ....115 D1
Orbain Rd *FUL/PGN* SW6 ....113 E3
Orbel St *BTSEA* SW11 ....115 E4
Orb St *WALW* SE17 ....48 A5
Orchard Cl *CRICK* NW2 ....52 A5
   FSTH SE23 ....138 C4
   NKENS W10 ....89 E4
Orchard Dr *BKHTH/KID* SE3 ......123 E5
Orchard Hl *LEW* SE13 ....122 B5
Orchard Ms *IS* N1 ....77 D4
Orchard Pl *POP/IOD* E14 ....105 E1
Orchard Ri *RCHPK/HAM* TW10 ....128 B2
Orchard Ri East *BFN/LL* DA15 ....145 E3
Orchard Ri West *BFN/LL* DA15 ....145 E5
Orchard Rd *HGT* N6 ....56 B2
   RCH/KEW TW9 ....128 A1
   SCUP DA14 ....163 E4
Orchardson St *STJWD* NW8 ....16 A1
Orchard Sq *WKENS* * W14 ....113 F1
Orchard St *MBLAR* W1H 18 A5
Orchard Ter *WLSDN* * NW10 ....69 F1
The Orchard *BKHTH/KID* SE3 ......123 D5
   CHSWK W4 ....99 D5
Orchid St *SHB* W12 ....100 A1
Orde Hall St *BMSBY* * WC1N 21 E2
Ordell Rd *BOW* E3 ....91 F1
Ordnance Crs *GNWCH* SE10 ....105 E3
Ordnance Hl *STJWD* NW8 ....73 D5
Ordnance Ms *STJWD* NW8 ....4 B1
Ordnance Rd *CAN/RD* E16 ....93 F4
   WOOL/PLUM SE18 ....126 A2
Oregon Av *MNPK* E12 ....83 F1
Orestes Ms *KIL/WHAMP* * NW6 ....72 A2
Orford Rd *CAT* SE6 ....158 B3
Oriel Ct *HAMP* NW3 ....72 C1
Oriel Dr *BARN* SW13 ....112 C2
Oriel Rd *HOM* E9 ....79 D3
Oriental Rd *CAN/RD* E16 ....107 D2
Orient St *LBTH* SE11 ....46 C4
Orient Wy *CLPT* E5 ....61 D5
   LEY E10 ....62 A5
Orissa Rd *WOOL/PLUM* SE18 ......127 E1
Orkney St *BTSEA* SW11 ....116 A1

Orlando Rd *CLAP* SW4 ....134 C1
Orleston Ms *HOLWY* N7 ....76 A3
Orleston Rd *HOLWY* N7 ....76 A3
Ormanton Rd *SYD* SE26 ....156 A4
Orme Ct *BAY/PAD* W2 ....26 C2
Orme Court Ms *BAY/PAD* * W2 ......27 D2
Orme La *BAY/PAD* W2 ....26 C2
Ormeley Rd *BAL* SW12 ....134 B5
Orme Sq *BAY/PAD* W2 ....26 C2
Orme Square Ga *KENS* W8 ....26 C2
Ormiston Gv *SHB* W12 ....100 B2
Ormiston Rd *GNWCH* SE10 ....124 A1
Ormond Cl *BMSBY* WC1N 21 D2
Ormonde Ct *STJWD* * NW8 ....73 F5
Ormonde Ga *CHEL* * SW3 ....115 F1
Ormonde Rd *MORT/ESHN* SW14 ..128 B1
Ormonde Ter *STJWD* NW8 ....73 F5
Ormond Rd *ARCH* N19 ....57 E3
Ormond Yd *STJS* SW1Y 31 F3
Ormsby Pl *STNW/STAM* N16 ....59 F5
Ormsby St *BETH* E2 ....13 E1
Ormside St *PECK* SE15 ....120 C2
Ornan Rd *HAMP* NW3 ....73 E2
Oronsay Wk *IS* * N1 ....76 C3
Orpheus St *CMBW* SE5 ....119 D4
Orsett Ms *BAY/PAD* W2 ....15 E4
Orsett St *LBTH* SE11 ....117 F1
Orsett Ter *BAY/PAD* W2 ....15 E4
Orsman Rd *IS* N1 ....77 E5
Orton St *WAP* E1W 102 A2
Orville Rd *BTSEA* SW11 ....115 D5
Orwell Rd *PLSTW* E13 ....94 C1
Osbaldeston Rd *STNW/STAM* N16 ..60 A4
Osberton Rd *LEE/GVPK* SE12 ......142 A3
Osbert St *WEST* SW1P 44 A5
Osborn Cl *HACK* E8 ....78 A5
Osborne Rd *ACT* W3 ....98 B3
   CRICK NW2 ....70 B3
   FSBYPK N4 ....58 A3
   FSTGT E7 ....82 B2
   HOM E9 ....79 F3
   LEY E10 ....62 B5
Osborne Ter *TOOT* * SW17 ....152 A5
Osborn La *FSTH* SE23 ....139 E5
Osborn St *WCHPL* E1 ....25 F3
Osborn Ter *BKHTH/KID* SE3 ......141 F2
Oscar Faber Pl *IS* * N1 ....77 E4
Oscar St *DEPT* SE8 ....122 A4
Oseney Crs *KTTN* NW5 ....74 C3
O'Shea Gv *BOW* E3 ....79 F5
Osiers Rd *WAND/EARL* SW18 ......132 A2
Osier St *WCHPL* E1 ....90 C3
Osier Wy *LEY* E10 ....62 B5
Oslac Rd *CAT* SE6 ....158 B5
Osman Rd *HMSMTH* * W6 ....100 C4
Osmund St *SHB* W12 ....87 F5
Osnaburgh St *CAMTN* NW1 ....19 D1
Osnaburgh Ter *CAMTN* NW1 ....7 D5
Osprey Cl *EHAM* E6 ....95 E4
Osprey Est *BERM/RHTH* SE16 ......103 D5
Ospringe Rd *KTTN* NW5 ....74 C1
Ossian Rd *FSBYPK* N4 ....57 F2
Ossington Buildings *MHST* * W1U ..18 A3
Ossington Cl *BAY/PAD* * W2 ....26 B2
Ossington St *BAY/PAD* W2 ....26 B1
Ossory Rd *STHWK* SE1 ....120 A2
Ossulston St *CAMTN* NW1 ....8 B2
Ostade Rd *BRXS/STRHM* SW2 ......135 F5
Osten Ms *SKENS* SW7 ....39 D3
Osterley Rd *STNW/STAM* N16 ....77 E1
Oswald's Md *CLPT* E5 ....79 E1
Oswald St *CLPT* E5 ....61 D5
Oswald Ter *CRICK* * NW2 ....52 C5

Osward Rd *BAL* SW12 ....151 F2
Oswin St *LBTH* SE11 ....47 D4
Oswyth Rd *CMBW* SE5 ....119 E5
Otford Cls *BROCKY* SE4 ....139 F4
Othello Cl *LBTH* SE11 ....118 B1
Otis St *BOW* E3 ....92 C2
Otley Dr *GNTH/NBYPK* IG2 ....66 B1
Otley Rd *CAN/RD* E16 ....94 C5
Otley Ter *CLPT* E5 ....60 C4
Ottaway St *CLPT* E5 ....60 A5
Otterden St *CAT* SE6 ....158 A4
Otto Cl *SYD* * SE26 ....156 B2
Otto St *WALW* SE17 ....118 B2
Oulton Crs *BARK* IG11 ....85 F3
Ouseley Rd *BAL* SW12 ....151 F1
Outer Cir *CAMTN* NW1 ....5 F1
Outgate Rd *WLSDN* NW10 ....69 F4
Outram Pl *IS* N1 ....75 E5
Outram Rd *EHAM* E6 ....83 E5
Outwich St *HDTCH* * EC3A 25 D4
Oval *VX/NE* SW8 ....117 F3
Oval Rd *CAMTN* NW1 ....74 B5
The Oval *BETH* E2 ....90 B1
Oval Wy *LBTH* SE11 ....117 F1
Overbury Rd *FSBYPK* N4 ....59 D1
Overbury St *CLPT* E5 ....79 D1
Overcliff Rd *LEW* SE13 ....140 A1
Overdown Rd *CAT* SE6 ....158 A4
Overhill Rd *EDUL* SE22 ....138 A5
Overlea Rd *CLPT* E5 ....60 A2
Overmead *ELTH/MOT* SE9 ....145 D5
Overstone Rd *HMSMTH* W6 ....100 C5
Overton Cl *WLSDN* NW10 ....68 C3
Overton Dr *WAN* E11 ....64 B2
Overton Rd *BRXN/ST* SW9 ....118 A5
   LEY E10 ....61 E3
Ovex Cl *POP/IOD* E14 ....104 C1
Ovington Gdns *CHEL* SW3 ....41 D3
Ovington Ms *CHEL* SW3 ....41 D3
Ovington Sq *CHEL* SW3 ....41 D3
Ovington St *CHEL* SW3 ....41 D3
Owen's Ct *FSBYE* EC1V 10 C3
Owen's Rw *FSBYE* EC1V 10 C3
Owen St *FSBYE* EC1V 10 C2
Owens Wy *FSTH* SE23 ....139 E5
Owen Wy *WLSDN* NW10 ....68 C3
Owgan Cl *CMBW* SE5 ....119 D3
Oxberry Av *FUL/PGN* SW6 ....113 E5
Oxendon St *SOHO/SHAV* * W1D 32 A2
Oxenford St *PECK* SE15 ....137 F1
Oxestalls Rd *DEPT* SE8 ....121 E1
Oxford Ct *MANHO* EC4N 36 A1
Oxford Gdns *CHSWK* W4 ....110 A1
   NKENS W10 ....89 D5
Oxford Ga *HMSMTH* * W6 ....101 D5
Oxford Rd *FSBYPK* N4 ....58 A3
   IL IG1 ....84 C1
   KIL/WHAMP NW6 ....2 B1
   PUT/ROE SW15 ....131 E2
   SRTFD E15 ....81 D3
Oxford Rd North *CHSWK* W4 ....110 B1
Oxford Rd South *CHSWK* W4 ....110 A1
Oxford Sq *BAY/PAD* W2 ....16 C5
Oxford St *MYFR/PKLN* W1K 18 A5
Oxgate Court Pde *CRICK* * NW2 ....52 B4
Oxgate Gdns *CRICK* NW2 ....52 B5
Oxgate La *CRICK* NW2 ....52 B4
Oxleas *EHAM* E6 ....96 B5
Oxleas Cl *WELL* DA16 ....127 D5
Oxley Cl *STHWK* SE1 ....119 F1
Oxleys Rd *CRICK* NW2 ....52 B5
Oxonian St *EDUL* SE22 ....137 F2
Oyster Catchers Cl *CAN/RD* E16 ....94 B5

Oyster Rw *WCHPL* E1 ....90 C5
Ozolins Wy *CAN/RD* E16 ....93 F5

P

Pace Pl *WCHPL* E1 ....90 B5
Pacific Rd *CAN/RD* E16 ....94 A5
Packington Sq *IS* N1 ....76 C5
Packington St *IS* N1 ....76 B5
Packmores Rd *ELTH/MOT* SE9 ....145 D3
Padbury Ct *BETH* E2 ....13 F4
Paddenswick Rd *HMSMTH* W6 ....100 A4
Paddington Gn *BAY/PAD* W2 ....16 A3
Paddington St *MHST* W1U 18 A2
Paddock Cl *BKHTH/KID* SE3 ....142 A1
   SYD SE26 ....157 D4
Paddock Rd *CRICK* NW2 ....52 A5
The Paddocks *WBLY* HA9 ....50 B4
Padfield Rd *CMBW* SE5 ....136 C1
Pagden St *VX/NE* SW8 ....116 B4
Pageant Crs *BERM/RHTH* SE16 ....103 F2
Page St *WEST* SW1P 44 B4
Page's Wk *STHWK* SE1 ....48 C4
Pages Yd *CHSWK* * W4 ....111 E2
Paget Ri *WOOL/PLUM* SE18 ....126 A3
Paget Rd *IL* IG1 ....84 B1
   STNW/STAM N16 ....59 D3
Paget St *FSBYE* EC1V 10 C3
Paget Ter *WOOL/PLUM* SE18 ....126 B2
Pagnell St *NWCR* SE14 ....121 F3
Pagoda Gdns *BKHTH/KID* SE3 ....123 D5
Paignton Rd *SEVS/STOTM* N15 ....59 E1
Painsthorpe Rd *STNW/STAM* N16 ....59 E5
Pakeman St *HOLWY* N7 ....58 A5
Pakenham Cl *BAL* SW12 ....152 A1
Pakenham St *FSBYW* WC1X 9 F4
Palace Av *KENS* W8 ....27 D4
Palace Ct *BAY/PAD* W2 ....26 C1
Palace Garden Ms *KENS* W8 ....26 B3
Palace Gardens Ter *KENS* W8 ....26 B3
Palace Ga *KENS* W8 ....39 E1
Palace Gn *KENS* W8 ....26 C4
Palace Ms *FUL/PGN* * SW6 ....113 F3
Palace Pl *WESTW* SW1E 43 F3
Palace Rd *BRXS/STRHM* SW2 ....153 F1
Palace St *WESTW* SW1E 43 E2
Palace Vw *LEE/GVPK* SE12 ....160 A2
Palamos Rd *LEY* E10 ....62 A3
Palatine Av *STNW/STAM* N16 ....77 E1
Palatine Rd *STNW/STAM* N16 ....77 E1
Palemead Cl *FUL/PGN* SW6 ....113 D4
Palermo Rd *WLSDN* NW10 ....88 C3
Palewell Common Dr
   MORT/ESHN SW14 ....129 D3
Palewell Pk *MORT/ESHN* SW14 ....129 D3
Palfrey Pl *BRXN/ST* SW9 ....117 F3
Palgrave Gdns *CAMTN* NW1 ....5 D5
Palgrave Rd *SHB* W12 ....99 F4
Palissy St *BETH* E2 ....13 E4
Pallet Wy *WOOL/PLUM* SE18 ....125 E4
Palliser Rd *HMSMTH* W6 ....113 E1
Pall Ml *STJS* SW1Y 32 A4
Pall Ml East *STJS* SW1Y 32 A3
Pall Mall Pl *STJS* SW1Y 31 F4
Palm Cl *LEY* E10 ....62 B5
Palmer Pl *HOLWY* N7 ....76 A2
Palmer Rd *PLSTW* E13 ....94 B3
Palmers Rd *BETH* E2 ....91 D1
   MORT/ESHN SW14 ....128 C1
Palmerston Crs *WOOL/PLUM* SE18 ....126 C2

Palmerston Rd *ACT* W3 ....98 C4
  FSTGT E7 ....82 B2
  KIL/WHAMP NW6 ....71 F4
  MORT/ESHN SW14 ....128 C2
Palmerston Wy *VX/NE* * SW8 ....116 B3
Palmer St *STJSPK* SW1H 44 A2
Pancras La *MANHO* EC4N 25 F5
Pancras St *CAMTN* NW1 ....8 A1
Pandora Rd *KIL/WHAMP* NW6 .....72 A3
Panfield Ms *GNTH/NBYPK* IG2 ....66 A1
Pangbourne Av *NKENS* * W10 .....88 C4
Panmure Cl *HBRY* N5 ....76 B1
Panmure Rd *SYD* SE26 ....156 B3
Pansy Gdns *SHB* W12 ....100 A1
Panther Dr *WLSDN* NW10 ....69 D2
Panton St *LSQ/SEVD* WC2H 32 B2
Paper Buildings *EMB* * EC4Y 34 B1
Papillons Wk *BKHTH/KID* SE3 ...124 A5
Papworth Gdns *HOLWY* N7 ....75 F2
Papworth Wy *BRXS/STRHM* SW2 .136 A5
Parade Ms *BRXS/STRHM* SW2 ....154 B2
Parade Ter *CDALE/KGS* * NW9 ....52 A1
The Parade *BROCKY* * SE4 ....121 F4
  BTSEA * SW11 ....133 D2
  CMBW * SE5 ....137 E1
  FSBYPK * N4 ....58 A4
  RCH/KEW * TW9 ....128 A1
  SYD * SE26 ....156 B3
Paradise Pas *HOLWY* N7 ....76 A2
Paradise Rd *CLAP* SW4 ....117 E5
Paradise Rw *BETH* * E2 ....90 B2
Paradise St *BERM/RHTH* SE16 ...102 B3
Paradise Wk *CHEL* SW3 ....115 F2
Paragon Cl *CAN/RD* E16 ....94 A5
Paragon Ms *WALW* SE17 ....48 B4
Paragon Pl *BKHTH/KID* SE3 ....123 F5
Paragon Rd *HACK* E8 ....78 B3
The Paragon *BKHTH/KID* SE3 ....124 A5
Parbury Rd *FSTH* SE23 ....139 E4
Pardoner St *STHWK* SE1 ....48 B2
Pardon St *FSBYE* EC1V 11 D5
Parfett St *WCHPL* E1 ....90 A4
Parfrey St *HMSMTH* W6 ....112 C2
Parham Dr *GNTH/NBYPK* IG2 ......66 B1
Paris Gdn *STHWK* SE1 ....34 C3
Parish Gate Dr *BFN/LL* DA15 .....145 E4
Parish Whf *WOOL/PLUM* SE18....107 E5
Park Ap *BERM/RHTH* * SE16 ......102 C4
Park Av *CRICK* NW2 ....70 C3
  EHAM E6 ....84 A5
  GLDGN NW11 ....54 B3
  IL IG1 ....66 A4
  MORT/ESHN SW14 ....129 D2
Park Av North *WLSDN* NW10 ......70 B2
Park Cl *CRICK* NW2 ....52 A5
  HOM E9 ....78 C5
  SKENS * SW7 ....41 E1
  WKENS W14 ....101 F4
Park Ct *DUL* * SE21 ....155 D3
Park Crs *REGST* W1B 18 C1
Park Crescent Ms East *REGST* W1B ...19 D1
Park Crescent Ms West
  CAVSQ/HST W1G 18 C1
Parkcroft Rd *LEE/GVPK* SE12 ....141 F5
Parkdale Rd *WOOL/PLUM* SE18...127 E4
Park Dr *ACT* W3 ....98 A4
  CHARL SE7 ....125 E1
  GLDGN NW11 ....54 B3
  MORT/ESHN SW14 ....129 D3
Park End *HAMP* NW3 ....73 E1
Parker Cl *CAN/RD* E16 ....107 E2
Parker Ms *HOL/ALD* * WC2B 21 D4
Parke Rd *BARN* SW13 ....112 A4

Parker's Rw *STHWK* SE1 ....49 F1
Parker St *CAN/RD* E16 ....107 E2
  HOL/ALD WC2B 21 D4
Parkfield Av *MORT/ESHN* SW14 ..129 E2
Parkfield Rd *NWCR* SE14 ....121 F4
  WLSDN NW10 ....70 A4
Parkfields *PUT/ROE* SW15 ....130 C2
Parkfields Av *CDALE/KGS* NW9 ...51 D3
Parkfield St *IS* N1 ....10 B1
Parkgate *BKHTH/KID* SE3 ....141 F1
Parkgate Gdns *MORT/ESHN* SW14 .129 D3
Parkgate Rd *BTSEA* SW11 ....115 E3
Park Gv *SRTFD* E15 ....82 A5
Park Grove Rd *WAN* E11 ....63 E4
Park Hall Rd *DUL* SE21 ....155 D2
Parkham St *BTSEA* SW11 ....115 D4
Park Hl *CLAP* SW4 ....135 D3
  FSTH SE23 ....156 B2
Parkhill Rd *BFN/LL* DA15 ....163 E3
  HAMP NW3 ....73 F2
Parkhill Wk *HAMP* NW3 ....73 F2
Parkholme Rd *HACK* E8 ....78 A3
Parkhouse St *CMBW* SE5 ....119 D3
Parkhurst Rd *HOLWY* N7 ....75 E1
  MNPK E12 ....84 A1
Parklands *HGT* N6 ....56 B2
Parklands Cl *MORT/ESHN* SW14 .128 C3
Parklands Rd *TOOT* SW17 ....152 B5
Park La *MBLAR* W1H 29 F1
  SRTFD * E15 ....80 C5
Parkmead *PUT/ROE* SW15 ....130 B4
Park Ms *NKENS* W10 ....89 E1
Park Pde *ACT* * W3 ....98 A4
  WLSDN NW10 ....87 F1
Park Pl *ACT* W3 ....98 A5
  POP/IOD E14 ....104 A2
  WHALL SW1A 31 E4
Park Place Vls *BAY/PAD* W2 ....15 F2
Park Rise Rd *FSTH* SE23 ....157 E1
Park Rd *CAMTN* NW1 ....17 F1
  CDALE/KGS NW9 ....51 D3
  CDALE/KGS NW9 ....52 A2
  CHSWK W4 ....111 D2
  EHAM E6 ....82 C5
  IL IG1 ....67 D5
  LEY E10 ....62 A3
  MNPK E12 ....83 D1
  SRTFD E15 ....82 A5
  STJWD NW8 ....5 D4
  WAN E11 ....64 B3
  WLSDN * NW10 ....69 E5
Park Rd East *ACT* W3 ....98 C3
Park Rd North *ACT* W3 ....98 B3
  CHSWK W4 ....111 D2
Park Rw *GNWCH* SE10................123 D2
Park Royal Rd *WLSDN* NW10 ......86 C2
Park Side *CRICK* NW2 ....52 A5
Parkside *BKHTH/KID* * SE3 ....123 F3
  WIM/MER SW19 ....149 D4
Parkside Av *WIM/MER* SW19 .....149 D5
Parkside Crs *HOLWY* N7 ....58 A5
Parkside Est *HOM* * E9 ....79 D5
Parkside Gdns *WIM/MER* SW19 ..149 D4
Parkside St *BTSEA* SW11 ....116 A4
Park Sq East *CAMTN* NW1 ....6 C5
Park Square Ms *CAMTN* NW1 .....18 C1
Park Sq West *CAMTN* NW1 ....6 C5
Parkstead Rd *PUT/ROE* SW15 ...130 A3
Park Steps *BAY/PAD* * W2 ....29 D1
Parkstone Rd *PECK* * SE15 ....120 A5
Park St *MYFR/PKLN* W1K 30 A2
  STHWK SE1 ....35 E3

The Park GLDGN NW11 ....54 B3
HGT N6 ....56 A2
SCUP DA14 ....163 F5
Parkthorne Rd BAL SW12 ....135 D5
Park Vw ACT W3 ....86 C4
WBLY HA9 ....68 B2
Park View Est HBRY * N5 ....76 C1
Park View Rd CRICK NW2 ....69 F1
ELTH/MOT SE9 ....162 B1
Park Village East CAMTN NW1 ....6 C1
Park Village West CAMTN NW1 ....6 C1
Park Vls TOOT * SW17 ....151 E5
Parkville Rd FUL/PGN SW6 ....113 F3
Park Vis GNWCH SE10 ....123 D2
Park Wk WBPTN SW10 ....114 C2
Parkway CAMTN NW1 ....74 B5
GDMY/SEVK IG3 ....67 F5
Park West BAY/PAD W2 ....17 D4
Park West Pl BAY/PAD W2 ....17 D4
Parkwood Ms HGT N6 ....56 B1
Parkwood Rd WIM/MER SW19 ....149 F5
Parliament Ct WCHPL * E1 ....25 D3
Parliament Hl HAMP NW3 ....73 E1
Parliament Hill Flds KTTN * NW5 ....56 A5
Parliament Sq WEST SW1P 44 C5
Parliament St WHALL SW1A 32 C5
Parma Crs BTSEA SW11 ....133 F2
Parmiter St BETH E2 ....90 B1
Parnell Cl SHB W12 ....100 B4
Parnell Rd BOW E3 ....79 F5
Parnham St POP/IOD * E14 ....91 E5
Parolles Rd ARCH N19 ....56 C3
Parr Rd EHAM E6 ....83 D5
Parr St IS N1 ....12 A1
Parry Av EHAM E6 ....95 F5
Parry Pl WOOL/PLUM SE18 ....108 B5
Parry Rd NKENS W10 ....89 E2
Parry St VX/NE SW8 ....117 E2
Parsifal Rd KIL/WHAMP NW6 ....72 A2
Parsonage St POP/IOD E14 ....104 C5
Parsons Gn FUL/PGN SW6 ....114 A4
Parsons Green La FUL/PGN SW6 ......114 A4
Parsons Rd PLSTW E13 ....94 C1
Parthenia Rd FUL/PGN SW6 ....114 A4
Partridge Cl CAN/RD E16 ....95 D4
Partridge Gn ELTH/MOT SE9 ....162 A3
Partridge Rd SCUP DA14 ....163 E3
Pascal St VX/NE SW8 ....117 D3
Pascoe Rd LEW SE13 ....141 D3
Pasley Cl WALW SE17 ....118 B1
Passey Pl ELTH/MOT SE9 ....143 F4
Passfield Dr POP/IOD * E14 ....92 B1
Passmore St BGVA SW1W 42 A5
Paston Crs LEE/GVPK SE12 ....142 B5
Pastor St LBTH SE11 ....47 D4
Pasture Rd CAT SE6 ....159 E1
Patcham Ter VX/NE SW8 ....116 B4
Paternoster Rw STP EC4M 23 D5
Pater St KENS W8 ....38 A3
Patience Rd BTSEA SW11 ....115 E5
Patio Cl CLAP SW4 ....135 D4
Patmore St VX/NE SW8 ....116 C4
Patmos Rd BRXN/ST SW9 ....118 B3
Paton Cl BOW E3 ....92 A2
Patrick Rd PLSTW E13 ....94 C2
Patriot Sq BETH E2 ....90 B1
Patrol Pl CAT SE6 ....140 B4
Patshull Pl KTTN NW5 ....74 C3
Patshull Rd KTTN NW5 ....74 C3
Pattenden Rd FSTH SE23 ....157 F1
Patten Rd WAND/EARL SW18 ....133 E5
Patterdale Rd PECK SE15 ....120 C3
Pattina Wk BERM/RHTH SE16 ....103 E2

Pattison Rd CRICK NW2 ....54 A5
Paul Cl SRTFD E15 ....81 E4
Paulet Rd CMBW SE5 ....118 B5
Paul Julius Cl POP/IOD E14 ....105 D1
Paul Robeson Cl EHAM E6 ....96 A2
Paul St SDTCH EC2A 12 C5
SRTFD E15 ....81 E5
Paultons Sq CHEL SW3 ....115 D2
Paultons St CHEL SW3 ....115 D2
Pauntley St ARCH N19 ....56 C3
Paveley Dr BTSEA SW11 ....115 E3
Paveley St CAMTN NW1 ....5 D5
The Pavement CLAP SW4 ....134 C2
WAN * E11 ....62 C3
WNWD * SE27 ....154 C4
Pavilion Pde SHB * W12 ....88 C5
Pavilion Rd IL IG1 ....66 F2
KTBR SW1X 41 F1
Pavilion St KTBR SW1X 41 F3
The Pavilion VX/NE SW8 ....117 D3
Pavillion Ter SHB * W12 ....88 C5
Pawsey Cl PLSTW E13 ....82 A5
Paxton Pl WNWD SE27 ....155 E4
Paxton Rd CHSWK W4 ....111 E2
FSTH SE23 ....157 E3
Paxton Ter PIM SW1V 116 B2
Payne Cl BARK IG11 ....85 E4
Paynell Ct BKHTH/KID SE3 ....141 E1
Payne Rd BOW E3 ....92 B1
Paynesfield Av MORT/ESHN SW14 ...129 D1
Payne St DEPT SE8 ....121 F2
Paynes Wk HMSMTH W6 ....113 E2
Peabody Av PIM * SW1V 116 B1
Peabody Cl GNWCH * SE10 ....122 B4
PIM SW1V 116 B1
Peabody Cottages HNHL * SE24 ......136 C5
Peabody Est BTSEA * SW11 ....133 E2
CHEL * SW3 ....115 E2
CLKNW * EC1R 22 B1
CMBW * SE5 ....119 D4
FUL/PGN * SW6 ....114 A2
HMSMTH * W6 ....112 C1
HNHL SE24 ....136 B5
NKENS * W10 ....88 C4
STHWK * SE1 ....34 B3
STHWK * SE1 ....35 E3
STLK * EC1Y 23 F1
Peabody Hl DUL SE21 ....154 B1
Peabody Sq IS * N1 ....76 C5
Peabody Ter CLKNW * EC1R 22 B1
Peace Gv WBLY HA9 ....50 B5
Peace St WOOL/PLUM SE18 ....126 A2
Peach Rd NKENS W10 ....89 D2
Peachum Rd BKHTH/KID SE3 ....123 F2
Peacock St WALW SE17 ....47 D5
Peacock Yd WALW SE17 ....47 D5
Peak Hl SYD SE26 ....156 C4
Peak Hill Av SYD SE26 ....156 C4
Peak Hill Gdns SYD SE26 ....156 C4
The Peak SYD SE26 ....156 C3
Pearcefield Av FSTH SE23 ....156 C1
Pear Cl NWCR SE14 ....121 E3
Pearcroft Rd WAN E11 ....63 D4
Peardon St VX/NE SW8 ....116 B5
Pearfield Rd FSTH SE23 ....157 E3
Pear Gv WAN E11 ....63 D5
Pearl Cl CRICK NW2 ....53 D2
EHAM E6 ....96 A5
Pearl St WAP E1W 102 B2
Pearman St STHWK SE1 ....46 B2
Pear Pl STHWK SE1 ....34 A5
Pearscroft Ct FUL/PGN SW6 ....114 B4
Pearscroft Rd FUL/PGN SW6 ....114 B5

Pearson's Av *NWCR* SE14 ....**122** A4
Pearson St *BETH* E2 ....**13** E1
Pear Tree Cl *BETH* E2 ....**77** F5
Pear Tree La *CLKNW* EC1R **22** B1
Peartree La *WAP* * E1W **102** C1
Peartree St *FSBYE* EC1V **11** D5
Peartree Wy *GNWCH* SE10 ....**106** A5
Peary Pl *BETH* E2 ....**90** C2
Peatfield Cl *BFN/LL* DA15 ....**163** B5
Peckarmans Wd *DUL* SE21 ....**156** A3
Peckett Sq *HBRY* * N5 ....**76** C1
Peckford Pl *BRXN/ST* SW9 ....**118** A3
Peckham Gv *PECK* SE15 ....**119** E3
Peckham High St *PECK* SE15 ....**120** A4
Peckham Hill St *PECK* SE15 ....**120** A3
Peckham Park Rd *PECK* SE15 ....**120** A3
Peckham Rd *CMBW* SE5 ....**119** E4
Peckham Rye *EDUL* SE22 ....**138** A2
Pecks Yd *WCHPL* * E1 ....**25** E2
Peckwater St *KTTN* NW5 ....**74** C2
Pedlars Wk *HOLWY* * N7 ....**75** E2
Pedley St *BETH* E2 ....**90** A3
  WCHPL E1 ....**25** F1
Pedro St *CLPT* E5 ....**61** D3
Peek Crs *WIM/MER* SW19 ....**149** D5
Peel Gv *BETH* E2 ....**90** C1
Peel Pas *KENS* * W8 ....**26** A4
Peel Prec *KIL/WHAMP* NW6 ....**89** F1
Peel St *KENS* W8 ....**26** A4
Peerless St *FSBYE* EC1V **12** A4
Pegasus Cl *STNW/STAM* * N16 ....**77** D1
Pegasus Pl *FUL/PGN* SW6 ....**114** A4
  LBTH * SE11 ....**118** A2
Pegley Gdns *LEE/GVPK* SE12 ....**160** A2
Pegwell St *WOOL/PLUM* SE18 ....**127** E3
Pekin St *POP/IOD* E14 ....**92** A5
Peldon Wk *IS* * N1 ....**76** B5
Pelham Av *BARK* IG11 ....**85** F5
Pelham Cl *CMBW* SE5 ....**137** E1
Pelham Crs *SKENS* SW7 ....**40** C5
Pelham Pl *SKENS* SW7 ....**40** C5
Pelham Rd *IL* IG1 ....**67** D2
Pelham St *SKENS* SW7 ....**40** B4
Pelier St *WALW* SE17 ....**118** C2
Pelinore Rd *CAT* SE6 ....**159** E2
Pellant Rd *FUL/PGN* SW6 ....**113** E3
Pellatt Rd *EDUL* SE22 ....**137** F3
Pellerin Rd *STNW/STAM* N16 ....**77** E2
Pelling St *POP/IOD* E14 ....**91** F5
Pellipar Rd *WOOL/PLUM* SE18 ....**125** F1
Pelly Rd *PLSTW* E13 ....**82** A3
Pelter St *BETH* E2 ....**13** E5
Pelton Rd *GNWCH* SE10 ....**123** E1
Pember Rd *WLSDN* NW10 ....**89** D2
Pemberton Gdns *ARCH* N19 ....**56** C5
Pemberton Pl *HACK* E8 ....**78** B4
Pemberton Rw *FLST/FETLN* EC4A **22** B4
Pemberton Ter *ARCH* N19 ....**56** C5
Pembridge Crs *NTGHL* W11 ....**101** F1
Pembridge Gdns *BAY/PAD* W2 ....**26** A2
Pembridge Ms *NTGHL* W11 ....**26** A1
Pembridge Pl *BAY/PAD* W2 ....**26** B1
Pembridge Rd *NTGHL* W11 ....**26** A2
Pembridge Sq *BAY/PAD* W2 ....**26** A2
Pembridge Vls *NTGHL* W11 ....**26** A1
Pembroke Cl *KTBR* SW1X **42** B1
Pembroke Gdns *KENS* W8 ....**101** F4
Pembroke Gardens Cl *KENS* W8 ....**101** F4
Pembroke Ms *KENS* * W8 ....**38** A3
Pembroke Pl *KENS* * W8 ....**38** A3
Pembroke Rd *ECT* SW5 ....**38** A4
  EHAM E6 ....**95** F4
  GDMY/SEVK IG3 ....**67** D3
Pembroke Sq *KENS* W8 ....**38** A3
Pembroke St *IS* N1 ....**75** E4
Pembroke Ter *STJWD* * NW8 ....**73** D5
Pembroke Vls *KENS* W8 ....**38** A3
Pembroke Wk *KENS* W8 ....**38** A4
Pembrook Ms *BTSEA* * SW11 ....**133** D2
Pembury Cl *CLPT* * E5 ....**78** B2
Pembury Rd *CLPT* E5 ....**78** B2
Pemell Cl *WCHPL* E1 ....**90** C3
Penally Pl *IS* N1 ....**77** D5
Penang St *WAP* E1W **102** B2
Penarth St *PECK* SE15 ....**120** C2
Penberth Rd *CAT* SE6 ....**158** C2
Pencombe Ms *NTGHL* W11 ....**101** F1
Pencraig Wy *PECK* * SE15 ....**120** B2
Penda's Md *HOM* E9 ....**79** E1
Pendennis Rd *STRHM/NOR* SW16 ....**153** E4
Penderry Ri *CAT* SE6 ....**159** D2
Penderyn Wy *HOLWY* N7 ....**75** D1
Pendragon Rd *BMLY* BR1 ....**160** A3
Pendrell Rd *BROCKY* SE4 ....**139** E1
Pendrell St *WOOL/PLUM* SE18 ....**127** D2
Pendulum Ms *HACK* * E8 ....**77** F2
Penerley Rd *CAT* SE6 ....**158** B1
Penfold Pl *BAY/PAD* W2 ....**16** C2
Penfold St *STJWD* NW8 ....**16** B1
Penford Gdns *ELTH/MOT* SE9 ....**143** D2
Penford St *CMBW* SE5 ....**118** B5
Penge Rd *PLSTW* E13 ....**82** C4
Penhall Rd *CHARL* SE7 ....**107** D5
Peninsular Park Rd *CHARL* SE7 ....**124** A1
Pennack Rd *PECK* SE15 ....**119** F2
Pennant Ms *KENS* W8 ....**38** C4
Pennard Rd *SHB* W12 ....**100** C3
Penner Cl *WIM/MER* SW19 ....**149** E2
Pennethorne Cl *HOM* E9 ....**78** C5
Pennethorne Rd *PECK* SE15 ....**120** B3
Pennine Dr *CRICK* NW2 ....**53** D4
Pennine La *CRICK* NW2 ....**53** E4
Pennine Pde *CRICK* * NW2 ....**53** E4
Pennington St *WAP* E1W **102** B1
Pennington Wy *LEE/GVPK* SE12 ....**160** B2
Penn Rd *HOLWY* N7 ....**75** E2
Penn St *IS* N1 ....**77** D5
Pennyfields *POP/IOD* E14 ....**104** A1
Pennymoor Wk *MV/WKIL* W9 ....**89** F3
Pennyroyal Av *EHAM* E6 ....**96** A5
Penpoll Rd *HACK* E8 ....**78** B3
Penrhyn Crs
  MORT/ESHN * SW14 ....**128** C2
Penrith Cl *PUT/ROE* SW15 ....**131** E3
Penrith Pl *STRHM/NOR* SW16 ....**154** B1
Penrose Gv *WALW* SE17 ....**118** C1
Penrose St *WALW* SE17 ....**118** C1
Penryn St *CAMTN* NW1 ....**8** A1
Penry St *STHWK* SE1 ....**49** D5
Pensbury Pl *VX/NE* SW8 ....**116** C5
Pensbury St *VX/NE* SW8 ....**116** C5
Pensford Av *RCH/KEW* TW9 ....**110** A5
Penshurst Rd *HOM* E9 ....**79** D4
Pentland Cl *CRICK* NW2 ....**53** E4
Pentland St *WAND/EARL* SW18 ....**132** C4
Pentlow St *PUT/ROE* SW15 ....**112** C5
Pentney Rd *BAL* SW12 ....**152** C1
Penton Gv *IS* N1 ....**10** A2
Penton Pl *WALW* SE17 ....**47** D5
Penton Ri *FSBYW* WC1X **9** F3
Penton St *IS* N1 ....**10** A1
Pentonville Rd *IS* N1 ....**9** E2
Pentridge St *PECK* SE15 ....**119** F3
Penwith Rd *WAND/EARL* SW18 ....**150** B2
Penywern Rd *ECT* SW5 ....**114** A1
Penzance Pl *NTGHL* W11 ....**101** E2

Penzance St *NTGHL* W11	**101**	E2
Peony Gdns *SHB* W12	**100**	A1
Peploe Rd *KIL/WHAMP* NW6	**89**	D1
Pepper Cl *EHAM* E6	**95**	F4
Peppermead Sq *BROCKY* * SE4	**140**	A3
Peppermint Pl *WAN* E11	**63**	E5
Pepper St *POP/IOD* E14	**104**	B4
STHWK SE1	**35**	E5
Peppie Cl *STNW/STAM* N16	**59**	E4
Pepys Est *DEPT* SE8	**103**	E5
Pepys Park Est *DEPT* SE8	**103**	F5
Pepys Rd *NWCR* SE14	**121**	D4
Pepys St *TWRH* EC3N	**37**	D1
Perceval Av *HAMP* NW3	**73**	E2
Perch St *HACK* E8	**77**	F1
Percival Rd *MORT/ESHN* SW14	**128**	C3
Percival St *FSBYE* EC1V	**10**	C5
Percy Ms *FITZ* W1T	**20**	A3
Percy Rd *CAN/RD* E16	**93**	E4
SHB W12	**100**	A3
WAN E11	**63**	E2
Percy St *FITZ* W1T	**20**	A3
Peregrine Cl *WLSDN* NW10	**69**	D2
Peregrine Ct *WELL* DA16	**127**	F4
Perham Rd *WKENS* W14	**113**	E1
Peridot St *EHAM* E6	**95**	E4
Perifield *DUL* SE21	**154**	C1
Periton Rd *ELTH/MOT* SE9	**143**	D2
Perkin's Rents *WEST* SW1P	**44**	A2
Perkins Sq *STHWK* SE1	**35**	F3
Perks Cl *BKHTH/KID* SE3	**123**	E5
Perpins Rd *ELTH/MOT* SE9	**145**	E4
Perran Rd *BRXS/STRHM* SW2	**154**	B2
Perrers Rd *HMSMTH* W6	**100**	B4
Perrin's Ct *HAMP* * NW3	**72**	C1
Perrin's Wk *HAMP* NW3	**72**	C1
Perry Av *ACT* W3	**87**	D5
Perry Ct *SEVS/STOTM* * N15	**59**	E1
Perryfield Wy *CDALE/KGS* NW9	**51**	E1
Perry Hl *CAT* SE6	**157**	F2
Perrymans Farm Rd		
GNTH/NBYPK IG2	**67**	D1
Perrymead St *FUL/PGN* SW6	**114**	A4
Perryn Rd *ACT* W3	**99**	D1
BERM/RHTH SE16	**102**	B4
Perry Ri *FSTH* SE23	**157**	E3
Perry V *FSTH* SE23	**156**	C2
Persant Rd *CAT* SE6	**159**	E3
Perseverance Pl *BRXN/ST* * SW9	**118**	A3
Perth Av *CDALE/KGS* NW9	**51**	D2
Perth Rd *BARK* IG11	**97**	D1
FSBYPK N4	**58**	A3
GNTH/NBYPK IG2	**66**	B1
LEY E10	**61**	E3
PLSTW E13	**94**	B1
Perth Ter *GNTH/NBYPK* IG2	**66**	C2
Peter Av *WLSDN* NW10	**70**	B4
Peterboat Cl *GNWCH* SE10	**105**	E5
Peterborough Ms *FUL/PGN* SW6	**114**	A5
Peterborough Rd *FUL/PGN* SW6	**114**	A5
Peterborough Vls *FUL/PGN* SW6	**114**	B4
Petergate *BTSEA* SW11	**132**	C2
Peters Cl *WELL* DA16	**127**	E5
Petersfield Ri *PUT/ROE* SW15	**148**	B1
Petersfield Rd *ACT* W3	**98**	C3
Petersham La *SKENS* SW7	**39**	E2
Petersham Ms *SKENS* SW7	**39**	E3
Petersham Pl *SKENS* SW7	**39**	E3
Peter's Hl *BLKFR* EC4V	**35**	E1
Peterstow Cl *WIM/MER* SW19	**149**	E2
Peter St *SOHO/CST* W1F	**32**	A1
Petherton Rd *HBRY* N5	**76**	C2
Petiver Cl *HOM* * E9	**78**	C4
Petley Rd *HMSMTH* W6	**112**	C2
Peto Pl *CAMTN* NW1	**7**	D5
Petrie Cl *CRICK* * NW2	**71**	E3
Petros Gdns *HAMP* * NW3	**72**	B2
Petticoat Sq *WCHPL* E1	**25**	E4
Petticoat Tower *WCHPL* * E1	**25**	E4
Pettiward Cl *PUT/ROE* SW15	**130**	C2
Pettman Crs *THMD* SE28	**109**	D4
Pett St *CHARL* SE7	**107**	E5
Petty France *STJSPK* SW1H	**43**	F2
Petworth St *BTSEA* SW11	**115**	E4
Petyt Pl *CHEL* * SW3	**115**	E2
Petyward *CHEL* SW3	**41**	D5
Pevensey Rd *FSTGT* E7	**82**	A1
TOOT SW17	**151**	D4
Peyton Pl *GNWCH* SE10	**122**	C3
Pheasant Cl *CAN/RD* E16	**94**	B5
Phelp St *WALW* SE17	**119**	D2
Phene St *CHEL* SW3	**115**	E2
Philbeach Gdns *ECT* SW5	**114**	A1
Philchurch Pl *WCHPL* E1	**90**	A5
Philimore Cl *WOOL/PLUM* SE18	**127**	E1
Philippa Gdns *ELTH/MOT* SE9	**143**	D3
Philip Rd *PECK* SE15	**138**	A1
Philip St *PLSTW* E13	**94**	A3
Phillimore Gdns *KENS* W8	**38**	A1
WLSDN NW10	**70**	C5
Phillimore Gardens Cl *KENS* * W8	**38**	A2
Phillimore Pl *KENS* W8	**38**	A1
Phillimore Wk *KENS* W8	**38**	A2
Phillipp St *IS* N1	**77**	E5
Philpot La *FENCHST* EC3M	**36**	C1
Philpot St *WCHPL* * E1	**90**	B5
Phineas Pett Rd *ELTH/MOT* SE9	**143**	E1
Phipp St *SDTCH* EC2A	**12**	C5
Phoebeth Rd *LEW* SE13	**140**	A3
Phoenix Cl *HACK* * E8	**77**	F5
Phoenix Pl *FSBYW* WC1X	**9**	F4
Phoenix Rd *CAMTN* NW1	**8**	A3
Phoenix St *LSQ/SEVD* WC2H	**20**	B5
Phoenix Wharf Rd *STHWK* SE1	**49**	F1
Physic Pl *CHEL* SW3	**115**	F2
The Piazza *COVGDN* WC2E	**33**	D1
Piccadilly *MYFR/PICC* W1J	**30**	C4
Piccadilly Ar *MYFR/PICC* W1J	**31**	E3
Piccadilly Circ *MYFR/PICC* W1J	**32**	A2
Pickard St *FSBYE* EC1V	**11**	D3
Pickering Av *EHAM* E6	**96**	A1
Pickering Pl *STJS* * SW1Y	**31**	F4
Pickering St *IS* N1	**76**	B5
Pickets St *BAL* SW12	**134**	A5
Pickfords Whf *IS* * N1	**11**	D2
Pickwick Rd *DUL* SE21	**137**	D5
Pickwick St *STHWK* SE1	**47**	E1
Pickworth Cl *VX/NE* * SW8	**117**	E3
Picton Pl *MBLAR* W1H	**18**	B5
Picton St *CMBW* SE5	**119**	D3
Piedmont Rd *WOOL/PLUM* SE18	**127**	D1
Pier Head *WAP* * E1W	**102**	B2
Piermont Rd *EDUL* SE22	**138**	B3
Pierrepoint Ar *IS* * N1	**10**	C1
Pierrepoint Rd *ACT* W3	**98**	B1
Pierrepoint Rw *IS* N1	**10**	C1
Pier Rd *CAN/RD* E16	**107**	F3
Pier St *POP/IOD* E14	**104**	C5
Pier Ter *WAND/EARL* SW18	**132**	B2
Pier Wy *WOOL/PLUM* SE18	**109**	D4
Pigott St *POP/IOD* E14	**92**	A5
Pike Cl *BMLY* BR1	**160**	B5
Pilgrimage St *STHWK* SE1	**48**	A1
Pilgrim Hl *WNWD* SE27	**154**	C1
Pilgrim's La *HAMP* NW3	**73**	D1
Pilgrims Ms *POP/IOD* E14	**105**	D1

Pilgrim St *BLKFR* * EC4V 22 C5
Pilgrims Wy *ARCH* N19 ....57 D3
    WBLY HA9 ....50 B3
Pilkington Rd *PECK* SE15 ....120 B5
Pilot Cl *DEPT* SE8 ....121 F2
Pilsden Cl *WIM/MER* * SW19 ....149 D1
Pilton Pl *WALW* SE17 ....118 C1
Pimlico Rd *BGVA* SW1W 116 A1
Pinchin & Johnsons Yd
    WCHPL * E1 ....102 A1
Pinchin St *WCHPL* E1 ....102 A1
Pincott Pl *BROCKY* SE4 ....139 D1
Pindar St *SDTCH* EC2A 24 C2
Pindock Ms *MV/WKIL* W9 ....15 D1
Pine Apple Ct *WESTW* * SW1E 43 E2
Pine Av *SRTFD* E15 ....81 D2
Pine Cl *LEY* E10 ....62 A4
Pinefield Cl *POP/IOD* * E14 ....104 A1
Pine Gv *FSBYPK* N4 ....57 E4
    WIM/MER SW19 ....149 F5
Pinelands Cl *BKHTH/KID* * SE3 ....123 F3
Pinelees Ct *MORT/ESHN* * SW14 ......128 C2
Pinemartin Cl *CRICK* NW2 ....52 C5
Pine Rd *CRICK* NW2 ....70 C1
Pine St *CLKNW* EC1R 10 A5
Pinewood Av *BFN/LL* DA15 ....163 E1
Pinfold Rd *STRHM/NOR* SW16 ....153 E4
Pinnell Rd *ELTH/MOT* SE9 ....143 D2
Pintail Cl *EHAM* E6 ....95 E4
Pinto Wy *BKHTH/KID* SE3 ....142 B2
Pioneer Cl *SHB* W12 ....88 B5
Pioneer St *PECK* SE15 ....120 A4
Pioneer Wy *SHB* W12 ....88 B5
Piper Cl *HOLWY* N7 ....75 F2
Pippin Cl *CRICK* NW2 ....52 A5
Pirbright Rd *WAND/EARL* SW18 ....149 F1
Pirie St *CAN/RD* E16 ....106 B2
Pitchford St *SRTFD* E15 ....81 D4
Pitfield St *IS* N1 ....12 C2
Pitfield Wy *WLSDN* NW10 ....68 C3
Pitfold Rd *LEE/GVPK* SE12 ....142 A5
Pitman St *CMBW* SE5 ....118 C3
Pitsea Pl *WCHPL* E1 ....91 D5
Pitsea St *WCHPL* E1 ....91 D5
Pitt Crs *WIM/MER* SW19 ....150 B4
Pittman Gdns *IL* IG1 ....84 C2
Pitt's Head Ms *MYFR/PKLN* W1K 30 B4
Pitt St *KENS* W8 ....26 B5
Pixley St *POP/IOD* E14 ....91 F5
Plaistow Gv *SRTFD* E15 ....81 F5
Plaistow Park Rd *PLSTW* E13 ....94 B1
Plaistow Rd *PLSTW* E13 ....94 A4
    SRTFD E15 ....81 F5
Plane St *SYD* SE26 ....156 B3
Plantain Gdns *WAN* * E11 ....63 D5
Plantain Pl *STHWK* SE1 ....36 A5
The Plantation *BKHTH/KID* SE3 ....124 A5
Plashet Gv *EHAM* E6 ....82 C5
Plashet Rd *PLSTW* E13 ....82 A5
Plassy Rd *CAT* SE6 ....140 B5
Platina St *SDTCH* EC2A 12 B5
Plato Rd *CLAP* SW4 ....135 E2
Platt's La *HAMP* NW3 ....54 A5
Platt St *CAMTN* NW1 ....8 A1
Playfair St *HMSMTH* * W6 ....112 C1
Playfield Crs *EDUL* SE22 ....137 E3
Playford Rd *FSBYPK* N4 ....57 F4
Playgreen Wy *ELTH/MOT* SE9 ....158 A4
Playhouse Yd *BLKFR* EC4V 22 C5
Pleasance Rd *PUT/ROE* SW15 ....130 B3
The Pleasance *PUT/ROE* SW15 ....130 B2
Pleasant Pl *IS* N1 ....76 B4
Plender St *CAMTN* NW1 ....74 C1

Pleshey Rd *HOLWY* N7 ....75 D1
Plevna Crs *SEVS/STOTM* N15 ....59 E1
Plevna St *POP/IOD* E14 ....104 C4
Pleydell Av *HMSMTH* W6 ....99 F4
Pleydell Est *FSBYE* * EC1V 11 F4
Pleydell St *EMB* EC4Y 22 B5
Plimsoll Cl *POP/IOD* E14 ....92 B5
Plimsoll Rd *FSBYPK* N4 ....58 B5
Plough La *EDUL* SE22 ....137 F4
    WIM/MER SW19 ....150 B5
Ploughmans Cl *CAMTN* NW1 ....75 D5
Plough Pl *FLST/FETLN* * EC4A 22 B4
Plough Rd *BTSEA* SW11 ....133 D1
Plough St *WCHPL* * E1 ....90 A5
Plough Ter *BTSEA* SW11 ....133 D2
Plough Wy *BERM/RHTH* SE16 ....103 D5
Plough Yd *SDTCH* EC2A 25 D1
Plover Wy *BERM/RHTH* SE16 ....103 E4
Plowden Buildings *EMB* * EC4Y 34 A1
Plumbers Rw *WCHPL* E1 ....90 A4
Plumbridge St *GNWCH* * SE10 ....122 C4
Plum La *WOOL/PLUM* SE18 ....126 B3
Plummer Rd *CLAP* SW4 ....134 C4
Plumstead Common Rd
    WOOL/PLUM SE18 ....126 C2
Plumstead High St
    WOOL/PLUM SE18 ....109 D5
Plumstead Rd *WOOL/PLUM* SE18 ......108 C5
Plumtree Ct *FLST/FETLN* EC4A 22 B4
Plymouth Rd *CAN/RD* E16 ....94 A4
Plymouth Whf *POP/IOD* E14 ....105 D5
Plympton Av *KIL/WHAMP* NW6 ....71 F4
Plympton Pl *STJWD* * NW8 ....16 C1
Plympton Rd *KIL/WHAMP* NW6 ....71 F4
Plympton St *STJWD* NW8 ....16 C1
Pocock St *STHWK* SE1 ....34 C5
Podmore Rd *WAND/EARL* SW18 ....132 C2
Poet's Rd *HBRY* N5 ....77 D2
Point Cl *GNWCH* SE10 ....122 C4
Pointers Cl *POP/IOD* E14 ....122 B1
Point Hl *GNWCH* SE10 ....122 C4
Point Pl *WBLY* HA9 ....68 B4
Point Pleasant *WAND/EARL* SW18 .....132 A2
Poland St *SOHO/CST* W1F 19 F4
Polebrook Rd *BKHTH/KID* SE3 ....142 C1
Polecroft La *CAT* SE6 ....157 F2
Pollard Cl *CAN/RD* E16 ....106 A1
    HOLWY N7 ....75 F1
Pollard Rw *BETH* E2 ....90 A2
Pollard St *BETH* * E2 ....90 A2
Pollen St *CONDST* W1S 19 D5
Pollitt Dr *STJWD* NW8 ....4 C3
Polperro Ms *LBTH* SE11 ....46 C4
Polsted Rd *CAT* SE6 ....139 F5
Polthorne Gv *WOOL/PLUM* SE18 ....108 C5
Polworth Rd *STRHM/NOR* SW16 ....153 F1
Polygon Rd *CAMTN* NW1 ....8 A3
The Polygon *CLAP* * SW4 ....134 C2
Polytechnic St *WOOL/PLUM* SE18 .....108 A5
Pomell Wy *WCHPL* E1 ....25 F4
Pomeroy St *NWCR* SE14 ....120 C3
Pomfret Rd *CMBW* SE5 ....136 B1
Pomoja La *ARCH* N19 ....57 D3
Pond Cl *BKHTH/KID* SE3 ....124 A5
Ponder St *HOLWY* * N7 ....75 F4
Pond Farm Est *CLPT* * E5 ....60 C5
Pond Md *DUL* SE21 ....137 D4
Pond Pl *CHEL* SW3 ....40 C5
Pond Rd *BKHTH/KID* SE3 ....141 F1
    SRTFD E15 ....93 E1
Ponler St *WCHPL* E1 ....90 B5
Ponsard Rd *WLSDN* NW10 ....88 B2

Ponsford St *HOM* E9 ....**78** C3
Ponsonby Pl *WEST* SW1P **117** D1
Ponsonby Rd *PUT/ROE* SW15 ....**130** B5
Ponsonby Ter *WEST* SW1P **117** D1
Pontefract Rd *BMLY* BR1 ....**160** A5
Ponton Rd *VX/NE* SW8 ....**117** D3
Pont St *KTBR* SW1X **41** E3
Pont Street Ms *CHEL* SW3 ....**41** E3
Pool Cl *BECK* BR3 ....**158** A5
Pool Ct *CAT* SE6 ....**158** A2
Poole Rd *HOM* E9 ....**79** D3
Pooles Buildings *FSBYW* WC1X **22** A1
Pooles La *WBPTN* * SW10 ....**114** C3
Pooles Pk *FSBYPK* N4 ....**58** A4
Poole St *IS* N1 ....**77** D5
Poolmans St *BERM/RHTH* SE16 ....**103** D3
Poonah St *STHWK* SE1 ....**90** C5
Pope's Rd *BRXN/ST* * SW9 ....**136** A2
Pope St *STHWK* SE1 ....**49** D1
Popham Gdns *RCH/KEW* * TW9 ....**128** D1
Popham Rd *IS* N1 ....**76** C5
Popham St *IS* N1 ....**76** B5
Poplar Bath St *POP/IOD* E14 ....**104** B1
Poplar Cl *HOM* E9 ....**79** F2
Poplar Crs *HMSMTH* W6 ....**100** C3
Poplar Gv *WBLY* HA9 ....**50** C5
Poplar High St *POP/IOD* E14 ....**104** B1
Poplar Ms *SHB* W12 ....**100** C2
Poplar Pl *BAY/PAD* W2 ....**26** C1
Poplar Rd *HNHL* SE24 ....**136** C2
Poplars Rd *LEY* E10 ....**62** B3
Poplar Wk *HNHL* SE24 ....**136** C2
Poppins Ct *FLST/FETLN* EC4A **22** C5
Poppleton Rd *WAN* E11 ....**63** F1
Porchester Garden Ms
  BAY/PAD * W2 ....**15** D5
Porchester Gdns *BAY/PAD* W2 ....**27** D1
Porchester Ga *BAY/PAD* * W2 ....**27** E2
Porchester Pl *BAY/PAD* W2 ....**17** E5
Porchester Rd *BAY/PAD* W2 ....**15** D4
Porchester Sq *BAY/PAD* W2 ....**15** D4
Porchester Square Ms
  BAY/PAD * W2 ....**15** D4
Porchester Ter *BAY/PAD* W2 ....**15** D4
Porchester Ter North *BAY/PAD* W2 .**15** D4
Porcupine Cl *ELTH/MOT* SE9 ....**161** E2
Porden Rd *BRXN/ST* SW9 ....**135** F2
Porlock Rd *STHWK* SE1 ....**36** B5
Portal Cl *WNWD* SE27 ....**154** A3
Portbury Cl *PECK* SE15 ....**120** A4
Portchester Cl *CMBW* SE5 ....**136** C2
Portchester Ga *BAY/PAD* W2 ....**27** E2
Portelet Rd *WCHPL* E1 ....**91** D2
Porten Houses *WKENS* * W14 ....**101** E4
Porten Rd *WKENS* W14 ....**101** E4
Porter Rd *EHAM* E6 ....**95** F5
Porter St *MHST* W1U **17** F2
  STHWK SE1 ....**35** F3
Porters Wk *WAP* * E1W **102** B1
Porteus Rd *BAY/PAD* W2 ....**15** F3
Portgate Cl *MV/WKIL* W9 ....**89** D2
Porthcawe Rd *SYD* SE26 ....**157** E4
Portia Wy *BOW* E3 ....**91** F3
The Portico *WBPTN* * SW10 ....**115** D2
Portinscale Rd *PUT/ROE* SW15 .....**131** E3
Portland Av *STNW/STAM* N16 ....**59** F3
Portland Crs *ELTH/MOT* SE9 ....**161** D2
Portland Gdns *FSBYPK* N4 ....**58** B1
Portland Gv *VX/NE* SW8 ....**117** F4
Portland Ms *SOHO/CST* W1F **19** F5
Portland Pl *CAVSQ/HST* W1G **18** C1
Portland Ri *FSBYPK* N4 ....**58** B3
Portland Rd *BMLY* BR1 ....**160** C4

NTGHL W11 ....**101** E1
Portland Sq *WAP* E1W **102** B2
Portland St *WALW* SE17 ....**119** D1
Portman Av *MORT/ESHN* SW14 ....**129** D1
Portman Ga *CAMTN* NW1 ....**17** D1
Portman Cl *MBLAR* W1H **18** A4
Portman Ms South *MBLAR* W1H **18** A5
Portman Pl *BETH* E2 ....**90** C2
Portman Sq *MBLAR* W1H **17** F4
Portman St *MBLAR* W1H **18** A5
Portman Towers *MBLAR* W1H **17** F4
Portmeers Cl *WALTH* * E17 ....**61** F1
Portnall Rd *MV/WKIL* W9 ....**89** F2
Portobello Ct *NTGHL* * W11 ....**101** F1
Portobello Ms *NTGHL* * W11 ....**26** A2
Portobello Rd *NKENS* W10 ....**89** E4
  NTGHL W11 ....**101** F1
Portpool La *FSBYW* WC1X **22** A2
Portree St *POP/IOD* E14 ....**93** D5
Portsdown Av *GLDGN* NW11 ....**53** F1
Portsdown Ms *GLDGN* NW11 ....**53** F1
Portsea Ms *BAY/PAD* W2 ....**17** D5
Portsea Pl *BAY/PAD* W2 ....**17** D5
Portslade Rd *VX/NE* SW8 ....**116** C5
Portsmouth Rd *PUT/ROE* SW15 .....**130** B5
Portsmouth St *LINN* WC2A **21** E4
Portsoken St *TWRH* EC3N **37** E1
Portugal St *LINN* WC2A **21** F5
Portway *SRTFD* E15 ....**81** F5
Portway Gdns *WOOL/PLUM* SE18 ..**125** D4
The Postern *BARB* * EC2Y **23** F3
Post Office Ap *FSTGT* E7 ....**82** B2
Postway Ms *IL* IG1 ....**66** B5
Potier St *STHWK* SE1 ....**48** B3
Potterne Cl *WIM/MER* SW19 ....**131** D5
Potters Flds *STHWK* SE1 ....**37** D4
Potters Rd *FUL/PGN* SW6 ....**114** C5
Pottery La *NTGHL* W11 ....**101** E2
Pottery Rd *BERM/RHTH* * SE16 .....**102** B3
Pott St *BETH* E2 ....**90** B2
Poulett Rd *EHAM* E6 ....**95** F1
Poulton Cl *HACK* E8 ....**78** B3
Poultry *LOTH* EC2R **24** A5
Pound La *WLSDN* NW10 ....**70** A3
Pound Park Rd *CHARL* SE7 ....**107** D5
Pound Pl *ELTH/MOT* SE9 ....**144** A4
Pountney Rd *BTSEA* SW11 ....**134** A1
Powell Rd *CLPT* E5 ....**60** B5
Power Rd *CHSWK* W4 ....**98** A5
Powerscroft Rd *CLPT* E5 ....**78** C1
Powis Gdns *GLDGN* NW11 ....**53** F2
  NTGHL W11 ....**89** F5
Powis Ms *NTGHL* W11 ....**89** F5
Powis Pl *BMSBY* WC1N **21** D1
Powis Rd *BOW* E3 ....**92** B2
Powis Sq *NTGHL* W11 ....**89** F5
Powis St *WOOL/PLUM* SE18 ....**108** A4
Powis Ter *NTGHL* W11 ....**89** F5
Powlett Pl *CAMTN* * NW1 ....**74** B4
Pownall Rd *HACK* E8 ....**78** A5
Pownsett Ter *IL* IG1 ....**84** C2
Powster Rd *BMLY* BR1 ....**160** A5
Poynders Rd *CLAP* SW4 ....**134** C5
Poynings Rd *ARCH* N19 ....**56** C5
Poyntz Rd *BTSEA* SW11 ....**115** F5
Poyser St *BETH* E2 ....**90** B2
Praed Ms *BAY/PAD* W2 ....**16** B4
Praed St *BAY/PAD* W2........................**16** B4
Pragel St *PLSTW* E13 ....**94** B1
Pragnell Rd *LEE/GVPK* SE12 ....**160** B2
Prague Pl *BRXS/STRHM* SW2 ....**135** E3
Prah Rd *FSBYPK* N4 ....**58** A4
Prairie St *VX/NE* SW8 ....**116** A5

The Priory *BKHTH/KID* SE3...........**141** F1
Priory Wk *WBPTN* SW10................**114** C1
Pritchard's Rd *BETH* E2 ....**90** A1
Priter Rd *BERM/RHTH* * SE16 ....**102** A4
Probert Rd *BRXS/STRHM* SW2.......**136** A3
Probyn Rd *BRXS/STRHM* SW2 ....**154** B2
Procter St *GINN* WC1R **21** E3
Promenade Approach Rd
   CHSWK W4.................................**111** E3
The Promenade *CHSWK* W4 ....**111** E4
Prospect Cl *SYD* SE26 ....**156** B4
Prospect Cottages
   WAND/EARL SW18 ....**132** A2
Prospect Pl *CHSWK* W4 ....**111** D1
   CRICK NW2....................................**53** F5
   WAP E1W **102** C2
Prospect Rd *CRICK* NW2.................**53** F5
Prospect St *BERM/RHTH* SE16 ......**102** B3
Prospect V *CHARL* SE7 ....**107** E5
Prospero Rd *ARCH* N19 ....**57** D3
Prothero Rd *FUL/PGN* SW6 ....**113** E3
Prout Gv *WLSDN* NW10..................**69** E1
Prout Rd *CLPT* E5 ....**60** B5
Providence Cl *HOM* * E9.................**79** D5
Providence Ct *MYFR/PKLN* W1K ...**30** B1
Providence Pl *IS* * N1 ....**76** B5
Providence Row Cl *BETH* E2 ....**90** B2
Providence Sq *STHWK* SE1............**36** C5
Providence Yd *BETH* * E2 ....**90** A2
Provost Est *IS* N1 ....**12** A3
Provost Rd *HAMP* NW3 ....**73** F4
Provost St *IS* N1 ....**12** A2
Prowse Pl *CAMTN* NW1 ....**74** C4
Prusom St *WAP* E1W.........................**102** B2
Pudding La *MON* EC3R **36** B1
Pudding Mill La *SRTFD* E15 ....**80** B5
Puddle Dock *BLKFR* EC4V **35** D1
Pulborough Rd *WAND/EARL* SW18..**131** F5
Pulford Rd *SEVS/STOTM* N15 ....**59** D3
Pulleyns Av *EHAM* E6.......................**95** E2
Pullman Gdns *PUT/ROE* SW15.......**130** C4
Pullman Ms *LEE/GVPK* SE12..........**160** B5
Pullman Pl *ELTH/MOT* SE9 ....**143** E3
Pulross Rd *BRXN/ST* SW9................**135** F1
Pulteney Cl *BOW* E3 ....**79** F5
Pulton Pl *FUL/PGN* SW6 ....**114** A3
Puma Ct *WCHPL* E1..........................**25** E2
Pump Ct *EMB* * EC4Y **22** A5
Pumping Station Rd *CHSWK* W4.....**111** E3
Pump La *NWCR* SE14........................**120** C3
Punderson's Gdns *BETH* E2..............**90** B2
Purbeck Dr *CRICK* NW2....................**53** D4
Purbrook St *STHWK* SE1..................**49** D2
Purcell Crs *FUL/PGN* * SW6 ....**113** D2
Purcell Ms *WLSDN* * NW10.............**69** E4
Purcell St *IS* N1 ....**12** C1
Purchese St *CAMTN* NW1 ....**8** A1
Purdy St *BOW* E3 ....**92** B3
Purelake Ms *LEW* * SE13.................**141** F1
Purland Rd *THMD* SE28 ....**109** F3
Purley Av *CRICK* NW2.......................**53** E4
Purley Pl *IS* N1 ....**76** B4
Purneys Rd *ELTH/MOT* SE9 ....**143** D2
Purrett Rd *WOOL/PLUM* SE18 ....**127** F1
Pursers Cross Rd *FUL/PGN* * SW6...**113** F4
Purves Rd *WLSDN* NW10 ....**88** B2
Putney Br *PUT/ROE* SW15................**131** E1
Putney Bridge Ap *PUT/ROE* SW15 ..**131** E1
Putney Bridge Rd *PUT/ROE* SW15 ..**131** E2
Putney Common *PUT/ROE* SW15 ....**130** C1
Putney Ex *PUT/ROE* * SW15............**131** D2
Putney Heath *PUT/ROE* SW15.........**130** B4
Putney Heath La *PUT/ROE* SW15 ....**131** D4

Putney High St *PUT/ROE* SW15.........**131** E2
Putney Hl *PUT/ROE* SW15................**131** D4
Putney Park Av *PUT/ROE* SW15 ......**130** A2
Putney Park La *PUT/ROE* SW15 ......**130** B2
Pymers Md *DUL* SE21 ....**154** C1
Pyrland Rd *HBRY* N5.........................**77** D2
Pyrmont Gv *WNWD* SE27 ....**154** B3
Pyrmont Rd *CHSWK* W4 ....**110** A2
Pytchley Rd *CMBW* SE5 ....**137** E1

Q

The Quadrangle *BAY/PAD* W2 ....**16** C4
   HNHL * SE24 ....**136** C3
   WBPTN SW10 ....**114** C4
Quadrant Ar *REGST* W1B **31** F2
Quadrant Gv *HAMP* NW3 ....**73** F2
The Quadrant *NKENS* * W10............**89** D2
Quaggy Wk *BKHTH/KID* SE3............**142** A2
Quainton St *WLSDN* NW10 ....**51** D5
Quakers Pl *FSTGT* E7 ....**83** D2
Quaker St *WCHPL* E1........................**25** E1
Quality Ct *LINN* WC2A **22** A4
Quantock Gdns *CRICK* * NW2..........**53** D4
Quarley Wy *PECK* SE15 ....**119** F3
Quarrendon St *FUL/PGN* SW6 ....**114** A4
Quarry Rd *WAND/EARL* SW18 ....**132** C4
Quartermile La *LEY* E10....................**80** B1
Quay House *POP/IOD* * E14..............**104** A3
Quebec Ms *MBLAR* W1H **17** F5
Quebec Rd *GNTH/NBYPK* IG2..........**66** C2
Quebec Wy *BERM/RHTH* SE16.........**103** D3
Queen Anne Ms *CAVSQ/HST* W1G ..**19** D3
Queen Anne Rd *HOM* E9 ....**79** D3
Queen Anne's Gdns *CHSWK* W4 ......**99** E4
Queen Anne's Ga *STJSPK* SW1H.......**44** A1
Queen Anne's Gv *CHSWK* W4...........**99** E4
Queen Anne St *CAVSQ/HST* W1G.....**18** C3
Queen Anne Ter *WAP* * E1W.............**102** B1
Queen Caroline Est *HMSMTH* W6....**112** C1
Queen Caroline St *HMSMTH* W6 .....**112** C1
Queen Elizabeth Buildings
   EMB * EC4Y **34** A1
Queen Elizabeth's Cl
   STNW/STAM N16........................**59** D4
Queen Elizabeth St *STHWK* SE1 ......**37** D5
Queen Elizabeth's Wk
   STNW/STAM N16........................**59** D3
Queenhithe *BLKFR* EC4V **35** F2
Queen Margaret's Gv *IS* N1 ....**77** E2
Queen Mother Ga *BAY/PAD* W2 ......**30** B4
Queensberry Ms West
   SKENS * SW7 ....**40** A4
Queensberry Pl *SKENS* SW7.............**40** A4
Queensberry Wy *SKENS* * SW7 ....**40** A4
Queensborough
   Ms *BAY/PAD* * W2.......................**27** E1
Queensborough Pas *BAY/PAD* W2 ...**27** E1
Queensborough Studios
   BAY/PAD W2 ....**27** E1
Queensborough Ter *BAY/PAD* W2 ....**27** E1
Queensbridge Rd *HACK* E8 ....**77** F3
Queensbury Rd *CDALE/KGS* NW9 ....**51** D2
Queensbury St *IS* N1 ....**76** C4
Queens Circ *VX/NE* SW8 ....**116** B3
Queen's Club Gdns *WKENS* W14 ......**113** E2
   WKENS * W14 ....**113** E2
Queens Club Ter *WKENS* * W14 ....**113** F2
Queens Crs *KTTN* NW5......................**74** A2
Queenscroft Rd *ELTH/MOT* SE9 ......**143** D3

Queensdale Crs *NTGHL* W11 ....**101** D2
Queensdale Pl *NTGHL* W11 ....**101** E2
Queensdale Rd *NTGHL* W11 ....**101** D2
Queensdale Wk *NTGHL* W11 ....**101** E2
Queens Down Rd *CLPT* E5 ....**78** B1
Queen's Dr *FSBYPK* N4 ....**58** B4
LEY E10 ....**62** A2
Queen's Elm Sq *CHEL* SW3 ....**115** D1
Queen's Gdns *BAY/PAD* W2 ....**27** E1
Queens Garth *FSTH* * SE23 ....**156** C2
Queens Ga *SKENS* SW7 ....**39** F1
Queensgate Gdns
PUT/ROE SW15 ....**130** B2
Queen's Gate Gdns *SKENS* SW7 ....**39** E3
Queen's Gate Ms *SKENS* SW7 ....**39** E2
Queensgate Pl *KIL/WHAMP* NW6 ....**72** A4
Queen's Gate Pl *SKENS* SW7 ....**39** F3
Queen's Gate Place Ms *SKENS* SW7 ...**39** F3
Queen's Gate Ter *SKENS* SW7 ....**39** E2
Queen's Gv *STJWD* NW8 ....**73** D5
Queen's Head St *IS* N1 ....**76** B5
Queensland Pl *HOLWY* N7 ....**76** A1
Queensland Rd *HOLWY* N7 ....**76** A1
Queensmead *STJWD* NW8 ....**73** D5
Queensmere Cl *WIM/MER* SW19 ....**149** D2
Queensmere Rd *WIM/MER* SW19 ....**149** D2
Queen's Ms *BAY/PAD* W2 ....**26** C1
Queensmill Rd *FUL/PGN* SW6 ....**113** D3
Queens Pde *CRICK* * NW2 ....**70** C3
Queen Sq *BMSBY* WC1N **21** D1
Queen's Ride *BARN* SW13 ....**130** A1
Queen's Rd *BARK* IG11 ....**84** C4
MORT/ESHN SW14 ....**129** D1
PECK SE15 ....**120** C4
PLSTW E13 ....**82** B5
WALTH E17 ....**61** F1
WAN E11 ....**63** D2
WIM/MER SW19 ....**150** B5
Queen's Rd West *PLSTW* E13 ....**94** A1
Queens Rw *WALW* SE17 ....**119** D2
WALW * SE17 ....**119** D2
Queens Ter *PLSTW* E13 ....**82** B5
STJWD NW8 ....**73** D5
WCHPL * E1 ....**90** C3
Queensthorpe Ms *SYD* * SE26 ....**157** D4
Queensthorpe Rd *SYD* SE26 ....**157** D4
Queenstown Rd *VX/NE* SW8 ....**116** B5
Queen St *MYFR/PICC* W1J **30** C3
Queen Street Pl *CANST* EC4R **35** F2
Queensville Rd *CLAP* SW4 ....**135** D5
Queens Wk *CDALE/KGS* NW9 ....**50** C4
Queensway *BAY/PAD* W2 ....**15** D4
Queenswood Gdns *WAN* E11 ....**64** A3
Queenswood Rd *BFN/LL* DA15 ....**145** E3
FSTH SE23 ....**157** E3
Queen Victoria St *BLKFR* EC4V **34** C1
MANHO EC4N **23** F5
Queen Victoria Ter *E1W* * E1W **102** B1
Quemerford Rd *HOLWY* N7 ....**75** F2
Quentin Pl *LEW* SE13 ....**141** E1
Quentin Rd *BKHTH/KID* SE3 ....**141** E1
Quernmore Rd *FSBYPK* N4 ....**58** A1
Querrin St *FUL/PGN* SW6 ....**114** C5
Quex Ms *KIL/WHAMP* NW6 ....**72** A5
Quex Rd *KIL/WHAMP* NW6 ....**72** A5
Quick Rd *CHSWK* W4 ....**111** E1
Quick St *IS* N1 ....**11** D2
Quickswood *HAMP* NW3 ....**73** E4
Quill St *FSBYPK* N4 ....**58** A5
Quilp St *STHWK* SE1 ....**35** E5

Quilter St *BETH* E2 ....**90** A2
WOOL/PLUM SE18 ....**127** F1
Quinton St *WAND/EARL* SW18 ....**150** C2
Quixley St *POP/IOD* E14 ....**105** D1
Quorn Rd *EDUL* SE22 ....**137** E2

R

Rabbit Rw *KENS* * W8 ....**26** B3
Rabbits Rd *MNPK* E12 ....**83** E1
Raby St *POP/IOD* * E14 ....**91** E5
Racton Rd *FUL/PGN* SW6 ....**114** A2
Radbourne Cl *CLPT* E5 ....**79** D1
Radbourne Rd *BAL* SW12 ....**134** C5
Radcliffe Av *WLSDN* NW10 ....**88** A1
Radcliffe Rd *STHWK* SE1 ....**49** D2
Radcot St *LBTH* SE11 ....**118** A1
Raddington Rd *NKENS* W10 ....**89** E4
Radfield Wy *ELTH/MOT* SE9 ....**145** D5
Radford Est *WLSDN* * NW10 ....**87** E2
Radford Rd *LEW* SE13 ....**140** C4
Radford Wy *BARK* IG11 ....**97** F2
Radipole Rd *FUL/PGN* SW6 ....**113** F4
Radland Rd *CAN/RD* E16 ....**94** A5
Radlet Av *FSTH* SE23 ....**156** B3
Radlett Cl *FSTGT* E7 ....**81** F3
Radlett Pl *STJWD* NW8 ....**73** E5
Radley Av *GDMY/SEVK* IG3 ....**85** F1
Radley Ct *BERM/RHTH* SE16 ....**103** D3
Radley Ms *KENS* W8 ....**38** B3
Radley Sq *CLPT* * E5 ....**60** C4
Radley Ter *CAN/RD* * E16 ....**93** F4
Radlix Rd *LEY* E10 ....**62** A3
Radnor Ms *BAY/PAD* W2 ....**16** B5
Radnor Pl *BAY/PAD* W2 ....**16** C5
Radnor Rd *KIL/WHAMP* NW6 ....**71** E5
PECK SE15 ....**120** A3
Radnor St *FSBYE* EC1V **11** F1
Radnor Ter *WKENS* W14 ....**101** F5
Radnor Wk *CHEL* SW3 ....**115** E1
Radnor Wy *WLSDN* NW10 ....**86** B3
Radstock St *BTSEA* * SW11 ....**115** E3
Raeburn Cl *EFNCH* N2 ....**54** C1
Raeburn Rd *BFN/LL* DA15 ....**145** E4
Raeburn St *BRXS/STRHM* SW2 ....**135** E2
Raglan Rd *WOOL/PLUM* SE18 ....**126** C1
Raglan St *KTTN* NW5 ....**74** B3
Ragley Cl *ACT* W3 ....**98** C3
Railey Ms *KTTN* NW5 ....**74** C2
Railton Rd *HNHL* SE24 ....**136** A3
Railway Ap *STHWK* SE1 ....**36** B3
Railway Ar *BRXN/ST* * SW9 ....**136** A1
Railway Av *BERM/RHTH* SE16 ....**102** C3
Railway Cottages *SHB* * W12 ....**100** B3
SRTFD * E15 ....**93** E1
WIM/MER * SW19 ....**150** B4
Railway Gv *NWCR* SE14 ....**121** F3
Railway Ri *EDUL* SE22 ....**137** E2
Railway Side *BARN* SW13 ....**129** E3
Railway Station Whf *LEY* * E10 ....**61** D3
Railway St *IS* N1 ....**9** D2
Railway Ter *LEW* SE13 ....**140** B3
Rainborough Cl *WBLY* HA9 ....**68** C3
Rainbow Av *POP/IOD* E14 ....**122** B1
Rainbow St *CMBW* SE5 ....**119** E3
Raine St *WAP* E1W **102** B2
Rainham Cl *BTSEA* SW11 ....**133** E4
ELTH/MOT SE9 ....**145** E4
Rainham Rd *WLSDN* NW10 ....**88** C2
Rainhill Wy *BOW* E3 ....**92** A2
Rainsborough Av *DEPT* SE8 ....**103** E5

Rainsford Rd *WLSDN* NW10 ....**86** B2
Rainsford St *BAY/PAD* W2 ....**16** C4
Rainton Rd *CHARL* SE7 ....**124** A1
Rainville Rd *HMSMTH* W6 ....**112** C2
Raleigh Ms *IS* N1 ....**76** B5
Raleigh St *IS* N1 ....**76** B5
Ralston St *CHEL* SW3 ....**115** F1
Ramac Wy *CHARL* SE7 ....**106** B3
Rambler Cl *STRHM/NOR* SW16 ....**152** C4
Rame Cl *TOOT* SW17 ....**152** A5
Ramillies Cl *BRXS/STRHM* SW2 ....**135** E4
Ramillies Pl *SOHO/CST* W1F **19** D5
Ramillies Rd *CHSWK* W4 ....**99** D5
Ramillies St *SOHO/CST* W1F **19** D5
Rampart St *WCHPL* E1 ....**90** B5
Rampayne St *PIM* SW1V **117** D1
Ramsay Rd *ACT* W3 ....**98** C4
   FSTGT E7 ....**81** F1
Ramsdale Rd *TOOT* SW17 ....**152** A5
Ramsden Ga *BAL* SW12 ....**134** A5
Ramsden Rd *BAL* SW12 ....**134** A5
Ramsey Cl *CDALE/KGS* NW9 ....**51** E1
Ramsey St *BETH* E2 ....**90** A3
Ramsey Wk *IS* * N1 ....**77** D3
Ramsgate St *HACK* * E8 ....**77** F3
Ram St *WAND/EARL* SW18 ....**132** A3
Rancliffe Gdns *ELTH/MOT* SE9 ....**143** F2
Rancliffe Rd *EHAM* E6 ....**95** E1
Randall Av *CRICK* NW2 ....**51** E4
Randall Cl *BTSEA* SW11 ....**115** E4
Randall Pl *GNWCH* SE10 ....**122** C3
Randall Rd *LBTH* SE11 ....**117** F1
Randall Rw *LBTH* SE11 ....**45** E1
Randell's Rd *IS* N1 ....**75** E5
Randisbourne Gdns *CAT* * SE6 ....**158** B3
Randlesdown Rd *CAT* SE6 ....**158** A4
Randolph Ap *CAN/RD* E16 ....**94** C5
Randolph Av *KIL/WHAMP* NW9 ....**2** C2
Randolph Cl *KUTN/CMB* * KT2 ....**146** C5
Randolph Crs *MV/WKIL* W9 ....**15** E1
Randolph Gdns *KIL/WHAMP* NW9 ....**2** C2
Randolph Ms *MV/WKIL* W9 ....**15** F1
Randolph Rd *MV/WKIL* W9 ....**15** E1
Randolph St *CAMTN* NW1 ....**74** C4
Ranelagh Av *BARN* SW13 ....**112** A5
   FUL/PGN SW6 ....**131** F1
Ranelagh Gdns *CHSWK* W4 ....**110** C3
   FUL/PGN SW6 ....**131** E1
   IL IG1 ....**66** A3
Ranelagh Gv *BCVA* SW1W **116** A1
Ranelagh Rd *EHAM* E6 ....**84** A5
   PIM SW1V **116** C1
   WAN E11 ....**81** E1
   WLSDN NW10 ....**87** F1
Rangeworth Pl *BFN/LL* DA15 ....**163** F3
Rangoon St *TWRH* * EC3N **25** C1
Ranmere St *BAL* SW12 ....**152** B1
Rannoch Rd *HMSMTH* W6 ....**112** C2
Rannock Av *CDALE/KGS* NW9 ....**51** D2
Ransom Rd *CHARL* * SE7 ....**124** C1
Ranston St *CAMTN* NW1 ....**16** C2
Ranulf Rd *CRICK* NW2 ....**71** F1
Raphael St *SKENS* SW7 ....**41** E1
Rastell Av *BAL* SW12 ....**153** D2
Ratcliffe Cl *LEE/GVPK* SE12 ....**142** A5
Ratcliffe Cross St *WCHPL* * E1 ....**91** D5
Ratcliffe La *POP/IOD* E14 ....**91** E5
Ratcliff Rd *FSTGT* E7 ....**82** C2
Rathbone Market *CAN/RD* * E16 ....**93** F4
Rathbone Pl *FITZ* W1T **20** A1
Rathbone St *CAN/RD* E16 ....**93** F4
   FITZ W1T **19** F3

Rathfern Rd *FSTH* SE23 ....**157** F1
Rathgar Rd *BRXN/ST* SW9 ....**136** B1
Rathmell Dr *CLAP* SW4 ....**135** D4
Rathmore Rd *CHARL* SE7 ....**124** B1
Rattray Rd *BRXS/STRHM* SW2 ....**136** A2
Raul Rd *PECK* SE15 ....**120** A5
Raveley St *KTTN* NW5 ....**74** C1
Ravencroft Crs *ELTH/MOT* SE9 ....**161** F3
Ravenet St *BTSEA* SW11 ....**116** B4
Ravenfield Rd *TOOT* SW17 ....**151** F3
Ravenhill Rd *PLSTW* E13 ....**82** C5
Ravenna Rd *PUT/ROE* SW15 ....**131** D3
Raven Rw *WCHPL* E1 ....**90** B4
Ravensbourne Pk *BROCKY* SE4 ....**140** A5
Ravensbourne Park Crs *CAT* SE6 ....**139** F5
Ravensbourne Pl *DEPT* SE8 ....**122** B5
Ravensbourne Rd *FSTH* SE23 ....**139** F5
Ravensbury Rd *WAND/EARL* SW18 .....**150** B2
Ravensbury Ter
   WAND/EARL SW18 ....**150** B2
Ravenscar Rd *BMLY* BR1 ....**159** E4
Ravenscourt Av *HMSMTH* W6 ....**100** A5
Ravenscourt Gdns *HMSMTH* W6 ....**99** F5
Ravenscourt Pk *HMSMTH* W6 ....**100** A5
Ravenscourt Pl *HMSMTH* W6 ....**100** B5
Ravenscourt Rd *HMSMTH* W6 ....**100** B5
Ravenscourt Sq *HMSMTH* W6 ....**100** A4
Ravenscroft Av *GLDGN* NW11 ....**53** F2
Ravenscroft Cl *CAN/RD* E16 ....**94** A4
Ravenscroft Rd *CAN/RD* E16 ....**94** A4
   CHSWK W4 ....**98** C5
Ravenscroft St *BETH* E2 ....**13** F2
Ravensdale Rd *STNW/STAM* N16 ....**59** F3
Ravensdon St *LBTH* SE11 ....**118** A1
Ravenshaw St *KIL/WHAMP* NW6 ....**71** F2
Ravenslea Rd *BAL* SW12 ....**133** F5
Ravensmede Wy *CHSWK* W4 ....**99** F5
Ravens Ms *BKHTH/KID* * SE3 ....**142** A3
Ravenstone Rd *CDALE/KGS* * NW9 ......**51** F1
Ravenstone St *BAL* SW12 ....**152** A1
Ravens Wy *LEE/GVPK* SE12 ....**142** A3
Ravenswood Rd *BAL* SW12 ....**134** B5
Ravensworth Rd *ELTH/MOT* SE9 ....**161** F4
   WLSDN * NW10 ....**88** B2
Ravent Rd *LBTH* SE11 ....**45** F5
Ravey St *SDTCH* EC2A **12** C5
Ravine Gv *WOOL/PLUM* SE18 ....**127** E2
Rav Pinter Cl *STNW/STAM* N16 ....**59** E2
Rawlings St *CHEL* SW3 ....**41** E4
Rawreth Wk *IS* * N1 ....**76** C3
Rawson St *BTSEA* SW11 ....**116** A4
Rawsthorne Cl *CAN/RD* E16 ....**107** F3
Rawstorne Pl *FSBYE* * EC1V **10** C3
Rawstorne St *FSBYE* EC1V **10** C3
Ray Bell Ct *BROCKY* * SE4 ....**121** F5
Raydon St *KTTN* NW5 ....**56** B4
Rayford Av *LEE/GVPK* SE12 ....**141** F5
Rayleas Cl *WOOL/PLUM* SE18 ....**126** A4
Rayleigh Rd *CAN/RD* E16 ....**106** B2
Raymere Gdns *WOOL/PLUM* SE18 .....**127** D3
Raymond Buildings *GINN* * WC1R **21** F2
Raymond Cl *SYD* SE26 ....**156** C5
Raymond Rd *GNTH/NBYPK* IG2 ....**67** D2
   PLSTW E13 ....**82** C4
Raymouth Rd *BERM/RHTH* SE16 ....**102** B5
Rayner's Rd *PUT/ROE* SW15 ....**131** E3
Raynes Av *WAN* E11 ....**64** C3
Raynham Rd *HMSMTH* W6 ....**100** B5
Raynor Pl *IS* N1 ....**76** C5
Ray St *CLKNW* EC1R **22** B1
Ray Street Br *CLKNW* * EC1R **22** B1
Reachview Cl *CAMTN* NW1 ....**74** C4
Reading La *HACK* E8 ....**78** B3

Reads Cl IL IG1 .... 66 B5
Reapers Cl CAMTN NW1 .... 75 D5
Reardon Pth WAP E1W 102 B3
Reardon St WAP E1W 102 B2
Reaston St NWCR SE14 .... 120 C3
Reckitt Rd CHSWK W4 .... 111 E1
Record St PECK SE15 .... 120 C2
Recovery St TOOT SW17 .... 151 E5
Rector St IS N1 .... 76 C5
Rectory Field Crs CHARL SE7 .... 124 C3
Rectory Gv CLAP SW4 .... 134 C1
Rectory La TOOT SW17 .... 152 A5
Rectory Orch WIM/MER SW19 .... 149 E4
Rectory Pl WOOL/PLUM SE18 .... 108 A5
Rectory Rd ACT W3 .... 98 B2
    BARN SW13 .... 112 A5
    MNPK E12 .... 83 F2
    STNW/STAM N16 .... 59 F4
Rectory Sq WCHPL E1 .... 91 D4
Reculver Rd BERM/RHTH SE16 .... 120 C1
Red Anchor Cl CHEL * SW3 .... 115 D5
Redan Pl BAY/PAD W2 .... 14 C5
Redan St WKENS W14 .... 101 E4
Redan Ter CMBW SE5 .... 118 B5
Red Barracks Rd
    WOOL/PLUM SE18 .... 107 F5
Redberry Gv SYD SE26 .... 156 C3
Redbridge Gdns CMBW SE5 .... 119 E3
Redbridge La East REDBR IG4 .... 65 D1
Redbridge La West WAN E11 .... 64 B1
Redburn St CHEL SW3 .... 115 F2
Redcar St CMBW * SE5 .... 118 C3
Redcastle Cl WCHPL E1 .... 102 C1
Redchurch St BETH E2 .... 13 E5
Redcliffe Ct ECT SW5 .... 114 B1
Redcliffe Gdns IL IG1 .... 66 A3
    WBPTN SW10 .... 114 B1
Redcliffe Ms WBPTN SW10 .... 114 B1
Redcliffe Pl WBPTN SW10 .... 114 C2
Redcliffe Rd WBPTN SW10 .... 114 C1
Redcliffe Sq WBPTN SW10 .... 114 B1
Redcliffe St WBPTN * SW10 .... 114 B2
Redclyffe Rd EHAM E6 .... 82 C5
Redcross Wy STHWK SE1 .... 35 H4
Reddins Rd PECK SE15 .... 120 A3
Rede Pl BAY/PAD W2 .... 14 B5
Redesdale St CHEL SW3 .... 115 F2
Redfern Rd CAT SE6 .... 140 C5
    WLSDN NW10 .... 69 E4
Redfield La ECT SW5 .... 38 C4
Redford Wk IS * N1 .... 76 B5
Redgate Ter PUT/ROE SW15 .... 131 D4
Redgrave Rd PUT/ROE SW15 .... 131 D1
Redgrave Ter BETH * E2 .... 90 A2
Redhall Ter ACT * W3 .... 98 A1
Red Hl CHST SR7 .... 162 A5
Red House Sq IS * N1 .... 76 C4
Redington Gdns HAMP NW3 .... 72 B1
Redington Rd HAMP NW3 .... 54 B5
Redlands Wy BRXS/STRHM SW2 ..... 135 E5
Red Lion Cl WALW SE17 .... 119 D2
Red Lion Ct FLST/FETLN EC4A 22 B5
Red Lion La WOOL/PLUM SE18 .... 126 A5
Red Lion Pl WOOL/PLUM * SE18 ...... 126 A4
Red Lion Rw WALW SE17 .... 118 C3
Red Lion Sq BMSBY WC1N 21 E3
    WAND/EARL * SW18 .... 132 A3
Red Lion St GINN WC1R 21 E3
Red Lion Yd MYFR/PKLN * W1K 30 B3
Redman's Rd WCHPL E1 .... 90 C4
Redmead La WAP E1W 102 A2

Redmore Rd HMSMTH * W6 .... 100 B5
Red Pl MYFR/PKLN W1K 30 A1
Red Post Hl HNHL SE24 .... 137 D3
Redriffe Rd PLSTW E13 .... 93 F1
Redriff Rd BERM/RHTH SE16 .... 103 E4
Redruth Rd HOM E9 .... 78 C5
Redstart Cl EHAM E6 .... 95 E4
    NWCR * SE14 .... 121 E3
Redvers St IS N1 .... 13 D3
Redwald Rd CLPT E5 .... 79 D1
Redwood Cl BERM/RHTH SE16 .... 103 E2
Reece Ms SKENS SW7 .... 40 A4
Reed Cl CAN/RD E16 .... 94 A4
    LEE/GVPK SE12 .... 142 A3
Reedham St PECK * SE15 .... 120 A5
Reedholm Vls STNW/STAM N16 .... 77 D1
Reed's Pl CAMTN NW1 .... 74 C4
Reedworth St LBTH SE11 .... 46 B5
Reesland Cl MNPK SE12 .... 84 A3
Rees St IS N1 .... 76 C5
Reets Farm Cl CDALE/KGS NW9 .... 51 E1
Reeves Av CDALE/KGS NW9 .... 51 D2
Reeves Ms MYFR/PKLN W1K 30 A2
Reeves Rd BOW E3 .... 92 B3
    WOOL/PLUM SE18 .... 126 B2
Reform St BTSEA SW11 .... 115 F5
Regal Cl WCHPL E1 .... 90 A4
Regal La CAMTN NW1 .... 74 A5
Regan Wy IS N1 .... 12 C2
Regency Lawn KTTN * NW5 .... 56 B5
Regency Ms WLSDN NW10 .... 70 A3
Regency Pde HAMP * NW3 .... 73 D4
Regency Pl WEST * SW1P 44 A4
Regency St WEST SW1P 44 B5
Regency Ter HGT * N6 .... 55 F1
    SKENS * SW7 .... 115 D1
Regent Pde STNW/STAM * N16 .... 59 F2
Regent Pl WIM/MER SW19 .... 150 C5
Regent Rd HNHL SE24 .... 136 B4
Regents Bridge Gdns VX/NE SW8 .... 117 E2
Regents Ms STJWD NW8 .... 3 F1
Regents Pk CAMTN NW1 .... 6 B3
Regent's Park Rd HAMP NW3 .... 73 F4
Regent's Park Ter CAMTN NW1 .... 74 B5
Regents Plaza KIL/WHAMP * NW6 .... 2 C1
Regent Sq STPAN WC1H 9 D4
Regent's Rw HACK E8 .... 78 A5
Regent St CHSWK W4 .... 110 A1
    CONDST W1S 19 E5
    STJS SW1Y 32 A2
    WLSDN NW10 .... 89 D2
Regents Whf IS * N1 .... 9 E1
Reginald Rd DEPT SE8 .... 122 A3
    FSTGT E7 .... 82 A4
Reginald Sq DEPT SE8 .... 122 A3
Regina Rd FSBYPK N4 .... 57 F3
Regis Rd KTTN NW5 .... 74 B2
Regnart Buildings CAMTN NW1 .... 7 F4
Reidhaven Rd WOOL/PLUM SE18 .... 109 E5
Reigate Rd BMLY BR1 .... 160 A3
    GDMY/SEVK IG3 .... 67 F4
Reighton Rd CLPT E5 .... 60 C5
Relay Rd SHB W12 .... 100 C1
Relf Rd PECK SE15 .... 138 A1
Reliance Ar BRXN/ST * SW9 .... 136 A2
Relton Ms SKENS SW7 .... 41 D2
Rembrandt Cl BGVA * SW1W 116 A1
    POP/IOD E14 .... 105 D4
Rembrandt Rd LEW SE13 .... 141 D3
Remington Rd EHAM E6 .... 95 E5
    SEVS/STOTM N15 .... 59 D1
Remington St IS N1 .... 11 D2
Remnant St HOL/ALD WC2B 21 E4

Remus Rd *BOW* E3 ....80 A4
Rendlesham Rd *CLPT* E5 ....78 A1
Renforth St *BERM/RHTH* SE16 ......102 C3
Renfrew Cl *EHAM* E6 ....108 A1
Renfrew Rd *LBTH* SE11 ....46 C4
Rennell St *LEW* SE13 ....140 C1
Rennets Cl *ELTH/MOT* SE9 ....145 D3
Rennets Wood Rd *ELTH/MOT* SE9 ....145 D3
Rennie Est *BERM/RHTH* SE16 ....102 A3
Rennie St *STHWK* SE1 ....34 C3
Renters Av *HDN* NW4 ....52 C1
Renton Cl *BRXS/STRHM* SW2 ....135 F4
Rephidim St *STHWK* SE1 ....48 B3
Replingham Rd *WAND/EARL* SW18 ...149 F1
Reporton Rd *FUL/PGN* SW6 ....113 E4
Repository Rd *WOOL/PLUM* SE18 ...125 F2
Repton St *POP/IOD* E14 ....91 E5
Reservoir Rd *BROCKY* SE4 ....121 E5
Restell Cl *BKHTH/KID* SE3 ....123 D4
Reston Pl *SKENS* SW7 ....39 E1
Restons Crs *ELTH/MOT* SE9 ....145 D4
Retford St *BETH* * E2 ....13 D2
Retreat Pl *HOM* E9 ....78 C3
The Retreat *BARN* SW13 ....129 E1
Reunion Rd *WAP* * E1W 102 B1
Reveley Sq *BERM/RHTH* SE16 ....103 E3
Revell Ri *WOOL/PLUM* SE18 ....127 F2
Revelon Rd *BROCKY* SE4 ....139 E2
Revelstoke Rd *WIM/MER* SW19 .....150 A2
Reventlow Rd *ELTH/MOT* SE9 ....162 C1
Reverdy Rd *STHWK* SE1 ....102 A5
Review Rd *CRICK* NW2 ....51 F4
Rewell St *FUL/PGN* * SW6 ....114 C3
Rex Pl *MYFR/PKLN* W1K 30 B5
Reydon Av *WAN* E11 ....64 C1
Reynard St *NWCR* * SE14 ....121 E2
Reynolds Av *MNPK* E12 ....84 A2
Reynolds Cl *GLDGN* NW11 ....54 B2
Reynolds Pl *BKHTH/KID* SE3 ....124 B3
Reynolds Rd *CHSWK* W4 ....98 C4
PECK SE15 ....138 C3
Rheidol Ms *IS* N1 ....11 E1
Rheidol Ter *IS* N1 ....11 D1
Rhoda St *BETH* E2 ....13 F5
Rhodesia Rd *BRXN/ST* SW9 ....117 E5
WAN E11 ....63 D4
Rhodes St *HOLWY* N7 ....75 F2
Rhodeswell Rd *BOW* E3 ....91 E4
Rhondda Gv *BOW* E3 ....91 E2
Rhyl St *KTTN* NW5 ....74 A3
Ribblesdale Rd *STRHM/NOR* SW16 ...152 B5
Ribbon Dance Ms *CMBW* SE5 ....119 D4
Ricardo St *POP/IOD* E14 ....92 B5
Ricards Rd *WIM/MER* SW19 ....149 F5
Richard Cl *WOOL/PLUM* SE18 ....107 E5
Richard House Dr *CAN/RD* E16 ....95 D3
Richardson Cl *HACK* * E8 ....77 F5
Richardson's Ms *FITZ* W1T 19 E1
Richard's Pl *CHEL* SW3 ....41 D4
Richard St *WCHPL* E1 ....90 B5
Richbell Pl *BMSBY* WC1N 21 E2
Richborne Ter *VX/NE* SW8 ....117 F3
Richborough Rd *CRICK* NW2 ....71 D1
Riches Rd *IL* IG1 ....66 C4
Richford Ga *HMSMTH* * W6 ....100 C4
Richford St *SRTFD* E15 ....81 F5
Richford St *HMSMTH* W6 ....100 C3
Richmond Av *IS* N1 ....75 F5
WLSDN NW10 ....70 B3

Richmond Buildings
SOHO/CST W1F 20 A5
Richmond Cl *WALTH* E17 ....61 F1

Richmond Crs *IS* N1 ....75 F5
Richmond Gv *IS* N1 ....76 B4
Richmond Ms *SOHO/CST* W1F 20 A5
Richmond Park Rd
MORT/ESHN SW14 ....128 C3
Richmond Pl *WOOL/PLUM* SE18 ....108 C5
Richmond Rd *FSTGT* E7 ....82 B2
HACK E8 ....77 F4
IL IG1 ....66 C5
SEVS/STOTM N15 ....59 E1
WAN E11 ....63 D4
Richmond St *PLSTW* E13 ....94 A1
Richmond Ter *WHALL* SW1A 32 C5
Richmond Wy *SHB* W12 ....101 D3
WAN E11 ....64 A4
Richmount Gdns *BKHTH/KID* SE3 ...142 A1
Rich St *POP/IOD* E14 ....103 F5
Rickard Cl *BRXS/STRHM* SW2 ....154 A1
Rickett St *FUL/PGN* SW6 ....114 A2
Rickman St *WCHPL* E1 ....90 C3
Rick Roberts Wy *SRTFD* E15 ....81 D5
Rickthorne Rd *ARCH* N19 ....57 E4
Riddons Rd *LEE/GVPK* SE12 ....160 C3
Rideout St *WOOL/PLUM* SE18 ....107 F5
Rider Cl *BFN/LL* DA15 ....145 E4
Ridgdale St *BOW* E3 ....92 A1
Ridgebrook Rd *ELTH/MOT* SE9 .....142 C2
Ridge Cl *THMD* SE28 ....109 D3
Ridge Hl *GLDGN* NW11 ....53 E3
Ridge Rd *CEND/HSY/T* N8 ....57 F1
CRICK NW2 ....53 F5
Ridgeway Dr *BMLY* BR1 ....160 B4
Ridgeway East *BFN/LL* DA15 ....145 F3
The Ridgeway *ACT* W3 ....98 A4
GLDGN NW11 ....53 F3
Ridgeway West *BFN/LL* DA15 ....145 E3
Ridgewell Cl *IS* N1 ....76 C5
SYD SE26 ....157 F4
Ridgmount Gdns *GWRST* WC1E 20 A2
Ridgmount Rd *WAND/EARL* SW18 ...132 B3
Ridgmount St *GWRST* WC1E 20 A2
Ridgway Rd *BRXN/ST* SW9 ....136 B1
Ridgwell Rd *CAN/RD* E16 ....94 C4
Riding House St *GTPST* W1W 19 E3
The Riding *GLDGN* NW11 ....53 F2
Ridley Rd *FSTGT* E7 ....82 C1
HACK E8 ....77 F2
WLSDN NW10 ....88 A1
Riefield Rd *ELTH/MOT* SE9 ....144 C2
Riffel Rd *CRICK* NW2 ....70 C2
Rifle Pl *NTGHL* W11 ....101 D2
Rifle St *POP/IOD* E14 ....92 B4
Rigault Rd *FUL/PGN* SW6 ....113 E5
Rigby Ms *IL* IG1 ....66 A4
Rigden St *POP/IOD* E14 ....92 B5
Rigeley Rd *WLSDN* NW10 ....88 A2
Rigg Ap *LEY* E10 ....61 D3
Rigge Pl *CLAP* SW4 ....135 D2
Riggindale Rd *STRHM/NOR* SW16 ...153 D3
Riley Rd *STHWK* SE1 ....49 E2
Riley St *WBPTN* SW10 ....115 D3
Rinaldo Rd *BAL* SW12 ....134 B5
Ringcroft St *HOLWY* N7 ....76 A2
Ringford Rd *WAND/EARL* SW18 .....131 F3
Ringlet Cl *CAN/RD* E16 ....94 B4
Ringmer Av *FUL/PGN* SW6 ....113 E4
Ringmore Ri *FSTH* SE23 ....138 B5
Ringstead Rd *CAT* SE6 ....140 B5
Ringwood Gdns *PUT/ROE* SW15 ....148 A2
Ringwood Rd *WALTH* E17 ....61 F1
Ripley Gdns *MORT/ESHN* SW14 .....129 D1
Ripley Ms *WAN* * E11 ....63 E1

Ripley Rd CAN/RD E16 ....94 C5
  GDMY/SEVK IG3 ....67 F4
Ripon Gdns IL IG1 ....65 E1
Ripon Rd WOOL/PLUM SE18 ....126 B2
Ripple Rd BARK IG11 ....84 C4
Ripplevale Gv IS N1 ....75 F4
Rippolson Rd WOOL/PLUM SE18 ....127 F1
Risborough St STHWK SE1 ....35 D5
Risdon St BERM/RHTH SE16 ....102 C3
Riseldine Rd FSTH SE23 ....139 E4
The Rise WLSDN NW10 ....51 D5
Risinghill St IS N1 ....10 A1
Rita Rd VX/NE SW8 ....117 E3
Ritchie St IS N1 ....10 B1
Ritherdon Rd TOOT SW17 ....152 A2
Ritson Rd HACK E8 ....77 F3
Ritter St WOOL/PLUM SE18 ....126 A2
Rivaz PI HOM E9 ....78 C3
Riverbank Rd BMLY BR1 ....160 A3
River Barge CI POP/IOD E14 ....104 C3
River CI WAN E11 ....64 C1
Rivercourt Rd HMSMTH W6 ....100 B5
Riverdale Dr WAND/EARL SW18 ....150 B1
Riverdale Rd WOOL/PLUM SE18 ....127 F1
Riverdene Rd IL IG1 ....66 A5
River PI IS N1 ....76 C4
River Rd BARK IG11 ....97 E1
Riversdale Rd HBRY N5 ....58 B5
Riverside CHARL SE7 ....106 B4
  HDN NW4 ....52 B2
  RCH/KEW * TW9 ....110 A2
Riverside CI CLPT E5 ....60 C3
Riverside Dr CHSWK W4 ....111 D3
  GLDGN * NW11 ....53 E1
Riverside Gdns HMSMTH W6 ....112 B1
Riverside Rd IL IG1 ....66 B5
  SEVS/STOTM N15 ....60 A1
  SRTFD E15 ....92 C1
  TOOT SW17 ....150 B4
River St CLKNW EC1R 10 A3
River Ter HMSMTH W6 ....112 C1
Riverton CI MV/WKIL * W9 ....89 F2
Riverview Gdns BARN SW13 ....112 B3
Riverview Pk CAT SE6 ....158 A2
Riverview Rd CHSWK W4 ....110 B3
River Wy GNWCH SE10 ....105 F4
Rivington PI SDTCH EC2A 13 D4
Rivington St SDTCH EC2A 13 D4
Rivington Wk HACK * E8 ....78 A5
Rixon St HOLWY N7 ....58 A5
Rixsen Rd MNPK E12 ....83 E2
Roach Rd HOM E9 ....80 A4
Roads PI ARCH N19 ....57 E4
Roan St GNWCH SE10 ....122 C1
Robert Adam St MBLAR W1H 18 A4
Roberta St BETH E2 ....90 A2
Robert CI MV/WKIL W9 ....15 F1
Robert Keen CI PECK SE15 ....120 A4
Robert Lowe CI NWCR SE14 ....121 D3
Roberts CI ELTH/MOT SE9 ....163 D1
Roberts Ct WLSDN NW10 ....69 E3
Roberts Ms KTBR * SW1X 42 A3
Robertson Rd SRTFD E15 ....80 C5
Robertson St VX/NE SW8 ....134 B1
Robert's PI CLKNW * EC1R 10 B5
Robert St CAMTN NW1 ....7 D4
  CHCR WC2N 33 D2
  WOOL/PLUM SE18 ....109 D5
Robeson St BOW E3 ....91 F4
Robin Gv HGT N6 ....56 A4
Robin Hood Gdns POP/IOD * E14 ....104 C3
Robin Hood La POP/IOD E14 ....104 C3
  PUT/ROE SW15 ....147 E3

Robin Hood Rd PUT/ROE SW15 ....147 E4
Robin Hood Wy
(Kingston By Pass)
  PUT/ROE SW15 ....147 E4
Robinia Crs LEY E10 ....62 B4
Robinson Rd BETH E2 ....90 C1
Robinson St CHEL SW3 ....115 F2
Robinwood PI
  RCHPK/HAM TW10 ....147 D4
Robsart St BRXN/ST SW9 ....117 F5
Robson Av WLSDN NW10 ....70 A5
Robson CI EHAM E6 ....95 E5
Robson Rd WNWD SE27 ....154 B3
Rochdale Wy DEPT SE8 ....122 A3
Rochelle CI BTSEA SW11 ....133 D2
Rochelle St BETH E2 ....13 E4
Rochemont Wk HACK * E8 ....77 F5
Rochester Av PLSTW E13 ....82 C5
Rochester Gdns IL IG1 ....65 F2
Rochester Ms CAMTN NW1 ....74 C3
Rochester PI CAMTN NW1 ....74 C3
Rochester Rd CAMTN NW1 ....74 C3
Rochester Rw WEST SW1P 43 F4
Rochester Sq CAMTN NW1 ....74 C4
Rochester St WEST SW1P 44 A3
Rochester Ter CAMTN NW1 ....74 C3
Rochester Wk STHWK * SE1 ....36 A3
Rochester Wy BKHTH/KID SE3 ....124 B4
Rochester Way Relief Rd
  ELTH/MOT SE9 ....143 E3
Rochford CI EHAM E6 ....95 D1
Rochford Wk HACK * E8 ....78 A4
Rock Av MORT/ESHN SW14 ....129 D1
Rockbourne Rd FSTH SE23 ....157 D1
Rockell's PI EDUL SE22 ....138 B4
Rock Grove Wy BERM/RHTH SE16 ....102 A5
Rockhall Rd CRICK NW2 ....71 D1
Rockhampton Rd
  STRHM/NOR SW16 ....154 A4
Rock HI NRWD SE19 ....155 F4
Rockingham CI PUT/ROE SW15 ....129 F2
Rockingham St STHWK SE1 ....47 E3
Rockland Rd PUT/ROE SW15 ....131 E2
Rockley Rd SHB W12 ....101 D3
Rockmount Rd WOOL/PLUM SE18 ....127 F1
Rocks La BARN SW13 ....130 A1
Rock St FSBYPK N4 ....58 A4
Rockwell Gdns NRWD SE19 ....155 E4
Rocliffe St IS N1 ....11 D2
Rocombe Crs FSTH * SE23 ....138 C5
Rocque La BKHTH/KID SE3 ....141 F1
Rodborough Rd GLDGN NW11 ....54 A3
Rodenhurst Rd CLAP SW4 ....134 C5
Roden St HOLWY N7 ....57 F5
  IL IG1 ....66 A5
Roderick Rd HAMP NW3 ....73 F1
Roding Ms WAP E1W 102 A2
Roding Rd CLPT E5 ....79 D1
  EHAM E6 ....96 B4
Rodmarton St MHST W1U 17 F3
Rodmere St GNWCH SE10 ....123 E1
Rodmill La BRXS/STRHM SW2 ....135 E5
Rodney PI STHWK SE1 ....47 E4
Rodney Rd WALW SE17 ....47 F5
Rodney St IS N1 ....9 F1
Rodway Rd PUT/ROE SW15 ....130 A5
Rodwell Rd EDUL SE22 ....137 F4
Roedean Crs PUT/ROE SW15 ....129 E4
Roehampton CI PUT/ROE SW15 ....130 A2
Roehampton Ga PUT/ROE SW15 ....129 E4
Roehampton High St
  PUT/ROE SW15 ....130 A3
Roehampton La PUT/ROE SW15 ....130 A3

Roehampton V *PUT/ROE* SW15 ....**147** F3
Roffey St *POP/IOD* E14....................**104** C3
Rogers Rd *CAN/RD* E16 ....**93** F5
   TOOT SW17 ....**151** D4
Roger St *BMSBY* WC1N....................**21** F1
Rojack Rd *FSTH* SE23 ....**157** D1
Rokeby Rd *BROCKY* * SE4..............**121** F5
Rokeby St *SRTFD* E15 ....**81** E5
Rokesby Cl *WELL* DA16...................**127** D5
Roland Gdns *SKENS* SW7 ....**114** C1
Roland Ms *WCHPL* * E1...................**91** D4
Roland Wy *WALW* SE17 ....**119** D1
   WBPTN SW10 ....**114** C1
Rollins St *PECK* SE15 ....**120** C2
Rollit St *HOLWY* N7.........................**76** A2
Rolls Buildings *FLST/FETLN* EC4A ...**22** A4
Rollscourt Av *HNHL* SE24................**136** C3
Rolls Rd *STHWK* SE1 ....**119** F1
Rolt St *DEPT* SE8 ....**121** E2
Roman Cl *ACT* W3 ....**98** B3
Romanfield Rd *BRXS/STRHM* SW2 ...**135** F1
Roman Rd *BETH* E2...........................**91** D1
   CHSWK W4.....................................**99** E5
   EHAM E6...**95** E4
   IL IG1..**84** B3
Roman Wy *HOLWY* N7.......................**75** F3
Romberg Rd *TOOT* SW17 ....**152** A3
Romborough Gdns *LEW* SE13 ....**140** C3
Romborough Wy *LEW* SE13 ....**140** C3
Romero Sq *ELTH/MOT* SE9...............**142** C2
Romeyn Rd *STRHM/NOR* SW16.........**153** F3
Romford Rd *MNPK* E12 ....**66** A5
   SRTFD E15 ....**81** E4
Romford St *WCHPL* E1......................**90** A4
Romilly Rd *FSBYPK* N4 ....**58** B1
Romilly St *SOHO/SHAV* W1D............**32** B1
Rommany Rd *WNWD* SE27 ....**155** D4
Romney Cl *GLDGN* NW11..................**54** B3
Romney Rd *GNWCH* SE10..................**122** C2
   WOOL/PLUM SE18...........................**108** B4
Romney Rw *CRICK* * NW2 ....**53** D4
Romola Rd *BRXS/STRHM* SW2.........**154** B1
Ronald Av *SRTFD* E15 ....**93** E2
Ronalds Rd *HBRY* N5.........................**76** A2
Ronaldstone Rd *BFN/LL* DA15.........**145** E4
Ronald St *WCHPL* E1.........................**90** C5
Rona Rd *HAMP* NW3 ....**74** A1
Rona Wk *IS* N1 ....**77** D3
Rondu Rd *CRICK* NW2 ....**71** E2
Ron Leighton Wy *EHAM* E6...............**83** D4
Ronver Rd *LEE/GVPK* SE12...............**160** A1
Rood La *FENCHST* EC3M **36** C1
Rook Cl *WBLY* HA9............................**50** B5
Rookery La *CLAP* SW4 ....**134** C4
Rookstone Rd *TOOT* SW17 ....**151** F5
Rookwood Rd *STNW/STAM* N16.......**59** F1
Rootes St *NKENS* W10.......................**89** D3
Ropemaker Rd *BERM/RHTH* SE16 .....**103** E3
Ropemaker's Flds *POP/IOD* * E14 ...**103** F1
Ropemaker St *BARB* EC2Y **24** A2
Roper La *STHWK* SE1.........................**49** D1
Ropers Orch *CHEL* * SW3 ....**115** C2
Roper St *ELTH/MOT* SE9...................**143** F3
Ropery St *BOW* E3.............................**91** F3
Rope St *BERM/RHTH* SE16 ....**103** E4
Ropewalk Gdns *WCHPL* E1...............**90** A5
Ropewalk Ms *HACK* * E8...................**77** F4
Rope Yard Rails
   WOOL/PLUM SE18...........................**108** B4
Ropley St *BETH* E2............................**90** A1
Rosa Alba Ms *HBRY* N5.....................**76** C1
Rosaline Rd *FUL/PGN* SW6...............**113** E3
Rosaline Ter *FUL/PGN* * SW6 ....**113** E3

Rosamond St *SYD* SE26 ....**156** B3
Rosamond Vls *MORT/ESHN* * SW14...**129** D2
Rosary Gdns *SKENS* SW7 ....**39** F5
Rosaville Rd *FUL/PGN* SW6 ....**113** F3
Roscoe St *STLK* EC1Y **23** F1
Rose Aly *STHWK* SE1..........................**35** F3
Rosebank Est *BOW* E3........................**91** F1
Rosebank Gdns *ACT* * W3..................**87** D5
   BOW * E3..**91** E1
Rosebank Rd *LEY* E10........................**62** A1
Rosebank Wk *CAMTN* * NW1..............**75** D4
Rosebank Wy *ACT* W3........................**87** D5
Roseberry Gdns *FSBYPK* N4 ....**58** B1
Roseberry Pl *HACK* E8.......................**77** F3
Roseberry St *BERM/RHTH* SE16 ....**102** B5
Rosebery Av *BFN/LL* DA15................**145** E5
   CLKNW EC1R **10** A5
   MNPK E12.......................................**83** E3
Rosebery Ct *CLKNW* EC1R **10** A5
Rosebery Rd *CLAP* SW4 ....**135** E4
Rosebury Rd *FUL/PGN* SW6..............**114** B5
Rose Ct *WCHPL* E1.............................**25** E3
Rosecroft Av *HAMP* NW3...................**54** A5
Rose Croft Gdns *CRICK* NW2............**52** A5
Rose & Crown Yd *STJS* * SW1Y.........**31** F4
Rosedale Rd *FSTGT* E7......................**82** C2
Rosedene Av *STRHM/NOR* SW16.......**153** F3
Rosedene Ter *LEY* E10.......................**62** B4
Rosedew Rd *HMSMTH* W6.................**113** D2
Rosefield *POP/IOD* E14......................**104** A1
Rosefield Gdns *POP/IOD* E14 ....**104** A1
Rosehart Ms *NTGHL* * W11................**14** A5
Rosehill Rd *WAND/EARL* SW18.........**132** C4
Roseleigh Av *HBRY* N5.......................**76** B1
Rosemary Dr *POP/IOD* E14 ....**93** D5
Rosemary La *MORT/ESHN* SW14.......**128** C1
Rosemary Rd *PECK* SE15 ....**119** F3
   TOOT SW17 ....**150** B3
   WELL DA16 ....**127** F4
Rosemary St *IS* N1 ....**77** D5
Rosemead *CDALE/KGS* NW9...............**51** F2
Rosemont Rd *ACT* W3........................**98** B3
   HAMP NW3.....................................**72** C3
Rosemoor St *CHEL* SW3 ....**41** E5
Rosenau Crs *BTSEA* SW11................**115** F4
Rosenau Rd *BTSEA* SW11.................**115** E4
Rosendale Rd *DUL* SE21 ....**154** C1
   HNHL SE24 ....**136** C5
Roseneath Rd *BTSEA* SW11..............**134** A4
Rosenthal Rd *CAT* SE6......................**140** B4
Rosenthorpe Rd *PECK* SE15 ....**139** D3
Roserton St *POP/IOD* E14.................**104** C3
Rosery Ga *BTSEA* SW11....................**116** B3
Rose Sq *CHEL* * SW3 ....**115** D1
Rose St *COVGDN* WC2E.....................**32** C1
Rosethorn Cl *BAL* SW12...................**134** C5
Rosetta Cl *VX/NE* SW8.....................**117** E3
Roseveare Rd *LEE/GVPK* SE12.........**160** C4
Roseway *DUL* SE21............................**137** D4
Rose Wy *LEE/GVPK* SE12 ....**142** A3
Rosher Cl *SRTFD* E15........................**81** D4
Rosina St *HOM* E9.............................**79** D2
Roskell Rd *PUT/ROE* SW15...............**131** E1
Roslin Rd *ACT* W3.............................**98** A4
Roslin Wy *BMLY* BR1.........................**160** A5
Rosmead Rd *NTGHL* W11..................**101** E1
Rosoman Pl *CLKNW* EC1R.................**10** B5
Rosoman St *CLKNW* EC1R.................**10** B4
Rossdale Dr *CDALE/KGS* NW9...........**50** C3
Rossdale Rd *PUT/ROE* SW15............**130** C2
Rosse Ms *BKHTH/KID* SE3................**124** B4
Rossendale St *CLPT* E5.....................**60** B4
Rossendale Wy *CAMTN* NW1.............**74** C5

Rossetti Rd *BERM/RHTH* SE16..........**120** B1
Rossington St *CLPT* * E5.....................**60** B4
Rossiter Rd *BAL* SW12.......................**152** B1
Rosslyn Av *BARN* SW13.....................**129** E1
Rosslyn Hl *HAMP* NW3.........................**73** D2
Rosslyn Park Ms *HAMP* NW3................**73** D2
Rosslyn Rd *BARK* IG11.........................**85** D4
Rossmore Cl *CAMTN* * NW1.................**17** D1
Rossmore Rd *CAMTN* NW1......................**5** D5
Ross Wy *ELTH/MOT* SE9.....................**143** E1
Rostella Rd *TOOT* SW17.....................**151** D4
Rostrevor Av *SEVS/STOTM* N15..........**59** F1
Rostrevor Rd *FUL/PGN* SW6...............**113** F4
    WIM/MER SW19.............................**150** A5
Rotary St *STHWK* SE1...........................**46** C2
Rothbury Rd *HOM* E9...........................**79** F4
Rotherfield St *IS* N1.............................**76** C4
Rotherham Wk *STHWK* * SE1...............**35** D3
Rotherhithe New Rd
    BERM/RHTH SE16..........................**120** B3
Rotherhithe Old Rd
    BERM/RHTH SE16..........................**103** D5
Rotherhithe St
    BERM/RHTH SE16..........................**102** B3
Rotherhithe Tnl *BERM/RHTH* SE16....**102** C3
Rotherwick Rd *GLDGN* NW11................**54** A2
Rotherwood Rd *PUT/ROE* SW15.........**131** D1
Rothery St *IS* N1....................................**76** B5
Rothery Ter *BRXN/ST* * SW9..............**118** B3
Rothesay Av *RCHPK/HAM* TW10.........**128** B2
Rothsay Rd *FSTGT* E7............................**82** C4
Rothsay St *STHWK* SE1..........................**48** C2
Rothschild Rd *CHSWK* W4.....................**98** C5
Rothschild St *WNWD* SE27.................**154** B4
Rothwell St *CAMTN* NW1.......................**73** F5
Rotterdam Dr *POP/IOD* E14................**104** C4
Rouel Rd *BERM/RHTH* SE16................**102** A4
Roundel Cl *BROCKY* SE4......................**139** F2
Roundhay Cl *FSTH* SE23......................**157** D2
Round Hl *FSTH* SE23............................**156** B2
Roundtable Rd *BMLY* BR1....................**159** F3
Roundwood Pk *WLSDN* * NW10............**70** A5
Roundwood Rd *WLSDN* NW10................**69** E3
Rounton Rd *BOW* E3..............................**92** A3
Roupell Rd *BRXS/STRHM* SW2............**153** F1
Roupell St *STHWK* SE1..........................**34** B4
Rousden St *CAMTN* * NW1.....................**74** C4
Rouse Gdns *DUL* SE21.........................**155** E4
Routemaster Cl *PLSTW* E13.................**94** B2
Routh Rd *WAND/EARL* SW18...............**133** E5
Routh St *EHAM* E6..................................**95** F4
Rowallan Rd *FUL/PGN* SW6................**113** E3
Rowan Cl *IL* IG1......................................**85** D2
Rowan Wk *HMSMTH* W6......................**101** D5
Rowan Wk *EFNCH* N2..............................**54** C1
    NKENS * W10....................................**89** E3
Rowberry Cl *FUL/PGN* SW6................**113** D3
Rowcross St *STHWK* SE1.....................**119** F1
Rowditch La *BTSEA* SW11....................**116** A5
Rowdon Av *WLSDN* NW10.......................**70** B4
Rowe Gdns *BARK* IG11............................**97** F1
Rowe La *HOM* E9.....................................**78** C2
Rowena Crs *BTSEA* SW11....................**115** E5
Rowfant Rd *TOOT* SW17......................**152** A2
Rowhill Rd *CLPT* E5................................**78** B1
Rowington Cl *BAY/PAD* W2....................**14** C2
Rowland Gv *SYD* SE26.........................**156** B3
Rowland Hill St *HAMP* NW3...................**73** E2
Rowlands Rd *HGT* * N6............................**56** A1
Rowley Cottages *WKENS* * W14..........**101** F5
Rowley Gdns *FSBYPK* N4.......................**58** C2
Rowley Wy *STJWD* NW8..........................**72** C5
Rowntree Cl *KIL/WHAMP* * NW6............**72** A3

PLSTW E13...**94** B3
Rowse Cl *SRTFD* E15..............................**80** C5
Rowstock Gdns *HOLWY* N7....................**75** D2
Rowton Rd *WOOL/PLUM* SE18............**126** C3
Roxburgh Rd *WNWD* SE27...................**154** B5
Roxby Pl *FUL/PGN* SW6.......................**114** A2
Roxley Rd *LEW* SE13............................**140** B4
Roxwell Rd *SHB* W12............................**100** A3
Royal Albert Rd *EHAM* E6...................**108** A1
Royal Albert Wy *CAN/RD* E16.............**107** D1
Royal Ar *CONDST* W1S............................**31** E2
Royal Arsenal West
    WOOL/PLUM * SE18.......................**126** A1
Royal Av *CHEL* SW3.............................**115** F1
Royal Circ *WNWD* SE27.......................**154** A3
Royal Cl *DEPT* SE8...............................**121** F2
    STNW/STAM * N16............................**59** E3
Royal College St *CAMTN* NW1..............**74** C4
Royal Ct *BANK* EC3V.............................**24** B5
    ELTH/MOT * SE9.............................**161** F1
Royal Crs *NTGHL* W11.........................**101** D3
Royal Crescent Ms *NTGHL* W11.........**101** D3
Royal Docks Rd *EHAM* E6.....................**96** B4
Royal Herbert Pavilions
    WOOL/PLUM * SE18.......................**125** F4
Royal Hl *GNWCH* SE10........................**122** C3
Royal Hospital Rd *CHEL* SW3.............**115** F2
Royal Ms *BAL* SW12.............................**134** B5
The Royal Ms *WHALL* SW1A....................**43** D2
Royal Mint Pl *WCHPL* E1........................**37** F1
Royal Mint St *TWRH* EC3N......................**37** F1
Royal Naval Pl *NWCR* SE14.................**121** F3
Royal Oak Pl *EDUL* SE22.....................**138** B4
Royal Oak Rd *HACK* E8...........................**78** B3
Royal Opera Ar *STJS* * SW1Y.................**32** A3
Royal Orchard Cl
    WAND/EARL SW18.........................**131** E5
Royal Pde *BKHTH/KID* SE3..................**123** F5
    FUL/ * SW6....................................**113** E3
Royal Pl *GNWCH* SE10.........................**122** C3
Royal Rd *CAN/RD* E16............................**94** C5
    WALW SE17....................................**118** B2
Royal St *STHWK* SE1..............................**45** F2
Royal Victor Pl *BOW* E3.........................**91** D1
Roycraft Av *BARK* IG11...........................**97** F1
Roycroft Cl *BRXS/STRHM* * SW2.........**154** A1
Roydene Rd *WOOL/PLUM* SE18..........**127** E2
Royston Gdns *IL* IG1...............................**65** D3
Royston St *BETH* E2................................**90** C1
Rozel Rd *CLAP* SW4.............................**116** C5
Rubens St *CAT* SE6..............................**157** F2
Ruby Rd *PECK* SE15.............................**120** B2
Ruby Triangle *PECK* * SE15.................**120** B2
Ruckholt Cl *LEY* E10...............................**62** B5
Ruckholt Rd *LEY* E10..............................**62** C5
Rucklidge Av *WLSDN* NW10...................**87** F1
Rudall Crs *HAMP* NW3............................**73** D1
Ruddington Cl *CLPT* E5..........................**79** E1
Ruddstreet Cl *WOOL/PLUM* SE18......**108** B5
Rudgwick Ter *STJWD* * NW8..................**73** E5
Rudloe Rd *BAL* SW12...........................**134** C5
Rudolf Pl *VX/NE* SW8...........................**117** E2
Rudolph Rd *KIL/WHAMP* NW6..................**2** B2
    PLSTW E13......................................**93** F1
Rufford Cl *IS* N1......................................**75** E5
Rufus St *IS* N1.......................................**12** C4
Rugby Rd *CHSWK* W4.............................**99** E3
Rugby St *BMSBY* WC1N..........................**21** E1
Rugg St *POP/IOD* E14...........................**104** A1
Ruislip St *TOOT* SW17..........................**151** F4
Rumbold Rd *FUL/PGN* SW6.................**114** B3
Rum Cl *WAP* E1W..................................**102** B1
Rumsey Rd *BRXN/ST* SW9...................**135** F1

Runbury Cir *CDALE/KGS* NW9 ....**51** D4
Runcorn Pl *NTGHL* W11 ....**101** E1
Rupack St *BERM/RHTH* * SE16 ....**102** C3
Rupert Gdns *BRXN/ST* SW9 ....**118** B5
Rupert Rd *ARCH* N19 ....**57** D5
  CHSWK W4 ....**99** E4
  KIL/WHAMP NW6 ....**89** F1
Rupert St *SOHO/SHAV* W1D **32** A1
Rusbridge Cl *HACK* E8 ....**78** A2
Ruscoe Rd *CAN/RD* E16 ....**93** F5
Rusham Rd *BAL* SW12 ....**133** F4
Rushbrook Rd *ELTH/MOT* SE9 ....**162** C2
Rushcroft Rd *BRXS/STRHM* SW2 ....**136** A2
Rushey Gn *CAT* SE6 ....**140** B5
Rushey Md *BROCKY* SE4 ....**140** A3
Rushford Rd *BROCKY* SE4 ....**139** F4
Rushgrove St *WOOL/PLUM* SE18 ....**107** F5
Rush Hill Ms *BTSEA* SW11 ....**134** A1
Rush Hill Rd *BTSEA* SW11 ....**134** A1
Rushmead *BETH* E2 ....**90** B2
Rushmere Pl *WIM/MER* SW19 ....**149** D5
Rushmore Rd *CLPT* E5 ....**78** C1
Rusper Cl *CRICK* NW2 ....**52** C5
Russell Cl *WHALL* SW1A **31** F4
Russell Gdns *GLDGN* NW11 ....**53** E1
  WKENS * W14 ....**101** E1
Russell Gardens Ms *WKENS* W14 ....**101** E3
Russell Gv *BRXN/ST* SW9 ....**118** A4
Russell Kerr Cl *CHSWK* * W4 ....**110** C3
Russell Pde *GLDGN* * NW11 ....**53** E1
Russell Pl *HAMP* NW3 ....**73** E2
Russell Rd *CAN/RD* E16 ....**94** A5
  CDALE/KGS NW9 ....**51** F1
  CEND/HSY/T N8 ....**57** D1
  LEY E10 ....**62** B1
  WKENS W14 ....**101** E4
Russell Sq *GWRST* WC1E **20** B2
Russell St *HOL/ALD* WC2B **21** E5
Russet Crs *HOLWY* * N7 ....**75** F2
Russia Dock Rd
  BERM/RHTH * SE16 ....**103** D2
Russia La *BETH* E2 ....**90** C1
Russia Rw *CITYW* EC2V **23** F5
Rusthall Av *CHSWK* W4 ....**99** D4
Ruston Ms *NTGHL* * W11 ....**89** D4
Ruston Rd *WOOL/PLUM* SE18 ....**107** E4
Ruston St *BOW* E3 ....**79** F5
Rust Sq *CMBW* SE5 ....**119** D3
Rutford Rd *STRHM/NOR* SW16 ....**153** E5
Rutherford St *WEST* SW1P **44** A4
Rutherford Wy *WBLY* HA9 ....**50** A5
Ruthin Cl *CDALE/KGS* NW9 ....**51** F3
Ruthin Rd *BKHTH/KID* SE3 ....**124** A2
Ruthven St *HOM* E9 ....**79** D5
Rutland Cl *MORT/ESHN* SW14 ....**128** B3
Rutland Ct *SKENS* SW7 ....**41** D1
Rutland Gdns *FSBYPK* N4 ....**58** B3
  SKENS SW7 ....**41** D1
Rutland Ga *SKENS* SW7 ....**40** C1
Rutland Gate Ms *SKENS* * SW7 ....**40** C1
Rutland Gv *HMSMTH* W6 ....**112** B3
Rutland Ms *STJWD* * NW8 ....**72** B5

Rutland Ms South *SKENS* * SW7 ....**40** C2
Rutland Pk *CAT* SE6 ....**157** F2
  CRICK NW2 ....**70** C2
Rutland Pl *FARR* * EC1M **23** D2
Rutland Rd *FSTGT* E7 ....**83** D4
  HOM E9 ....**79** D5
  IL IG1 ....**84** B1
  WALTH E17 ....**62** A1
Rutland St *SKENS* SW7 ....**41** D2
Rutland Wk *CAT* SE6 ....**157** F2
Rutley Cl *LBTH* SE11 ....**118** B2
Rutt's Ter *NWCR* SE14 ....**121** D4
Ruvigny Gdns *PUT/ROE* SW15 ....**131** D1
Ryan Cl *ELTH/MOT* SE9 ....**142** B2
Ryculff Sq *BKHTH/KID* SE3 ....**123** F5
Rydal Gdns *PUT/ROE* SW15 ....**147** E5
Rydal Rd *STRHM/NOR* SW16 ....**153** D5
Ryder Dr *BERM/RHTH* SE16 ....**120** B1
Ryder's Ter *STJWD* NW8 ....**3** E1
Ryder St *STJS* SW1Y **31** E3
Ryde Vale Rd *BAL* SW12 ....**152** B2
Rydon St *IS* N1 ....**76** C5
Rydston Cl *HOLWY* N7 ....**75** F4
Ryecotes Md *DUL* SE21 ....**155** F1
Ryecroft Rd *LEW* SE13 ....**140** C3
Ryecroft St *FUL/PGN* SW6 ....**114** B4
Ryedale *EDUL* SE22 ....**138** B4
Rye Hill Pk *PECK* SE15 ....**138** C2
Ryelands Crs *LEE/GVPK* SE12 ....**142** C4
Rye La *PECK* SE15 ....**120** A4
Rye Rd *PECK* SE15 ....**139** D2
Rye Wk *PUT/ROE* SW15 ....**131** D3
Ryfold Rd *WIM/MER* SW19 ....**150** A3
Rylandes Rd *CRICK* NW2 ....**52** A5
Ryland Rd *KTTN* * NW5 ....**74** B3
Rylett Crs *SHB* W12 ....**99** F4
Rylett Rd *SHB* W12 ....**99** F3
Rylston Rd *FUL/PGN* SW6 ....**113** F2
Rymer St *HNHL* SE24 ....**136** B4
Rymill St *CAN/RD* E16 ....**108** A2
Rysbrack St *CHEL* SW3 ....**41** E2

S

Sabbarton St *CAN/RD* E16 ....**93** F5
Sabine Rd *BTSEA* SW11 ....**133** F1
Sable St *IS* N1 ....**76** B4
Sach Rd *CLPT* E5 ....**60** B4
Sackville Est *STRHM/NOR* SW16 ....**153** E3
Sackville Gdns *IL* IG1 ....**65** F3
Sackville St *MYFR/PICC* W1J **31** F2
Saffron Av *POP/IOD* E14 ....**105** D1
Saffron Hl *HCIRC* EC1N **22** B2
Saffron St *FARR* EC1M **22** B2
Sage Cl *EHAM* E6 ....**95** F4
Sage St *WCHPL* E1 ....**102** C1
Sage Wy *FSBYW* WC1X **9** E4
Saigasso Cl *CAN/RD* E16 ....**95** D5
Sail St *LBTH* SE11 ....**45** F4
Sainfoin Rd *TOOT* SW17 ....**152** A2
Sainsbury Rd *NRWD* SE19 ....**155** E5
St Agnes Cl *HOM* * E9 ....**78** C5
St Agnes Pl *CMBW* SE5 ....**118** B5
St Agnes Well *STLK* EC1Y **12** B5
St Aidan's Rd *EDUL* SE22 ....**138** C4
St Albans Av *CHSWK* W4 ....**99** D4
  EHAM E6 ....**95** F2
St Albans Gv *KENS* W8 ....**39** D2
  KENS W8 ....**39** D2
St Albans La *GLDGN* NW11 ....**54** A3
St Alban's Ms *BAY/PAD* W2 ....**16** B2

St Alban's Pl *IS* N1.....................................**76** B5
St Albans Rd *GDMY/SEVK* IG3.............**67** F3
   KTTN NW5...**56** A5
   WLSDN NW10..................................**69** E5
St Alban's St *STJS* SW1Y........................**32** A2
St Albans Ter *HMSMTH* * W6..............**113** E2
St Alfege Rd *CHARL* SE7......................**125** D2
St Alphage Gdn *BARB* EC2Y..................**23** F3
St Alphage Gdns *BARB* *........................**23** F3
St Alphage Highwalk *BARB* EC2Y.......**23** F3
St Alphonsus Rd *CLAP* SW4................**134** C2
St Amunds Cl *CAT* SE6.........................**158** A4
St Andrews Cl *BERM/RHTH* * SE16....**120** B1
   CRICK * NW2.....................................**52** B5
St Andrew's Ct *WAND/EARL* SW18....**150** C2
St Andrew's Gv *STNW/STAM* N16........**59** D3
St Andrew's Hl *BLKFR* EC4V..................**35** D1
St Andrew's Ms *STNW/STAM* * N16......**59** D3
St Andrew's Pl *CAMTN* NW1....................**6** C5
St Andrew's Rd *ACT* W3........................**87** E5
   CDALE/KGS NW9...............................**51** D3
   GLDGN NW11...................................**53** F1
   IL IG1...**65** F2
   PLSTW E13.......................................**94** B2
   WAN E11...**63** E1
   WKENS W14...................................**113** E2
   WLSDN NW10..................................**70** B3
St Andrew's Sq *NTGHL* * W11...............**89** E5
St Andrew St *HCIRC* EC1N......................**22** B3
St Andrews Wy *BOW* E3..........................**92** B3
St Anne's Cl *HGT* N6...............................**56** A5
St Annes Ct *SOHO/CST* W1F....................**20** A5
St Anne's Pas *POP/IOD* * E14...............**91** F5
St Anne's Rw *WAN* E11...........................**63** D4
St Anne's Rw *POP/IOD* E14.....................**91** F5
St Anne St *POP/IOD* E14.........................**91** F5
St Ann's *BARK* IG11.................................**84** C5
St Ann's Crs *WAND/EARL* SW18.........**132** B4
St Ann's Gdns *HAMP* NW3....................**74** A3
St Ann's Hl *WAND/EARL* SW18...........**132** B3
St Ann's Park Rd
   WAND/EARL SW18.........................**132** C3
St Ann's Rd *BARK* IG11...........................**84** C5
   BARN * SW13..................................**111** F5
   NTGHL W11.....................................**101** D1
   SEVS/STOTM N15..............................**59** E1
St Ann's St *WEST* SW1P..........................**44** B2
St Ann's Ter *STJWD* NW8...........................**4** B1
St Ann's Vls *NTGHL* W11.......................**101** D2
St Anselm's Pl *MYFR/PKLN* W1K..........**30** C1
St Anthonys Cl *TOOT* SW17.................**151** E2
   WAP * E1W......................................**102** A2
St Antony's Rd *FSTGT* E7........................**82** B4
St Asaph Rd *PECK* SE15........................**139** D1
St Aubyn's Av *WIM/MER* SW19............**149** F5
St Augustine's Rd *CAMTN* NW1.............**75** D4
St Austell Rd *LEW* SE13........................**122** C5
St Awdry's Rd *BARK* IG11......................**85** D5
St Barnabas Rd *WALTH* E17....................**62** A1
St Barnabas Ter *HOM* E9.........................**79** D2
St Barnabas Vls *VX/NE* SW8.................**117** E4
St Barnabus St *BGVA* SW1W..................**116** A1
St Bartholomew's Cl *SYD* SE26............**156** C4
St Bartholomew's Rd *EHAM* E6.............**83** E5
St Benets Cl *TOOT* * SW17....................**151** E2
St Bernards Cl *WNWD* SE27.................**155** D4
St Bernard's Rd *EHAM* E6.......................**83** D5
St Botolph St *HDTCH* EC3A.....................**25** E4
St Bride St *FLST/FETLN* EC4A.................**22** C1
St Catherines Cl *TOOT* * SW17.............**151** E2
St Catherine's Dr *NWCR* SE14.............**121** D3
St Catherines Ms *CHEL* SW3...................**41** E4
St Chad's Pl *FSBYW* WC1X........................**9** D3

St Chad's St *STPAN* WC1H..........................**9** D3
St Charles Pl *NKENS* W10.......................**89** E4
St Charles Sq *NKENS* W10......................**89** D4
St Christopher's Pl *MHST* W1U..............**18** B5
St Clair Rd *PLSTW* E13............................**94** B1
St Clare St *TWRH* EC3N..........................**25** E5
St Clement's La *LINN* WC2A.....................**21** F5
St Clements St *HOLWY* N7.....................**76** A4
St Clements Yd *EDUL* SE22...................**137** E5
St Cloud Rd *WNWD* SE27.....................**154** C4
St Crispins Cl *HAMP* NW3.......................**73** E1
St Cross St *HCIRC* EC1N..........................**22** B2
St Cuthbert's Rd *CRICK* NW2...................**71** F3
St Cyprian's St *TOOT* SW17..................**151** F4
St Davids Cl *BERM/RHTH* * SE16.........**120** B1
   WBLY HA9..**50** C5
St Davids Dr *BOW* * E3.............................**91** E2
St David's Pl *HDN* NW4............................**52** B2
St Davids Sq *POP/IOD* E14...................**122** B1
St Denis Rd *WNWD* SE27.......................**155** D4
St Dionis Rd *FUL/PGN* SW6...................**113** F5
St Donatt's Rd *NWCR* SE14...................**121** F4
St Dunstan's Av *ACT* W3.........................**99** D1
St Dunstan's Gdns *ACT* W3.....................**99** D1
St Dunstan's Hl *MON* * EC3R...................**36** C2
St Dunstan's La *MON* * EC3R...................**36** C2
St Dunstans Rd *FSTGT* E7........................**82** B3
   HMSMTH W6...................................**113** D1
St Edmund's Cl *STJWD* NW8....................**73** F5
   TOOT SW17....................................**151** E2
St Edmund's Rd *IL* IG1.............................**65** F1
St Edmunds Sq *BARN* SW13..................**112** C2
St Edmund's Ter *STJWD* NW8....................**5** D1
St Edward's Cl *GLDGN* NW11..................**54** A1
St Elmo Rd *ACT* W3..................................**99** D1
St Elmos Rd *BERM/RHTH* SE16.............**103** E3
St Erkenwald Ms *BARK* IG11...................**85** D5
St Erkenwald Rd *BARK* IG11....................**85** D5
St Ervans Rd *NKENS* W10........................**89** E4
St Faith's Rd *HNHL* SE24.......................**154** B1
St Fillans Rd *CAT* SE6...........................**158** C1
St Francis Rd *EDUL* SE22......................**137** D2
St Francis Wy *IL* IG1.................................**85** D1
St Gabriel's Cl *WAN* E11..........................**64** B3
St Gabriel's Rd *CRICK* NW2.....................**71** D2
St George's Av *FSTGT* E7........................**82** B4
   HOLWY N7......................................**75** D1
St George's Circ *STHWK* SE1..................**46** C5
St George's Cl *GLDGN* NW11...................**53** F1
St George's Dr *PIM* SW1V.....................**116** B2
   PIM * SW1V....................................**116** B1
St George's La *MON* * EC3R.....................**36** C1
St Georges Ms *CAMTN* NW1....................**73** F4
   CHSWK * W4...................................**110** C2
St Georges Pde *CAT* * SE6....................**157** F2
St Georges Rd *CHSWK* W4.......................**99** D3
   FSTGT E7...**82** B4
   IL IG1...**65** F2
   LEY E10..**62** C5
   STHWK SE1.......................................**46** C3
St George's Ct *STP* * EC4M......................**22** C4
St George's Sq *FSTGT* E7........................**82** B4
   PIM SW1V.......................................**117** D1
   PIM * SW1V....................................**117** D1
St George's Square Ms *PIM* SW1V.......**117** D1
St George's Ter *CAMTN* NW1...................**73** F4
   PECK * SE15..................................**120** A3
St George St *CONDST* W1S......................**31** D1
St George's Wy *PECK* SE15...................**119** E2
   PECK * SE15..................................**119** E2
St Gerards Cl *CLAP* SW4.......................**134** C3

St German's Pl *BKHTH/KID* SE3 ....**124** A4
St German's Rd *FSTH* SE23.................**157** E1
St Giles Churchyard *BARB* * EC2Y.......**23** F3
St Giles High St *LSQ/SEVD* WC2H........**20** B4
St Giles Rd *CMBW* SE5.......................**119** E4
St Gothard Rd *WNWD* SE27 ....**155** D3
St Helena Rd *BERM/RHTH* SE16 ....**103** D5
St Helena St *WCHPL* * WC1X.................**10** A4
St Helen's Gdns *NKENS* W10 ....**89** D4
St Helen's Pl *OBST* EC2N...................**24** C4
St Helen's Rd *IL* IG1 ....**65** F1
St Helier's Rd *LEY* E10.........................**62** B1
St Hildas Cl *KIL/WHAMP* * NW6 ....**71** D5
   TOOT SW17 ....**151** E2
St Hilda's Rd *BARN* SW13 ....**112** B2
St Hughes Cl *TOOT* * SW17 ....**151** E2
St James Cl *STJWD* NW8 ....**5** E1
St James' Ct *WESTW* * SW1E **43** F3
St James Ms *POP/IOD* * E14 ....**104** C4
St James' Rd *FSTGT* E7 ....**81** F2
St James's *NWCR* SE14 ....**121** E4
St James's Av *BETH* E2 ....**90** C1
St James's Chambers *STJS* * SW1Y **31** F3
St James's Cl *TOOT* * SW17 ....**151** E2
   WOOL/PLUM SE18 ....**126** C1
St James's Ct *WESTW* SW1E **43** F2
St James's Crs *BRXN/ST* SW9 ....**136** A1
St James's Dr *BAL* SW12 ....**151** E1
St James's Gdns *CAMTN* * NW1 ....**7** E4
   NTGHL W11 ....**101** E2
St James's Gv *BTSEA* * SW11 ....**115** F5
St James's Market *STJS* * SW1Y **32** A2
St James's Pl *WHALL* SW1A..................**31** E3
St James's Sq *STJS* SW1Y **32** A3
St James's St *WHALL* SW1A **31** E3
St James's Terrace Ms *STJWD* NW8 .....**73** D5
St James St *HMSMTH* W6 ....**112** C1
St James Ter *BAL* * SW12 ....**152** A1
St James Wk *CLKNW* EC1R **10** C5
St John Cl *FUL/PGN* SW6 ....**114** C5
St John's Av *PUT/ROE* SW15 ....**131** D3
   WLSDN NW10 ....**69** F5
St John's Church Rd *HACK* * E8...........**78** C2
St John's Cl *FUL/PGN* SW6 ....**114** A3
St John's Crs *BRXN/ST* SW9 ....**136** A1
St John's Dr *WAND/EARL* SW18 ....**150** B1
St John's Gdns *NTGHL* W11 ....**101** E1
St John's Gv *ARCH* N19 ....**56** C4
   BARN SW13 ....**111** F5
St John's Hl *BTSEA* SW11 ....**133** E2
St John's Hill Gv *BTSEA* SW11 ....**133** D2
St John's La *FARR* EC1M **22** C1
St John's Pk *BKHTH/KID* SE3 ....**124** A3
St John's Pl *FARR* EC1M **22** C1
St John's Rd *BARK* IG11......................**85** E5
   BTSEA SW11..................................**133** E2
   CAN/RD E16...................................**94** A5
   EHAM E6 ....**83** E5
   GLDGN NW11 ....**53** F1
   GNTH/NBYPK IG2 ....**67** E3
   SEVS/STOTM N15 ....**59** E1
St John's Sq *FARR* EC1M **22** C1
St John's Ter *FSTGT* E7 ....**82** B3
   NKENS W10 ....**89** D3
   WOOL/PLUM SE18 ....**126** C1
St John St *FSBYE* EC1V **10** B2
St John's V *BROCKY* SE4 ....**122** A5
St John's Vls *ARCH* N19 ....**57** D4
   KENS W8 ....**39** D3
   KENS * W8 ....**39** D3
St John's Wy *ARCH* N19 ....**56** C4

St John's Wood High St
   STJWD NW8...**4** B2
St John's Wood Pk *STJWD* NW8 ....**73** D5
St John's Wood Rd *STJWD* NW8 ....**4** A5
St John's Wood Ter *STJWD* NW8 ....**4** C1
St Josephs Cl *NKENS* W10...................**89** E4
St Joseph's St *VX/NE* * SW8 ....**116** B4
St Joseph's V *BKHTH/KID* SE3 ....**123** D5
St Jude's Rd *BETH* E2 ....**90** B1
St Jude St *STNW/STAM* N16 ....**77** E2
St Julian's Cl *STRHM/NOR* * SW16 ....**154** A4
St Julian's Farm Rd *WNWD* SE27 ....**154** A4
St Julian's Rd *KIL/WHAMP* NW6 ....**71** F4
St Katharine's Prec *CAMTN* * NW1 ....**6** C1
St Katharine's Wy *TWRH* EC3N **37** F3
St Katherines Wk *NTGHL* * W11 ....**101** D1
St Keverne Rd *ELTH/MOT* SE9 ....**161** E4
St Kilda's Rd *STNW/STAM* N16...........**59** D3
St Kitts Ter *NRWD* SE19 ....**155** E5
St Laurence's Cl *KIL/WHAMP* NW6 ......**71** D5
St Lawrence Cottages
   POP/IOD * E14 ....**104** C2
St Lawrence St *POP/IOD* E14 ....**104** C2
St Lawrence Ter *NKENS* W10...............**89** E4
St Lawrence Wy *BRXN/ST* * SW9 ......**118** A5
St Leonards Gdns *IL* IG1 ....**84** C2
St Leonards Pl *KTTN* NW5 ....**74** A3
St Leonards Rd *MORT/ESHN* SW14 ...**128** C3
   POP/IOD E14...................................**92** C4
   WLSDN NW10 ....**87** D3
St Leonard's St *BOW* E3 ....**92** B2
St Leonard's Ter *CHEL* SW3 ....**115** F1
   CHEL * SW3 ....**115** F1
St Loo Av *CHEL* SW3 ....**115** E2
St Louis Rd *WNWD* SE27 ....**154** C4
St Lucia Dr *SRTFD* E15........................**81** F5
St Luke's Av *CLAP* SW4 ....**135** D2
   IL IG1 ....**84** B2
St Luke's Est *FSBYE* EC1V **12** A4
St Luke's Ms *NTGHL* W11 ....**89** F5
St Luke's Rd *NTGHL* W11 ....**89** F4
St Lukes's Cl *FSBYE* EC1V **11** F5
St Luke's Sq *CAN/RD* E16 ....**93** F5
St Luke's St *CHEL* SW3 ....**115** E1
St Lukes Yd *MV/WKIL* * W9 ....**89** F1
St Margarets *BARK* IG11......................**85** D5
   RCHPK/HAM * TW10........................**146** C5
St Margarets Av *BFN/LL* DA15............**163** D3
St Margarets Ct *PUT/ROE* * SW15......**130** B2
St Margaret's Crs *PUT/ROE* * SW15 ...**130** B3
St Margaret's Gv *WAN* E11....................**63** F5
   WOOL/PLUM SE18 ....**126** C2
St Margarets La *KENS* W8 ....**38** C3
St Margarets Ms
   RCHPK/HAM * TW10........................**146** C5
St Margaret's Rd *BROCKY* SE4............**139** F2
   MNPK E12 ....**64** C2
   WLSDN NW10 ....**88** C2
St Margaret's Ter
   WOOL/PLUM SE18 ....**126** C1
St Margaret St *WEST* SW1P **44** C1
St Marks Cl *FUL/PGN* SW6 ....**114** A4
St Mark's Crs *CAMTN* * NW1 ....**74** A5
St Marks Ga *HOM* E9............................**79** E4
St Mark's Gv *WBPTN* * SW10 ....**114** B3
St Mark's Pl *NTGHL* W11 ....**89** D5
St Mark's Ri *HACK* E8...........................**77** F2
St Mark's Rd *NKENS* W10 ....**89** D4
St Mark's Sq *CAMTN* NW1 ....**74** A5
St Mark St *WCHPL* E1 ....**25** F5
St Marks Vls *HOLWY* * N7 ....**57** F4
St Martin's Av *EHAM* E6 ....**95** D1
St Martin's Cl *CAMTN* NW1 ....**74** C5

St Martin's Ct LSQ/SEVD * WC2H **32** C1
   LSQ/SEVD WC2H **32** C1
St Martin's La CHCR WC2N **32** C1
St Martin's Le Grand STBT EC1A **23** E4
St Martin's Pl CHCR WC2N **32** C2
St Martin's Rd BRXN/ST SW9 ....**117** F5
St Martin's Wy TOOT SW17 ....**150** C3
St Mary Abbot's Pl KENS W8 ....**101** F4
   KENS W8 ....**101** F4
St Mary Abbots Ter WKENS * W14 .....**101** F4
St Mary At Hl MON EC3R **36** C2
St Mary Axe HDTCH EC3A **24** C5
St Marychurch St
   BERM/RHTH SE16 ....**102** C3
St Mary Graces Ct TWRH * EC3N........**37** F2
St Mary Newington Cl
   WALW * SE17 ....**119** E1
St Marys Bark IG11 ....**97** D1
St Mary's Ap MNPK E12 ....**83** F2
St Mary's Av WAN E11 ....**64** B1
St Marys Ct SHB * W12 ....**99** E4
St Marys Est BERM/RHTH SE16 ....**102** C3
St Marys Gdns LBTH * SE11 ....**46** B4
   LBTH SE11 ....**46** B4
St Mary's Ga KENS W8 ....**38** C3
   KENS * W8 ....**38** C3
St Mary's Gv BARN SW13 ....**130** B1
   CHSWK W4 ....**110** B2
   IS N1 ....**76** B3
St Mary's Man BAY/PAD W2 ....**15** F2
St Mary's Ms KIL/WHAMP * NW6 ....**72** B4
St Marys Pl KENS W8 ....**38** C3
   KENS * W8 ....**39** D3
St Mary's Rd GLDGN NW11 ....**53** E2
   IL IG1 ....**66** C4
   LEY E10 ....**62** C5
   PECK SE15 ....**120** C4
   PLSTW E13 ....**94** B1
   WIM/MER SW19 ....**149** E5
   WLSDN NW10 ....**69** E5
St Mary's Sq BAY/PAD W2 ....**16** A3
St Mary's Ter BAY/PAD W2 ....**16** A2
St Mary St WOOL/PLUM SE18 ....**107** F1
St Marys Wk LBTH * SE11 ....**46** B4
   LBTH SE11 ....**46** B4
St Matthew's Rd
   BRXS/STRHM SW2 ....**135** F3
St Matthew's Rw BETH E2 ....**90** A2
St Matthew St WEST SW1P **44** A2
St Maur Rd FUL/PGN SW6 ....**113** F4
St Merryn Cl WOOL/PLUM SE18...........**127** D3
St Michael's Aly BANK EC3V **24** B5
St Michaels Av WBLY HA9 ....**68** A3
St Michaels Cl CAN/RD E16 ....**95** D4
St Michaels Ct GLDGN * NW11 ....**53** E2
St Michael's Gdns NKENS W10 ....**89** D4
St Michael's Rd BRXN/ST SW9 ....**117** F5
   CRICK NW2 ....**70** A3
St Michael's St BAY/PAD W2 ....**16** A4
St Michaels Ter HGT * N6 ....**56** A3
St Mildred's Ct LOTH * EC2R **24** A5
St Mildreds Rd CAT SE6 ....**141** E5
St Nicholas Rd WOOL/PLUM SE18.......**127** F1
St Nicholas St DEPT SE8 ....**121** F4
St Norbert Rd BROCKY SE4 ....**139** E2
St Olaf's Rd FUL/PGN SW6 ....**113** E3
St Olave's Rd EHAM E6 ....**84** A1
St Oswald's Pl LBTH SE11 ....**117** F1
   LBTH * SE11 ....**117** F1
St Oswulf St WEST * SW1P **44** B5
St Pancras Gdns CAMTN * NW1................**8** A1

St Pancras Wy CAMTN NW1.....................**74** C4
St Paul's Av BERM/RHTH * SE16 ....**103** D2
   CRICK NW2 ....**70** B3
St Paul's Church Yd BLKFR * EC4V **23** D5
St Paul's Cl CHARL SE7 ....**125** D1
St Pauls Crs CAMTN NW1 ....**75** D4
   CAMTN NW1 ....**75** D4
St Paul's Dr SRTFD E15 ....**81** D2
St Pauls Ms CAMTN NW1 ....**75** D4
St Paul's Pl IS N1 ....**77** D3
St Pauls Rd BARK IG11 ....**84** C5
   IS N1 ....**76** B3
St Pauls Ter WALW * SE17 ....**118** B2
St Paul St IS N1 ....**76** C5
St Peter's Av BETH E2 ....**90** A1
St Petersburgh Ms BAY/PAD W2 ....**26** A1
St Petersburgh Pl BAY/PAD W2 ....**26** C1
St Peter's Cl BETH E2 ....**90** A1
   TOOT SW17 ....**151** E2
St Peters Crs LEE/GVPK * SE12 ....**141** F3
St Peter's Gdns WNWD * SE27 ....**154** A3
St Peter's Gv HMSMTH W6 ....**100** A5
St Peters Pl MV/WKIL W9 ....**14** C1
St Peter's Rd HMSMTH * W6 ....**112** A1
   HMSMTH W6 ....**100** A5
St Peter's Sq BETH * E2 ....**90** A1
   HMSMTH W6 ....**100** A5
St Peter's St IS N1 ....**76** B5
St Peter's Ter FUL/PGN SW6 ....**113** E3
St Peter's Vls HMSMTH W6 ....**100** A5
St Peter's Wy IS * N1 ....**77** E4
St Philip Sq VX/NE * SW8 ....**116** B5
St Philip's Rd HACK E8 ....**78** A3
St Philip St VX/NE SW8 ....**116** B5
St Philip's Wy IS N1 ....**76** C5
St Quentin Rd WELL DA16 ....**145** F1
St Quintin Av NKENS W10 ....**88** C4
St Quintin Rd PLSTW E13 ....**94** B2
St Raphael's Wy WLSDN NW10 ....**68** C2
St Rule St VX/NE SW8 ....**116** C5
St Saviour's Est STHWK SE1 ....**49** E2
St Saviour's Rd BRXS/STRHM SW2 ......**135** F3
Saints Cl WNWD SE27 ....**154** B4
Saints Dr FSTGT E7 ....**83** D2
St Silas Pl KTTN NW5 ....**74** A3
St Simon's Av PUT/ROE SW15 ....**130** C3
St Stephens Cl KTTN * NW5 ....**73** F2
St Stephen's Crs BAY/PAD * W2 ....**14** B4
St Stephen's Gdns BAY/PAD W2 ....**14** A4
St Stephen's Gv LEW SE13 ....**140** C1
St Stephen's Ms BAY/PAD W2 ....**14** A3
St Stephens Pde WEST SW1A **32** C5
St Stephen's Rd BOW E3 ....**79** E5
   EHAM E6 ....**82** C4
St Stephens Ter VX/NE * SW8 ....**117** E4
   VX/NE SW8 ....**117** F3
St Stephen's Wk SKENS SW7 ....**39** E4
St Swithin's La MANHO EC4N **36** A1
St Swithun's Rd LEW * SE13 ....**141** D3
St Thomas Gdns IL IG1 ....**84** C3
St Thomas Rd CAN/RD E16 ....**94** A5
   CHSWK W4 ....**110** C3
St Thomas's Gdns HAMP NW3...............**74** A3
St Thomas's Pl HOM * E9 ....**78** C4
St Thomas's Rd FSBYPK N4 ....**58** A4
   WLSDN NW10 ....**69** E5
St Thomas's Sq HACK E8 ....**78** B4
St Thomas St STHWK SE1 ....**36** B4
St Thomas's Wy FUL/PGN SW6 ....**113** E3
St Vincent Cl WNWD SE27 ....**154** B5
St Vincent St MHST W1U **18** B3
St Winefride's Av MNPK E12 ....**83** F2

Salamanca Pl *LBTH* SE11 ....**45** E5
Salamanca Rd *LBTH* SE11 ....**45** E5
Salcombe Rd *STNW/STAM* N16 ....**77** F2
    WALTH E17 ....**61** F2
Salcott Rd *BTSEA* SW11 ....**133** E3
Salehurst Rd *BROCKY* SE4 ....**139** F4
Salem Rd *BAY/PAD* W2 ....**27** D1
Sale Pl *BAY/PAD* W2 ....**16** C1
Sale St *BETH* E2 ....**90** A3
Salford Rd *BAL* SW12 ....**153** D1
Salisbury Av *BARK* IG11 ....**85** D4
Salisbury Cl *WALW* SE17 ....**48** A4
Salisbury Ct *EC4Y* **22** B5
Salisbury Pavement
    FUL/PGN * SW6 ....**114** A3
Salisbury Pl *BRXN/ST* SW9 ....**118** B3
    MBLAR W1H **17** E2
Salisbury Rd *FSTGT* E7 ....**82** A3
    GDMY/SEVK IG3 ....**67** E4
    LEY E10 ....**62** C4
Salisbury Sq *EMB* * EC4Y **22** B5
Salisbury St *ACT* W3 ....**98** C3
    STJWD NW8 ....**16** B1
Salisbury Ter *PECK* SE15 ....**138** C1
Sally Murray Cl *MNPK* E12 ....**84** A1
Salmen Rd *PLSTW* E13 ....**93** F1
Salmon La *POP/IOD* E14 ....**91** E5
Salmon Ms *KIL/WHAMP* * NW6 ....**72** A2
Salmon St *POP/IOD* * E14 ....**91** F5
    WBLY HA9 ....**50** C4
Salomons Rd *PLSTW* E13 ....**94** C4
Salop Rd *WALTH* E17 ....**61** D1
Saltcoats Rd *CHSWK* W4 ....**99** E3
Saltcroft Cl *WBLY* HA9 ....**50** B3
Salter Rd *BERM/RHTH* SE16 ....**103** D2
Salters' Hall Ct *MANHO* * EC4N **36** A1
Salter's Hl *NRWD* SE19 ....**155** D5
Salters Rd *NKENS* W10 ....**89** D3
Salters Rw *IS* * N1 ....**77** D3
Salter St *POP/IOD* E14 ....**104** A1
    WLSDN NW10 ....**88** A2
Salterton Rd *HOLWY* N7 ....**57** E5
Saltley Cl *EHAM* E6 ....**95** E5
Saltram Crs *MV/WKIL* W9 ....**89** F2
Saltwell St *POP/IOD* E14 ....**104** A1
Saltwood Gv *WALW* * SE17 ....**119** D5
Salusbury Rd *KIL/WHAMP* NW6 ....**71** E5
Salvador *TOOT* SW17 ....**151** E4
Salvin Rd *PUT/ROE* SW15 ....**131** D1
Salway Pl *SRTFD* E15 ....**81** D5
Salway Rd *SRTFD* E15 ....**81** D5
Samantha Cl *WALTH* E17 ....**61** F2
Sam Bartram Cl *CHARL* SE7 ....**124** C2
Samels Ct *HMSMTH* W6 ....**112** A1
Samford St *STJWD* NW8 ....**16** C1
Sampson St *WAP* * E1W **102** A2
Samson St *PLSTW* E13 ....**94** C1
Samuel Cl *HACK* E8 ....**77** F5
    NWCR SE14 ....**121** D2
    WOOL/PLUM SE18 ....**107** E5
Samuel St *WOOL/PLUM* SE18 ....**107** F5
Sancroft Cl *CRICK* NW2 ....**52** B5
Sancroft Rd *LBTH* SE11 ....**118** A1
Sanctuary St *STHWK* SE1 ....**47** F1
The Sanctuary *WEST* SW1P **44** B1
Sandall Rd *KTTN* NW5 ....**74** C3
Sandal St *SRTFD* E15 ....**81** D5
Sandalwood Cl *WCHPL* E1 ....**91** E3
Sandbach Pl *WOOL/PLUM* SE18 ....**126** A5
Sandbourne Rd *BROCKY* SE4 ....**121** E5
Sandbrook Rd *STNW/STAM* N16 ....**59** E5
Sandby Gn *ELTH/MOT* SE9 ....**143** E1
Sandell St *STHWK* SE1 ....**34** A5

Sanderson Cl *KTTN* * NW5 ....**74** B1
Sanderstead Av *CRICK* NW2 ....**53** E4
Sanderstead Cl *BAL* SW12 ....**134** C5
Sanderstead Rd *LEY* E10 ....**61** E3
Sandford Rd *EHAM* E6 ....**95** F2
Sandford Rw *WALW* SE17 ....**119** D1
Sandford St *FUL/PGN* SW6 ....**114** B3
Sandgate La *WAND/EARL* SW18 ....**151** E1
Sandgate St *PECK* SE15 ....**120** B2
Sandhurst Dr *GDMY/SEVK* IG3 ....**85** F1
Sandhurst Market *CAT* * SE6 ....**158** C1
Sandhurst Pde *CAT* * SE6 ....**158** C1
Sandhurst Rd *BFN/LL* DA15 ....**163** F3
    CAT SE6 ....**159** D1
Sandifer Dr *CRICK* NW2 ....**53** D5
Sandilands Rd *FUL/PGN* SW6 ....**114** B4
Sandison St *PECK* SE15 ....**137** F1
Sandland St *GINN* WC1R **21** F3
Sandling Ri *ELTH/MOT* SE9 ....**162** A3
Sandlings Cl *PECK* SE15 ....**120** B5
Sandmere Rd *CLAP* SW4 ....**135** E2
Sandown St *SYD* SE26 ....**156** B3
Sandpiper Cl *BERM/RHTH* SE16 ....**103** F3
Sandpit Pl *CHARL* SE7 ....**125** E1
Sandpit Rd *BMLY* BR1 ....**159** E5
Sandridge St *ARCH* N19 ....**56** C4
Sandringham Cl *WIM/MER* * SW19 .....**149** E1
Sandringham Dr *WELL* DA16 ....**127** E5
Sandringham Gdns
    CEND/HSY/T N8 ....**57** E1
Sandringham Rd *BARK* IG11 ....**85** F3
    BMLY BR1 ....**160** A5
    CRICK NW2 ....**70** B2
    FSTGT E7 ....**82** C2
    GLDGN NW11 ....**53** E2
    HACK E8 ....**77** F2
    LEY E10 ....**63** D2
Sandrock Rd *LEW* SE13 ....**140** A1
Sands End La *FUL/PGN* SW6 ....**114** B4
Sandstone Rd *LEE/GVPK* SE12 ....**160** B2
Sandtoft Rd *CHARL* SE7 ....**124** B2
Sandwell Crs *KIL/WHAMP* NW6 ....**72** A3
Sandwich St *STPAN* WC1H **8** C4
Sandycombe Rd *RCH/KEW* TW9 ....**110** A5
Sandy Hill Av *WOOL/PLUM* SE18 ....**126** B1
Sandy Hill La *WOOL/PLUM* SE18 ....**108** B5
Sandyhill Rd *IL* IG1 ....**84** B1
Sandy Hill Rd *WOOL/PLUM* SE18 ....**126** B1
Sandy Rd *GLDGN* NW11 ....**54** B4
Sandy's Rw *WCHPL* E1 ....**25** D3
Sanford La *STNW/STAM* N16 ....**59** F4
Sanford St *NWCR* SE14 ....**121** E2
Sanford Ter *STNW/STAM* N16 ....**59** F5
Sangley Rd *CAT* SE6 ....**140** B5
Sangora Rd *BTSEA* SW11 ....**133** D2
Sansom Rd *WAN* * E11 ....**63** F4
Sansom St *CMBW* SE5 ....**119** D3
Sans Wk *CLKNW* EC1R **10** C5
Santley Rd *BRXS/STRHM* SW2 ....**135** E2
Santos Rd *PUT/ROE* SW15 ....**132** A3
Saperton Wk *LBTH* SE11 ....**45** F4
Sapphire Rd *DEPT* SE8 ....**103** E5
Saracen St *POP/IOD* E14 ....**92** A5
Sarah St *BETH* E2 ....**13** D3
Saratoga Rd *CLPT* E5 ....**78** C1
Sardinia St *HOL/ALD* WC2B **21** E5
Sarre Rd *CRICK* NW2 ....**71** F2
Sarsfeld Rd *BAL* SW12 ....**151** F1
Sartor Rd *PECK* SE15 ....**139** D2
Sarum Ter *BOW* * E3 ....**91** F3
Satanita Cl *CAN/RD* E16 ....**95** D5
Satchwell Rd *BETH* E2 ....**90** A2

Sattar Ms *STNW/STAM* * N16 ....**59** D5
Sauls Gn *WAN* E11 ....**63** E5
Saunders Cl *POP/IOD* * E14 ....**103** F1
Saunders Ness Rd *POP/IOD* E14 ......**105** D5
Saunders Rd *WOOL/PLUM* SE18 ......**127** F1
Saunders St *LBTH* SE11 ....**46** A4
Savage Gdns *EHAM* E6 ....**95** F5
   TWRH EC3N **37** D1
Savernake Rd *HAMP* NW3 ....**73** F1
Savile Rw *CONDST* W1S **31** E1
Saville Rd *CAN/RD* E16 ....**107** E2
   CHSWK W4 ....**99** D4
Savona St *VX/NE* SW8 ....**116** C3
Savoy Cl *SRTFD* E15 ....**81** E5
Savoy Ct *TPL/STR* * WC2R **33** D2
Savoy Hl *TPL/STR* WC2R **33** E2
Savoy Pl *CHCR* WC2N **33** D2
Savoy Rw *TPL/STR* * WC2R **33** E2
Savoy Steps *TPL/STR* * WC2R **33** E2
Savoy St *TPL/STR* WC2R **33** E1
Savoy Wy *TPL/STR* WC2R **33** E2
Sawkins Cl *WIM/MER* SW19 ....**149** D2
Sawley Rd *SHB* W12 ....**100** A3
Sawyer St *STHWK* SE1 ....**35** E5
Saxby Rd *BRXS/STRHM* SW2 ....**135** E5
Saxham Rd *BARK* IG11 ....**85** E5
Saxon Cl *WALTH* E17 ....**62** A2
Saxon Dr *ACT* W3 ....**86** B5
Saxonfield Cl *BRXS/STRHM* SW2 ......**135** F5
Saxon Rd *BOW* E3 ....**91** F1
   EHAM E6 ....**95** F3
   IL IG1 ....**84** B3
   WBLY HA9 ....**50** C5
Saxton Cl *LEW* SE13 ....**141** D1
Sayes Court St *DEPT* SE8 ....**121** F1
Scala St *FITZ* W1T **19** F2
Scampston Ms *NKENS* W10 ....**89** D5
Scandrett St *WAP* * E1W **102** B2
Scarba Wk *IS* N1 ....**77** D3
Scarborough Rd *FSBYPK* N4 ....**58** A2
   WAN E11 ....**63** D3
Scarborough St *WCHPL* E1 ....**25** F5
Scarlet Rd *CAT* SE6 ....**159** E3
Scarsbrook Rd *BKHTH/KID* SE3 ......**143** D1
Scarsdale Pl *KENS* * W8 ....**38** C2
Scarsdale Vls *KENS* W8 ....**38** B3
Scarth Rd *BARN* SW13 ....**129** F1
Scawen Rd *DEPT* SE8 ....**121** E1
Scawfell St *BETH* E2 ....**13** F2
Sceptre Rd *BETH* E2 ....**90** C2
Scholars Rd *BAL* SW12 ....**152** C1
Scholefield Rd *ARCH* N19 ....**57** D3
Schonfeld Sq *STNW/STAM* N16 ....**59** D4
Schoolhouse La *WAP* * E1W **103** D1
School Rd *WLSDN* NW10........................**87** D3
Schooner Cl *POP/IOD* E14 ....**105** D4
Schubert Rd *PUT/ROE* SW15 ....**131** F3
Sclater St *WCHPL* E1 ....**13** E5
Scoles Crs *BRXS/STRHM* SW2 ....**154** A1
Scoresby St *STHWK* SE1 ....**34** C4
Scotia Rd *BRXS/STRHM* SW2 ....**136** B3
Scotsdale Rd *LEE/GVPK* SE12 ....**142** B3
Scotswood St *CLKNW* * EC1R **10** B5
Scott Ellis Gdns *STJWD* NW8 ....**4** A4
Scott Lidgett Crs
   BERM/RHTH SE16 ....**102** A3
Scotts Pas *WOOL/PLUM* * SE18 ......**108** B5
Scott's Rd *LEY* E10 ....**62** C3
   SHB W12 ....**100** B3
Scott St *WCHPL* E1 ....**90** B3
Scoulding Rd *CAN/RD* E16 ....**93** F3
Scouler St *POP/IOD* E14 ....**105** D1
Scout La *CLAP* SW4 ....**134** C1

Scovell Crs *STHWK* * SE1 ....**47** E1
Scovell Rd *STHWK* SE1 ....**47** E1
Scriven St *HACK* E8 ....**77** F5
Scrooby St *CAT* SE6 ....**140** B4
Scrubs La *WLSDN* NW10 ....**88** A2
Scrutton St *SDTCH* EC2A **24** C1
Scutari Rd *EDUL* SE22 ....**138** B3
Scylla Rd *PECK* SE15 ....**138** B1
Seabright St *BETH* E2 ....**90** B2
Seacole Cl *ACT* W3 ....**87** D5
Seaford St *STPAN* WC1H **9** D4
Seaforth Crs *HBRY* N5 ....**76** C2
Seager Buildings *DEPT* * SE8 ....**122** A4
Seager Pl *BOW* E3 ....**91** F4
Seagrave Cl *WCHPL* * E1 ....**91** D4
Seagrave Rd *FUL/PGN* SW6 ....**114** A2
Seagry Rd *WAN* E11 ....**64** A1
Seal St *HACK* E8 ....**77** F1
Searles Cl *BTSEA* SW11 ....**115** E3
Searles Dr *EHAM* E6 ....**96** B4
Searles Rd *STHWK* SE1 ....**48** B4
Sears St *CMBW* SE5 ....**119** D3
Seaton Av *GDMY/SEVK* IG3 ....**85** E2
Seaton Cl *LBTH* SE11 ....**118** B1
   PLSTW E13 ....**94** A3
   PUT/ROE SW15 ....**130** B5
Sebastian St *FSBYE* EC1V **11** D4
Sebbon St *IS* N1 ....**76** B4
Sebert Rd *FSTGT* E7 ....**82** B2
Secker St *STHWK* SE1 ....**34** A4
Second Av *ACT* W3 ....**99** F2
   MNPK E12 ....**83** E1
   MORT/ESHN SW14 ....**129** E1
   NKENS W10 ....**89** E3
   PLSTW E13 ....**94** A3
Second Wy *WBLY* HA9 ....**68** B1
Sedan Wy *WALW* SE17 ....**119** E1
Sedding St *KTBR* SW1X **42** A4
Seddon St *FSBYW* WC1X **9** E4
Sedgebrook Rd *BKHTH/KID* SE3 ......**125** D5
Sedgeford Rd *SHB* W12 ....**99** F3
Sedgehill Rd *CAT* SE6 ....**158** A5
Sedgeway *CAT* SE6 ....**159** F1
Sedgmoor Pl *CMBW* SE5 ....**119** E3
Sedgwick Rd *LEY* E10 ....**62** C4
Sedgwick St *HOM* E9 ....**79** D2
Sedleigh Rd *WAND/EARL* SW18 ......**131** F4
Sedlescombe Rd *FUL/PGN* SW6 ......**113** F2
Sedley Pl *MYFR/PKLN* W1K **18** C5
Seeley Dr *DUL* SE21 ....**155** E4
Seelig Av *CDALE/KGS* NW9 ....**52** A2
Seething La *TWRH* EC3N **37** D1
Sefton St *PUT/ROE* SW15 ....**112** C5
Sekforde St *CLKNW* EC1R **22** C1
Selbie Av *WLSDN* NW10 ....**69** F2
Selborne Av *MNPK* E12 ....**84** A1
Selborne Rd *CMBW* SE5 ....**119** D5
   IL IG1 ....**66** A4
Selby Rd *PLSTW* E13 ....**94** B4
   WAN E11 ....**63** E5
Selby St *WCHPL* E1 ....**90** A3
Selden Rd *PECK* SE15 ....**120** C5
Selhurst Cl *WIM/MER* SW19 ....**149** D1
Selkirk Rd *TOOT* SW17 ....**151** E4
Sellincourt Rd *TOOT* SW17 ....**151** E5
Sellons Av *WLSDN* NW10 ....**69** F5
Selsdon Rd *CRICK* NW2 ....**51** F4
   PLSTW E13 ....**82** C5
   WAN E11 ....**64** A2
   WNWD SE27 ....**154** B3
Selsdon Wy *POP/IOD* E14 ....**104** B3
Selsea Pl *STNW/STAM* N16 ....**77** E2
Selsey St *POP/IOD* E14 ....**92** A4

Selwood Pl *SKENS* SW7..................**115** D1
Selwood Ter *SKENS* SW7 ....**115** D1
Selworthy Rd *CAT* SE6................**157** F3
Selwyn Av *GDMY/SEVK* IG3...........**67** F1
Selwyn Rd *BOW* E3........................**91** F1
   PLSTW E13............................**82** B3
   WLSDN NW10.........................**69** E4
Semley Pl *BGVA* SW1W **42** B5
Senate St *PECK* SE15...................**120** C5
Senior St *BAY/PAD* W2 ....**14** C2
Senlac Rd *LEE/GVPK* SE12............**160** B1
Senrab St *WCHPL* E1......................**91** D5
Serbin Cl *WAN* E11.........................**62** C2
Serpentine Rd *BAY/PAD* W2 ....**29** D4
Service Route No 1 *SRTFD* E15.......**81** D4
Service Route No 2 *SRTFD* E15.......**81** D4
Service Route No 3 *SRTFD* E15.......**81** D3
Setchell Est *STHWK* SE1..............**49** E4
Setchell Rd *STHWK* SE1...............**49** E4
Setchell Wy *STHWK* SE1..............**49** E4
Settles St *WCHPL* E1......................**90** A5
Settrington Rd *FUL/PGN* SW6......**114** B5
Seven Kings Rd *GDMY/SEVK* IG3.....**67** E3
Sevenoaks Rd *BROCKY* SE4 ....**139** F4
Seven Sisters Rd *HOLWY* N7 ....**57** F5
Seventh Av *MNPK* E12...................**83** F1
Severnake Cl *POP/IOD* E14 ....**104** A3
Severn Av *NKENS* W10....................**89** E2
Severn Wy *WLSDN* NW10.................**69** F2
Severus Rd *BTSEA* SW11.............**133** E2
Seville Ms *IS* N1............................**77** E4
Seville St *KTBR* SW1X **41** E3
Sevington Rd *HDN* NW4.................**52** B1
Sevington St *MV/WKIL* W9..............**14** C1
Sewardstone Rd *BETH* E2 ....**90** C1
Seward St *FSBYE* EC1V **11** D5
Sewdley St *CLPT* E5........................**61** D5
Sewell St *PLSTW* E13 ....**94** A2
Sextant Av *POP/IOD* E14 ....**105** D5
Seymour Gdns *BROCKY* SE4........**139** D1
   IL IG1....................................**65** F3
Seymour Ms *MBLAR* W1H...............**18** A4
Seymour Pl *MBLAR* W1H **17** D3
Seymour Rd *CHSWK* W4..................**98** C5
   EHAM E6...............................**83** D5
   LEY E10................................**61** F3
   WAND/EARL SW18................**131** F5
   WIM/MER SW19...................**149** D3
Seymour St *BAY/PAD* W2...............**17** E5
   WOOL/PLUM SE18................**108** C5
Seymour Wk *WBPTN* SW10..........**114** C5
Seyssel St *POP/IOD* E14..............**104** C5
Shaa Rd *ACT* W3............................**99** D1
Shackleton Cl *SYD* SE23..............**156** B2
Shacklewell La *HACK* E8.................**77** F1
Shacklewell Rd *STNW/STAM* N16...**77** F1
Shacklewell Rw *HACK* E8................**77** F1
Shacklewell St *BETH* E2.................**13** F5
Shad Thames *STHWK* SE1...............**37** E4
Shadwell Gdns *WCHPL* E1............**102** C3
Shadwell Pierhead *WAP* E1W.........**90** C1
Shaftesbury Av *LSQ/SEVD* WC2H......**20** C4
   MYFR/PICC W1J.....................**32** A1
Shaftesbury Gdns *WLSDN* NW10....**87** E3
Shaftesbury Ms *KENS* W8..............**38** B3
Shaftesbury Pl *BARB* EC2Y............**23** E3
Shaftesbury Rd *ARCH* N19.............**57** E3
   FSTGT E7..............................**82** C4
   LEY E10................................**62** A3
The Shaftesburys *BARK* IG11.........**96** E3

Shaftesbury St *IS* N1.....................**11** F2
Shaftesbury Ter *HMSMTH* W6 ....**99** F5
Shafto Ms *KTBR* SW1X....................**41** E3
Shafton Ms *HOM* E9.......................**79** D5
Shafton Rd *HOM* E9........................**79** D5
Shakespeare Av *WLSDN* NW10........**68** C5
   WLSDN NW10.........................**69** D5
Shakespeare Crs *MNPK* E12...........**83** F4
   WLSDN NW10.........................**69** D5
Shakespeare Rd *ACT* W3................**98** C2
   HNHL SE24...........................**136** B3
Shakespeare Ter *RCH/KEW* TW9...**128** A1
Shakspeare Ms *STNW/STAM* N16....**77** E1
Shakspeare Wk *STNW/STAM* N16...**77** E1
Shalcomb St *WBPTN* SW10..........**114** C2
Shalfleet Dr *NKENS* W10...............**101** D1
Shalford Ct *IS* * N1........................**10** C1
Shalimar Gdns *ACT* W3...................**98** C1
Shalimar Rd *ACT* W3.......................**98** C1
Shallons Rd *ELTH/MOT* SE9..........**162** B4
Shalstone Rd *MORT/ESHN* SW14...**128** B1
Shamrock St *CLAP* SW4................**135** D1
Shandon Rd *CLAP* SW4.................**134** C4
Shand St *STHWK* SE1.....................**37** D5
Shandy St *WCHPL* E1......................**91** D4
Shannon Cl *CRICK* NW2...................**53** D5
Shannon Gv *BRXN/ST* SW9...........**135** F2
Shannon Pl *STJWD* NW8...................**5** D1
Shardcroft Av *HNHL* SE24............**136** B3
Shardeloes Rd *BROCKY* SE4.........**121** F5
   BROCKY * SE4........................**139** F3
Shard's Sq *PECK* SE15..................**120** A2
Sharon Gdns *HOM* E9......................**78** C5
Sharon Rd *CHSWK* W4...................**111** D1
Sharples Hall St *CAMTN* NW1.........**73** F4
Sharratt St *PECK* SE15.................**120** C2
Sharsted St *WALW* SE17...............**118** B1
Shavers Pl *MYFR/PICC* W1J............**32** A2
Shawbrooke Rd *ELTH/MOT* SE9....**143** D2
Shawbury Rd *EDUL* SE22..............**137** E3
Shawfield St *CHEL* SW3................**115** E1
Shaw Rd *BMLY* BR1.......................**159** F3
   EDUL SE22...........................**137** E2
Shaws Cottages *FSTH* * SE23.......**157** E3
Shearling Wy *HOLWY* N7................**75** E3
Shearman Rd *BKHTH/KID* SE3......**141** F2
Sheen Common Dr
   RCHPK/HAM TW10...............**128** A2
Sheen Court Rd
   RCHPK/HAM TW10...............**128** A2
Sheenewood *SYD* SE26.................**156** B5
Sheen Gate Gdns
   MORT/ESHN SW14................**128** C2
Sheen Gv *IS* N1..............................**76** A5
Sheen La *MORT/ESHN* SW14..........**128** C2
Sheen Wd *MORT/ESHN* SW14........**128** C3
Sheepcote La *BTSEA* SW11...........**115** F5
Sheep La *HACK* E8..........................**78** B5
Sheerwater Rd *CAN/RD* E16...........**95** D4
Sheffield St *LINN* * WC2A................**21** E5
Sheffield Ter *KENS* W8....................**26** A5
Shelburne Rd *HOLWY* N7................**75** E3
Shelbury Rd *EDUL* SE22................**138** B3
Sheldon Av *HGT* N6.........................**55** F3
Sheldon Cl *LEE/GVPK* SE12..........**142** B3
Sheldon Rd *CRICK* NW2..................**71** D1
Sheldrake Cl *CAN/RD* E16.............**107** F2
Sheldrake Pl *KENS* W8..................**101** F3
Shelduck Cl *FSTGT* E7.....................**81** F2
Shelford Pl *STNW/STAM* N16..........**59** D5
Shelgate Rd *BTSEA* SW11............**133** F3
Shelley Av *MNPK* E12......................**83** E3
Shelley Dr *WELL* DA16..................**127** E4
Shelley Rd *WLSDN* NW10................**69** D5

Shellgrove Rd *STNW/STAM* * N16......**77** E2
Shellness Rd *CLPT* E5 ......**78** B2
Shell Rd *LEW* SE13 ......**140** B1
Shellwood Rd *BTSEA* SW11 ......**115** F5
Shelmerdine CI *BOW* E3 ......**92** A4
Shelton St *LSQ/SEVD* * WC2H......**20** C5
Shenfield St *IS* N1 ......**13** D2
Shenley Rd *CMBW* SE5 ......**119** E4
Shepherdess PI *FSBYE* EC1V **11** F3
Shepherdess Wk *IS* N1 ......**11** F1
Shepherd Market
MYFR/PICC * W1J **30** C4
Shepherd's Bush Gn *SHB* W12 ......**100** C3
Shepherd's Bush Market
SHB W12 ......**100** C3
Shepherd's Bush PI *SHB* * W12 ......**101** D3
Shepherd's Bush Rd
HMSMTH W6 ......**100** C4
Shepherd's CI *HGT* N6......**56** B1
Shepherd's HI *HGT* N6 ......**56** B1
Shepherd's La *HOM* * E9 ......**79** D2
Shepherd's Leas *ELTH/MOT* * SE9...**145** D2
Shepherds Rd *FSTGT* E7......**30** A1
Shepherd St *MYFR/PICC* W1J **30** C4
Shepherds Wk *CRICK* NW2 ......**52** A4
HAMP NW3 ......**73** D2
Sheppard Dr *BERM/RHTH* SE16 ......**120** B1
Sheppard St *CAN/RD* E16......**93** F3
Shepperton Rd *IS* N1 ......**77** D5
Sheppey Wk *IS* * N1 ......**76** C4
Shepton Houses *BETH* * E2 ......**90** C2
Sherard Rd *ELTH/MOT* SE9......**143** E3
Sherborne La *MANHO* EC4N **36** A1
Sherborne St *IS* N1 ......**77** D5
Sherboro Rd *SEVS/STOTM* N15 ......**59** F1
Sherbrooke Rd *FUL/PGN* SW6 ......**113** E3
Sherbrooke Ter *FUL/PGN* * SW6 ......**113** E3
Sherfield Gdns *PUT/ROE* SW15 ......**129** F4
Sheridan Rd *FSTGT* E7......**63** F5
MNPK E12 ......**83** E2
Sheridan St *WCHPL* E1 ......**90** B5
Sheridan Wk *GLDGN* NW11 ......**54** A1
Sheringham Av *MNPK* E12......**83** F1
Sheringham Dr *BARK* IG11 ......**85** F2
Sheringham Rd *HOLWY* N7 ......**76** A3
Sherington Rd *CHARL* SE7 ......**124** B2
Sherlock Ms *MHST* W1U **18** A2
Sherrard Rd *FSTGT* E7......**82** C3
Sherrick Green Rd *WLSDN* NW10 ......**70** B2
Sherriff Rd *KIL/WHAMP* NW6......**72** A3
Sherry Ms *BARK* IG11......**85** D4
Sherwin Rd *NWCR* SE14 ......**121** D4
Sherwood Ct *MBLAR* W1H **17** E3
Sherwood Gdns *BARK* IG11 ......**85** D4
POP/IOD E14......**104** A5
STHWK SE1 ......**120** A1
Sherwood Rd *WELL* DA16 ......**145** E1
Sherwood St *SOHO/SHAV* W1D **31** F1
Shetland Rd *BOW* E3 ......**91** F1
Shifford Pth *FSTH* * SE23 ......**157** D3
Shillibeer PI *MBLAR* W1H **17** D3
Shillingford St *IS* N1 ......**76** B5
Shinfield St *SHB* W12 ......**88** C5
Shipka Rd *BAL* SW12 ......**152** B1
Shipman Rd *CAN/RD* E16 ......**94** B5
FSTH SE23 ......**157** D2
Ship & Mermaid Rw *STHWK* * SE1...**36** B5
Ship St *DEPT* SE8 ......**122** A4
Ship Tavern Pas *BANK* EC3V **36** C1
Shipton St *BETH* E2 ......**13** F3
Shipwright Rd *BERM/RHTH* SE16 ......**103** E3
Shipwright Yd *STHWK* * SE1 ......**36** C1

Shirburn CI *FSTH* SE23 ......**138** C5
Shirbutt St *POP/IOD* E14 ......**104** A1
Shirebrook Rd *BKHTH/KID* SE3 ......**125** D5
Shirehall CI *HDN* NW4 ......**53** D1
Shirehall Gdns *HDN* NW4 ......**53** D1
Shirehall La *HDN* NW4 ......**53** D1
Shirehall Pk *HDN* NW4 ......**53** D1
Shirland Ms *MV/WKIL* W9......**89** F2
Shirland Rd *MV/WKIL* W9 ......**2** A5
Shirley Gdns *BARK* IG11 ......**85** E3
Shirley Gv *BTSEA* SW11 ......**134** A1
Shirley Rd *BFN/LL* DA15 ......**163** E3
CHSWK W4......**99** D3
SRTFD E15 ......**81** E4
Shirley St *CAN/RD* E16 ......**93** F5
Shirlock Rd *HAMP* NW3 ......**73** F1
Shobroke CI *CRICK* NW2 ......**52** C5
Shoebury Rd *EHAM* E6 ......**83** F4
Shoe La *FLST/FETLN* EC4A **22** B4
Shooters HI *WOOL/PLUM* SE18 ......**125** F4
Shooters Hill Rd *BKHTH/KID* SE3 ...**123** E4
Shoot-up HI *CRICK* NW2 ......**71** E3
Shoreditch High St *BETH* E2 ......**13** D4
WCHPL E1 ......**25** D2
Shoreham CI *WAND/EARL* SW18 ...**132** B3
Shore PI *HOM* E9 ......**78** C4
Shore Rd *HOM* E9 ......**78** C4
Shorncliffe Rd *STHWK* SE1 ......**119** F1
Shorndean St *CAT* SE6 ......**158** C1
Shorrolds Rd *FUL/PGN* SW6 ......**114** A3
Shorter St *WCHPL* E1 ......**37** E1
Shortlands *HMSMTH* W6 ......**101** D5
Shortlands Rd *LEY* E10 ......**62** B2
Short Rd *CHSWK* W4 ......**111** E2
WAN E11 ......**63** E4
Shorts Gdns *LSQ/SEVD* * WC2H **20** C5
Short St *STHWK* SE1 ......**34** B5
Shortway *ELTH/MOT* SE9 ......**143** E1
Shottendane Rd *FUL/PGN* * SW6 ...**114** A3
Shottery CI *ELTH/MOT* SE9......**161** E3
Shottfield Av *MORT/ESHN* SW14 ...**129** E2
Shoulder of Mutton Aly
POP/IOD E14......**103** E1
Shouldham St *MBLAR* W1H **17** D3
Shrapnel CI *WOOL/PLUM* SE18 ......**125** E3
Shrapnel Rd *ELTH/MOT* SE9......**143** F1
Shrewsbury Av *MORT/ESHN* SW14 ...**128** C2
Shrewsbury Crs *WLSDN* NW10 ......**69** D5
Shrewsbury La *WOOL/PLUM* SE18 ...**126** B4
Shrewsbury Ms *BAY/PAD* W2 ......**14** A4
Shrewsbury Rd *BAY/PAD* W2 ......**14** A3
MNPK E12 ......**83** D3
Shrewsbury St *NKENS* W10 ......**88** C3
Shroffold Rd *BMLY* BR1 ......**159** E4
Shroton St *CAMTN* NW1 ......**16** C2
Shrubbery Rd *STRHM/NOR* SW16 ...**153** E4
Shrubland Rd *HACK* E8......**78** A5
LEY E10 ......**62** A2
Shrublands CI *SYD* SE26 ......**156** C3
Shrubsall CI *ELTH/MOT* SE9 ......**161** E1
Shuna Wk *IS* * N1 ......**77** D3
Shurland Gdns *PECK* * SE15 ......**119** F3
Shuters Sq *WKENS* * W14 ......**113** F1
Shuttle CI *BFN/LL* DA15 ......**145** F5
Shuttle St *WCHPL* E1......**90** A3
Shuttleworth Rd *BTSEA* SW11 ......**115** D5
Sibella Rd *CLAP* SW4 ......**117** D3
Sibley Gv *MNPK* E12 ......**83** E4
Sibthorpe Rd *LEE/GVPK* SE12 ......**142** B5
Sicilian Av *NOXST/BSQ* * WC1A **21** D3
Sicilion Av *NOXST/BSQ* WC1A......**21** D3
Sidbury St *FUL/PGN* SW6 ......**113** E4
Sidcup By-Pass Rd *SCUP* DA14 ......**163** E4

Sidcup Rd ELTH/MOT SE9..............161 D1
   LEE/GVPK SE12 ....142 B3
Siddons La WAND/EARL NW1..........17 F1
Siddons Rd FSTH SE23 ....157 E2
Sidewood Rd ELTH/MOT SE9...........163 D1
Sidford Pl STHWK SE1 ....45 F3
The Sidings WAN E11 ....62 C3
Sidmouth Pde CRICK * NW2............70 C4
Sidmouth Rd LEY E10......................62 C5
   PECK SE15 ....119 F4
   WLSDN NW10 ....70 C4
Sidmouth St STPAN WC1H 9 D4
Sidney Elson Wy EHAM E6...............96 A1
Sidney Gv FSBYE EC1V 10 C2
Sidney Rd BRXN/ST SW9.................117 F5
   FSTGT E7 ....64 A5
Sidney Sq WCHPL * E1 ....90 C4
Sidney St WCHPL E1 ....90 B4
Sidworth St HACK E8 ....78 B4
Siebert Rd BKHTH/KID SE3..............124 A2
Siemens Rd WOOL/PLUM SE18 ....107 D4
Sienna Ter CRICK * NW2..................52 A4
Sigdon Rd HACK E8 ....78 A2
Signmakers Yd CAMTN * NW1..........74 B5
Silbury St IS * N1 ....12 A3
Silchester Rd NKENS W10 ....89 D5
Silesia Buildings HACK E8................78 B4
Silex St STHWK SE1 ....47 D1
Silk Cl LEE/GVPK SE12 ....142 A3
Silk Mills Pth LEW SE13 ....140 C1
Silk St BARB EC2Y 23 F2
Silverbirch Wk HAMP * NW3............73 F3
Silver Cl NWCR * SE14 ....121 E3
Silver Crs CHSWK W4 ....98 B5
Silverdale CAMTN NW1 ....7 E2
   SYD SE26 ....156 C4
Silverdale Dr ELTH/MOT SE9 ....161 E2
Silver Dene PUT/ROE * SW15...........130 C3
Silvermere Rd LEW SE13 ....140 A4
Silver Rd SHB W12 ....101 D1
Silverthorne Rd VX/NE SW8 ....116 B5
Silverton Rd HMSMTH W6 ....113 D3
Silvertown Wy CAN/RD E16 ....93 F5
Silver Wk BERM/RHTH SE16 ....103 F2
Silvester Rd EDUL SE22 ....137 F3
Silvester St STHWK SE1...................48 A1
Silwood St BERM/RHTH SE16 ....121 D1
Simmons Rd WOOL/PLUM SE18 ......126 B1
Simms Rd STHWK SE1 ....102 A5
Simnel Rd LEE/GVPK SE12 ....142 B5
Simon Cl NTGHL W11.......................101 F1
Simonds Rd LEY E10 ....62 A4
Simons Wk SRTFD E15 ....81 D2
Simpson Dr ACT W3 ....87 D5
Simpson's Rd POP/IOD E14 ....104 B1
Simpson St BTSEA SW11 ....115 E5
Sinclair Gdns WKENS W14 ....101 D3
Sinclair Gv GLDGN NW11 ....53 D1
Sinclair Rd WKENS W14 ....101 E4
Singer St FSBYE EC1V 12 B4
Sir Abraham Dawes Cottages
   PUT/ROE * SW15......................131 E2
Sir Alexander Cl ACT W3..................99 F2
Sirdar Rd NTGHL W11......................101 D1
Sir Thomas Moore Est CHEL SW3 .....115 D2
Sise La MANHO * EC4N 24 A5
Sisley Rd BARK IG11........................85 E5
Sispara Gdns WAND/EARL SW18 ......131 F4
Sister Mabel's Wy PECK * SE15 ....120 A3
Sisters Av BTSEA SW11 ....133 F2
Sistova Rd BAL SW12 ....152 B1
Sisulu Pl BRXN/ST SW9 ....136 A1
Siward Rd TOOT SW17 ....150 B1

Sixth Av MNPK E12 ....83 F1
   NKENS W10 ....89 E3
Skardu Rd CRICK NW2 ....71 E2
Skeena Hl WIM/MER SW19 ....131 E5
Skeffington Rd EHAM E6..................83 F5
Skelbrook St WAND/EARL SW18 ....150 B2
Skelgill Rd PUT/ROE SW15 ....131 F2
Skelley Rd SRTFD E15 ....81 F4
Skelton Cl HACK * E8 ....77 F3
Skelton Rd FSTGT E7.......................82 A3
Skelton's La LEY E10........................62 B2
Skelwith Rd HMSMTH W6 ....112 C2
Sketchley Gdns BERM/RHTH SE16 ....121 D1
Skiers St SRTFD E15 ....81 E5
Skiffington Cl BRXS/STRHM SW2 .....154 A1
Skinner Rd * SW1W..........................42 A5
Skinners La BLKFR EC4V 35 F1
Skinner St CLKNW EC1R 10 B4
Skipsey Av EHAM E6 ....95 F2
Skipworth Rd HOM E9 ....78 C5
Skylines Village POP/IOD * E14........104 C3
Sladebrook Rd BKHTH/KID SE3........143 D1
Sladedale Rd WOOL/PLUM SE18 ......127 E1
Sladen Pl CLPT E5 ....78 B1
Slades Dr CHST BR7.........................162 C3
The Slade WOOL/PLUM SE18 ....127 E2
Slade Wk WALW SE17 ....118 B2
Slagrove Pl BROCKY SE4 ....140 A3
Slaidburn St WBPTN SW10...............114 C2
Slaithwaite Rd LEW SE13 ....140 C2
Slaney Pl HOLWY N7 ....76 A2
Sleaford St VX/NE SW8 ....116 C3
Slievemore Cl CLAP SW4 ....135 D1
Slingsby Pl COVGDN WC2E 32 C1
Slippers Pl BERM/RHTH SE16 ....102 B4
Sloane Av CHEL SW3 ....41 D5
Sloane Ct East CHEL SW3 ....116 A1
Sloane Ct West CHEL SW3 ....116 A1
Sloane Gdns BGVA SW1W 42 A5
Sloane Sq BGVA SW1W 41 F5
Sloane St KTBR SW1X 41 F3
Sloane Ter KTBR SW1X.....................41 F4
Sly St WCHPL * E1 ....90 B5
Smallbrook Ms BAY/PAD W2 ....16 A5
Smalley Cl STNW/STAM N16.............59 F5
Smallwood Rd TOOT SW17 ....151 D4
Smart's Pl HHOL WC1V 21 D4
Smart St BETH E2 ....91 D2
Smeaton Rd WAND/EARL SW18.........132 A5
Smeaton St WAP E1W......................102 B2
Smedley St VX/NE SW8....................117 D5
Smeed Rd BOW E3 ....80 A4
Smiles Pl LEW SE13 ....122 C5
Smith Cl BERM/RHTH SE16 ....103 D2
Smithfield St STBT EC1A..................22 C3
Smith's Ct SOHO/SHAV * W1D 32 A1
Smith St CHEL SW3 ....115 F1
Smith Ter CHEL SW3 ....115 F1
Smithwood Cl WIM/MER SW19 ....149 E1
Smithy St WCHPL E1........................90 C4
Smugglers Wy WAND/EARL SW18.....132 B2
Smyrks Rd WALW * SE17..................119 E1
   WALW SE17 ....119 E1
Smyrna Rd KIL/WHAMP NW6 ....72 A4
Smythe St POP/IOD E14....................104 B1
Snarsgate St NKENS W10.................88 C4
Sneath Av GLDGN NW11 ....53 F2
Sneyd Rd CRICK NW2 ....70 C2
Snowbury Rd FUL/PGN SW6 ....114 B5
Snowden Dr CDALE/KGS NW9 ....51 E1
Snowden St SDTCH EC2A.................24 C1
Snow Hl STBT EC1A 22 C3
Snowfields STHWK SE1 ....35 B5

Snowshill Rd MNPK E12 ....83 E2
Soames St PECK SE15 ....137 F1
Soho Sq SOHO/SHAV W1D 20 A4
Soho St SOHO/SHAV W1D 20 A4
Sojourner Truth Cl HACK * E8 ......78 B3
Solander Gdns WCHPL E1 ....102 B3
Solebay St WCHPL E1 ....91 E3
Solent Ri PLSTW E13 ....94 A2
Solent Rd KIL/WHAMP NW6 ....72 A2
Solna Av PUT/ROE SW15 ....130 C3
Solomon's Pas PECK SE15 ....138 E2
Solon New Rd CLAP SW4 ....135 E2
Solon Rd CLAP SW4 ....135 E2
Solway Cl HACK E8 ....77 F3
Solway Rd EDUL SE22 ....138 A3
Somali Rd CRICK NW2 ....71 F1
Somerby Rd BARK IG11 ....85 D4
Somerfield Rd FSBYPK N4 ....58 B4
Somerford Gv STNW/STAM N16 ......77 F3
Somerford St WCHPL * E1 ....90 B3
Somerford Wy BERM/RHTH SE16 ....103 E3
Somerleyton Rd BRXN/ST SW9 ....136 A2
Somers Cl CAMTN * NW1 ....8 A1
Somers Crs BAY/PAD W2 ....16 C5
Somerset Av WELL DA16 ....145 F3
Somerset Gdns HGT N6 ....56 A2
   LEW SE13 ....122 B5
Somerset Rd CHSWK W4 ....99 D4
   WIM/MER SW19 ....149 D3
Somerset Sq WKENS * W14 ....101 E4
Somerset Street Little TWRH EC3N ...25 E5
Somers Pl BRXS/STRHM SW2 ....135 F5
Somers Rd BRXS/STRHM SW2 ....135 F4
Somerton Av RCH/KEW TW9 ....128 B1
Somerton Rd CRICK NW2 ....53 D5
   PECK SE15 ....138 E2
Somertrees Av LEE/GVPK SE12 ......160 B2
Somerville Av BARN SW13 ....112 C2
Sonderburg Rd HOLWY N7 ....57 F4
Sondes St WALW SE17 ....119 D2
Sonia Gdns CRICK NW2 ....69 F1
Soper Cl FSTH SE23 ....157 D1
Sophia Cl HOLWY N7 ....75 F3
Sophia Rd CAN/RD E16 ....94 B5
   LEY E10 ....62 B3
Sophia Sq BERM/RHTH SE16 ....103 E1
Sopwith Wy VX/NE SW8 ....116 B3
Sorrel Gdns EHAM E6 ....95 E4
Sorrel La POP/IOD E14 ....93 D5
Sorrell Cl BRXN/ST * SW9 ....118 A5
   NWCR SE14 ....121 E3
Sotheby Rd HBRY N5 ....76 C1
Sotheran Cl HACK E8 ....78 A5
Soudan Rd BTSEA SW11 ....115 F4
Souldern Rd WKENS * W14 ....101 D4
South Access Rd WALTH E17 ....61 E2
South Africa Rd SHB W12 ....100 B1
Southall Pl STHWK SE1 ....48 A1
Southampton Buildings
   LINN * WC2A 22 A3
Southampton Pl NOXST/BSQ WC1A ...21 D3
Southampton Rd HAMP NW3 ....73 F2
Southampton Rw RSQ WC1B 21 D2
Southampton St COVGDN WC2E 33 D1
Southampton Wy CMBW SE5 ....119 D3
Southam St NKENS W10 ....89 E3
South Audley St MYFR/PKLN W1K 30 B2
South Av RCH/KEW * TW9 ....110 A3
South Bank STHWK SE1 ....34 B2
South Birkbeck Rd WAN E11 ....63 D5
South Black Lion La HMSMTH W6 ....112 A4
Southborough Rd HOM E9 ....78 C5

Southbourne Gdns IL IG1 ....84 C2
   LEE/GVPK SE12 ....142 B3
Southbrook Rd LEW SE13 ....141 E4
South Carriage Dr KTBR SW1X 29 C1
   SKENS SW7 ....40 C1
Southchurch Rd EHAM E6 ....95 F1
South Cl HGT N6 ....56 B1
South Colonnade POP/IOD E14 ....104 A2
Southcombe St WKENS W14 ....101 E5
Southcote Rd ARCH N19 ....74 C1
South Crs CAN/RD E16 ....93 D3
Southcroft Av WELL DA16 ....145 E1
South Croxted Rd DUL SE21 ....155 D3
Southdean Gdns WIM/MER SW19 ...149 F2
South Eaton Pl BGVA SW1W 42 B4
South Edwardes Sq KENS W8 ....101 F4
South End KENS W8 ....39 D2
Southend Cl ELTH/MOT SE9 ....144 B4
Southend Crs ELTH/MOT SE9 ....144 A4
Southend La CAT SE6 ....157 F4
South End Rd HAMP NW3 ....73 E1
South End Rw KENS W8 ....39 D2
Southerngate Wy NWCR SE14 ....121 E3
Southern Gv BOW E3 ....91 F2
Southern Rd PLSTW E13 ....94 B1
Southern Rw NKENS W10 ....89 D3
Southern St IS N1 ....9 E1
Southerton Rd HMSMTH * W6 ....100 C5
South Esk Rd FSTGT E7 ....82 C3
Southey Rd BRXN/ST SW9 ....118 A4
Southfield Rd CHSWK W4 ....99 D3
Southfields Ms WAND/EARL * SW18 ...132 A4
Southfields Rd WAND/EARL SW18 ...132 A4
South Gdns WBLY * HA9 ....50 A4
Southgate Gv IS N1 ....77 D4
Southgate Rd IS N1 ....77 D5
South Gv HGT N6 ....56 A3
South Hill Pk HAMP NW3 ....73 E1
South Hill Park Gdns HAMP NW3 ......73 E1
Southill St POP/IOD E14 ....92 B5
South Island Pl BRXN/ST SW9 ....117 F3
South Kensington Station Ar
   SKENS SW7 ....40 B4
South Lambeth Pl VX/NE SW8 ....117 E2
South Lambeth Rd VX/NE SW8 ....117 E2
Southland Rd WOOL/PLUM SE18 ....127 F3
Southlands Dr WIM/MER SW19 ....149 D2
Southmead Rd WIM/MER SW19 ......149 E1
South Molton La MYFR/PKLN W1K 18 C5
South Molton Rd CAN/RD E16 ....94 A5
South Molton St MYFR/PKLN W1K 18 C5
Southmoor Wy HOM E9 ....79 F1
South Oak Rd STRHM/NOR SW16 ...153 F4
Southold Ri ELTH/MOT SE9 ....161 F3
Southolm St VX/NE SW8 ....116 B4
Southover BMLY BR1 ....160 A5
South Pde CHEL SW3 ....115 D1
   CHSWK W4 ....99 D5
South Park Crs CAT SE6 ....159 E1
   IL IG1 ....67 D5
South Park Dr GDMY/SEVK IG3 ....85 E2
   IL IG1 ....67 E5
South Park Ms FUL/PGN SW6 ....132 B1
South Park Rd IL IG1 ....67 D5
South Park Ter IL IG1 ....67 D5
South Pl LVPST EC2M 24 B3
South Place Ms LVPST EC2M 24 B3
Southport Rd WOOL/PLUM SE18 ....109 F5
South Ri BAY/PAD * W2 ....29 D1
South Rd FSTH SE23 ....157 D2
South Rw BKHTH/KID SE3 ....124 A5
South Sea St BERM/RHTH SE16 ......103 F4
South Side HMSMTH W6 ....99 F4

Southspring *ELTH/MOT* SE9............**145** D5
South Sq *GINN* WC1R....................**22** A3
  GLDGN NW11..........................**54** A1
South St *MYFR/PKLN* W1K..............**30** B3
South Tenter St *WCHPL* E1.............**37** F1
South Ter *SKENS* SW7...................**40** C4
Southvale Rd *BKHTH/KID* SE3.......**123** E5
Southview Av *WLSDN* NW10............**69** F2
Southview Cl *TOOT* SW17..............**152** A5
South View Crs *CNTH/NBYPK* IG2.....**66** B1
Southview Rd *BMLY* BR1................**159** D4
South Vis *CAMTN* NW1...................**75** D3
Southville *VX/NE* SW8..................**117** D4
Southwark Br *CANST* EC4R.............**35** F2
Southwark Bridge Rd *STHWK* SE1.....**35** F3
Southwark Park Est
  BERM/RHTH * SE16..................**102** B5
Southwark Park Rd
  BERM/RHTH SE16....................**49** F4
Southwark St *STHWK* SE1..............**35** D3
Southway *GLDGN* NW11.................**54** B1
South Wy *WBLY* HA9......................**68** A2
Southwell Gdns *SKENS* SW7...........**39** E4
Southwell Grove Rd *WAN* E11.........**63** E4
Southwell Rd *CMBW* SE5..............**136** C1
Southwest Rd *WAN* E11.................**63** D3
South Wharf Rd *BAY/PAD* W2...........**16** A4
Southwick Ms *BAY/PAD* W2.............**16** B4
Southwick Pl *BAY/PAD* W2..............**16** C5
Southwick St *BAY/PAD* W2..............**16** C4
Southwick Yd *BAY/PAD* * W2...........**17** D5
Southwold Rd *CLPT* E5...................**60** B4
Southwood Av *HGT* N6...................**56** B2
Southwood La *HGT* N6...................**56** A2
Southwood Lawn Rd *HGT* N6..........**56** A2
Southwood Pk *HGT* * N6................**56** B2
Southwood Rd *ELTH/MOT* SE9........**162** B2
Southwood Smith St *IS* * N1..........**76** A5
South Worple Wy
  MORT/ESHN SW14...................**129** D1
Sovereign Cl *WAP* E1W..................**102** D1
Sovereign Crs *BERM/RHTH* SE16.....**103** E1
Sovereign Ms *BETH* * E2.................**13** E1
Sovereign Pk *WLSDN* * NW10..........**86** B3
Sowerby Cl *ELTH/MOT* SE9............**143** F3
Spafield St *CLKNW* * EC1R..............**10** A5
Spa Green Est *CLKNW* * EC1R..........**10** B3
Spalding Rd *HDN* NW4...................**52** C1
  TOOT SW17...........................**152** B5
Spanby Rd *BOW* E3......................**92** A3
Spaniards Cl *GLDGN* NW11.............**54** C3
Spaniards End *GLDGN* NW11...........**54** C3
Spaniards Rd *HAMP* NW3...............**54** C4
Spanish Pl *MHST* * W1U.................**18** B4
Spanish Rd *WAND/EARL* SW18........**132** C3
Sparke Ter *CAN/RD* * E16...............**93** F5
Sparks Cl *ACT* W3.......................**87** D5
Spa Rd *BERM/RHTH* SE16................**49** E3
Sparrows La *ELTH/MOT* SE9...........**144** C5
Sparsholt Rd *ARCH* N19.................**57** F3
  BARK IG11.............................**85** E5
Sparta St *LEW* SE13....................**122** C4
Spearman St *WOOL/PLUM* * SE18....**126** A2
Spear Ms *ECT* SW5.......................**38** B5
Spears Rd *ARCH* N19....................**57** E3
Spedan Cl *HAMP* NW3...................**54** B5
Speedwell St *DEPT* SE8................**122** A3
Spekehill *ELTH/MOT* SE9..............**161** F3
Speldhurst Rd *CHSWK* W4..............**99** D4
  HOM E9................................**79** D4
Spellbrook Wk *IS* * N1..................**76** C5
Spelman St *WCHPL* E1...................**90** A4
Spence Cl *BERM/RHTH* SE16..........**103** E1

Spencer Dr *EFNCH* N2...................**54** C1
Spencer Gdns *MORT/ESHN* SW14....**128** C3
Spencer Ms *HMSMTH* W6...............**113** E2
Spencer Pk *WAND/EARL* SW18.......**133** D3
Spencer Pl *IS* N1.........................**76** B4
  WEST SW1P............................**43** F3
Spencer Ri *KTTN* NW5...................**74** B1
Spencer Rd *ACT* W3......................**98** C2
  BTSEA SW11..........................**133** D2
  CHSWK W4.............................**110** C3
  EHAM E6................................**83** D5
  GDMY/SEVK IG3.......................**67** F3
Spencer St *FSBYE* EC1V................**10** C4
Spencer Wk *PUT/ROE* SW15..........**131** D2
Spenser Gv *STNW/STAM* N16...........**77** E1
Spenser Ms *DUL* SE21.................**155** D1
Spenser Rd *HNHL* SE24...............**136** B3
Spenser St *WESTW* SW1E...............**43** F2
Spensley Wk *STNW/STAM* N16.........**59** D5
Speranza St *WOOL/PLUM* SE18......**127** F1
Spert St *POP/IOD* E14..................**103** E1
Spey St *POP/IOD* E14....................**92** C4
Spezia Rd *WLSDN* NW10.................**88** A1
Spicer Cl *CMBW* SE5...................**118** B5
Spindle Cl *WOOL/PLUM* SE18.........**107** E4
Spindrift Av *POP/IOD* E14.............**104** B5
Spinel Cl *WOOL/PLUM* SE18...........**127** F1
Spinney Gdns *NRWD* SE19.............**155** F5
The Spinney *BARN* * SW13.............**112** B2
  STRHM/NOR SW16.....................**152** B3
Spirit Quay *WAP* E1W...................**102** A2
Spital Sq *WCHPL* E1......................**25** D2
Spital St *WCHPL* E1.......................**90** A4
Spital Yd *WCHPL* * E1....................**25** D2
Spode Wk *KIL/WHAMP* * NW6..........**72** B2
Sportsbank St *CAT* SE6...............**140** C5
Spratt Hall Rd *WAN* E11................**64** A1
Spray St *WOOL/PLUM* SE18............**108** B5
Sprimont Pl *CHEL* SW3.................**115** F1
Springall St *PECK* SE15................**120** B3
Springbank Rd *LEW* SE13.............**141** E4
Springbank Wk *CAMTN* NW1............**75** D4
Springdale Rd *STNW/STAM* N16.......**77** D1
Springfield *CLPT* E5......................**60** B3
Springfield Gdns *CLPT* E5..............**60** B3
Springfield Gv *CHARL* SE7.............**124** C2
Springfield La *KIL/WHAMP* NW6........**72** A5
Springfield Ri *SYD* SE26...............**156** B4
Springfield Rd *EHAM* E6.................**83** F4
  SRTFD * E15...........................**93** E2
  STJWD NW8............................**72** C5
  SYD SE26.............................**156** B5
  WALTH E17.............................**61** F1
  WIM/MER SW19........................**149** F5
Springfield Wk *KIL/WHAMP* NW6.......**72** B5
Spring Gdns *HBRY* N5....................**76** C2
  WHALL SW1A...........................**32** C3
Spring Gv *CHSWK* W4..................**110** A1
Spring Hl *CLPT* E5.......................**60** A2
  SYD SE26.............................**156** C2
Spring La *CLPT* E5........................**60** B3
Spring Ms *MHST* * W1U..................**17** F2
Springpark Dr *FSBYPK* N4...............**58** C3
Spring Pl *KTTN* NW5.....................**74** A2
Springrice Rd *LEW* SE13..............**140** C4
Spring St *BAY/PAD* W2....................**16** A5
Spring Tide Cl *PECK* * SE15...........**120** A4
Springvale Ter *WKENS* W14...........**101** D4
Spring Wk *WCHPL* E1.....................**90** A4
Springwater Cl
  WOOL/PLUM * SE18..................**126** A4
Springwell Av *WLSDN* NW10............**69** F5
Springwell Rd *STRHM/NOR* SW16....**154** A4

Sprowston Ms *FSTGT* E7 ....82 A3
Sprowston Rd *FSTGT* E7 ....82 A2
Sprules Rd *BROCKY* SE4 ....121 E5
Spurgeon St *STHWK* SE1 ....48 A3
Spurling Rd *EDUL* * SE22 ....137 F2
Spur Rd *BARK* IG11 ....96 C2
   STHWK SE1 ....46 A1
   WHALL SW1A 43 E1
Spurstowe Rd *HACK* E8 ....78 B3
Spurstowe Ter *HACK* E8 ....78 A2
The Square *HMSMTH* W6 ....112 C1
Squarey St *TOOT* SW17 ....150 C3
Squire Gdns *STJWD* NW8 ....4 A4
Squires Ct *WIM/MER* SW19 ....150 A4
Squire's Mt *HAMP* NW3 ....55 D5
The Squirrels *LEW* SE13 ....141 E1
Stable Ms *WNWD* SE27 ....154 C5
Stables Wy *LBTH* SE11 ....118 A1
Stable Wy *NKENS* W10 ....88 C5
Stable Yard Rd *WHALL* SW1A 31 F4
Stacey St *HOLWY* N7 ....58 A5
   LSQ/SEVD WC2H 20 B5
Stackhouse St *KTBR* SW1X 41 E2
Stacy Pth *CMBW* * SE5 ....119 E3
Stadium Rd *WOOL/PLUM* SE18 ....125 F3
Stadium St *WBPTN* SW10 ....114 C3
Staffa Rd *LEY* E10 ....61 E3
Stafford Cl *KIL/WHAMP* NW6 ....2 A4
   WALTH E17 ....61 F1
Stafford Pl *WESTW* SW1E 43 E2
Stafford Rd *BOW* E3 ....91 F1
   FSTGT E7 ....82 C4
   KIL/WHAMP NW6 ....2 A3
   SCUP DA14 ....163 E4
Staffordshire St *PECK* SE15 ....120 A4
Stafford Ter *KENS* W8 ....38 A2
Stag La *PUT/ROE* SW15 ....147 F3
Stag Pl *WESTW* SW1E 43 E2
Stainer St *STHWK* SE1 ....36 B4
Staines Rd *IL* IG1 ....85 D1
Stainforth Rd *GNTH/NBYPK* IG2 ....67 F2
Staining La *CITYW* EC2V 23 G4
Stainsbury St *BETH* E2 ....90 C1
Stainsby Pl *POP/IOD* * E14 ....92 A5
Stainsby Rd *POP/IOD* E14 ....92 A5
Stainton Rd *LEW* SE13 ....141 D5
Stalbridge St *CAMTN* NW1 ....17 D2
Stalham St *BERM/RHTH* SE16 ....102 B4
Stamford Brook Av *HMSMTH* W6 ....99 F4
Stamford Brook Gdns
   HMSMTH W6 ....99 F4
Stamford Brook Rd *HMSMTH* W6 ....99 F4
Stamford Cottages
   FUL/PGN * SW6 ....114 B3
Stamford Gv East
   STNW/STAM N16 ....60 A3
Stamford Gv West
   STNW/STAM N16 ....60 A3
Stamford Hl *STNW/STAM* N16 ....59 F3
Stamford Rd *EHAM* E6 ....83 E5
   IS N1 ....77 E4
Stamford St *STHWK* SE1 ....34 A4
Stamp Pl *BETH* E2 ....13 E3
Stanborough *HACK* E8 ....77 F3
Stanbridge Rd *PUT/ROE* SW15 ....130 C1
Stanbury Ct *HAMP* NW3 ....73 F3
Stanbury Rd *PECK* SE15 ....120 B4
Standard Pl *SDTCH* EC2A 13 D4
Standard Rd *WLSDN* NW10 ....86 C3
Standen Rd *WAND/EARL* SW18 ....132 A5
Standish Rd *HMSMTH* W6 ....100 A5
Stane Wy *WOOL/PLUM* SE18 ....125 D3

Stanfield Rd *BOW* E3 ....91 E1
Stanford Pl *STHWK* SE1 ....48 C5
Stanford Rd *KENS* W8 ....39 D3
Stanford St *WEST* SW1P 44 A5
Stanhope Cl *BERM/RHTH* * SE16 ....103 D3
Stanhope Gdns *FSBYPK* N4 ....58 B1
   HGT N6 ....56 B1
   IL IG1 ....65 F3
   SKENS SW7 ....39 F4
Stanhope Ga *BAY/PAD* W2 ....29 E1
   MYFR/PKLN W1K 30 B4
Stanhope Ms East *SKENS* SW7 ....39 F4
Stanhope Ms South *SKENS* SW7 ....39 F5
Stanhope Ms West *SKENS* SW7 ....39 F4
Stanhope Pde *CAMTN* NW1 ....7 D3
Stanhope Pl *BAY/PAD* W2 ....17 E5
Stanhope Rd *HGT* N6 ....56 C1
Stanhope Rw *MYFR/PICC* * W1J 30 C4
Stanhope St *CAMTN* NW1 ....7 E3
Stanhope Ter *BAY/PAD* W2 ....28 B1
Stanier Cl *ECT* SW5 ....113 F1
Staniake Rd *SHB* W12 ....100 C2
Stanlake Vls *SHB* W12 ....100 C2
Stanley Av *BARK* IG11 ....97 F2
Stanley Crs *NTGHL* W11 ....101 F1
Stanley Gdns *ACT* W3 ....99 E3
   CRICK NW2 ....70 C2
   NTGHL W11 ....101 F1
Stanley Gv *VX/NE* SW8 ....116 A5
Stanley Pas *CAMTN* NW1 ....8 C2
Stanley Rd *ACT* W3 ....98 B4
   IL IG1 ....67 D4
   LEY E10 ....62 B1
   MNPK E12 ....83 E2
   MORT/ESHN SW14 ....128 B2
   SRTFD E15 ....81 D5
Stanley St *DEPT* SE8 ....121 F3
Stanley Ter *ARCH* * N19 ....57 F3
Stanmer St *BTSEA* SW11 ....115 E4
Stanmore Rd *WAN* E11 ....63 F3
Stanmore St *IS* N1 ....75 F5
Stannard Ms *HACK* * E8 ....78 A3
Stannard Rd *HACK* E8 ....78 A3
Stannary St *LBTH* SE11 ....118 A2
Stansfeld Rd *CAN/RD* E16 ....95 D5
Stansfield Rd *BRXN/ST* SW9 ....135 F1
Stansted Gv *FSTH* SE23 ....157 F1
Stanstead Rd *FSTH* SE23 ....157 D1
Stanswood Gdns *CMBW* SE5 ....119 E3
Stanthorpe Cl *STRHM/NOR* * SW16 ....153 E5
Stanthorpe Rd *STRHM/NOR* SW16 ....153 E5
Stanton Rd *BARN* SW13 ....111 F3
Stanton St *PECK* * SE15 ....120 A4
Stanton Wy *SYD* SE26 ....157 F4
Stanway Gdns *ACT* W3 ....98 A2
Stanway St *IS* N1 ....13 D1
Stanwick Rd *WKENS* W14 ....101 F5
Stanworth St *STHWK* SE1 ....49 E1
Staplefield Cl *BRXS/STRHM* * SW2 ....153 E1
Stapleford Cl *WIM/MER* SW19 ....131 E5
Staplehurst Rd *LEW* SE13 ....141 D3
Staple Inn *HHOL* WC1V 22 A3
Staples Cl *BERM/RHTH* SE16 ....103 E2
Staple St *STHWK* SE1 ....48 B1
Stapleton Hall Rd *FSBYPK* N4 ....57 F2
Stapleton Rd *TOOT* SW17 ....152 A3
Stapleton Vls *STNW/STAM* * N16 ....77 E1
Starboard Wy *POP/IOD* E14 ....104 A4
Starcross St *CAMTN* NW1 ....7 F4
Starfield Rd *SHB* W12 ....100 A3
Star La *CAN/RD* E16 ....93 E3
Star Rd *WKENS* W14 ....113 F2
Star St *BAY/PAD* W2 ....16 B4

Star Yd *LINN* WC2A **22** A4
Statham Gv *STNW/STAM* N16 ......**59** D5
Station Ap *BKHTH/KID* SE3 ....**142** B1
  CAMTN * NW1 ....**18** A1
  CAT SE6 ....**157** F5
  FSTGT * E7 ....**82** B1
  FUL/PGN * SW6 ....**131** E1
  GLDGN * NW11 ....**53** D2
  RCH/KEW TW9 ....**110** A4
  STRHM/NOR SW16 ....**153** D5
  WAN * E11 ....**81** E1
  WELL DA16 ....**127** F5
  WLSDN NW10 ....**87** F2
Station Approach Rd *CHSWK* W4 ...**110** C3
Station Ar *GTPST* * W1W................**19** D1
Station Chambers *EA* * W5 ....**86** A3
Station Crs *BKHTH/KID* SE3 ....**124** A1
Stationers Hall Ct *STP* * EC4M **23** D5
Station Gdns *CHSWK* W4 ....**110** C3
Station Pde *ACT* * W3 ....**86** A5
  BAL * SW12 ....**152** A1
  BARK IG11 ....**84** C4
  CHSWK * W4 ....**98** C5
  CHSWK * W4 ....**110** C3
  CLPT * E5 ....**60** B5
  CRICK NW2 ....**70** A5
  EHAM * E6 ....**82** C5
  EHAM * E6 ....**83** E4
  RCH/KEW TW9 ....**110** A4
Station Pas *PECK* SE15 ....**120** C4
Station Pl *FSBYPK* N4 ....**58** A4
Station Ri *WNWD* SE27 ....**154** B2
Station Rd *ARCH* N19 ....**56** C5
  BARN SW13 ....**111** F5
  HDN NW4 ....**52** A1
  IL IG1 ....**66** B5
  LEW SE13 ....**140** C1
  MNPK E12 ....**83** D1
  WALTH E17 ....**61** E1
  WLSDN NW10 ....**87** F1
Station St *SRTFD* E15 ....**81** D4
Station Ter *CMBW* SE5 ....**118** C4
  WLSDN NW10 ....**89** D1
Staunton St *DEPT* SE8 ....**121** F2
Staveley Cl *HOLWY* * N7 ....**75** E1
  PECK SE15 ....**120** C4
Staveley Gdns *CHSWK* W4 ....**111** D4
Staveley Rd *CHSWK* W4 ....**110** C2
Staverton Rd *CRICK* NW2 ....**70** C4
Stave Yard Rd *BERM/RHTH* SE16 ...**103** E2
Stavordale Rd *HBRY* N5 ....**76** A1
Stayner's Rd *WCHPL* E1 ....**91** D3
Stead St *WALW* SE17 ....**48** A5
Stean St *HACK* E8 ....**77** F5
Stebondale St *POP/IOD* E14 ....**122** C1
Stedman St *WALW* SE17 ....**47** E5
Steele Rd *CHSWK* W4 ....**98** C4
  WAN E11 ....**81** E1
  WLSDN NW10 ....**86** C1
Steele's Ms North *HAMP* * NW3 ...**73** F3
Steele's Ms South *HAMP* NW3 .....**73** F3
Steele's Rd *HAMP* NW3..................**73** F3
Steeles Studios *HAMP* * NW3 ......**73** F3
Steel's La *WCHPL* E1 ....**90** C5
Steelyard Pas *CANST* EC4R............**36** A2
Steep Hl *STRHM/NOR* SW16.........**153** D3
Steeple Cl *FUL/PGN* SW6 ....**131** E1
  WIM/MER SW19 ....**149** E4
Steeple Wk *IS* * N1 ....**76** C5
Steerforth St *WAND/EARL* SW18 ...**150** B2
Steers Wy *BERM/RHTH* SE16 ......**103** E3
Stellman Cl *CLPT* E5 ....**60** A5
Stephan Cl *HACK* E8 ....**78** A5

Stephendale Rd *FUL/PGN* SW6 .....**114** B5
Stephen Ms *FITZ* W1T....................**20** A3
Stephen Pl *CLAP* SW4 ....**134** C1
Stephenson St *CAN/RD* E16.........**93** E4
  WLSDN NW10 ....**87** E2
Stephenson Wy *CAMTN* NW1 ....**7** F5
Stephen's Rd *SRTFD* E15 ....**81** E5
Stephen St *FITZ* W1T......................**20** A4
Stepney Cswy *WCHPL* E1...............**91** D5
Stepney Gn *WCHPL* E1 ....**90** C4
Stepney High St *WCHPL* E1 ....**91** D4
Stepney Wy *WCHPL* E1 ....**90** B4
Sterling Cl *WLSDN* NW10 ....**70** A4
Sterling Gdns *NWCR* SE14 ....**121** E2
Sterling St *SKENS* SW7 ....**41** D1
Sterndale Rd *WKENS* * W14 ....**101** D4
Sterne St *SHB* W12 ....**101** D3
Sternhall La *PECK* SE15...............**138** A1
Sternhold Av *BRXS/STRHM* SW2 ...**153** D2
Sterry Rd *BARK* IG11 ....**85** F5
Sterry St *STHWK* SE1 ....**48** A1
Steucers La *FSTH* SE23 ....**157** E1
Steve Biko La *CAT* SE6 ....**158** A4
Steve Biko Rd *HOLWY* N7 ....**58** A5
Stevedore St *WAP* E1W **102** B2
Stevenage Rd *EHAM* E6 ....**84** A3
  FUL/PGN SW6 ....**113** D4
Stevens Av *HOM* E9 ....**78** C3
Stevenson Crs *BERM/RHTH* SE16 ...**120** A1
Stevens St *STHWK* SE1 ....**49** D2
Steventon Rd *SHB* W12 ....**99** F1
Steward St *WCHPL* E1 ....**25** D2
Stewart Cl *CDALE/KGS* * NW9 ......**50** C1
  CHST BR7 ....**162** B5
Stewart Rd *WAN* E11 ....**81** D1
Stewart's Gv *CHEL* SW3 ....**115** D1
  CHEL * SW3 ....**115** D1
Stewart's La *VX/NE* SW8 ....**116** B3
Stewarts Rd *VX/NE* SW8 ....**116** C3
  VX/NE SW8 ....**116** C4
Stewart St *POP/IOD* E14 ....**104** C3
Stew La *BLKFR* EC4V **35** E1
Steyne Rd *ACT* W3 ....**98** B2
Steyning Gv *ELTH/MOT* SE9 ....**161** F4
Stile Hall Gdns *CHSWK* W4 ....**110** A1
Stillingfleet Rd *BARN* SW13 ....**112** A3
Stillington St *WEST* SW1P...............**43** F4
Stillness Rd *FSTH* SE23 ....**139** E4
Stirling Rd *ACT* W3 ....**98** B4
  BRXN/ST SW9 ....**117** E5
  PLSTW E13 ....**94** B1
St John's Est *IS* N1 ....**12** B1
  STHWK SE1 ....**37** E5
Stockfield Rd *STRHM/NOR* SW16 ...**153** F4
Stockholm Rd *BERM/RHTH* SE16 ...**120** C2
Stockholm Wy *WAP* * E1W **102** A2
Stockhurst Cl *PUT/ROE* SW15 .....**112** C5
Stock Orchard Crs *HOLWY* * N7 ...**75** F1
Stock Orchard St *HOLWY* N7 ....**75** F2
Stocks Pl *POP/IOD* E14 ....**103** F1
Stock St *PLSTW* E13 ....**94** A1
Stockwell Av *BRXN/ST* SW9 ....**135** F1
Stockwell Gdns *BRXN/ST* SW9......**117** F4
Stockwell Gn *BRXN/ST* SW9 ....**117** F5
Stockwell La *BRXN/ST* SW9 ....**117** F5
Stockwell Park Crs *BRXN/ST* SW9 ...**117** F4
Stockwell Park Rd *BRXN/ST* SW9 ...**117** F4
Stockwell Park Wk *BRXN/ST* SW9 ...**135** F1
Stockwell Rd *BRXN/ST* SW9...........**117** F5
Stockwell St *GNWCH* SE10 ....**122** C2
Stockwell Ter *BRXN/ST* SW9 ....**117** F4
Stoford Cl *WIM/MER* SW19 ....**149** E1
Stokenchurch St *FUL/PGN* SW6 ....**114** B4

Stoke Newington Church St
  STNW/STAM N16 ....**59** D5
Stoke Newington Common
  STNW/STAM N16 ....**59** F5
Stoke Newington High St
  STNW/STAM N16 ....**59** F5
Stoke Newington Rd
  STNW/STAM N16 ....**77** F2
Stoke Pl *WLSDN NW10* **87** F2
Stokesley St *SHB W12* **87** F5
Stokes Rd *EHAM E6* **95** E3
Stoll Cl *CRICK NW2* **52** C5
Stondon Pk *FSTH SE23* **139** F3
Stonebridge Pk *WLSDN NW10* **69** D4
Stonebridge Wy *WBLY HA9* **68** B3
Stone Buildings *LINN WC2A* **21** F3
Stone Cl *CLAP SW4* **116** C5
Stonecutter St *FLST/FETLN EC4A* ...**22** C4
Stonefield St *IS N1* **76** A5
Stonefield Wy *CHARL SE7* **125** D3
Stonehall Av *IL IG1* **65** E1
Stone Hall Gdns *KENS * W8* **38** C3
Stone Hall Pl *KENS * W8* **38** C3
Stonehill Cl *MORT/ESHN SW14* **129** D3
Stonehill Rd *CHSWK W4* **110** A1
  MORT/ESHN SW14 ....**128** C3
Stonehills Ct *DUL SE21* **155** E3
Stone House Ct *HDTCH EC3A* **25** D4
Stoneleigh Pl *NTGHL W11* **101** F1
Stoneleigh St *NTGHL W11* **101** F1
Stonenest St *FSBYPK N4* **57** F3
Stones End St *STHWK SE1* **47** E1
Stonewall *EHAM E6* **96** A4
Stoney Aly *WOOL/PLUM SE18* **126** A5
Stoneyard La *POP/IOD E14* **104** B1
Stoneycroft Cl *LEE/GVPK SE12* **141** F5
Stoney La *HDTCH EC3A* **25** D4
Stoney St *STHWK SE1* **36** A3
Stonhouse St *CLAP SW4* **134** C1
Stonnell's Rd *BTSEA SW11* **133** F3
Stonor Rd *WKENS W14* **101** F5
Stopes St *PECK SE15* **119** F3
Stopford Rd *PLSTW E13* **82** A5
  WALW SE17 ....**118** B1
Store Rd *CAN/RD E16* **108** A3
Storers Quay *POP/IOD E14* **105** D5
Store St *GWRST WC1E* **20** A3
  SRTFD E15 ....**81** D2
Storey Rd *HGT N6* **55** F1
Storeys Ga *STJSPK * SW1H* **44** B3
  WEST SW1P **44** B3
Stories Ms *CMBW * SE5* **119** E5
Stories Rd *CMBW SE5* **137** E1
Stork Rd *FSTGT E7* **81** F3
Storks Rd *BERM/RHTH * SE16* **102** A4
Stormont Rd *BTSEA SW11* **134** A2
  HGT N6 ....**55** F2
Story St *IS N1* **75** F4
Stothard St *WCHPL E1* **90** C3
Stott Cl *WAND/EARL SW18* **133** D4
Stoughton Cl *PUT/ROE SW15* **148** A1
Stourcliffe St *BAY/PAD W2* **17** E5
Stourhead Cl *WIM/MER SW19* **131** D3
Stour Rd *BOW E3* **80** A4
Stowage *DEPT SE8* **122** A2
Stowe Rd *SHB W12* **100** B3
Stracey Rd *WLSDN NW10* **69** D5
Stradbroke Rd *HBRY N5* **76** C1
Stradella Rd *HNHL SE24* **136** C4
Strafford Rd *ACT W3* **98** C3
Strafford St *POP/IOD E14* **104** A3
Strahan Rd *BOW E3* **91** E2
Straightsmouth *GNWCH SE10* **122** C3

Strait Rd *EHAM E6* **107** E1
Straker's Rd *EDUL SE22* **138** B2
Strand *CHCR WC2N* **32** C3
Strandfield Cl *WOOL/PLUM SE18* ...**127** E1
Strand-on-the-Green *CHSWK W4* ...**110** A2
Strangways Ter *WKENS W14* **101** F4
Stranraer Wy *IS N1* **75** E4
Strasburg Rd *BTSEA SW11* **116** A4
Stratford Gv *PUT/ROE SW15* **131** D2
Stratford Pl *MHST W1U* **18** B5
Stratford Rd *KENS W8* **38** B3
  PLSTW E13 ....**82** A5
Stratford Vls *CAMTN NW1* **74** C4
Strathan Cl *WAND/EARL SW18* **131** E4
Strathaven Rd *LEE/GVPK SE12* **142** B4
Strathblaine Rd *BTSEA SW11* **133** D3
Strathdale *STRHM/NOR SW16* **153** F5
Strathdon Dr *TOOT SW17* **151** D3
Strathearn Pl *BAY/PAD W2* **28** C1
Strathearn Rd *WIM/MER SW19* **150** A5
Stratheden Rd *BKHTH/KID SE3* **124** A4
Strathfield Gdns *BARK IG11* **85** D3
Strathleven Rd *BRXS/STRHM SW2* ..**135** E3
Strathmore Rd *WIM/MER SW19* **150** A3
Strathnairn St *STHWK SE1* **102** A5
Strathray Gdns *HAMP * NW3* **73** E3
Strath Ter *BTSEA SW11* **133** E2
Strathville Rd *WAND/EARL SW18* ...**150** A1
Strattondale St *POP/IOD E14* **104** C4
Stratton Dr *BARK IG11* **85** E2
Stratton St *MYFR/PICC W1J* **31** D3
Strauss Rd *CHSWK * W4* **99** D3
Streakes Field Rd *CRICK NW2* **52** A4
Streatfeild Av *EHAM E6* **83** F5
Streatham Cl *STRHM/NOR * SW16* ...**153** E2
Streatham Common North
  STRHM/NOR SW16 ....**153** F5
Streatham Ct *STRHM/NOR SW16* ...**153** F5
Streatham Gn *STRHM/NOR * SW16* ..**153** E4
Streatham High Rd
  STRHM/NOR SW16 ....**153** E4
Streatham Hl *BRXS/STRHM SW2* **153** E1
Streatham Pl *BRXS/STRHM SW2* **135** E3
Streatham St *NOXST/BSQ WC1A* **20** C4
Streathbourne Rd *TOOT SW17* **152** A2
Streatleigh Pde
  *STRHM/NOR * SW16* **153** E2
Streatley Pl *HAMP NW3* **73** D1
Streatley Rd *KIL/WHAMP NW6* **71** F3
Streetfield Ms *BKHTH/KID SE3* **124** A5
Streimer Rd *SRTFD E15* **92** C1
Strelley Wy *ACT W3* **99** E1
Strickland Rw *WAND/EARL SW18* ...**133** D5
Strickland St *DEPT SE8* **122** A5
Stride Rd *PLSTW E13* **93** F1
Strode Rd *FSTGT E7* **82** A1
  FUL/PGN SW6 ....**113** D3
  WLSDN NW10 ....**70** B3
Strone Rd *FSTGT E7* **82** C3
Strongbow Crs *ELTH/MOT SE9* **143** F3
Strongbow Rd *ELTH/MOT SE9* **143** F3
Stronsa Rd *SHB W12* **99** F3
Stroud Crs *PUT/ROE SW15* **147** F3
Stroud Green Rd *FSBYPK N4* **57** F3
Stroud Rd *WIM/MER SW19* **150** A3
Stroughton Cl *LBTH SE11* **45** F5
Strout's Pl *BETH E2* **13** E3
Strutton Gnd *WEST SW1P* **44** A2
Strype St *WCHPL E1* **25** E3
Stuart Av *CDALE/KGS NW9* **52** A2
Stuart Rd *ACT W3* **98** C2
  BARK IG11 ....**85** F3
  KIL/WHAMP NW6 ....**2** A4

PECK SE15	138	C2
WIM/MER SW19	150	A3
Stubbs Dr *BERM/RHTH* SE16	120	B1
Stucley Pl *CAMTN* NW1	74	B4
Studdridge St *FUL/PGN* SW6	114	A5
Studd St *IS* N1	76	B5
Studholme Ct *KIL/WHAMP* * NW6	72	A1
Studholme St *PECK* SE15	120	B3
Studio Pl *KTBR* * SW1X	41	F1
Studland Cl *BFN/LL* DA15	163	F3
Studland Rd *SYD* SE26	157	D5
Studland St *HMSMTH* W6	100	B5
Studley Cl *CLPT* E5	79	E2
Studley Dr *REDBR* IG4	65	D1
Studley Rd *CLAP* SW4	117	E4
FSTGT E7	82	B3
Stukeley Rd *FSTGT* E7	82	B4
Stukeley St *HOL/ALD* WC2B	21	D4
Sturdy Rd *PECK* SE15	120	B5
Sturgeon Rd *WALW* SE17	118	C1
Sturgess Av *HDN* NW4	52	B2
Sturge St *STHWK* SE1	47	E1
Sturmer Wy *HOLWY* N7	75	F2
Sturry St *POP/IOD* E14	92	B5
Sturt St *IS* N1	11	F2
Stutfield St *WCHPL* E1	90	A5
Styles Gdns *BRXN/ST* SW9	136	B1
Sudbourne Rd *BRXS/STRHM* SW2	135	E3
Sudbrooke Rd *BAL* SW12	133	F4
Sudbury *EHAM* E6	96	A5
Sudbury Crs *BMLY* BR1	160	A5
Sudbury Rd *BARK* IG11	85	F2
Sudeley St *IS* N1	11	D2
Sudlow Rd *WAND/EARL* SW18	132	A2
Sudrey St *STHWK* SE1	47	E1
Suffolk La *CANST* EC4R	36	A1
Suffolk Rd *BARK* IG11	85	D4
BARN SW13	111	F3
GDMY/SEVK IG3	67	E3
PLSTW E13	93	F2
SEVS/STOTM N15	59	D1
WLSDN NW10	69	E4
Suffolk Rd *FSTGT* E7	82	A2
STJS SW1Y	32	B3
Suffolk Vls *WAND/EARL* * SW18	132	A5
Sugar House La *SRTFD* E15	92	C1
Sugar Loaf Wk *BETH* * E2	90	C2
Sugden Rd *BTSEA* SW11	134	A1
Sugden Wy *BARK* IG11	97	F1
Sulgrave Gdns *SHB* W12	100	A3
Sulgrave Rd *HMSMTH* W6	100	C3
Sulina Rd *BRXS/STRHM* SW2	135	E5
Sulivan Ct *FUL/PGN* SW6	114	A5
Sulivan Rd *FUL/PGN* SW6	132	A1
Sullivan Av *CAN/RD* E16	95	D4
Sullivan Cl *BTSEA* SW11	133	E1
Sullivan Rd *LBTH* SE11	46	B4
Sultan St *CMBW* SE5	118	C3
Sumatra Rd *KIL/WHAMP* NW6	72	A3
Sumburgh Rd *BAL* SW12	134	A4
Summercourt Rd *WCHPL* E1	90	C5
Summerfield Av *KIL/WHAMP* NW6	89	E1
Summerfield St *LEE/GVPK* SE12	141	F5
Summerhouse Rd *STNW/STAM* N16	59	E4
Summerlands Av *ACT* W3	98	C3
Summerley St *WAND/EARL* SW18	150	B2
Summersby Rd *HGT* N6	56	B1
Summers Cl *WBLY* HA9	50	B3
Summers St *CLKNW* EC1R	22	A1
Summerstown *TOOT* SW17	150	C3
Summit Est *STNW/STAM* * N16	60	A2
Sumner Av *PECK* SE15	119	F4
Sumner Pl *SKENS* SW7	28	A5
Sumner Place Ms *SKENS* SW7	40	B5
Sumner Rd *PECK* SE15	119	F4
Sumner St *STHWK* SE1	35	E3
Sumpter Cl *HAMP* NW3	72	C3
Sunbeam Crs *NKENS* W10	88	C3
Sunbeam Rd *WLSDN* NW10	86	C3
Sunbury Av *MORT/ESHN* SW14	129	D2
Sunbury La *BTSEA* SW11	115	D4
Sunbury St *WOOL/PLUM* SE18	107	F4
Suncroft Pl *SYD* SE26	156	C3
Sunderland Mt *FSTH* * SE23	157	D2
Sunderland Rd *FSTH* SE23	157	D1
Sunderland Ter *BAY/PAD* W2	14	C4
Sunderland Wy *MNPK* E12	65	D4
Sundew Av *SHB* W12	100	A1
Sundorne Rd *CHARL* SE7	124	B1
Sundridge Av *WELL* DA16	127	D5
Sunfields Pl *BKHTH/KID* SE3	124	B3
Sun in Sands Rbt *BKHTH/KID* SE3	124	B3
Sun La *BKHTH/KID* SE3	124	B3
Sunlight Sq *BETH* E2	90	B2
Sunningdale Av *ACT* W3	99	E1
BARK IG11	85	D5
Sunningdale Cl		
BERM/RHTH * SE16	120	B1
Sunningdale Gdns *KENS* W8	38	B3
Sunninghill Ct *ACT* * W3	98	C3
Sunninghill Rd *LEW* SE13	122	B5
Sunny Crs *WLSDN* NW10	68	C4
Sunnydale Rd *LEE/GVPK* SE12	142	B3
Sunnydene St *SYD* SE26	157	E4
Sunnyhill Cl *CLPT* E5	79	E1
Sunnyhill Rd *STRHM/NOR* SW16	153	E4
Sunnymead Rd *CDALE/KGS* NW9	51	D2
PUT/ROE SW15	130	B3
Sunnyside *CRICK* NW2	53	F5
FSTH * SE23	139	F5
Sunnyside Rd *ARCH* N19	57	D2
IL IG1	66	C5
LEY E10	62	A3
Sun Pas *BERM/RHTH* SE16	102	A4
Sunray Av *CMBW* SE5	137	D2
Sun Rd *WKENS* W14	113	F1
Sunset Rd *CMBW* SE5	136	C2
WIM/MER SW19	148	B5
Sun St *SDTCH* EC2A	24	B2
Surma Cl *WCHPL* E1	90	A3
Surrendale Pl *MV/WKIL* W9	14	B1
Surrey Canal Rd		
BERM/RHTH SE16	120	C2
Surrey Crs *CHSWK* W4	110	A1
Surrey Gdns *FSBYPK* N4	58	C2
Surrey Gv *WALW* SE17	119	E1
Surrey La *BTSEA* SW11	115	E4
Surrey Ms *WNWD* SE27	155	E4
Surrey Quays Rd		
BERM/RHTH SE16	102	C4
Surrey Rd *BARK* IG11	85	E4
PECK SE15	139	D3
Surrey Rw *STHWK* SE1	34	C5
Surrey Sq *WALW* SE17	119	E1
Surrey St *PLSTW* E13	94	B2
TPL/STR WC2R	33	F1
Surrey Ter *WALW* SE17	49	D5
Surrey Water Rd		
BERM/RHTH SE16	103	D2
Surr St *HOLWY* N7	75	E2
Susannah St *POP/IOD* E14	92	B5
Susan Rd *BKHTH/KID* SE3	124	B5
Sussex Cl *ARCH* * N19	57	E4
REDBR IG4	65	F1
Sussex Gdns *BAY/PAD* W2	16	B5
Sussex Ms East *BAY/PAD* * W2	28	B1

Sussex Ms West *BAY/PAD* W2 ....**28** B1
Sussex Pl *BAY/PAD* W2 ....**16** B5
   CAMTN NW1 ....**5** E5
   HMSMTH W6 ....**112** C1
Sussex Rd *EHAM* E6 ....**96** A1
Sussex Sq *BAY/PAD* W2 ....**28** B1
Sussex St *PIM* SW1V **116** B1
   PLSTW E13 ....**94** B2
Sussex Wy *ARCH* N19 ....**57** D3
Sutcliffe Rd *WOOL/PLUM* SE18 ....**127** E2
Sutherland Av *MV/WKIL* W9 ....**3** E4
   MV/WKIL W9 ....**14** B1
   WELL DA16..**145** D2
Sutherland Gdns
   MORT/ESHN SW14 ....**129** E1
Sutherland Gv *WAND/EARL* SW18.....**131** F5
Sutherland Pl *BAY/PAD* W2 ....**14** A4
Sutherland Rd *BOW* E3 ....**91** F1
   CHSWK W4 ....**111** D2
Sutherland Rw *PIM* * SW1V.................**116** B1
Sutherland Sq *WALW* SE17 ....**118** C1
Sutherland St *PIM* SW1V **116** B1
Sutherland Wk *WALW* SE17 ....**118** C1
Sutlej Rd *CHARL* SE7 ....**124** C3
Sutterton St *HOLWY* N7 ....**75** F3
Sutton Cl *CHSWK* * W4 ....**110** C1
Sutton Ct *CHSWK* * W4 ....**110** C1
Sutton Court Rd *CHSWK* W4 ....**110** C1
   PLSTW E13 ....**94** C2
Sutton Est *CHEL* * SW3 ....**115** E1
   IS * N1 ....**76** B4
The Sutton Est *IS* * N1 ....**76** B4
Sutton La *CHSWK* W4 ....**110** C1
Sutton La South *CHSWK* W4 ....**110** C1
Sutton Pl *HOM* E9 ....**78** C2
Sutton Rd *BARK* IG11 ....**97** E1
   PLSTW E13 ....**93** F3
Sutton Rw *SOHO/SHAV* W1D **20** A4
Sutton Sq *HOM* * E9 ....**78** C2
Sutton St *WCHPL* E1 ....**90** C5
Sutton Wy *NKENS* W10 ....**88** C4
Swaby Rd *WAND/EARL* SW18 ....**150** C2
Swaffield Rd *WAND/EARL* SW18 ....**132** C5
Swain's La *KTTN* NW5 ....**56** A5
Swainson Rd *ACT* W3 ....**99** F3
Swain St *STJWD* NW8 ....**16** B1
Swallands Rd *CAT* SE6...........................**158** A3
Swallow Cl *NWCR* SE14 ....**120** C4
Swallow Dr *WLSDN* NW10 ....**69** D3
Swallowfield Rd *CHARL* SE7 ....**124** B1
Swallow Gdns *STRHM/NOR* SW16......**153** D5
Swallow Pl *REGST* W1B.........................**19** D5
Swallow St *CONDST* W1S **31** F2
   EHAM E6 ....**95** E4
Swanage Rd *WAND/EARL* SW18 ....**132** C4
Swan Ap *EHAM* E6...................................**95** E4
Swandon Wy *WAND/EARL* SW18.......**132** B2
Swanfield St *BETH* E2 ....**13** G4
Swan La *CANST* EC4R **36** B2
Swan Md *STHWK* SE1 ....**48** C3
Swan Ms *BRXN/ST* SW9 ....**117** F3
Swan Pas *WCHPL* E1 ....**37** F2
Swan Pl *BARN* SW13 ....**111** F5
Swan Rd *BERM/RHTH* SE16 ....**102** C3
Swanscombe Rd *CHSWK* W4 ....**111** D1
   NTGHL W11 ....**101** D2
Swan St *STHWK* SE1 ....**47** F1
Swanton Gdns *WIM/MER* SW19 ....**149** D1
Swan Wk *CHEL* SW3 ....**115** F2
Swanwick Cl *PUT/ROE* SW15 ....**129** F5
Swan Yd *IS* N1 ....**76** B3
Swaton Rd *BOW* E3...................................**92** A3
Sweden Ga *BERM/RHTH* SE16............**103** E5

Sweeney Crs *STHWK* SE1 ....**49** F1
Swete St *PLSTW* E13 ....**94** A1
Sweyn Pl *BKHTH/KID* SE3....................**124** A5
Swift Cl *FUL/PGN* SW6 ....**113** E4
Swinbrook Rd *NKENS* W10.....................**89** E4
Swinburne Rd *PUT/ROE* SW15 ....**130** A2
Swindon Cl *GDMY/SEVK* IG3................**67** E4
Swindon St *SHB* * W12 ....**100** B2
Swinford Gdns *BRXN/ST* SW9 ....**136** B1
Swingate La *WOOL/PLUM* SE18 ....**127** E3
Swinnerton St *HOM* E9 ....**79** E2
Swinton Cl *WBLY* HA9 ....**50** B3
Swinton Pl *FSBYW* WC1X **9** E3
Swinton St *FSBYW* WC1X **9** E3
Swithland Gdns *ELTH/MOT* SE9 ....**161** F4
Sybil Phoenix Cl *DEPT* SE8..................**121** D1
Sybourn St *WALTH* E17 ....**61** F2
Sycamore Av *BFN/LL* DA15 ....**145** F4
   BOW E3 ....**79** F5
Sycamore Cl *ACT* W3 ....**99** E2
   CAN/RD E16..**93** E2
Sycamore Gdns *SHB* W12 ....**100** B3
Sycamore Gv *CAT* SE6 ....**140** C4
   CDALE/KGS NW9 ....**50** C2
Sycamore Ms *CLAP* SW4 ....**134** C1
Sycamore St *FSBYE* EC1V **23** E1
Sycamore Wk *NKENS* W10 ....**89** E3
Sydcote *DUL* * SE21 ....**154** C2
Sydenham Av *SYD* SE26 ....**156** B5
Sydenham Cottages
   LEE/GVPK * SE12 ....**160** C2
Sydenham Hl *SYD* SE26 ....**156** A3
Sydenham Pk *SYD* SE26 ....**156** C3
Sydenham Park Rd *SYD* SE26 ....**156** C3
Sydenham Ri *FSTH* SE23.......................**156** B2
Sydenham Rd *SYD* SE26 ....**156** C3
Sydenham Station Ap *SYD* SE26........**156** C4
Sydmons Ct *FSTH* * SE23 ....**138** C5
Sydner Rd *STNW/STAM* N16 ....**77** F1
Sydney Cl *SKENS* SW7 ....**40** B5
Sydney Ms *SKENS* SW7 ....**40** B5
Sydney Pl *SKENS* SW7 ....**40** B5
Sydney Rd *SCUP* DA14 ....**163** E4
   WAN E11 ....**64** B1
Sydney St *CHEL* SW3 ....**115** E1
Sylvan Gv *CRICK* NW2 ....**71** D1
   PECK SE15 ....**120** B3
Sylvan Rd *FSTGT* E7 ....**82** A3
   IL IG1...**66** C4
Sylvan Ter *PECK* * SE15 ....**120** B3
Sylvester Pth *HACK* * E8..........................**78** B3
Sylvester Rd *HACK* * E8 ....**78** B3
   WALTH * E17 ....**61** F2
Sylvia Gdns *WBLY* HA9 ....**68** B4
Symes Ms *CAMTN* NW1...........................**7** E1
Symington Ms *HOM* * E9 ....**79** D2
Symister Ms *IS* * N1................................**12** C4
Symons St *CHEL* SW3 ....**41** F5
Symphony Ms *NKENS* * W10 ....**89** E2

T

Tabard Garden Est *STHWK* SE1 ....**36** A5
Tabard St *STHWK* SE1 ....**48** A2
Tabernacle Av *PLSTW* E13 ....**94** A3
Tabernacle St *SDTCH* EC2A **24** C1
Tableer Av *CLAP* SW4 ....**134** C3
Tabley Rd *HOLWY* N7 ....**75** E1
Tabor Rd *HMSMTH* W6 ....**100** B4
Tachbrook St *PIM* SW1V **43** F5

Tack Ms *BROCKY* SE4 ....140 A1
Tadema Rd *WBPTN* SW10 ....114 C3
Tadmor St *SHB* W12 ....101 D2
Tadworth Rd *CRICK* NW2 ....52 A4
Taeping St *POP/IOD* E14 ....104 B5
Talacre Rd *KTTN* NW5 ....74 A3
Talbot Ct *BANK* EC3V 36 B1
Talbot Pl *BKHTH/KID* SE3 ....123 E5
Talbot Rd *BAY/PAD* W2 ....14 B4
   EDUL SE22 ....137 E2
   EHAM E6 ....95 F1
   FSTGT E7 ....82 A1
   HGT N6 ....56 A1
   NTGHL W11 ....89 F5
Talbot Sq *BAY/PAD* W2 ....16 A5
Talbot Wk *NTGHL* W11 ....89 E5
   WLSDN * NW10 ....69 E3
Talbot Yd *STHWK* SE1 ....36 A4
Talcott Pth *BRXS/STRHM* * SW2 ...154 A1
Talfourd Pl *PECK* SE15 ....119 E4
Talfourd Rd *PECK* SE15 ....119 F4
Talgarth Rd *HMSMTH* W6 ....113 D1
Talisman Sq *SYD* SE26 ....156 A4
Tallack Rd *LEY* E10 ....61 F3
Tallis Cl *CAN/RD* E16 ....94 B5
Tallis Gv *CHARL* SE7 ....124 B2
Tallis St *EMB* EC4Y 34 B1
Tallis Vw *WLSDN* NW10 ....69 D3
Talmage Cl *FSTH* SE23 ....138 C5
Talma Rd *BRXS/STRHM* SW2 ....136 A3
Talwin St *BOW* E3 ....92 B2
Tamar Cl *BOW* * E3 ....79 F5
Tamarind Yd *WAP* E1W 102 A3
Tamarisk Sq *SHB* W12 ....99 F1
Tamar St *CHARL* SE7 ....107 E5
Tamworth St *FUL/PGN* SW6 ....114 A2
Tancred Rd *FSBYPK* N4 ....58 B1
Tanfield Av *CRICK* NW2 ....69 F1
Tangier Rd *RCHPK/HAM* TW10 ......128 B1
Tangley Gv *PUT/ROE* SW15 ....129 F5
Tanhouse Fld *KTTN* * NW5 ....75 D2
Tankerton Houses *STPAN* * WC1H ...9 D4
Tankerton St *STPAN* WC1H 9 D4
Tankridge Rd *CRICK* NW2 ....52 B4
The Tanneries *WCHPL* * E1 ....90 C3
Tanner's Hl *DEPT* SE8 ....122 A4
Tanner St *BARK* IG11 ....84 C3
   STHWK SE1 ....49 D1
Tannington Ter *FSBYPK* * N4 ....58 A5
Tannsfeld Rd *SYD* SE26 ....157 D5
Tansley Cl *HOLWY* * N7 ....75 D2
Tanswell St *STHWK* * SE1 ....46 A1
Tansy Cl *EHAM* E6 ....96 A5
Tantallon Rd *BAL* SW12 ....152 A1
Tant Av *CAN/RD* E16 ....93 F5
Tanza Rd *HAMP* NW3 ....73 F1
Taplow St *IS* N1 ....11 F2
Tappesfield Rd *PECK* SE15 ....138 C1
Tapp St *BETH* * E2 ....90 B3
Taransay Wk *IS* N1 ....77 D3
Tara Ter *BROCKY* * SE4 ....139 E1
Tarbert Rd *EDUL* SE22 ....137 E3
Tarbert Wk *WCHPL* E1 ....102 C1
Tarleton Gdns *FSTH* SE23 ....156 B1
Tarling Rd *CAN/RD* E16 ....93 F5
Tarling St *WCHPL* E1 ....90 B5
Tarn St *STHWK* SE1 ....47 E3
Tarnwood Pk *ELTH/MOT* SE9 ....161 F1
Tarragon Cl *NWCR* * SE14 ....121 E3
Tarrant Pl *MBLAR* W1H 17 E3
Tarriff Crs *DEPT* SE8 ....103 F5
Tarrington Cl
   STRHM/NOR * SW16 ....153 D4

Tarver Rd *WALW* SE17 ....118 B1
Tarves Wy *GNWCH* SE10 ....122 B3
Tasker Rd *HAMP* NW3 ....73 F2
Tasman Rd *BRXN/ST* SW9 ....135 E1
Tasso Rd *HMSMTH* W6 ....113 E2
Tate Rd *CAN/RD* E16 ....107 F2
Tatnell Rd *FSTH* SE23 ....139 E4
Tattersall Cl *ELTH/MOT* SE9 ....143 E3
Tatton Crs *CLPT* E5 ....59 F2
Tatum Rd *WLSDN* NW10 ....68 C4
Tatum St *WALW* SE17 ....48 B5
Tauheed Cl *FSBYPK* N4 ....58 C4
Taunton Ms *CAMTN* NW1 ....17 E1
Taunton Pl *CAMTN* NW1 ....5 E5
Taunton Rd *LEW* SE13 ....141 E3
Taverners Cl *NTGHL* * W11 ....101 E2
Taverner Sq *HBRY* * N5 ....76 C1
Tavistock Cl *STNW/STAM* * N16 ....77 E2
Tavistock Ct *COVGDN* * WC2E 33 D1
Tavistock Crs *NTGHL* W11 ....89 F4
Tavistock Gdns *GDMY/SEVK* IG3 ....85 E1
Tavistock Ms *NTGHL* * W11 ....89 F5
Tavistock Pl *STPAN* WC1H 8 B5
Tavistock Rd *FSBYPK* N4 ....59 D1
   NTGHL W11 ....89 F4
   SRTFD E15 ....81 F3
   WLSDN NW10 ....87 F1
Tavistock Sq *STPAN* WC1H 8 B5
Tavistock St *COVGDN* WC2E 33 D1
Tavistock Ter *ARCH* N19 ....57 D5
Taviton St *STPAN* WC1H 8 A5
Tavy Cl *LBTH* SE11 ....118 A1
Tawny Wy *BERM/RHTH* SE16 ....103 D5
Taybridge Rd *BTSEA* SW11 ....134 A1
Tayburn Cl *POP/IOD* E14 ....92 C5
Taylor Av *RCH/KEW* TW9 ....110 B5
Taylor's Buildings
   WOOL/PLUM SE18 ....108 B5
Taylors Cl *SCUP* DA14 ....163 F4
Taylor's Gn *ACT* * W3 ....87 E5
Taylor's La *SYD* SE26 ....156 B4
   WLSDN NW10 ....69 E3
Taymount Ri *FSTH* SE23 ....156 C2
Tayport Cl *IS* N1 ....75 F4
Teak Cl *BERM/RHTH* SE16 ....103 E2
Teal Cl *CAN/RD* E16 ....95 D4
Teale St *BETH* E2 ....90 A1
Teasel Wy *SRTFD* E15 ....93 E2
Tedworth Gdns *CHEL* SW3 ....115 F1
Tedworth Sq *CHEL* * SW3 ....115 F1
Teesdale Cl *BETH* E2 ....90 A1
Teesdale Rd *WAN* E11 ....63 F1
Teesdale St *BETH* E2 ....90 B1
Teesdale Yd *BETH* * E2 ....90 B1
The Tee *ACT* W3 ....87 E5
Teignmouth Cl *CLAP* SW4 ....135 D2
Teignmouth Rd *CRICK* NW2 ....71 D2
Telegraph Hl *HAMP* NW3 ....54 B5
Telegraph Pl *POP/IOD* E14 ....104 B5
Telegraph Rd *PUT/ROE* SW15 ....130 B5
Telegraph St *LOTH* EC2R 24 A4
Telephone Pl *FUL/PGN* * SW6 ....113 F1
Telferscot Rd *BAL* SW12 ....153 D1
Telford Av *BAL* SW12 ....153 D1
Telford Cl *WALTH* E17 ....61 E2
Telford Rd *CDALE/KGS* NW9 ....51 F1
   CHST BR7 ....163 D2
   NKENS W10 ....89 E4
Telfords Yd *WAP* * E1W....................102 A3
Telford Ter *PIM* * SW1V...................116 C2
Telford Wy *ACT* W3 ....87 E4
Telham Rd *EHAM* E6 ....96 A1
Tell Gv *EDUL* SE22 ....137 F2

Tellson Av *WOOL/PLUM* SE18...........**125** E4
Temeraire St *BERM/RHTH* SE16 ......**102** C3
Tempelhof Av *HDN* NW4 ....**52** C2
Temperley Rd *BAL* SW12 ....**134** A5
Templars Av *GLDGN* NW11 ....**53** F1
Templar St *CMBW* SE5 ....**118** B5
Temple Av *EMB* EC4Y **34** B1
Temple Cl *WAN* E11 ....**63** E2
   WOOL/PLUM SE18 ....**108** C4
Templecombe Rd *HOM* E9 ....**78** C5
Temple Dwellings *BETH* * E2 ....**90** B1
Temple Fortune La *GLDGN* NW11 ....**53** F1
Temple Gdns *EMB* * EC4Y **34** A1
   GLDGN NW11 ....**53** F1
Temple Gv *GLDGN* NW11 ....**54** A1
Temple La *EMB* EC4Y **22** B5
Templemead Cl *ACT* W3 ....**87** E5
Temple Mills La *LEY* E10 ....**80** B1
Temple Pl *TPL/STR* WC2R **33** F1
Temple Rd *CHSWK* W4 ....**98** C4
   CRICK NW2 ....**70** C1
   EHAM E6 ....**83** E5
Temple Sheen Rd
   MORT/ESHN SW14 ....**128** C2
Temple St *BETH* E2 ....**90** B1
Templeton Cl *STNW/STAM* * N16....**77** E2
Templeton Pl *ECT* SW5 ....**38** D5
Templeton Rd *SEVS/STOTM* N15 ....**59** C1
Templewood Av *HAMP* NW3 ....**54** B5
Templewood Gdns *HAMP* NW3........**54** B5
Temple Yd *BETH* E2 ....**90** A2
Tenbury Cl *FSTGT* E7 ....**83** D2
Tenbury Ct *BAL* SW12 ....**153** D1
Tench St *WAP* * E1W **102** B2
Tenda Rd *BERM/RHTH* SE16 ....**102** B5
Tenham Av *BRXS/STRHM* SW2.......**153** D2
Tenniel Cl *BAY/PAD* W2 ....**15** E5
Tennis St *STHWK* SE1 ....**36** A5
Tennyson Av *MNPK* E12 ....**83** E4
   WAN E11 ....**64** A2
Tennyson Cl *WELL* DA16 ....**127** E4
Tennyson Rd *KIL/WHAMP* NW6 ....**71** F5
   SRTFD E15 ....**81** E4
   WALTH E17 ....**61** F1
Tennyson St *VX/NE* SW8 ....**116** B5
Tenterden Cl *ELTH/MOT* SE9 ....**161** F4
Tenterden St *CONDST* W1S **19** D5
Tenter Gnd *WCHPL* * E1 ....**25** E3
Tent St *WCHPL* E1 ....**90** B3
Terling Cl *WAN* E11 ....**63** E2
Terling Wk *IS* * N1 ....**76** C5
Terminus Pl *PIM* SW1V **43** D3
Terrace Gdns *BARN* SW13 ....**111** F5
Terrace Rd *HOM* E9 ....**79** D4
   PLSTW E13 ....**82** A5
The Terrace *BARN* SW13 ....**111** E5
   BETH * E2 ....**90** C2
   DEPT * SE8...................................**105** F5
   FSTH * SE23 ....**139** E5
   KIL/WHAMP NW6 ....**72** A5
Terrace Vls *HMSMTH* * W6 ....**112** A1
Terrapin Rd *TOOT* SW17 ....**152** B3
Terretts Pl *IS* N1 ....**76** B4
Terrick St *SHB* W12 ....**88** B5
Testerton Wk *NTGHL* * W11 ....**101** D1
Tetcott Rd *WBPTN* SW10 ....**114** C3
Teversham La *VX/NE* SW8 ....**117** D1
Teviot St *POP/IOD* E14 ....**92** C4
Tewkesbury Av *FSTH* SE23 ....**156** B1
Tewkesbury Rd *FSBYPK* N15 ....**59** D2
Tewson Rd *WOOL/PLUM* SE18.......**127** F5
Thackeray Ms *HACK* * E8 ....**78** A3
Thackeray Rd *EHAM* E6 ....**95** D4

   VX/NE SW8 ....**116** B5
Thackeray St *KENS* W8 ....**39** D2
Thakeham Cl *SYD* SE26 ....**156** B5
Thalia Cl *GNWCH* SE10 ....**123** D2
Thame Rd *BERM/RHTH* SE16 ....**103** D3
Thames Av *WBPTN* * SW10 ....**114** C4
Thames Bank *MORT/ESHN* SW14 ...**110** C5
Thames Cir *POP/IOD* E14 ....**104** A5
Thames Pth *BERM/RHTH* SE16 ....**103** F4
   BOW E3 ....**92** C1
   CHSWK W4 ....**111** F4
   CLPT E5 ....**61** D5
   GNWCH SE10 ....**106** A4
   LBTH SE11 ....**117** E1
   WEST SW1P **45** D4
Thames Pl *PUT/ROE* SW15 ....**131** D1
Thames Quay *WBPTN* * SW10 ....**114** C4
Thames Rd *CAN/RD* E16 ....**107** D3
   CHSWK W4 ....**110** B2
Thames St *GNWCH* SE10 ....**122** B2
Thames Village *CHSWK* W4 ....**110** C4
Thanet St *STPAN* WC1H **8** C4
Thane Vls *HOLWY* N7 ....**57** F5
Thant Cl *LEY* E10 ....**80** B1
Thaxted Rd *ELTH/MOT* SE9 ....**162** C2
Thaxton Rd *WKENS* W14 ....**113** F2
Thayer St *MHST* W1U **18** B3
Theatre St *BTSEA* SW11 ....**133** F1
Theberton St *IS* N1 ....**76** A5
Theed St *STHWK* SE1 ....**34** A4
Theobald Rd *WALTH* E17 ....**61** F2
Theobald's Rd *FSBYW* WC1X **21** E2
Theobald St *STHWK* SE1 ....**48** A3
Theodore Rd *LEW* SE13 ....**141** D4
Therapia Rd *EDUL* SE22 ....**138** C2
Theresa Rd *HMSMTH* W6 ....**100** A5
Thermopylae Ga *POP/IOD* E14 ....**104** B5
Theseus Wk *IS* N1 ....**11** D2
Thessaly Rd *VX/NE* SW8 ....**117** D1
Theydon Rd *CLPT* E5 ....**60** C4
Theydon St *WALTH* E17 ....**61** F2
Third Av *ACT* W3 ....**99** F2
   MNPK E12 ....**83** E1
   NKENS W10 ....**89** E2
   PLSTW E13 ....**94** A2
Third Wy *WBLY* HA9 ....**68** B1
Thirleby Rd *WEST* SW1P **43** F3
Thirlmere Rd *STRHM/NOR* SW16...**153** D3
Thirsk Rd *BTSEA* SW11 ....**134** A1
Thistle Gv *WBPTN* * SW10 ....**114** C1
Thistlewaite Rd *CLPT* E5 ....**60** B5
Thistlewood Cl *HOLWY* N7 ....**57** F1
Thomas Baines Rd *BTSEA* SW11 ....**133** D1
Thomas Cribb Ms *EHAM* E6 ....**95** F4
Thomas Dean Rd *SYD* * SE26 ....**157** F4
Thomas Dinwiddy Rd
   LEE/GVPK SE12 ....**160** B2
Thomas Doyle St *STHWK* SE1 ....**46** C2
Thomas' La *CAT* SE6 ....**140** B5
Thomas More St *WAP* * E1W **102** A1
Thomas North Ter *CAN/RD* * E16 ....**93** F4
Thomas Pl *KENS* W8 ....**38** C3
Thomas Rd *POP/IOD* E14 ....**91** F5
Thomas St *WOOL/PLUM* SE18 ....**108** A5
Thompson Av *RCH/KEW* TW9 ....**128** C4
Thompson Cl *IL* IG1 ....**66** C4
Thompson Rd *EDUL* SE22 ....**137** F4
Thompson's Av *CMBW* * SE5 ....**118** C3
   CMBW SE5....................................**118** C3
Thorburn Sq *STHWK* SE1 ....**102** A5
Thoresby St *IS* N1 ....**11** F3
Thornbury Cl *STNW/STAM* N16 ....**77** E2
Thornbury Rd *CLAP* SW4 ....**135** E4

Thornby Rd *CLPT* E5 ....60 C5
Thorncliffe Rd *CLAP* SW4 ....135 D4
Thorncombe Rd *EDUL* SE22 ....137 E3
Thorncroft St *VX/NE* SW8 ....117 E3
Thorndean St *WAND/EARL* SW18 ....150 C2
Thorndike Cl *WBPTN* SW10 ....114 C3
Thorndike St *PIM* * SW1V 44 A5
  WAN * E11 ....81 E1
Thorne Cl *CAN/RD* E16 ....94 A5
Thorne Rd *VX/NE* SW8 ....117 E3
Thorne St *BARN* SW13 ....129 E1
Thorney Crs *BTSEA* * SW11 ....115 D3
Thorney Hedge Rd *CHSWK* W4 ....98 B5
Thorney St *WEST* SW1P 44 C4
Thornfield Rd *SHB* W12 ....100 B3
Thornford Rd *LEW* SE13 ....140 C3
Thorngate Rd *MV/WKIL* W9 ....2 B3
Thorngrove Rd *PLSTW* E13 ....82 B5
Thornham Gv *SRTFD* E15 ....81 D2
Thornham St *GNWCH* SE10 ....122 B3
Thornhaugh St *STPAN* WC1H 20 B1
Thornhill Av *WOOL/PLUM* SE18 ....127 E3
Thornhill Bridge Whf *IS* * N1 ....75 F5
Thornhill Crs *IS* N1 ....75 F4
Thornhill Gdns *BARK* IG11 ....85 E4
  LEY E10 ....62 B4
Thornhill Gv *IS* N1 ....75 F4
Thornhill Rd *IS* N1 ....76 A4
  LEY E10 ....62 B4
Thornhill Sq *IS* N1 ....75 F5
Thornlaw Rd *WNWD* SE27 ....154 A4
Thornsbeach Rd *CAT* SE6 ....158 C1
Thornsett Rd *WAND/EARL* SW18 ....150 B4
Thornton Av *BAL* SW12 ....153 D1
  CHSWK W4 ....99 E5
Thornton Gdns *BAL* SW12 ....153 D1
Thornton Pl *MBLAR* W1H 17 E2
Thornton Rd *BAL* SW12 ....135 D5
  BMLY BR1 ....160 A5
  IL IG1 ....84 B1
  MORT/ESHN SW14 ....129 D1
  WAN E11 ....63 D4
Thornton St *BRXN/ST* SW9 ....118 A5
Thorntree Rd *CHARL* SE7 ....125 D1
Thornville St *DEPT* SE8 ....122 A4
Thornwood Rd *LEW* SE13 ....141 E3
Thorogood Gdns *SRTFD* E15 ....81 E2
Thorold Rd *IL* IG1 ....66 B4
Thorparch Rd *VX/NE* SW8 ....117 D4
Thorpebank Rd *SHB* W12 ....100 A2
Thorpe Cl *NKENS* W10 ....89 E5
  SYD * SE26 ....157 D4
Thorpedale Rd *FSBYPK* N4 ....57 E3
Thorpe Rd *BARK* IG11 ....85 D4
  EHAM E6 ....83 F5
  FSTGT E7 ....64 A5
  SEVS/STOTM N15 ....59 E1
Thorpewood Av *FSTH* SE23 ....156 B2
Thorsden Wy *NRWD* * SE19 ....155 E5
Thorverton Rd *CRICK* NW2 ....53 E5
Thoydon Rd *BOW* E3 ....91 E1
Thrale Rd *STRHM/NOR* SW16 ....152 C5
Thrale St *STHWK* SE1 ....35 F4
Thrasher Cl *HACK* * E8 ....77 F5
Thrawl St *WCHPL* E1 ....25 F3
Threadneedle St *LOTH* EC2R 24 B5
Three Colts La *BETH* E2 ....90 B3
Three Colt St *POP/IOD* * E14 ....103 F5
Three Kings Yd *MYFR/PKLN* W1K 30 C1
Three Mill La *BOW* E3 ....92 C2
Three Oak La *STHWK* SE1 ....37 E5
Threshers Pl *NTGHL* W11 ....101 E1
Thriffwood *FSTH* SE23 ....156 B5

Throckmorten Rd *CAN/RD* E16 ....94 B5
Throgmorton Av *OBST* EC2N 24 B4
Throgmorton St *LOTH* EC2R 24 A5
Thrush St *WALW* SE17 ....118 C5
Thurbarn Rd *CAT* SE6 ....158 B5
Thurland Rd *BERM/RHTH* SE16 ....102 A4
Thurlby Rd *WNWD* SE27 ....154 A4
Thurleigh Av *BAL* SW12 ....134 A4
Thurleigh Rd *BAL* SW12 ....133 F4
Thurlestone Av *GDMY/SEVK* IG3 ......85 F1
Thurlestone Rd *WNWD* SE27 ....154 A3
Thurloe Cl *SKENS* SW7 ....40 C4
Thurloe Pl *SKENS* SW7 ....40 B4
Thurloe Place Ms *SKENS* * SW7 ....40 B4
Thurloe Sq *SKENS* SW7 ....40 C4
Thurloe St *SKENS* SW7 ....40 B4
Thurlow Hl *DUL* SE21 ....154 C1
Thurlow Park Rd *DUL* SE21 ....154 B2
Thurlow Rd *HAMP* NW3 ....73 D2
Thurlow St *WALW* SE17 ....119 E1
Thurlow Ter *KTTN* NW5 ....73 F2
Thurlow Wk *WALW* SE17 ....119 E1
Thursley Gdns *WIM/MER* SW19 ....149 D2
Thursley Rd *ELTH/MOT* SE9 ....161 F3
Thurso St *TOOT* SW17 ....151 D4
Thurston Rd *DEPT* SE8 ....122 B5
Thurtle Rd *BETH* E2 ....13 F1
Tibbatt's Rd *BOW* E3 ....92 B3
Tibbenham Pl *CAT* * SE6 ....158 B1
Tibberton Sq *IS* * N1 ....76 C4
Tibbets Cl *WIM/MER* SW19 ....149 D1
Tibbet's Ride *PUT/ROE* SW15 ....131 D5
Tiber Gdns *IS* N1 ....75 E5
Ticehurst Rd *FSTH* SE23 ....157 E2
Tidal Basin Rd *CAN/RD* E16 ....105 F1
Tideswell Rd *PUT/ROE* SW15 ....130 C2
Tideway Wk *VX/NE* * SW8 ....116 C2
Tidey St *BOW* E3 ....92 A4
Tidford Rd *WELL* DA16 ....127 F5
Tidworth Rd *BOW* E3 ....92 A3
Tierney Rd *BRXS/STRHM* SW2 ....153 E1
Tierney Ter *BRXS/STRHM* * SW2 .....153 E1
Tiger Wy *CLPT* E5 ....78 B1
Tilbrook Rd *BKHTH/KID* SE3 ....142 C1
Tilbury Cl *PECK* SE15 ....119 F3
Tilbury Rd *EHAM* E6 ....95 F1
  LEY E10 ....62 C2
Tildesley Rd *PUT/ROE* SW15 ....130 C4
Tilehurst Rd *WAND/EARL* SW18 ......151 F1
Tile Kiln La *HGT* N6 ....56 B3
Tileyard Rd *HOLWY* N7 ....75 E4
Tilford Gdns *WIM/MER* SW19 ....149 D1
Tilia Rd *CLPT* E5 ....78 B1
Tiller Rd *POP/IOD* E14 ....104 A4
Tillett Cl *WLSDN* NW10 ....68 C3
Tillet Wy *BETH* E2 ....90 A2
Tilling Rd *CRICK* NW2 ....52 B3
Tillman St *WCHPL* E1 ....90 B5
Tilloch St *IS* * N1 ....75 F4
Tillotson Rd *IL* IG1 ....66 A2
Tilney Gdns *IS* N1 ....77 D3
Tilney St *MYFR/PKLN* W1K 30 B3
Tilson Cl *CMBW* * SE5 ....119 E3
Tilson Gdns *CLAP* SW4 ....135 E5
Tilston Cl *WAN* E11 ....63 F5
Tilton St *FUL/PGN* SW6 ....113 E2
The Tiltwood *ACT* W3 ....98 C1
Tilt Yard Ap *ELTH/MOT* SE9 ....143 F4
Timbercroft La
  WOOL/PLUM SE18 ....127 E2
Timberland Cl *PECK* * SE15 ....120 A3
Timberland Rd *WCHPL* * E1 ....90 B5
Timber Mill Wy *CLAP* SW4 ....135 D1

Timber Pond Rd
  BERM/RHTH SE16.........................**103** D3
Timber St *FSBYE* * EC1V **11** E5
Timberwharf Rd
  SEVS/STOTM N15.........................**60** A1
Time Sq *HACK* * E8 ....**77** F2
Timothy Rd *POP/IOD* E14 ....**91** F4
Tindal St *BRXN/ST* SW9 ....**118** B4
Tinniswood Cl *HOLWY* * N7 ....**76** A2
Tinsley Rd *WCHPL* E1 ....**90** C4
Tintagel Crs *EDUL* SE22 ....**137** F2
Tintern Cl *PUT/ROE* SW15 ....**131** E3
Tintern St *CLAP* SW4 ....**135** E2
Tinto Rd *CAN/RD* E16 ....**94** A4
Tinworth St *LBTH* SE11 ....**117** E1
Tipthorpe Rd *BTSEA* SW11 ....**134** A1
Tisdall Pl *WALW* SE17 ....**48** B5
Titchborne Rw *BAY/PAD* W2 ....**17** D5
Titchfield Rd *STJWD* NW8 ....**73** E5
Titchwell Rd *WAND/EARL* SW18 ....**133** E1
Tite St *CHEL* SW3 ....**115** F2
Titmuss St *SHB* * W12 ....**100** B3
Tiverton Dr *ELTH/MOT* SE9 ....**162** C1
Tiverton Rd *SEVS/STOTM* N15 ....**59** D1
  WLSDN NW10 ....**71** D5
Tiverton St *STHWK* SE1 ....**47** E2
Tivoli Gdns *CHARL* SE7 ....**107** E5
Tivoli Rd *WNWD* SE27 ....**154** C5
Tobago St *POP/IOD* * E14 ....**104** A3
Tobin Cl *HAMP* NW3 ....**73** E4
Tokenhouse Yd *LOTH* EC2R **24** A4
Tokyngton Av *WBLY* HA9 ....**68** A3
Toland Sq *PUT/ROE* SW15 ....**130** A3
Tollbridge Cl *NKENS* W10 ....**89** E3
Tollet St *WCHPL* E1 ....**91** D3
Tollgate Dr *DUL* SE21 ....**155** E2
Tollgate Gdns *KIL/WHAMP* NW6 ....**2** C1
Tollgate Rd *EHAM* E6 ....**95** E4
Tollhouse Wy *ARCH* N19 ....**56** C4
Tollington Pk *HOLWY* N7 ....**57** F4
Tollington Pl *FSBYPK* N4 ....**57** F4
Tollington Rd *HOLWY* N7 ....**75** F1
Tollington Wy *HOLWY* N7 ....**57** E5
Tolmer's Sq *CAMTN* NW1 ....**7** F5
Tolpuddle Av *PLSTW* E13 ....**82** C5
Tolpuddle St *IS* N1 ....**10** A1
Tolsford Rd *CLPT* E5 ....**78** B2
Tom Cribb Rd *WOOL/PLUM* SE18 ......**108** C4
Tom Jenkinson Rd *CAN/RD* E16 ....**106** A2
Tomlin's Gv *BOW* E3 ....**92** A2
Tomlinson Cl *BETH* E2 ....**13** F4
  CHSWK W4.....................................**110** B1
Tomlins Orch *BARK* IG11 ....**84** C5
Tomlin's Ter *POP/IOD* E14 ....**91** E5
Tom Mann Cl *BARK* IG11 ....**85** E5
Tom Nolan Cl *SRTFD* E15 ....**93** E1
Tompion St *FSBYE* EC1V **10** C4
Tom Smith Cl *GNWCH* SE10 ....**123** E2
Tonbridge St *STPAN* WC1H **8** C1
Tonsley Hl *WAND/EARL* SW18 ....**132** B3
Tonsley Pl *WAND/EARL* SW18.............**132** B3
Tonsley Rd *WAND/EARL* SW18 ....**132** B3
Tonsley St *WAND/EARL* SW18 ....**132** B3
Took's Ct *FLST/FETLN* EC4A **22** A4
Tooley St *STHWK* SE1 ....**36** B3
Tooting Bec Gdns
  STRHM/NOR SW16.......................**153** D4
Tooting Bec Rd *TOOT* SW17 ....**152** A3
Tooting Gv *TOOT* SW17 ....**151** E5
Tooting High St *TOOT* SW17 ....**151** E4
Tooting Market *TOOT* * SW17 ....**151** F5
Topham St *CLKNW* * EC1R **10** A5
Topley St *ELTH/MOT* SE9 ....**142** C1

Topmast Point *POP/IOD* * E14 ....**104** A3
Topsham Rd *TOOT* SW17 ....**151** F3
Torbay Rd *KIL/WHAMP* NW6 ....**71** F4
Torbay St *CAMTN* * NW1 ....**74** B4
Torcross Dr *FSTH* SE23 ....**156** C2
Tor Gdns *KENS* W8 ....**26** A5
Tormount Rd *WOOL/PLUM* SE18 ....**127** E2
Toronto Av *MNPK* E12 ....**83** F1
Toronto Rd *IL* IG1 ....**66** B3
Torquay St *BAY/PAD* W2 ....**14** C3
Torrens Rd *BRXS/STRHM* SW2 ....**135** F3
Torrens Sq *SRTFD* E15.........................**81** F3
Torrens St *FSBYE* EC1V **10** C2
Torriano Av *KTTN* NW5 ....**75** D2
Torriano Ms *KTTN* NW5 ....**74** C2
Torridge Gdns *PECK* SE15 ....**138** C2
Torridon Rd *CAT* SE6 ....**159** D1
  LEW SE13.....................................**141** D5
Torrington Pl *FITZ* W1T **19** F2
  WAP E1W **102** A2
Torrington Sq *GWRST* WC1E **20** B1
Torwood Rd *PUT/ROE* SW15 ....**130** A3
Tothill St *STJSPK* SW1H **44** A1
Tottan Ter *WCHPL* * E1 ....**91** D5
Tottenham Court Rd *FITZ* W1T **19** F1
Tottenham La *CEND/HSY/T* N8 ....**57** E1
Tottenham Ms *FITZ* * W1T **19** F2
Tottenham Rd *IS* N1 ....**77** E3
Tottenham St *GTPST* W1W **19** F3
Totterdown St *TOOT* SW17 ....**151** F4
Toulmin St *STHWK* SE1 ....**47** E1
Toulon St *CMBW* SE5 ....**118** C3
Tournay Rd *FUL/PGN* SW6 ....**113** F3
Toussaint Wk *BERM/RHTH* SE16 ....**102** A4
Towcester Rd *BOW* E3 ....**92** B3
Tower Br *TWRH* EC3N **37** E3
Tower Bridge Ap *TWRH* EC3N **37** E3
Tower Bridge Rd *STHWK* SE1 ....**48** C4
Tower Buildings *WAP* * E1W **102** B2
Tower Cl *HAMP* NW3 ....**73** D2
Tower Ct *LSQ/SEVD* * WC2H **20** C5
Tower Hamlets Rd *FSTGT* E7 ....**81** F2
Tower Hl *TWRH* EC3N **37** D2
Tower Hill Ter *MON* EC3R **37** D2
Tower Ms *CLPT* * E5 ....**79** E2
Tower Mill Rd *PECK* * SE15 ....**119** E3
Tower Pl *MON* EC3R **37** D2
Tower Rd *WLSDN* NW10 ....**70** A4
Tower Royal *MANHO* * EC4N **35** F1
Tower St *LSQ/SEVD* * WC2H **20** B5
Towncourt Pth *FSBYPK* N4 ....**58** C3
Townhall Av *CHSWK* W4 ....**111** D1
Town Hall Pde *BRXS/STRHM* * SW2 ...**135** F2
Town Hall Rd *BTSEA* SW11 ....**133** F1
Townley Ct *SRTFD* E15 ....**81** F3
Townley Rd *DUL* SE21 ....**137** E3
Townley St *WALW* * SE17 ....**119** D1
Townmead Rd *FUL/PGN* SW6 ....**114** C5
  RCH/KEW TW9.............................**110** B5
Town Quay *BARK* IG11 ....**84** B5
Townsend La *CDALE/KGS* NW9 ....**51** D2
Townsend Rd *WOOL/PLUM* SE18 ....**108** B4
Townsend St *WALW* SE17 ....**48** B5
Townsend Yd *HGT* N6 ....**56** B3
Townshend Est *STJWD* NW8 ....**4** C1
Townshend Rd *CHST* BR7 ....**162** B5
  STJWD NW8 ....**73** E5
Towton Rd *WNWD* SE27 ....**154** C5
Toynbee Cl *CHST* BR7 ....**162** B4
Toynbee St *WCHPL* E1 ....**25** E3
Toyne Wy *HGT* N6 ....**55** F1
Tracey Av *CRICK* * NW2 ....**70** C2
Trader Rd *EHAM* E6 ....**96** B5

Tradescant Rd *VX/NE* SW8 ....**117** E3
Trading Estate Rd *WLSDN* * NW10 ...**86** C3
Trafalgar Av *PECK* SE15 ....**119** F4
Trafalgar Chambers *CHEL* * SW3 .....**115** D1
Trafalgar Gdns *WCHPL* E1 ....**91** D4
Trafalgar Gv *GNWCH* SE10 ....**123** D2
Trafalgar Rd *GNWCH* SE10 ....**123** E1
Trafalgar St *WALW* SE17 ....**119** D1
Trafalgar Sq *CHCR* WC2N **32** B3
Trafalgar Wy *POP/IOD* E14 ....**104** C2
Trafford Cl *SRTFD* E15 ....**80** B2
Tramway Av *SRTFD* E15 ....**81** D4
Tranley Ms *HAMP* * NW3 ....**73** E1
Tranmere Rd
  WAND/EARL SW18 ....**150** C2
Tranquil V *BKHTH/KID* SE3 ....**123** E5
Transept St *CAMTN* NW1 ....**17** D3
Transom Sq *POP/IOD* E14 ....**122** D1
Tranton Rd *BERM/RHTH* SE16 ....**102** B4
Travers Rd *HOLWY* N7 ....**58** A5
Treadgold St *NTGHL* W11 ....**101** D1
Treadway St *BETH* E2 ....**90** B1
Treaty St *IS* N1 ....**75** F5
Trebeck Rd *MYFR/PICC* W1J **30** C3
Trebovir Rd *ECT* SW5 ....**114** A1
Treby St *BOW* E3 ....**91** F3
Trecastle Wy *HOLWY* * N7 ....**75** D1
Tredegar Rd *BOW* E3 ....**91** F1
Tredegar Sq *BOW* E3 ....**91** F2
Trederwen Rd *HACK* E8 ....**78** A5
Tredwell Rd *WNWD* SE27 ....**154** B4
Treen Av *BARN* SW13 ....**129** E1
Tree Rd *CAN/RD* E16 ....**94** C5
Treewall Gdns *BMLY* BR1 ....**160** B4
Trefoil Rd *WAND/EARL* SW18 ....**132** C3
Tregaron Av *CEND/HSY/T* N8 ....**57** E2
Tregarvon Rd *BTSEA* SW11 ....**134** A2
Trego Rd *HOM* E9 ....**80** A4
Tregothnan Rd *BRXN/ST* SW9 ....**135** E1
Tregunter Rd *WBPTN* SW10 ....**114** C1
Treherne Ct *BRXN/ST* * SW9 ....**118** B4
Trehern Rd *MORT/ESHN* SW14 ....**129** D1
Trehurst St *CLPT* E5 ....**79** E2
Trelawney Est *HOM* * E9 ....**78** C3
Trelawn Rd *BRXS/STRHM* SW2 ....**136** A3
  LEY E10 ....**62** C5
Tremadoc Rd *CLAP* SW4 ....**135** D2
Tremlett Gv *ARCH* N19 ....**56** C5
Tremlett Ms *ARCH* * N19 ....**56** C5
Trenchard St *GNWCH* SE10 ....**123** D1
Trenchold St *VX/NE* * SW8 ....**117** E2
Trenmar Gdns *WLSDN* NW10 ....**88** B2
Trentham St *WAND/EARL* SW18 ....**150** A1
Trent Rd *BRXS/STRHM* SW2 ....**135** F3
Treport St *WAND/EARL* SW18 ....**132** B5
Tresco Gdns *GDMY/SEVK* IG3 ....**67** F4
Tresco Rd *PECK* SE15 ....**138** B3
Tresham Crs *STJWD* NW8 ....**4** C4
Tresham Rd *BARK* IG11 ....**85** F4
Tressell Cl *IS* N1 ....**76** B4
Tressillian Crs *BROCKY* SE4 ....**140** A1
Tressillian Rd *BROCKY* SE4 ....**140** A1
Trevanion Rd *WKENS* * W14 ....**113** E1
Trevelyan Av *MNPK* E12 ....**83** F1
Trevelyan Gdns *WLSDN* * NW10 ....**70** C5
Trevelyan Rd *FSTGT* E7 ....**81** E3
Treveris St *STHWK* SE1 ....**35** D4
Treverton St *NKENS* W10 ....**89** D3
Treville St *PUT/ROE* SW15 ....**130** B5
Treviso Rd *FSTH* SE23 ....**157** D2
Trevithick St *DEPT* SE8 ....**122** A2
Trevor Pl *SKENS* SW7 ....**41** D1

Trevor Sq *SKENS* SW7 ....**41** D1
Trevor St *SKENS* SW7 ....**41** D1
Trewint St *WAND/EARL* SW18 ....**150** C2
Trewsbury Rd *SYD* SE26 ....**157** D5
Triangle Est *LBTH* * SE11 ....**117** F1
Triangle Pl *CLAP* SW4 ....**135** D2
Triangle Rd *HACK* E8 ....**78** B5
Trident Pl *CHEL* * SW3 ....**115** D2
Trident St *BERM/RHTH* SE16 ....**103** D5
Trig La *BLKFR* EC4V **35** E1
Trigon Rd *VX/NE* SW8 ....**117** F3
Trilby Rd *FSTH* SE23 ....**157** D2
Trim St *NWCR* SE14 ....**121** F2
Trinder Rd *ARCH* N19 ....**57** E3
Tring Av *WBLY* HA9 ....**68** A3
Trinidad St *POP/IOD* E14 ....**103** F1
Trinity Buoy Whf *POP/IOD* * E14 ....**93** D4
Trinity Church Rd *BARN* SW13 ....**112** B2
Trinity Church Sq *STHWK* SE1 ....**47** F2
Trinity Cl *CLAP* * SW4 ....**134** C2
  HACK * E8 ....**77** F3
  LEW SE13 ....**141** D2
  WAN E11 ....**63** E4
Trinity Ct *ELTH/MOT* SE9 ....**144** B4
Trinity Crs *TOOT* SW17 ....**151** F2
Trinity Gdns *BRXN/ST* SW9 ....**135** F2
  CAN/RD E16 ....**93** F4
Trinity Gn *WCHPL* * E1 ....**90** C4
Trinity Gv *GNWCH* SE10 ....**122** C4
Trinity Ri *HNHL* SE24 ....**136** B5
Trinity Rd *TOOT* SW17 ....**151** F2
  WAND/EARL SW18 ....**133** D4
Trinity Sq *TWRH* EC3N **37** D2
Trinity St *CAN/RD* E16 ....**93** F4
  STHWK SE1 ....**47** F1
Trinity Wy *ACT* W3 ....**99** E1
Trio Pl *STHWK* SE1 ....**47** F1
Tristan Sq *BKHTH/KID* SE3 ....**141** E1
Tristram Rd *BMLY* BR1 ....**159** F4
Triton Sq *CAMTN* NW1 ....**7** E5
Tritton Rd *WNWD* SE27 ....**155** D3
Triumph Rd *EHAM* E6 ....**95** F5
Troon Cl *BERM/RHTH* * SE16 ....**120** B1
Troon St *WCHPL* E1 ....**91** E5
Trossachs Rd *EDUL* SE22 ....**137** E3
Trothy Rd *STHWK* SE1 ....**102** A5
Trott St *BTSEA* SW11 ....**115** D4
Troughton Rd *CHARL* SE7 ....**124** B1
Troutbeck Rd *NWCR* SE14 ....**121** E4
Trouville Rd *BAL* SW12 ....**134** C4
Trowbridge Rd *HOM* E9 ....**79** F3
Troy Ct *KENS* W8 ....**38** A2
Troy Town *PECK* SE15 ....**138** A1
Truman's Rd *STNW/STAM* N16 ....**77** E2
Trumpington Rd *FSTGT* E7 ....**81** F1
Trump St *CITYW* EC2V **23** F5
Trundle St *STHWK* SE1 ....**35** E5
Trundleys Rd *DEPT* SE8 ....**121** E2
  DEPT SE8 ....**121** D1
Trundley's Ter *DEPT* SE8 ....**103** D5
Truro Gdns *IL* IG1 ....**65** D2
Truro St *KTTN* NW5 ....**74** A3
Trusedale Rd *EHAM* E6 ....**95** F5
Truslove Rd *WNWD* SE27 ....**154** A5
Trussley Rd *HMSMTH* W6 ....**100** C4
Tryon Crs *HOM* E9 ....**78** C5
Tryon St *CHEL* SW3 ....**115** F1
Tuam Rd *WOOL/PLUM* SE18 ....**127** D2
Tubbs Rd *WLSDN* NW10 ....**87** F1
Tudor Cl *BRXS/STRHM* * SW2 ....**135** F4
  CDALE/KGS NW9 ....**50** C4
  HAMP NW3 ....**73** E2
  HGT N6 ....**56** C2

Tudor Ct *ELTH/MOT* * SE9............143 E2
  WALTH 61 F2
Tudor Ct North *WBLY* HA9 ....68 A2
Tudor Ct South *WBLY* HA9 ....68 A2
Tudor Est *WLSDN* * NW10 ....86 B1
Tudor Gdns *ACT* W3....................86 A5
  BARN SW13 ....129 E1
  CDALE/KGS NW9 ....50 C4
Tudor Gv *HOM* E9 ....78 C4
Tudor Pde *ELTH/MOT* * SE9 ....143 E2
Tudor Rd *BARK* IG11 ....85 F4
  EHAM E6 ....82 C5
  HACK E8 ....78 B5
Tudor St *EMB* EC4Y 34 B1
Tudor Wy *ACT* W3.......................98 A3
Tudway Rd *ELTH/MOT* SE9 ....142 C2
Tufnell Park Rd *HOLWY* N7 ....75 D1
Tufton St *WEST* SW1P...................44 C3
Tugboat St *THMD* SE28 ....109 E3
Tugela St *CAT* SE6 ....157 F2
Tulip Cl *EHAM* E6 ....95 F4
Tulip Gdns *IL* IG1 ....84 B3
Tulse HI *BRXS/STRHM* SW2.............136 A5
Tulsemere Rd *WNWD* SE27 ....154 C2
Tunis Rd *SHB* W12 ....100 C2
Tunley Rd *BAL* SW12 ....152 A2
  WLSDN NW10 ....69 E5
Tunmarsh La *PLSTW* E13 ....94 C2
Tunnan Leys *EHAM* E6 ....96 A5
Tunnel Av *GNWCH* SE10 ....105 D3
Tunnel Rd *BERM/RHTH* SE16 ....102 C3
Tunstall Rd *BRXN/ST* SW9 ....135 F2
Tunworth Cl *CDALE/KGS* NW9 ....50 C1
Tunworth Crs *PUT/ROE* SW15 ....129 F4
Tupelo Rd *LEY* E10.....................62 B4
Turene Cl *BTSEA* SW11 ....132 C2
Turin St *BETH* E2 ....90 A2
Turks Rw *CHEL* SW3 ....115 F1
Turle Rd *FSBYPK* * N4 ....57 F4
Turlewray Cl *FSBYPK* N4 ....57 F3
Turley Cl *SRTFD* E15 ....81 E5
Turnagain La *STP* EC4M 22 C4
Turnberry Cl *BERM/RHTH* * SE16 .....120 B1
Turner Cl *CMBW* SE5 ....118 B4
  GLDGN NW11 ....54 B1
Turner Ct *CMBW* * SE5 ....137 D2
Turner Dr *GLDGN* NW11 ....54 B1
Turner's Rd *POP/IOD* E14...............91 F4
Turner St *CAN/RD* E16 ....93 F5
  WCHPL E1 ....90 B4
Turner's Wd *GLDGN* NW11 ....54 C3
Turneville Rd *WKENS* W14 ....113 F2
Turney Rd *DUL* SE21 ....136 C5
Turnham Green Ter *CHSWK* W4 ....99 D1
Turnham Rd *BROCKY* SE4 ....139 E3
Turnmill St *FARR* EC1M 22 B1
Turnpike Cl *DEPT* SE8 ....121 F3
Turnstone Cl *PLSTW* E13 ....94 A2
Turpentine La *PIM* SW1V 116 B1
Turpins Yd *CRICK* * NW2 ....52 B4
Turquand St *WALW* SE17 ....47 F5
Turret Gv *CLAP* SW4 ....134 C1
Turville St *BETH* * E2 ....15 E5
Tuscan Rd *WOOL/PLUM* SE18 ....127 D1
Tuskar St *GNWCH* SE10 ....123 E1
Tweedmouth Rd *PLSTW* E13 ....94 B1
Twelvetrees Crs *BOW* E3 ....92 C3
Twickenham Rd *WAN* E11 ....63 D4
Twig Folly Cl *BOW* E3 ....91 D1
Twig Folly Whf *BETH* * E2 ....91 D1
Twilley St *WAND/EARL* SW18 ....132 B5
Twine Ct *WCHPL* E1 ....102 C1
Twine Ter *BOW* * E3 ....91 D1

Twisden Rd *KTTN* NW5 ....74 B1
Twybridge Wy *WLSDN* NW10............68 C4
Twyford Av *ACT* W3 ....98 A1
Twyford Crs *ACT* W3 ....98 A2
Twyford Rd *IL* IG1 ....84 C2
Twyford St *IS* N1 ....75 F5
Tyas Rd *CAN/RD* E16 ....93 F3
Tyburn Wy *MBLAR* W1H 29 F1
Tyers Ga *STHWK* SE1 ....48 C1
Tyers St *LBTH* SE11 ....117 F1
Tyers Ter *LBTH* SE11 ....117 F1
Tylehurst Gdns *IL* IG1 ....84 C2
Tyler Cl *BETH* E2.......................13 E1
Tyler St *GNWCH* SE10 ....123 E1
Tylney Av *NRWD* SE19 ....155 F5
Tylney Rd *FSTGT* E7 ....82 C1
Tyndale La *IS* N1 ....76 B4
Tyndale Ter *IS* N1 ....76 B3
Tyndall Rd *LEY* E10 ....62 C4
  WELL DA16...........................145 F1
Tyneham Cl *BTSEA* * SW11 ....134 A1
Tyneham Rd *BTSEA* SW11 ....116 A5
Tynemouth Cl *EHAM* E6 ....96 B5
Tynemouth Rd *WOOL/PLUM* SE18 .....127 E1
Tynemouth St *FUL/PGN* SW6 ....114 C5
Tyne St *WCHPL* E1 ....25 F4
Type St *BETH* E2 ....91 D1
Tyrawley Rd *FUL/PGN* SW6 ....114 B4
Tyrone Rd *EHAM* E6 ....95 F1
Tyron Wy *SCUP* DA14 ....163 E4
Tyrrell Rd *EDUL* SE22 ....138 A2
Tyrrel Wy *CDALE/KGS* NW9 ....51 F2
Tyrwhitt Rd *BROCKY* SE4 ....140 F1
Tysoe St *CLKNW* EC1R 10 A4
Tyson Gdns *FSTH* SE23 ....138 C5
Tyson Rd *FSTH* SE23 ....138 C5
Tyssen Rd *STNW/STAM* * N16 ....59 F5
Tyssen St *HACK* E8 ....77 F3
Tytherton Rd *ARCH* N19 ....57 D5

U

Uamvar St *POP/IOD* E14 ....92 B4
Udall St *WEST* SW1P 43 F5
Uffington Rd *WLSDN* NW10 ....70 A5
  WNWD SE27..........................154 A4
Ufford St *STHWK* SE1 ....34 B5
Ufton Gv *IS* N1 ....77 E4
Ufton Rd *IS* N1 ....77 E4
Uhura Sq *STNW/STAM* * N16 ....59 E5
Ullathorne Rd *STRHM/NOR* SW16......152 C4
Ullin St *POP/IOD* E14...................92 C4
Ullswater Cl *KUTN/CMB* * KT2 ....147 D4
Ullswater Crs *PUT/ROE* SW15 ....147 D4
Ullswater Rd *BARN* SW13 ....112 A3
  WNWD SE27..........................154 B3
Ulster Pl *CAMTN* NW1 ....18 C1
Ulundi Rd *BKHTH/KID* SE3 ....123 E2
Ulva Rd *PUT/ROE* SW15 ....131 D2
Ulverscroft Rd *EDUL* SE22 ....138 A3
Ulysses Rd *KIL/WHAMP* NW6 ....71 F2
Umberston St *WCHPL* * E1..............90 A5
Umbria St *PUT/ROE* SW15 ....130 A4
Umfreville Rd *FSBYPK* N4 ....58 B1
Undercliff Rd *LEW* SE13 ....140 A1
Underhill Rd *EDUL* SE22 ....138 A3
Underhill St *CAMTN* NW1 ....74 B5
Undershaft *HDTCH* EC3A 24 C5
Undershaw Rd *BMLY* BR1 ....159 E3
Underwood Rd *WCHPL* E1 ....90 A3
Underwood Rw *IS* N1 ....11 F3

Underwood St *IS* N1 ....11 F3
The Underwood St *ELTH/MOT* SE9 ....161 F2
Undine Rd *POP/IOD* E14 ....104 B5
Undine St *TOOT* SW17 ....151 F5
Union Cl *WAN* E11 ....81 D1
Union Ct *CLAP* SW4 ....117 E5
Union Dr *WCHPL* * E1 ....91 E3
Union Gv *VX/NE* SW8 ....117 D5
Union Rd *CLAP* SW4 ....117 D5
Union Sq *IS* N1 ....76 C5
Union St *SRTFD* E15 ....81 D5
    STHWK SE1 ....35 D4
Union Wk *BETH* E2 ....13 E3
Unity Cl *WLSDN* NW10 ....70 A3
    WNWD SE27 ....154 C5
Unity Ms *CAMTN* NW1 ....8 A1
Unity Wy *WOOL/PLUM* SE18 ....107 D4
University St *FITZ* W1T 19 F1
University Wy *EHAM* E6 ....108 A1
Unwin Cl *PECK* SE15 ....120 A2
Unwin Rd *SKENS* SW7 ....40 B2
Upbrook Ms *BAY/PAD* W2 ....15 F5
Upcerne Rd *WBPTN* SW10 ....114 C3
Updale Rd *SCUP* DA14 ....163 F4
Uphall Rd *IL* IG1 ....84 B2
Upham Park Rd *CHSWK* W4 ....99 E5
Upland Rd *EDUL* SE22 ....138 A5
    PLSTW E13 ....94 A3
Uplands Cl *MORT/ESHN* SW14 ....128 B3
Upney La *BARK* IG11 ....85 F4
Upnor Wy *WALW* SE17 ....119 E1
Uppark Dr *GNTH/NBYPK* IG2 ....66 C1
Upper Addison Gdns
    WKENS W14 ....101 E3
Upper Bardsey Wk *IS* * N1 ....76 C3
Upper Belgrave St *KTBR* SW1X 42 B2
Upper Berenger Wk
    WBPTN * SW10 ....115 D3
Upper Berkeley St *BAY/PAD* W2 ....17 E5
Upper Blantyre Wk *WBPTN* * SW10 ...115 D3
Upper Brockley Rd *BROCKY* SE4 ......121 F5
Upper Brook St *MYFR/PKLN* W1K 30 A1
Upper Caldy Wk *IS* * N1 ....76 C3
Upper Camelford Wk
    NTGHL * W11 ....89 E5
Upper Cheyne Rw *CHEL* SW3 ....115 E2
Upper Clapton Rd *CLPT* E5 ....60 B4
Upper Clarendon Wk
    NTGHL * W11 ....89 E5
Upper Dartrey Wk *WBPTN* * SW10 ...114 C3
Upper Dengie Wk *IS* * N1 ....76 C5
Upper Grosvenor St
    MYFR/PKLN W1K 30 A2
Upper Gnd *STHWK* SE1 ....34 A3
Upper Gulland Wk *IS* * N1 ....76 C3
Upper Handa Wk *IS* * N1 ....77 D3
Upper Harley St *CAMTN* NW1 ....18 B1
Upper Hawkwell Wk *IS* * N1 ....76 C5
Upper John St *REGST* W1B 31 F1
Upper Lismore Wk *IS* * N1 ....76 C3
Upper Ldg *KENS* * W8 ....27 D4
Upper Ml *HMSMTH* W6 ....112 A1
Upper Marsh *STHWK* SE1 ....45 F2
Upper Montagu St *MBLAR* W1H 17 E2
Upper North St *POP/IOD* E14 ....92 A4
Upper Park Rd *HAMP* NW3 ....73 F3
Upper Phillimore Gdns *KENS* W8 ......38 A1
Upper Ramsey Wk *IS* * N1 ....77 D3
Upper Rawreth Wk *IS* * N1 ....76 C5
Upper Richmond Rd
    PUT/ROE SW15 ....130 B2
Upper Richmond Rd West
    RCHPK/HAM TW10 ....128 A2

Upper Rd *PLSTW* E13 ....94 A2
Upper St Martin's La
    LSQ/SEVD WC2H 20 C5
Upper Sheppey Wk *IS* N1 ....76 C3
Upper St *IS* N1 ....10 B1
Upper Tachbrook St *PIM* SW1V 43 F4
Upper Talbot Wk *NTGHL* * W11 ....89 E5
Upper Ter *HAMP* NW3 ....54 C5
Upper Thames St *BLKFR* EC4V 35 E1
Upper Tollington Pk *FSBYPK* N4 ....58 A3
Upperton Rd *SCUP* DA14 ....163 F5
Upperton Rd East *PLSTW* E13 ....94 C2
Upperton Rd West *PLSTW* E13 ....94 C2
Upper Tooting Pk *TOOT* SW17 ....151 F2
Upper Tooting Rd *TOOT* SW17 ....151 F4
Upper Tulse Hl *BRXS/STRHM* SW2 ....135 F5
Upper Whistler Wk *WBPTN* * SW10 ..114 C3
Upper Wimpole St
    CAVSQ/HST W1G 18 B2
Upper Woburn Pl *CAMTN* NW1 ....8 B4
Upstall St *CMBW* SE5 ....118 B4
Upton Av *FSTGT* E7 ....82 A4
Upton La *FSTGT* E7 ....82 B3
Upton Park Rd *FSTGT* E7 ....82 B4
Upton Rd *WOOL/PLUM* SE18 ....126 C2
Upwood Rd *LEE/GVPK* SE12 ....142 A4
Urlwin St *CMBW* SE5 ....118 C2
Urlwin Wk *BRXN/ST* SW9 ....118 A4
Urmston Dr *WIM/MER* SW19 ....149 E1
Ursula Ms *FSBYPK* N4 ....58 B3
Ursula St *BTSEA* SW11 ....115 E4
Urswick Rd *CLPT* E5 ....78 C2
Usborne Ms *VX/NE* SW8 ....117 F3
Usher Rd *BOW* E3 ....79 F5
Usk Rd *BTSEA* SW11 ....132 C2
Usk St *BETH* E2 ....91 D2
Uverdale Rd *WBPTN* SW10 ....114 C3
Uxbridge Rd *SHB* W12 ....100 A2
Uxbridge St *KENS* W8 ....26 A3

V

Vale Cl *MV/WKIL* W9 ....3 E4
Vale Cottages *PUT/ROE* * SW15 ......147 E3
Vale Ct *ACT* * W3 ....99 F2
Vale Crs *PUT/ROE* SW15 ....147 E4
Vale End *EDUL* SE22 ....137 F2
Vale Gv *ACT* W3 ....99 D2
    FSBYPK N4 ....58 C2
Vale La *ACT* W3 ....86 A4
Valentia Pl *BRXN/ST* SW9 ....136 A2
Valentine Pl *STHWK* SE1 ....34 C5
Valentine Rd *HOM* * E9 ....79 D3
Valentines Rd *IL* IG1 ....66 B3
Vale of Health *HAMP* NW3 ....54 C5
Valerian Wy *SRTFD* E15 ....93 E2
Vale Ri *GLDGN* NW11 ....53 F3
Vale Rd *FSBYPK* N4 ....58 C2
    FSTGT E7 ....82 B3
Vale Royal *HOLWY* N7 ....75 E4
Valeswood Rd *BMLY* BR1 ....159 F5
Vale Ter *FSBYPK* N4 ....58 C1
Valetta Gv *PLSTW* E13 ....94 A1
Valetta Rd *ACT* W3 ....99 E3
Valette St *HACK* * E8 ....78 B3
Valiant Wy *EHAM* E6 ....95 F4
Vallance Rd *WCHPL* E1 ....90 A3
Valleyfield Rd *STRHM/NOR* SW16 ...153 F5

Valley Gv *CHARL* SE7 ....124 C1
Valley Rd *STRHM/NOR* SW16 ....153 F4
Valliere Rd *WLSDN* NW10 ....88 A2
Valliers Wood Rd *BFN/LL* DA15 ....163 D1
Valmar Rd *CMBW* SE5 ....118 C4
Valnay St *TOOT* SW17 ....151 F5
Valonia Gdns *WAND/EARL* SW18 ...131 F4
Vambery Rd *WOOL/PLUM* SE18 .....126 C2
Vanbrugh Flds *BKHTH/KID* SE3 ....123 F2
Vanbrugh HI *GNWCH* SE10 ....123 E1
Vanbrugh Pk *BKHTH/KID* SE3 ....123 F3
Vanbrugh Park Rd
    BKHTH/KID SE3 ....123 F3
Vanbrugh Park Rd West
    BKHTH/KID SE3 ....123 F3
Vanbrugh Rd *CHSWK* W4 ....99 D4
Vanbrugh Ter *BKHTH/KID* SE3 ......123 F4
Vanburgh CI *CAN/RD* E16 ....95 D4
Vancouver Rd *FSTH* SE23 ....157 E2
Vanderbilt Rd *WAND/EARL* SW18 ..150 B1
Vanderbilt VIs *SHB* * W12 ....101 D3
Vandome CI *CAN/RD* E16 ....94 B5
Vandon St *STJSPK* SW1H 43 F2
Vandyke CI *PUT/ROE* SW15 ....131 D4
Vandyke Cross *ELTH/MOT* SE9 .....143 E3
Vandy St *SDTCH* EC2A 24 C1
Vane CI *HAMP* NW3 ....73 D2
Vanguard CI *CAN/RD* E16 ....94 A4
Vanguard St *DEPT* SE8 ....122 A4
Vanneck Sq *PUT/ROE* * SW15 ......130 A3
Vanoc Gdns *BMLY* BR1 ....160 A4
Vansittart Rd *FSTGT* E7 ....82 A1
Vansittart St *NWCR* SE14 ....121 E3
Vanston PI *FUL/PGN* SW6 ....114 A3
Vant Rd *TOOT* SW17 ....151 F5
Varcoe Rd *BERM/RHTH* SE16 ....120 B3
Vardens Rd *BTSEA* SW11 ....133 D2
Varden St *WCHPL* E1 ....90 B5
Varley Rd *CAN/RD* E16 ....94 B5
Varna Rd *FUL/PGN* SW6 ....113 E3
Varndell St *CAMTN* NW1 ....7 E3
Varsity Rw *MORT/ESHN* SW14 ......110 C5
Vartry Rd *SEVS/STOTM* N15 ....59 E1
Vassall Rd *BRXN/ST* SW9 ....118 A3
Vauban Est *BERM/RHTH* SE16 ....49 F3
Vauban St *BERM/RHTH* SE16 ....49 F3
Vaughan Av *HMSMTH* W6 ....99 F5
Vaughan Est *BETH* * E2 ....13 E3
Vaughan Gdns *IL* IG1 ....65 F2
Vaughan Rd *CMBW* SE5 ....118 C5
    SRTFD E15 ....81 E3
    WELL DA16 ....127 F5
Vaughan St *BERM/RHTH* SE16 ......103 F3
Vaughan Wy *WAP* E1W 102 A3
Vaughan Williams CI *DEPT* SE8 ....122 A3
Vauxhall Br *VX/NE* SW8 ....117 E1
Vauxhall Bridge Rd *PIM* SW1V 43 E3
Vauxhall Gv *VX/NE* SW8 ....117 F2
Vauxhall St *LBTH* SE11 ....117 F1
Vauxhall Wk *LBTH* SE11 ....117 F1
Vawdrey CI *WCHPL* E1 ....90 C3
Veda Rd *LEW* SE13 ....140 A2
Venables St *STJWD* NW8 ....16 B1
Vencourt PI *HMSMTH* W6 ....112 A1
Venetian Rd *CMBW* SE5 ....118 C5
Venetia Rd *FSBYPK* N4 ....58 B1
Venn St *CLAP* SW4 ....134 C2
Ventnor Gdns *BARK* IG11 ....85 E3
Ventnor Rd *NWCR* SE14 ....121 D3
Venue St *POP/IOD* E14 ....92 B4
Venus Rd *WOOL/PLUM* SE18 ....107 F3
Vera Lynn CI *FSTGT* E7 ....82 A1
Vera Rd *FUL/PGN* SW6 ....113 E4

Verbena CI *CAN/RD* E16 ....93 E3
Verbena Gdns *HMSMTH* W6 ....112 A1
Verdant La *CAT* SE6 ....159 E1
Verdun Rd *BARN* SW13 ....112 A3
Vereker Rd *WKENS* * W14 ....113 E1
Vere St *MHST* W1U 18 C5
Vermont Rd *WAND/EARL* SW18 .....132 B4
Verney Rd *BERM/RHTH* SE16 ....120 B1
Verney St *WLSDN* NW10 ....51 D5
Verney Wy *BERM/RHTH* SE16 ....120 B1
Vernham Rd *WOOL/PLUM* SE18 .....126 C2
Vernon Av *MNPK* E12 ....83 F1
Vernon PI *BMSBY* WC1N 21 D3
Vernon Ri *FSBYW* WC1X 9 F3
Vernon Rd *BOW* E3 ....91 F1
    GDMY/SEVK IG3 ....67 F3
    MORT/ESHN SW14 ....129 D1
    SRTFD E15 ....81 E4
    WAN E11 ....63 E3
Vernon Sq *FSBYW* * WC1X 9 F3
Vernon St *WKENS* W14 ....101 E5
Vernon Yd *NTGHL* W11 ....101 F1
Veronica Rd *TOOT* SW17 ....152 B3
Verran Rd *BAL* * SW12 ....134 B5
Verulam Av *WALTH* E17 ....61 F2
Verulam Ct *CDALE/KGS* * NW9 ....52 A2
Verulam St *FSBYW* WC1X 22 A1
Vespan Rd *SHB* W12 ....100 A3
Vesta Rd *BROCKY* SE4 ....121 E5
Vestris Rd *FSTH* SE23 ....157 D2
Vestry Rd *CMBW* SE5 ....119 E4
Vestry St *IS* N1 ....12 A3
Vevey St *FSTH* SE23 ....157 D2
Viaduct PI *BETH* E2 ....90 B2
Viaduct St *BETH* E2 ....90 B2
Vian St *LEW* SE13 ....140 B1
Vibart Gdns *BRXS/STRHM* SW2 ....135 F1
Vibart Wk *IS* * N1 ....75 E5
Vicarage Crs *BTSEA* SW11 ....115 D4
Vicarage Dr *BARK* IG11 ....84 C4
    MORT/ESHN SW14 ....129 D3
Vicarage Gdns *KENS* * W8 ....26 B5
Vicarage Ga *KENS* W8 ....26 C4
Vicarage Gv *CMBW* SE5 ....119 D4
Vicarage La *EHAM* E6 ....95 F2
    IL IG1 ....67 D3
    SRTFD E15 ....81 E3
Vicarage Ms *CHSWK* * W4 ....111 E2
Vicarage Pk *WOOL/PLUM* SE18 ....126 C1
Vicarage Rd *HDN* NW4 ....52 A1
    LEY E10 ....62 B2
    MORT/ESHN SW14 ....128 C3
    SRTFD E15 ....81 F4
    WOOL/PLUM SE18 ....126 C1
Vicarage Wk *BTSEA* * SW11 ....115 D4
Vicarage Wy *WLSDN* NW10 ....51 D5
Vicar's CI *HACK* E8 ....78 C5
    SRTFD E15 ....82 A5
Vicars HI *LEW* SE13 ....140 B2
Vicar's Rd *KTTN* NW5 ....74 A2
Viceroy Rd *VX/NE* SW8 ....117 E4
Victoria Ar *PIM* SW1V 43 D3
Victoria Av *EHAM* E6 ....83 D5
    WBLY HA9 ....68 B3
Victoria Cottages *WCHPL* * E1 ....90 A4
Victoria Ct *WBLY* HA9 ....68 A3
Victoria Dock Rd *CAN/RD* E16 ....93 F5
Victoria Dr *WIM/MER* SW19 ....131 D5
Victoria Emb *TPL/STR* WC2R 33 E2
    WHALL SW1A 45 D1
Victoria Embankment Gdns
    CHCR * WC2N 33 D2
Victoria Ga *BAY/PAD* W2 ....28 B1

Victoria Gv KENS W8 ....39 E2
Victoria Grove Ms NTCHL * W11 ....26 C2
Victoria Ms KIL/WHAMP NW6 ....72 A5
  WAND/EARL SW18 ....150 C1
Victorian Gv STNW/STAM N16 ....59 E5
Victorian Rd STNW/STAM N16 ....59 E5
Victoria Pde RCH/KEW * TW9 ....110 A4
Victoria Park Rd HOM E9 ....79 D5
Victoria Park Sq BETH E2 ....90 C2
Victoria Park Studios HOM * E9 ....78 C3
Victoria Ri CLAP SW4 ....134 B1
Victoria Rd ACT W3 ....87 D4
  BARK IG11 ....84 B3
  BFN/LL DA15 ....163 F3
  CHST BR7 ....162 A5
  FSBYPK N4 ....57 F2
  KENS W8 ....39 E3
  KIL/WHAMP NW6 ....89 F1
  MORT/ESHN SW14 ....129 D1
  PLSTW E13 ....94 A1
  WAN E11 ....81 D1
Victoria Sq BGVA SW1W 43 D2
Victoria St PIM SW1V 43 D3
  SRTFD E15 ....81 E4
Victoria Ter FSBYPK N4 ....58 A3
Victoria Wy CHARL SE7 ....124 B1
Victoria Yd WCHPL * E1 ....90 A5
Victor Rd WLSDN NW10 ....88 B2
Victory Pl WALW SE17 ....47 F4
Victory Wy BERM/RHTH SE16 ....103 E3
View Cl HGT N6 ....55 F2
Viewfield Rd WAND/EARL SW18 ....131 F4
Viewland Rd WOOL/PLUM SE18 ....127 F1
View Rd HGT N6 ....55 F2
Vigilant Cl SYD SE26 ....156 A4
Vigo St MYFR/PICC W1J 31 E2
Viking Gdns EHAM E6 ....95 E4
Viking Pl LEY E10 ....61 F3
Village Cl HAMP * NW3 ....73 D2
Village Ms CDALE/KGS * NW9 ....51 D4
Village Mt HAMP * NW3 ....72 C1
The Village CHARL SE7 ....124 C2
  GLDGN * NW11 ....54 C4
Village Wy HNHL SE24 ....137 D4
  WLSDN NW10 ....69 D1
Villa Rd BRXN/ST SW9 ....136 A1
Villas Rd WOOL/PLUM SE18 ....108 C5
Villa St WALW SE17 ....119 E5
Villiers Rd CRICK NW2 ....70 A3
Villiers St CHCR WC2N 33 D3
Vincennes Est WNWD * SE27 ....155 D4
Vincent Cl BFN/LL DA15 ....163 E5
Vincent Gdns CRICK NW2 ....51 F5
Vincent Pde ARCH * N19 ....57 D3
Vincent Rd ACT W3 ....98 C4
  WOOL/PLUM * SE18 ....108 B5
Vincents Cl BERM/RHTH SE16 ....103 E3
Vincent Sq WEST SW1P 43 F4
Vincent St CAN/RD E16 ....94 A4
  WEST SW1P 44 A4
Vincent Ter IS N1 ....10 C1
Vince Sq FSBYE EC1V 12 B4
Vine Cottages WCHPL * E1 ....90 A5
Vine Ct WCHPL E1 ....90 A4
Vine Gdns IL IG1 ....84 C2
Vinegar St WAP E1W 102 B2
Vinegar Yd STHWK SE1 ....36 C5
Vine Hl CLKNW EC1R 22 A1
Vine La STHWK SE1 ....37 D4
The Vineries CAT * SE6 ....158 A4
Vine Rd BARN SW13 ....129 D1
  SRTFD E15 ....81 F4
Vine Sq WKENS * W14 ....113 F1

Vine St CONDST W1S 31 F2
  TWRH EC3N 25 E5
Vine Street Br FARR EC1M 22 B1
Vine Street Crs TWRH * EC3N 37 E1
Vine Yd STHWK SE1 ....35 F5
Vineyard Cl CAT SE6 ....158 A1
Vineyard Hill Rd WIM/MER SW19 ......150 A4
Vineyard Ms CLKNW * EC1R 10 A5
Vineyard Pth MORT/ESHN SW14 ....129 D1
Vineyard Wk CLKNW EC1R 10 A5
Viney Rd LEW SE13 ....140 B1
Vining St BRXN/ST SW9 ....136 A2
Viola Sq SHB W12 ....99 F1
Violet Cl CAN/RD E16 ....93 E3
  DEPT SE8 ....121 F2
Violet Hl STJWD NW8 ....3 E2
Violet Rd BOW E3 ....92 B3
  LEY E10 ....62 A1
Violet St BETH E2 ....90 B3
Virgil St STHWK SE1 ....45 F2
Virginia Rd BETH E2 ....13 E4
Virginia St WAP * E1W 102 A1
Viscount Dr EHAM E6 ....96 F4
Viscount St STLK EC1Y 23 E1
The Vista ELTH/MOT SE9 ....143 D4
Vivian Av WBLY HA9 ....68 A3
Vivian Gdns WBLY HA9 ....68 A2
Vivian Rd BOW E3 ....91 E1
Vivian Sq PECK SE15 ....138 B1
Vixen Ms HACK * E8 ....77 F5
Voce Rd WOOL/PLUM SE18 ....127 D3
Voltaire Rd CLAP SW4 ....135 D1
Volt Av WLSDN NW10 ....87 D2
Voluntary Pl WAN E11 ....64 A1
Vorley Rd ARCH N19 ....56 C4
Voss St BETH E2 ....90 A2
Vulcan Cl EHAM E6 ....96 F5
Vulcan Rd BROCKY SE4 ....121 F5
Vulcan Ter BROCKY SE4 ....121 F5
Vulcan Wy HOLWY N7 ....75 F3
Vyner Rd ACT W3 ....99 D1
Vyner St BETH E2 ....90 B1

W

Wadding St WALW SE17 ....48 A5
Waddington Rd SRTFD E15 ....81 D2
Waddington St SRTFD E15.....................81 D3
Wade House STHWK * SE1 ....102 A3
Wadeson St BETH E2 ....90 B1
Wade's Pl POP/IOD E14 ....104 C1
Wadham Gdns HAMP NW3 ....73 E4
Wadham Rd PUT/ROE SW15 ....131 E2
Wadhurst Rd CHSWK W4 ....99 D4
Wadley Rd WAN E11 ....63 E2
Wager St BOW E3 ....91 F3
Waghorn Rd PLSTW E13.........................82 C5
Waghorn St PECK SE15 ....138 A1
Wagner St PECK SE15 ....120 C3
Wainford Cl WIM/MER SW19 ....149 D1
Waite Davies Rd LEE/GVPK SE12 ....141 F5
Waite St PECK SE15 ....119 F2
Wakefield Gdns IL IG1 ....65 E1
Wakefield Ms STPAN WC1H 9 D4
Wakefield St BMSBY WC1N 9 D5
  EHAM E6 ....83 D5
Wakeham St IS N1 ....77 D3
Wakehurst Rd BTSEA SW11 ....133 E5
Wakeling St WCHPL * E1 ....91 E5
Wakelin Rd SRTFD E15 ....93 E1

Wakeman Rd *WLSDN* NW10......**88** C2
Wakering Rd *BARK* IG11......**84** C4
Wakerly Cl *EHAM* E6......**95** F5
Wakley St *FSBYE* EC1V......**10** C3
Walberswick St *VX/NE* SW8......**117** E3
Walbrook *MANHO* EC4N......**36** A1
Walburgh St *WCHPL* E1......**90** B5
Walcorde Av *WALW* SE17......**47** F5
Walcot Sq *LBTH* SE11......**46** B4
Walcott St *WEST* SW1P......**43** F4
Waldeck Gv *WNWD* SE27......**154** B3
Waldeck Rd *CHSWK* W4......**110** A2
MORT/ESHN SW14......**128** C1
Waldemar Av *FUL/PGN* SW6......**113** E4
Waldemar Rd *WIM/MER* SW19......**150** A5
Waldenshaw Rd *FSTH* SE23......**156** C1
Walden St *WCHPL* * E1......**90** B5
Waldo Cl *CLAP* SW4......**134** C3
Waldo Rd *WLSDN* NW10......**88** A2
Waldram Crs *FSTH* SE23......**156** C1
Waldram Park Rd *FSTH* SE23......**157** D1
Waldron Ms *CHST* SW3......**115** D2
Waldron Rd *WAND/EARL* SW18......**150** C3
Walerand Rd *LEW* SE13......**122** C5
Wales Farm Rd *ACT* W3......**87** D4
Waley St *WCHPL* * E1......**91** D4
Walford Rd *STNW/STAM* N16......**77** E1
Walham Green Ct *FUL/PGN* * SW6 ...**114** B3
Walham Gv *FUL/PGN* SW6......**114** A3
Walham Yd *FUL/PGN* SW6......**114** A3
Walkden Rd *CHST* BR7......**162** A4
Walker Cl *WOOL/PLUM* SE18......**108** C5
Walker's Ct *SOHO/CST* W1F......**32** A1
Walkerscroft Md *DUL* SE21......**154** C1
Walker's Pl *PUT/ROE* * SW15......**131** E2
Wallace Rd *IS* N1......**76** C3
Wallbutton Rd *BROCKY* SE4......**121** E5
Wallcote Av *CRICK* NW2......**53** D3
Wall End Rd *EHAM* E6......**84** A4
Waller Rd *NWCR* SE14......**121** D4
Wallflower St *SHB* W12......**99** F1
Wallgrave Rd *ECT* SW5......**38** C1
Wallingford Av *NKENS* W10......**89** D4
Wallington Rd *GDMY/SEVK* IG3......**67** F2
Wallis Cl *BTSEA* SW11......**133** D1
Wallis Rd *HOM* E9......**79** F3
Wallorton Gdns
MORT/ESHN SW14......**129** D2
Wallside *BARB* * EC2Y......**23** F3
Wall St *IS* N1......**77** D3
Wallwood Rd *WAN* E11......**63** D2
Wallwood St *POP/IOD* E14......**91** F4
Walmer Rd *NTGHL* W11......**101** E1
Walmer St *WOOL/PLUM* SE18......**108** C5
Walm La *CRICK* NW2......**71** D2
Walney Wk *IS* * N1......**76** C3
Walnut Cl *DEPT* SE8......**121** F2
Walnut Gdns *SRTFD* E15......**81** E2
Walnut Rd *LEY* E10......**62** A4
Walnut Tree Cl *BARN* SW13......**111** F4
Walnut Tree Rd *GNWCH* * SE10 ...**123** E1
Walnut Tree Wk *LBTH* SE11......**46** B4
Walpole Gdns *CHSWK* W4......**110** C1
Walpole Ms *STJWD* NW8......**73** D2
Walpole Rd *EHAM* E6......**82** C4
Walpole St *CHEL* SW3......**115** F1
Walsham Cl *STNW/STAM* N16......**60** A3
Walsham Rd *NWCR* SE14......**121** D5
Walsingham Rd *BTSEA* SW11......**134** A4
CLPT E5......**60** A3
Walter St *BETH* E2......**91** D2
Walters Wy *FSTH* SE23......**139** D1

Walter Ter *WCHPL* E1......**91** D5
Walterton Rd *MV/WKIL* W9......**89** F3
Waltham Av *CDALE/KGS* NW9......**50** A1
VX/NE SW8......**117** E3
Walton Dr *WLSDN* NW10......**69** D3
Walton Gdns *ACT* W3......**86** B5
Walton Pl *CHEL* SW3......**41** E2
Walton Rd *MNPK* E12......**84** A1
PLSTW E13......**94** C1
Walton St *CHEL* SW3......**41** D4
Walton Vls *IS* * N1......**77** E4
Walton Wy *ACT* W3......**86** B5
Walt Whitman Cl *HNHL* * SE24 ...**136** B2
Walworth Pl *WALW* SE17......**118** C1
Walworth Rd *WALW* SE17......**47** E4
Wanborough Dr *PUT/ROE* SW15...**148** B1
Wandle Rd *TOOT* SW17......**151** E2
Wandle Wy *WAND/EARL* SW18 ...**150** B1
Wandon Rd *FUL/PGN* SW6......**114** B3
Wandsworth Br
WAND/EARL SW18......**132** C1
Wandsworth Bridge Rd
FUL/PGN SW6......**114** B4
Wandsworth Common West Side
WAND/EARL SW18......**132** C3
Wandsworth High St
WAND/EARL SW18......**132** A3
VX/NE SW8......**117** E3
Wanless Rd *HNHL* SE24......**136** C1
Wanley Rd *CMBW* SE5......**137** D2
Wansbeck Rd *HOM* E9......**79** F4
Wansdown Pl *FUL/PGN* SW6......**114** A3
Wansey St *WALW* SE17......**47** F5
Wanstead La *IL* IG1......**65** E1
Wanstead Park Av *MNPK* E12......**65** D4
Wanstead Park Rd *IL* IG1......**65** E3
Wanstead Pl *WAN* E11......**64** A1
Wantage Rd *LEE/GVPK* SE12......**141** F3
Wapping Dock St *WAP* * E1W ...**102** B2
Wapping High St *WAP* E1W......**102** A2
Wapping La *WAP* E1W......**102** B1
Wapping Wall *WAP* E1W......**102** C2
Warbeck Rd *SHB* W12......**100** B3
Warburton Cl *IS* N1......**77** E3
Warburton Rd *HACK* E8......**78** B5
Warburton St *HACK* E8......**78** B5
Wardalls Gv *NWCR* * SE14......**120** C3
Warden Rd *KTTN* NW5......**74** A3
Wardens Gv *STHWK* SE1......**35** E4
Wardle St *HOM* E9......**79** D2
Wardley St *WAND/EARL* SW18 ...**132** B5
Wardo Av *FUL/PGN* SW6......**113** E4
Wardour Ms *SOHO/CST* W1F......**19** F5
Wardour St *SOHO/CST* W1F......**19** F4
Ward Rd *ARCH* N19......**74** C1
SRTFD * E15......**81** D5
Wardrobe Pl *BLKFR* * EC4V......**23** D5
Wards Rd *GNTH/NBYPK* IG2......**67** D2
Warepoint Dr *THMD* SE28......**109** D3
Warfield Rd *WLSDN* NW10......**89** D3
Warfield Yd *WLSDN* * NW10......**89** D2
Wargrave Av *SEVS/STOTM* N15...**59** F1
Warham Rd *CMBW* SE5......**118** B3
Waring St *WNWD* SE27......**154** C4
Warland Rd *WOOL/PLUM* SE18 ...**127** D3
Warley St *BETH* E2......**91** D2
Warlock Rd *MV/WKIL* W9......**89** F3
Warlters Cl *HOLWY* * N7......**75** E1
Warlters Rd *HOLWY* N7......**75** E1
Warltersville Rd *ARCH* N19......**57** E2

Warming Cl *CLPT* * E5..................................**61** D5
Warmington Rd *HNHL* SE24..............**136** C4
Warmington St *PLSTW* E13.................**94** A3
Warndon St *BERM/RHTH* SE16.......**102** C5
Warneford St *HOM* E9..........................**78** B5
Warner Cl *CDALE/KGS* NW9.................**51** F2
  SRTFD E15..**81** E2
Warner Pl *BETH* E2..................................**90** A1
Warner Rd *CMBW* SE5.......................**118** C4
Warner St *CLKNW* EC1R.......................**22** A1
Warner Ter *POP/IOD* * E14...................**92** A4
Warner Yd *CLKNW* EC1R.......................**22** A1
Warple Ms *ACT* * W3..............................**99** E3
Warple Wy *ACT* W3.................................**99** E3
Warrender Rd *ARCH* N19......................**56** C5
The Warren Dr *WAN* E11.......................**64** C2
Warren La *WOOL/PLUM* SE18..........**108** B4
Warren Ms *GTPST* W1W.........................**19** E1
Warren Rd *CRICK* NW2...........................**51** F4
  LEY E10..**62** D3
  WAN E11..**64** C1
Warren St *FITZ* W1T...............................**19** E1
The Warren *MNPK* E12...........................**83** F1
Warriner Gdns *BTSEA* SW11...............**115** F4
Warrington Crs *MV/WKIL* W9...............**15** E1
Warrington Gdns *MV/WKIL* W9.............**15** E1
Warrington Pl *POP/IOD* * E14............**104** C2
Warrior Sq *MNPK* E12.............................**84** A1
Warspite Rd *WOOL/PLUM* SE18.......**107** E4
Warton Rd *SRTFD* E15.............................**80** C5
Warwall *EHAM* E6.....................................**96** B5
Warwick Av *MV/WKIL* W9......................**15** D1
Warwick Cl *HHOL* WC1V.......................**21** F3
Warwick Crs *BAY/PAD* W2....................**15** E2
Warwick Dr *BARN* SW13.....................**130** B1
Warwick Gdns *IL* IG1..............................**66** B3
  WKENS W14...................................**101** F4
Warwick Gv *CLPT* E5...............................**60** B3
Warwick House St *STJS* SW1Y.............**32** B3
Warwick La *STP* EC4M.............................**23** D4
Warwick Pl *MV/WKIL* W9......................**15** D1
Warwick Pl North *PIM* * SW1V..............**43** E5
Warwick Pl *FSTGT* E7...............................**81** F3
  MNPK E12.......................................**83** E2
  WKENS W14...................................**101** F5
Warwick Rw *WESTW* SW1E.....................**43** E2
Warwick Sq *PIM* SW1V.........................**116** C1
  STP * EC4M.......................................**23** D4
Warwick Square Ms *PIM* SW1V............**43** E5
Warwick St *REGST* W1B..........................**31** F1
Warwick Ter *WOOL/PLUM* SE18.......**127** D2
Warwick Wy *PIM* SW1V..........................**43** D5
Warwick Yd *STLK* * EC1Y.......................**23** F1
Washington Av *MNPK* E12......................**83** F1
Washington Cl *BOW* E3...........................**92** B2
Washington Rd *BARN* SW13...............**112** A3
  EHAM E6..**82** C4
Wastdale Rd *FSTH* SE23.......................**157** D1
Watchfield Ct *CHSWK* * W4................**110** C1
Waterbank Rd *CAT* SE6.......................**158** B3
Watercress Pl *IS* N1.................................**77** E4
Waterden Rd *SRTFD* E15.........................**80** A3
Waterfield Cottages
  MORT/ESHN * SW14......................**128** B2
Waterford Rd *FUL/PGN* SW6..............**114** B3
The Water Gdns *BAY/PAD* W2.............**16** C4
Watergate St *DEPT* SE8........................**122** C2
Waterhouse Cl *HAMP* NW3....................**73** D2
Water La *CAMTN* NW1.........................**74** B4
  GDMY/SEVK IG3...............................**67** F5
  PECK SE15......................................**120** C3

SRTFD E15...**81** E3
Waterloo Br *STHWK* SE1.......................**33** F2
Waterloo Gdns *BETH* E2.........................**90** C1
Waterloo Pl *RCH/KEW* TW9................**110** A2
  STJS SW1Y.......................................**32** A3
Waterloo Rd *CRICK* NW2........................**52** A4
  EHAM E6..**82** C4
  FSTGT E7...**81** F2
  LEY E10..**62** A2
  STHWK SE1..**33** F3
Waterloo Ter *IS* N1..................................**76** B4
Waterlow Rd *ARCH* N19.........................**56** C3
Waterman St *PUT/ROE* SW15.............**131** D1
Waterman Wy *WAP* E1W.....................**102** B2
Watermeadow La *FUL/PGN* SW6......**114** C5
Watermead Rd *CAT* SE6......................**158** C4
Water Ms *PECK* SE15...........................**138** C2
Watermint Quay *CLPT* E5.......................**60** A2
Water's Edge *FUL/PGN* * SW6............**113** D4
Waterside *WALTH* E17..............................**60** C1
Waterside Cl *BERM/RHTH* SE16........**102** A3
  HOM E9..**79** F5
Waterside Cl *LEW* * SE13......................**141** D2
Waterside Wy *TOOT* SW17....................**150** C4
Waterson St *BETH* E2..............................**13** D3
Waters Rd *CAT* SE6...............................**159** E3
Water St *TPL/STR* WC2R.........................**34** A1
Waterworks La *CLPT* E5..........................**61** D4
Waterworks Rd
  BRXS/STRHM SW2..........................**135** E4
Watford Cl *BTSEA* SW11......................**115** E4
Watford Rd *CAN/RD* E16........................**94** A4
Watkin Rd *WBLY* HA9.............................**50** B5
Watkinson Rd *HOLWY* N7.......................**75** F3
Watling St *STP* EC4M..............................**23** E5
Watling St *STP* EC4M..............................**23** E5
Watlington Gv *SYD* SE26.....................**157** E5
Watney Market *WCHPL* E1......................**90** B5
Watney Rd *MORT/ESHN* SW14...........**128** C1
Watney St *WCHPL* E1..............................**90** B5
Watson Av *EHAM* E6................................**84** A4
Watson Cl *STNW/STAM* N16..................**77** D2
Watson's Ms *CAMTN* NW1.....................**17** D3
Watson's St *DEPT* SE8..........................**122** A3
Wattisfield Rd *CLPT* E5...........................**60** C1
Watts Gv *BOW* E3.....................................**92** A4
Watts St *E1W*...**102** B2
Wat Tyler Rd *BKHTH/KID* SE3.............**122** C5
Wavell Dr *BFN/LL* DA15........................**145** E4
Wavel Ms *KIL/WHAMP* NW6...................**72** B4
Wavel Pl *NRWD* SE19............................**155** F4
Wavendon Av *CHSWK* W4.....................**111** D1
Waveney Av *PECK* SE15........................**138** B2
Waveney Cl *WAP* E1W...........................**102** A2
Waverley Crs *WOOL/PLUM* SE18........**127** D2
Waverley Gdns *BARK* IG11.....................**97** E1
  EHAM E6..**95** E4
Waverley Pl *FSBYPK* * N4.......................**58** B3
  STJWD NW8...**4** A1
Waverley Rd *CEND/HSY/T* N8................**57** D1
  WOOL/PLUM SE18..........................**126** C1
Waverton Rd *WAND/EARL* SW18.......**132** C5
Waverton St *MYFR/PICC* W1J...............**30** B3
Wavertree Rd *BRXS/STRHM* SW2......**153** F1
Waxlow Rd *WLSDN* NW10......................**86** B5
Wayford St *BTSEA* SW11.....................**115** E5
Wayland Av *HACK* E8................................**78** A3
Waylett Pl *WNWD* SE27.......................**154** B3
Waynflete Sq *NKENS* W10....................**101** D1
Waynflete St *WAND/EARL* SW18.......**150** C2
Wayside *CRICK* NW2...............................**53** E3
  MORT/ESHN SW14........................**128** C2
Wayside Gv *CHST* BR7..........................**161** F4

Wayside Ms GNTH/NBYPK IG2 ....66 A1
Weald Cl BERM/RHTH SE16 ....120 B1
Weald Sq CLPT * E5 ....60 B4
Weardale Rd LEW SE13 ....141 D3
Wearside Rd LEW SE13 ....140 B2
Weaver Cl EHAM E6 ....108 B1
Weaver's La STHWK SE1 ....37 D4
Weavers Ter FUL/PGN * SW6 ....114 A2
Weaver St WCHPL E1 ....90 A3
Weavers Wy CAMTN NW1 ....75 D5
Weaver Wk WNWD SE27 ....154 B4
Webb Cl NKENS W10 ....88 C3
Webber Rw STHWK SE1 ....46 B1
Webber St STHWK SE1 ....34 B5
Webb Est CLPT * E5 ....60 A2
Webb Pl WLSDN NW10 ....87 F2
Webb Rd BKHTH/KID SE3 ....123 F2
Webb's Rd BTSEA SW11 ....133 F3
Webb St STHWK SE1 ....48 C3
Webster Rd BERM/RHTH SE16 ....102 A4
    LEY E10 ....62 C5
Wedderburn Rd BARK IG11 ....85 D5
    HAMP NW3 ....73 D2
Wedgwood Wk
    KIL/WHAMP * NW6 ....72 B2
Wedlake St NKENS W10 ....89 E3
Wedmore Gdns ARCH N19 ....57 E4
Wedmore St ARCH N19 ....57 D5
Weech Rd KIL/WHAMP NW6 ....72 A1
Weedington Rd KTTN NW5 ....74 A2
Weekley Sq BTSEA * SW11 ....133 D1
Weigall Rd LEE/GVPK SE12 ....142 A2
Weighhouse St MYFR/PKLN W1K ..30 B1
Weimar St PUT/ROE SW15 ....131 E1
Weir Rd BAL SW12 ....152 C1
    WIM/MER SW19 ....150 B3
Weirs Pas CAMTN NW1 ....8 B3
Weiss Rd PUT/ROE SW15 ....131 D1
Welbeck Av BMLY BR1 ....160 A4
Welbeck Rd EHAM E6 ....95 D2
Welbeck St MHST W1U 18 B3
Welbeck Wy MHST W1U 18 A3
Welby St CMBW SE5 ....118 B4
Welford Cl CLPT E5 ....61 D5
Welford Pl WIM/MER SW19 ....149 E4
Welham Rd TOOT SW17 ....152 A5
Welland Ms WAP E1W 102 A2
Welland St GNWCH SE10 ....122 C2
Well Cl STRHM/NOR SW16 ....153 F4
Wellclose Sq WAP E1W 102 A1
Wellclose St WAP E1W 102 A1
Well Cottage Cl WAN E11 ....64 C2
Well Ct MANHO EC4N 23 F5
Wellers Ct CAMTN NW1 ....8 C2
Weller St STHWK SE1 ....35 E5
Wellesley Av HMSMTH W6 ....100 B4
Wellesley Cl CHARL * SE7 ....124 C1
Wellesley Ct MV/WKIL W9 ....3 E1
Wellesley Pl CAMTN * NW1 ....8 A4
    KTTN NW5 ....74 A2
Wellesley Rd CHSWK W4 ....110 A1
    IL IG1 ....66 B4
    KTTN NW5 ....74 A2
    WALTH E17 ....62 A1
Wellesley St WCHPL E1 ....91 D4
Wellesley Ter IS N1 ....11 F3
Wellfield Rd STRHM/NOR SW16 ......153 E4
Wellfit St HNHL SE24 ....136 B1
Wellgarth Rd GLDGN NW11 ....54 B3
Well Hall Pde ELTH/MOT SE9 ....143 F2
Well Hall Rd ELTH/MOT SE9 ....143 F1

Wellington Av SEVS/STOTM N15 ......60 A1
    WOOL/PLUM SE18 ....108 C4
Wellington Cl NTGHL W11 ....14 A5
    NWCR SE14 ....121 D4
Wellington Gdns CHARL SE7 ....124 C1
Wellington Gv GNWCH SE10 ....123 D3
Wellington Ms HOLWY N7 ....75 F3
Wellington Park Est CRICK * NW2 ....52 A4
Wellington Pl STJWD NW8 ....4 B3
    LEY E10 ....61 E3
Wellington Rd FSTGT E7 ....82 A2
    STJWD NW8 ....4 B2
    WIM/MER SW19 ....150 A2
    WLSDN * NW10 ....89 D2
Wellington Rw BETH E2 ....13 F3
Wellington Sq CHEL SW3 ....115 F1
Wellington St COVGDN WC2E 33 D1
    WOOL/PLUM SE18 ....108 A5
Wellington Ter NTGHL W11 ....26 B2
    WAP * E1W 102 B2
Wellington Wy BOW E3 ....92 A2
Welling Wy ELTH/MOT SE9 ....145 D1
Well La MORT/ESHN SW14 ....128 C3
Wellmeadow Rd LEW SE13 ....141 E4
Well Rd HAMP NW3 ....55 D5
Wells Dr CDALE/KGS NW9 ....51 D3
Wells Gdns IL IG1 ....65 E2
Wells House Rd WLSDN NW10 ....87 F4
Wellside Gdns MORT/ESHN SW14 ..128 C2
Wells Ms FITZ * W1T 19 F3
Wells Park Rd SYD SE26 ....156 A3
Wells Pl CMBW SE5 ....119 E3
Wellsprings Crs WBLY HA9 ....50 B5
Wells Ri STJWD NW8 ....73 F5
Wells Rd HMSMTH W6 ....100 C3
Wells Sq FSBYW WC1X 9 E4
Wells St GTPST W1W 19 E3
Wellstead Rd EHAM E6 ....96 A1
Wells Ter FSBYPK N4 ....58 A4
Well St HOM E9 ....78 C4
    SRTFD E15 ....81 E3
Wells Wy CMBW SE5 ....119 D2
    SKENS SW7 ....40 A2
Well Wk HAMP NW3 ....55 D5
Welsford St STHWK SE1 ....120 A1
Welsh Cl PLSTW E13 ....94 A2
Welshpool St HACK * E8 ....78 A5
Welstead Wy CHSWK W4 ....99 F4
Weltje Rd HMSMTH W6 ....112 A1
Welton Rd WOOL/PLUM SE18 ....127 E3
Welwyn St BETH E2 ....90 C2
Wembley Pk WBLY HA9 ....68 B3
Wembury Rd HGT N6 ....56 B2
Wemyss Rd BKHTH/KID SE3 ....123 F5
Wendell Rd SHB W12 ....99 F3
Wendon St BOW E3 ....79 B3
Wendover Rd ELTH/MOT SE9 ....143 D1
    WLSDN NW10 ....87 F1
Wenlock Rd IS N1 ....11 E2
Wenlock St IS N1 ....11 F2
Wennington Rd BOW E3 ....91 D1
Wensley Cl ELTH/MOT SE9 ....143 F4
Wentland Cl CAT SE6 ....159 D2
Wentland Rd CAT SE6 ....159 D2
Wentworth Crs PECK SE15 ....120 A3
Wentworth Ms BOW E3 ....91 E3
Wentworth Rd GLDGN NW11 ....53 F1
    MNPK E12 ....83 D1
Wentworth St WCHPL E1 ....25 E4
Wernbrook St WOOL/PLUM SE18 ....126 C2
Werrington St CAMTN NW1 ....7 F2
Werter Rd PUT/ROE SW15 ....131 E2
Wesleyan Pl KTTN NW5 ....74 B1

Wesley Av CAN/RD E16.....................**106** A2
   WLSDN NW10..............................**87** D2
   WALW SE17...................................**47** D5
Wesley Cl HOLWY N7.......................**57** F4
Wesley Rd LEY E10..........................**62** C2
   WLSDN NW10..............................**68** C5
Wesley Sq NTGHL W11.....................**89** D5
Wesley St CAVSQ/HST W1G..............**18** B3
Wessex Cl GDMY/SEVK IG3................**67** E1
Wessex Gdns CRICK NW2...................**53** E3
Wessex St BETH E2...........................**90** D4
Wessex Wy GLDGN NW11..................**53** E2
Wesson Md CMBW * SE5...................**118** C3
West Arbour St WCHPL E1.................**91** D5
West Bank BARK IG11.......................**84** B5
   STNW/STAM N16...........................**59** E2
Westbere Rd CRICK NW2...................**71** E1
Westbourne Av ACT W3.....................**87** D5
Westbourne Crs BAY/PAD W2.............**28** A1
Westbourne Crescent Ms
   BAY/PAD W2..................................**28** A1
Westbourne Dr FSTH SE23................**157** D1
Westbourne Gdns BAY/PAD W2..........**14** C4
Westbourne Ga BAY/PAD W2..............**28** B2
Westbourne Gv BAY/PAD W2.............**14** B5
   NTGHL * W11..............................**101** F1
Westbourne Grove Ms
   NTGHL * W11................................**14** A5
Westbourne Grove Ter
   BAY/PAD W2..................................**14** C4
Westbourne Park Rd BAY/PAD W2....**14** A4
   NTGHL W11...................................**89** F5
Westbourne Park Vls BAY/PAD W2.....**14** B3
Westbourne Rd HOLWY N7................**75** F3
Westbourne St BAY/PAD W2...............**28** A1
Westbourne Ter BAY/PAD W2.............**15** E3
Westbourne Terrace Ms
   BAY/PAD W2..................................**15** E4
Westbourne Terrace Rd
   BAY/PAD W2..................................**15** D3
Westbridge Cl SHB W12...................**100** A2
Westbridge Rd BTSEA SW11.............**115** D4
Westbrooke Rd BFN/LL DA15............**163** D2
Westbrook Rd BKHTH/KID SE3..........**124** A4
Westbury Rd BARK IG11....................**85** D5
   FSTGT E7.......................................**82** B2
Westbury Ter FSTGT E7.....................**82** B3
West Carriage Dr BAY/PAD W2...........**28** B5
West Central St NOXST/BSQ WC1A.....**20** C4
Westcombe Hl BKHTH/KID SE3..........**124** A2
Westcombe Park Rd
   BKHTH/KID SE3............................**124** A3
Westcote Rd STRHM/NOR SW16........**152** C5
Westcott Cl SEVS/STOTM N15............**59** F1
Westcott House POP/IOD * E14..........**104** A1
Westcott Rd WALW SE17..................**118** B2
Westcroft Cl CRICK NW2....................**71** E1
Westcroft Ms HMSMTH * W6.............**100** A5
Westcroft Sq HMSMTH W6................**100** A5
Westcroft Wy CRICK NW2..................**71** E1
West Cross Route NTGHL W11...........**101** D1
Westdale Rd WOOL/PLUM SE18.........**126** B2
Westdean Av LEE/GVPK SE12............**160** B1
Westdean Cl WAND/EARL SW18.........**132** B4
Westdown Rd CAT SE6.....................**140** A5
   SRTFD E15....................................**80** C1
West Dr TOOT SW17..........................**152** B4
West Eaton Pl KTBR SW1X.................**42** A4
West Eaton Place Ms KTBR * SW1X.....**42** A4
West Ella Rd WLSDN NW10................**69** E4
West End Cl WLSDN NW10.................**68** C4
West End La KIL/WHAMP NW6.............**72** A2
Westerdale Rd GNWCH SE10.............**124** A1

Westerham Rd LEY E10......................**62** B1
Westerley Crs SYD * SE26................**157** F5
Western Av ACT W3...........................**86** B3
   GLDGN NW11.................................**53** D1
Western Gdns ACT W3.......................**98** A1
Western Gtwy CAN/RD E16................**106** B1
Western La BAL SW12.......................**134** A5
Western Ms MV/WKIL W9....................**89** F3
Western Rd BRXN/ST SW9.................**136** A1
   PLSTW E13....................................**82** B5
   WLSDN NW10................................**86** C3
Western Ter HMSMTH * W6...............**112** A1
Westernville Gdns
   GNTH/NBYPK IG2..........................**66** C2
Western Wy THMD SE28..................**109** E3
Westferry Circ POP/IOD E14.............**104** A2
Westferry Rd POP/IOD E14...............**103** F1
Westfield Cl FUL/PGN * SW6.............**114** C3
Westfields BARN SW13....................**129** F1
Westfields Av BARN SW13................**129** E1
Westfields Rd ACT W3.......................**86** B4
Westfield St WOOL/PLUM SE18.........**107** D4
Westfield Wy WCHPL E1.....................**91** E2
West Gdns WAP E1W........................**102** B3
Westgate St HACK E8.........................**78** B5
Westgate Ter WBPTN SW10..............**114** B1
West Gv GNWCH SE10.....................**122** C4
Westgrove La GNWCH SE10..............**122** C4
West Halkin St KTBR SW1X................**42** A2
West Hallowes ELTH/MOT SE9..........**161** D1
West Hall Rd RCH/KEW TW9.............**110** B4
West Ham La SRTFD E15....................**81** D4
West Hampstead Ms
   KIL/WHAMP NW6..........................**72** B3
West Harding St
   FLST/FETLN * EC4A........................**22** B4
Westhay Gdns
   MORT/ESHN SW14........................**128** B3
West Heath Av GLDGN NW11.............**54** A3
West Heath Cl HAMP NW3..................**54** A5
West Heath Dr GLDGN NW11.............**54** A3
West Heath Gdns HAMP NW3.............**54** A4
West Heath Rd HAMP NW3.................**54** A4
West Hl HGT N6.................................**56** A3
   PUT/ROE SW15............................**131** D5
Westhill Pk HGT N6............................**55** F4
West Hill Rd WAND/EARL SW18.........**131** F4
Westhorne Av ELTH/MOT SE9............**142** C4
Westhorpe Rd PUT/ROE SW15..........**130** C1
West House Cl WIM/MER SW19..........**149** E1
Westhurst Dr CHST BR7...................**162** B5
West India Av POP/IOD E14...............**104** A2
West India Dock Rd POP/IOD E14......**91** F5
Westland Pl FSBYE EC1V....................**12** A1
Westlands Ter BAL SW12.................**134** C4
West La BERM/RHTH SE16................**102** B3
Westleigh Av PUT/ROE SW15............**130** C3
West Lodge Av ACT W3......................**98** A3
West Lodge Ct ACT * W3....................**98** A2
Westmead PUT/ROE SW15................**130** B5
West Ms PIM SW1V............................**43** D5
Westminster Br WEST SW1P..............**45** D1
Westminster Bridge Rd
   STHWK SE1...................................**45** E1
Westminster Gdns BARK IG11............**97** E1
Westmoor St CHARL SE7..................**107** D5
Westmoreland Av WELL DA16............**145** E1
Westmoreland Pl PIM * SW1V............**116** B1
Westmoreland Rd BARN SW13..........**111** F4
   WALW SE17...................................**119** D2
Westmoreland St CAVSQ/HST W1G.....**18** B3
Westmoreland Ter PIM SW1V............**116** B1
Westmorland Cl MNPK E12................**65** D4

Westmorland Rd *LEY* E10 ....62 A1
Westmount Rd *ELTH/MOT* SE9 ..125 F5
Weston Pk *CEND/HSY/T* N8 ....57 E1
Weston Ri *FSBYW* WC1X 9 F3
Weston Rd *CHSWK* W4 ....98 C4
Weston St *STHWK* SE1 ....48 B1
Westover HI *HAMP* NW3 ....54 A4
Westover Rd *WAND/EARL* SW18 ..132 C5
West Pk *ELTH/MOT* SE9 ....161 E2
West Park Av *RCH/KEW* TW9 ....110 A4
West Park Rd *RCH/KEW* TW9 ....110 A4
West Parkside *GNWCH* SE10 ....105 E3
West PI *WIM/MER* SW19 ....148 C5
Westport Rd *PLSTW* E13 ....94 B3
Westport St *WCHPL* E1 ....91 D5
West Poultry Av *FARR* EC1M 22 C3
West Quarters *SHB* W12 ....88 A5
West Ri *BAY/PAD* * W2 ....29 D1
West Rd *CHEL* SW3 ....115 F1
   CLAP SW4 ....135 D3
   SRTFD E15 ....81 F5
West Rw *NKENS* W10 ....89 E3
Westrow Dr *BARK* IG11 ....85 F3
Westrow Gdns *GDMY/SEVK* IG3 ....67 F3
West Side Common
   WIM/MER SW19 ....148 C5
West Smithfield *STBT* EC1A 22 C3
West Sq *LBTH* SE11 ....46 C3
West St *BETH* E2 ....90 B1
   WAN E11 ....63 E5
West Temple Sheen
   MORT/ESHN SW14 ....128 B3
West Tenter St *WCHPL* E1 ....25 F5
West Ter *BFN/LL* * DA15 ....163 E1
Westview CI *NKENS* W10 ....88 C5
   WLSDN NW10 ....69 F2
Westville Rd *SHB* W12 ....100 A3
West Warwick PI *PIM* * SW1V 43 E1
Westway *NTGHL* W11 ....89 F4
   SHB W12 ....99 F1
West Wy *WLSDN* NW10 ....69 D1
Westwick Gdns *HMSMTH* W6 ....101 D3
Westwood Gdns *BARN* SW13 ....129 F1
Westwood Hl *SYD* SE26 ....156 A5
Westwood Pk *FSTH* SE23 ....138 B5
Westwood PI *SYD* * SE26 ....156 A5
Westwood Rd *BARN* SW13 ....129 F1
   CAN/RD E16 ....106 B2
   GDMY/SEVK IG3 ....67 F3
Wetherby Gdns *ECT* SW5 ....39 E5
Wetherby Ms *ECT* SW5 ....114 B1
Wetherby PI *ECT* SW5 ....39 E5
Wetherden St *WALTH* E17 ....61 F2
Wetherell Rd *HOM* E9 ....79 D5
Wexford St *BAL* SW12 ....133 F5
Weybourne St *WAND/EARL* SW18 ..150 C2
Weybridge Ct *STHWK* * SE1 ....120 B1
Weydown CI *WIM/MER* SW19 ....149 E1
Weyhill Rd *WCHPL* * E1 ....90 A5
Weyman Rd *BKHTH/KID* SE3 ....124 C4
Weymouth CI *EHAM* E6 ....96 B5
Weymouth Ms *CAVSQ/HST* W1G 18 C2
Weymouth St *CAVSQ/HST* W1G 18 B2
Weymouth Ter *BETH* E2 ....13 F1
Weymouth VIs *HOLWY* * N7 ....57 F4
Whadcoat St *FSBYPK* N4 ....58 A4
Whales Yd *SRTFD* * E15 ....81 E4
Wharfdale Rd *IS* N1 ....9 D1
Wharfedale St *WBPTN* SW10 ....114 B1
Wharf PI *BETH* E2 ....78 A5
Wharf Rd *IS* N1 ....11 E2
   SRTFD E15 ....81 D5

Wharfside Rd *CAN/RD* E16 ....93 E5
Wharf St *CAN/RD* E16 ....93 E4
Wharton CI *WLSDN* NW10 ....69 E3
Wharton Cottages *FSBYW* * WC1X 9 F4
Wharton St *FSBYW* WC1X 9 F4
Whateley Rd *EDUL* SE22 ....137 F3
Whatman Rd *FSTH* SE23 ....139 D5
Wheastone Rd *NKENS* * W10 ....89 E4
Wheatlands Rd *TOOT* SW17 ....152 A3
Wheatley St *CAVSQ/HST* W1G 18 B3
Wheat Sheaf La *FUL/PGN* SW6 .....112 C3
   VX/NE SW8 ....117 E3
Wheatsheaf Ter *FUL/PGN* * SW6 ...113 F3
Wheeler Gdns *IS* N1 ....75 E5
Wheeler La *WCHPL* E1 ....25 E2
Wheelers Cross *BARK* IG11 ....97 D1
Wheelwright St *HOLWY* N7 ....75 F4
Wheler St *WCHPL* E1 ....25 E1
Whellock Rd *CHSWK* W4 ....99 E4
Whetstone Pk *LINN* WC2A 21 E4
Whetstone Rd *BKHTH/KID* SE3 .....124 C5
Whewell Rd *ARCH* N19 ....57 E4
Whichcote St *STHWK* * SE1 ....34 A4
Whidborne CI *DEPT* SE8 ....122 A5
Whidborne St *STPAN* WC1H 9 D4
Whinchat Rd *THMD* SE28 ....109 D4
Whinfell CI *STRHM/NOR* SW16 .....153 D5
Whinyates Rd *ELTH/MOT* SE9 ......143 E1
Whiskin St *CLKNW* EC1R 10 C4
Whistlers Av *BTSEA* * SW11 ....115 D3
Whistler St *HBRY* N5 ....76 B1
Whistler Wk *WBPTN* * SW10 ....114 C3
Whiston Rd *BETH* E2 ....13 E1
Whitbread Rd *BROCKY* SE4 ....139 E2
Whitburn Rd *LEW* SE13 ....140 B3
Whitby Av *WLSDN* NW10 ....86 B2
Whitby Rd *WOOL/PLUM* SE18 ....107 F5
Whitby St *WCHPL* E1 ....13 E1
Whitcher CI *NWCR* SE14 ....121 E2
Whitcher PI *CAMTN* NW1 ....74 C3
Whitchurch Rd *NKENS* W10 ....101 D1
Whitcomb St *SOHO/SHAV* W1D 32 A1
Whitear Wk *SRTFD* E15 ....81 D3
Whitebeam CI *BRXN/ST* * SW9 .....117 E3
White Bear PI *HAMP* * NW3 ....73 D1
White Bear Yd *CLKNW* * EC1R 22 A1
Whitechapel High St *WCHPL* E1 ......25 F4
Whitechapel Rd *WCHPL* E1 ....90 A5
White Church La *WCHPL* E1 ....90 A5
White City CI *SHB* W12 ....100 C1
White City Rd *SHB* W12 ....100 B1
White Conduit St *IS* N1 ....10 B1
Whitecross St *STLK* EC1Y 11 F5
Whitefield Av *CRICK* NW2 ....52 C2
Whitefield CI *WAND/EARL* SW18 ...131 E4
Whitefoot La *CAT* SE6 ....159 D4
Whitefoot Ter *BMLY* BR1 ....159 F3
Whitefriars St *EMB* EC4Y 22 B5
Whitehall *WHALL* SW1A 32 C4
Whitehall Ct *WHALL* SW1A 32 C4
Whitehall Gdns *ACT* W3 ....98 A2
   CHSWK W4 ....110 B2
   WHALL SW1A 32 C4
Whitehall Pk *ARCH* N19 ....56 C3
Whitehall Park Rd *CHSWK* W4 ....110 B2
Whitehall PI *WHALL* SW1A 32 C4
White Hart La *BARN* SW13 ....111 E5
White Hart Rd
   WOOL/PLUM SE18 ....109 E5
White Hart St *LBTH* SE11 ....118 A4
White Hart Yd *STHWK* SE1 ....36 A4
Whitehaven St *STJWD* NW8 ....16 C1

Whitehead Cl *WAND/EARL* SW18........**132** C5
Whiteheads Gv *CHEL* SW3..................**41** D5
   CHEL SW3.................................**115** E1
White Horse La *WCHPL* E1.................**91** D3
White Horse Rd *EHAM* E6....................**95** F2
Whitehorse Rd *WCHPL* E1...................**91** E4
White Horse St *MYFR/PICC* W1J **31** D4
White Kennett St *WCHPL* E1..............**25** D4
Whitelegg Rd *PLSTW* E13...................**93** F1
Whiteley Rd *NRWD* SE19...................**155** D5
White Lion Ct *BANK* EC3V..................**24** C5
   PECK * SE15................................**120** C2
White Lion Hl *BLKFR* EC4V.................**35** D1
White Lion St *IS* N1............................**10** A2
White Lodge Cl *EFNCH* N2..................**55** D1
White Lyon Ct *BARB* EC2Y..................**23** E2
White Oak Gdns *BFN/LL* DA15........**145** F5
White Post La *HOM* E9........................**79** F4
White Post St *PECK* SE15.................**120** C4
White Rd *SRTFD* E15...........................**81** E4
Whites Av *GNTH/NBYPK* IG2..............**67** E3
White's Grounds *STHWK* SE1..............**37** D5
Whites Grounds Est *STHWK* SE1.........**37** D5
White's Rw *WCHPL* E1.........................**25** E3
White's Sq *CLAP* SW4.......................**135** D2
Whitestone La *HAMP* NW3...................**54** C5
Whitestone Wk *HAMP* NW3..................**54** C5
Whitethorn St *BOW* E3.........................**92** A3
Whitfield Pl *FITZ* W1T..........................**19** E1
Whitfield Rd *EHAM* E6..........................**82** C4
   GNWCH SE10............................**123** D4
Whitfield St *FITZ* W1T..........................**19** F2
Whitgift St *LBTH* SE11..........................**45** E4
Whitings Wy *EHAM* E6..........................**96** A4
Whitlock Dr *WIM/MER* SW19.............**131** E5
Whitman Rd *BOW* E3............................**91** E3
Whitmore Est *IS* N1..............................**77** E5
Whitmore Gdns *WLSDN* NW10.............**88** C2
Whitmore Rd *IS* N1...............................**77** E5
Whitnell Wy *PUT/ROE* * SW15..........**130** C3
Whitney Rd *LEY* E10.............................**62** A2
Whittaker Rd *EHAM* E6.........................**82** C4
Whittaker St *BGVA* SW1W....................**42** A5
Whitta Rd *MNPK* E12............................**83** D1
Whittell Gdns *SYD* SE26...................**156** C3
Whittingstall Rd *FUL/PGN* SW6........**113** F4
Whittington Av *BANK* EC3V..................**24** C5
Whittle Cl *WALTH* E17...........................**61** E1
Whittlesey St *STHWK* SE1....................**34** B4
Whitwell Rd *PLSTW* E13........................**94** A2
Whitworth Rd
   WOOL/PLUM SE18.....................**126** A3
Whitworth St *GNWCH* SE10...............**123** E1
Whorlton Rd *PECK* SE15.....................**138** A1
Whyteville Rd *FSTGT* E7........................**82** B3
Wickersley Rd *BTSEA* SW11..............**116** A5
Wickers Oake *NRWD* * SE19.............**155** F4
Wicker St *WCHPL* * E1..........................**90** A5
Wickford St *WCHPL* E1..........................**90** C3
Wickham Gdns *BROCKY* SE4.............**139** F1
Wickham Rd *BROCKY* SE4..................**139** F1
Wickham St *LBTH* SE11.......................**117** F1
   WELL DA16.................................**127** E5
Wick La *BOW* E3....................................**80** A5
Wickliffe Gdns *WBLY* HA9....................**50** A4
Wicklow St *FSBYW* WC1X........................**9** E3
Wick Rd *HOM* E9...................................**79** D3
Wicks Cl *LEE/GVPK* SE12..................**161** D4
Wickwood St *CMBW* SE5....................**118** B5
Widdenham Rd *HOLWY* N7....................**75** F1
Widdin St *SRTFD* E15............................**81** E4
Widecombe Rd *ELTH/MOT* SE9.........**161** D4

Widegate St *WCHPL* E1........................**25** D3
Widgeon Cl *CAN/RD* E16.......................**94** B5
Widley Rd *MV/WKIL* W9...........................**2** B4
Wigginton Av *WBLY* HA9........................**68** A3
Wigmore Pl *CAVSQ/HST* * W1G..........**18** C4
Wigmore St *MBLAR* W1H.......................**18** B4
Wigram Rd *WAN* E11...............................**64** C1
Wigston Rd *PLSTW* E13.........................**94** B3
Wigton Pl *LBTH* SE11..........................**118** A1
Wilberforce Rd *FSBYPK* N4...................**58** B4
Wilbraham Pl *KTBR* SW1X.....................**41** E5
Wilby Ms *NTGHL* W11...........................**101** F1
Wilcox Cl *VX/NE* SW8..........................**117** E3
Wilcox Rd *VX/NE* SW8.........................**117** E3
Wild Ct *HOL/ALD* WC2B.........................**21** E4
Wildcroft Rd *PUT/ROE* SW15.............**130** C5
Wilde Cl *HACK* E8...................................**78** A5
Wilderton Rd *STNW/STAM* N16.............**59** E2
Wildfell Rd *CAT* SE6.............................**140** B5
Wild Goose Dr *PECK* SE15.................**120** C4
Wild Hatch *GLDGN* NW11........................**54** A1
Wild's Rents *STHWK* SE1.......................**48** C3
Wild St *HOL/ALD* WC2B...........................**21** D5
Wildwood Cl *LEE/GVPK* SE12............**141** F5
Wildwood Gv *GLDGN* NW11....................**54** C3
Wildwood Ri *GLDGN* NW11.....................**54** C3
Wildwood Rd *GLDGN* NW11....................**54** C2
Wilfred St *WESTW* SW1E........................**43** E2
Wilfrid Gdns *ACT* W3.............................**86** C4
Wilkes St *WCHPL* E1..............................**25** F2
Wilkinson Rd *CAN/RD* E16.....................**94** C5
Wilkinson St *VX/NE* SW8......................**117** F3
Wilkinson Wy *CHSWK* W4.......................**99** D3
Wilkin St *LTTN* NW5................................**74** A3
Wilkin Street Ms *KTTN* * NW5................**74** B3
Wilks Pl *IS* N1..**13** D2
Willan Wall *CAN/RD* E16......................**105** F1
Willard St *VX/NE* SW8.........................**134** B1
Willcott Rd *ACT* W3................................**98** B2
Will Crooks Gdns *ELTH/MOT* SE9......**143** D2
Willenhall Rd *WOOL/PLUM* SE18.......**126** B1
Willerfield Rd *WLSDN* NW10..................**86** C2
Willersley Av *BFN/LL* DA15.................**163** F1
Willersley Cl *BFN/LL* DA15..................**163** F1
Willesden La *KIL/WHAMP* NW6..............**71** D4
Willes Rd *KTTN* * NW5............................**74** B3
William Barefoot Dr
   ELTH/MOT SE9.........................**162** A4
William Cl *LEW* SE13...........................**140** C1
William Ellis Wy
   BERM/RHTH * SE16..................**102** A4
William Gdns *PUT/ROE* SW15............**130** B3
William Guy Gdns *BOW* E3....................**92** B2
William IV St *CHCR* WC2N......................**32** C2
William Margrie Cl *PECK* * SE15.........**120** A5
William Ms *KTBR* SW1X.........................**41** E1
William Morley Cl *EHAM* E6...................**83** D5
William Morris Wy *FUL/PGN* SW6......**132** C1
William Rd *CAMTN* NW1...........................**7** E4
William's Buildings *BETH* * E2...............**90** C3
Williams Cl *CEND/HSY/T* * N8...............**57** D1
   FUL/PGN SW6..........................**113** E3
Williams La *MORT/ESHN* SW14..........**128** C1
Williamson Cl *GNWCH* SE10...............**123** F1
Williamson Rd *FSBYPK* N4.....................**58** B1
Williamson St *HOLWY* * N7.....................**75** E1
William Sq *BERM/RHTH* SE16.............**103** E2
William St *BARK* IG11.............................**84** C4
   KTBR SW1X...............................**41** F1
   LEY E10.......................................**62** B1
Willingham Cl *KTTN* NW5.......................**74** C2
Willingham Ter *KTTN* * NW5...................**74** C2
Willington Rd *BRXN/ST* SW9..............**135** E1

Willis Rd *SRTFD* E15.....................**93** F1
Willis St *POP/IOD* E14..................**92** B5
Willoughby Rd *HAMP* NW3............**73** D1
Willoughby Wy *CHARL* SE7...........**106** B5
Willow Av *BARN* SW13..................**111** F5
Willow Bridge Rd *IS* * N1...............**76** C3
Willowbrook Est *PECK* * SE15........**119** F3
Willowbrook Rd *PECK* SE15...........**119** F2
Willowdene *HGT* * N6.....................**55** F2
Willow La *WOOL/PLUM* SE18.........**107** F5
Willow Pl *WEST* SW1P....................**43** F4
Willow Rd *HAMP* NW3....................**73** D1
Willows Ter *WLSDN* * NW10...........**87** F1
Willow St *SDTCH* EC2A..................**12** C5
Willow Tree Cl *HOM* E9..................**79** E5
   WAND/EARL SW18...............**150** B1
Willow V *SHB* W12.........................**100** A2
Willow Wk *STHWK* SE1...................**49** D4
Willow Wy *NTGHL* W11....................**101** D1
   SYD SE26.................................**156** B3
Willshaw St *NWCR* SE14................**122** A4
Wilman Gv *HACK* E8.......................**78** A4
Wilmer Gdns *IS* N1.........................**77** E5
Wilmer Lea Cl *SRTFD* E15..............**80** C3
Wilmer Pl *STNW/STAM* N16............**59** F4
Wilmington Av *CHSWK* W4.............**111** D3
Wilmington Gdns *BARK* IG11..........**85** D4
Wilmington Sq *FSBYW* WC1X..........**10** A1
Wilmington St *FSBYW* WC1X...........**10** A1
Wilmot Cl *PECK* * SE15..................**120** F3
Wilmot Pl *CAMTN* NW1...................**74** C4
Wilmot Rd *LEY* E10.........................**62** B4
Wilmot St *BETH* E2.........................**90** A3
Wilmount St *WOOL/PLUM* SE18......**108** B5
Wilna Rd *WAND/EARL* SW18...........**132** C5
Wilsham St *NTGHL* W11...................**101** D2
Wilson Gv *BERM/RHTH* SE16..........**102** B3
Wilson Rd *CMBW* SE5.....................**119** D4
   IL IG1......................................**65** F2
   PLSTW E13.............................**95** D2
Wilson's Pl *POP/IOD* E14................**91** F1
Wilson's Rd *HMSMTH* W6...............**113** D1
Wilson St *SDTCH* EC2A...................**24** B3
Wilson Wk *HMSMTH* * W6................**99** F5
Wilton Av *CHSWK* W4......................**111** E1
Wilton Crs *KTBR* SW1X....................**42** A1
Wilton Est *HACK* * E8......................**78** A3
Wilton Ms *HACK* * E8......................**78** B3
   KTBR SW1X.............................**42** B2
Wilton Pl *KTBR* SW1X......................**30** A3
Wilton Rd *PIM* SW1V........................**43** E3
Wilton Rw *KTBR* SW1X.....................**42** A1
Wilton Sq *IS* N1...............................**77** D5
Wilton St *KTBR* SW1X......................**42** C2
Wilton Ter *KTBR* SW1X.....................**42** A2
Wilton Vls *IS* N1...............................**77** D5
Wilton Wy *HACK* E8..........................**78** A3
Wiltshire Cl *CHEL* SW3....................**41** D5
Wiltshire Gdns *FSBYPK* N4..............**58** C1
Wiltshire Rd *BRXN/ST* SW9.............**136** A1
Wiltshire Rw *IS* N1...........................**77** D5
Wimbart Rd *BRXS/STRHM* * SW2.....**135** F5
Wimbledon Park Rd
   WIM/MER SW19......................**149** E3
Wimbledon Park Side
   WIM/MER SW19......................**149** D2
Wimbledon Rd *TOOT* SW17.............**150** C4
Wimbolt St *BETH* E2.........................**90** A2
Wimborne Cl *LEE/GVPK* SE12..........**141** D3
Wimbourne St *IS* N1.........................**12** A1
Wimpole Ms *CAVSQ/HST* W1G.........**18** C2
Wimpole St *CAVSQ/HST* W1G...........**18** C3
Winans Wk *BRXN/ST* SW9................**118** A5

Wincanton Rd *WAND/EARL* SW18....**131** F5
Winchcomb Gdns *ELTH/MOT* SE9....**143** D1
Winchelsea Cl *PUT/ROE* SW15........**131** D3
Winchelsea Rd *WLSDN* NW10..........**69** D5
Winchendon Rd *FUL/PGN* SW6........**113** F3
Winchester Av *KIL/WHAMP* NW6......**71** E5
Winchester Cl *LBTH* * SE11.............**47** D5
Winchester Pl *HACK* E8....................**77** F2
   HGT N6....................................**56** B3
Winchester Rd *HAMP* NW3...............**73** D4
   HGT N6....................................**56** B3
   IL IG1......................................**67** D5
Winchester Sq *STHWK* SE1...............**36** A3
Winchester St *ACT* W3.....................**98** C2
   PIM SW1V................................**116** B1
Winchester Wk *STHWK* SE1..............**36** A3
Winchfield Rd *SYD* SE26..................**157** E5
Wincott St *LBTH* SE11......................**46** B4
Wincrofts Dr *ELTH/MOT* SE9...........**145** D2
Windermere Av *KIL/WHAMP* NW6.....**71** E5
Windermere Rd *ARCH* * N19.............**56** C4
   PUT/ROE SW15.......................**147** E4
Winders Rd *BTSEA* * SW11...............**115** E5
Windfield Cl *SYD* SE26.....................**157** D4
Windlass Pl *DEPT* SE8......................**103** E5
Windlesham Gv
   WIM/MER SW19......................**149** D1
Windley Cl *FSTH* SE23.....................**156** C2
Windmill Cl *BERM/RHTH* * SE16......**102** A5
   LEW SE13................................**122** C3
Windmill Dr *CLAP* SW4....................**134** B3
Windmill Hl *HAMP* * NW3..................**54** C5
Windmill La *SRTFD* E15...................**81** D3
Windmill Pas *CHSWK* * W4...............**99** E5
Windmill Rd *CHSWK* W4...................**99** E5
   WAND/EARL SW18...................**133** D4
   WIM/MER SW19.......................**148** B5
Windmill Rw *LBTH* * SE11................**118** A1
Windmill St *FITZ* W1T.......................**20** A3
Windmill Wk *STHWK* * SE1................**34** B4
Windrose Cl *BERM/RHTH* SE16........**103** D3
Windrush Cl *BTSEA* * SW11..............**133** D2
   CHSWK * W4...........................**110** C3
Windrush La *FSTH* SE23...................**157** D3
Windrush Rd *WLSDN* NW10..............**69** D5
Windsor Cl *CHST* BR7.......................**162** B5
   WNWD SE27............................**154** C4
Windsor Crs *WBLY* HA9....................**50** A5
Windsor Gdns *MV/WKIL* * W9............**14** A1
Windsor Gv *WNWD* SE27...................**154** C4
Windsor Ms *CAT* SE6.......................**158** C1
Windsor Rd *CRICK* NW2...................**70** B3
   FSTGT E7................................**82** B2
   HOLWY N7...............................**57** E5
   IL IG1......................................**84** C1
   LEY E10...................................**62** B4
   WAN E11..................................**64** A3
Windsor St *IS* N1..............................**76** B5
Windsor Ter *IS* N1.............................**11** F3
Windsor Wk *CMBW* SE5....................**119** D5
Windsor Wy *HMSMTH* W6.................**101** D5
Windspoint Dr *PECK* * SE15.............**120** A2
Windus Rd *STNW/STAM* N16............**59** F3
Windy Ridge Cl *WIM/MER* SW19.......**149** D5
Wine Cl *WAP* E1W.............................**102** C1
Winforton St *GNWCH* SE10..............**122** C4
Winfrith Rd *WAND/EARL* SW18.........**132** C5
Wingate Rd *HMSMTH* W6..................**100** B4
   IL IG1......................................**84** B2
Wingfield Ms *PECK* * SE15..............**138** A1
Wingfield Rd *SRTFD* E15..................**81** E2
Wingfield St *PECK* SE15...................**138** A1
Wingford Rd *CLAP* SW4....................**135** E4

Wingmore Rd *HNHL* SE24 ....**136** C1
Wingrave Rd *HMSMTH* W6 ....**112** C2
Wingrove Rd *CAT* SE6 ....**159** E2
Winifred St *CAN/RD* E16 ....**107** F2
Winkley St *BETH* E2 ....**90** B1
Winkworth Cottages *WCHPL* * E1 ......**90** C3
Winlaton Rd *BMLY* BR1 ....**159** D4
Winn Common Rd
  WOOL/PLUM SE18 ....**127** E2
Winnett St *SOHO/SHAV* W1D **32** A1
Winnington Cl *EFNCH* N2 ....**55** D1
Winnington Rd *EFNCH* N2 ....**55** D1
Winn Rd *LEE/GVPK* SE12 ....**160** A1
Winscombe St *KTTN* NW5 ....**56** B5
Winsford Rd *CAT* SE6 ....**157** F3
Winsham Gv *BTSEA* SW11 ....**134** A3
Winslade Rd *BRXS/STRHM* SW2 ....**135** E3
Winsland Ms *BAY/PAD* W2 ....**16** A4
Winsland St *BAY/PAD* W2 ....**16** A4
Winsley St *GTPST* W1W **19** E4
Winslow Cl *WLSDN* NW10 ....**51** E5
Winslow Rd *HMSMTH* W6 ....**112** C2
Winsor Ter *EHAM* E6 ....**96** A4
Winstanley Rd *BTSEA* SW11 ....**133** D1
Winston Av *CDALE/KGS* NW9 ....**51** E2
Winston Rd *STNW/STAM* N16 ....**77** D1
Winston Wy *IL* IG1 ....**66** B5
Winter Av *EHAM* E6 ....**83** E5
Winterbourne Rd *FSTH* SE23 ....**157** F1
Winterbrook Rd *HNHL* SE24 ....**136** C4
Winterfold Cl *WIM/MER* SW19 ....**149** E2
Winterstoke Rd *FSTH* SE23 ....**157** F1
Winterton Pl *WBPTN* SW10 ....**114** C2
Winterwell Rd *BRXS/STRHM* SW2 ....**135** E3
Winthorpe Rd *PUT/ROE* SW15 ....**131** E2
Winthrop St *WCHPL* * E1 ....**90** B4
Winton Wy *STRHM/NOR* SW16 ....**154** A5
Wiseman Rd *LEY* * E10 ....**62** A4
Wise Rd *SRTFD* E15 ....**80** C5
Wiseton Rd *TOOT* SW17 ....**151** E1
Wishart Rd *BKHTH/KID* SE3 ....**125** D4
Wisley Rd *BTSEA* SW11 ....**133** F3
Wisteria Cl *IL* IG1 ....**84** B2
Wisteria Rd *LEW* SE13 ....**141** D2
Witan St *BETH* E2 ....**90** B2
Witherington Rd *HBRY* * N5 ....**76** A2
Witherston Wy *ELTH/MOT* SE9 ....**162** A2
Witley Rd *ARCH* N19 ....**56** C4
Witney Pth *FSTH* * SE23 ....**157** D3
Wittersham Rd *BMLY* BR1 ....**159** F5
Wivenhoe Cl *PECK* SE15 ....**138** A1
Wix's La *BTSEA* SW11 ....**134** B2
Woburn Pl *STPAN* WC1H **8** B5
Woburn Sq *STPAN* WC1H **20** B1
Woburn Wk *STPAN* WC1H **8** B4
Wodehouse Av *PECK* SE15 ....**119** F4
Woking Cl *PUT/ROE* SW15 ....**129** F2
Wolfe Crs *CHARL* SE7 ....**125** D1
Wolferton Rd *MNPK* E12 ....**83** F1
Wolfington Rd *WNWD* SE27 ....**154** B4
Wolfram Cl *LEW* SE13 ....**141** E3
Wolftencroft Cl *BTSEA* SW11 ....**133** E1
Wollaston Cl *WALW* SE17 ....**47** D5
Wolseley Av *WAND/EARL* SW18 ....**150** A2
Wolseley Gdns *CHSWK* W4 ....**110** B2
Wolseley Rd *CEND/HSY/T* N8 ....**57** D1
  CHSWK W4 ....**98** C5
  FSTGT E7 ....**82** B4
Wolseley St *STHWK* SE1 ....**49** F1
Wolsey Av *EHAM* E6 ....**96** A2
Wolsey Ct *ELTH/MOT* * SE9 ....**143** F4
Wolsey Ms *KTTN* NW5 ....**74** C3
Wolsey Rd *IS* N1 ....**77** D2

Wolsey St *WCHPL* E1 ....**90** C4
Wolverley St *BETH* * E2 ....**90** B2
Wolverton Gdns *HMSMTH* W6 ....**101** D5
Womersley Rd *CEND/HSY/T* N8 ....**57** F1
Wontner Cl *IS* * N1 ....**76** C4
Wontner Rd *BAL* SW12 ....**151** F2
Woodbank Rd *BMLY* BR1 ....**159** F5
Woodberry Down *FSBYPK* N4 ....**58** C3
Woodberry Gv *FSBYPK* N4 ....**58** C2
Woodbine Pl *WAN* E11 ....**64** A1
Woodbine Rd *BFN/LL* DA15 ....**163** E1
Woodbine Ter *HOM* E9 ....**78** C3
Woodborough Rd
  PUT/ROE SW15 ....**130** B2
Woodbourne Av
  STRHM/NOR SW16 ....**153** D3
Woodbridge Cl *HOLWY* N7 ....**57** F4
Woodbridge Rd *BARK* IG11 ....**85** F2
Woodbridge St *CLKNW* EC1R **10** C5
Woodbury Rd *TOOT* SW17 ....**151** E5
Woodchester Sq *BAY/PAD* W2 ....**14** C2
Woodchurch Cl *BFN/LL* DA15 ....**163** D1
Woodchurch Rd *KIL/WHAMP* NW6 ....**72** A2
Wood Cl *BETH* E2 ....**90** A3
  CDALE/KGS NW9 ....**51** D2
Woodcocks *CAN/RD* E16 ....**94** C4
Woodcombe Crs *FSTH* SE23 ....**156** C1
Woodcote Pl *WNWD* * SE27 ....**154** B5
Woodcote Rd *WAN* E11 ....**64** A2
Woodcroft *ELTH/MOT* SE9 ....**161** F3
Woodcroft Ms *DEPT* SE8 ....**103** E5
Wood Dene *PECK* * SE15 ....**120** B4
Wooden Bridge Ter *WNWD* * SE27 ....**154** B3
Wooder Gdns *FSTGT* E7 ....**81** F1
Woodfall Rd *FSBYPK* N4 ....**58** A3
Woodfall St *CHEL* SW3 ....**115** F1
Woodfarrs *CMBW* SE5 ....**137** D2
Wood Fld *HAMP* * NW3 ....**73** F2
Woodfield Av *STRHM/NOR* SW16 ....**153** D3
Woodfield Gv *STRHM/NOR* SW16 ....**153** D3
Woodfield Pl *MV/WKIL* W9 ....**89** F3
Woodfield Rd *MV/WKIL* W9 ....**89** F4
Woodford Rd *FSTGT* E7 ....**82** B1
Woodger Rd *SHB* W12 ....**100** C3
Woodget Cl *EHAM* E6 ....**95** E5
Woodhall Av *DUL* SE21 ....**155** F3
Woodhall Dr *DUL* SE21 ....**155** F3
Woodham Rd *CAT* SE6 ....**158** C3
Woodhatch Cl *EHAM* E6 ....**95** E4
Woodheyes Rd *WLSDN* NW10 ....**69** E3
Woodhill *CHARL* SE7 ....**107** E5
Woodhouse Gv *MNPK* E12 ....**83** E3
Woodhouse Rd *WAN* E11 ....**63** F5
Woodhurst Rd *ACT* W3 ....**98** C2
Woodington Cl *ELTH/MOT* SE9 ....**144** A4
Woodison St *BOW* E3 ....**91** E3
Woodland Cl *CDALE/KGS* NW9 ....**50** C1
Woodland Crs *GNWCH* SE10 ....**123** E2
Woodland Rd *NRWD* SE19 ....**155** E5
Woodlands Av *ACT* W3 ....**98** B2
  BFN/LL DA15 ....**163** E1
  WAN E11 ....**64** B3
Woodlands Gv *GNWCH* SE10 ....**123** E1
Woodlands Park Rd
  BKHTH/KID SE3 ....**123** E2
Woodlands Rd *BARN* SW13 ....**129** F1
  IL IG1 ....**66** C5
  WAN * E11 ....**63** G4
Woodlands St *LEW* SE13 ....**141** D5
The Woodlands *CMBW* * SE5 ....**118** B3
  LEW SE13 ....**141** D5
Woodland St *HACK* * E8 ....**77** F3
Woodlands Wy *PUT/ROE* SW15 ....**131** F3

Woodland Ter *CHARL* SE7.................**107** E5
Woodland Wk *HAMP* NW3....................**73** E2
Wood La *CDALE/KGS* NW9..................**51** D2
  HGT N6...................................**56** B1
  SHB W12.................................**88** C5
Woodlawn Cl *PUT/ROE* SW15..........**131** F3
Woodlawn Rd *FUL/PGN* SW6............**113** D3
Woodlea Rd *STNW/STAM* N16............**59** E5
Woodleigh Gdns
  STRHM/NOR SW16......................**153** E3
Woodmans Gv *WLSDN* NW10............**69** F2
Woodman Rd *CAN/RD* E16...............**108** A2
Woodmere *ELTH/MOT* SE9..............**143** F5
Woodmere Cl *BTSEA* SW11.............**134** A1
Woodnook Rd
  STRHM/NOR SW16......................**152** B5
Woodquest Av *HNHL* SE24.............**136** B3
Woodriffe Rd *WAN* E11..................**63** D2
Woodrow *WOOL/PLUM* SE18...........**107** E5
Woodrush Cl *NWCR* SE14...............**121** E3
Woodseer St *WCHPL* E1....................**25** F2
Woodsford Sq *WKENS* W14.............**101** E3
Woodside *WIM/MER* SW19..............**149** F5
Woodside Av *CHST* BR7.................**162** C5
Woodside Crs *BFN/LL* DA15............**163** E3
Woodside Pde *BFN/LL* * DA15..........**163** E3
Woodside Rd *BFN/LL* DA15..............**163** E3
  PLSTW E13..............................**94** C3
Woodspring Rd
  WIM/MER SW19.........................**149** E2
Wood's Rd *PECK* SE15...................**120** B4
Woodstock Av *GLDGN* NW11...........**53** E2
Woodstock Gv *SHB* W12..................**101** D3
Woodstock Ms *CAVSQ/HST* W1G.......**18** B3
Woodstock Rd *CHSWK* W4..............**99** E5
  FSBYPK N4.............................**58** A3
  FSTGT E7...............................**82** C4
  GLDGN NW11...........................**53** F2
Woodstock St *CAN/RD* E16..............**93** F5
  MYFR/PKLN W1K......................**18** C5
Woodstock Ter *POP/IOD* E14...........**104** B1
Wood St *BARB* EC2Y.......................**23** F3
  CAN/RD E16............................**106** B1
  CHSWK W4.............................**111** E1
Woodsyre *NRWD* SE19...................**155** F4
Wood Ter *CRICK* * NW2...................**51** F4
Woodthorpe Rd *PUT/ROE* SW15.......**130** B2
Wood V *EDUL* SE22.......................**156** B1
Woodvale Wy *CRICK* NW2................**53** D5
Woodview Cl *KUTN/CMB* KT2...........**147** D4
Woodville Cl *LEE/GVPK* SE12..........**142** A1
Woodville Rd *GLDGN* NW11.............**53** E2
  KIL/WHAMP * NW6....................**89** D1
  STNW/STAM N16......................**77** E2
  WAN E11................................**63** F3
Woodville St *CHARL* SE7................**107** E5
Woodwarde Rd *EDUL* SE22.............**137** E4
Woodwell St *WAND/EARL* SW18........**132** C3
Wood Whf *GNWCH* SE10.................**122** B2
Woodyard Cl *KTTN* NW5..................**74** A2
Woodyard La *DUL* SE21..................**137** E5
Woodyates Rd *LEE/GVPK* SE12........**142** A4
Woolacombe Rd *BKHTH/KID* SE3.......**124** C5
Woolands Rd *WAN* E11..................**63** E4
Wooler St *WALW* SE17...................**119** D1
Woolf Ms *STPAN* WC1H....................**8** C5
Woollaston Rd *FSBYPK* N4................**58** B1
Woolmead Av *CDALE/KGS* NW9........**52** A2
Woolmore St *POP/IOD* E14..............**104** C1
Woolneigh St *FUL/PGN* SW6............**132** B1

Woolridge Wy *HOM* * E9..................**78** C4
Woolstaplers Wy
  BERM/RHTH SE16......................**102** A4
Woolstone Rd *FSTH* SE23..............**157** E2
Woolwich Church St *CHARL* SE7.......**107** D5
Woolwich Common
  WOOL/PLUM SE18.....................**126** A2
Woolwich High St
  WOOL/PLUM SE18.....................**108** A4
Woolwich Manorway
  CAN/RD E16............................**108** B3
Woolwich Manor Wy
  CAN/RD E16............................**108** B2
  EHAM E6................................**95** F3
Woolwich New Rd
  WOOL/PLUM SE18.....................**126** A1
Woolwich Rd *CHARL* SE7...............**106** C5
  CHARL SE7............................**124** B1
Wooster Gdns *POP/IOD* E14............**93** D5
Wootton St *STHWK* SE1..................**34** B5
Worcester Cl *CRICK* NW2.................**52** A5
Worcester Dr *CHSWK* W4................**99** E4
Worcester Gdns *IL* IG1....................**65** E2
Worcester Ms *KIL/WHAMP* NW6........**72** B3
Worcester Rd *MNPK* E12.................**65** F5
  WIM/MER SW19........................**149** F5
Wordsworth Av *MNPK* E12..............**83** E4
Wordsworth Pl *HAMP* NW3..............**73** F2
Wordsworth Rd *STHWK* SE1.............**49** E5
  STNW/STAM N16.......................**77** E1
  WELL DA16.............................**127** E4
Worfield St *BTSEA* SW11................**115** E3
Worgan St *BERM/RHTH* SE16...........**103** D4
  LBTH SE11.............................**117** F1
Worland Rd *SRTFD* E15..................**81** E4
Worlds End Est *WBPTN* * SW10.........**115** D3
Worlds End Pas *WBPTN* * SW10........**115** D3
Worlidge St *HMSMTH* W6................**112** C1
Worlingham Rd *EDUL* SE22.............**137** F2
Wormholt Rd *SHB* W12...................**100** A2
Wormholt Ter *SHB* * W12................**100** A2
Wormwood St *LVPST* EC2M..............**24** C4
Wornington Rd *NKENS* W10.............**89** E4
Woronzow Rd *STJWD* NW8..............**73** D5
Worple St *MORT/ESHN* SW14..........**129** D1
Worship St *SDTCH* EC2A..................**24** B1
Worslade Rd *TOOT* SW17................**151** D4
Worsley Bridge Rd *CAT* SE6............**157** F5
Worsley Rd *WAN* E11......................**81** E1
Worsopp Dr *CLAP* SW4...................**134** C3
Worth Gv *WALW* * SE17..................**119** D1
Worthing Rd *SRTFD* E15.................**81** E5
Wortley Rd *EHAM* E6.......................**83** D4
Wotton Rd *CRICK* NW2...................**70** C1
Wouldham Rd *CAN/RD* E16.............**93** F5
Wragby Rd *WAN* * E11....................**63** E5
Wray Crs *FSBYPK* N4.....................**57** E4
Wrekin Rd *WOOL/PLUM* SE18.........**126** C3
Wren Av *CRICK* NW2.......................**70** C1
Wren Cl *CAN/RD* E16.......................**93** F5
Wren Ms *LEW* * SE13.....................**141** E2
Wren Rd *CMBW* SE5.......................**119** D4
Wren St *FSBYW* WC1X.......................**9** F5
Wrentham Av *WLSDN* NW10............**89** D1
Wrenthorpe Rd *BMLY* BR1..............**159** E4
Wrexham Rd *BOW* E3.......................**92** A1
Wricklemarsh Rd *BKHTH/KID* SE3....**124** B5
Wrigglesworth St *NWCR* SE14..........**121** D3
Wright Cl *LEW* SE13.......................**141** D2
Wrights La *KENS* * W8.....................**38** B2
  KENS W8...............................**38** C2
Wrights Pl *WLSDN* * NW10...............**68** C3
Wright's Rd *BOW* E3........................**91** F1

Wrotham Rd *CAMTN* * NW1......................**74** C4
Wrottesley Rd *WLSDN* NW10..................**88** C4
  WOOL/PLUM SE18.........................**126** C2
Wroughton Rd *BTSEA* SW11................**133** F4
Wroxton Rd *PECK* SE15........................**120** B5
Wulfstan St *SHB* W12..............................**87** F5
Wyatt Dr *BARN* SW13............................**112** B2
Wyatt Park Rd
  BRXS/STRHM SW2...........................**153** F2
Wyatt Rd *FSBYPK* N4..............................**58** C5
  FSTGT E7...**82** A3
Wybert St *CAMTN* NW1..............................**7** D5
Wyborne Wy *WLSDN* NW10....................**68** C4
Wycherley Cl *BKHTH/KID* SE3..........**123** F3
Wychcombe Studios *HAMP* * NW3....**73** F3
Wychwood End *HGT* N6...........................**56** C2
Wycliffe Cl *WELL* DA16............................**127** F4
Wycliffe Rd *BTSEA* SW11......................**116** A5
Wyclif St *FSBYE* EC1V..............................**10** C4
Wycombe Gdns *CRICK* NW2....................**53** F4
Wycombe Pl *WAND/EARL* * SW18....**132** C4
Wycombe Rd *ALP/SUD* HA0......................**68** A5
Wydeville Manor Rd
  LEE/GVPK SE12..................................**160** B4
Wye St *BTSEA* SW11..............................**133** D1
Wyfold Rd *FUL/PGN* SW6......................**113** E4
Wyke Rd *BOW* E3..**80** A4
Wyldes Cl *GLDGN* NW11..........................**54** C3
Wyld Wy *WBLY* HA9..................................**68** B3
Wyleu St *FSTH* SE23................................**139** E5
Wyllen Cl *WCHPL* E1..................................**90** C1
Wymering Rd *MV/WKIL* W9..........................**2** B4
Wymond St *PUT/ROE* SW15................**130** C1
Wynan Rd *POP/IOD* E14........................**122** B1
Wyncham Av *BFN/LL* DA15....................**163** E1
Wyndale Av *CDALE/KGS* NW9................**50** A1
Wyndcliff Rd *CHARL* SE7.......................**124** B2
Wyndham Crs *KTTN* NW5........................**56** C5
Wyndham Est *CMBW* SE5......................**118** C3
Wyndham Ms *MBLAR* W1H........................**17** E3
Wyndham Pl *MBLAR* W1H..........................**17** E3
Wyndham Rd *CMBW* SE5.......................**118** C3
  EHAM E6...**83** D2
Wyndham St *MBLAR* W1H..........................**17** E2
Wyneham Rd *HNHL* SE24......................**137** D3
Wynell Rd *FSTH* SE23............................**157** D3
Wynford Rd *IS* N1..**9** E1
Wynford Wy *ELTH/MOT* SE9................**161** F3
Wynne Rd *BRXN/ST* SW9......................**118** A5
Wynnstay Gdns *KENS* W8........................**38** B2
Wynter St *BTSEA* SW11.........................**132** C2
Wynton Pl *ACT* W3....................................**86** B5
Wynyard Ter *LBTH* * SE11......................**117** F1
Wynyatt St *FSBYE* EC1V..........................**10** C5
Wythburn Pl *MBLAR* W1H..........................**17** E5
Wythes Rd *CAN/RD* E16........................**107** D3
Wythfield Rd *ELTH/MOT* SE9................**143** F4
Wyvil Rd *VX/NE* SW8..............................**117** E3
Wyvis St *POP/IOD* E14............................**92** B4

WLSDN NW10..**69** E3
Yeldham Rd *HMSMTH* W6......................**113** D1
Yeldham Vls *HMSMTH* * W6..................**113** D1
Yelverton Rd *BTSEA* SW11....................**115** D5
Yeoman Cl *EHAM* E6................................**108** B1
Yeoman's Rw *CHEL* SW3..........................**41** D3
Yeoman St *BERM/RHTH* SE16..............**103** E5
Yeo St *BOW* E3..**92** B4
Yerbury Rd *ARCH* N19..............................**57** D5
Yewfield Rd *WLSDN* NW10......................**69** F4
Yew Gv *NW2*..**71** D1
Yew Tree Rd *SHB* W12..............................**99** F1
Yoakley Rd *STNW/STAM* N16..................**59** E4
Yoke Cl *HOLWY* N7....................................**75** E3
Yolande Gdns *ELTH/MOT* SE9..............**143** E3
Yonge Pk *HOLWY* N7................................**58** A5
York Av *BFN/LL* DA15..............................**163** E2
  MORT/ESHN SW14..........................**128** C3
York Br *CAMTN* NW1....................................**6** A5
York Buildings *CHCR* WC2N....................**33** D2
York Cl *CMBW* * SE5................................**118** C5
  EHAM E6...**95** F5
York Ga *CAMTN* NW1..................................**18** B1
York Gv *PECK* SE15................................**120** C4
York Hl *STRHM/NOR* SW16..................**154** B3
York House Pl *KENS* W8............................**26** C5
Yorkland Av *WELL* DA16........................**145** E3
York Ms *IL* IG1..**66** A4
  KTTN NW5...**74** B2
York Pde *CDALE/KGS* * NW9..................**52** A1
York Pl *BTSEA* SW11..............................**132** C1
  IL IG1...**66** A4
York Ri *KTTN* NW5....................................**56** B5
York Rd *ACT* W3..**86** C5
  BTSEA SW11..**132** C2
  FSTGT E7...**82** A3
  IL IG1...**66** A5
  LEY E10...**62** C5
  STHWK SE1..**33** F5
Yorkshire Cl *STNW/STAM* N16..............**59** E5
Yorkshire Grey Yd *HHOL* * WC1V..........**21** E3
Yorkshire Rd *POP/IOD* E14....................**91** E5
York Sq *POP/IOD* * E14............................**91** E5
York St *BARK* IG11....................................**84** B5
  MBLAR W1H..**17** F2
York Street Chambers *MHST* * W1U....**17** F2
York Ter East *CAMTN* NW1........................**18** B1
York Ter West *CAMTN* NW1........................**18** A1
Yorkton St *BETH* E2....................................**90** A1
York Wy *IS* N1..**9** D1
York Way Ct *IS* N1....................................**75** E5
York Way Est *HOLWY* N7..........................**75** E3
Young Rd *CAN/RD* E16..............................**94** C3
Young St *KENS* W8....................................**38** C1
Yoxley Ap *GNTH/NBYPK* IG2....................**66** C1
Yoxley Dr *GNTH/NBYPK* IG2....................**66** C1
Yukon Rd *BAL* SW12..............................**134** B5
Yuletide Cl *WLSDN* NW10........................**69** E3

Y

Yabsley St *POP/IOD* E14........................**104** C2
Yalding Rd *BERM/RHTH* SE16..............**102** A4
Yardley St *FSBYW* WC1X..........................**10** A4
Yarmouth Pl *MYFR/PICC* W1J................**30** C4
Yarrow Crs *EHAM* E6................................**95** E4
Yateley St *WOOL/PLUM* SE18..............**107** D4
Yeate St *IS* N1..**77** D4
Yeatman Rd *HGT* N6................................**55** F1
Yeats Cl *BKHTH/KID* * SE3....................**123** D5

Z

Zampa Rd *BERM/RHTH* SE16................**120** C1
Zander Ct *BETH* E2....................................**90** A2
Zangwill Rd *BKHTH/KID* SE3................**125** D4
Zealand Rd *BOW* E3..................................**91** E1
Zennor Rd *BAL* SW12..............................**152** C1
Zenoria St *EDUL* SE22............................**137** F2
Zetland St *POP/IOD* E14..........................**92** C4
Zoar St *STHWK* SE1..................................**35** E3
Zoffany St *ARCH* N19................................**57** D4

Abbey Business Centre
VX/NE SW8 .... 116 C4
Abbey Medical Centre
STJWD NW8 .... 72 B5
Abbey Park Industrial Estate
BARK IG11 .... 96 B1
Abbey Road Health Centre
SRTFD E15 .... 81 E5
**Abbey School for the
English Language**
STJWD NW8 .... 3 F2
Abbey Trading Estate
SYD SE26 .... 157 E5
Abbey Tutorial College
BAY/PAD W2 .... 14 B5
Abbey Wharf Industrial Estate
BARK IG11 .... 97 D2
ABC Cinema
CAT SE6 .... 158 B1
HAMP NW3 .... 73 E2
PUT/ROE SW15 .... 131 E1
STRHM/NOR SW16 .... 153 E1
Abercorn Place School
STJWD NW8 .... 3 F2
Aberdeen Wharf
WAP E1W 102 B2
Abney Park Cemetery
STNW/STAM N16 .... 59 E4
Acacia Business Centre
WAN E11 .... 63 E5
Acland Burghley School
KTTN NW5 .... 74 B1
Acton Business Centre
WLSDN NW10 .... 87 D3
Acton Central Industrial Estate
ACT W3 .... 98 B1
Acton Health Centre
ACT W3 .... 98 C2
Acton High School
ACT W3 .... 98 A3
Acton Hospital
ACT W3 .... 98 A3
Acton Lane Medical Centre
CHSWK W4 .... 99 D3
Acton Park Industrial Estate
ACT W3 .... 99 F2
CHSWK W4 .... 99 D3
Acton Superbowl
ACT W3 .... 86 A3
Acton Swimming Baths
ACT W3 .... 98 C2
Adams Bridge Business Centre
WBLY HA9 .... 68 B2
Adamsrill Primary School
SYD SE26 .... 157 E3
Addey & Stanhope School
NWCR SE14 .... 121 F4
Addison Primary School
WKENS W14 .... 101 D4
Adelphi Theatre
COVGDN WC2E 33 D2
Admiral Hyson Industrial Estate
BERM/RHTH SE16 .... 102 B5
Admiralty Arch
STJS SW1Y 32 B3
ADT Technology College
PUT/ROE SW15 .... 131 F3
**The Adult College of
Barking & Dagenham**
BARK IG11 .... 85 E3
Adult Education Centre
POP/IOD E14 .... 104 C4

Africa Centre
COVGDN WC2E 33 D1
Agora Shopping Centre
PECK SE15 .... 120 A5
Airedale Physiotherapy Clinic
CHSWK W4 .... 111 F1
AIU London
MHST W1U 18 B3
Aksaray Sports Club
STNW/STAM N16 .... 77 D1
Albany Centre & Theatre
DEPT SE8 .... 121 F3
Albemarle Independant College
BAY/PAD W2 .... 27 D1
Albemarle Primary School
WIM/MER SW19 .... 149 E2
Albert Memorial
SKENS SW7 .... 28 A5
Albery Theatre
CHCR WC2N 32 C1
Albion Health Centre
WCHPL E1 .... 90 B4
Albion Junior & Infant School
BERM/RHTH SE16 .... 102 C3
Albion Street Health Centre
BERM/RHTH SE16 .... 102 C3
The Alchemy Gallery
CLKNW EC1R 10 A5
Alderbrook Primary School
BAL SW12 .... 134 B5
**Aldersbrook County
Secondary School**
MNPK E12 .... 64 C3
Aldersbrook Primary School
WAN E11 .... 64 C3
Alderwood Primary School
ELTH/MOT SE9 .... 145 D4
Aldwych Theatre
HOL/ALD WC2B 21 E5
Alfred Salter Primary School
BERM/RHTH SE16 .... 103 D3
Allegery Clinic
CAVSQ/HST W1G 18 C4
Allen Edwards Primary School
CLAP SW4 .... 117 E4
**The All England Lawn Tennis &
Croquet Club**
WIM/MER SW19 .... 149 D3
Alleyns School
EDUL SE22 .... 137 E3
Allfarthing JMI School
WAND/EARL SW18 .... 132 C4
All Saints CE Primary School
BKHTH/KID SE3 .... 123 E5
CRICK NW2 .... 53 F5
FUL/PGN SW6 .... 113 E5
PUT/ROE SW15 .... 130 C1
All Souls CE Primary School
GTPST W1W 19 E3
Allum Medical Centre
WAN E11 .... 63 D2
Alma Primary School
BERM/RHTH SE16 .... 102 A5
Almeida Theatre
IS N1 .... 76 B4
Al Muntada Islamic School
FUL/PGN SW6 .... 113 F4
Alpine Business Centre
EHAM E6 .... 96 A4
Alscot Road Industrial Estate
STHWK SE1 .... 49 F4
Altmore Infant School
EHAM E6 .... 83 F4

The Alton School
PUT/ROE SW15 .... **129** F5

Ambler Primary School
FSBYPK N4 .... **58** B5

AMC Business Centre
WLSDN NW10 .... **86** B2

AMF Bowling
LEW SE13 .... **140** C1

Amherst Primary School
HACK E8 .... **78** A2

Ampthill Square Medical Centre
CAMTN NW1 .... **7** E2

Anchorage Point Industrial Estate
CHARL SE7 .... **106** C4

Anchor Retail Park
WCHPL E1 .... **90** C3

Andover Medical Centre
HOLWY N7 .... **57** F5

Andrew Sketchley Theatre
WCHPL E1 .... **90** A4

Angerstein Business Park
GNWCH SE10 .... **106** A5

Angerstein Works
BKHTH/KID SE3 .... **124** A2

Anglian Industrial Estate
BARK IG11 .... **97** F3

Annandale Primary School
GNWCH SE10 .... **123** F1

The Anna Scher Theatre
IS N1 .... **76** A5

Annemount School
EFNCH N2 .... **54** C1

Anson Primary School
CRICK NW2 .... **71** D2

Apex Industrial Estate
WLSDN NW10 .... **87** F3

Apollo Theatre
SOHO/SHAV W1D **32** A1

Apollo Victoria Theatre
PIM SW1V **43** E3

Apostolic Nuncio
WIM/MER SW19 .... **148** C3

Apsley House, The Wellington Museum
BAY/PAD W2 .... **30** A5

Aquarius Business Park
CRICK NW2 .... **52** A3

Aquarius Golf Club
EDUL SE22 .... **138** C3

Archbishop Michael Ramsey Technology College
CMBW SE5 .... **118** B3

Archbishop Sumners CE Primary School
LBTH SE11 .... **46** B5

Archbishop Tenison's School
VX/NE SW8 .... **117** F2

Arches Leisure Centre
GNWCH SE10 .... **123** D2

Archway Business Centre
ARCH N19 .... **57** D5

Arena Estate
FSBYPK N4 .... **58** B1

Argyle Primary School
STPAN WC1H **8** C3

Arklow Trading Estate
NWCR SE14 .... **121** E2

Armchair Theatre
LBTH SE11 .... **118** A2

Armourers & Braziers' Hall
LOTH EC2R **24** A3

Arndale Health Centre
WAND/EARL SW18 .... **132** A4

Arnhem Wharf Primary School
POP/IOD E14 .... **103** F4

Arnold House School
STJWD NW8 .... **4** A1

Arnot Abbey
FARR EC1M **22** C2

Arsenal FC (Highbury)
HBRY N5 .... **58** A5

Arts Centre
HAMP NW3 .... **72** B2

Arts Theatre
LSQ/SEVD WC2H **32** B1
PUT/ROE SW15 .... **131** D2

Ashbourne Independent Sixth Form College
KENS W8 .... **27** D5

Ashburnham Primary School
WBPTN SW10 .... **115** D3

Ashby Mill School
CLAP SW4 .... **135** E3

Ashleigh Commercial Estate
CHARL SE7 .... **106** C5

Ashmead Primary School
BROCKY SE4 .... **122** A5

Ashmole Primary School
VX/NE SW8 .... **117** F2

Ashmount Primary School
ARCH N19 .... **56** C2

Aspen House Secondary & Primary School
BRXS/STRHM SW2 .... **135** E5

Associated Newspapers
BERM/RHTH SE16 .... **103** D4

The Association of British Language Schools
WCHPL E1 .... **90** B4

Astor College
FITZ W1T **19** F2

Athelney Primary School
CAT SE6 .... **158** A3

Athena Medical Centre
CLPT E5 .... **78** C1

Atherton Leisure Centre
FSTGT E7 .... **81** F3

Athlone House Hospital
HGT N6 .... **55** F3

Atlas Business Centre
CRICK NW2 .... **52** B4

Atlas Transport Estate
BTSEA SW11 .... **114** C5

Australia House
HOL/ALD WC2B **21** F5

Avenue Primary School
KIL/WHAMP NW6 .... **71** E4
MNPK E12 .... **83** E1

Avigdor Primary School
STNW/STAM N16 .... **59** D4

Avondale Park Primary School
NTGHL W11 .... **101** D1

Avon Trading Estate
WKENS W14 .... **101** F5

Axis Business Centre
SRTFD E15 .... **80** B5

The Aylesham Centre
PECK SE15 .... **120** A4

Aylwin Girls School
BERM/RHTH SE16 .... **49** F4

Bacons City Technology College
BERM/RHTH SE16 .... **103** D3

Bacon's College
BERM/RHTH SE16 .... **103** E2

Baden Powell House
  SKENS SW7 .... **39** F4
Baden Powell Primary School
  CLPT E5 .... **60** B5
Bakers Hall
  MON EC3R **37** D2
Balaam Leisure Centre
  PLSTW E13 .... **94** A3
Bales College
  NKENS W10 .... **89** D2
Balham Health Centre
  BAL SW12 .... **152** B2
Balmoral Trading
  BARK IG11 .... **97** F4
Baltic Exchange
  HDTCH EC3A **25** D4
Bangabandhu Primary School
  BETH E2 .... **90** C2
Bank of England
  LOTH EC2R **24** A5
Bank of England Extension
  STP EC4M **23** E5
Bank of England Museum
  LOTH EC2R **24** A5
Bankside Jetty
  STHWK SE1 .... **35** E2
Bannockburn Primary School
  WOOL/PLUM SE18 .... **109** F5
Banqueting House
  WHALL SW1A **32** C4
Barber Surgeons' Hall
  BARB EC2Y **23** F3
Barbican Cinema
  BARB EC2Y **23** E2
The Barbican
  BARB EC2Y **23** E2
Barbican Theatre
  BARB EC2Y **23** F2
Barclay Junior & Infant School
  LEY E10 .... **63** D1
Baring Primary School
  LEE/GVPK SE12 .... **142** A5
Baring Road Medical Centre
  LEE/GVPK SE12 .... **160** A2
Barkantine Clinic
  POP/IOD E14 .... **104** A3
Barking Abbey
  Comprehensive School
  BARK IG11 .... **85** F3
  BARK IG11 .... **85** D2
Barking Abbey Industrial Estate
  BARK IG11 .... **84** B5
Barking Hospital
  BARK IG11 .... **85** F4
Barking Industrial Park
  BARK IG11 .... **85** F5
Barlby Primary School
  NKENS W10 .... **89** D3
Barn Croft Primary School
  WALTH E17 .... **61** E1
Barn Elms Athletics Track
  BARN SW13 .... **112** B5
Barn Elms Water Sports Centre
  BARN SW13 .... **112** C5
Barnes Hospital
  MORT/ESHN SW14 .... **129** E1
Barnes Sports Club
  BARN SW13 .... **111** F4
Barnsbury School for Girls
  IS N1 .... **76** A3
Barons Court Theatre
  WKENS W14 .... **113** E1

Barratt Industrial Park
  BOW E3 .... **92** C3
Barrow Hill Junior School
  STJWD NW8 .... **4** C2
Barton House Health Centre
  STNW/STAM N16 .... **59** D5
Bath Factory Estate
  HNHL SE24 .... **136** C4
Battersea Business Centre
  BTSEA SW11 .... **134** A1
Battersea Dogs' Home
  VX/NE SW8 .... **116** B3
Battersea Power Station (disused)
  VX/NE SW8 .... **116** B2
Battersea Sports Centre
  BTSEA SW11 .... **133** D1
Battersea Technology College
  BTSEA SW11 .... **115** F4
Battersea Tutorial College
  TOOT SW17 .... **152** A2
BBC Studios
  MV/WKIL W9 .... **2** C5
BBC Television Centre
  SHB W12 .... **100** C1
Beatrix Potter Primary School
  WAND/EARL SW18 .... **150** C1
Beaumont Primary School
  LEY E10 .... **62** B2
Beckford Primary School
  KIL/WHAMP NW6 .... **71** F2
Beckton Ski Centre
  EHAM E6 .... **96** A3
Beckton Special School
  CAN/RD E16 .... **95** D4
Beckton Triangle Retail Park
  EHAM E6 .... **96** B2
Bective House Clinic
  PUT/ROE SW15 .... **131** F2
Beis Rochel D'satmar Girls School
  STNW/STAM N16 .... **59** E2
Bellamy's Wharf
  BERM/RHTH SE16 .... **103** D2
Bellenden Primary School
  PECK SE15 .... **138** A1
Bellenden Road Business Centre
  PECK SE15 .... **119** F5
Bellenden Road Retail Park
  PECK SE15 .... **119** F4
Belleville Primary School
  BTSEA SW11 .... **133** F3
Belle Vue Cinema
  WLSDN NW10 .... **70** B4
Bell Industrial Estate
  CHSWK W4 .... **98** C5
Bellingham Trading Estate
  CAT SE6 .... **158** B3
Belmont Park School
  LEY E10 .... **62** C1
Belmont Primary School
  CHSWK W4 .... **99** D5
Belvedere Day Hospital
  WLSDN NW10 .... **70** A5
Ben Jonson Primary School
  WCHPL E1 .... **91** E3
Benthal Primary School
  STNW/STAM N16 .... **60** A5
Bentworth Primary School
  SHB W12 .... **88** B5
Beormund School
  STHWK SE1 .... **48** A1
Berger Primary School
  HOM E9 .... **79** D3

Berlitz Schools of Languages
LINN WC1V **21** F3
Bermondsey Town Hall
STHWK SE1 .... **49** F3
Bermondsey Trading Estate
BERM/RHTH SE16 .... **102** C5
Berrymede Junior School
ACT W3 .... **98** B3
Bertram House School
TOOT SW17 .... **152** A2
Bessemer Grange Junior &
Infant School
CMBW SE5 .... **137** E2
Bessemer Park Industrial Estate
HNHL SE24 .... **136** B2
Bethnal Green
Museum of Childhood
BETH E2 .... **90** B2
Bethnal Green Technology College
BETH E2 .... **13** F4
Bevington Primary School
NKENS W10 .... **89** E4
BFI London IMAX Cinema
STHWK SE1 .... **33** F4
Big Ben
WEST SW1P **45** D1
Bigland Green Primary School
WCHPL E1 .... **90** B5
Billingsgate Fish Market
POP/IOD E14 .... **104** B2
Birkbeck College
STPAN WC1H **8** A5
Bishop Challoner RC
Secondary School
WCHPL E1 .... **90** C5
Bishop Gilpin Primary School
WIM/MER SW19 .... **149** F5
Bishopsgate Institute
WCHPL E1 .... **25** D3
Bishop Thomas Grant School
STRHM/NOR SW16 .... **153** F5
Blackfriars Millennium Pier
EMB EC4Y **34** B1
Blackfriars Pier
BLKFR EC4V **35** D1
Blackfriars Station
BLKFR EC4V **34** C1
Blackheath Bluecoat CE School
BKHTH/KID SE3 .... **124** B3
Blackheath Business Estate
GNWCH SE10 .... **122** C4
The Blackheath Clinic
BKHTH/KID SE3 .... **142** A2
Blackheath High School GDST
BKHTH/KID SE3 .... **123** F5
Blackheath High Senior School
BKHTH/KID SE3 .... **124** A3
Blackheath Hospital
BKHTH/KID SE3 .... **141** F1
Blackwall Trading Estate
POP/IOD E14 .... **93** D4
Blake College
GTPST W1W **19** E2
Blessed John Roche
Catholic School
POP/IOD E14 .... **92** A5
Blessed Sacrament
RC Primary School
IS N1 .... **75** F5
Bloomfield Clinic (Guys Hospital)
STHWK SE1 .... **36** B5
Bloomsbury College
FUL/PGN SW6 .... **114** A3

Bloomsbury Theatre
STPAN WC1H **8** A5
Blossoms Inn Medical Centre
BLKFR EC4V **35** F1
Blue Gate Fields Primary School
WCHPL E1 .... **102** C1
BMI Medical Centre
CAVSQ/HST W1G **18** B3
Bnois Jerusalem School
STNW/STAM N16 .... **59** D2
The Bob Hope Theatre
ELTH/MOT SE9 .... **143** F4
Bodywise Natural Health Centre
BETH E2 .... **90** C2
Boleyn Cinema
EHAM E6 .... **95** D1
Bolingbroke Hospital
BTSEA SW11 .... **133** E3
Bolingbroke Primary School
BTSEA SW11 .... **115** D4
Bonner Primary School
BETH E2 .... **91** D1
Bonneville Primary School
CLAP SW4 .... **134** C4
Bonus Pastor School
BMLY BR1 .... **159** E4
Borough Market
STHWK SE1 .... **36** A3
Bousfield Primary School
ECT SW5 .... **114** B1
Boutcher CE Primary School
STHWK SE1 .... **49** E3
Bowater House
SKENS SW7 .... **41** E1
Bow County Court
SRTFD E15 .... **81** F3
Bow County Secondary School
BOW E3 .... **92** A2
Bow Industrial Park
SRTFD E15 .... **80** A4
Bow Street Magistrates Court
HOL/ALD WC2B **21** D5
Bow Triangle Business Centre
BOW E3 .... **92** A3
Brackenbury Health Centre
HMSMTH W6 .... **100** B4
Brackenbury Primary School
HMSMTH W6 .... **100** B4
Brady Recreation Centre
WCHPL E1 .... **90** A4
Braincroft Primary School
CRICK NW2 .... **51** F5
Bramah Tea & Coffee Museum
STHWK SE1 .... **37** F5
Brampton Manor School
PLSTW E13 .... **95** D3
Brampton Primary School
EHAM E6 .... **95** E2
Brandlehow Primary School
PUT/ROE SW15 .... **131** F2
Branollys Health Centre
PLSTW E13 .... **94** A3
Brecknock Primary School
HOLWY N7 .... **75** D3
Bredinghurst School
PECK SE15 .... **138** C2
Brent Adult College
WLSDN NW10 .... **69** D5
Brent Arts Council
CRICK NW2 .... **52** A5
Brent Child & Family Clinic
WLSDN NW10 .... **69** F2

Brent Cross Shopping Centre
HDN NW4 .... **52** C2
Brentfield Medical Centre
WLSDN NW10 .... **69** D3
Brentfield Primary School
WLSDN NW10 .... **69** D3
Brentford Fountain
Leisure Centre
CHSWK W4 .... **110** A1
Brent Knoll School
SYD SE26 .... **157** D3
Brent Magistrates Court House
WLSDN NW10 .... **69** E3
Brent Trading Estate
WLSDN NW10 .... **69** E2
Brewers' Hall
CITYW EC2V **23** F3
Brewery Industrial Estate
IS N1 .... **11** E2
Brick Lane Music Hall
SDTCH EC2A **13** D4
Brick Lane Music House
WCHPL E1 .... **25** F1
Bricklayer Arms Industrial Estate
STHWK SE1 .... **49** E5
The Bridewell Theatre
EMB EC4Y **22** C5
Bridge Lane Theatre
BTSEA SW11 .... **115** E4
Bright Sparks Montessori School
WKENS W14 .... **101** D3
Bright Sparks School
STRHM/NOR SW16 .... **153** E4
Brindishe Primary School
LEE/GVPK SE12 .... **141** F3
Britannia Business Centre
CRICK NW2 .... **71** D1
Britannia Village Primary School
CAN/RD E16 .... **106** B2
British Airways London Eye
WHALL SW1A **33** D5
British Dental Association
CAVSQ/HST W1G **18** C3
British Friends of
Diaspora Museum
KTTN NW5 .... **74** A3
British Library
CAMTN NW1 .... **8** B3
British Medical Association
STPAN WC1H **8** B5
British Museum
RSQ WC1B **20** C3
British Telecom Tower
GTPST W1W **19** E2
Brixton Academy
BRXN/ST SW9 .... **136** A1
Brixton College for
Further Education
BRXS/STRHM SW2 .... **135** F3
Brixton Recreation Centre
BRXN/ST SW9 .... **136** A1
Broadgate
LVPST EC2M **24** B2
Broadgate Ice Arena
LVPST EC2M **24** C3
Broadhurst School
KIL/WHAMP NW6 .... **72** C4
Broadwater Primary School
TOOT SW17 .... **151** D4
Broadway Retail Park
CRICK NW2 .... **71** D1
Broadway Shopping Centre
HMSMTH W6 .... **112** C1

Brocklebank Health Centre
WAND/EARL SW18 .... **132** B5
Brocklebank Industrial Estate
GNWCH SE10 .... **106** A5
Brockley Cross Business Centre
BROCKY SE4 .... **139** E1
Brockley Primary School
BROCKY SE4 .... **139** F3
Brockwell Lido
HNHL SE24 .... **136** B4
Brockwell Primary School
BRXS/STRHM SW2 .... **136** A4
Bromley Road Retail Park
CAT SE6 .... **158** B2
Brompton Cemetery
WBPTN SW10 .... **114** B2
Brompton Medical Centre
WBPTN SW10 .... **114** B1
Brompton Oratory
SKENS SW7 .... **40** C3
Bromyard Leisure Centre
ACT W3 .... **99** E2
Brondesbury College for Boys
KIL/WHAMP NW6 .... **71** D4
Brookfield Primary School
ARCH N19 .... **56** B4
Brooklands Primary School
BKHTH/KID SE3 .... **142** A1
Brookmarsh Trading Estate
DEPT SE8 .... **122** B3
Broomsleigh Business Park
CAT SE6 .... **157** F5
Broomwood Hall School
BAL SW12 .... **134** A5
Brunel Engine House
BERM/RHTH SE16 .... **102** C3
Brunswick Housing &
Shopping Centre
BMSBY WC1N **21** D1
Brunswick Medical Centre
BMSBY WC1N **8** C5
Brunswick Park Primary School
CMBW SE5 .... **119** D3
BT Centre
STBT EC1A **23** E4
Buckingham Palace
WHALL SW1A **43** D1
Buckingham Road Cemetery
IL IG1 .... **67** D4
Building Centre
GWRST WC1E **20** A3
Burbage School
IS N1 .... **12** C1
Burdett Coutts CE Primary School
WEST SW1P **44** A4
Burgess Industrial Park
CMBW SE5 .... **119** D3
Burlington Danes School
SHB W12 .... **88** B5
Burnley Road Clinic
WLSDN NW10 .... **70** A2
Burnt Ash Infant School
BMLY BR1 .... **160** A5
Burnt Ash School
BMLY BR1 .... **159** F5
Burntwood School
TOOT SW17 .... **151** D2
Burrels Wharf
POP/IOD E14 .... **122** B1
Burwell Industrial Estate
LEY E10 .... **61** E3
Bush House (BBC)
HOL/ALD WC2B **21** E5

Bush Industrial Estate
 ARCH N19 .... 56 C5
Bush Industrial Estate
 WLSDN NW10 .... 87 D2
The Business Centre
 IL IG1 .... 66 B4
The Business Design Centre
 IS N1 .... 76 A5
Bute House Preparatory School
 for Girls
 HMSMTH W6 .... 100 C5
Butler's Wharf
 STHWK SE1 .... 37 F4
Butler's Wharf Business Centre
 STHWK SE1 .... 37 F5
Butler's Wharf Pier
 STHWK SE1 .... 37 F4
Butterfly Sports Club
 ELTH/MOT SE9 .... 144 B4
Buzzard Creek Industrial Estate
 BARK IG11 .... 97 F2
Byam Shaw School of Art
 ARCH N19 .... 56 C4
Bygrove JMI School
 POP/IOD E14 .... 92 B5
Cabinet War Rooms
 WHALL SW1A 32 B5
Calder House School
 BTSEA SW11 .... 115 F4
Caledonian Market
 STHWK SE1 .... 49 D2
Calverton Primary School
 CAN/RD E16 .... 95 D5
Camberwell Business Centre
 CMBW SE5 .... 119 D3
Camberwell College of Arts
 CMBW SE5 .... 119 E4
Camberwell New Cemetery
 FSTH SE23 .... 139 D4
Camberwell Trading Estate
 CMBW SE5 .... 118 B5
Cambridge School
 HMSMTH W6 .... 100 B5
Cambridge Theatre
 LSQ/SEVD WC2H 20 C5
Camden Community Trust
 Day Hospital
 CAMTN NW1 .... 74 C3
Camden House Clinic
 BKHTH/KID SE3 .... 123 E5
Camden Market
 CAMTN NW1 .... 74 A4
Camden Peoples Theatre
 CAMTN NW1 .... 7 E4
Camden School for Girls
 CAMTN NW1 .... 74 C3
Camden Theatre
 CAMTN NW1 .... 7 E1
Camden Town Hall &
 St Pancras Library
 CAMTN NW1 .... 8 C3
Camelot Primary School
 PECK SE15 .... 120 B3
Cameron House School
 CHEL SW3 .... 115 D2
Camperdown House
 WCHPL E1 .... 25 F5
Canada House
 STJS SW1Y 32 B3
Canada Square
 POP/IOD E14 .... 104 A2
Canada Water Retail Park
 BERM/RHTH SE16 .... 103 D4

Canada Wharf Museum
 BERM/RHTH SE16 .... 103 F2
Canal Cafe Theatre
 BAY/PAD W2 .... 15 D2
Canary Riverside
 BERM/RHTH SE16 .... 103 F2
Canary Wharf Pier
 BERM/RHTH SE16 .... 103 F2
Canary Wharf Tower
 POP/IOD E14 .... 104 B2
Canberra Primary School
 SHB W12 .... 100 B1
Cann Hall Primary School
 WAN E11 .... 63 F5
The Canning School
 KENS W8 .... 38 A2
Cannon Sports Club
 CANST EC4R 35 F1
Cannon Street Station
 CANST EC4R 36 A1
Cannon Trading Estate
 WBLY HA9 .... 68 B1
Cannon Wharf Business Centre
 DEPT SE8 .... 103 E5
Cannon Workshops
 POP/IOD E14 .... 104 A1
Canon Barnett Primary School
 WCHPL E1 .... 25 F4
Canonbury Business Centre
 IS N1 .... 76 C5
Canonbury Primary School
 IS N1 .... 76 B3
Canon Palmer RC High School
 IL IG1 .... 67 E3
Canterbury Industrial Estate
 PECK SE15 .... 121 D2
Cantium Retail Park
 STHWK SE1 .... 120 A2
Capital Radio
 LSQ/SEVD WC2H 32 B2
Capital Wharf
 WAP E1W 102 A2
Cardinal Hinsley High School
 WLSDN NW10 .... 70 A5
Cardinal Pole RC School
 HOM E9 .... 79 E3
Cardinal Pole
 RC Secondary Lower School
 HOM E9 .... 79 D4
Cardinal Vaughan
 Memorial School
 WKENS W14 .... 101 E3
Cardwell Primary School
 WOOL/PLUM SE18 .... 107 F5
Carlton Gate Development
 MV/WKIL W9 .... 14 B2
Carlton House
 STJS SW1Y 32 A4
Carlton Primary School
 KTTN NW5 .... 74 A2
Carlton Vale Infant School
 MV/WKIL W9 .... 89 F2
Carlyle's House (NT)
 CHEL SW3 .... 115 E2
Carnwath Road Industrial Estate
 FUL/PGN SW6 .... 132 B1
Carpenters Business Park
 HOM E9 .... 80 A3
Carpenters' Hall
 LVPST EC2M 24 B3
Carpenters Primary School
 SRTFD E15 .... 80 C5

Cassidy Medical Centre
FUL/PGN SW6 .... **114** A3
Castlecombe Primary School
ELTH/MOT SE9 .... **161** E5
Castle Industrial Estate
WALW SE17 .... **47** E4
Catford & Bromley Synagogue
CAT SE6 .... **158** B2
Catford Cricket & Sports Club
CAT SE6 .... **158** B1
Catford Cyphers Cricket Club
CAT SE6 .... **157** F2
Catford Girls School
CAT SE6 .... **159** D3
Catford Trading Estate
CAT SE6 .... **158** B2
Catford Wanderers Sports Club
CAT SE6 .... **158** C4
Cathall Leisure Centre
WAN E11 .... **63** D5
Cathedral School of
St Saviour & St Mary Overie
STHWK SE1 .... **35** F5
Cavendish College
FITZ W1T **20** A3
Cavendish Primary School
CHSWK W4 .... **111** E3
The Cavendish School
CAMTN NW1 .... **74** B5
Caxton Hall
STJSPK SW1H **44** A2
Cayley Primary School
POP/IOD E14 .... **91** E4
The Cedar School
FSTGT E7 .... **82** C3
Cedar Way Industrial Estate
CAMTN NW1 .... **75** D4
Cenotaph
WHALL SW1A **32** C5
Central Business Centre
WLSDN NW10 .... **69** E2
Central Criminal Court
STP EC4M **22** C4
Central Foundation Boys School
SDTCH EC2A **12** B5
Central Foundation Girls School
BOW E3 .... **91** E2
Central Hall
STJSPK SW1H **44** B1
Central London County Court
CAVSQ/HST W1G **18** C1
Central London Golf Club
TOOT SW17 .... **151** D2
Central London Markets
FARR EC1M **22** C3
Central Middlesex Hospital
WLSDN NW10 .... **86** C2
Central Park Primary School
EHAM E6 .... **95** D1
Central St Martins College of
Art and Design
RSQ WC1B **21** D3
Central School of Ballet
CLKNW EC1R **22** B1
Central School of Fashion
GTPST W1W **19** E3
Central School of Speech & Drama
HAMP NW3 .... **73** D4
CAMTN NW1 .... **75** D5
Centre Point
LSQ/SEVD WC2H **20** B4
Chalcot School
CAMTN NW1 .... **74** B3

Chalkhill Primary School
WBLY HA9 .... **50** B5
Chambers Wharf
BERM/RHTH SE16 .... **102** A3
Channelsea Business Centre
SRTFD E15 .... **93** D1
Channing School
HGT N6 .... **56** B3
Chapman Park Industrial Estate
WLSDN NW10 .... **69** F3
Charing Cross Hospital
HMSMTH W6 .... **113** D2
Charing Cross Station
CHCR WC2N **33** D3
Charing Cross &
Westminster Medical School
HMSMTH W6 .... **113** D1
Charles Dickens Primary School
STHWK SE1 .... **47** E1
Charles Edward Brook
Lower School
CMBW SE5 .... **118** B4
Charles Edward Brook
Upper School
CMBW SE5 .... **118** B4
Charles Lamb Primary School
IS N1 .... **76** C5
Charlotte Sharman
Primary School
LBTH SE11 .... **46** C3
Charlton Athletic FC (The Valley)
CHARL SE7 .... **124** C1
Charlton House
CHARL SE7 .... **125** D2
Charlton RFC
ELTH/MOT SE9 .... **144** B5
Charlton School
CHARL SE7 .... **125** E2
Charter Clinic
CHEL SW3 .... **115** F1
Charterhouse
FARR EC1M **23** D2
Charterhouse Works
WAND/EARL SW18 .... **132** C2
The Charter School
HNHL SE24 .... **137** D3
Chartfield School
PUT/ROE SW15 .... **130** B3
Chase Road Trading Estate
WLSDN NW10 .... **87** D3
Chelsea Barracks
BGVA SW1W **116** A1
Chelsea Bridge Business Centre
VX/NE SW8 .... **116** B3
Chelsea Centre & Theatre
WBPTN SW10 .... **115** D3
Chelsea Cinema
CHEL SW3 .... **115** E1
Chelsea College of Art & Design
CHEL SW3 .... **115** D1
FUL/PGN SW6 .... **114** C5
Chelsea FC (Stamford Bridge)
FUL/PGN SW6 .... **114** B3
Chelsea Old Town Hall
CHEL SW3 .... **115** E1
Chelsea Physic Garden
CHEL SW3 .... **115** F2
Chelsea Sports Centre
CHEL SW3 .... **115** E1
Chelsea & Westminster Hospital
WBPTN SW10 .... **114** C2
Chelsea Wharf
WBPTN SW10 .... **115** D3

Cherry Garden School
BERM/RHTH SE16 .... **102** A5
Cherry Orchard Primary School
CHARL SE7 .... **124** C3
Chesterton Primary School
BTSEA SW11 .... **116** A4
Chestnut Grove School
BAL SW12 .... **152** A1
Cheyne Centre
CHEL SW3 .... **115** E2
Childeric Primary School
NWCR SE14 .... **121** E3
Childs Hill Clinic
CRICK NW2 .... **53** F4
Childs Hill Primary School
CRICK NW2 .... **53** E5
Chiltonian Industrial Estate
LEE/GVPK SE12 .... **141** F4
Chimnocks Wharf
POP/IOD E14 .... **103** E1
Chisenhale Primary School
BOW E3 .... **91** E1
Chislehurst Cemetery
CHST BR7 .... **163** E5
**Chiswick & Bedford Park
Preparatory School**
CHSWK W4 .... **99** E5
Chiswick Community School
CHSWK W4 .... **111** D3
Chiswick House
CHSWK W4 .... **111** D2
Chrisp Street Health Centre
POP/IOD E14 .... **92** B5
**Christ Church Bentinck
CE Primary School**
CAMTN NW1 .... **16** C2
**Christ Church Brondesbury
CE J & I School**
KIL/WHAMP NW6 .... **71** F5
Christ Church CE Primary School
BRXN/ST SW9 .... **118** A4
BRXS/STRHM SW2 .... **153** F1
CHEL SW3 .... **115** F2
FSTH SE23 .... **157** D2
WCHPL E1 .... **25** F3
WOOL/PLUM SE18 .... **126** A4
CHEL SW3 .... **115** F2
Christchurch Industrial Centre
STHWK SE1 .... **34** C3
Christ Church Primary School
BTSEA SW11 .... **133** E1
IL IG1 .... **66** C3
Christ Church School
CAMTN NW1 .... **7** D2
**Christopher Hutton
Primary School**
FSBYW WC1X **22** A1
Christs College
BKHTH/KID SE3 .... **124** A4
Christ the King RC Primary School
FSBYPK N4 .... **57** F4
Chrysalis Theatre
BAL SW12 .... **152** A1
Chrysanthemum Clinic
CHSWK W4 .... **110** C3
Church Down Adult School
LEE/GVPK SE12 .... **160** A2
Church End Medical Centre
WLSDN NW10 .... **69** E2
Churchfield School
WOOL/PLUM SE18 .... **109** F5
Churchill Clinic
STHWK SE1 .... **46** B2

Churchill College
TOOT SW17 .... **151** F2
Churchill Gardens Primary School
PIM SW1V **116** C1
Church Mead Infant School
LEY E10 .... **62** A3
Church Mead Junior School
LEY E10 .... **62** A3
Church Stairs
BERM/RHTH SE16 .... **102** B3
City Banking College
STHWK SE1 .... **36** B5
City Business Centre
BERM/RHTH SE16 .... **102** C3
City Business College
FSBYE EC1V **11** D4
City Central Estate
FSBYE EC1V **11** E4
City College of Higher Education
IS N1 .... **12** B3
**City & Guilds of London
Art School**
LBTH SE11 .... **118** B1
City Health Centre
FSBYE EC1V **12** A5
City & Islington College
FSBYPK N4 .... **58** B4
HOLWY N7 .... **75** E1
IS N1 .... **76** C5
STLK EC1Y **24** A1
**City & Islington College
Sixth Form Centre**
HOLWY N7 .... **75** F1
City of London Cemetery
MNPK E12 .... **65** E4
City of London Crematorium
MNPK E12 .... **65** D5
City of London Club
OBST EC2N **24** C4
City of London College
WCHPL E1 .... **90** A5
City of London Magistrates Court
MANHO EC4N **24** A5
**City of London Polytechnic
Sports Ground**
ELTH/MOT SE9 .... **160** C2
City of London School
BLKFR EC4V **35** D1
City of London School for Girls
BARB EC2Y **23** E2
City of Westminster College
BAY/PAD W2 .... **16** A2
MV/WKIL W9 .... **2** A4
**City of Westminster
Vehicle Pound**
BAY/PAD W2 .... **15** F3
City Thameslink Station
STP EC4M **22** C4
City University
FSBYE EC1V **10** C3
FSBYE EC1V **10** C4
City University Business School
BARB EC2Y **23** F2
Civil Service Recreation Centre
WEST SW1P **44** B3
Civil Service Sports Ground
ELTH/MOT SE9 .... **142** C4
Clapham Common Clinic
CLAP SW4 .... **135** D2
Clapham Manor Primary School
CLAP SW4 .... **134** C1

Clapham Manor Street
Public Baths
CLAP SW4 .... **135** D1
Clapham North Business Centre
CLAP SW4 .... **135** D1
Clapham Park School
CLAP SW4 .... **135** D3
Clapham Picture House
CLAP SW4 .... **134** C2
Clapton Girls' Technology College
CLPT E5 .... **78** C1
Clapton Jewish Boys School
STNW/STAM N16 .... **59** F2
Clara Grant Primary School
BOW E3 .... **92** A3
Claremont Clinic
FSTGT E7 .... **82** B2
Claremont Way Industrial Estate
CRICK NW2 .... **52** C3
Clarence House
WHALL SW1A **31** F5
Claridges Hotel
MYFR/PKLN W1K **30** C1
Cleopatra's Needle
CHCR WC2N **33** E3
Clerkenwell County Court
IS N1 .... **10** C1
Clerkenwell Heritage Centre
FARR EC1M **22** C1
Clerkenwell Parochial
CE Primary School
CLKNW EC1R **10** A4
Cleveland Primary School
IL IG1 .... **84** B1
Cleves Primary School
EHAM E6 .... **83** D5
Clink Exhibition
STHWK SE1 .... **36** A3
Clissold Park Natural Health Centre
STNW/STAM N16 .... **59** E4
Clitterhouse Primary School
CRICK NW2 .... **53** D4
Clock Museum
CITYW EC2V **23** F4
Cloisters Business Centre
VX/NE SW8 .... **116** B3
Clore Gallery
WEST SW1P **44** C5
Clothworkers' Hall
FENCHST EC3M **37** D1
Clouster's Green
WAP E1W **102** A2
Cobbold Estate
WLSDN NW10 .... **69** F3
Cobourg Primary School
CMBW SE5 .... **119** F1
Cochrane Theatre
GINN WC1R **21** E3
The Cockpit Theatre
STJWD NW8 .... **16** C1
Coldharbour Industrial Estate
CMBW SE5 .... **118** C5
Coldharbour Sports Ground
ELTH/MOT SE9 .... **162** A2
Colebrooke Primary School
IS N1 .... **10** C1
Colebrooke Works
IS N1 .... **10** C1
Colegrave Primary School
SRTFD E15 .... **81** D2
Coleridge Primary School
HGT N6 .... **57** D2

Colfes Preparatory School
LEE/GVPK SE12 .... **142** B4
Coliseum Theatre
CHCR WC2N **32** C2
College of Arms
BLKFR EC4V **23** E5
College of Fuel Technology
HGT N6 .... **56** A1
The College of Law
FLST/FETLN EC4A **22** A4
GWRST WC1E **20** C3
College of North West London
KIL/WHAMP NW6 .... **72** A5
WBLY HA9 .... **50** A5
WLSDN NW10 .... **69** F2
College of Organists
FLST/FETLN EC4A **22** B4
College Park School
BAY/PAD W2 .... **14** B5
Collingwood Business Centre
ARCH N19 .... **57** E5
Collins Method School
CRICK NW2 .... **70** C3
The Colonnades Shopping Centre
BCVA SW1W **42** C4
Columbia Primary School
BETH E2 .... **13** F3
Colvestone Primary School
HACK E8 .... **77** F2
Colville Primary School
NTGHL W11 .... **89** F5
Comber Grove Primary School
CMBW SE5 .... **118** C3
Comedy Theatre
STJS SW1Y **32** A2
Comelle House Trading Estate
DEPT SE8 .... **121** E1
Commonwealth Institute
KENS W8 .... **38** A2
Community Arts Centre
GNWCH SE10 .... **122** B3
Community Centre
(Island History Trust)
POP/IOD E14 .... **104** C5
Community College and School
GNWCH SE10 .... **122** C3
Community Mental Health Centre
BRXN/ST SW9 .... **118** A3
Complementary Health Centre
LEW SE13 .... **141** E4
Concord Business Centre
ACT W3 .... **86** B4
Concord Shopping Centre
WKENS W14 .... **101** D3
Connaught Girls School
WAN E11 .... **63** E3
Consort Clinic
PECK SE15 .... **138** B1
Consulate General of Monaco
SKENS SW7 .... **40** A4
Consulate General of the
Republic of Guinea Bissau
KENS W8 .... **39** E2
Consulate of Burkina Faso
BTSEA SW11 .... **132** C1
Consulate of Chile
CAVSQ/HST W1G **18** C1
Consulate of Colombia
GTPST W1W **19** E4
Consulate of Eritrea
IS N1 .... **10** B1
Consulate of Guinea
MYFR/PKLN W1K **30** A2

Consulate of Panama
MYFR/PICC W1J 30 C4
Convent of Jesus &
Mary Infant School
CRICK NW2 .... 70 C3
Convent of Jesus &
Mary Language College
WLSDN NW10 .... 69 F5
Conway Hall
FSBYW WC1X 21 E2
Conway Medical Centre
WOOL/PLUM SE18 .... 127 D1
Conway Primary School
WOOL/PLUM SE18 .... 109 E5
Coopers' Hall
LVPST EC2M 25 D3
Coopers Lane Primary School
LEE/GVPK SE12 .... 160 A2
Copenhagen Primary School
IS N1 .... 9 E1
Copper Mills Works
WALTH E17 .... 60 C1
Cordwainers College
HOM E9 .... 78 C4
Cornhill Sports Club
BECK BR3 .... 158 A5
Coronet Cinema
NTGHL W11 .... 26 A3
Corpus Christi RC Primary School
BRXS/STRHM SW2 .... 135 F3
Cosmopolitan College
IS N1 .... 9 E2
Council of Mosques
FITZ W1T 19 F3
Counterpoint Theatre
STPAN WC1H 9 D3
Courtauld Institute Galleries
HOL/ALD WC2B 33 E1
Courtfield Medical Centre
ECT SW5 .... 39 D5
Covent Garden Flower Market
VX/NE SW8 .... 117 E2
Covent Garden Medical Centre
LSQ/SEVD WC2H 20 C5
CPFC Soccer & Sports Centre
BRXN/ST SW9 .... 135 F1
Crampton Primary School
WALW SE17 .... 47 D5
Cranbrook College
IL IG1 .... 66 A4
The Craven Clinic
HMSMTH W6 .... 100 B5
Craven Park Health Centre
WLSDN NW10 .... 69 D5
Craven Park Medical Centre
WLSDN NW10 .... 69 D5
Craven Park Primary School
SEVS/STOTM N15 .... 60 A1
Crawford Primary School
CMBW SE5 .... 118 C4
Crawford Upper School
MBLAR W1H 17 E3
Creekmouth Industrial Estate
BARK IG11 .... 97 F3
Creek Road Health Centre
DEPT SE8 .... 122 A2
Creek Road Industrial Estate
DEPT SE8 .... 122 B2
Cremer Business Centre
BETH E2 .... 13 E2
Crewe House
MYFR/PICC W1J 30 C3

Cricket Pavilion
WEST SW1P 44 A4
Cricklefield Stadium
IL IG1 .... 67 E4
Cricklewood Trading Estate
CRICK NW2 .... 53 E5
Criterion Theatre
MYFR/PICC W1J 31 F2
Crofton Leisure Centre
BROCKY SE4 .... 140 A4
Crofton School
BROCKY SE4 .... 140 A4
Cromwell Business Centre
BARK IG11 .... 97 E2
Cromwell Hospital
KENS W8 .... 38 C4
Cromwell Industrial Estate
LEY E10 .... 61 E3
Crouch Hill Recreation Centre
ARCH N19 .... 57 E2
Crown Close Business Centre
BOW E3 .... 80 A5
Crown Court at the Borough
STHWK SE1 .... 35 D5
Crowndale Health Centre
CAMTN NW1 .... 7 F1
Crown Lane Primary School
WNWD SE27 .... 154 B5
Crown Woods School
ELTH/MOT SE9 .... 144 C3
Crusader Industrial Estate
FSBYPK N4 .... 58 C1
Crusoe House School
IS N1 .... 12 A3
Cubitt Town Primary School
POP/IOD E14 .... 104 C4
Culloden Primary School
POP/IOD E14 .... 93 D5
Cumberland Business Park
WLSDN NW10 .... 86 B2
Cumberland Comprehensive School
CAN/RD E16 .... 93 F4
Cumberland Park Industrial Estate
WLSDN NW10 .... 88 A2
The Cuming Museum
WALW SE17 .... 47 E5
Curwen Primary School
PLSTW E13 .... 94 A1
Curzon Mayfair Cinema
MYFR/PICC W1J 30 C4
Curzon Soho Cinema
SOHO/SHAV W1D 32 B1
Cutlers' Hall
STP EC4M 23 D4
Cutty Sark
GNWCH SE10 .... 122 C2
Cygnet Clinic Beckton
EHAM E6 .... 96 B5
Cygnus Business Centre
WLSDN NW10 .... 69 F2
Cyprus College of Art
WNWD SE27 .... 154 B4
Cyril Jackson Primary School
POP/IOD E14 .... 103 F1
Daily Mirror Office
FLST/FETLN EC4A 22 B3
Daily Telegraph
POP/IOD E14 .... 104 A4
Dali Universal Exhibition
STHWK SE1 .... 33 D5
Dallington School
FSBYE EC1V 11 D5

Dulwich & Sydenham
  Hill Golf Club
  DUL SE21...................................... **156** A2
Dulwich Village CE Infant School
  DUL SE21...................................... **137** E3
Dunbar Wharf
  POP/IOD E14................................ **103** F1
Duncombe Primary School
  ARCH N19...................................... **57** F1
Dundee Wharf
  POP/IOD E14................................ **103** F1
Dunraven School (Lower School)
  STRHM/NOR SW16...................... **153** F3
Dunraven School (Upper School)
  STRHM/NOR SW16...................... **153** F3
Durand Primary School
  BRXN/ST SW9................................ **117** F4
Eaglesfield School
  WOOL/PLUM SE18........................ **126** A4
Ealdham Primary School
  ELTH/MOT SE9.............................. **142** C2
Earlham Primary School
  FSTGT E7...................................... **81** F2
Earl's Court Exhibition Centre
  ECT SW5.. **114** A1
Earlsfield Primary School
  WAND/EARL SW18........................ **150** C2
Earth Gallery (Geological Museum)
  SKENS SW7.................................... **40** A3
East Acton Primary School
  ACT W3.. **99** E1
East Beckton District Centre
  EHAM E6.. **95** F3
Eastbury Comprehensive School
  BARK IG11...................................... **85** D4
  BARK IG11...................................... **85** F5
Eastbury Infant School
  BARK IG11...................................... **85** F4
Eastcote Primary School
  ELTH/MOT SE9.............................. **145** D1
East Dulwich Baths
  EDUL SE22.................................... **137** F2
East Greenwich Christ Church
  CE Primary School
  GNWCH SE10................................ **105** E5
East Ham Industrial Estate
  CAN/RD E16.................................. **95** D3
East Ham Jewish Cemetery
  EHAM E6.. **95** E2
East Ham Memorial Hospital
  FSTGT E7...................................... **83** D4
East Ham Nature Reserve
  EHAM E6.. **95** F3
Eastlea Community School
  CAN/RD E16.................................. **93** E3
East London Business College
  WAN E11.. **63** E3
East London Cemetery
  PLSTW E13.................................... **93** F2
East London Crematorium
  PLSTW E13.................................... **93** F2
East London RFC
  EHAM E6.. **95** F4
East London RUFC
  PLSTW E13.................................... **93** F1
Eastman Dental Hospital
  FSBYW WC1X................................ **9** E4
East Sheen Cemetery
  RCHPK/HAM TW10........................ **128** A3
East Sheen Primary School
  MORT/ESHN SW14........................ **129** E3
East Wickham Primary School
  WELL DA16.................................... **127** F4

Eaton House School
  KTBR SW1X.................................... **42** A4
Eaton Square Preparatory School
  BGVA SW1W.................................. **42** C4
Eaton Square School
  PIM SW1V...................................... **43** E5
Ecclesbourne Primary School
  IS N1.. **77** D4
Eckerd College
  GWRST WC1E................................ **20** A2
Ecole De Mime Corporel
  Theatre De Lange Fou
  ARCH N19...................................... **57** E4
Eden College
  STHWK SE1.................................... **47** D2
Eden Medical Centre
  WKENS W14.................................. **101** F5
Edgebury Primary School
  CHST BR7...................................... **162** C4
Edge Business Centre
  CRICK NW2.................................... **52** B4
Edgware College
  HAMP NW3.................................... **72** C3
Edith Neville Primary School
  CAMTN NW1.................................. **8** A2
Edmund Waller Primary School
  NWCR SE14.................................... **121** D5
Education Centre
  WOOL/PLUM SE18........................ **126** B1
Edward Wilson Primary School
  BAY/PAD W2.................................. **14** C2
Effra Primary School
  BRXS/STRHM SW2........................ **136** A3
Effra Road Retail Park
  BRXS/STRHM SW2........................ **136** A3
Eglinton Infant School
  WOOL/PLUM SE18........................ **126** A3
Eglinton Junior School
  WOOL/PLUM SE18........................ **126** A2
Eleanor Palmer Primary School
  KTTN NW5...................................... **74** C1
Eleanor Smith Special School &
  Primary Support Service
  PLSTW E13.................................... **94** A1
Electric Cinema
  NTGHL W11.................................... **89** F5
Elephant & Castle
  Shopping Centre
  STHWK SE1.................................... **47** D3
Elfrida Primary School
  CAT SE6.. **158** B4
Eliot Bank Primary School
  FSTH SE23.................................... **156** B2
Elizabeth Garrett
  Anderson Hospital
  CAMTN NW1.................................. **8** B4
Elizabeth Garrett Anderson School
  IS N1.. **9** F1
Elizabeth Selby Infant School
  BETH E2.. **90** A2
Elizabeth Trading Estate
  NWCR SE14.................................... **121** D2
Ellen Wilkinson Primary School
  EHAM E6.. **95** D4
Ellerslie Square Industrial Estate
  CLAP SW4...................................... **135** E2
Elliott Foundation School
  PUT/ROE SW15.............................. **130** C4
Elm Court School
  WNWD SE27.................................. **154** B2
Elmhurst Primary School
  FSTGT E7...................................... **82** B4

Elm Wood Primary School
WNWD SE27 .... **155** D3

Elsdale Street Health Centre
HOM E9 .... **78** C4

Elsley School
BTSEA SW11 .... **134** A1

Eltham Baths
ELTH/MOT SE9 .... **143** E3

Eltham Cemetery
ELTH/MOT SE9 .... **144** C2

Eltham CE Primary School
ELTH/MOT SE9 .... **143** F3

Eltham College
ELTH/MOT SE9 .... **161** D2

Eltham College Junior School
ELTH/MOT SE9 .... **161** D1

Eltham Crematorium
ELTH/MOT SE9 .... **145** D2

Eltham Green School
ELTH/MOT SE9 .... **143** D4

Eltham Health Clinic
ELTH/MOT SE9 .... **143** E3

Eltham Hill Technology College
ELTH/MOT SE9 .... **143** E4

Eltham Palace (Remains)
ELTH/MOT SE9 .... **143** E5

Eltham Warren Golf Club
ELTH/MOT SE9 .... **144** B3

Emanuel School
WAND/EARL SW18 .... **133** D3

Embankment Pier
CHCR WC2N **33** E3

Embassy of Afghanistan
SKENS SW7 .... **40** A1

Embassy of Albania
BGVA SW1W **43** D3

Embassy of Algeria
NTGHL W11 .... **101** E2

Embassy of Angola
MYFR/PKLN W1K **30** A2

Embassy of Argentina
MYFR/PKLN W1K **30** C1

Embassy of Armenia
KENS W8 .... **38** C2

Embassy of Austria
KTBR SW1X **42** A2

Embassy of Bahrain
SKENS SW7 .... **39** E3

Embassy of Belarus
KENS W8 .... **39** D1

Embassy of Belgium
KTBR SW1X **42** B3

Embassy of Bolivia
KTBR SW1X **42** B3

Embassy of Bosnia-Herzegovina
CAVSQ/HST W1G **19** D4

Embassy of Brazil
MYFR/PKLN W1K **30** A1

Embassy of Bulgaria
SKENS SW7 .... **39** F2

Embassy of Cameroon
WKENS W14 .... **101** E2

Embassy of China
CAVSQ/HST W1G **18** C2

Embassy of Costa Rica
BAY/PAD W2 .... **27** F1

Embassy of Cote d'Ivoire
KTBR SW1X **42** B2

Embassy of Croatia
GTPST W1W **19** D1

Embassy of Cuba
HHOL WC1V **20** C4

**Embassy of The Democratic
Republic of the Congo**
KTBR SW1X **41** F3

Embassy of Denmark
KTBR SW1X **41** E2

Embassy of The Dominican Republic
BAY/PAD W2 .... **15** D5

Embassy of Ecuador
KTBR SW1X **41** E2

Embassy of Egypt
MYFR/PICC W1J **30** C3

Embassy of Estonia
SKENS SW7 .... **39** F1

Embassy of Ethiopia
SKENS SW7 .... **40** B1

Embassy of Finland
KTBR SW1X **42** A2

Embassy of France
KTBR SW1X **29** F5

Embassy of Gabon
SKENS SW7 .... **39** F3

Embassy of Georgia
KENS W8 .... **38** C1

Embassy of Germany
KTBR SW1X **42** A2

Embassy of Ghana
HGT N6 .... **56** B3

Embassy of Greece
KENS W8 .... **101** F2

Embassy of Guatemala
WBPTN SW10 .... **114** B2

Embassy of Honduras
MBLAR W1H **17** F2

Embassy of Hungary
KTBR SW1X **42** B3

Embassy of Iceland
KTBR SW1X **42** A4

Embassy of Indonesia
MYFR/PKLN W1K **30** B2

Embassy of Iran
SKENS SW7 .... **40** B1

Embassy of Iraq
SKENS SW7 .... **39** F2

Embassy of Ireland
KTBR SW1X **42** C1

Embassy of Israel
KENS W8 .... **27** D5

Embassy of Italy
MYFR/PKLN W1K **30** B1

Embassy of Japan
MYFR/PICC W1J **31** D4

Embassy of Jordan
KENS W8 .... **38** A1

Embassy of Korea
WESTW SW1E **43** F2

Embassy of Krygyzstan
MBLAR W1H **17** E3

Embassy of Kuwait
KTBR SW1X **29** F5

Embassy of Latvia
CAMTN NW1 .... **18** A1

Embassy of Lebanon
KENS W8 .... **26** C3

Embassy of Liberia
BAY/PAD W2 .... **26** B1

Embassy of Lithuania
MBLAR W1H **17** E3

Embassy of Luxembourg
KTBR SW1X **42** A1

Embassy of Mexico
MYFR/PICC W1J **30** C4

Embassy of Mongolia
KENS W8 .... **39** D1

Embassy of Morocco
SKENS SW7 .... **39** E4
Embassy of Mozambique
FITZ W1T **19** E1
Embassy of Myanmar
MYFR/PICC W1J **30** C3
Embassy of Nepal
KENS W8 .... **26** C3
Embassy of The Netherlands
SKENS SW7 .... **39** F1
Embassy of Norway
KTBR SW1X **42** B2
Embassy of Paraguay
SKENS SW7 .... **39** D3
Embassy of Peru
KTBR SW1X **41** F2
Embassy of The Philippines
KENS W8 .... **26** C4
Embassy of Poland
CAVSO/HST W1G **18** C2
Embassy of Portugal
KTBR SW1X **42** A1
Embassy of Qatar
MYFR/PKLN W1K **30** B3
Embassy of The Republic of Senegal
CRICK NW2 .... **70** C4
Embassy of Romania
KENS W8 .... **26** C5
Embassy of Russian Federation
KENS W8 .... **26** C4
Embassy of Saudi Arabia
MYFR/PICC W1J **30** C3
Embassy of Slovak Republic
KENS W8 .... **26** C3
Embassy of Slovenia
CAVSO/HST W1G **18** C4
Embassy of South Vietnam
KENS W8 .... **39** D2
Embassy of Spain
KTBR SW1X **42** B2
Embassy of Sudan
WHALL SW1A **31** E4
Embassy of Sweden
MBLAR W1H **17** E3
Embassy of Switzerland
MBLAR W1H **17** E3
Embassy of Syria
KTBR SW1X **42** A1
Embassy of Thailand
SKENS SW7 .... **39** F3
Embassy of Tunisia
SKENS SW7 .... **40** B1
Embassy of Turkey
KTBR SW1X **42** B1
Embassy of Turkmenistan
GTPST W1W **19** F3
Embassy of Ukraine
NTGHL W11 .... **101** E2
Embassy of The United
Arab Emirates
SKENS SW7 .... **28** B5
Embassy of Uruguay
SKENS SW7 .... **41** D2
Embassy of USA
MYFR/PKLN W1K **30** A1
Embassy of Uzbekistan
NTGHL W11 .... **101** F2
Embassy of Venezuela
SKENS SW7 .... **40** B3
Embassy of Yemen
SKENS SW7 .... **40** A4
Emery Theatre
POP/IOD E14 .... **92** B5

Emmanuel CE Primary School
KIL/WHAMP NW6 .... **72** A2
Empire Cinema
LSQ/SEVD WC2H **32** B1
English Martyrs RC Primary School
WALW SE17 .... **48** A5
WCHPL E1 .... **25** F5
Ennersdale Primary School
LEW SE13 .... **141** D3
Ensham Secondary School
TOOT SW17 .... **151** F5
Enterprise Business Park
POP/IOD E14 .... **104** B3
Enterprise Industrial Estate
BERM/RHTH SE16 .... **120** C1
Ernest Bevin School
TOOT SW17 .... **151** E3
Eros
MYFR/PICC W1J **32** A2
Essendine Primary School
KIL/WHAMP NW6 .... **2** B4
Essex Primary School
MNPK E12 .... **83** E3
Ethelburga GM School
BTSEA SW11 .... **115** E4
Euro Business Centre
SRTFD E15 .... **81** F5
Eurolink Business Centre
BRXS/STRHM SW2 .... **136** A2
European School of Economics
KTBR SW1X **42** B1
European Vocational College
HDTCH EC3A **25** D5
Euro Way School London
FSBYPK N4 .:........................... **58** B2
Euston Centre
CAMTN NW1 .... **7** E5
Euston Station
CAMTN NW1 .... **8** A4
Euston Tower
CAMTN NW1 .... **7** E5
Eveline Lowe Primary School
STHWK SE1 .... **120** A1
Evendine College
SOHO/SHAV W1D **20** A4
Everyman Cinema
HAMP NW3 .... **72** C1
EW Fact/Emile Woolf Colleges
HOLWY N7 .... **75** E3
Excel Exhibition Centre
CAN/RD E16 .... **106** A1
Exchange Square
SDTCH EC2A **24** C2
The Exchange
IL IG1 .... **66** B4
Exhibition Halls
STLK EC1Y **23** F2
WBLY HA9 .... **68** A1
Eye Clinic
LSQ/SEVD WC2H **20** B4
Eye Hospital
HHOL WC1V **20** C4
Faircharm Trading Estate
DEPT SE8 .... **122** B3
IS N1 .... **11** E1
The Faircross Complementary
Medical Centre
BARK IG11 .... **85** E3
Fairlawn Primary School
FSTH SE23 .... **138** C5
Fairley House School
WEST SW1P **44** A5

Fairways Business Park
LEY E10 .... 61 E4
Falconbrook JMI School
BTSEA SW11 .... 115 D5
Falcon Business Centre
BTSEA SW11 .... 133 E2
Falcon Park Industrial Estate
WLSDN NW10 .... 69 E2
Falkner House School
SKENS SW7 .... 114 C1
Fanmakers' Hall
LVPST EC2M 24 C4
Fan Museum
GNWCH SE10 .... 122 C3
Faraday Building
BLKFR EC4V 23 D5
Farm Lane Trading Estate
FUL/PGN SW6 .... 114 A2
Farringdon Station
FARR EC1M 22 C2
Fashion & Textile Design Museum
STHWK SE1 .... 49 D1
Fenchurch Street Station
MON EC3R 37 D1
**Fenstanton Junior &
Infant School**
BRXS/STRHM SW2 .... 154 A1
Fenton House
HAMP NW3 .... 54 C5
Ferrier Industrial Estate
WAND/EARL SW18 .... 132 B2
Festival Pier
STHWK SE1 .... 33 F3
Financial Times
POP/IOD E14 .... 92 C5
STHWK SE1 .... 35 F3
Fine Arts College
HAMP NW3 .... 73 E3
Finsbury Circus Medical Centre
LVPST EC2M 24 B3
Finsbury Health Centre
CLKNW EC1R 10 A5
Finsbury Leisure Complex
FSBYE EC1V 11 E5
Finsbury Park Track
FSBYPK N4 .... 58 B2
Finton House School
TOOT SW17 .... 151 E2
Fircroft Primary School
TOOT SW17 .... 151 F1
Fire Brigade HQ
STHWK SE1 .... 45 E4
Fire Brigade Museum
STHWK SE1 .... 35 E5
Firepower (Museum of Artillery)
WOOL/PLUM SE18 .... 108 B4
Fisher Athletic FC
BERM/RHTH SE16 .... 103 D2
Fishmonger's Hall
CANST EC4R 36 A2
Fitness Unlimited Leisure Centre
BOW E3 .... 92 A1
Fitzjohns Primary School
HAMP NW3 .... 73 D2
Fitzrovia Medical Centre
GTPST W1W 19 E1
Fitzroy Nuffield Hospital
MBLAR W1H 17 E4
Flamsteed House Museum
GNWCH SE10 .... 123 D3
Flaxman Sports Centre
CMBW SE5 .... 118 C5

Fleet Primary School
HAMP NW3 .... 73 F2
Fleming Lab Museum
BAY/PAD W2 .... 16 B4
Flora Gardens Primary School
HMSMTH W6 .... 100 B5
Florence Nightingale Museum
STHWK SE1 .... 45 E1
Florida State University
RSQ WC1B 20 B3
Flutters Leisure Centre
FUL/PGN SW6 .... 114 A3
FOB School
CLPT E5 .... 60 A2
The Foot Clinic
WIM/MER SW19 .... 149 E5
The Ford College
CONDST W1S 31 D1
Foreign & Commonwealth Office
WHALL SW1A 32 B5
Foreland Medical Centre
NTGHL W11 .... 101 E1
Forest Business Park
WALTH E17 .... 61 D2
Forest Gate Community School
FSTGT E7 .... 82 A2
Forest Hill Business Centre
FSTH SE23 .... 156 C2
Forest Hill Industrial Estate
FSTH SE23 .... 156 C2
Forest Hill School
SYD SE26 .... 157 D3
Forest House Business Centre
WAN E11 .... 63 F2
The Former Health Centre
CHARL SE7 .... 107 D5
Forster Park Primary School
CAT SE6 .... 159 E3
Fortune Theatre
HOL/ALD WC2B 21 D5
Fossdene Primary School
CHARL SE7 .... 124 B1
The Foundling Museum
BMSBY WC1N 9 D5
Fountayne Road Health Centre
CLPT E5 .... 60 A4
Fox Primary School
KENS W8 .... 26 A4
Frances King School of English
SKENS SW7 .... 39 E4
Franciscan Primary School
TOOT SW17 .... 152 A4
Francis Holland School
BGVA SW1W 42 B5
CAMTN NW1 .... 17 E1
Frank Barnes Primary School
STJWD NW8 .... 73 D4
Free Trade Wharf
WAP E1W 103 D1
Fresh Wharf Estate
BARK IG11 .... 84 B5
Freuchen Medical Centre
WLSDN NW10 .... 87 F1
Freud Museum
HAMP NW3 .... 73 D3
Friars Primary Foundation School
STHWK SE1 .... 34 C5
Friends House
CAMTN NW1 .... 8 A4
Friends of Bar Ilan University
GLDGN NW11 .... 54 A3
Friends of the Hebrew University
CAMTN NW1 .... 74 B5

Froebel College
PUT/ROE SW15.............................. **130** A4

Frogmore Industrial Estate
HBRY N5 .... **76** C1
WLSDN NW10 .... **86** C2

Fryent Country Park
WBLY HA9 .... **50** A3

Fryent Medical Centre
CDALE/KGS NW9 .... **50** C2

Fryent Primary School
CDALE/KGS NW9 .... **50** C2

Fulham Clinic
FUL/PGN SW6 .... **113** F2

Fulham Cross School
FUL/PGN SW6 .... **113** D3

Fulham FC (Craven Cottage)
BARN SW13 .... **112** C4

Fulham Medical Centre
FUL/PGN SW6 .... **114** B3

Fulham Palace
FUL/PGN SW6 .... **113** E5

Fulham Preparatory School
FUL/PGN SW6 .... **113** E5

Fulham Prep School
FUL/PGN SW6 .... **113** E5

Fulham Primary School
FUL/PGN SW6 .... **114** A2

Fulham & South RC Primary School Kensington Institute
WBPTN SW10 .... **114** C1

Fuller Smith & Turner Sports Club
CHSWK W4 .... **111** E4

Future Business College
CONDST W1S.................................. **19** D5

Gainsborough Primary School
HOM E9 .... **79** F3
SRTFD E15 .... **93** E2

Galleywall Primary School
BERM/RHTH SE16 .... **102** B5

Gallions Mount Primary School
WOOL/PLUM SE18 .... **127** F1

Gants Hill Medical Centre
GNTH/NBYPK IG2 .... **66** A1

Gardener Industrial Estate
BECK BR3 .... **157** E5

Garratt Park Secondary School Special Sch
WAND/EARL SW18 .... **150** B3

Garrick Theatre
LSQ/SEVD WC2H............................ **32** C2

Gascoigne Primary School
BARK IG11 .... **84** C5

Gate Cinema
NTGHL W11 .... **26** A3

Gatehouse School
BETH E2 .... **91** D1

The Gatehouse Theatre
HGT N6 .... **56** A2

The Gate Theatre
NTGHL W11 .... **26** A3

Gateway Industrial Estate
WLSDN NW10 .... **87** F2

Gateway Primary School
STJWD NW8 .... **4** B5

Gayhurst Primary School
HACK E8 .... **78** A4

Geffrye Museum
BETH E2 .... **13** D2

Gemini Business Estate
NWCR SE14 .... **121** D1

General Medical Clinics
WCHPL E1 .... **25** E2

Genesis Cinema
WCHPL E1 .... **90** C3

Geoffrey Chaucer School
STHWK SE1 .... **48** A3

The Geoffrey Lloyd Foulkes Clinic
IL IG1 .... **66** A4

George Eliot Junior & Infant School
STJWD NW8 .... **72** C5

George Green Mixed School
POP/IOD E14 .... **122** C1

George Lowe Court
BAY/PAD W2 .... **14** C2

George Mitchell School
LEY E10 .... **62** B3

George Mitchell School Annexe
LEY E10 .... **62** B3

George Tomlinson Primary School
WAN E11 .... **63** E3

The Gielgud Theatre
SOHO/SHAV W1D **32** A1

Giffin Business Centre
DEPT SE8.. **122** A3

Gilbert Collection
TPL/STR WC2R **33** E1

Gilbert Collection
WAP E1W **102** B1

Gillespie Primary School
FSBYPK N4 .... **58** B5

Girdlers' Hall
CITYW EC2V **23** F3

Gladstone Court Business Centre
VX/NE SW8 .... **116** C4

Gladstone Medical Centre
CRICK NW2 .... **69** F1

Gladstone Park Primary School
WLSDN NW10 .... **70** B2

Glaziers/Scientific Instrument Makers Hall
STHWK SE1 .... **36** A3

Gleen Lecky Health Centre
PUT/ROE SW15.............................. **131** D2

Glenbrook Primary School
CLAP SW4 .... **135** D4

Glendower Preparatory School
SKENS SW7 .... **39** F4

Glenham College
IL IG1 .... **66** B4

Globe Primary School
BETH E2 .... **90** C2

Globe Theatre
STHWK SE1 .... **35** D2

Globe Wharf
BERM/RHTH SE16 .... **103** D1

Gloucester Primary School
PECK SE15.................................... **119** E3

Godolphin & Latymer School
HMSMTH W6 .... **100** B5

Godwin Junior School
FSTGT E7 .... **82** B1

Golborne Medical Centre
NKENS W10 .... **89** F3

Golden Hinde
STHWK SE1 .... **36** A2

Golders Green Crematorium
GLDGN NW11 .... **54** A2

Golders Green Health Centre
GLDGN NW11 .... **54** B3

Golders Hill Health Centre
EFNCH N2 .... **54** C1

Golders Hill School
GLDGN NW11 .... **54** A2

Goldhawk Industrial Estate
  SHB W12 .... **100** B4
Goldsmiths College
  BROCKY SE4 .... **139** F1
  DEPT SE8 .... **122** A2
  LEW SE13 .... **141** E2
  NWCR SE14 .... **121** E4
Goldsmiths Hall
  STBT EC1A **23** E4
Gooding Health Centre
  HOLWY N7 .... **75** E3
Goodrich Junior & Infant School
  EDUL SE22 .... **138** A4
Good Shepherd RC Primary School
  BMLY BR1 .... **159** F4
**The Good Shepherd
RC Primary School**
  SHB W12 .... **99** F3
Goose Green Trading Estate
  EDUL SE22 .... **138** A2
Gordonbrock Primary School
  BROCKY SE4 .... **140** A3
Gordon Hospital
  WEST SW1P **44** A5
Gordon Infant School
  IL IG1 .... **67** D5
Gordon Primary School
  ELTH/MOT SE9 .... **143** F2
Gospel Oak Primary School
  HAMP NW3 .... **74** A1
Gower House School
  CDALE/KGS NW9 .... **50** C4
Grace Theatre at the Latchmere
  BTSEA SW11 .... **115** F5
Grafton Primary School
  HOLWY N7 .... **57** E5
Granard Primary School
  PUT/ROE SW15 .... **130** B4
Granby Sports Club
  ELTH/MOT SE9 .... **161** E5
Grande Vitesse Industrial Centre
  STHWK SE1 .... **35** D4
Grand Union Industrial Estate
  WLSDN NW10 .... **86** B1
Grange Infant School
  CAN/RD E16 .... **93** F2
The Grange Museum
  CRICK NW2 .... **69** F1
Grange Primary School
  STHWK SE1 .... **48** C3
Grangewood Independent School
  FSTGT E7 .... **83** D4
Granville Road Industrial Estate
  CRICK NW2 .... **53** F4
Grasmere Primary School
  STNW/STAM N16 .... **77** D1
Grazebrook Primary School
  STNW/STAM N16 .... **59** E4
Great Chapel Street Medical Centre
  SOHO/SHAV W1D **20** A4
Great Jubilee Wharf
  WAP E1W **102** C2
**Greater London Authority
Headquarters (City Hall)**
  STHWK SE1 .... **37** D4
Greenacres Primary School
  ELTH/MOT SE9 .... **162** A4
Greenfield Medical Centre
  CRICK NW2 .... **53** E5
Greenfields Junior School
  SHB W12 .... **99** F1
Greengate Medical Centre
  PLSTW E13 .... **94** B2

Greenheath Business Centre
  BETH E2 .... **90** B2
Greenhill Park Medical Centre
  WLSDN NW10 .... **69** E5
Greenland Pier
  BERM/RHTH SE16 .... **103** F4
Green Lane Business Park
  ELTH/MOT SE9 .... **162** A2
Greenmead Primary School
  PUT/ROE SW15 .... **130** B3
Greenshields Industrial Estate
  CAN/RD E16 .... **106** A2
Greenside Primary School
  SHB W12 .... **100** A3
Greenslade Primary School
  WOOL/PLUM SE18 .... **127** D2
Greenwich Centre Business Park
  DEPT SE8 .... **122** B3
Greenwich Cinema
  GNWCH SE10 .... **122** C3
Greenwich College
  GNWCH SE10 .... **122** C3
Greenwich Community College
  WOOL/PLUM SE18 .... **108** B5
  WOOL/PLUM SE18 .... **127** D2
Greenwich Hospital
  GNWCH SE10 .... **123** F1
Greenwich Industrial Estate
  CHARL SE7 .... **106** B5
  GNWCH SE10 .... **122** B3
Greenwich Natural Health Centre
  GNWCH SE10 .... **122** C3
Greenwich School of English
  GNWCH SE10 .... **122** C2
Greenwich Theatre & Art Gallery
  GNWCH SE10 .... **123** D3
Greenwich University Library
  GNWCH SE10 .... **122** C2
Greenwood School
  WOOL/PLUM SE18 .... **127** E4
Greenwood Theatre
  STHWK SE1 .... **36** B5
Grenfell Primary School
  WCHPL E1 .... **90** B5
Gresham College
  FLST/FETLN EC4A **22** A3
Gresham Way Industrial Estate
  WIM/MER SW19 .... **150** B3
The Greycoat Hospital
  WEST SW1P **44** A5
Grey Coat Hospital Upper School
  WEST SW1P **44** A3
Griffen Manor School
  WOOL/PLUM SE18 .... **127** E4
Grinling Gibbons Primary School
  DEPT SE8 .... **121** F2
Grocers' Hall
  CITYW EC2V **24** A5
Grove Health Centre
  KENS W8 .... **26** B3
The Grove Health Centre
  HMSMTH W6 .... **100** B3
Grove House School
  WNWD SE27 .... **154** B2
Grove Medical Centre
  DEPT SE8 .... **103** E5
The Grove Medical Centre
  ARCH N19 .... **56** C4
Grove Park Primary School
  CHSWK W4 .... **110** C2
Grove Vale Primary School
  EDUL SE22 .... **137** F2

Guardian Angels
RC Primary School
BOW E3 .... **91** E3

Guardian Newspapers
POP/IOD E14 .... **104** B3

Guards' Chapel and Museum
WHALL SW1A **44** A1

Guildhall School
BARB EC2Y **23** F2

Guildhall School of Music & Drama
STLK EC1Y **23** F1

Guildhall University
WCHPL E1 .... **90** A5

Gunnersbury Park Museum
ACT W3 .... **98** A4

Guys Hospital
STHWK SE1 .... **36** B4

Guys Kings & St Thomas
School of Medicine
CMBW SE5 .... **118** C5

Gwyn Jones Primary School
WAN E11 .... **63** D2

GX Superbowl
EHAM E6 .... **96** A4

Gypsy Moth IV
GNWCH SE10 .... **122** C2

Haberdashers Askes
Hatcham College
NWCR SE14 .... **121** E4
NWCR SE14 .... **121** E5

Haberdashers' Hall
CITYW EC2Y **23** F4

Hackney Business Centre
HACK E8 .... **78** B3

Hackney Community College
CLPT E5 .... **60** B5
IS N1 .... **12** C2

Hackney Empire Variety Theatre
HACK E8 .... **78** B3

Hackney Free &
Parochial CE School
HOM E9 .... **78** C3

Hackney Hospital
HOM E9 .... **79** E2

The Hackney Museum
HOM E9 .... **78** C5

Hackney Sports Centre
HOM E9 .... **80** A1

The Haelan Clinic
CEND/HSY/T N8 .... **57** D1

Haggerston School
BETH E2 .... **13** F1

Haggerston Swimming Pool
BETH E2 .... **77** F5

Hague Primary School
BETH E2 .... **90** B3

Haimo Primary School
ELTH/MOT SE9 .... **143** D3

The Hale Clinic
REGST W1B **19** D1

Half Moon Theatre
WCHPL E1 .... **91** D3

Halley Primary School
POP/IOD E14 .... **91** E4

Hallfield Clinic
BAY/PAD W2 .... **15** E5

Hallfield Junior & Infant School
BAY/PAD W2 .... **15** D5

The Hall Junior School
HAMP NW3 .... **73** D3

Hallmark Trading Estate
WBLY HA9 .... **68** C1

Hall School Wimbledon
PUT/ROE SW15 .... **148** A3

The Hall Senior School
HAMP NW3 .... **73** D3

Hallsville Primary School
CAN/RD E16 .... **94** A5

Halstow Primary School
GNWCH SE10 .... **123** F1

Hamer Indoor Market
BOW E3 .... **91** F1

Hamilton Road Industrial Estate
WNWD SE27 .... **155** D4

Hammersmith Apollo
HMSMTH W6 .... **112** C1

Hammersmith Cemetery
HMSMTH W6 .... **113** D1

The Hammersmith Hospitals
SHB W12 .... **88** A5

Hammersmith Industrial Estate
HMSMTH W6 .... **112** C2

Hammersmith New Cemetery
RCH/KEW TW9 .... **110** B5

Hammersmith Palais
HMSMTH W6 .... **100** C5

Hammersmith Physio &
Sports Injury Clinic
HMSMTH W6 .... **100** C5

Hammersmith & West
London College
WKENS W14 .... **101** D5

Hampden Gurney School
MBLAR W1H **17** D4

The Hampshire School
(Knightsbridge)
SKENS SW7 .... **40** C1

The Hampshire School
BAY/PAD W2 .... **27** D1

Hampstead Cricket Club
KIL/WHAMP NW6 .... **72** B2

Hampstead Golf Club
EFNCH N2 .... **54** C2

Hampstead Medical Centre
HAMP NW3 .... **72** C1

Hampstead Parochial CE School
HAMP NW3 .... **72** C1

Hampstead School
CRICK NW2 .... **71** E1

Hampstead School of English
KIL/WHAMP NW6 .... **72** A1

Hanover Primary School
IS N1 .... **11** D1

Hanover Trading Estate
HOLWY N7 .... **75** E2

Hanover West Industrial Estate
WLSDN NW10 .... **86** C2

Harbinger Primary School
POP/IOD E14 .... **104** A5

Harborough School
ARCH N19 .... **57** D4

Hargrave Park Primary School
ARCH N19 .... **56** C4

Haringey Magistrates Court
HGT N6 .... **56** A1

Harlesden Primary School
WLSDN NW10 .... **87** E1

Harley Medical Centre
CAVSQ/HST W1G **18** C4

The Harley Medical Centre
CANST EC4R **35** F1

Harley Street Clinic
CAVSQ/HST W1G **18** C2
CAVSQ/HST W1G **18** C3

Harp Business Centre
CRICK NW2 .... **52** A4

Harpley School
WCHPL E1 .... **90** C3

Harrington Hill Primary School
CLPT E5 .... **60** B3

Harrodian School
BARN SW13 .... **111** F3

Harrods Store
CHEL SW3 .... **41** E2

Harrow Road Health Centre
BAY/PAD W2 .... **14** B2

Harry Gosling Primary School
WCHPL E1 .... **90** A5

Hartley Primary School
EHAM E6 .... **83** E5

Haselrigge School
CLAP SW4 .... **135** D2

Haseltine Primary School
CAT SE6 .... **157** F4

Haslemere Industrial Estate
WAND/EARL SW18 .... **150** B2

Hastings Clinic
BRXS/STRHM SW2 .... **135** F3

Hatcham Mews Business Centre
NWCR SE14 .... **121** D3

Haverstock School
CAMTN NW1 .... **74** A3

Hawkins Clinic
PUT/ROE SW15 .... **131** D2

Hawley Infant School
CAMTN NW1 .... **74** B4

Haymerle School
PECK SE15 .... **120** A2

Hays Galleria
STHWK SE1 .... **36** C3

Hayward Gallery
STHWK SE1 .... **33** F4

Hazeldene Medical Centre
WBLY HA9 .... **68** B3

Healy Medical Centre
CLPT E5 .... **60** B3

The Heart Hospital
CAVSQ/HST W1G **18** B3

Heathbrook Primary School
VX/NE SW8 .... **116** C5

Heath House Preparatory School
BKHTH/KID SE3 .... **123** F5

Heathmere Primary School
PUT/ROE SW15 .... **148** A1

Heathside Preparatory School
HAMP NW3 .... **72** C1

Heber Primary School
EDUL SE22 .... **137** F4

Heckford Street Business Centre
WAP E1W **103** D1

Hedges & Butler Estate
SRTFD E15 .... **92** C1

Helena Road Clinic
WLSDN NW10 .... **70** B1

Heliport Industrial Estate
BTSEA SW11 .... **115** D5

Hellenic College of London
KTBR SW1X **41** E3

Helston Court Business Centre
WIM/MER SW19 .... **148** B5

Hendon FC
CRICK NW2 .... **53** D4

Hendon Youth Sports Centre
CRICK NW2 .... **53** D2

Henry Cavendish Primary School
BAL SW12 .... **152** C1

Henry Compton School
FUL/PGN SW6 .... **113** D4

Henry Fawcett Primary School
LBTH SE11 .... **118** A2

Henwick Primary School
ELTH/MOT SE9 .... **143** D1

Herbert Morrison Primary School
VX/NE SW8 .... **117** E3

Hereward House School
HAMP NW3 .... **73** E3

Her Majestys' Theatre
STJS SW1Y **32** B3

Hermitage Primary School
WAP E1W **102** A2

Herne Hill School
HNHL SE24 .... **136** C3

Heron Industrial Estate
SRTFD E15 .... **92** B1

Heronsgate Primary School
THMD SE28 .... **109** D4

Heron Trading Estate
ACT W3 .... **86** B5

HGS Institute Centre
GLDGN NW11 .... **54** B1

Higgs Industrial Estate
BRXN/ST SW9 .... **136** B1

**Highbury Corner
Magistrates Court**
HOLWY N7 .... **76** A3

Highbury Fields School
HBRY N5 .... **76** B2

Highbury Grove School
HBRY N5 .... **76** C2

Highbury Park Clinic
HBRY N5 .... **58** B5

**Highbury Quadrant
Primary School**
HBRY N5 .... **76** C1

High Commission of Angola
MYFR/PKLN W1K **30** B1

**High Commission of
Antigua & Barbuda**
MHST W1U **18** A4

High Commission of Bahamas
MYFR/PICC W1J **30** B3

High Commission of Bangladesh
SKENS SW7 .... **39** F2

High Commission of Barbados
FITZ W1T **20** A4

High Commission of Belize
CAVSQ/HST W1G **18** C4

High Commission of Botswana
OXSTW W1C **18** C5

High Commission of Brunei
BAY/PAD W2 .... **16** B4
KTBR SW1X **42** A2

High Commission of Cyprus
CONDST W1S **19** D5
MYFR/PKLN W1K **30** A1

High Commission of Dominica
ECT SW5 .... **39** D5

High Commission of Fiji
SKENS SW7 .... **39** E1

High Commission of the Gambia
KENS W8 .... **39** D1

High Commission of Grenada
ECT SW5 .... **114** B1

High Commission of Guyana
NTGHL W11 .... **26** C2

High Commission of Jamaica
SKENS SW7 .... **40** A1

High Commission of Kenya
CAVSQ/HST W1G **18** C2

High Commission of Lesotho
KTBR SW1X **42** A2

High Commission of Malawi
MYFR/PKLN W1K **30** C1

High Commission of Malaysia
KTBR SW1X **42** B1
MBLAR W1H **17** E4

High Commission of the Maldives
MHST W1U **18** A2

High Commission of Malta
MYFR/PICC W1J **31** F2

High Commission of Mauritius
SKENS SW7 .... **39** F2

High Commission of Namibia
CAVSO/HST W1G **19** D3

High Commission of New Zealand
STJS SW1Y **32** A3

High Commission of Nigeria
CHCR WC2N **32** C3
EMB EC4Y **22** B5

High Commission of Pakistan
KTBR SW1X **41** F1

High Commission of
Papua New Guinea
STJS SW1Y **32** A3

High Commission of St Vincent &
The Grenadines
KENS W8 .... **39** D1

High Commission of Seychelles
MBLAR W1H **17** F2

High Commission of Sierra Leone
OXSTW W1C **19** E4

High Commission of Singapore
KTBR SW1X **41** F1
STJS SW1Y **32** A3
WEST SW1P **43** F4

High Commission of South Africa
CHCR WC2N **32** B3

High Commission of Sri Lanka
BAY/PAD W2 .... **28** B1

High Commission of Swaziland
WESTW SW1E **43** E2

High Commission of Tonga
MBLAR W1H **17** D3

High Commission of
Trinidad & Tobago
KTBR SW1X **42** A2

High Commission of Uganda
STJS SW1Y **32** B3

High Commission of Zambia
SKENS SW7 .... **39** E1

High Commission of Zimbabwe
CHCR WC2N **32** C2

Highfield School
WAND/EARL SW18 .... **133** E5

Highgate Cemetery
HGT N6 .... **56** A3

Highgate Golf Club
HGT N6 .... **55** E1

Highgate Junior School
HGT N6 .... **55** F2

Highgate Pre-Preparatory School
HGT N6 .... **55** F2

Highgate Primary School
HGT N6 .... **55** F1

Highgate Private Hospital
HGT N6 .... **55** F1

Highgate School
HGT N6 .... **55** F2

Highlands Junior & Infant School
IL IG1 .... **65** F3

Highlands Primary School
IL IG1 .... **65** F3

High Road Swimming Baths
IL IG1 .... **67** D4

Highshore School
PECK SE15 .... **119** F4

High View Primary School
BTSEA SW11 .... **133** D2

The Highway Trading Centre
WAP E1W **103** D1

Hillbrook Primary School
TOOT SW17 .... **151** F4

Hill House International School
KTBR SW1X **41** E3

Hill House School
CHEL SW3 .... **115** E2

Hill Mead Infant School
HNHL SE24 .... **136** B2

Hillmead Primary School
BRXN/ST SW9 .... **136** B2

Hilly Fields Medical Centre
BROCKY SE4 .... **140** A3

Hinley Clinic
LBTH SE11 .... **46** C5

Hispaniola
WHALL SW1A **33** D4

Hitherfield Primary School
STRHM/NOR SW16 .... **154** A2

Hither Green Cemetery
CAT SE6 .... **159** F2

Hither Green Primary School
LEW SE13 .... **141** D4

HM Prison
CLAP SW4 .... **135** E4
HOLWY N7 .... **75** F3
HOLWY N7 .... **75** E1
SHB W12 .... **88** A5
WAND/EARL SW18 .... **133** D4

HMS Belfast
STHWK SE1 .... **37** D3

HMS President
EMB EC4Y **34** B1

Hogarth Business Park
CHSWK W4 .... **111** E2

Hogarth Industrial Estate
WLSDN NW10 .... **88** A3

Hogarth Primary School
CHSWK W4 .... **111** E1

Hogarth's House
CHSWK W4 .... **111** D2

Holbeach Primary School
CAT SE6 .... **140** A5

Holborn College
WKENS W14 .... **113** E2

Holborn Medical Centre
BMSBY WC1N **21** E1

Holborn Town Hall
HHOL WC1V **21** D4

Holland Park School
KENS W8 .... **101** F3

Holland Park Theatre
KENS W8 .... **101** F3

Holland Street Clinic
KENS W8 .... **38** B1

Holloway School
HOLWY N7 .... **75** D2

Hollydale Primary School
PECK SE15 .... **120** C5

The Holme
CAMTN NW1 .... **5** F4

Holmleigh Primary School
STNW/STAM N16 .... **59** F3

Holy Cross RC Primary School
CAT SE6 .... **158** C1

Holy Family RC Primary School
  ELTH/MOT SE9 .... **142** B2
  POP/IOD E14 .... **104** A1
Holy Ghost RC Primary School
  BAL SW12 .... **133** F5
Holy Trinity CE Primary School
  BGVA SW1W **42** A4
  BRXS/STRHM SW2 .... **135** F5
  FSTH SE23 .... **156** C2
  KIL/WHAMP NW6 .... **72** C3
  RCHPK/HAM TW10 .... **128** A2
Holy Trinity Haverstock Hill
  CE Primary School
  CAMTN NW1 .... **74** B4
Holy Trinity Primary School
  HACK E8 .... **77** F3
Holy Trinity School
  CHEL SW3 .... **41** F4
Home Office
  STJSPK SW1H **43** F1
Homerton Hospital
  CLPT E5 .... **79** D2
Homerton House School
  HOM E9 .... **78** C2
Homoeopathic Health Centre
  PLSTW E13 .... **94** A3
Honeywell Primary School
  BTSEA SW11 .... **133** F5
Honor Oak Crematorium
  FSTH SE23 .... **139** D3
Honor Oak Gallery
  FSTH SE23 .... **139** D4
Honor Oak Health Centre
  BROCKY SE4 .... **139** E2
Honourable Artillery
  Company HQ
  STLK EC1Y **24** A1
Horizon Industrial Estate
  PECK SE15 .... **120** A2
Horizon School
  STNW/STAM N16 .... **77** E1
The Horniman Museum & Gardens
  FSTH SE23 .... **156** B1
Horniman Primary School
  FSTH SE23 .... **156** B1
Horn Park Primary School
  LEE/GVPK SE12 .... **142** B5
Hornsby House School
  BAL SW12 .... **152** A1
Hornsey Rise Health Centre
  ARCH N19 .... **57** D2
Horseferry Road
  Magistrates Court
  WEST SW1P **44** B3
Horse Guards Parade
  WHALL SW1A **32** B4
Hospital & Counselling Centre
  CAMTN NW1 .... **17** D2
Hospital of St John &
  St Elizabeth
  STJWD NW8 .... **4** A2
Hotham Primary School
  PUT/ROE SW15 .... **131** D2
House of Detention
  CLKNW EC1R **10** B5
House of St Barnabus
  SOHO/SHAV W1D **20** A5
Houses of Parliament
  WEST SW1P **45** D1
Howland Quay
  BERM/RHTH SE16 .... **103** D4
Hoxton Hall Community Theatre
  IS N1 .... **12** C1

HQS Wellington (Master Mariners)
  TPL/STR WC2R **34** A2
Hughesfields Primary School
  DEPT SE8 .... **122** A2
Hugh Myddelton Primary School
  CLKNW EC1R **10** B4
The Humana Wellington Hospital
  STJWD NW8 .... **4** B3
Humber Trading Estate
  CRICK NW2 .... **52** B4
Hungerford Primary School
  HOLWY N7 .... **75** D3
Hunter Street Health Centre
  STPAN WC1H **8** C5
Huntsman Sports Club
  BKHTH/KID SE3 .... **142** A2
Hurlingham Business Park
  FUL/PGN SW6 .... **132** A1
Hurlingham & Chelsea School
  FUL/PGN SW6 .... **132** A1
Hurlingham House
  FUL/PGN SW6 .... **131** F1
Huron College
  SKENS SW7 .... **39** F4
Huron University
  SKENS SW7 .... **40** B2
Hyleford School
  IL IG1 .... **85** E2
Hythe Road Industrial Estate
  WLSDN NW10 .... **88** A3
Ibstock Place School
  PUT/ROE SW15 .... **129** E4
ICA Cinema
  STJS SW1Y **32** B4
Ichthus Primary School
  CMBW SE5 .... **119** D3
Ickburgh School
  CLPT E5 .... **60** B5
Ihlara Sport FC
  HBRY N5 .... **76** C1
Ikra Primary School
  STNW/STAM N16 .... **77** E1
Ilderton Primary School
  BERM/RHTH SE16 .... **120** C2
Ilford County Court
  IL IG1 .... **67** D4
Ilford Golf Club
  IL IG1 .... **65** F3
Ilford Medical Centre
  IL IG1 .... **66** B5
Ilford Preparatory School
  GDMY/SEVK IG3 .... **67** F3
Ilford Retail Park
  IL IG1 .... **66** C4
Imperial College
  PUT/ROE SW15 .... **113** D5
  SKENS SW7 .... **40** A2
Imperial College of Science
  FUL/PGN SW6 .... **114** A2
Imperial College of
  Science & Technology
  SKENS SW7 .... **40** B1
Imperial College of
  Science Technology & Medicine
  SKENS SW7 .... **39** F2
Imperial College School of Medicine
  PIM SW1V **44** A5
Imperial War Museum
  STHWK SE1 .... **46** B3
Imperial War Museum Annexe
  STHWK SE1 .... **46** B3
India House
  HOL/ALD WC2B **33** E1

Infant College
IL IG1 .... **66** A4
Inner London Sessions House
(Crown Court)
STHWK SE1 .... **47** E2
Inner Temple
EMB EC4Y **34** B1
Innholders Hall
CANST EC4R **35** F1
Inns of Court and Chancery
TPL/STR WC2R **22** A5
Inns of Court School of Law
GINN WC1R **21** F2
Institut Francais
SKENS SW7 .... **40** A4
International Community School
CAMTN NW1 .... **18** A4
International Financial Centre
OBST EC2N **24** C4
International Medical Centre
ECT SW5 .... **38** B5
International School of London
ACT W3 .... **98** A5
Invicta Industrial Estate
SRTFD E15 .... **92** C2
Invicta Primary School
BKHTH/KID SE3 .... **124** A2
Ironmongers Hall
STBT EC1A **23** E3
Islamia Girls School
KIL/WHAMP NW6 .... **71** E5
Islamic College for
Advanced Studies
WLSDN NW10 .... **70** B4
The Islamic Grammar School
WAND/EARL SW18 .... **131** F5
Island Clinic
POP/IOD E14 .... **104** C3
Islington Arts & Media School
FSBYPK N4 .... **57** F3
Islington Business Centre
IS N1 .... **76** C5
Islington Green Medical Centre
IS N1 .... **76** B5
Islington Green School
IS N1 .... **76** B5
Islington Town Hall
IS N1 .... **76** B4
Ismaili Centre
SKENS SW7 .... **40** B4
Italia Conti Academy of
Theatre Arts
BRXN/ST SW9 .... **135** E1
Italian Hospital
WEST SW1P **43** E4
Ivydale Primary School
PECK SE15 .... **139** D2
Jack Taylor School
KIL/WHAMP NW6 .... **72** C5
Jack Tizzard School
FUL/PGN SW6 .... **113** D4
Jamahiriya School
CHEL SW3 .... **115** E2
James Allens Preparatory
Girls School
HNHL SE24 .... **137** D3
Jamestown Mental Health Centre
HAMP NW3 .... **73** F4
James Wolfe Primary School
GNWCH SE10 .... **122** B3
Janet Adegoke Leisure Centre
SHB W12 .... **100** A1

The Japanese School
ACT W3 .... **98** A1
Japan Green Medical Centre
ACT W3 .... **98** B2
Jenner Health Centre
FSTH SE23 .... **157** E1
Jermyn Street Theatre
STJS SW1Y **31** F2
Jessop Primary School
HNHL SE24 .... **136** B2
Jewel Tower
WEST SW1P **44** C2
Jewish Cemetery
GLDGN NW11 .... **54** A1
Jewish Community Theatre
CMBW SE5 .... **137** D1
The Jewish Museum
CAMTN NW1 .... **74** B5
Johanna Primary School
STHWK SE1 .... **46** A1
John Ball Primary School
BKHTH/KID SE3 .... **123** E5
John Betts Primary School
HMSMTH W6 .... **100** A4
John Burns Primary School
BTSEA SW11 .... **116** A5
John Dixon Clinic
BERM/RHTH SE16 .... **102** B4
John Donne Primary School
PECK SE15 .... **120** B4
John F Kennedy Special School
SRTFD E15 .... **81** D5
John Keble CE Primary School
WLSDN NW10 .... **69** F5
John Kelly Boys & Girls
Technology College
CRICK NW2 .... **51** F5
John Milton Primary School
VX/NE SW8 .... **116** C3
John Orwell Sports Centre
WAP E1W **102** A2
John Paul II RC School
WIM/MER SW19 .... **131** D5
John Perryn Primary School
ACT W3 .... **87** E4
John Roan Lower School
BKHTH/KID SE3 .... **123** F2
John Roan School
BKHTH/KID SE3 .... **123** E3
John Ruskin Primary School
WALW SE17 .... **118** C2
John Scott Health Centre
FSBYPK N4 .... **58** C3
John Scurr JMI School
WCHPL E1 .... **90** C3
John Smith House
WALW SE17 .... **47** E5
John Stainer Primary School
BROCKY SE4 .... **139** E1
Joseph Lancaster School
STHWK SE1 .... **47** F3
Joseph Tritton Primary School
BTSEA SW11 .... **132** C2
Jubilee JMI School
STNW/STAM N16 .... **60** A3
Jubilee Market
COVGDN WC2E **33** D1
Julians Primary School
STRHM/NOR SW16 .... **154** A4
Junior & Youth Centre
POP/IOD E14 .... **91** F4
Juno Way Industrial Estate
NWCR SE14 .... **121** D2

JVC Business Park
CRICK NW2 .... 52 A3
Kangley Business Centre
SYD SE26 .... 157 F5
Katella Trading Estate
BARK IG11 .... 97 E2
Katherine Road Medical Centre
FSTGT E7 .... 82 C3
Keats House Museum
HAMP NW3 .... 73 D1
Keen Students
Supplementary School
WCHPL E1 .... 90 A4
Keir Hardie Primary School
CAN/RD E16 .... 94 A4
Kelmscott Leisure Centre
WALTH E17 .... 61 F1
Kelmscott School
WALTH E17 .... 61 F1
Kelvin Grove Primary School
SYD SE26 .... 156 B3
Kemnal Technology College
CHST BR7 .... 163 D5
Ken Barrington Centre
LBTH SE11 .... 117 F2
Kender Primary School
NWCR SE14 .... 120 C4
Kenmont Primary School
WLSDN NW10 .... 88 A2
Kenneth More Theatre
IL IG1 .... 66 C5
Kensal Rise Primary School
WLSDN NW10 .... 89 D1
Kensington and Chelsea Town Hall
KENS W8 .... 38 B1
Kensington Business Centre
SKENS SW7 .... 41 D2
Kensington & Chelsea College
NKENS W10 .... 89 E4
WBPTN SW10 .... 114 C3
The Kensington Clinic
KENS W8 .... 38 C3
Kensington Market
KENS W8 .... 38 C1
Kensington Palace State Apartments
& Royal Ceremonial
Dress Collection
KENS W8 .... 27 D4
Kensington Park School
REGST W1B 19 D2
Kensington Preparatory School
FUL/PGN SW6 .... 113 F4
Kensington Primary School
MNPK E12 .... 83 F3
Kensington School of Business
HCIRC EC1N 22 B2
Kensington Wharf
WBPTN SW10 .... 115 D3
Kentish Town Church
CE Primary School
KTTN NW5 .... 74 C2
Kentish Town Health Centre
KTTN NW5 .... 74 C3
Kentish Town Industrial Estate
KTTN NW5 .... 74 B2
Kent Park Industrial Estate
PECK SE15 .... 120 B2
Kenwood House
HGT N6 .... 55 E3
Kew College
RCH/KEW TW9 .... 110 A3
Kew Retail Park
RCH/KEW TW9 .... 110 B4

Keyplan & Roxburghe College
FITZ W1T 19 F1
Keyworth Primary School
WALW SE17 .... 118 B1
Kidbrooke Park Primary School
BKHTH/KID SE3 .... 124 C5
Kidbrooke School
BKHTH/KID SE3 .... 125 D5
Kilburn Park Junior School
KIL/WHAMP NW6 .... 2 A2
Killick Street Medical Centre
IS N1 .... 9 E1
Kilmorie Primary School
FSTH SE23 .... 157 E2
King Alfred School
GLDGN NW11 .... 54 B3
King Edward VII
Hospital for Officers
MHST W1U 18 B2
The Kingfisher Medical Centre
DEPT SE8 .... 121 F2
Kingford Community School
PLSTW E13 .... 94 C3
Kingham Industrial Estate
WLSDN NW10 .... 87 D2
King Henry's Reach Development
BARN SW13 .... 112 C2
King & Queen Wharf
BERM/RHTH SE16 .... 103 D1
Kings Acre Primary School
CLAP SW4 .... 135 E3
Kingsbury Trading Estate
CDALE/KGS NW9 .... 50 C1
Kings College Hospital
CMBW SE5 .... 136 C1
EDUL SE22 .... 137 E2
Kings College London
CMBW SE5 .... 119 D5
HAMP NW3 .... 72 A1
STHWK SE1 .... 35 D3
TPL/STR WC2R 33 F1
WBPTN SW10 .... 114 C3
WEST SW1P 43 F4
Kings College School of
Medicine & Dentistry
HNHL SE24 .... 137 D4
Kings Cross Station
CAMTN NW1 .... 8 C2
Kings Cross Thameslink Station
FSBYW WC1X 9 D3
Kingsdale School
DUL SE21 .... 155 E3
Kingsgate Primary School
KIL/WHAMP NW6 .... 72 A4
Kings Head Theatre
IS N1 .... 76 A5
Kingsland Health Centre
HACK E8 .... 77 F4
Kingsland School
HACK E8 .... 77 F2
Kingsland Shopping Centre
HACK E8 .... 77 F3
Kings Mall Shopping Centre
HMSMTH W6 .... 100 C5
Kingsmead Primary School
CLPT E5 .... 79 E1
Kings Private Clinic
GDMY/SEVK IG3 .... 67 F3
MHST W1U 18 A2
Kings Stairs
BERM/RHTH SE16 .... 102 B3
Kingston University
KUTN/CMB KT2 .... 147 D5

King Street College
  HMSMTH W6 .... **100** C5
Kingsway College
  CLKNW EC1R **10** B5
  KTTN NW5 .... **74** B3
  STPAN WC1H **9** E4
Kingswood Primary School
  WNWD SE27 .... **155** D4
Kisharon School
  GLDGN NW11 .... **53** F1
KLC School of Design
  WBPTN SW10 .... **114** C4
Knightsbridge Barracks
  SKENS SW7 .... **41** D1
Knightsbridge Medical Centre
  KTBR SW1X **41** F2
Knowledge Point School
  HOLWY N7 .... **75** F3
Kobi Nazrul Primary School
  WCHPL E1 .... **90** A5
Kubrick Business Estate
  FSTGT E7 .... **82** B1
Laban Centre
  DEPT SE8 .... **122** B3
Laburnum Primary School
  HACK E8 .... **77** F5
Lady Edens School
  KENS W8 .... **39** E2
Lady Margaret School
  FUL/PGN SW6 .... **114** A4
Ladywell Arena
  LEW SE13 .... **140** B4
Ladywell Cemetery
  BROCKY SE4 .... **139** F3
Ladywell Leisure Centre
  LEW SE13 .... **140** C3
Laker Industrial Estate
  BECK BR3 .... **157** E5
Lambeth Cemetery
  TOOT SW17 .... **150** C5
Lambeth College
  CLAP SW4 .... **134** C3
  STHWK SE1 .... **37** D4
Lambeth Crematorium
  TOOT SW17 .... **150** C5
Lambeth Palace
  STHWK SE1 .... **45** E3
Lambs Court
  POP/IOD E14 .... **103** E1
The Lanark Medical Centre
  MV/WKIL W9 .... **3** D3
Lancaster House
  WHALL SW1A **31** E5
Langbourne Primary School
  DUL SE21 .... **155** E3
Langdon Park Secondary School
  POP/IOD E14 .... **92** B5
Langdon School
  EHAM E6 .... **96** B1
Langford Primary School
  FUL/PGN SW6 .... **114** B5
Langthorne Health Centre
  WAN E11 .... **63** D5
Langthorne Hospital
  WAN E11 .... **81** D1
Lansbury Lawrence
  Primary School
  POP/IOD E14 .... **92** B5
Lansdowne College
  BAY/PAD W2 .... **26** C2
Lansdowne School
  BRXN/ST SW9 .... **135** F1

La Retraite RC Girls School
  BAL SW12 .... **134** C5
Lark Hall Junior School
  CLAP SW4 .... **117** D5
Lark Hall Primary School
  CLAP SW4 .... **117** D5
Larmenier Infant School
  HMSMTH W6 .... **101** D5
La Sainte Union Convent School
  KTTN NW5 .... **56** A5
Latchmere Leisure Centre
  BTSEA SW11 .... **115** F5
Lathom Junior School
  EHAM E6 .... **83** E4
Latimer Industrial Estate
  SHB W12 .... **88** C5
Latymer Upper School
  HMSMTH W6 .... **100** A5
Launcelot Primary School
  BMLY BR1 .... **160** A4
Lauriston Primary School
  HOM E9 .... **79** D5
Lawdale Junior School
  BETH E2 .... **90** A2
Lawrence Trading Estate
  GNWCH SE10 .... **105** E5
Lawrence University
  SKENS SW7 .... **39** F5
Lawrence Wharf
  BERM/RHTH SE16 .... **103** F2
Laycock Primary School
  IS N1 .... **76** A3
Lea Bridge Industrial Estate
  LEY E10 .... **61** E3
Leadenhall Market
  BANK EC3V **24** C5
Lea Park Trading Estate
  LEY E10 .... **61** F2
Lea Valley Ice Centre
  LEY E10 .... **61** D4
Leathermarket Gardens
  STHWK SE1 .... **48** C1
Leathersellers Sports Ground
  ELTH/MOT SE9 .... **142** C5
Leathers Hall
  HDTCH EC3A **24** C4
L'écoles Des Petits
  FUL/PGN SW6 .... **114** B5
Lee Manor Primary School
  LEW SE13 .... **141** E4
Leeside Court
  BERM/RHTH SE16 .... **103** D2
Leighton House Museum &
  Art Gallery
  WKENS W14 .... **101** F4
Lena Gardens Primary School
  HMSMTH W6 .... **100** C4
Leopold Primary School
  WLSDN NW10 .... **69** F4
Leopold Street Clinic
  BOW E3 .... **91** F4
Lewisham Bridge Primary School
  LEW SE13 .... **140** B1
Lewisham Business Centre
  NWCR SE14 .... **121** D2
Lewisham College
  DEPT SE8 .... **122** A4
  LEW SE13 .... **140** C1
Lewisham Crematorium
  CAT SE6 .... **159** F2
Leyton Business Centre
  LEY E10 .... **61** F4

Leyton FC
LEY E10 .... **61** F3

Leyton Industrial Village
LEY E10 .... **61** D2

**Leyton Orient FC
(Matchroom Stadium)**
LEY E10 .... **62** B5

Leytonstone School
WAN E11 .... **63** E1

Leyton VI Form College
LEY E10 .... **63** D1

Leyton Youth Sports Ground
LEY E10 .... **62** B3

The Liberty City Clinic
SDTCH EC2A **12** C5

Library and Community Centre
BTSEA SW11 .... **133** H1

Lillian Baylis School
LBTH SE11 .... **45** F5

Lillian Baylis Theatre
FSBYE EC1V **10** C3

Lillian Bishop School of English
SKENS SW7 .... **40** A4

Limehouse Town Hall
POP/IOD E14 .... **91** F5

Lincoln's Inn
LINN WC2A **21** F4

Linden Lodge School
WIM/MER SW19 .... **149** E1

Linford Christie Stadium
SHB W12 .... **88** A4

Linley Sambourne House
KENS W8 .... **38** A1

Linnet House Clinic
STJWD NW8 .... **4** C2

Lion House School
PUT/ROE SW15.................................. **131** D2

Lisson Grove Health Centre
STJWD NW8 .... **4** C5

Lister Community School
PLSTW E13 .... **94** B1

The Lister Hospital
BGVA SW1W **116** B1

Lister House Clinic
CAVSQ/HST W1G................................. **18** C4

Little Angel Theatre
IS N1 .... **76** B5

Little Ilford School
MNPK E12 .... **83** F2

Little Wandsworth School
TOOT SW17 .... **152** A2

Liverpool Street Station
LVPST EC2M **24** C3

Livesey Museum
PECK SE15 .... **120** B2

Lloyds Register Cricket Club
DUL SE21... **155** D1

Locks View Court
POP/IOD E14 .... **103** E1

Lombard Business Centre
BTSEA SW11 .... **115** D5

Lombard Business Park
WAND/EARL SW18 .... **133** D4

Lombard Trading Estate
CHARL SE7.. **106** B5

London Aquarium
STHWK SE1 .... **33** E5

London Arena
POP/IOD E14 .... **104** B4

London Ballet Theatre
HAMP NW3 .... **73** D4

London Balloon
LBTH SE11 .... **117** F1

London Bridge City Pier
STHWK SE1 .... **36** C3

London Bridge Hospital
STHWK SE1 .... **36** B3

London Bridge Sports Centre
CANST EC4R **36** A2

London Bridge Station
STHWK SE1 .... **36** C4

London Bubble Theatre
BERM/RHTH SE16 .... **102** B3

London Business School
CAMTN NW1 .... **5** E5

The London Canal Museum
IS N1 .... **9** D1

London Capital College
CAMTN NW1 .... **74** B5

London City Airport
CAN/RD E16 .... **107** F2

London City Mission
STHWK SE1 .... **37** D5

The London Clinic
MHST W1U **18** B1

**London College of
Business & Computing**
BETH E2 .... **90** B1

London College of Fashion
CAVSQ/HST W1G................................ **19** D4
MHST W1U **18** B5
SDTCH EC2A **13** D5

**London College of
Further Education**
LBTH SE11 .... **46** C5

**London College of
Higher Education**
CLAP SW4 .... **134** B1

**London College of
International Business Studies**
HHOL WC1V **21** D3

London College of Printing
LBTH SE11 .... **47** D3

The London College
KENS W8 .... **26** A3

London Commodity Exchange
WAP E1W **37** F2

London Dungeon
STHWK SE1 .... **36** B3

London Electronics College
ECT SW5 .... **114** A1

London Executive College
TOOT SW17 .... **152** A3

London Eye Clinic
CAVSQ/HST W1G................................ **18** C3

London Fields Primary School
HACK E8 .... **78** B5

London Foot Hospital
FITZ W1T **19** E1

London Gender Clinic
HDN NW4 .... **52** B1

London Group Business Park
CRICK NW2 .... **51** F3

London Guildhall University
LVPST EC2M **24** B3
TWRH EC3N **25** E5

**London Guildhall
University Sports Ground**
LEE/GVPK SE12................................. **160** C2

London Heart Clinic
CAVSQ/HST W1G................................ **18** C3

London Hospital Medical College
WCHPL E1 .... **90** B4

The London Industrial Estate
EHAM E6 .... **96** A4

London Industrial Park
EHAM E6 .... **96** B4
The London Institute
MYFR/PKLN W1K **30** C1
WEST SW1P.................................... **117** E1
The London Irish Youth Theatre
HGT N6 .... **56** B3
London Ladies & Girls FC
CAT SE6 .... **158** B5
London Lighthouse
NTGHL W11 .... **89** E5
London Living Theatre
SYD SE26 .... **157** D4
London Nautical School
STHWK SE1 .... **34** B3
London Open College
FSBYE EC1V **11** D3
London Oratory School
FUL/PGN SW6.................................. **114** A3
London Pavilion
REGST W1B...................................... **32** A2
London School of Economics
HHOL WC1V **20** C4
LINN WC2A **21** F5
STHWK SE1 .... **35** E3
London School of Hygiene &
  Tropical Medicine
GWRST WC1E **20** B2
London Silver Vaults
LINN WC2A **22** A3
The London Television Centre (LWT)
STHWK SE1 .... **34** A3
London Tourist Board &
  Convention Centre
BGVA SW1W **42** C2
London Toy & Model Museum
BAY/PAD W2.................................... **27** F1
SHB W12 .... **88** C5
London Transport Museum
COVGDN WC2E **33** D1
London Underwriting Centre
MON EC3R.. **37** D1
London Weather Centre
CLKNW EC1R.................................... **22** A2
London Welsh School
CRICK NW2 .... **70** C3
London Zoo
CAMTN NW1 .... **6** A1
Longlands Primary School
BFN/LL DA15.................................... **163** E3
Long Lane AFC
BKHTH/KID SE3 .... **124** C5
Lord Lister Health Centre
FSTGT E7 .... **82** A1
Lord's Tour & MCC Museum
STJWD NW8 .... **4** A4
Loughborough Primary School
BRXN/ST SW9 .... **118** B5
Lower Clapton Health Centre
CLPT E5 .... **78** C2
Lower Place Business Centre
WLSDN NW10 .... **86** C1
Lower Sydenham
  Industrial Estate
CAT SE6 .... **157** F5
Low Hall Sports Ground
WALTH E17 .... **61** D1
Lowther Primary School
BARN SW13 .... **112** A2
Loxford School of Science
  and Technology
IL IG1 .... **85** D2

LT Lost Property Office
CAMTN NW1 .... **17** F1
LTR Depot
SHB W12 .... **101** D2
Lucas Vale Primary School
DEPT SE8.. **122** A4
Lucie Clayton Secretarial/Fashion
  Design College
SKENS SW7 .... **39** E3
Lutomer House Business Centre
POP/IOD E14 .... **104** B2
Lux Cinema
IS N1 .... **12** C4
Lycee Francais
SKENS SW7 .... **40** A4
The Lyceum Theatre
TPL/STR WC2R **33** E1
Lyndhurst House
  Preparatory School
HAMP NW3 .... **73** D2
Lyndhurst Primary School
CMBW SE5 .... **119** D5
Lyon Business Park
BARK IG11 .... **97** E1
Lyric Theatre
HMSMTH W6 .... **100** C5
SOHO/SHAV W1D **32** A1
Macaulay CE Primary School
CLAP SW4 .... **134** B2
Madame Tussaud's
CAMTN NW1 .... **18** A1
Mahatma Gandhi
  Industrial Estate
BRXN/ST SW9 .... **136** B1
Maida Vale Hospital
MV/WKIL W9.................................... **3** F5
Maida Vale Medical Centre
MV/WKIL W9.................................... **2** C4
Malham Road Industrial Estate
FSTH SE23 .... **157** D1
Mall Galleries
STJS SW1Y.. **32** B3
Malmesbury Primary School
BOW E3 .... **91** F2
Malorees Junior & Infant School
KIL/WHAMP NW6............................ **71** D4
Malory School
BMLY BR1 .... **160** A4
Mandeville Primary School
CLPT E5 .... **61** E5
Manor Brook Medical Centre
BKHTH/KID SE3 .... **124** B5
Manorfield Primary School
POP/IOD E14 .... **92** B4
Manor House Hospital
GLDGN NW11 .... **54** B3
Manor Park Cemetery
FSTGT E7 .... **83** D1
Manor Park Crematorium
FSTGT E7 .... **82** C1
Manor Park Methodist School
MNPK E12.. **83** E1
Manor Primary School
SRTFD E15.. **93** E1
Manor Special School
WLSDN NW10 .... **89** D1
Mansion House
MANHO EC4N **24** A5
Mapledown School
CRICK NW2 .... **53** D2
Maples Business Centre
IS N1 .... **76** A4

Marble Arch
BAY/PAD W2.................................. **29** F1

**Maria Fidelis Convent
Lower School**
CAMTN NW1................................... **7** F4

**Maria Fidelis Convent
Upper School**
CAMTN NW1................................... **8** A3

**Marion Richardson
Primary School**
WCHPL E1.................................... **91** D5

Maritime Industrial Estate
CHARL SE7................................ **106** B5

Maritime Museum
GNWCH SE10.............................. **105** E5

Marlborough Cricket Club
DUL SE21.................................. **156** A1

Marlborough Day Hospital
STJWD NW8.................................... **3** B1

Marlborough House
STJS SW1Y.................................. **31** F4

Marlborough Primary School
CHEL SW3.................................. **41** D5

Marlborough Trading Estate
RCH/KEW TW9............................ **110** B4

Marlowe Business Centre
NWCR SE14................................ **121** E3

Marner Primary School
BOW E3...................................... **92** B3

Marshall Street Leisure Centre
SOHO/CST W1F........................... **19** E5

Marsh Gate Business Centre
SRTFD E15.................................. **92** C1

Marshgate Trading Estate
SRTFD E15.................................. **80** B4

Martan College
HOL/ALD WC2B............................ **21** D4

Marvels Lane Primary School
LEE/GVPK SE12.......................... **160** C4

Mary Boone School
WKENS W14................................ **101** E5

Maryland Industrial Estate
SRTFD E15.................................. **81** E2

Maryland Primary School
SRTFD E15.................................. **81** E2

Marylebone Health Centre
MHST W1U.................................. **18** B1

Marylebone Magistrates Court
CAMTN NW1................................ **17** D2

Marylebone Station
CAMTN NW1................................ **17** E1

Maudlin's Green
WAP E1W.................................. **102** A2

The Maudsley Hospital
CMBW SE5................................ **119** D5

Mawbrey Brough Health Centre
VX/NE SW8................................ **117** E3

Mayfair Medical Centre
MYFR/PKLN W1K........................... **18** B5

Mayflower Primary School
POP/IOD E14............................... **92** A5

Maytime School
IL IG1...................................... **66** A5

Mayville Infant School
WAN E11.................................... **63** E5

Mayville Junior School
WAN E11.................................... **63** E4

Maze Hill School
GNWCH SE10.............................. **123** E2

Mazenod RC Primary School
KIL/WHAMP NW6........................... **72** A4

Mckay Trading Estate
NKENS W10................................. **89** E3

Mead Road Infant School
CHST BR7.................................. **162** C5

Meadowgate School
PECK SE15................................ **139** D1

Medical Express Clinic
CAVSQ/HST W1G........................... **18** C2

Mednurs Clinic
SEVS/STOTM N15.......................... **59** D1

Megabowl
BRXS/STRHM SW2......................... **153** E2

Melcombe Primary School
HMSMTH W6................................ **113** D2

Mellish Industrial Estate
WOOL/PLUM SE18........................ **107** D4

Memorial Hospital
WOOL/PLUM SE18........................ **126** A5

Menorah Grammar School
GLDGN NW11............................... **53** E2

Mercers' Hall
CITYW EC2V................................ **23** F5

The Merchant Taylors Hall
BANK EC3V.................................. **24** B5

Mercury Theatre
LSQ/SEVD WC2H........................... **20** C5

Meridian Clinic
BRXN/ST SW9............................. **136** A1

**Meridian Locality Mental
Health Centre**
CHARL SE7................................ **124** C2

Meridian Primary School
GNWCH SE10.............................. **123** D1

Meridian Sports Club
CHARL SE7................................ **125** E2

Meridian Trading Estate
CHARL SE7................................ **106** B5

Merlin Primary School
BMLY BR1................................ **160** A3

Merlin School
PUT/ROE SW15............................ **131** D3

Mermaid Theatre
BLKFR EC4V................................ **35** D1

Merton Road Industrial Estate
WAND/EARL SW18......................... **132** A5

Metropolitan Business Centre
HACK E8.................................... **77** E4

Metropolitan Hospital
STHWK SE1.................................. **46** B2

Metropolitan Tabernacle
LBTH SE11.................................. **47** D4

Metro Trading Centre
WBLY HA9................................... **68** B1

Michael Faraday Primary School
WALW SE17................................ **119** D1

Michael Manley Industrial Estate
VX/NE SW8................................ **116** C5

Michael Sobell Sinai School
KTN/HRWW/W HA3........................ **50** A1

Michael Sobell Sports Centre
HOLWY N7.................................. **57** F5

The Michael Tippett School
LBTH SE11.................................. **46** B5

Middle Park Primary School
ELTH/MOT SE9............................ **143** D5

Middle Row Primary School
NKENS W10................................. **89** E3

**Middlesex CCC
(Lord's Cricket Ground)**
STJWD NW8.................................... **4** B3

Middlesex Guildhall
WEST SW1P................................. **44** B1

Middlesex Hospital
GTPST W1W................................ **19** F3

Middlesex Hospital
  Medical School
    FITZ W1T **19** F2
Middlesex Hospital
  Nurses Home
    GTPST W1W **19** E2
Middlesex Hospital School of
  Physiotherapy
    FITZ W1T **19** F2
Middlesex Hospital
  Sports Ground
    CHST BR7 .... **163** F5
Middlesex University
    GLDGN NW11 .... **54** B3
Middle Temple Hall
    TPL/STR WC2R **34** A1
Midway Mission Hospital
    BETH E2 .... **13** E4
Mile End & Bow Business Centre
    WCHPL E1 .... **90** B4
Mile End Hospital
    WCHPL E1 .... **91** D2
Mile End Stadium
    BOW E3 .... **91** F4
Miles Coverdale Primary School
    SHB W12 .... **100** C3
Millbank Millennium Pier
    WEST SW1P **45** D5
Millbank Primary School
    WEST SW1P **44** B5
Millbank Tower
    WEST SW1P **44** C5
Millennium Arena
    BTSEA SW11 .... **116** A3
Millennium Balloon
    STHWK SE1 .... **37** D4
Millennium Harbour Development
    POP/IOD E14 .... **103** F3
Millennium Quay
    DEPT SE8 .... **122** B2
Millennium Wharf Development
    POP/IOD E14 .... **105** D4
Millfields Junior & Infant School
    CLPT E5 .... **78** C1
Mill Lane Medical Centre
    KIL/WHAMP NW6 .... **72** A2
Mill Street Clinic
    STHWK SE1 .... **37** F5
Mill Trading Estate
    WLSDN NW10 .... **86** B1
Millwall FC (The New Den)
    BERM/RHTH SE16 .... **120** C1
Milton Natural Health Centre
    HGT N6 .... **56** C2
Minerva Works
    CAN/RD E16 .... **105** F2
Ministry of Defence
    WHALL SW1A **32** C4
Mini Town Hall
    WOOL/PLUM SE18 .... **127** F1
Mint Business Park
    CAN/RD E16 .... **94** A4
Mitchell Brook Primary School
    WLSDN NW10 .... **69** D3
Mitre Bridge Industrial Park
    WLSDN NW10 .... **88** B3
Moatbridge School
    ELTH/MOT SE9 .... **143** D4
Monega Primary School
    MNPK E12 .... **83** D2
Monson Primary School
    NWCR SE14 .... **121** D3

Montbelle Primary School
    ELTH/MOT SE9 .... **162** B3
Montem Primary School
    HOLWY N7 .... **57** F5
The Monument
    MON EC3R **36** B2
Moorfields Eye Hospital
    FSBYE EC1V **12** A4
Moorfields Primary School
    STLK EC1Y **12** A5
Mora Primary School
    CRICK NW2 .... **70** C1
Morden College Homes
    BKHTH/KID SE3 .... **124** A5
Morden Mount Primary School
    LEW SE13 .... **122** B5
More House School
    KTBR SW1X **41** F3
Moreland Primary School
    FSBYE EC1V **11** D4
Morningside Primary School
    HOM E9 .... **78** C3
Mornington Leisure Centre
    CAMTN NW1 .... **74** B5
Morpeth School
    BETH E2 .... **90** C2
Mortimer Road Clinic
    WLSDN NW10 .... **88** C2
Mortimer School
    STRHM/NOR SW16 .... **153** D2
Mortlake Cemetery
    MORT/ESHN SW14 .... **129** E1
Mortlake Crematorium
    RCH/KEW TW9 .... **110** B5
Mosiah Foundation
  Supplementary School
    STNW/STAM N16 .... **59** E3
The Mother & Baby Clinic
    HOM E9 .... **78** C3
Mottingham Community
  Health Clinic
    ELTH/MOT SE9 .... **161** E4
Mottingham Primary School
    ELTH/MOT SE9 .... **161** F3
Mowlem Primary School
    BETH E2 .... **90** C1
MSP Business Centre
    WBLY HA9 .... **68** B1
Mudchute City Farm
    POP/IOD E14 .... **104** C5
Mulberry Business Centre
    BERM/RHTH SE16 .... **103** D3
Mulberry House School
    CRICK NW2 .... **71** E2
Mulberry School for Girls
    WCHPL E1 .... **90** B5
Mulgrave Primary School
    WOOL/PLUM SE18 .... **108** B4
Museum in Docklands
    POP/IOD E14 .... **104** A1
Museum of Artillery
  in the Rotunda
    CHARL SE7 .... **125** F1
Museum of Fulham Palace
    FUL/PGN SW6 .... **113** D5
Museum of Garden History
    STHWK SE1 .... **45** D3
Museum of London
    STBT EC1A **23** E3
Museum of the Order of St John
    FARR EC1M **23** D1

Museums of the Royal College of Surgeons
LINN WC2A **21** F4

Myatt Garden Primary School
BROCKY SE4 .... **121** F5

Myatts Field Clinic
BRXN/ST SW9 .... **118** B4

Nags Head Shopping Centre
HOLWY N7 .... **75** F1

Naima Jewish Preparatory School
KIL/WHAMP NW6 .... **2** C1

National Army Museum
CHEL SW3 .... **115** F2

National Film Theatre
STHWK SE1 .... **33** F3

National Gallery
LSQ/SEVD WC2H **32** B2

National Hospital for Neurology & Neurosurgery
BMSBY WC1N **20** C1

National Hospital for Sick Children (Great Ormond Street)
BMSBY WC1N **21** D1

National Maritime Museum
GNWCH SE10 .... **123** D2

National Portrait Gallery
LSQ/SEVD WC2H **32** B2

National Temperance Hospital
CAMTN NW1 .... **7** F4

National Youth Theatre of GB
HOLWY N7 .... **57** E5

Natural History Museum
SKENS SW7 .... **40** A3

Natural Therapy Clinic
TOOT SW17 .... **152** B5

Navigation College
MANHO EC4N **35** F1

Nelson Dock Museum
BERM/RHTH SE16 .... **103** F2

Nelson Primary School
EHAM E6 .... **96** A1

Nelson's Column
CHCR WC2N **32** C3

Neo Clinic
PIM SW1V **43** E5

Netley Primary School
CAMTN NW1 .... **7** E4

The New Ambassadors Theatre
LSQ/SEVD WC2H **20** C5

New Atlas Wharf Development
POP/IOD E14 .... **103** F4

Newbury Park Health Centre
GNTH/NBYPK IG2 .... **67** D1

Newbury Park Primary School
GNTH/NBYPK IG2 .... **67** D1

The New Business Centre
WLSDN NW10 .... **87** F2

New Caledonian Wharf
BERM/RHTH SE16 .... **103** F4

New Chiswick Swimming Pool
CHSWK W4 .... **111** E3

New City Primary School
PLSTW E13 .... **94** C2

New Connaught Rooms
HOL/ALD WC2B **21** D4

New Covent Garden Market
VX/NE SW8 .... **117** D2

New Crane Wharf
WAP E1W **102** C2

New Cross Sports Arena
NWCR SE14 .... **121** E3

New End Primary School
HAMP NW3 .... **72** C1

New End Theatre
HAMP NW3 .... **54** C5

New England Industrial Estate
BARK IG11 .... **96** C1

Newfield Primary School
WLSDN NW10 .... **69** F4

The New Furness Primary School
WLSDN NW10 .... **88** A1

Newham College of Further Education
EHAM E6 .... **95** F1

Newham College of Further Education
SRTFD E15 .... **81** E4

Newham Community College
CAN/RD E16 .... **93** E3

Newham General Hospital
PLSTW E13 .... **94** C3

Newham Leisure Centre
PLSTW E13 .... **94** C4

Newham Medical Centre
PLSTW E13 .... **94** C1

Newham Museum Service
SRTFD E15 .... **81** D4

Newham Sixth Form College
PLSTW E13 .... **94** B3

Newington Court Business Centre
STHWK SE1 .... **47** E3

Newington Green Primary School
STNW/STAM N16 .... **77** E2

Newington Industrial Estate
WALW SE17 .... **47** D5

New Kings Primary School
FUL/PGN SW6 .... **113** F5

New London Theatre
LSQ/SEVD WC2H **21** D4

Newport Junior & Infant School
WAN E11 .... **62** C4

New Rush Hall School
IL IG1 .... **66** C4

New School
FUL/PGN SW6 .... **113** F4

New Scotland Yard
STJSPK SW1H **44** A2

News International
WAP E1W **102** B1

Newton Medical Centre
BAY/PAD W2 .... **14** B4

Newton Preparatory School
VX/NE SW8 .... **116** B3

New Woodlands School
BMLY BR1 .... **159** E4

Nightingale Clinic
PLSTW E13 .... **94** C1

Nightingale Primary School
WOOL/PLUM SE18 .... **126** B1

Nightingale School
STHWK SE1 .... **45** E1
TOOT SW17 .... **151** E2

Nineacres School
WOOL/PLUM SE18 .... **127** D1

Norlington School
LEY E10 .... **63** D3

Normand Park Primary School
FUL/PGN SW6 .... **113** F2

Norman Shaw Building (MP's Offices)
WHALL SW1A **32** C5

North Acton Business Park
ACT W3 .... **87** D5

North Beckton Primary School
EHAM E6 .... **95** F4

North Bridge House
HAMP NW3 .... **72** C3
North Bridge House School
CAMTN NW1 .... **74** A5
HAMP NW3 .... **73** D3
Northbrook CE School
LEW SE13 .... **141** E3
Northbury Primary School
BARK IG11 .... **84** B3
Northcote Lodge School
BTSEA SW11 .... **133** E4
Northfields Industrial Estate
ALP/SUD HA0 .... **68** A5
Northfields Prospect
Business Centre
WAND/EARL SW18 .... **131** F2
Northgate Clinic
CDALE/KGS NW9 .... **51** E1
North London
School of Physiotherapy
ARCH N19 .... **56** C3
North London Tutorial College
HDN NW4 .... **52** C1
The North Street Health Centre
CLAP SW4 .... **134** C1
Northview Primary School
WLSDN NW10 .... **69** E1
North West London
Jewish J & I School
CRICK NW2 .... **71** E4
North West London
Medical Centre
MV/WKIL W9 .... **3** E2
North Westminster
Community School
BAY/PAD W2 .... **16** A3
North Westminster
Community School
STJWD NW8 .... **16** C2
North Westminster Community
Secondary School
MV/WKIL W9 .... **2** B5
Northwold Primary School
CLPT E5 .... **60** A4
Norwegian/British Monument
BAY/PAD W2 .... **29** D4
Norwood Park Primary School
WNWD SE27 .... **154** C4
Norwood School
WNWD SE27 .... **154** C5
Notre Dame RC Girls School
STHWK SE1 .... **46** C2
Notre Dame RC Primary School
WOOL/PLUM SE18 .... **126** B2
N1 Shopping Centre
IS N1 .... **10** B1
NTGB Sports Ground
EHAM E6 .... **84** A3
Nutrition Clinic
MHST W1U **18** A2
NW5 Theatre School
KTTN NW5 .... **74** C2
Oakfield Preparatory School
DUL SE21 .... **155** D2
Oakington Manor School
WBLY HA9 .... **68** B2
Oaklands Secondary School
BETH E2 .... **90** A2
Oak Lodge School
BAL SW12 .... **133** F5
Oak Tree Medical Centre
GDMY/SEVK IG3 .... **67** E4

Oakwood Business Park
WLSDN NW10 .... **87** D2
Oasis Sports Centre
LSQ/SEVD WC1E **20** C4
Obstetrics Hospital
GWRST WC1E **19** F1
Odeon Cinema
CAMTN NW1 .... **74** B5
ELTH/MOT SE9 .... **143** E2
FITZ W1T **20** A3
GNTH/NBYPK IG2 .... **66** A1
HOLWY N7 .... **57** E5
KENS W8 .... **38** A2
KIL/WHAMP NW6 .... **73** D4
LSQ/SEVD WC2H **20** B5
LSQ/SEVD WC2H **32** B2
MBLAR W1H **17** F5
SOHO/SHAV W1D **32** A1
STJS SW1Y **32** A2
STRHM/NOR SW16 .... **153** E3
Odessa Infant School
FSTGT E7 .... **82** A2
Old Admiralty
WHALL SW1A **32** B4
Old Barnes Cemetery
BARN SW13 .... **112** B5
Old Bellgate Wharf Development
POP/IOD E14 .... **103** F4
Old Brockleians Sports Ground
ELTH/MOT SE9 .... **142** C4
Old Cemetery
EDUL SE22 .... **138** B4
Old Colfeian Sports Club
LEE/GVPK SE12 .... **142** A3
Old Curiosity Shop
LINN WC2A **21** E4
Old Ford Primary School
BOW E3 .... **91** F1
Oldhill Medical Centre
STNW/STAM N16 .... **59** F3
Old Jamaica Business Estate
BERM/RHTH SE16 .... **49** F2
Old Oak Primary School
SHB W12 .... **87** F5
Old Operating Theatre Museum
STHWK SE1 .... **36** A4
Old Palace Primary School
BOW E3 .... **92** B2
Old Royal Naval College
GNWCH SE10 .... **123** D2
Old Royal Observatory Greenwich
GNWCH SE10 .... **123** D3
Old Station Museum
CAN/RD E16 .... **108** A3
Old Sun Wharf
POP/IOD E14 .... **103** E1
Old Treasury
WHALL SW1A **32** C5
Old Vic Theatre
STHWK SE1 .... **34** B5
Old War Office
WHALL SW1A **32** C4
Olga Primary School
BOW E3 .... **91** E1
Oliver Business Park
WLSDN NW10 .... **86** C1
Oliver Goldsmith Primary School
CMBW SE5 .... **119** E4
Olympia
WKENS W14 .... **101** E4
Olympic Industrial Estate
WBLY HA9 .... **68** B1

Olympic Retail Park
WBLY HA9 .... **68** A1
Olympic Trading Estate
WBLY HA9 .... **68** B1
On Sai Clinic
ECT SW5 .... **38** C5
On the Road Tours CC
WAND/EARL SW18 .... **132** C4
Open Air Theatre
CAMTN NW1 .... **6** A4
The Open University
FSBYW WC1X **9** E3
KIL/WHAMP NW6 .... **72** A1
Ophaboom Theatre
WLSDN NW10 .... **88** B2
Optimax Laser Eye Clinic
HAMP NW3 .... **72** C3
Oratory RC Primary School
CHEL SW3 .... **115** E1
Orchard Business Centre
SYD SE26 .... **157** F5
The Orchard Health Centre
BARK IG11 .... **96** C1
Orchard Primary School
HOM E9 .... **78** C4
Orient Industrial Park
LEY E10 .... **62** A4
Orion Business Centre
BERM/RHTH SE16 .... **121** D1
Osmani Primary School
WCHPL E1 .... **90** A4
Our Lady of Dolours
RC Primary School
BAY/PAD W2 .... **14** C2
Our Lady of Grace
RC Junior School
CRICK NW2 .... **52** B5
Our Lady of Lourdes
RC Primary School
LEW SE13 .... **141** D1
WAN E11 .... **63** F1
WLSDN NW10 .... **68** C5
Our Lady of the Rosary
RC Primary School
BFN/LL DA15 .... **145** E4
Our Lady of the Sacred
Heart School
HOLWY N7 .... **75** F3
Our Lady of Victories
RC Primary School
PUT/ROE SW15 .... **131** D2
SKENS SW7 .... **40** A5
Our Lady Queen of Heaven
RC Primary School
WIM/MER SW19 .... **131** D5
Our Lady RC Primary School
POP/IOD E14 .... **91** F5
Our Lady & St Joseph
Primary School
IS N1 .... **77** E3
Our Lady & St Philip Neri
RC Primary School
FSTH SE23 .... **157** D3
Our Ladys Convent High School
STNW/STAM N16 .... **59** E2
Our Ladys RC Primary School
CAMTN NW1 .... **74** C5
Oval Business Centre
LBTH SE11 .... **117** F1
Oval House Theatre
LBTH SE11 .... **118** A2
Oxford Gardens Primary School
NKENS W10 .... **89** D5

Oxford House College
SOHO/SHAV W1D **20** A4
Oxo Tower Wharf
STHWK SE1 .... **34** B2
Paddington Bowling & Sports Club
MV/WKIL W9 .... **2** C5
Paddington Community Hospital
MV/WKIL W9 .... **14** A2
Paddington Green Primary School
BAY/PAD W2 .... **16** A1
Paddington Recreation
Ground Athletics Track
KIL/WHAMP NW6 .... **2** B3
Paddington Station
BAY/PAD W2 .... **16** A4
Paddock School
PUT/ROE SW15 .... **129** F2
Pain Relief Clinic
HDN NW4 .... **52** B1
Pakeman Primary School
HOLWY N7 .... **57** F5
Palladium Theatre
REGST W1B **19** E5
Panorama Pier
STHWK SE1 .... **35** D2
Parayhouse School
WBPTN SW10 .... **114** C3
Parent Infant Clinic
HAMP NW3 .... **72** C2
Park Business Centre
KIL/WHAMP NW6 .... **2** A4
Parkfield Industrial Estate
BTSEA SW11 .... **116** A5
Parkfield JMI School
HDN NW4 .... **52** B2
Parkgate House School
CLAP SW4 .... **134** A2
Park Hall Trading Estate
WNWD SE27 .... **154** C3
Park House Medical Centre
KIL/WHAMP NW6 .... **89** E1
Parkhouse Middle School
WIM/MER SW19 .... **149** F4
Park Medical Centre
BERM/RHTH SE16 .... **103** D5
Park Mews Small Business Centre
HNHL SE24 .... **136** C4
Park Primary School
SRTFD E15 .... **81** F4
Park Royal Business Centre
WLSDN NW10 .... **86** C3
Park School for Girls
IL IG1 .... **66** B3
Parkside Business Estate
DEPT SE8 .... **121** F2
Parkside Clinic
NTGHL W11 .... **89** E5
Parkside Health
NTGHL W11 .... **89** E5
Parkside Hospital
WIM/MER SW19 .... **149** D3
Park Walk Primary School
WBPTN SW10 .... **115** D2
Parkwood Primary School
FSBYPK N4 .... **58** A4
Parliament Hill Fields
Athletics Track
KTTN NW5 .... **73** F1
Parliament Hill School
KTTN NW5 .... **74** A1
Parmiter Industrial Centre
BETH E2 .... **90** B1

Parsons Green Health Clinic
 FUL/PGN SW6 .... **114** A4
Patent Office
 HHOL WC1V **22** A3
Peace Pagoda
 BTSEA SW11 .... **115** F3
The Peacock Theatre
 HOL/ALD WC2B **21** E5
Peckham Park Primary School
 PECK SE15 .... **120** A3
The Peckham Pulse Health &
 Leisure Centre
 PECK SE15 .... **120** A4
Peckham Rye Primary School
 PECK SE15 .... **138** B1
Pendragon Secondary School
 BMLY BR1 .... **160** A3
Penton Primary School
 IS N1 .... **10** B1
Percival David Foundation of
 Chinese Art
 STPAN WC1H **8** B5
Perrymount Primary School
 FSTH SE23 .... **157** D2
Peterborough Primary School
 FUL/PGN SW6 .... **114** A5
Peter Hills School
 BERM/RHTH SE16 .... **103** D2
Peterley Business Centre
 BETH E2 .... **90** B1
Peter Pan Statue
 BAY/PAD W2 .... **28** A3
Pewterers' Hall
 CITYW EC2V **23** F3
Phoenix Business Centre
 POP/IOD E14 .... **92** A4
Phoenix College
 TOOT SW17 .... **151** E2
Phoenix Court
 POP/IOD E14 .... **104** A5
Phoenix High School
 SHB W12 .... **100** A1
Phoenix Leisure Centre
 CAT SE6 .... **140** B5
Phoenix School
 BOW E3 .... **91** F2
 HAMP NW3 .... **73** D4
Phoenix Theatre
 LSQ/SEVD WC2H **20** B5
Physical Energy Statue
 BAY/PAD W2 .... **28** A4
Piccadilly Theatre
 SOHO/SHAV W1D **32** A1
Picture House Cinema
 SRTFD E15 .... **81** D3
Pilgrims Way Junior
 & Infant School
 PECK SE15 .... **120** C2
Pilot Industrial Centre
 WLSDN NW10 .... **87** E3
Pimlico School
 PIM SW1V **116** C1
Plaisterers Hall
 CITYW EC2V **23** E3
Plaistow Hospital
 PLSTW E13 .... **94** B1
Planetarium
 CAMTN NW1 .... **18** A1
Plantation House Medical Centre
 LOTH EC2R **24** B4
Plashet Jewish Cemetery
 MNPK E12 .... **83** D3

Plashet Road Medical Centre
 FSTGT E7 .... **82** B4
Plashet School
 EHAM E6 .... **83** E4
Players Theatre
 CHCR WC2N **32** C3
The Playhouse
 CHCR WC2N **33** D3
Pleasance Theatre
 HOLWY N7 .... **75** E3
Plumcroft Primary School
 WOOL/PLUM SE18 .... **126** C2
Plumstead Manor School
 WOOL/PLUM SE18 .... **127** D1
The Pointer School
 BKHTH/KID SE3 .... **124** A4
Police Cadet School
 WAN E11 .... **64** A3
The Polish Institute &
 Sikorski Museum
 SKENS SW7 .... **40** B1
Pollock's Toy Museum
 FITZ W1T **19** F2
Poole's Park Primary School
 HOLWY N7 .... **57** F4
Pope John Primary School
 SHB W12 .... **100** B1
Pop In Business Centre
 WBLY HA9 .... **68** B2
Poplar Business Park
 POP/IOD E14 .... **104** C1
Poplar Coroners Court
 POP/IOD E14 .... **104** B1
Pop Up Theatre
 FSBYE EC1V **10** C2
Porchester Leisure Centre
 BAY/PAD W2 .... **14** C4
Portcullis House
 WHALL SW1A **45** D1
The Portland Hospital
 REGST W1B **19** D1
Portland Place School
 REGST W1B **19** D2
The Portman Clinic
 HAMP NW3 .... **73** D3
Portobello Market
 NKENS W10 .... **89** E4
Portobello Medical Centre
 NTGHL W11 .... **89** E5
Portway Primary School
 SRTFD E15 .... **82** A5
Pound Park Nursery School
 CHARL SE7 .... **125** D1
Powergate Business Park
 WLSDN NW10 .... **87** D2
Premier Cinema
 PECK SE15 .... **120** A5
Prendergast School
 BROCKY SE4 .... **140** A2
PR for Schools
 SYD SE26 .... **156** C3
Primrose Hill School
 CAMTN NW1 .... **74** A5
Primrose Montessori School
 HBRY N5 .... **58** C5
Prince Charles Cinema
 SOHO/SHAV W1D **32** B1
Prince Edward Theatre
 SOHO/SHAV W1D **20** A5
Prince of Wales Theatre
 STJS SW1Y **32** A2
Princes College
 NOXST/BSQ WC1A **20** C4

Princes Court Business Centre
WAP E1W 102 B1
Princess Frederica CE J & I School
WLSDN NW10 .... 88 B1
Princess Grace Hospital
MHST W1U 18 A1
Princess Louise Hospital
NKENS W10 .... 88 C4
Prior Western Primary School
STLK EC1Y 23 F1
Priory Boys & Infant School
ACT W3 .... 98 C3
Priory CE Middle School
WIM/MER SW19 .... 150 B5
Priory House School
CAT SE6 .... 158 B1
Privy Council
STJS SW1Y 32 A4
Privy Council Office
WHALL SW1A 32 C4
Prospect House School
PUT/ROE SW15 .... 131 D5
Prospect of Whitby
WAP E1W 102 C2
Proud Gallery
CHCR WC2N 32 C2
Psychiatric Home
BRXN/ST SW9 .... 135 E1
Public Record Office
LINN WC2A 22 A4
Public Record Office Museum
RCH/KEW TW9 .... 110 B3
Pump House
BERM/RHTH SE16 .... 103 E2
Purdy Hicks Gallery
STHWK SE1 .... 34 C3
Pursuit Centre
WAP E1W 102 C1
Putney Animal Hospital
PUT/ROE SW15 .... 131 D2
Putney Exchange
Shopping Centre
PUT/ROE SW15 .... 131 D2
Putney High School
PUT/ROE SW15 .... 131 D3
Putney Hospital
PUT/ROE SW15 .... 130 C1
Putney Leisure Centre
PUT/ROE SW15 .... 130 C2
Putney Lower Common Cemetery
PUT/ROE SW15 .... 112 B5
Putneymead Medical Centre
PUT/ROE SW15 .... 130 C2
Putney Park School
PUT/ROE SW15 .... 130 B2
Putney School of Art
PUT/ROE SW15 .... 131 E2
Putney Vale Cemetery
PUT/ROE SW15 .... 148 A2
Putney Vale Crematorium
PUT/ROE SW15 .... 148 A2
Pylon Trading Estate
CAN/RD E16 .... 93 D3
Quadrant Business Park
KIL/WHAMP NW6 .... 71 E5
Quebec Industrial Estate
BERM/RHTH SE16 .... 103 E3
Queen Charlottes &
Chelsea Hospital
HMSMTH W6 .... 100 A4
Queen Elizabeth College
KENS W8 .... 26 A5

Queen Elizabeth
Conference Centre
WEST SW1P 44 B1
Queen Elizabeth Hall
STHWK SE1 .... 33 E3
Queen Elizabeth Hospital
CHARL SE7 .... 125 F2
Queen Elizabeth II School
MV/WKIL W9 .... 89 F3
Queenhithe Stairs
BLKFR EC4V 35 E2
Queen Mary's
Royal Free Hospital
HAMP NW3 .... 54 C5
Queen Mary's University Hospital
PUT/ROE SW15 .... 130 A4
Queen Mary & Westfield College
WCHPL E1 .... 91 D3
Queen Mother Sports Centre
PIM SW1V 43 E4
Queensbridge Infant School
HACK E8 .... 77 F4
Queen's Club
WKENS W14 .... 113 E1
Queens College
CAVSQ/HST W1G 18 C3
Queen's Gallery
WHALL SW1A 43 D1
The Queens House
GNWCH SE10 .... 123 D2
Queens Ice Skating Club
BAY/PAD W2 .... 27 D2
Queens Manor Primary School
FUL/PGN SW6 .... 112 C3
Queens Park
Community School GM
WLSDN NW10 .... 70 C5
Queens Park Health Centre
NKENS W10 .... 89 E2
Queens Park Primary School
NKENS W10 .... 89 E2
Queens Park Rangers FC
(Loftus Road Stadium)
SHB W12 .... 100 B1
Queens Road Practice
NWCR SE14 .... 121 D4
Queens Theatre
SOHO/SHAV W1D 32 A1
Queen Victoria Memorial
WHALL SW1A 43 E1
Quicksilver Theatre
IS N1 .... 77 E4
Quintin Kynaston School
STJWD NW8 .... 73 D5
Radcliffe College
SOHO/CST W1F 19 E5
Ragged School Museum Trust
BOW E3 .... 91 E4
Railton Road Clinic
HNHL SE24 .... 136 B3
Rainbow Quay
BERM/RHTH SE16 .... 103 E4
Raines Foundation School
BETH E2 .... 90 B2
Ramac Industrial Estate
CHARL SE7 .... 124 A1
Ram Brewery & Visitor Centre
WAND/EARL SW18 .... 132 B3
RAM College
WEST SW1P 117 E1
Rams Episcopal Primary School
HACK E8 .... 78 C2

Randal Cremer Primary School
  BETH E2 .... **13** E1
Ranelagh Gardens
  (Site of Chelsea Flower Show)
  CHEL SW3 .... **116** A2
Ranelagh Primary School
  SRTFD E15 .... **93** E1
Rangefield Primary School
  BMLY BR1 .... **159** E5
Rangers House
  GNWCH SE10 .... **123** D4
Ransomes Dock Business Centre
  BTSEA SW11 .... **115** E3
Rathfern Primary School
  FSTH SE23 .... **157** F1
Ravensbourne College of
  Design & Communication
  CHST BR7 .... **161** F5
Ravenscourt Park
  Preparatory School
  HMSMTH W6 .... **100** A5
Ravenscraft Medical Centre
  GLDGN NW11 .... **53** F2
Ravenscroft Primary School
  PLSTW E13 .... **94** A3
Ravenstone Primary School
  BAL SW12 .... **152** A1
RCA
  SKENS SW7 .... **39** F1
RCA Sculpture School
  BTSEA SW11 .... **115** E3
Reay Primary School
  BRXN/ST SW9 .... **117** F3
Records Office
  CLKNW EC1R **10** B5
Recreation Centre
  LBTH SE11 .... **47** D4
Redbridge Museum Service
  IL IG1 .... **66** C4
Redcliffe School
  WBPTN SW10 .... **114** C2
Redhill Junior School
  CHST BR7 .... **162** B5
Redlands Primary School
  WCHPL E1 .... **90** C4
Redriff Community
  Primary School
  BERM/RHTH SE16 .... **103** E2
Regent Clinic
  CAVSQ/HST W1G................................. **18** C3
Regent's College
  CAMTN NW1 .... **6** A3
Regent's Park Barracks
  CAMTN NW1 .... **6** C1
Regents Park Clinic
  CAMTN NW1 .... **5** E5
Regents Park Medical Centre
  CAMTN NW1 .... **7** D3
Renoir Cinema
  BMSBY WC1N **9** D5
Rhyl Primary School
  KTTN NW5 .... **74** A3
Riba Drawings Collection &
  Heinz Gallery
  MBLAR W1H **17** F4
Ricards Lodge High School
  WIM/MER SW19 .... **149** F5
Richard Atkins Primary School
  BRXS/STRHM SW2 .... **135** E5
Richard Cloudesley School
  STLK EC1Y **23** E1
Richard Cobden Primary School
  CAMTN NW1 .... **74** C5

Rich Industrial Estate
  PECK SE15 .... **120** B2
  STHWK SE1 .... **49** D3
Richmond College
  KENS W8 .... **38** C2
Richmond Park Golf Club
  PUT/ROE SW15 .... **129** E5
Rio Cinema
  HACK E8 .... **77** F2
Ripple Junior & Infant School
  BARK IG11 .... **85** D5
Ritzy Cinema
  BRXN/ST SW9 .... **136** A2
River Place Health Centre
  IS N1 .... **76** C4
River Road Business Park
  BARK IG11 .... **97** E2
Riversdale Primary School
  WAND/EARL SW18 .... **150** A1
Riverside Business Centre
  WAND/EARL SW18 .... **150** B1
Riverside Community Health Care
  WKENS W14 .... **101** D4
Riverside Primary School
  BERM/RHTH SE16 .... **102** A3
Riverside Studios Cinema
  BARN SW13 .... **112** C1
Riverston School
  LEE/GVPK SE12 .... **142** A3
Robert Blair Primary School
  HOLWY N7 .... **75** E3
Robert Browning Primary School
  WALW SE17 .... **119** D1
Robin Hood Primary School
  KUTN/CMB KT2 .... **147** D5
Robinsfield Infant School
  STJWD NW8 .... **4** B1
The Roche School
  WAND/EARL SW18 .... **132** A3
Rockcliffe Manor
  Primary School
  WOOL/PLUM SE18 .... **127** E3
Roehampton Church School
  PUT/ROE SW15 .... **130** B5
Roehampton Golf Club
  PUT/ROE SW15 .... **129** F2
Roehampton Institute
  PUT/ROE SW15 .... **129** F3
  WAND/EARL SW18 .... **131** E4
The Roehampton Priory Hospital
  PUT/ROE SW15 .... **129** F2
Roehampton Recreation Centre
  PUT/ROE SW15 .... **130** A5
Rokeby School
  SRTFD E15 .... **81** D4
Roman Bath
  TPL/STR WC2R **33** F1
Roman Road Primary School
  EHAM E6 .... **95** D3
Roman Wall Remains
  BARB EC2Y **23** E3
Ronald Rose Primary School
  WIM/MER SW19 .... **131** D5
Rood Lane Medical Centre
  FENCHST EC3M **36** C1
Roosevelt Memorial
  MYFR/PKLN W1K **30** B1
Ropery Business Park
  CHARL SE7 .... **106** C5
The Rosary RC Primary School
  HAMP NW3 .... **73** E2
Rose Bruford College
  DEPT SE8 .... **122** A2

Rosemary School (Primary)
IS N1 .... **76** C5
Rosemary Secondary School
CLKNW EC1R **10** C5
Rose McAndrew Clinic
BRXN/ST SW9 .... **117** F5
Rosemead Preparatory School
DUL SE21 .... **154** C2
Rosendale Primary School
DUL SE21 .... **136** C5
Rose Theatre Exhibition
STHWK SE1 .... **35** E3
Rosetta Primary School
CAN/RD E16 .... **94** B4
Rosslyn Park RFC
PUT/ROE SW15 .... **129** F2
Rotherhithe Civic Centre
BERM/RHTH SE16 .... **102** C3
Rotherhithe Primary School
BERM/RHTH SE16 .... **102** C5
The Roundhouse Theatre
CAMTN NW1 .... **74** A4
Roundwood Park Medical Centre
WLSDN NW10 .... **70** A4
Rowan High School
CLAP SW4 .... **135** D4
Rowley Industrial Park
ACT W3 .... **98** B4
Roxwell Trading Park
LEY E10 .... **61** E2
Royal Academy of Arts
MYFR/PICC W1J **31** E2
Royal Academy of Dramatic Art
GWRST WC1E **20** B1
Royal Academy of Music
CAMTN NW1 .... **18** B1
Royal Albert Hall
SKENS SW7 .... **40** A1
Royal Arsenal
WOOL/PLUM SE18 .... **108** B4
The Royal Ballet School
HMSMTH W6 .... **113** D1
Royal Blackheath Golf Club
ELTH/MOT SE9 .... **143** F5
Royal Brompton & National Heart
Hospitals
CHEL SW3 .... **115** D1
Royal College of Anaesthetists
RSQ WC1B **20** C2
Royal College of Art
SKENS SW7 .... **39** F1
Royal College of Music
SHB W12 .... **100** D3
SKENS SW7 .... **40** A2
Royal College of Nursing
CAMTN NW1 .... **7** F5
IS N1 .... **76** B5
Royal College of Obstetricians &
Gynaecologists
CAMTN NW1 .... **5** E5
Royal College of Ophthalmologists
CAMTN NW1 .... **18** A1
Royal College of Paediatrics &
Child Health
GTPST W1W **19** D2
The Royal College of Pathology
STJS SW1Y **32** A4
Royal College of Physicians
CAMTN NW1 .... **6** C5
Royal College of Surgeons
LINN WC2A **21** F4
Royal Courts of Justice
LINN WC2A **21** F5

Royal Court Theatre
BGVA SW1W **42** A5
Royal Court Young
Peoples Theatre
NKENS W10 .... **89** E4
The Royal Dock
Community School
CAN/RD E16 .... **94** C5
Royal Docks Medical Centre
EHAM E6 .... **96** A5
Royal Exchange
LOTH EC2R **24** B5
Royal Festival Hall
STHWK SE1 .... **33** E4
Royal Foundation of
Grey Coat Hospital
WESTW SW1E **43** E2
Royal Free Hospital
HAMP NW3 .... **73** E2
Royal Free Hospital
School of Medicine
HAMP NW3 .... **73** E2
Royal Geographical Society
SKENS SW7 .... **40** A1
Royal Horticultural Society New Hall
WEST SW1P **44** A3
Royal Horticultural Society Old Hall
WEST SW1P **44** A4
Royal Hospital Chelsea
CHEL SW3 .... **115** F1
Royal Hospital for
Neuro-Disability
PUT/ROE SW15 .... **131** E4
Royal Hospital & Home
PUT/ROE SW15 .... **130** B5
Royal Hospital Museum
CHEL SW3 .... **116** A1
Royal Institute of
British Architects
REGST W1B **19** D2
Royal Institution
(Faraday Museum)
MYFR/PICC W1J **31** D2
Royal London Homeopathic Hospital
BMSBY WC1N **21** D2
Royal London Hospital
BETH E2 .... **90** C1
The Royal London Hospital
BOW E3 .... **91** F2
The Royal London Hospital
(Whitechapel)
WCHPL E1 .... **90** B4
Royal Marsden Hospital
CHEL SW3 .... **115** D1
The Royal Mews
WHALL SW1A **43** D2
Royal Mint Court
TWRH EC3N **37** F2
Royal National
Orthopaedic Hospital
GTPST W1W **19** D1
Royal National Theatre
BRXN/ST SW9 .... **118** A3
STHWK SE1 .... **34** A3
Royal National Throat Nose &
Ear Hospital
FSBYW WC1X **9** E3
Royal Observatory Greenwich
GNWCH SE10 .... **123** D2
Royal Opera House
COVGDN WC2E **21** D5
The Royal School
HAMP NW3 .... **73** D1

Royal Society of Arts
TPL/STR WC2R **33** D2
Royal Society of Medicine
CAVSQ/HST W1G **18** C4
Royal Veterinary College
CAMTN NW1 .... **75** D5
Royal Victoria Docks
  Watersports Centre
CAN/RD E16 .... **106** A1
Royal Wimbledon Golf Club
WIM/MER SW19 .... **148** B5
RSPCA Animal Hospital
HOLWY N7 .... **57** F4
Rudolph Steiner Hall
CAMTN NW1 .... **5** E5
Rufus Business Centre
WAND/EARL SW18 .... **150** B2
Rushey Green Primary School
CAT SE6 .... **158** B1
Rushmore Junior School
CLPT E5 .... **78** C1
Ruskin House School
HNHL SE24 .... **136** C3
Ruxley Manor School
ELTH/MOT SE9 .... **162** A4
Saatchi Gallery
KIL/WHAMP NW6 .... **72** B5
Sacred Heart High School
HMSMTH W6 .... **100** C5
Sacred Heart Junior School
HMSMTH W6 .... **101** D5
Sacred Heart RC Infant School
BTSEA SW11 .... **115** E5
Sacred Heart RC Junior &
  Middle School
BTSEA SW11 .... **133** E1
Sacred Heart RC School
CMBW SE5 .... **118** C4
Sacred Heart School
HOLWY N7 .... **75** F2
Saddlers Hall
CITYW EC2V **23** E5
Sadler's Wells Theatre
CLKNW EC1R **10** B3
SAE Technology College
HOLWY N7 .... **75** E2
Sai Medical Centre
POP/IOD E14 .... **104** C2
St Agnes RC Primary School
BOW E3 .... **92** A2
CRICK NW2 .... **53** E5
St Aidans Primary School
FSBYPK N4 .... **58** A2
St Aidans RC Primary School
IL IG1 .... **67** D3
St Albans CE Primary School
FSBYW WC1X **22** A2
St Albans Health Clinic
KTTN NW5 .... **56** A5
St Albans Junior & Infant
  RC School
PECK SE15 .... **119** F4
St Alfege with St Peter
  CE Primary School
GNWCH SE10 .... **122** C2
St Aloysius College
ARCH N19 .... **56** C3
St Aloysius RC Infant School
CAMTN NW1 .... **8** A3
St Aloysius RC Junior School
CAMTN NW1 .... **7** F2

St Andrew & St Francis
  CE JMI School
CRICK NW2 .... **70** A3
St Andrews CE Primary School
BRXN/ST SW9 .... **118** A4
St Andrews Greek School
CAMTN NW1 .... **74** B3
St Andrews Hospital
BOW E3 .... **92** B3
St Andrews Primary School
BRXN/ST SW9 .... **117** F5
IS N1 .... **75** F5
St Andrews School
WLSDN NW10 .... **70** B4
St Angelas RC School
FSTGT E7 .... **82** B3
St Annes CE Primary School
WAND/EARL SW18 .... **132** B3
St Annes RC Primary School
LBTH SE11 .... **117** F2
WCHPL E1 .... **90** A3
St Anne's Trading Estate
POP/IOD E14 .... **91** F5
St Anslems RC Primary School
TOOT SW17 .... **152** A3
St Anthonys RC Primary School
EDUL SE22 .... **137** F4
FSTGT E7 .... **82** A4
St Augustines CE School
KIL/WHAMP NW6 .... **2** B2
St Augustines Primary School
KIL/WHAMP NW6 .... **2** B1
St Augustines RC Primary School
CAT SE6 .... **158** B5
FUL/PGN SW6 .... **113** E2
St Barnabas & St Philips
  CE Primary School
KENS W8 .... **38** A3
St Bartholomews
  CE Primary School
SYD SE26 .... **156** C4
St Bartholomews Hospital
STBT EC1A **23** D3
St Bartholomews Medical School
FARR EC1M **23** D1
St Bartholomews & Royal
  London School of Medicine
FARR EC1M **23** E2
St Bartholomew's the Great
STBT EC1A **23** D3
St Bonaventure's School
FSTGT E7 .... **82** A4
St Boniface RC Primary School
TOOT SW17 .... **151** F5
St Charles Hospital
NKENS W10 .... **89** D4
St Charles RC Sixth Form College
NKENS W10 .... **89** D4
St Christophers School
HAMP NW3 .... **73** D2
St Christopher House
STHWK SE1 .... **35** E3
St Clement Danes
  CE Primary School
HOL/ALD WC2B **21** E5
St Clement & James
  CE Primary School
NTCHL W11 .... **101** E2
St Cuthbert With St Matthias
  CE Primary School
ECT SW5 .... **114** B1

St Dominics RC Junior
& Infant School
HOM E9 .... 79 D3
St Dominics RC Primary School
HAMP NW3 .... 73 F2
St Dunstans College
CAT SE6 .... 157 F1
St Edmunds RC Primary School
POP/IOD E14 .... 104 A5
St Edwards RC JMI School
STJWD NW8 .... 16 C1
St Faiths CE School
WAND/EARL SW18 .... 132 B3
St Francesca Cabrini
Primary School
FSTH SE23 .... 138 C4
St Francis of Assisi
Primary School
NTGHL W11 .... 101 D1
St Francis RC Primary School
PECK SE15 .... 120 A2
SRTFD E15 .... 81 E2
St Francis Xavier College
BAL SW12 .... 134 B4
St Gabriels CE Primary School
PIM SW1V 116 C1
St George's Cathedral
STHWK SE1 .... 46 B2
St George's Cathedral RC Primary
STHWK SE1 .... 46 C2
St Georges CE Primary School
PECK SE15 .... 119 E3
VX/NE SW8 .... 116 C3
St Georges College
HOLWY N7 .... 58 A5
St Georges Elizabethan Theatre
HOLWY N7 .... 75 D1
St Georges Hanover Square
CE Primary School
MYFR/PKLN W1K 30 B2
St Georges Hospital
TOOT SW17 .... 151 E5
St Georges RC School
MV/WKIL W9 .... 3 D2
St George the Martyr
CE Primary School
BMSBY WC1N 21 E1
St George Wharf
VX/NE SW8 .... 117 E2
St Gildas RC Junior School
CEND/HSY/T N8 .... 57 E2
St Giles College London Central
RSQ WC1B 20 C2
St Helens RC Primary School
BRXN/ST SW9 .... 136 A1
St Helens RC Primary School
PLSTW E13 .... 93 F3
St Ignatius RC Primary School
SEVS/STOTM N15 .... 59 E1
St James And St Michaels
CE Primary School
BAY/PAD W2 .... 27 F1
St James CE J&i School
BERM/RHTH SE16 .... 102 A4
St James CE Junior School
FSTGT E7 .... 81 F2
St James Hatcham
CE Primary School
NWCR SE14 .... 121 E4
St James's Palace
WHALL SW1A 31 F4

St John of Jerusalem
CE Primary School
HOM E9 .... 78 C4
St Johns Angell Town
CE Primary School
BRXN/ST SW9 .... 118 A5
St Johns CE Primary School
BETH E2 .... 90 C1
WALW SE17 .... 47 F5
St John's CE Walham Green
FUL/PGN SW6 .... 113 E4
St John's Concert Hall
WEST SW1P 44 C3
St Johns Highbury Vale
CE Primary School
HBRY N5 .... 58 B5
St John's Hospital
SOHO/SHAV W1D 32 A1
St John's Hospital Day Centre
BTSEA SW11 .... 133 D2
St Johns RC Primary School
BERM/RHTH SE16 .... 103 E3
St Johns Upper Holloway
CE Primary School
ARCH N19 .... 57 D5
St Johns Way Medical Centre
ARCH N19 .... 57 D3
St Johns Wood School of English
KIL/WHAMP NW6 .... 72 B5
St John the Baptist
CE Primary School
CAT SE6 .... 158 C4
St John the Baptist
CE Primary School
IS N1 .... 12 C2
St John the Divine
CE Primary School
CMBW SE5 .... 118 B3
St John the Evangelist
RC Primary School
IS N1 .... 10 C1
St Josephs Catholic Infant School
LEY E10 .... 61 F3
St Josephs Convent School
WAN E11 .... 64 A1
St Josephs Primary School
PUT/ROE SW15 .... 132 A3
St Josephs RC Junior School
CMBW SE5 .... 118 C3
LEY E10 .... 62 B3
ARCH N19 .... 56 B3
BARK IG11 .... 84 C5
BERM/RHTH SE16 .... 102 C4
CHEL SW3 .... 41 E5
DEPT SE8 .... 122 A3
GNWCH SE10 .... 123 E1
HOL/ALD WC2B 21 D4
MV/WKIL W9 .... 3 E4
STHWK SE1 .... 35 F5
STHWK SE1 .... 102 A3
WLSDN NW10 .... 69 E4
St Judes CE Primary School
STHWK SE1 .... 46 C3
St Judes & St Pauls
CE Primary School
IS N1 .... 77 E3
St Katharine Pier
WAP E1W 37 F3
St Lawrence University
FSBYW WC1X 21 F1
St Leonards CE Primary School
STRHM/NOR SW16 .... 153 D5

St Leonards Hospital
IS N1 .... **13** D1
St Lukes CE Primary School
CAN/RD E16 .... **93** F5
FSBYE EC1V **11** F4
MV/WKIL W9 .... **89** F1
POP/IOD E14 .... **105** D5
WNWD SE27 .... **154** C5
St Luke's Health Centre
CAN/RD E16 .... **93** F5
St Lukes Hospital for the Clergy
FITZ W1T **19** E1
St Margaret Lee
CE Primary School
LEW SE13 .... **141** E2
St Margarets Clitherow
RC Primary School
WLSDN NW10 .... **51** D5
St Margarets Primary School
BARK IG11 .... **84** B5
St Margarets School
HAMP NW3 .... **72** B1
St Marks CE Primary School
ARCH N19 .... **57** E4
St Marks Industrial Estate
CAN/RD E16 .... **107** D2
St Martin-in-the-Fields High School
BRXS/STRHM SW2 .... **154** B1
St Martins Hospital
MYFR/PKLN W1K **30** A1
St Martins School of Art
SOHO/SHAV W1D **20** B5
St Martins Theatre
LSQ/SEVD WC2H **32** B1
St Mary Abbots
CE Primary School
KENS W8 .... **38** C1
St Mary Abbots Church Hall
KENS W8 .... **26** C5
St Mary & St Josephs GM School
SCUP DA14 .... **163** F5
St Mary CE Primary School
PUT/ROE SW15 .... **131** D1
St Marylebone
CE Secondary School
MHST W1U **18** B2
St Mary Magdalene
CE Primary School
MV/WKIL W9 .... **14** C2
PECK SE15 .... **120** B5
WOOL/PLUM SE18 .... **107** F5
St Mary Magdalene Primary School
HOLWY N7 .... **76** A3
St Mary Magdalen RC Junior School
CRICK NW2 .... **70** B3
St Mary Magdalens
RC Primary School
MORT/ESHN SW14 .... **129** D1
St Mary of the Angels
RC Primary School
BAY/PAD W2 .... **14** A4
St Mary & St Pancras
CE Primary School
CAMTN NW1 .... **8** A2
St Marys Bryanston Square
CE Primary School
MBLAR W1H **17** E3
St Mary's Cemetery
BTSEA SW11 .... **133** E3
St Marys CE Primary School
IS N1 .... **76** B4

LEW SE13 .... **140** B3
WLSDN NW10 .... **69** E3
St Marys Hospital
BAY/PAD W2 .... **16** B4
St Marys Hospital Medical School
BAY/PAD W2 .... **16** B4
St Mary's Kilburn Primary School
KIL/WHAMP NW6 .... **72** A5
St Marys Magdalens
RC Primary School
BROCKY SE4 .... **139** E2
St Mary's Primary School
WKENS W14 .... **101** D4
St Marys RC Primary School
CHSWK W4 .... **111** D1
CLAP SW4 .... **134** C3
ELTH/MOT SE9 .... **144** A3
KIL/WHAMP NW6 .... **2** A1
NKENS W10 .... **89** E3
SEVS/STOTM N15 .... **59** D1
VX/NE SW8 .... **116** B4
St Marys School
HAMP NW3 .... **72** C2
St Marys Stoke Newington
CE Primary School
STNW/STAM N16 .... **59** E4
St Matthews CE Primary School
WEST SW1P **44** B3
St Matthias CE Primary School
BETH E2 .... **13** F5
STNW/STAM N16 .... **77** E2
St Michaels CE Primary School
HGT N6 .... **56** A2
WAND/EARL SW18 .... **131** F1
St Michaels RC Primary School
EHAM E6 .... **95** F1
St Michaels RC Secondary School
BERM/RHTH SE16 .... **102** A3
St Michaels Sydenham
CE Primary
SYD SE26 .... **157** E4
St Monica's RC Primary School
IS N1 .... **12** C3
St Olaves Preparatory School
ELTH/MOT SE9 .... **162** B2
St Osmunds RC Primary School
BARN SW13 .... **111** F4
St Pancras Hospital
CAMTN NW1 .... **75** D5
St Pancras Station
CAMTN NW1 .... **8** C3
St Patricks Church School
STHWK SE1 .... **34** A4
St Patricks Infants School
WAP E1W **102** B2
St Patricks International School
SOHO/CST W1F **19** F4
St Patricks Primary School
KTTN NW5 .... **74** B3
WAP E1W **102** B2
WOOL/PLUM SE18 .... **109** D5
St Paul's Cathedral
STP EC4M **23** D5
St Paul's Cathedral School
STP EC4M **23** E5
St Pauls CE Primary School
HAMP NW3 .... **73** E4
WALW SE17 .... **118** B1
WAP E1W **102** B2
St Pauls Girls School
HMSMTH W6 .... **101** D5
St Pauls Preparatory School
BARN SW13 .... **112** A1

St Paul's Primary School
HMSMTH W6 .... 112 C1

St Pauls Road Medical Centre
IS N1 .... 76 B3

St Pauls Way School
BOW E3 .... 92 A3

St Pauls with St Lukes
CE Primary School
BOW E3 .... 91 F4
POP/IOD E14 .... 91 F4

St Paul's with St Michael's
CE Primary School
HACK E8 .... 78 A5

St Peter & Pauls
RC Primary School
IL IG1 .... 67 D5
FSBYE EC1V 11 D5

St Peters CE Primary School
HMSMTH W6 .... 112 A1
MV/WKIL W9 .... 14 A1
WALW SE17 .... 119 D1

St Peters Eaton Square
CE Primary School
BGVA SW1W 42 C3

St Peter's Hospital
COVGDN WC2E 33 D1

St Peters Primary School
WAP E1W 102 C2

St Peters RC Primary School
WOOL/PLUM SE18 .... 126 B1

St Philips School
SKENS SW7 .... 39 F5

St Phillips Infant School
SYD SE26 .... 156 B4

St Quintins Health Centre
NKENS W10 .... 88 C4

St Raphaels Way Medical Centre
WBLY HA9 .... 68 C2

St Robert Southwell
RC Primary School
CDALE/KGS NW9 .... 50 C1

St Saviour & St Olaves School
STHWK SE1 .... 48 B3

St Saviours CE Primary School
HNHL SE24 .... 136 C1
MV/WKIL W9 .... 15 D1
POP/IOD E14 .... 92 B4

St Saviours RC Primary School
LEW SE13 .... 140 C2

St Scholastica's RC Primary School
STNW/STAM N16 .... 60 A5

St Stephens CE Primary School
BAY/PAD W2 .... 14 B3
DEPT SE8 .... 122 A5
SHB W12 .... 100 C2

St Stephens CE School
VX/NE SW8 .... 117 E3

St Stephens Primary School
EHAM E6 .... 82 C4

St Thomas CE Primary School
NKENS W10 .... 89 E3
STNW/STAM N16 .... 59 F3

St Thomas Hospital
Operation Theatre
STHWK SE1 .... 36 B4

St Thomas More
RC Primary School
ELTH/MOT SE9 .... 143 E1

St Thomas More RC School
CHEL SW3 .... 41 E5
ELTH/MOT SE9 .... 144 A4

St Thomas of Canterbury
RC Primary School
FUL/PGN SW6 .... 113 F3

St Thomas's Hospital
STHWK SE1 .... 45 E2

St Thomas the Apostle College
PECK SE15 .... 120 C4

St Ursulas Convent School
GNWCH SE10 .... 123 D3

St Vincent de Paul
RC Primary School
WEST SW1P 43 E3

St Vincents Catholic
Primary School
ELTH/MOT SE9 .... 161 E4

St Vincents RC Primary School
ACT W3 .... 98 B1
MHST W1U 18 A3

St Walter & St John
Sports Ground
TOOT SW17 .... 151 E1

St William of York
Primary School
FSTH SE23 .... 157 E1

St Winefrides Catholic
Primary School
MNPK E12 .... 83 F2

St Winifreds Junior School
LEE/GVPK SE12 .... 141 F4

St Winifreds RC Infant School
LEW SE13 .... 141 E3

Salesian College
BTSEA SW11 .... 115 E4

Salisbury Primary School
MNPK E12 .... 83 D2

Salters' Hall
BARB EC2Y 23 F3

Salusbury Primary School
KIL/WHAMP NW6 .... 71 E5

Salvation Army Heritage Centre
BLKFR EC4V 35 E1

Samaritan & Western Ophthalmic
Hospital
MBLAR W1H 17 E2

Samuel Jones Industrial Estate
PECK SE15 .... 119 E3

Samuel Rhodes School
IS N1 .... 76 A5

Sandgate Trading Estate
BERM/RHTH SE16 .... 120 B1

Sandhurst Primary School
CAT SE6 .... 141 E5

Sandringham Primary School
FSTGT E7 .... 82 C3

Sapcote Trading Centre
WLSDN NW10 .... 69 F2

Sarah Bonnell School
SRTFD E15 .... 81 E3

Sarum Hall School
HAMP NW3 .... 73 E4

Satmer Trust School
STNW/STAM N16 .... 60 A4

Savoy Pier
TPL/STR WC2R 33 E2

Savoy Theatre
TPL/STR WC2R 33 E2

Sayer Clinics
MBLAR W1H 17 F5

Scarsdale Place Medical Centre
KENS W8 .... 38 C2

Schiller International School
STHWK SE1 .... 34 A4

Skillion Business Park
BARK IG11 .... **97** F2

**Skinners Companys
Lower Girls School**
CLPT E5 .... **60** B3

**Skinners Companys
School for Girls**
STNW/STAM N16 .... **59** E2

Slade School of Fine Art
STPAN WC1H **8** B4

Sleaford Industrial Estate
VX/NE SW8 .... **116** C3

Smallwood Primary School
TOOT SW17 .... **151** D4

SMA Medical Centre
LEY E10 .... **62** B2

Smithy Street School
WCHPL E1 .... **90** C4

Snowsfields Primary School
STHWK SE1 .... **36** C5

Sobel Medical Centre
HOLWY N7 .... **76** A1

Soho Parish CE Primary School
SOHO/CST W1F **32** A1

Solent Road Health Centre
KIL/WHAMP NW6 .... **72** A3

Somerset House
COVGDN WC2E **33** E1

**Somers Town Community
Sports Centre**
CAMTN NW1 .... **7** F2

Sorsby Health Centre
CLPT E5 .... **79** D1

South Bank Business Centre
BTSEA SW11 .... **116** A4
VX/NE SW8 .... **117** D2

Southbank International School
NTGHL W11 .... **26** A2

Southbank University
STHWK SE1 .... **46** C1
STHWK SE1 .... **47** D2
STHWK SE1 .... **47** E2
STHWK SE1 .... **47** F3
VX/NE SW8 .... **117** D4

**South Camden
Community School**
CAMTN NW1 .... **7** F1

South Chelsea College
BRXN/ST SW9 .... **135** E2

South Eastern University
HOLWY N7 .... **57** F5

Southern Road Primary School
PLSTW E13 .... **94** B1

Southfield First & Middle School
CHSWK W4 .... **99** E3

Southfield Medical Centre
CHSWK W4 .... **99** D3

The Southfields Clinic
WAND/EARL SW18 .... **132** A4

Southfields Community School
WAND/EARL SW18 .... **150** A1

Southgate Road Medical Centre
IS N1 .... **77** D4

South Grove Primary School
WALTH E17 .... **61** E1

South Hampstead Cricket Club
CRICK NW2 .... **70** C4

**South Hampstead
High School (Senior)**
HAMP NW3 .... **73** D3

Southlands College
PUT/ROE SW15 .... **129** F2

South Lewisham Health Centre
CAT SE6 .... **158** C4

South London Montessori School
BTSEA SW11 .... **115** E4

**The South London
Natural Health Centre**
CLAP SW4 .... **134** C2

South London Theatre
WNWD SE27 .... **154** C3

Southmead Primary School
WIM/MER SW19 .... **149** E1

South Park Business Centre
IL IG1 .... **67** E4

South Park Clinic
IL IG1 .... **85** E1

South Park Primary School
GDMY/SEVK IG3 .... **67** E5

South Quay Plaza
POP/IOD E14 .... **104** B3

South Rise Primary School
WOOL/PLUM SE18 .... **127** D1

Southside Industrial Estate
VX/NE SW8 .... **116** C3

South Thames College
PUT/ROE SW15 .... **131** D3

**South Thames College/Wandsworth
Adult College**
PUT/ROE SW15 .... **129** F4

Southwark Bridge Business Centre
STHWK SE1 .... **35** F4

Southwark Bridge Stairs
BLKFR EC4V **35** E2

Southwark Cathedral
STHWK SE1 .... **36** A3

Southwark College
BERM/RHTH SE16 .... **102** B4
CMBW SE5 .... **119** E3
STHWK SE1 .... **34** C5
STHWK SE1 .... **49** D2

Southwark Coroners Court
STHWK SE1 .... **36** A5

Southwark Crown Court
STHWK SE1 .... **36** C3

Southwark Park Primary School
BERM/RHTH SE16 .... **102** B4

Southwark Park Running Track
BERM/RHTH SE16 .... **102** C5

Southwark Sports Ground
DUL SE21 .... **155** F1

Southwold Primary School
CLPT E5 .... **60** C4

Southwood Hospital
HGT N6 .... **56** A2

The Space Arts Centre Cinema
POP/IOD E14 .... **103** F5

The Spare Tyre Theatre Company
KTTN NW5 .... **74** A3

Speakers Corner
BAY/PAD W2 .... **29** F1

Speke's Monument
BAY/PAD W2 .... **27** F3

Spencer House
WHALL SW1A **31** E4

Spiritualist University
WLSDN NW10 .... **70** A4

Spitalfields Health Centre
WCHPL E1 .... **25** F3

Spitalfields Market
LEY E10 .... **62** A5

Spitalfields Market Hall
WCHPL E1 .... **25** E2

Springfield Hospital
TOOT SW17 .... **151** E3

Springfield Primary School
  VX/NE SW8 .... **117** D3
The Stables Gallery & Art Centre
  CRICK NW2 .... **70** A1
Stadium Business Centre
  WBLY HA9 .... **50** B5
Stadium Industrial Estate
  WBLY HA9 .... **68** B2
Stadium Retail Park
  WBLY HA9 .... **50** A5
Stamford Clinic
  HMSMTH W6 .... **100** A5
Stamford Hill Primary School
  SEVS/STOTM N15 .... **59** D1
Standard Industrial Estate
  CAN/RD E16 .... **107** D3
Stanton Square Industrial Estate
  CAT SE6 .... **157** F4
Staple Inn Buildings
  HHOL WC1V **22** A3
Staples Corner Business Park
  CRICK NW2 .... **52** A3
Star Primary School
  CAN/RD E16 .... **93** E3
Stationers Hall
  STP EC4M **23** D5
Stationery Office
  GINN WC1R **21** F3
Stephen Hawking Primary School
  POP/IOD E14 .... **91** E5
Stepney Day Hospital
  WCHPL E1 .... **90** C5
Stepney Greencoat
  CE Primary School
  POP/IOD E14 .... **91** F5
Stepney Green School
  WCHPL E1 .... **91** D4
Stewart Headlam Primary School
  WCHPL E1 .... **90** B3
Stillness Primary School
  BROCKY SE4 .... **139** E4
Stock Exchange
  OBST EC2N **24** B4
Stockwell Park School
  BRXN/ST SW9 .... **117** C4
Stockwell Primary School
  BRXN/ST SW9 .... **135** F1
Stoke Newington School
  STNW/STAM N16 .... **59** D5
The Stonebridge Primary School
  WLSDN NW10 .... **68** C5
Stonebridge Shopping Centre
  WLSDN NW10 .... **69** C5
Stone Lake Retail Park
  CHARL SE7 .... **106** C5
Storey Primary School
  CAN/RD E16 .... **108** B1
Stormont House School
  CLPT E5 .... **78** B1
Strand on the Green Junior
  & Infant School
  CHSWK W4 .... **110** A2
Strand Theatre
  HOL/ALD WC2B **33** E1
Stratford Magistrates Court
  SRTFD E15 .... **81** D4
Stratford School
  FSTGT E7 .... **82** A4
Stratford Shopping Centre
  SRTFD E15 .... **81** D4
Strawberry Fields School
  BAY/PAD W2 .... **14** B5

Streatham Cemetery
  TOOT SW17 .... **151** E3
Streatham & Clapham High School
  STRHM/NOR SW16 .... **152** C3
Streatham & Clapham High School
  Preparatory Site
  BRXS/STRHM SW2 .... **153** F1
Streatham Ice Rink
  STRHM/NOR SW16 .... **153** E5
Streatham Swimming Pool
  STRHM/NOR SW16 .... **153** E5
Streatham Wells Primary School
  BRXS/STRHM SW2 .... **153** F2
Stroud Green Primary School
  FSBYPK N4 .... **58** A3
The Study Preparatory School
  WIM/MER SW19 .... **149** D5
Sudbourne Primary School
  BRXS/STRHM SW2 .... **135** F3
Sulivan Primary School
  FUL/PGN SW6 .... **114** A5
Sunnyhill Primary School
  STRHM/NOR SW16 .... **153** F4
Surrey CCC (The Oval)
  LBTH SE11 .... **117** F2
Surrey Docks Farm
  BERM/RHTH SE16 .... **103** F3
Surrey Docks Health Centre
  BERM/RHTH SE16 .... **103** E3
Surrey Quays Leisure Park
  BERM/RHTH SE16 .... **103** D4
Surrey Quays Shopping Centre
  BERM/RHTH SE16 .... **103** D4
Surrey Square Junior
  & Infant School
  WALW SE17 .... **119** D1
Sussex House Preparatory School
  KTBR SW1X **41** E4
Sutcliffe Park Athletics Track
  ELTH/MOT SE9 .... **142** B3
Sutton House
  HOM E9 .... **78** C2
Swaffield Primary School
  WAND/EARL SW18 .... **132** C4
Swaminarayan School
  WLSDN NW10 .... **69** D3
Swan Business Centre
  CHSWK W4 .... **99** D5
Swan Lane Pier
  CANST EC4R **36** A2
Swanlea School
  WCHPL E1 .... **90** B3
Swedish School
  BARN SW13 .... **112** A2
Swiss Cottage School
  HAMP NW3 .... **73** D5
Sybourn Infant School
  LEY E10 .... **61** E3
Sybourn Junior School
  WALTH E17 .... **61** F2
Sydenham Girls School
  SYD SE26 .... **156** B3
Sydenham High School
  SYD SE26 .... **156** B5
Sydenham (Junior) High School
  SYD SE26 .... **156** B4
Syracuse University
  London Centre
  NTGHL W11 .... **101** F1
Tabard Theatre
  CHSWK W4 .... **99** E5
Tate Britain
  WEST SW1P **44** C5

Tate Modern
STHWK SE1 .... **35** D3

Tavistock Clinic
HAMP NW3 .... **73** D3

Telegraph Hill School
BROCKY SE4 .... **121** E5

Temple of Bacchus
CMBW SE5 .... **118** C5

Temple of Mithras
MANHO EC4N **24** A5

Terence McMillan Stadium
PLSTW E13 .... **94** C3

Thames Barrier
CAN/RD E16 .... **107** D3

Thames Barrier Visitor Centre
WOOL/PLUM SE18 .... **107** D4

Thames House
WEST SW1P **44** C4

Thameside Industrial Estate
CAN/RD E16 .... **107** D2

Thames Magistrates Court
BOW E3 .... **92** A2

Thames View Clinic
BARK IG11 .... **97** F1

Thames Water Tower
NTGHL W11 .... **101** D3

Théâtre De Complicité
HOLWY N7 .... **75** F2

Theatre for Mankind
FSBYPK N4 .... **57** F3

Theatre Museum Library & Archive
COVGDN WC2E **33** D1

Theatre of the Dispossessed
WIM/MER SW19 .... **149** D1

Theatre Royal
SRTFD E15 .... **81** D4

Theatre Royal, Drury Lane
HOL/ALD WC2B **21** D5

Theatre Royal Haymarket
STJS SW1Y **32** B2

Thomas Buxton Primary School
WCHPL E1 .... **90** A3

Thomas Fairchild Primary School
IS N1 .... **12** A1

Thomas Gamuel Primary School
WALTH E17 .... **62** A1

Thomas Road Industrial Estate
POP/IOD E14 .... **92** A4

Thomas's Preparatory School
BTSEA SW11 .... **115** D4

Thomas Tallis School
BKHTH/KID SE3 .... **142** B1

Thornhill Primary School
IS N1 .... **76** A4

Thorntree Primary School
CHARL SE7 .... **125** D1

Three Mills Heritage Centre
SRTFD E15 .... **92** C2

Thurlow Park School
WNWD SE27 .... **154** B2

Thurston Industrial Estate
LEW SE13 .... **140** B1

Tidemill Primary School
DEPT SE8 .... **122** A3

Tideway Industrial Estate
VX/NE SW8 .... **116** C2

Tiller Centre (Swimming Baths)
POP/IOD E14 .... **104** A4

Tiller Leisure Centre
POP/IOD E14 .... **104** A4

Timbercroft Primary School
WOOL/PLUM SE18 .... **127** E3

Tiverton Primary School
SEVS/STOTM N15 .... **59** D1

Tobacco Dock
WAP E1W **102** B1

Tokyngton Community Centre
WBLY HA9 .... **68** B2

Toldos School
STNW/STAM N16 .... **59** D3

Tollgate Primary School
PLSTW E13 .... **94** C3

Tom Hood School
WAN E11 .... **63** F5

Tonybee Hall & Curtain Theatre
WCHPL E1 .... **25** E4

Tooting Bec Athletics Track
TOOT SW17 .... **152** B4

Torriano Junior & Infant School
KTTN NW5 .... **74** C2

Torridon Primary School
CAT SE6 .... **159** D2

Total Health Clinic
SHB W12 .... **100** B3

The Tower Bridge Experience
STHWK SE1 .... **37** E4

Tower Bridge Museum
STHWK SE1 .... **37** E4

Tower Bridge Primary School
STHWK SE1 .... **37** E5

Tower Bridge Wharf
WAP E1W **102** A2

Tower Hamlets College
POP/IOD E14 .... **104** B1
WCHPL E1 .... **90** C4

Tower House School
MORT/ESHN SW14 .... **128** C2

Tower Medical Centre
WCHPL E1 .... **90** A5

Tower Millennium Pier
MON EC3R **37** D3

Tower of London
TWRH EC3N **37** E2

Towers Business Park
WBLY HA9 .... **68** B1

Tower Stairs
MON EC3R **36** C2

Tower Theatre
IS N1 .... **76** B4

Townmead Business Centre
FUL/PGN SW6 .... **132** C1

Townsend Industrial Estate
WLSDN NW10 .... **68** C5

Townsend Primary School
STHWK SE1 .... **48** C4

Trabzon Spor FC
STNW/STAM N16 .... **77** D1

Trade Union Congress
NOXST/BSQ WC1A **20** B4

Trafalgar Business Centre
BARK IG11 .... **97** F3

Tramshed Theatre
WOOL/PLUM SE18 .... **108** B5

Trans Atlantic College
BETH E2 .... **13** E1

Transport House
WEST SW1P **44** C3

Treasury
WHALL SW1A **44** C1

Trevor Roberts School
HAMP NW3 .... **73** D4

Tricycle Cinema
KIL/WHAMP NW6 .... **71** F4

Trident Business Centre
TOOT SW17 .... **151** F5

Trinity Business Centre
BERM/RHTH SE16 .... 103 F3
Trinity College Centre
PECK SE15 .... 119 E3
Trinity College of Music
MHST W1U 18 B3
Trinity Hospital
GNWCH SE10 .... 123 D1
Trinity House
TWRH EC3N 37 D1
Trinity St Marys Primary School
BAL SW12 .... 152 A1
Trocadero Centre
MYFR/PICC W1J 32 A2
Trojan Business Centre
WLSDN NW10 .... 69 F3
True Buddha School
IS N1 .... 75 F5
Tudor Lodge Health Centre
WIM/MER SW19 .... 131 D5
Tufnell Park Primary School
HOLWY N7 .... 75 D1
Tuke School
PECK SE15 .... 120 B4
Tulloch Clinic
SHB W12 .... 101 D2
Tunnel Avenue Trading Estate
GNWCH SE10 .... 105 D3
Turney School
DUL SE21 .... 136 C5
Turnham Primary School
BROCKY SE4 .... 139 E2
Twyford CE High School
ACT W3 .... 98 B2
Tyburn Infant School
STJWD NW8 .... 4 B5
**The Type Museum
Operation Hannibal**
BRXN/ST SW9 .... 117 F4
UCI Cinema
BAY/PAD W2 .... 15 D5
BERM/RHTH SE16 .... 103 D4
UCI Empire Cinema
LSQ/SEVD WC2H 32 B2
UCI Filmworks Cinema
GNWCH SE10 .... 105 F5
UCL Hospitals
FITZ W1T 19 F1
UGC Cinema
CHEL SW3 .... 115 D2
CRICK NW2 .... 52 B3
HMSMTH W6 .... 100 B5
SOHO/SHAV W1D 32 A1
United Medical & Dental Schools
STHWK SE1 .... 45 E2
United Services Sports Ground
CHSWK W4 .... 111 E4
Unity College
KTTN NW5 .... 74 B1
**University Church of
Christ the King**
STPAN WC1H 20 A1
University College Hospital
GWRST WC1E 19 F1
HAMP NW3 .... 73 D3
University College Junior School
HAMP NW3 .... 72 C1
University College London
FITZ W1T 19 F2
STPAN WC1H.. 8 A5

**University College London,
Department of Clinical
Haematology**
GWRST WC1E 20 A1
**University College London
Medical School**
FITZ W1T 19 E2
University College School
HAMP NW3 .... 72 C2
University Hospital Lewisham
LEW SE13 .... 140 B3
University of California
WHALL SW1A 31 E4
University of East London
EHAM E6 .... 108 A1
PLSTW E13 .... 94 B2
University of Greenwich
GNWCH SE10 .... 123 D1
WOOL/PLUM SE18 .... 108 A4
**University of Greenwich
(Mansion Site)**
ELTH/MOT SE9 .... 144 C4
**University of Greenwich
(Southwood Site)**
ELTH/MOT SE9 .... 144 C4
**University of Greenwich
Sports Ground**
ELTH/MOT SE9 .... 143 E2
ELTH/MOT SE9 .... 144 C5
University of London
BAY/PAD W2 .... 16 A5
BMSBY WC1N 21 D1
FITZ W1T 20 A4
NWCR SE14 .... 121 E4
STPAN WC1H.. 8 B5
University of North London
HOLWY N7 .... 75 F1
University of Notre Dame
LSQ/SEVD WC2H 32 B2
University of Westminster
CAMTN NW1 .... 7 E5
CHSWK W4 .... 110 C4
GTPST W1W 19 E2
HGT N6 .... 56 B3
MHST W1U 18 A2
Uphall Primary School
IL IG1 .... 84 B2
Upper Montagu Street Clinic
MBLAR W1H 17 E2
**Upper Tooting Independent
High School**
TOOT SW17 .... 151 E2
Upton Cross Primary School
PLSTW E13 .... 82 B5
Upton Lane Medical Centre
FSTGT E7 .... 82 B3
Ursuline High School
IL IG1 .... 66 B4
The Vale Medical Centre
FSTH SE23 .... 157 E2
Valentine High School
IL IG1 .... 66 A1
Vale Park Industrial
ACT W3 .... 99 E3
The Vale School
SKENS SW7 .... 39 E3
Valmar Trading Estate
CMBW SE5 .... 118 C4
Vanbrugh Theatre
GWRST WC1E 20 A1
Vanguard Trading Estate
SRTFD E15.. 80 C5

Vaudeville Theatre
COVGDN WC2E **33** D1

Vauxhall Primary School
LBTH SE11 .... **117** F1

Vernon House Special School
WLSDN NW10 .... **68** C2

Vicarage Fields Health Clinic
BARK IG11 .... **84** C4

The Vicarage Field
Shopping Centre
BARK IG11 .... **84** C4

Vicarage Primary School
EHAM E6 .... **95** F2

Victoria & Albert Museum
SKENS SW7 .... **40** B3

Victoria Chiropractic Clinic
CHEL SW3 .... **41** E4

Victoria Coach Station
BGVA SW1W **42** C5

Victoria Industrial Estate
ACT W3 .... **87** D4

Victoria Medical Centre
PIM SW1V **43** E5

Victoria Palace Theatre
WESTW SW1E **43** D3

Victoria Park Industrial Centre
HOM E9 .... **79** F4

Victoria Place Shopping Centre
PIM SW1V **43** D4

Victoria Rail/Air Terminal
PIM SW1V **43** D4

Victoria Station
PIM SW1V **43** D4

Victoria Wharf
POP/IOD E14 .... **103** E1

Victoria Wharf Industrial Estate
DEPT SE8 .... **121** F1

Victory Primary School
WALW SE17 .... **47** F4

Victory Works
HOM E9 .... **79** F3

The Village School
HAMP NW3 .... **73** F3

The Vines School
BTSEA SW11 .... **134** A2

Vinopolis, City of Wine
STHWK SE1 .... **35** F3

Vinters' Hall
BLKFR EC4V **35** F1

VIP Trading Estate
CHARL SE7 .... **106** C5

Virginia Primary School
BETH E2 .... **13** E4

Visitor Centre
STJS SW1Y **32** A3

Voyager Business Estate
BERM/RHTH SE16 .... **102** A4

Waldorf School of SW London
STRHM/NOR SW16 .... **152** C2

Waldorf Steiner School
of SW London
STRHM/NOR SW16 .... **153** D4

Wallace Collection
MHST W1U **18** A4

Walmer Road Clinic
NTGHL W11 .... **101** E1

Walm Lane Clinic
CRICK NW2 .... **71** D2

Walnut Tree Walk Primary School
LBTH SE11 .... **46** A4

Walworth Lower School
WALW SE17 .... **119** D1

Walworth Town Hall
WALW SE17 .... **47** E5

Walworth Upper School
WALW SE17 .... **119** E1

Wandle Primary School
WAND/EARL SW18 .... **150** B1

Wandle Recreation Centre
WAND/EARL SW18 .... **132** B4

Wandsworth Adult College
TOOT SW17 .... **151** E4

The Wandsworth Arndale Centre
WAND/EARL SW18 .... **132** B4

Wandsworth Cemetery
WAND/EARL SW18 .... **150** C1

Wandsworth Community
Health Trust
TOOT SW17 .... **152** A5

Wandsworth County Court
PUT/ROE SW15 .... **131** E3

Wandsworth Public Baths
TOOT SW17 .... **152** A2

Wandsworth Trading Estate
WAND/EARL SW18 .... **132** B5

Wanstead Cricket Club
WAN E11 .... **64** B2

Wanstead Golf Club
WAN E11 .... **64** C2

Wanstead High School
WAN E11 .... **64** C1

Wapping Sports Centre
WAP E1W **102** B2

Warner Village Cinema
ACT W3 .... **86** A3
FUL/PGN SW6 .... **114** A3
HAMP NW3 .... **72** B3
SHB W12 .... **101** D3
SOHO/SHAV W1D **32** B1

Warwick Estate
BAY/PAD W2 .... **15** D3

Warwick Leadlay Gallery
GNWCH SE10 .... **122** C2

Warwick Park School
PECK SE15 .... **119** F4

Watergate School
LEW SE13 .... **140** B2

Waterloo Health Centre
STHWK SE1 .... **46** A1

Waterloo Station
STHWK SE1 .... **34** A5

The Watermans Hall
MON EC3R **36** C2

Water Rats Theatre
STPAN WC1H **9** D3

Water Sports Centre
BERM/RHTH SE16 .... **103** E4

Waverley Lower
Secondary School
EDUL SE22 .... **138** B3

Waverley School
EDUL SE22 .... **138** C3

Waxchandlers' Hall
CITYW EC2V **23** F4

Weekend Arts College
KTTN NW5 .... **74** B3

Welbeck Clinic
CRICK NW2 .... **54** A5

Welfare Clinic
CMBW SE5 .... **137** D1
GNWCH SE10 .... **122** C3
HGT N6 .... **56** A1

Wellcome Institute
CAMTN NW1 .... **8** A5

Welling Medical Centre
  WELL DA16 .... **145** F2
Wellington Arch
  MYFR/PICC W1J **30** B5
Wellington Barracks
  STJSPK SW1H **43** F1
Wellington Primary School
  BOW E3 .... **92** A2
Wembley Arena
  WBLY HA9 .... **68** A1
Wembley Park Business Centre
  WBLY HA9 .... **50** B5
Wembley Stadium
  WBLY HA9 .... **68** A2
Wembley Stadium
  Industrial Estate
  WBLY HA9 .... **50** C5
  WBLY HA9 .... **68** A1
Wendell Park Primary School
  SHB W12 .... **99** F3
Wentworth Tutorial College
  GLDGN NW11 .... **53** D1
Wesley's Chapel; House & Museum
  STLK EC1Y **12** A5
Wessex Gardens Primary School
  CRICK NW2 .... **53** E3
West Acton Primary School
  ACT W3 .... **86** B5
West Becton Health Centre
  CAN/RD E16 .... **95** D5
Westbourne Green
  Sports Complex
  BAY/PAD W2 .... **14** B3
Westbridge College
  BTSEA SW11 .... **115** E4
Western Avenue Business Park
  ACT W3 .... **86** B3
Western Trading Estate
  WLSDN NW10 .... **86** C3
Westfields Primary School
  BARN SW13 .... **111** F5
Westgate Business Centre
  NKENS W10 .... **89** E3
West Ham Church Primary School
  SRTFD E15 .... **81** F5
West Ham Lane Clinic
  SRTFD E15 .... **81** E5
West Hampstead Medical Centre
  KIL/WHAMP NW6 .... **72** A4
West Ham United FC
  (Upton Park)
  EHAM E6 .... **95** D1
West Hendon Clinic
  CDALE/KGS NW9 .... **51** F1
West Hill Primary School
  WAND/EARL SW18 .... **132** A3
West India Pier
  POP/IOD E14 .... **103** F3
West India Shopping Centre
  POP/IOD E14 .... **104** A2
West Kensington Sports Centre
  NTGHL W11 .... **101** D1
Westland Heliport
  BTSEA SW11 .... **133** D1
West Lodge Preparatory School
  BFN/LL DA15 .... **163** F3
West London County Court
  WKENS W14 .... **101** E5
West London Magistrates Court
  HMSMTH W6 .... **113** D1
West London Tamil School
  WLSDN NW10 .... **87** F1

Westminster Abbey
  WEST SW1P **44** C2
Westminster Abbey Choir School
  WEST SW1P **44** B2
Westminster Business Square
  LBTH SE11 .... **117** F1
Westminster Cathedral
  WEST SW1P **43** E3
Westminster Cathedral
  Choir School
  WEST SW1P **43** F4
Westminster Cathedral
  RC Primary School
  PIM SW1V **117** D1
Westminster City Hall
  WESTW SW1E **43** F2
Westminster City School
  WESTW SW1E **43** F2
Westminster College
  BTSEA SW11 .... **116** A4
  SOHO/SHAV W1D **31** F1
Westminster Gallery
  STJSPK SW1H **44** B1
Westminster Industrial Estate
  WOOL/PLUM SE18 .... **107** D4
Westminster Natural
  Health Centre
  PIM SW1V **43** E5
Westminster Pier
  WHALL SW1A **45** D1
Westminster School
  WEST SW1P **44** C2
Westminster Technical College
  WEST SW1P **43** F4
Westminster Theatre
  WESTW SW1E **43** E2
Westminster Under School
  WEST SW1P **44** A5
Westmoor Community Clinic
  PUT/ROE SW15 .... **130** A5
West Norwood Clinic
  WNWD SE27 .... **154** C2
West Norwood Crematorium
  WNWD SE27 .... **154** C3
West One Shopping Centre
  MYFR/PKLN W1K **18** B5
Westpoint Trading Estate
  ACT W3 .... **86** B4
West Twyford Primary School
  WLSDN NW10 .... **86** A1
Westway Business Centre
  BAY/PAD W2 .... **14** C3
Westway Sports Centre
  NKENS W10 .... **89** D5
Westwood Primary School
  WELL DA16 .... **145** E2
Westwood Technology College
  WELL DA16 .... **145** D2
The Wetlands Centre
  BARN SW13 .... **112** B4
Whaddon House Clinic
  CMBW SE5 .... **137** E1
Whipps Cross Hospital
  LEY E10 .... **63** D1
Whitechapel Art Gallery
  WCHPL E1 .... **25** F4
Whitefield School
  CRICK NW2 .... **53** D2
Whitehall Theatre
  WHALL SW1A **32** B3
Whiteleys Shopping Centre
  BAY/PAD W2 .... **14** C5

Whitmore Primary School
IS N1 .... **77** D5

Whittington Hospital
ARCH N19 .... **56** B4

Wigmore Hall
MHST W1U **18** C4

Wilberforce Primary School
NKENS W10 .... **89** E2

Willesden Community Hospital
WLSDN NW10 .... **70** A4

Willesden County Court
WLSDN NW10 .... **87** E1

Willesden High School
WLSDN NW10 .... **70** B5

Willesden Medical Centre
CRICK NW2 .... **70** B3

Willesden Sports Stadium
WLSDN NW10 .... **70** B5

William Davies Primary School
FSTGT E7 .... **83** D3

William Ellis School
KTTN NW5 .... **56** A5

William Tyndale Primary School
IS N1 .... **76** B4

Willington School
WIM/MER SW9 .... **149** F5

Willoughby Hall School
HAMP NW3 .... **73** D1

Willow Business Park
SYD SE26 .... **156** C3

Willowfield School
HNHL SE24 .... **136** C2

The Willows Clinic
CHST BR7 .... **162** A5

Wimbledon Common Golf Club
WIM/MER SW19 .... **148** A5

Wimbledon (Gap Road) Cemetery
WIM/MER SW19 .... **150** B4

Wimbledon Park Athletics Track
WIM/MER SW19 .... **149** F2

Wimbledon Park Golf Club
WIM/MER SW19 .... **149** F3

Wimbledon Park Primary School
WIM/MER SW19 .... **150** A2

Wimbledon Stadium
TOOT SW17 .... **150** B4

**Wimbledon Stadium
Business Centre**
WIM/MER SW19 .... **150** B3

Winchcombe Business Centre
PECK SE15 .... **119** E2

Windmill School
BRXS/STRHM SW2 .... **135** E3

Winfield House
CAMTN NW1 .... **5** D3

Wingfield Primary School
BKHTH/KID SE3 .... **142** A1

Winsor Primary School
EHAM E6 .... **95** F5

**Winston Churchill's Britain at
War Experience**
STHWK SE1 .... **36** B4

Winton Primary School
IS N1 .... **9** E2

Witnitz School
STNW/STAM N16 .... **59** F3

Wix Primary School
BTSEA SW11 .... **134** B1

Women's Theatre Workshop
REGST W1B **31** F2

Woodbury Down Primary School
FSBYPK N4 .... **58** C2

Woodentops School
BAL SW12 .... **153** D1

Woodfield School
CDALE/KGS NW9 .... **51** E3

Woodgrange Infant School
FSTGT E7 .... **82** B1

Woodgrange Park Cemetery
FSTGT E7 .... **83** D2

Woodhill Primary School
CHARL SE7 .... **107** E5

Woodlands Infant & Junior School
IL IG1 .... **85** D2

Wood Lane School
FUL/PGN SW6 .... **114** C4

Wood Wharf
POP/IOD E14 .... **104** B2

Wood Wharf Business Park
POP/IOD E14 .... **104** C3

Woolmore Primary School
POP/IOD E14 .... **104** C1

Woolwich Cemetery
WOOL/PLUM SE18 .... **127** F3

Woolwich College
WOOL/PLUM SE18 .... **107** D5
WOOL/PLUM SE18 .... **108** C5

Woolwich County Court
WOOL/PLUM SE18 .... **108** A4

Woolwich Crown Court
THMD SE28 .... **109** E3

Working Mens College
CAMTN NW1 .... **7** F1

World of Football Hall of Fame
STHWK SE1 .... **45** E1

Worlds End Place
WBPTN SW10 .... **114** C3

World Trade Centre
TWRH EC3N **37** F2

World University Service
STLK EC1Y **24** A1

Wormholt Park Primary School
SHB W12 .... **100** A1

Wyborne Primary School
ELTH/MOT SE9 .... **162** B1

Wykeham Primary School
WLSDN NW10 .... **51** D5

Wyndhams Theatre
LSQ/SEVD WC2H **32** B1

Wyvil Primary School
VX/NE SW8 .... **117** E3

Yale University Press
HAMP NW3 .... **73** E1

Yerbury Primary School
ARCH N19 .... **57** D5

Yeshivo Horomo Talmudical College
STNW/STAM N16 .... **59** D3

Yesodey Hatorah Jewish School
STNW/STAM N16 .... **59** F2

Yetev Lev Day School for Boys
STNW/STAM N16 .... **60** A3

York Clinic
STHWK SE1 .... **36** A4

York Hall
BETH E2 .... **90** B1

York Water Gate
CHCR WC2N **33** D3

Young England RFC
VX/NE SW8 .... **117** E2

Young Victoria Theatre
STHWK SE1 .... **34** B5

Zennor Road Industrial Estate
BAL SW12 .... **152** C1

Ziam Trading Estate
WALTH E17 .... **60** C3

AA **Street by Street**   QUESTIONNAIRE

Dear Atlas User
Your comments, opinions and recommendations are very
important to us. So please help us to improve our street atlases
by taking a few minutes to complete this simple questionnaire.

You do NOT need a stamp (unless posted outside the UK). If you do not want to remove this page from your street atlas, then photocopy it or write your answers on a plain sheet of paper.

Send to: The Editor, AA Street by Street, FREEPOST SCE 4598,
Basingstoke RG21 4GY

ABOUT THE ATLAS...

Which city/town/county did you buy?

_____

Are there any features of the atlas or mapping that you find particularly
useful?

_____
_____
_____

Is there anything we could have done better?

_____
_____
_____

Why did you choose an AA Street by Street atlas?

_____
_____
_____

Did it meet your expectations?

Exceeded ☐   **Met all** ☐   **Met most** ☐   **Fell below** ☐

Please give your reasons

_____
_____
_____
_____

MN   *continued overleaf*

Where did you buy it?

_____

For what purpose? (please tick all applicable)

To use in your own local area ☐   To use on business or at work ☐

Visiting a strange place ☐   In the car ☐   On foot ☐

Other (please state)

_____

LOCAL KNOWLEDGE...

Local knowledge is invaluable. Whilst every attempt has been made to
make the information contained in this atlas as accurate as possible,
should you notice any inaccuracies, please detail them below (if necessary,
use a blank piece of paper) or e-mail us at _streetbystreet@theAA.com_

_____

_____

_____

_____

ABOUT YOU...

Name (Mr/Mrs/Ms)
_____
Address
_____
                                         Postcode
_____
Daytime tel no
_____
E-mail address
_____

Which age group are you in?

Under 25 ☐   25-34 ☐   35-44 ☐   45-54 ☐   55-64 ☐   65+ ☐

Are you an AA member?   YES ☐   NO ☐

Do you have Internet access?   YES ☐   NO ☐